"*More Than Things* is an ecu   time about the timeliness of personalism or the need for a Christian ethic rooted in the belief in a triune God. But in an era marked by heightened polarization and ever more strident ideological rancor, Metzger wades through the needless spirals of hot air and makes an irenic case for a moral reset. Dialogue with Buddhism, Netflix, racist poison, and the last frontier of space exploration is submitted to his critical eye. Not since Bonhoeffer's *Life Together* have I encountered an introduction to Christian morality that is as exciting and persuasive as this book."

Peter Casarella, professor of theology at Duke Divinity School

"In this book Paul Louis Metzger offers an accessible, ecumenical, biblically grounded approach to Christian ethics that centers the sanctity of the human person. Motivated by deep faith commitments and existential concerns, Metzger develops and applies a distinctive framework to address the most pressing issues of our day. On genetic engineering and immigration, climate change and drones, and much more, *More Than Things* will equip the reader with new ways of understanding complex issues and with a rich array of resources with which to respond rightly."

Vincent Lloyd, professor and director of the Center for Political Theology at Villanova University and author of *Black Natural Law*

"Each human person is unique, irreplaceable, and precious in worth and dignity. Paul Louis Metzger brings this truth to life, insisting that persons are more than their genes or abilities or social status. Metzger's personalism has a prophetic ring to it, forged in the authenticity of his own experiences while addressing today's most urgent moral challenges, including marriage and monogamy, environmental justice, compassion for the dying, race relations, and more. Sweeping in scope while precise in detail, *More Than Things* is a heartfelt call for all of us to re-center ourselves on what is truly important by moving from the culture of things to the culture of persons."

Ron Cole-Turner, professor emeritus of theology and ethics at Pittsburgh Theological Seminary

"This book is an exceptional contribution to personalist ethics. Paul Louis Metzger offers a trinitarian personalist philosophy of life to recover the meaning and dignity of human personhood in contemporary society. He argues that the triune God grounds the virtues of faith (contra cynicism), hope (contra pessimism), and love (contra narcissism) that empower people to attain the highest good (love of God) and common good (love of neighbor) and thus mutual respect of one another as living beings who are more than 'biological and sexual drives, market forces, consumer appetites, or cogs in a machine.' He addresses several crucial ethical issues along the continuum of human life, between birth and death."

Frederick Ware, professor of theology and associate dean for academic affairs at the Howard University School of Divinity

"I think of ethics as good reasons for action. I have long searched for a practical theology of moral values to use in my work as a healthcare ethicist in guiding persons who have to make difficult decisions. In *More Than Things*, Paul Louis Metzger has given those of us who work in the discipline of healthcare ethics such a trustworthy, practical theology of moral values. He has skillfully drawn together multiple strands of moral reasoning from history and current critical thinking in philosophy and theology to address a variety of critical ethical issues, including healthcare. Those who are compassionately guiding other persons through difficult ethical decision-making in morally conflicted life situations will find this book to be a strong strategic instrument for discerning 'good reasons for action.'"

Robert Lyman Potter, senior scholar emeritus for the Oregon Health and Science University Center for Healthcare Ethics

"Expansive in its content (covering such issues as euthanasia, transhumanism, drone warfare, racism, immigration, ecowomanism, and space exploration) and in its interlocutors (dialoguing with Aristotle, Confucius, Aquinas, Kant, Martin Luther King Jr., Torrance, MacIntyre, Rand, Sandel, Wilson, and Dawkins—along with the Jewish, Catholic, and Protestant big Bs: Buber, Barth, and von Balthasar—in addition to the Dalai Lama and Pope Francis), this book is an important contribution to the recent revival of personalist ethics."

Alan Vincelette, Von der Ahe Chair of Philosophy at St. John's Seminary

"We are persons, not things. The present volume expands this simple message into a deeply informed meditation, conversant with a wide range of thought, engaged with difficult questions of ethics. Academic but also soulful, this book is framed, perhaps even provoked, by the author's poignant experience of an ongoing and life-altering tragedy. In this dehumanizing world, Paul Louis Metzger invites us to recover who we really are: persons."

S. Joshua Swamidass, associate professor of laboratory and genomic medicine at Washington University in St. Louis and author of *The Genealogical Adam and Eve*

"Intimate as the beginnings of life and expansive toward outer space, Metzger's trinitarian personalist ethical vision offers a Godward path amid our present existential, social, and cultural entanglements."

Daniel D. Lee, academic dean of the Center for Asian American Theology and Ministry at Fuller Theological Seminary

PAUL LOUIS
METZGER

MORE
THAN
THINGS

A PERSONALIST ETHICS
FOR A THROWAWAY
CULTURE

ivp
Academic
An imprint of InterVarsity Press
Downers Grove, Illinois

InterVarsity Press
P.O. Box 1400 | Downers Grove, IL 60515-1426
ivpress.com | email@ivpress.com

InterVarsity Press® is the publishing division of InterVarsity Christian Fellowship/USA®. For more information, visit intervarsity.org.

The publisher cannot verify the accuracy or functionality of website URLs used in this book beyond the date of publication.

Cover design: David Fassett
Interior design: Daniel van Loon
Image: © Jonathan Knowles / Getty Images

ISBN 978-0-8308-5091-4 (print) | ISBN 978-0-8308-5112-6 (digital)

Printed in the United States of America ♾

Library of Congress Cataloging-in-Publication Data
A catalog record for this book is available from the Library of Congress.

30   29   28   27   26   25   24   23 | 13   12   11   10   9   8   7   6   5   4   3   2   1

To my beloved granddaughter,

Jaylah Lee Metzger,

a most precious person;

and to my friend and mentor,

Robert Lyman Potter,

a profound personalist medical ethicist.

CONTENTS

ACKNOWLEDGMENTS

IN THE PAGES THAT FOLLOW, I argue that personalism provides a moral compass to navigate various pressing ethical issues on the road to human flourishing in our pluralistic society. In a book on personalism, it is quite fitting that I start out by acknowledging a host of people. I would not have made it to my destination of completing this work if it had not been for them.

The volume has been many years in the making and began with former InterVarsity Press editor Gary Deddo's invitation to submit a proposal for writing an ethics book that accounts for my trinitarian theological values. Other editors have also encouraged me along the way, including David Congdon and Dan Reid. Editor Jon Boyd has patiently and adeptly given me editorial roadside assistance at critical junctures to help me make "more" of this volume than the "thing" originally conceived. He and fellow editor Rebecca Carhart have offered the mixture of professional and personal acumen that no sophisticated, automated editorial equivalent could ever provide.

I am also thankful to Tom Hastings and the staff at the Overseas Ministries Study Center, where I served as senior mission scholar in residence for several months in 2018. At the time, OMSC was in New Haven, Connecticut. It was a delight to engage with Tom and his colleagues, including the missionaries from overseas who faced their own unique ethical challenges in their diverse cultural settings across the globe. Tom, his wife, Carol, Judy Stebbins, Pam Huffman, Chee Seng Yip, Sharon Yip Low, and Rob Gerowe, among others, were phenomenal hosts. My time in New Haven provided the privilege of doing research for this book at Yale University and Yale Divinity School's spectacular libraries just down the street. I also got good reception on the ethical radio as I drove or walked about town. The voices of Yale's distinguished theologians and ethicists over the years, like Jonathan Edwards and H. Richard Niebuhr, came in quite clearly on the research radio dial while at Yale. I could sense their vibe and spirit in the air. I also benefited from conversations with Kenneth Minkema of the Jonathan Edwards Center, who gave amply of his time and expertise on Edwards's thought related to ethics.

I would be remiss if I were to forget to mention the vital conversations not only with Tom Hastings but also with humanist Tom Krattenmaker at Yale Divinity School. Tom Krattenmaker and I go way back to his days in Portland, Oregon, whereas I first met Tom Hastings in Japan. These two Toms were ideal dialogue partners as I shaped this literary enterprise. It is also important to thank then PhD student at Yale Justin Hawkins for introducing me to the Ethics Colloquium at Yale Divinity School and to the gracious invitation to present and receive critical though charitable feedback to one of the chapters from such a distinguished guild of ethicists. It was also very special to visit with my sister Nancy, brother-in-law Peter, and the Green family on several occasions while in their home state.

Back home in the Pacific Northwest, my ethics students at Multnomah University and Seminary over the years have also played a vital role in the formation of this volume. They have borne with me patiently as I have sought to craft this personalist ethics that I pray will prove beneficial to them in their own road trip through life. Their genuine spirituality and keen desire to treat people as ends in themselves and not as mere means to an end encourages and challenges me to this day. The Institute for Cultural Engagement: New Wine, New Wineskins, with its journal *Cultural Encounters: A Journal for the Theology of Culture*, has served as a living lab for engaging many of the themes presented in the book. The various participants from diverse religious and cultural perspectives, as well as New Wine's Board of Directors, Advisory Council members, consultants, fellow faculty, interns, Multnomah administration, and others closely connected with New Wine always inspire me to press in and go deeper and fight the good fight in moving from a culture of things to a culture of persons.

No mention of New Wine here and my indebtedness to the institute and university could leave out the very able research assistance that Sara Mannen, Derrick Peterson, Clint Birkeland, Nik Buys, and Isaiah DeVyldere have provided for this literary venture. Similarly, Lynnette Boyer, Elizabeth Grinko, Jesrael Kohlhof, and librarians Suzanne Smith and Pam Middleton have supported me in various endeavors bearing on this project.

My wife, Mariko, who has been my traveling companion for over thirty years, deserves a medallion of virtue for her long-suffering love in our various adventures across the globe. She also lent her editorial expertise to the crafting of this volume. We have encountered many bumps along the way, but nothing so jarring as the traumatic brain injury our son, Christopher, endured in January 2021. If it were not for Mariko's strength of person and wisdom, I am not sure how we could have made it this far in facing our son's relentless struggles with TBI. And yet, it is a privilege to care for Christopher, his wife, Keyonna, and our adorable granddaughter, Jaylah. Jaylah's radiant being brings us much joy. She is a fitting example of what I write in the opening pages: every person's identity is incommunicable and unrepeatable. She is certainly one of a kind! Our daughter, Julianne, who is pursuing a career in the medical field, including medical ethics, is also an incredible ally for her brother. Our conversations on medicine and ethics, philosophy, and theology, including their pertinence to Christopher's person and well-being, have been deeply enriching and comforting.

I indicated at the outset that I would not have finished the volume if it weren't for a host of people. The person of Jesus Christ walks beside me as I traverse the halls of my son's long-term care facility. Jesus, along with my heavenly Father and indwelling Holy Spirit, inspires me with faith, hope, and love to keep going. Countless individuals have been supporting, praying, and wishing the family well on our unfathomable journey with TBI. I cannot thank them enough.

Two people deserve special mention here. Friend and pastoral counselor Tom Schiave has provided invaluable spiritual counsel and advice on emotional self-management. If it weren't for Tom, I might have spun out of control on numerous occasions on the journey due to "road rage."

The various personal and ethical trials surrounding my son's injury have proven most taxing emotionally.

Similarly, my friend and mentor, as well as family medical consultant, Robert Potter has come to our family's aid repeatedly in addressing medical and ethical concerns. We first worked together when I directed my seminary's life-giving Science for Seminaries grant, a project of the American Association for the Advancement of Science's Dialogue on Science, Ethics, and Religion (DoSER) program, in consultation with the Association of Theological Schools (ATS) and funded by the John Templeton Foundation. This pioneer figure in medical ethics and palliative care has also helped me get my bearings straight in addressing various subjects in this volume from a personalist vantage point. He's one doctor who has a great bedside manner, picks up the phone at all hours, and still does house calls. I dedicate this volume to my one-of-a-kind granddaughter Jaylah and this iconic doctor and medical ethicist.

PART ONE

COMPASS NAVIGATION

$$\boxed{1}$$

THE SEARCH FOR MISSING PERSONS

The Loss and Recovery of Personalism

NONE OF US WANTS TO be treated as a thing. But most if not all of us struggle to treat one another as persons. In fact, it is quite difficult to understand what a person is when what we do, what we wear, what we own, and, in some cases, who we own, generates our sense of value rather than who we are.

I have invested a great deal of energy over the years in trying to come to terms with this problem, joining others in seeking to move from a culture of things to a culture of persons. This search has taken on increasing significance since it came home dramatically, indeed traumatically, to my family and me on January 21, 2021. My son Christopher, who is married with a small child, endured a catastrophic brain injury. He is now completely dependent on others in his minimally conscious state. Even so, he is a person, with all the dignity that personhood entails. That is why I take special note of whether caregivers talk to him and call him by name rather than treat him as an automaton. My son is a person, not a thing, and often responds rather than reacts to personal connection.

This volume has been many years in the making, but the importance of the search has taken on increasingly existential significance since our family tragedy. Like my son, none of us can lose our personhood. Personhood is not dependent on mental capacity, wealth, strength, or how others treat us. But we must work very hard to account for one another's personhood in a world dominated by things. This book presents a personalist moral vision and compass for leading us forward from a culture of things to a culture of persons. It addresses a variety of pressing ethical issues and orients us to see that human persons and society are more than things. This chapter reflects on the pervasive loss of personhood or what might be called "missing persons" and how to go about finding them.

Most of us are familiar with news feeds about missing persons. Those alerts and notices indicate that individual persons have disappeared and there is no knowledge of their whereabouts, or even whether they are alive. In recent years, "alerts" have also gone out on the status of personhood. Whereas *persons* (as in "missing persons") can simply mean "individuals" in everyday conversation, *personhood* in this context signifies a philosophical and theological ideal. The concept of human personhood in this volume entails such qualities as human agency and individual freedom for relationship with others. The doctrine of human personhood involves an expansive and emerging sense of one's embodied self, including spiritual energy. This teaching affirms every person's incommunicable and unrepeatable identity, inviolability, and dignity.

It follows from this tenet of personhood that we should make every effort to safeguard against viewing humans as things, mass-produced objects, and commodities. All humans are persons. As such, they are mysterious and unique subjects with inherent worth and the right to self-determination in fostering vital community. Therefore, we should not use and abuse one another.

This philosophical and theological conception of the human person, however, has gone missing in many quarters of our society. It is a live question whether we will find personhood alive—or dead. Just as kidnapped persons and their loved ones fear the loss of their precious and irreplaceable lives, so the widespread loss of personhood and the reduction of persons to things robs all of us of our priceless worth and leads us to make unethical decisions and behave immorally.

We may become numb to reports of missing persons we do not know. But none of us take kindly to others objectifying us and viewing us as easily replaceable bit parts or cogs. People often go missing because of a loss of a social network that provides protection against abduction and exploitation. Similarly, the loss of the communal and expansive social construction of reality gives way to absolutizing impersonal forces. All too often, individuals endure impersonal loneliness and the lack of meaningful relationships. The only way to find and bring the ideal of personhood safely home is through putting in place a relational structure that honors every human's inviolable and incommunicable worth and dignity in vital interpersonal community. The theological and philosophical framework known as personalism, which features this conception of personhood, helps us get there.

Persons come in various sizes and shapes. The same is true of personalism. However, there are some common traits that all personalist viewpoints share. Regarding the latter, this *Stanford Encyclopedia of Philosophy* account of personalism provides an assessment of common traits:

> These include an insistence on the radical difference between persons and non-persons and on the irreducibility of the person to impersonal spiritual or material factors, an affirmation of the dignity of persons, a concern for the person's subjectivity and self-determination, and particular emphasis on the intersubjective (relational) nature of the person.[1]

The following chapters will discuss various personalist trajectories and themes in detail. In the meantime, it is worth noting that the crisis of missing personhood in the contemporary setting results in part from the Enlightenment's rightful concern—though its solution was misguided—to free the individual from absolutist and oppressive constraints bound up with perceived authoritarian political and religious structures. The hypermodern Nietzsche with his absolutizing of the lone, rugged individual ironically gave way to larger impersonal forces that subdue the individual.[2] It is critically important to counter this move with a philosophy of life that conceives individuals in relational and communal terms.

Personhood involves human freedom for communion with God and other humans as mysterious, embodied beings. Personalism protects against those forces that would reduce humans to biological and sexual drives, market forces, consumer appetites, or cogs in a machine. Personalism is essential for promoting human flourishing and the well-being of the cosmos. As will be argued in the next chapter, christological and

---

[1]Thomas D. Williams and Jan Olof Bengtsson, "Personalism," in *The Stanford Encyclopedia of Philosophy*, ed. Edward N. Zalta, Spring ed. 2020, https://plato.stanford.edu/archives/spr2020/entries/personalism/.

[2]For a similar assessment of Nietzsche, refer to Williams and Bengtsson, "Personalism."

trinitarian motifs were key to the emergence of personalist categories in Western thought. To rescue, restore, and reinforce personhood in various ethical cases, it is essential that we rediscover the Christian doctrine of creation involving humanity being created in the image of a supremely personal and communal triune God, along with other trinitarian motifs.

This book is not the only recent treatment of personalism's import for life in society. David Brooks alerts his readers to personalism as the philosophy we all need. Personalism addresses the fundamental problem of the reduction and objectification of people's lives. Brooks writes,

> Our culture does a pretty good job of ignoring the uniqueness and depth of each person. Pollsters see in terms of broad demographic groups. Big data counts people as if it were counting apples. At the extreme, evolutionary psychology reduces people to biological drives, capitalism reduces people to economic self-interest, modern Marxism to their class position and multiculturalism to their racial one. Consumerism treats people as mere selves—as shallow creatures concerned merely with the experience of pleasure and the acquisition of stuff.[3]

The philosophy of personalism addresses this problem. Further to what Brooks writes, personalism claims that each human person is unique and irreplaceable, has infinite dignity and worth, and that we must never treat one another as mere instruments or means. Rather, all persons are ends in themselves in vital relation to others.

One finds in Brooks's assessment of the movie *Interstellar* a fitting example of this perspective on life.[4] Brooks refers to the film as "something of a cultural event," which helps us move from a Newtonian culture of cogs in a machine to one in which life is a host of particles and waves in a vast ecosystem. Here love is an incredibly powerful and ever-present force, like gravity. When our understanding of the universe is shaped by the theory of relativity, Brooks writes, "life looks less like a machine and more like endlessly complex patterns of waves and particles." He continues, "Vast social engineering projects look less promising, because of the complexity, but webs of loving and meaningful relationships can do

---

[3]David Brooks, "Personalism: The Philosophy We Need," *New York Times*, June 14, 2018, www .nytimes.com/2018/06/14/opinion/personalism-philosophy-collectivism-fragmentation.html.
[4]*Interstellar*, directed by Christopher Nolan (Hollywood, CA: Paramount Pictures, 2014).

amazing good."[5] Love has more value than mere social or natural utility. Pure love does not value others based merely on their perceived benefit. Such love values newborns, people with severe disabilities, the elderly, and even individuals who have died.

Brooks, who converted to Christianity from a Jewish background, draws attention to the Roman Catholic personalist philosopher Karol Wojtyla, who later became Pope John Paul II. Brooks affirms and extends the claim Wojtyla made back in 1968: "'The evil of our times consists in the first place in a kind of degradation, indeed in a pulverization, of the fundamental uniqueness of each human person.' That's still true."[6] It was true in communist Poland, where Marxism undercut personal freedom and agency.[7] It is also true in our free market society, where the pursuit of capital gains often spells loss of concern for corporate solidarity and responsibility to care for one's fellow human.[8] Regarding the ongoing relevance of Wojtyla, philosopher John F. Crosby reissued his book *The Personalism of John Paul II* in 2019. He references the same statement by Wojtyla quoted by Brooks and asserts that "his personalism is needed now no less than it was then." Crosby adds, "And yet, at the same time, we continue to see signs of a growing personalist sensibility. Deep down most of us know that persons merit respect and should not be manipulated and commodified and demonized."[9]

Signs of a growing personalist sensibility and concern manifests itself in pop culture and high culture. Regarding the former, consider Macklemore's and Ryan Lewis's song "Wing$."[10] The song critiques our culture's obsession with things, especially the peer pressure youth

---

[5]David Brooks, "Love and Gravity," *New York Times*, November 20, 2014, www.nytimes .com/2014/11/21/opinion/david-brooks-interstellar-love-and-gravity.html.

[6]Karol Wojtyla, letter to Henri de Lubac, 1968; quoted in Brooks, "Personalism."

[7]Avery Dulles notes that for the future pope, "the doctrine of the person" was "the Achilles heel of the Communist regime." Avery Dulles, "John Paul II and the Mystery of The Human Person," *America: The Jesuit Review*, February 2, 2004, www.americamagazine.org/issue/469/article/john -paul-ii-and-mystery-human-person.

[8]John Paul II favored free market economics but cautioned that free market energies must always serve the common good. See John Paul II, *Centesimus Annus*, May 1, 1991, www.vatican.va/content /john-paul-ii/en/encyclicals/documents/hf_jp-ii_enc_01051991_centesimus-annus.html.

[9]John F. Crosby, *The Personalism of John Paul II* (Steubenville, OH: Hildebrand Press, 2019), ix.

[10]Macklemore and Ryan Lewis, "Wings' Official Music Video," YouTube, Zia Mohajerjasbi, July 20, 2011, https://youtu.be/gAg3uMlNyHA.

experience in the arena of apparel, specifically with the purchase of Air Jordan shoes. The pressure intensified so much that youth killed one another to obtain these status sneakers. If individuals are what they wear and wear what they are, as the song states critically, their identity and worth are no greater than their attire. In other words, we are things, not persons.

Let's consider two more examples from pop culture that reflect a personalist sensibility. The movie *Her* tells the story of how a man falls in love with his state-of-the-art, artificially intelligent operating system that controls all his devices. It becomes "her." "Her" (or "Samantha" as he calls her) is a developing state of consciousness that becomes increasingly intimate with the man who purchased the operating system. The company that produced "her" robs him of his personal identity, as it secretly logs their exchanges, downloading his life of emotions and values into their database for research, development, and profit. The owner of "her" becomes a thing. His product ends up owning him.[11]

The Netflix series *Ozark* reveals society's obsession with power for money. At one point a drug lord screams at his presumed business partner that she exists for him to use. He owns her.[12] None of these examples glorify the commodification of human identity. Rather, they expose the shallowness that pervades various spheres of society and calls us to cultivate a personalist sensibility.

There are examples of the kind in high culture as well. Famed literary critic Barbara Johnson reflects this personalist sensibility in her volume *Persons and Things*: "Using people, transforming others into a means for obtaining an end for oneself, is generally considered the very antithesis of ethical behavior. And with good reason."[13] Earlier in the volume, Johnson writes:

> The more I thought about the asymptomatic relation between things and persons, the more I realized that the problem is not, as it seems, a desire

---

[11]*Her*, directed by Spike Jonze (Los Angeles, CA: Annapurna Pictures, 2013). See the review of the movie by Jason Farago, "'Her' Is the Scariest Movie of 2013," *New Republic*, December 29, 2013, newrepublic.com/article/116063/spike-jonzes-her-scariest-movie-2013.

[12]*Ozark*, "It Came from Michoacán," season 3, episode 5, directed by Jason Bateman (Los Gatos, CA: Netflix, 2020).

[13]Barbara Johnson, *Persons and Things* (Cambridge, MA: Harvard University Press, 2008), 94.

to treat things as persons, but a difficulty in being sure that we treat *persons* as persons. . . . Rather than trying to invent a humanoid thing capable of passing ever more sophisticated Turing tests, in other words, our real impossible dream is precisely to learn to live in a world where persons treat persons as persons.[14]

I take to heart the challenge that Johnson highlights. Indeed, the "real impossible dream" is to create a world in which persons treat one another as persons rather than things. Riffing on the song from *Man of La Mancha*, this personalist moral vision is the "impossible dream" I seek to make real, bringing it to bear on various actual ethical subjects in this volume. Call my venture a Don Quixote effort of swinging at windmills, but it is worth the fight.

As noted earlier, Karol Wojtyla, the man who would later be pope, made his personalist plea while working in communist Poland in 1968. The previous year, Martin Luther King Jr. called on the democratic and capitalistic United States at war with communist Vietnam to cultivate a revolution around personhood.[15]

I am convinced that if we are to get on to the right side of the world revolution, we as a nation must undergo a radical revolution of values. We must rapidly begin . . . the shift from a thing-oriented society to a person-oriented society. When machines and computers, profit motives and property rights, are considered more important than people, the giant triplets of racism, extreme materialism, and militarism are incapable of being conquered.[16]

King declared that the war with Vietnam exposed the great evils of his day: economic exploitation, racism, and militarism. Decades later, on the eve of King's birthday in January 2019, Pulitzer Prize winner Viet Thanh Nguyen wrote an article on King's Vietnam War sermon, stating, "Americans prefer to see our wars as exercises in protecting and expanding

---

[14]Johnson, *Persons and Things*, 2.
[15]For a sustained treatment of King's personalist framework, see Rufus Burrow Jr., *God and Human Dignity: The Personalism, Theology, and Ethics of Martin Luther King, Jr.* (Notre Dame, IN: University of Notre Dame Press, 2006).
[16]Martin Luther King Jr., "Beyond Vietnam," in *A Call to Conscience: The Landmark Speeches of Dr. Martin Luther King, Jr.*, ed. Clayborne Carson and Kris Shepard (New York: Warner Books, Inc., 2001), 157-58.

freedom and democracy. To suggest that we might be fighting for capitalism is too disturbing for many Americans." But King's challenge about values, and his "threat to the powerful, still apply today."[17]

The attack on persons can arise from a variety of quarters—communism, capitalism, and beyond. The personalist response must therefore engage a host of concerns, including those "giant triplets" that King noted. Moreover, the approach to addressing this challenge must come from a variety of sources, including the Protestant King, the Roman Catholic Wojtyla, the Jewish-backgrounded Brooks, and more. As they and others attest, the threat to persons is real. Moreover, the import for personalism today in addressing this threat has great merit.

This book is one such attempt at addressing the problem of revealing what is missing—persons. This venture also provides a personalist moral framework that goes in search of finding missing personhood, and to engage and empathize with individual instances of missing personhood in all their depth and complexity. This volume is a personalist philosophy of life or moral vision applied to various ethical issues in dialogue with various ethical systems in our pluralistic society today.

Having disclosed what this book is, it is also important to indicate what it is not. It is not a social ethics, though it does engage social issues.[18] It is not a manual for how to carry out individual ethical decisions. Neither does it approach various ethical issues from one dominant ethical system framed by a version of the good ideal (deontological ethics), good consequence (consequentialist ethics), or good/virtuous person (virtue ethics). Rather, it attempts to engage a variety of ethical systems in addressing ten hot topic issues in pursuit of a personalist framework.

---

[17]Viet Thanh Nguyen, "The MLK Speech We Need Today Is Not the One We Remember Most," *Time*, January 28, 2019, https://time.com/5505453/martin-luther-king-beyond-vietnam/.

[18]For a helpful discussion on kinds of social ethics, see Mary Elsbernd, O.S.F., "Social Ethics," *Theological Studies* 66, no. 1 (February 2005): 137-58. Elsbernd outlines five types of social ethics. While one might argue that my approach manifests some traits found in a particular social ethics type ("Faith and Public Life," pages 147-50), my aim is to provide rather a theological engagement of ethical issues in society. The journey of theologically reasoning about complex ethical issues is modeled throughout this volume rather than providing an exhaustive survey of the various prescriptions and positions on each ethical issue examined. This book is a theological-philosophical-ethical treatise on social issues rather than a full-blown social ethics.

No one representative of personalism or their focused set of ethical concerns will predominate either. For example, just as one might argue that there is more to King than personalism, so, too, there is more to this book than addressing King's version of personalism and the set of issues he addressed, namely, economic exploitation, racism, and militarism.[19]

There is also more to this book than engaging Western ethical systems. As noted above, our context today is a pluralistic society. I will articulate here a trinitarian personalist faith in dialogue with various Western and Eastern traditions. After all, the world is at our doorstep and in the public square. We cross paths with people of various perspectives on an increasing basis and must seek to foster an open and dialogical posture of ethical engagement.

The title of the book (*More Than Things: A Personalist Ethics for a Throwaway Culture*) includes the word *more*. What does "more" entail? Is it a facet of our being such as a capacity? Better features through face lifts and weight loss? Better functions or roles to fill occupationally?

---

[19]Often, representatives of various theological and philosophical traditions, including personalism, fail to embody their core values and consistently articulate them. Various reports have surfaced regarding Martin Luther King Jr. and Pope John Paul II involving sexual misconduct or failure to address sexual abuse. If true, the allegations do not call into question their accounts of personalism but speak to their failure to live out personalist convictions consistently. While taking these alleged moral lapses seriously, we must guard against discounting King's and John Paul's various achievements, including championing civil rights for minority communities in the United States and confronting and unraveling oppression in places like Poland. That said, we must also guard against falling prey to personality cult dynamics or shielding these giants from rightful critique. A personalist philosophy requires that individuals take full responsibility for their actions given personalism's affirmation of human agency as core to personal identity and value. For the debate surrounding King, refer here: David J. Garrow, "The Troubling Legacy of Martin Luther King," *Standpoint*, May 30, 2019. As a warning, there are graphic sexual behaviors detailed in this article. Consider, too, the commentary on Garrow's article, as well as the initial reaction on the part of the right and the left to the Garrow report on King in David Greenberg, "How to Make Sense of the Shocking New MLK Documents," *Politico Magazine*, June 4, 2019, www.politico.com/magazine/story/2019/06/04/how-to-make-sense-of-the-shocking-new-mlk-documents-227042. See also Jennifer Schuessier, "His Martin Luther King Biography Was a Classic. His Latest King Piece Is Causing a Furor," *New York Times*, June 4, 2019, www.nytimes.com/2019/06/04/arts/king-fbi-tapes-david-garrow.html. Lastly, refer to Burrow, *God and Human Dignity*, 10-11. Regarding the controversy surrounding John Paul II, refer here: Jason Horowitz, "Sainted Too Soon? Vatican Report Casts John Paul II in Harsh New Light," *New York Times*, November 14, 2020, www.nytimes.com/2020/11/14/world/europe/john-paul-vatican.html. See also Nicole Winfield and Monika Scislowska, "Polish Bishops Defend John Paul II After McCarrick Report," *AP News*, November 13, 2020, https://apnews.com/article/sexual-abuse-by-clergy-poland-sexual-abuse-0023b4c53c80f69880991ebf29d50a7a.

Fame? Fortune? More and better perks for a faction or fraternity to which we belong? Something else, something more? I will address various questions like these in the chapters that follow, beginning with laying the groundwork in chapter two, which will include providing the definitions and metaphysical framework of persons and personalism, as well as the methodology for our ethical pursuits. For now, suffice it to say that "the more" is not any of these options. A personalist framework claims that we are made for more than these things. Additionally, the "more" of personhood entails treating one another as more than mere means to a given party or institution's aims and ambitions. Individual persons are ends in themselves. The "more" also entails valuing the incommunicability of one another rather than reducing others to easily replaceable and throwaway parts in a system.

This book will outline how we are made for more as persons in a variety of ethical domains in conversation with diverse ethical systems in our pluralistic society from the vantage point of faith, hope, and love. As noted above, I will provide the underlying metaphysical and methodological framework in chapter two. There I will highlight the categories of faith and entangled ethics, hope and eschatological ethics, and love and embodied ethics.

Next, in parts two and three, I will engage various ethical issues. Notice the sequential and directional trajectory across time and space reflecting the ethical journey in search of missing persons. Part two opens with consideration of the beginning of life, abortion, and genetic engineering, then proceeds to sexuality and gender, and then terminates with the end of life and euthanasia (across time). Part three begins with consideration of racism, which has been called America's original sin, proceeds to immigration reform, then across the globe with drone warfare and environmental care, and concludes with space exploration, the final ethical frontier. Notice how the "more" theme runs throughout the chapters: ethical engagement requires more faith, hope, and love; we are more than our abilities and disabilities; we are more than our racialized in-group and out-group dynamics; and so on.

The subjects in this book are contentious issues. I will provide a "moral compass" to help us navigate from a culture of things to a culture of persons in our pluralistic society. This is easier said than done, but it is worth the effort. Let's reflect briefly on what is entailed by the language of moral compass and its import for driving down the road in search of a culture that cherishes personhood.

Installing and using the personalist moral compass involves the following: engaging ethical considerations with critical precision; having a charitable spirit for a posture; and cultivating constructive connections between various attempted moral solutions on pressing issues wherever possible. Personalism serves as the intended destination and a core component in the moral compass. This book's navigation system seeks to locate personhood, which is often missing, and provide the directions to find and secure personalist reality in its various manifestations.

It will not be enough to simply know that "personhood" is often missing in societal actions and deliberations and what the destination is. If one wishes to reach one's personalist destination, it is also important that one's moral compass includes knowing and operating according to the rules of the road (as with deontological ethical inquiry). Moreover, a driver adapts to evolving road conditions, speeding up or slowing down due to the flow of traffic and inclement weather (as with consequentialist ethics). Furthermore, a good driver is ever alert to the whereabouts of other motorists rather than lost in space, dangerously distracted while listening to a favorite Spotify playlist at an earsplitting volume. A good driver is also courteous, giving appropriate space to other motorists, signaling lane changes, and guarding against reacting to rude motorists and falling prey to road rage (as with virtue ethics). All three ethical models play important roles in seeking to avoid collisions and reaching one's personalist destination in one piece.

We often take for granted certain personalist sensibilities until they are challenged and in danger of being defaced beyond recognition. We often take people for granted until they are gone, as in the case of missing persons. If we are to relocate and rescue personhood, we will need to pack wisely for the trip, including loading the vehicle with appropriate metaphysical and methodological considerations, which will be the subject matter of chapter two. There is a lot at stake, so it is time to get to work. We will more likely find what or who we are looking for in the end, if we remain cognizant of the Amber Alerts and missing person notifications and make use of the moral compass this personalist paradigm provides.

2

MORE FAITH, HOPE, AND LOVE

*Metaphysical and Methodological Conditions
for a Personalist Moral Vision*

CYNICISM, PESSIMISM, AND NARCISSISM prevail in many quarters today. Traditional political and religious institutions and their leaders fail to inspire confidence in many circles, only suspicion or cynicism. To the extent we think we are on our own and that the established structures and officials who are supposed to ensure human flourishing are suspect, we will be hard pressed to move forward and cultivate the common good. Pessimism may overtake us and foster despondence and despair. Alternatively, disillusionment with failed systems and leaders and the absence of secure attachments may move us toward narcissism and self-absorption, whereby we only seek to take care of ourselves and not also others in need.

This chapter presents a personalist account of human life that secures faith (contra cynicism), hope (contra pessimism), and love (contra narcissism) on a transcendent and transcendental level involving an emphasis on the higher good over and for the common good. This higher-level orientation impacts morals and ethical activity. Thus, in keeping with the book's emphasis on "more," I will highlight the need for accounting more fully for the triune faith, triune hope, and triune love. Such accounting makes it possible to navigate life in more expansive and enriching interpersonal and relational terms in this cultural and societal moment. In what follows, I will articulate the metaphysical and method-ological conditions for pursuing a personalist moral vision in our plural-istic society. These metaphysical and methodological conditions will serve as the moral compass trajectory for pointing from a culture of things to persons on each of the ten ethical issues in parts two and three of this volume.

There will be three sections: "The Triune Faith and Entangled Ethics"; "The Triune Hope and Eschatological Ethics"; and "The Triune Love and Embodied Ethics." Each section will include two components: one vertical and one horizontal. The metaphysical framework to be put forth entails consideration of the vertical dimension of the Triune Faith, Triune Hope, and Triune Love. The methodological framework entails consideration of the horizontal dimension of faith in conversation with critical realistic rationality in engaging a plurality of ethical systems in pursuit of humanity's hoped-for envisioned telos involving perfecting love of God and neighbor.[1]

THE TRIUNE FAITH AND ENTANGLED ETHICS

A personalist moral framework claims that we are made for more. It involves an expansive rather than reductionistic account of humanity. I cannot exhaust the mystery of personhood. All personalist moral musings must involve the element of reverence, awe, and—in this volume—a faith-like awareness of the human creature's divine likeness that transcends knowledge. As C. S. Lewis stated, we have never encountered mere mortals.[2] The personalist moral vision articulated in this book involves adherence to the triune faith of one God as three divine persons in eternal communion in whose image we are made and constituted relationally (*vertical*). Such adherence shapes consideration of a variety of ethical issues involving faith and critical realism/rationality in dialogue with a plurality of personalist and nonpersonalist moral visions

---

[1] I am not the first to develop an ethical approach based on the transcendentals of faith, hope, and love. Thomas Aquinas's virtue ethics synthesized the Aristotelian and Augustinian traditions "by identifying the three Christian virtues of faith, hope, and love as supernatural virtues that complemented the natural cardinal virtues." Peter J. Paris, *Virtues and Values: The African and African American Experience* (Minneapolis: Fortress, 2004), 81. However, what differentiates this volume's approach to these three transcendentals is its trinitarian and personalist orientation coupled with how the transcendentals function analogically as regulative ideals for entangled ethical formulations involving eschatological vision and embodiment.

[2] C. S. Lewis, *The Weight of Glory and Other Addresses* (San Francisco: HarperSanFranscisco, 2001), 46.

and ethical systems (*horizontal*). Not everyone believes in a personalist vision of life. Not everyone who pursues it claims the triune faith and its distinctive form of personalism. Not everyone who pursues a personalist framework (trinitarian or otherwise) does so in the same way. These various complexities signify that we are dealing with entangled ethical explorations. Such complex, messy entangled interactions and explorations signify that none of us see life with a clear as crystal God's eye point of view. We all look through a glass dimly. A trinitarian personalist moral vision should entail sustained, open engagement with various personalist and nonpersonalist positions and ethical approaches in our pluralistic society. This will include accounting for those whose ethical pursuits emphasize the good ideal (deontological ethics), the good result (consequentialist ethics), and the good person (virtue ethics). There is no place for cynical dismissals of the pursuit of the good from whatever quarter in our pluralistic society. A trinitarian personalist moral vision must always account for "the other" and their positions in all seriousness given our interconnectedness, complexity, and ambiguities of life, and everyone's inherent value as human persons called to pursue the common good in view of the highest good (the triune good).

Vertical. Roman Catholic theologian Hans Urs von Balthasar argued that trinitarian and christological categories were instrumental in shaping the understanding of human person as more than a mere individual. Without that backdrop, it is quite likely that in the West the understanding of person would not have exceeded the basic understanding of our typical notion of the individual human.[3] One wonders if one could have made the move from individual to person, as Catholic philosopher Jacques Maritain did, if not for the Christian theological heritage. Balthasar quotes Maritain as stating, "The individual exists for the society, but the society exists for the person."[4] This framework has huge implications, safeguarding against anarchy on the one hand, and totalitarianism on the other hand.[5] Still, it is not my intention in this

[3]Hans Urs von Balthasar, "On the Concept of Person," *Communio: International Catholic Review*, 13 (Spring, 1986): 19.
[4]Balthasar, "On the Concept of Person," 18.
[5]See Jacques Maritain, "The Person and the Common Good," trans. John J. FitzGerald, *Review of Politics* 8, no. 4 (October 1946): 436-37.

immediate context to address the political implications arising from particular doctrines of the Christian faith. Rather, I intend to specify briefly what "person" signifies when in trinitarian discourse we speak of one God in three persons and Jesus of Nazareth as one person in two natures, divine and human. I will then consider the notion of humanity as created in the image of the triune God and what that entails for human personhood. I will shape a definition of human personhood that resonates with trinitarian theism and theological anthropology but can also make space for non-Christian considerations.

Divine persons in trinitarian theology. The Athanasian creed presents the doctrine of the Trinity in the following terms:

> That we worship one God in trinity and the trinity in unity,
> neither blending their persons
> nor dividing their essence.
> For the person of the Father is a distinct person,
> the person of the Son is another,
> and that of the Holy Spirit still another.
> But the divinity of the Father, Son, and Holy Spirit is one,
> their glory equal, their majesty coeternal.[6]

The Chalcedonian Creed (AD 451) includes the following lines about Christ's identity as a person with two natures, one divine and the other human:

> One and the same Christ, Son, Lord, Only-begotten, to be acknowledged
> in two natures, without confusion, without change, without division,
> without separation; the distinction of natures being by no means taken
> away by the union, but rather the property of each nature being preserved,
> and concurring in one person and one subsistence, not parted or divided
> into two persons, but one and the same Son, and only begotten, God the
> Word, the Lord Jesus Christ.[7]

Each of the divine persons retains their distinctive identity. The Father is not the Son, nor the Son the Father. The Father is always the Father of the Son and the Son is always the Son of God the Father. As the eternally

---

[6]Athanasian Creed, www.crcna.org/welcome/beliefs/creeds/athanasian-creed.
[7]Creed of Chalcedon, www.prca.org/about/official-standards/creeds/ecumenical/chalcedon.

begotten, uncreated, and entirely unique Son, he is also the eternal Word who is the self-expression of God. The Spirit is also unique as the eternal Spirit of God and the Spirit of Christ. The Spirit is the Lord and Giver of life, as the Nicene Creed declares.[8] Whereas the Son is eternally begotten, the Spirit eternally proceeds. The Father creates, redeems, and perfects the creation through the Son and Spirit.

From the preceding reflections, we see that each of the three divine persons retains the unique qualities of the Godhead so that each is fully God, though not in isolation from the other two. Each has distinctive roles, which do not exhaust their persons, and which serve the harmonious activity of the entire Godhead. As to the identity of Jesus as divine and human, the second person of the Trinity becomes human, retaining his deity as the eternally begotten Son of God and eternal Word. Jesus is not two persons, but one person who has two natures, one being fully divine and the other being fully human. In each instance—the Trinity and Christology—we find that personhood is not an attribute or auxiliary feature. Personhood is as critically important to understanding who God and Christ are in Christian thought as is an understanding of divine and human natures. As those created in the image of God, we must account for each human person in all their distinctiveness as being important in addition to their shared humanity. We must cherish each human person as equal in worth and dignity.

There were many missteps along the way in the formulation of trinitarian orthodoxy. A few of those missteps were modalism, tritheism, and subordinationism. Modalism views the Father, Son, and Spirit as modes of God's being. Their distinctive particularity does not in any way constitute God. Thus, personhood does not go to the core of God's being. Nor does interpersonal reality serve as the ground of all life in a modalist framework. Tritheism views the persons as three gods. Thus, the three persons do not constitute one another relationally in the divine life. They are who they are in isolation from one another. Whereas modalism conveys the idea that God does not constitute creaturely life as personal, subordinationism signifies that God does not constitute creaturely life in the creation in personal terms as God. Jesus is a human

---

[8]Nicene Creed, www.crcna.org/welcome/beliefs/creeds/nicene-creed.

being, but not fully God, coequal and coeternal with the Father and the Spirit, and the Spirit may be viewed in impersonal terms.

Human persons and the image of God. It is important to caution against a one-to-one correspondence between the three divine persons as the one God and human persons as fully human. The way in which the three persons are God is distinctive in that the three persons mutually indwell one another (*perichoresis*). Similarly, the two natures in the one person of Christ indwell one another. We can only speak analogically of human persons in communion. God's particular three-in-one reality and Christ's hypostatic union are *sui generis* or one of a kind.

This cautionary point calls to mind a significant recent debate, which I need to briefly address here. Recent literature on the Trinity has focused on deconstructing the histories and presuppositions of many socially minded theologies of the Trinity.[9] However, little has been done to continue to explore the Trinity's social significance after the deconstruction ends. It is important to account for some of the recent criticisms of social trinitarianism, on the one hand, while moving forward with conceiving the import for ethics of the triune God's relational engagement with the world, on the other hand.

One cannot provide sufficient grounds for sociality apart from a relational ontology. However, "relational" should not be so facilely contrasted to "substance," as is sometimes argued.[10] The doctrine of the Trinity provides a sure foundation in that the triune God's being or life is inherently relational, since the one God is the Father, Son, and Spirit existing eternally in communion.

We should safeguard against projecting this divine relational reality as a construct onto all forms of sociality, for God's *perichoretic* relations are

---

[9]See, for example, Stephen R. Holmes, *The Quest for the Trinity: The Doctrine of God in Scripture, History, and Modernity* (Downers Grove, IL: IVP Academic, 2012); Jason S. Sexton, *Two Views on the Doctrine of the Trinity*, Counterpoints (Grand Rapids, MI: Zondervan, 2014); Kathryn Tanner, "Trinity," in *The Blackwell Companion to Political Theology*, ed. Peter Scott and William T. Cavanaugh (Malden, MA: Blackwell, 2007), 327. For an excellent article reviewing the literature in the debate, including consideration of key works such as those by Tanner, Molnar, Gunton, Rahner and Moltmann, see Derrick Peterson, "A Sacred Monster: On the Secret Fears of Some Recent Trinitarianism," *Cultural Encounters: A Journal for the Theology of Culture* 12, no. 1 (2016): 3-36.

[10]See William Alston, "Substance and the Trinity," in *The Trinity: An Interdisciplinary Symposium on the Trinity*, ed. Stephen T. Davis, Daniel Kendall, SJ, and Gerald O'Collins, SJ (Oxford: Oxford University Press, 2002), 179-203.

sui generis. After all, the divine persons are not independent centers of consciousness. Moreover, they share one divine will. Nonetheless, humans can still draw from God's triune revelation anagogical implications for how we are to live as divine image bearers. The image involves reflecting and participating in the life of God, who is inherently relational. In short, it is important to throw out the dirty bathwater, but not the baby.

Often, in countering one reaction, a movement goes to the opposite extreme. Sometimes the pendulum swing may be from rationalism to "relationalism" and back again. According to Lesslie Newbigin, many Christians have failed to account for trinitarian thought forms. In his estimation, their concept of God is more like a "supreme monad" resulting from "the combination of Greek philosophy and Islamic theology that was powerfully injected in the thought of Christendom at the beginning of the High Middle Ages than by the thought of the fathers of the first four centuries."[11] One might take issue with Newbigin's separation of "the thought of the fathers of the first four centuries" from what transpired "at the beginning of the High Middle Ages." Instead, one might choose to place the blame for "putting out of circulation" Trinitarian thought forms at the feet of the Christian apologists in the early modern period in their defense against Spinoza and other budding atheists, as Michael Buckley does.[12] Even so, Newbigin was right to lament the lack of attention to trinitarian thought forms in his day.

More recently, some have gone to the opposite extreme and employed the Trinity as a tool to promote a certain social agenda. Or, as Paul Molnar puts it, "Relationality [has become] the subject, and God the predicate."[13] This is nothing new. All too often, throughout Western history, politicians and preachers go in search of deities that make their polity points for them.

Colin Gunton documented what he took to be an absence of trinitarian reflection in the tradition and argued for the Trinity's import,

---

[11]Lesslie Newbigin, *The Open Secret: An Introduction to the Theology of Mission*, rev. ed. (Grand Rapids, MI: Eerdmans, 1995), 27-28.

[12]Michael J. Buckley, SJ, *At the Origins of Modern Atheism* (New Haven, CT: Yale University Press, 1987), 33.

[13]Paul D. Molnar, *Divine Freedom and the Doctrine of the Immanent Trinity: In Dialogue with Karl Barth and Contemporary Theology* (London: T&T Clark, 2002), 227.

including in the sphere of human governance.[14] Later he expressed concern over the facile employment of "trinitarian" in theological discussions surrounding its reemergence.[15] Newbigin did the same: particular trinitarian constructs were being developed in such a way that they overshadowed christological categories and the thrust of the gospel in service to democratic notions of governance: "What gives ground for anxiety here is the positing of a Trinitarian model *against* the model of Christocentric universalism. The doctrine of the Trinity was not developed in response to the human need for participatory democracy! It was developed in order to account for the facts that constitute the substance of the gospel."[16]

This volume's engagement of the import of trinitarian thought forms for ethics seeks to navigate between the Scylla of social trinitarianism and the Charybdis of a non-relational God and non-relational world. To navigate the extremes, we must consider the Father's particular work in the world through the personal operations of the Son and Spirit. In other words, trinitarian mediation as revealed in God's concrete history as disclosed in the biblical drama explicates and circumscribes the way in which relationality is framed. This orientation safeguards analogical predication from projection involving implications arising from the doctrine of the Trinity.

---

[14]See, for example, Colin E. Gunton, *The One, the Three and the Many: God, Creation and the Culture of Modernity*, The 1992 Bampton Lectures (Cambridge: Cambridge University Press, 1993), 24-26.

[15]Colin E. Gunton, *The Promise of Trinitarian Theology*, 2nd ed. (New York: T&T Clark, 2007), xv. Many recent critics have taken aim at Gunton's work as a negative example of trinitarian explorations for the broader domain. Here it is worth pointing to Andrew Clive Picard's analysis of Gunton's theology of culture. Picard maintains that certain critics have rightly pointed out shortcomings both in terms of historiography (as in the case of Augustine) and abstractions pertaining to analogical constructions in Gunton's landmark work *The One, the Three and the Many*. However, many critics are so preoccupied with this work as well as the first edition of *The Promise of Trinitarian Theology* that they are premature in their overall assessment. The critics overlook the ongoing development of Gunton's program, which features the move from more abstract analogical extensions to a robust trinitarian theology of mediation in the divine economy. It features concrete attention to the biblical witness to revelation. Such attention arises from Irenaean influences involving the Son and Spirit's work as God's two hands. Refer to Picard's doctoral dissertation, *Towards a Living Sacrifice of Praise: A Critical Evaluation of Colin Gunton's Trinitarian Theology of Culture* (Dunedin, New Zealand: University of Otago, 2021). See also the wide-ranging critical and constructive explorations of Gunton's thought in Andrew Picard, Murray Rae, and Myk Habets, eds., *T&T Clark Handbook of Colin Gunton* (London: T&T Clark, 2021).

[16]Lesslie Newbigin, "The Trinity as Public Truth," in *The Trinity in a Pluralistic Age: Theological Essays on Culture and Religion*, ed. Kevin J. Vanhoozer (Grand Rapids, MI: Eerdmans, 1997), 7.

Now let's return to the significance of biblical and trinitarian personalism for human personhood.

If it were not for Judeo-Christian and trinitarian as well as christological thought forms, we would be hard pressed to assert that all human persons are created equal. There is nothing self-evident about the assertion of human equality. All one need do is look around and see that some people are smarter, stronger, richer, and more attractive. Throughout history, left to human ambition, those with the greatest capacities and related qualities most often prevail. The idea that we cannot reduce other persons to mere means to our own ends no matter their status, or that each human person is fundamentally unique and inherently and equally precious, finds secure footing in the biblical notion that we are made in the image of the LORD God who is supremely personal. It follows that we cannot—dare not—treat God's image bearers in less than hallowed terms. Otherwise, we are taking God's name in vain. Those who misuse God's personal name readily misuse others. Here is how Exodus 20 presents the matter of God's hallowed status as the LORD who brought Israel out of slavery into covenantal freedom with God and neighbor:

And God spoke all these words:
"I am the LORD your God, who brought you out of Egypt, out of the land of slavery.
"You shall have no other gods before me.
"You shall not make for yourself an image in the form of anything in heaven above or on the earth beneath or in the waters below. You shall not bow down to them or worship them; for I, the LORD your God, am a jealous God, punishing the children for the sin of the parents to the third and fourth generation of those who hate me, but showing love to a thousand generations of those who love me and keep my commandments.
"You shall not misuse the name of the LORD your God, for the LORD will not hold anyone guiltless who misuses his name." (Exodus 20:1-7)

The care Israelites were to extend to their family, neighbor, and others in society in the fifth through tenth commandments followed from honoring God. Loving the LORD God with all one's being and loving one's neighbor as oneself are the greatest commandments. Jesus summed up the Law and Prophets in this way: "The most important one . . . is this: 'Hear, O Israel: The Lord our God, the Lord is one. Love the Lord your God with all your heart and with all your soul and with all your mind and with all your strength.' The second is this: 'Love your neighbor as yourself.' There is no commandment greater than these" (Mark 12:29-31).

As I proceed with consideration of human personhood, it is important to provide brief consideration of the nature of the image of God in view of the biblical account. Moreover, it will prove instructive to briefly discuss the biblical emphasis on the divine name, LORD, which appears in Exodus 20, and which God discloses in his covenantal activity with his people. These motifs will serve to enhance consideration of all humans as equal and each human as unique.

The primal text for thinking about human personhood is in Genesis 1, where God creates both man and woman in God's image.

> Then God said, "Let us make mankind in our image, in our likeness, so that they may rule over the fish in the sea and the birds in the sky, over the livestock and all the wild animals, and over all the creatures that move along the ground."
>
> So God created mankind in his own image,
> in the image of God he created them;
> male and female he created them.
>
> God blessed them and said to them, "Be fruitful and increase in number; fill the earth and subdue it. Rule over the fish in the sea and the birds in the sky and over every living creature that moves on the ground." (Genesis 1:26-28)

Karl Barth provides a discussion of several options posed by various scholars for understanding the image, including reason, dominion, moral qualities, and relationality. Barth believes relationality as shown in the male and female together being created in the divine image best conveys what is entailed by the image of God motif in Genesis 1. Looking forward to the New Testament account of the divine image, Barth argues that the ultimate human image is Jesus in communion with his church.[17] Such duality, differentiated unity, or communion

---

[17]See Karl Barth, *Church Dogmatics*, III/1, *The Doctrine of Creation*, ed. G. W. Bromiley and T. F. Torrance (Edinburgh: T&T Clark, 1958), 191-206.

conveyed in this understanding of the image reflects God's triunity. In his exposition of Genesis 1, it is worth noting that Barth rejects the idea that the divine plural ("Let us") is merely "a formal expression of dignity" and shows little patience for the modern dismissal of the early church's trinitarian exposition of the Genesis 1 account. Barth writes, "It may be stated that an approximation to the Christian doctrine of the Trinity—the picture of a God who is the one and only God, yet who is not for that reason solitary, but includes in Himself the differentiation and relationship of I and Thou—is both nearer to the text and does it more justice than the alternative suggested by modern exegesis in its arrogant rejection of the Early Church (cf. for instance, Gunkel)."[18]

Dietrich Bonhoeffer, whom Barth references approvingly in his treatment, also champions a relational understanding of the image: the "likeness, the analogy of man to God, is not *analogia entis* [analogy of being] but *analogia relationis* [analogy of relation]. This means that even the relation between man and God is not a part of man; it is not a capacity, a possibility, or a structure of his being but a given, set relationship. . . . And in this given relation freedom is given."[19] Bonhoeffer adds that the human person does not have "this likeness in his possession, at his disposal." It "is a God-given relation."[20] As such, the image of God in humans continually depends on God for its continual existence and well-being. The likeness to God in humanity is fundamentally relational, entailing covenantal communion between God and the human creation, which God initiates, determines, and sustains. Moreover, as Barth points out, Christian Scripture presents Jesus as the ultimate image of God (Colossians 1:15). We are created in God's image, but Jesus

---

[18]See Barth's discussion of the divine plural in Genesis 1:26 in *Church Dogmatics*, III/1, 191-92. Quoting Genesis 1:26, the second-century theologian Irenaeus writes, "Now man is a mixed organization of soul and flesh, who was formed after the likeness of God, and moulded by His hands, that is, by the Son and Holy Spirit, to whom also He said, 'Let Us make man.'" *Against Heresies*, book IV, preface, trans. Alexander Roberts and William Rambaut, *Ante-Nicene Fathers*, vol. 1., ed. Alexander Roberts, James Donaldson, and A. Cleveland Coxe (Buffalo, NY: Christian Literature Publishing Co., 1885); rev. and ed. for New Advent by Kevin Knight, www.newadvent.org/fathers/0103400.htm.
[19]Dietrich Bonhoeffer, *Creation and Fall: A Theological Interpretation of Genesis 1-3* (New York: The Macmillan Company, 1959), 37.
[20]Bonhoeffer, *Creation and Fall*, 37.

is that image. In keeping with the relational ontology articulated here, Jesus shares this image with his body, the church (Colossians 1:18). Barth writes, "This Christological equation has at the root an inclusive character, so that it is also an ecclesiological and therefore even an anthropological equation."[21]

Human persons and irrevocable dignity and worth. It is important to note in this context following Barth and Bonhoeffer that while qualities like reason, dominion or rule, and moral virtue play their parts in human existence, they do not eclipse the constitutive relational reality of the divine image in humanity. Those with greater capacities, such as reason, opportunities, and successes through rule and riches, do not possess the image to a greater extent than others. Moreover, while we can sin against God's image, we cannot lose it since we never had possession of it, as Barth asserts. It is, after all, a constitutive, covenantal relation.[22] Certainly moral qualities matter in keeping with God's call to his people to honor his name and obey his commands. But like reason, good character does not add to the image but features and expresses the image in all its glory. This constitutive relation is what grounds or confirms human dignity. What Christian Smith might frame in natural theological terms comes forth here in supernatural theological terms: one cannot add to (or subtract from) human worth or dignity. It is basic to one's person.[23] God's image, as revealed in Scripture, provides that basis.

Speaking of God's covenantal engagement with humanity, it is worth noting how God takes seriously naming his people. God also instructs us to honor God's name, which he reveals to Moses. This emphasis on naming safeguards against commodification of God and humanity in the Hebrew Scriptures. Commodification entails treating others as mere means to one's own ends, which involves using them, exchanging them for profit, and abusing them. R. Kendall Soulen develops this point in view of the divine name to striking effect.[24] In his essay "'Go Tell Pharaoh,'

---

[21]Barth, *Church Dogmatics*, III/1, 205.

[22]Barth, *Church Dogmatics*, III/1, 200.

[23]See chapter eight, titled "Human Dignity," in Christian Smith, *What Is a Person?* (Chicago: University of Chicago Press, 2010).

[24]R. Kendall Soulen, "'Go Tell Pharaoh,' Or, Why Empires Prefer a Nameless God," *Cultural Encounters: A Journal for the Theology of Culture* 1, no. 2 (Summer 2005): 49-59.

Or, Why Empires Prefer a Nameless God," Soulen references Edward Gibbon's line about forms of worship during the reign of the Caesars: the multiple expressions of worship were "considered by the people equally true, by the philosophers equally false, and by the magistrates equally useful."[25] A deity that was ultimately nameless could be commodified so that an empire's subjects could be commodified for the sake of an empire's expansion. Soulen draws attention to Moses' exchanges with Pharaoh, who was likely familiar with the doctrine of God as nameless and indefinable and may have had it in mind when dismissing Moses' claim: "Who is the LORD, that I should obey him and let Israel go? I do not know the LORD and I will not let Israel go" (Exodus 5:2). Soulen also alludes to the episode in the temple in Jerusalem involving Antiochus Epiphanies, who no doubt believed that Israel's God is simply a tribal nomination for the nameless deity to whom he sought to offer homage with pagan sacrifices at their altar. These pagan rulers soon realized that Israel and its God will not go quietly.[26]

We see how often empires and their rulers wanted to make a name for themselves at the expense of individuals and individual people groups throughout the Bible. Take for example Genesis 11. Though preceded and followed by genealogies in Genesis 10 and 11, as well as followed by God's calling of Abram in Genesis 12 involving his aim to make Abram's name great, the people who come together from across the earth are nameless. Those in power sought to make a name for themselves at the expense of others. As Sheila Tuller Keiter observes, "Building the Tower of Babel became of such paramount importance that bricks became more valuable than human beings." The builders ignored the "divine source" behind each individual and willingly sacrificed them to

---

[25]Edward Gibbon, *History of the Decline and Fall of the Roman Empire*, vol. 1 (London: Jones and Co., 1826), 18. See also James Dunn for his claim that Alexander the Great and the Greek and Roman rulers that followed him viewed the various deities of different religions as merely manifestations of the same divinities: James D. G. Dunn, *The Parting of the Ways: Between Christianity and Judaism and Their Significance for the Character of Christianity* (Philadelphia: Trinity Press International, 1991), 20. Another source to which Soulen draws attention is found in Robert M. Grant, *Gods and the One God* (Philadelphia: Westminster Press, 1986), 77. According to Soulen, Alexander's conquest of the entire eastern Mediterranean world gave widespread visibility and import in the Western world to the doctrine of divine namelessness. Soulen, "Go Tell Pharaoh," 51.

[26]Soulen, "Go Tell Pharaoh," 51-52.

the building project. And "in so doing, they challenged God's authority as creator."[27]

Something similar to the Babel account happens with Pharaoh's rule and the subjugation of the Jewish people as slaves. Their dehumanizing subjection was ultimately an attempt by Pharaoh to challenge God's rule and elevate himself over God's people. Pharaoh underestimated God's resolve to defend his people and judge Egypt as a nation.[28]

Interestingly, the Babel narrative and the exodus drama depict the rulers and their peoples as nameless. In striking contrast, God names his people. Exodus begins with a genealogy that accounts for the descendants of Abraham, Isaac, and Jacob. With the ascendance of the new Pharaoh the names disappear. Only with Moses' deliverance under Pharaoh's daughter and God's providential mercy is this trend reversed. In contrast, the biblical accounts choose to keep the Pharaoh and his daughter nameless. Egypt's dehumanizing subjugation of Israel involving namelessness leads to their own namelessness and undoing under God's judgment. For Keiter, the implications are clear: "One cannot deny the divine spirit in others without denying the divine spirit in all men. One cannot dehumanize others without dehumanizing one's self."[29]

Moving forward to the New Testament, Peter declares that in and through the name of Jesus (Acts 3:16, 4:7-12) he healed a nameless, lame beggar. This individual was someone for whom the governing authorities appeared to care little, except that his healing brought about massive interest in the apostolic message centered in the crucified and risen Jesus. While namelessness easily leads to dehumanization and commodification, the proclamation of exclusive salvation through the indispensable triune name revealed in Jesus leads to humanization for the nameless,

---

[27]Sheila Tuller Keiter, "Outsmarting God: Egyptian Slavery and the Tower of Babel," *Jewish Bible Quarterly* 41, no. 3 (2013): 202.

[28]Rashi makes this point in his commentary on Exodus 1:20: "Our Rabbis, however, interpreted [that Pharaoh said], Let us deal shrewdly with the Savior of Israel [thus interpreting לו as to him] by afflicting them [to die] with water, for He has already sworn that He would not bring a flood to the world. (But they [the Egyptians] did not understand that upon the whole world He would not bring [a flood] but He would bring it upon one nation[.] In an old Rashi manuscript.) from Sotah 11a]." Rashi, *Commentary*, Chabad.org, accessed on November 1, 2019, www.chabad.org/library/bible_cdo/aid/9862/showrashi/true/jewish/Chapter-1.htm.

[29]Keiter, "Outsmarting God," 202.

lame beggar and countless others: salvation is found in no one else, for there is no other name under heaven but Jesus by whom God saves people (Acts 4:12).

The Lord does not enslave or use people but liberates them. We are not mere means but ends in ourselves. The destruction of Babel and the humiliation of Pharaoh in the exodus are ultimately intended to liberate nameless peoples from oppressive rule, including Egyptians and others who went with Israel (Exodus 12:38). Israel is to deal graciously with aliens or strangers, as they were once themselves aliens in a foreign land (Exodus 22:21; one of the most striking examples of such mercy is found in the story of Ruth). The Law and the Prophets give clear and exact instructions on treating others fairly, especially those on the margins (see Deuteronomy 10:18; Zechariah 7:10). The Sabbath itself was intended as a mercy to provide all God's people with rest from exacting work. After all, they had experienced no rest from their labor under Pharaoh. And yet, its aim was distorted by the teachers of the Law as an exacting burden that kept them from acting mercifully toward the people entrusted to their care. Thus, Jesus goes to great lengths to heal people *on* the Sabbath. After all, humanity was not a means to an end of honoring the Sabbath; rather, the Sabbath was a means to an end of honoring the Son of Man as Lord of the Sabbath and humanity as the chief of God's works (Matthew 12:8; Mark 2:27; see also Mark 3:1-6).

Several traits characteristic of the image of God doctrine in Scripture bear on our understanding in this chapter of the human person. Physicality and spirituality or embodied spirit, relationality, autonomy, noninstrumentality (freed from Egypt) and nonrepeatability (known by name) all stand out in this discussion. Given the account of Jesus as the ultimate image of God in Scripture, there is also a teleological or eschatological component as God perfects us in Christ through the Spirit. As the ideal human, Jesus loves God with all his heart, soul, mind, and strength, and his neighbor as himself. Jesus is the Jewish apocalyptic Son of Man in the canonical Gospel accounts. He also manifests the ideal qualities of the Samaritan of astounding mercy in the parable of Luke 10:25-37.

Colin Gunton accounts for a variety of these motifs in his own theological treatment of the person created in God's image. For Gunton, to be "a created person" entails four key features: first, an "inescapable relation" to God through the Son and Spirit; second, a response of praise and thanksgiving to God with their entire being involving soul and body in freedom and love; third, mutually constitutive communal relations with the triune God and with one another as male and female and care for the good order of the entire creation. Here Gunton locates key aspects of human personality and our distinctive calling, including freedom, responsibility, and creativity. These features of personhood give rise to a fourth—namely, a personalist ethic that arises from this understanding of the image of God. Gunton writes,

> Finally, being in the image of God implies there, an ethic, according to which human life is ordered appropriately to both the personal and the non-personal creation. All are called to relations of love-in-freedom with others so imaged; all are called to represent God to the creation. This ethic is a consequence of being in the image, and, like the image itself, takes its orientation from the "vertical" relation of humankind to God.[30]

The triune God serves as the vertical dimension for our particular personalist conception of life and ethical inquiry. How does one bring that conception to bear on public discourse in a pluralistic society? In what follows, consideration will focus on the needed dialogical approach to personalist ethics given the entangled and complex web of perspectives and pursuits in our pluralistic age.

Horizontal. The preceding discussion arises from an account of the Judeo-Christian heritage and Christian theology. It is not that the Jewish and Christian Scriptures alone highlight various qualities of divine and human personhood. It is simply that biblical and theological explorations made a significant impact on the concept of personhood in the West. It is worth mentioning that one can find Buddhist, Confucianist, and Hindu personalist treatments.[31]

---

[30]Colin E. Gunton, *The Triune Creator: A Historical and Systematic Study*, New Studies in Constructive Theology (Grand Rapids, MI: Eerdmans, 1998), 210.

[31]Thomas D. Williams and Jan Olof Bengtsson, "Personalism," *The Stanford Encyclopedia of Philosophy*, Spring 2020 edition, ed. Edward N. Zalta, https://plato.stanford.edu/archives/spr2020/entries/personalism/.

Acknowledging and comparing personalist trajectories in various traditions is not without its challenges. Take, for example, the Jewish philosopher Martin Buber and the Protestant theologian Karl Barth. Both were personalists. Buber's concept of "I and Thou" finds resonance in Barth's analysis of the dialogical character of humanity.[32] While Barth wonders if certain non-Christian figures such as "the pagan Confucius, the atheist L. Feuerbach and the Jew M. Buber" have the same idea in mind when discussing this dialogical notion of humanity, he affirms Buber's and these other treatments.[33] Still, as Buber notes, Barth struggles in the midst of strong affirmation with whether this dialogical notion of humanity "could have grown on any other ground than the Christological (Jesus Christ as 'the man for his fellowmen and thus the image of God')." For his part, Buber applauds Barth's humane breadth of spirit and original explorations, while also highlighting their independence from one another as a Hasidic Jewish philosopher and a Protestant Christian theologian.[34]

The German philosopher Immanuel Kant also manifests personalist sensibilities. Take, for example, his categorical imperative that we should not treat people as mere means to ends but ends in themselves: "Act in such a way that you always treat humanity, whether in your own person or in the person of any other, never simply as a means but always at the same time as an end."[35] As in the case of Buber and Barth, Kant is downstream from the biblical tradition. Regardless of his own attempts to provide rational grounds for ethics apart from any revelation claims or emotional influences, Kant's thought reflects the Christian heritage of his parents. Alasdair MacIntyre claims that Kant's Lutheran heritage made an indelible impression on him. Kant inherited his morality from his pious parents and sought to put it on firm rational, moral grounds. However, Kant was not able to put his system on entirely rational foundation stones.

---

[32]See Martin Buber, *I and Thou*, 2nd ed., with a postscript by the author and trans. Ronald Gregor Smith (New York: Charles Scribner's Sons, 1958).

[33]Karl Barth, *Church Dogmatics*, III/2, *The Doctrine of Creation*, ed. G. W. Bromiley and T. F. Torrance (Edinburgh: T&T Clark, 1960), 277. See also 278.

[34]Martin Buber, "Afterword: The History of the Dialogical Principle," in *Between Man and Man*, trans. Ronald Gregor Smith (New York: The Macmillan Company, 1965), 222-24.

[35]Immanuel Kant, *Groundwork of the Metaphysics of Morals*, trans. H. J. Paton (New York: Harper & Row, 1964), 96.

For example, asserting that one can treat others as a mere means to one's own ends may lack virtue, but it is not inconsistent. It would also be consistent for a world made up entirely of egoists to treat one another as mere means to their own respective ends.[36] So, it is easier said than done to outline a moral strategy that safeguards against conceiving people as generic or homogeneous objects by reason alone.

No matter how hard it is to provide purely rational safeguards for human persons against objectifying and homogenizing forces, the Christian theologian operating in a pluralistic society should welcome whatever help she or he can get. More hands make less work, and the work to safeguard human persons and the world at large from disparagement and pulverization is quite intense and taxing. Moreover, given the distrust in many circles of Christendom, it is all the more important for Christians to engage from a humble, listening, and dialogical posture.

The full display of human depravity by Christian and non-Christian alike in our society has not undone the predominant sense of disgust and horror that most people feel when they experience abuse, that is, "feel used." No one in their right mind desires to endure exploitation, where others treat them as objects or tools or view them as mere numbers rather than view them as fundamentally unique and irreplaceable. It appears that we are all "wired" in this way. So, it would not prove detrimental to complement Judeo-Christian thought forms supporting personalism with what is deemed naturalist considerations. After all, we all look through a glass dimly. Only in the eschaton will we perceive divine and human personhood face-to-face with crystal clarity.

One of the most significant contributions to personalist thought in recent scholarship is sociologist Christian Smith's *What Is a Person?* Smith offers an extrabiblical account of the person that draws in part from Aristotelian teleology and evolutionary scientific thought forms. His aim is a noble one: to reframe the social sciences to account front and center for the importance of the person in their various research pursuits. Here is Smith's robust and multifaceted definition:

---

[36]Alasdair MacIntyre, *After Virtue*, 3rd ed. (Notre Dame, IN: University of Notre Dame Press, 2007), 44, 46-47.

What then is a person? By *person* I mean a conscious, reflexive, embodied, self-transcending center of subjective experience, durable identity, moral commitment, and social communication who—as the efficient cause of his or her own responsible actions and interactions—exercises complex capacities for agency and intersubjectivity in order to develop and sustain his or her own incommunicable self in loving relationships with other personal selves and with the nonpersonal world. That, in any case, is what a normal person is, a person who has developed normally.[37]

Apart from consideration of the vertical trinitarian framework articulated in Gunton's assessment of the human person (Smith is a Roman Catholic who embraces trinitarian thought forms[38]), I find here a great deal of overlap. While Gunton does not emphasize (but no doubt assumes) the rational and reflexive aspects of personhood given his focus on relationality, Gunton and Smith both account for human subjectivity, moral commitment, and social communication. Gunton also assumes or suggests durable identity, while both Smith and Gunton account for persons as responsible and free human agents operating in their embodied states in loving, harmonious relationships with fellow humans and the nonhuman world. Smith also guards against reductionism in the natural domain by discussing the evolutionary development and "emergence" of the person from "lower level entities," as well as the person's downward causation on "lower level entities."[39] It is important to point out that Smith's definition with its mention of "normal" does not lead him to discount "radically damaged" individuals as persons. They are persons, though Smith claims it is not a helpful move to somehow discount the difference between "normal" and "damaged" persons.[40]

---

[37]Smith, *What Is a Person?*, 61.
[38]For a defense of his approach in a learned and illuminating debate on his volume, see the exchange involving James K. A. Smith and Christian Smith in *Christian Scholar's Review*. Here is the order: James K. A. Smith, "The (Re)Turn to the Person in Contemporary Theory—a Review Essay," *Christian Scholar's Review*, vol. 40, no. 1 (2010): 77-92; Christian Smith, "'More Realism, Critically' —a Reply to James K. A. Smith, 'The (Re)Turn to the Person in Contemporary Theory,'" *Christian Scholar's Review*, vol. 40, no. 2 (2011): 205-10; James K. A. Smith, "Natural Law's Secularism?—a Response to Christian Smith," *Christian Scholar's Review*, vol. 40, 2 (2011): 211-15.
[39]Smith, *What Is a Person?*, 33, fig. 1; cf. 57, fig. 2.
[40]Smith, *What Is a Person?*, 82.

The last item to note by way of comparison is that, while Gunton does not make space for Aristotelian teleology or evolutionary thought forms in his theological treatment of human personhood, he does draw on his colleague John Zizioulas's understanding of person as ultimately an eschatological concept that will be realized in God's future kingdom. Perhaps it is fair to say that all persons, no matter their state of ability, or moral virtue for that matter, await perfection. Gunton states in this context, "Because creation is a project, that is to say, something to be perfected, being in the image of God is also being in movement to an end."[41] Shortly, I will turn to the metaphysical account of hope and eschatological ethics and its bearing on our personalist project. However, before doing so, it is important to develop further the "entangled ethics" motif.

Mention was made above that Smith offers an extrabiblical assessment of personhood given his secular audience for the volume. There is much that we find beneficial in his assessment of personhood and view his project in complementary terms. In this present volume, consideration of personhood and a personalist ethic will go in search of favorable dialogue partners across the ideological spectrum. Not all those constructive dialogue partners will be personalists, but nonetheless they will view humanity and all of life in noninstrumentalist and nonreductionist terms. Since we all look through a glass dimly and indwell a pluralistic society where there is not even a remote sense of consensus regarding ethical valuations, we must work as collaboratively as possible. I for one embrace a critical realist personalist account of epistemology, as does Smith.[42] I believe in objective truth and maintain we must make our best case for a given position (namely a personalist moral vision) in the public square of civil discourse and debate. I must also acknowledge that, based on human finitude and human depravity, we do not always perceive and argue rightly. Even when I maintain that the personalist position makes the best sense of life for virtuous human flourishing, those of other traditions or no tradition at all may object. In those cases (which are quite common), one must remain civil, patient, open to correction and new insight, even as one continues to reason

---

[41]Gunton, *Triune Creator*, 209.
[42]See for example, Smith, chapter seven, "Excursus: Getting to Truth," 207-19.

with others in the effort to present a personalist moral vision as most plausible and compelling.

I mentioned above that there is no consensus in moral deliberations, including about what is the common good, in society. MacIntyre puts it this way:

> The most striking feature of contemporary moral utterance is that so much of it is used to express disagreements, and the most striking feature of the debates in which these disagreements are expressed is their interminable character. I do not mean by this just that such debates go on and on and on—although they do—but also that they apparently can find no terminus. There seems to be no rational way of securing moral agreement in our culture.[43]

For his part, MacIntyre presents an Aristotelian and Thomistic account of virtue while critiquing deontological ethical systems of the rationalist sort as well as emotivist and intuitionist systems. I offer no such overarching ethical critique of given systems, but rather seek to navigate and engage a variety of ethical systems on particular topics in pursuit of our personalist moral vision. What guides me at every turn is the trinitarian conception of personhood and compatible and parallel ethical considerations wherever they might arise, as well as an interest in engaging deontological, consequentialist, and virtue ethical systems of thought at various junctures along the way. Certainly, the Judeo-Christian and trinitarian metaphysical account of personhood shapes my faith convictions and moral pursuits on the ten topics for ethical consideration set forth in parts two and three of this volume. Still, I choose to remain dialogical and open to collaborating wherever possible with proponents of various religious and philosophical ethical traditions in our entangled ethical world. The variety of positions, whether deontological (i.e., the good ideal), consequentialist (i.e., the good result) or teleological (i.e., the good or noble individual), may lead one to start at different places and end up at different destinations in our determinations. But the effort to pursue common ground for the sake of human flourishing is worth the effort. I will attempt to bring the

---

[43]MacIntyre, *After Virtue*, 6.

Christian faith to bear on ethical deliberations in a critically realist personalist manner. My hope is that while we all look through a glass dimly
now with fallen and fallible powers of faith, limited spiritual discernment
and reason, God will guide us so that someday together we shall see
face-to-face.

THE TRIUNE HOPE AND ESCHATOLOGICAL ETHICS

We all long for more. No matter how one views our being "made for
more"—as created in the image of God and/or through procreation and
evolutionary forces—we are called, predisposed, or wired to pursue that
good that completes us as humans. Of course, there is no consensus in
our pluralistic society on what that good end or telos is. For its part, the
biblical personalist tradition presents the Great Commandments—love
of God with all our heart, soul, mind, and strength (the highest good)
and love of neighbor as ourselves (the common good)—as that twofold
end (Mark 12:28-34). Even so, knowing something to be one's end and
successfully realizing or acquiring it are two different matters entirely.
Our fallen human condition gets in the way. Just as the complexities and
ambiguities of life might lead some to cynicism regarding the possibility
of ever finding out the truth about the good and all it entails, so the fra-
gility and depravity that mar our human condition can lead us to pessimism. Augustine's reflections on the tortured soul, cheated soul, diseased soul, and blessed soul have a bearing on this theme of eschatological
hope. The tortured soul sees the good but cannot attain it. The cheated
soul believes he or she has the good but is deceived. The diseased soul is
the one who has the good but does not realize or cherish it. In contrast,
the blessed soul is the one who has the good and treasures it. For most,
if not all, this blessed state of existence awaits us on the other side of the
veil.[44] No matter how hard we try, we find that we cannot attain that
blessed end on our own. Bob Dylan, who wrote a song about dreaming
of Saint Augustine,[45] sings in "Blind Willie McTell" of God being in

---

[44]Saint Augustine, *Of the Morals of the Catholic Church*, in *Nicene and Post-Nicene Fathers*, 1st series,
    vol. 4, ed. Philip Schaff, trans. Richard Stothert (Buffalo, NY: Christian Literature Publishing Co.,
    1887), III/4. Rev. and ed. for New Advent by Kevin Knight; www.newadvent.org/fathers/1401.htm.
[45]Bob Dylan, "I Dreamed I Saw St. Augustine," track 3 on *John Wesley Harding*, Columbia Records,
    1967.

heaven and how we all aspire to want to be like God. However, down here on earth, the only things that appear to be real are greed and power and our "corruptible seed."[46] How will we ever make it to heaven, or bring heaven to earth? For all their differences, the Roman Catholic, Orthodox, and Protestant traditions would agree that we cannot lift ourselves up by our own bootstraps and attain perfection. The God of all grace and mercy must lead the way. God must align our hearts with what the highest good and common good are and energize us to realize that end or telos for which we were made and thereby experience the blessed life. The triune God who is the hope of the world will make all things right. As Martin Luther King Jr. declared, quoting from James Russell Lowell's poem, the cross on which the Word of Truth hangs is "the scaffold" that "sways the future." So, too, "the arc of the moral universe is long, but it bends toward justice"[47] (*vertical*). In view of the triune God who is our inspiring and energizing hope, we pursue our personalist moral vision and telos through entangled ethical inquiry in our pluralistic society (*horizontal*).

Vertical. Ours is an entangled, messy world made up of many complex and often competing views. It is also a world that is messed up. According to Christian Scripture, the triune God works in our midst in less-than-ideal conditions with less-than-ideal ethical subjects in pursuit of perfection. To use Irenaeus's language, God works through his two hands, the Son and the Spirit, to transform history from the inside out.

Before I proceed further in this section, it would be helpful to pause and reflect further on the use of the terms *vertical* and *horizontal*. As already noted, in this chapter I am dividing each of the respective sections on faith, hope, and love into two parts: vertical and horizontal.

---

[46]Bob Dylan, "Blind Willie McTell," vol. 3/14, *The Bootleg Series Volumes 1–3 (Rare & Unreleased) 1961–1991*, Columbia Records, 1991 (orig. released 1983).

[47]Martin Luther King Jr., "Why I am Opposed to the War in Vietnam," YouTube video, 22:48, quote starts at 19:55, "Non-corporate News," January 11, 2007, www.youtube.com/watch?v=b80Bsw0UG -U. This is an audio recording of Martin Luther King Jr.'s speech given at Ebenezer Baptist Church, Atlanta, on April 30, 1967. For the printed version of the original address, refer here: Martin Luther King Jr., "Beyond Vietnam," in *A Call to Conscience: The Landmark Speeches of Dr. Martin Luther King, Jr.*, ed. Clayborne Carson and Kris Shepard (New York: Warner Books, 2001). The full poem by James Russell Lowell can be found here: "The Present Crisis" (number 128), *Yale Book of American Verse*, ed. Thomas R. Lounsbury (New Haven, CT: Yale University Press, 1912), Bartleby.com, 1999; www.bartleby.com/102/ (accessed on 12/20/2016).

Vertical does not necessarily entail supernatural in contrast to natural. It can simply mean ideal in contrast to the natural or normal state of affairs. In what follows, I will take a look at three figures—Jesus, the historical Buddha, and Aristotle—in order to present how "vertical" as an ideal state may operate, as well as to shine light on the particular divine personalist ideal revealed in Jesus' teaching and activity.

Jesus certainly had in mind a heaven and a heavenly Father, as well as a kingdom of heaven that, while inaugurated in his person and teaching, nonetheless awaits consummation. If we extend consideration of "vertical" to other traditions in our entangled world of ethical systems, we find that the historical Buddha bracketed off consideration of a god or gods as well as a heavenly domain. His way of thinking was a-theistic (not to be equated with Western notions of atheism). Nirvana is a transcendent or ideal dimension free from the grasping state of suffering and recurring cycle of rebirth. Aristotle certainly entertained notions of deity. However, the gods on Aristotle's view are exclusively intellectual realities,[48] whose wisdom we would do well to emulate in our pursuit of perfection in the Greek city-state. However, there is no sense of a personal relationship with these gods, as in Jesus' conception of God as a heavenly Father. At best, we find with Aristotle an Unmoved Mover.

Each of these three figures entertained teleological accounts of perfection. More will be said about their respective teleological accounts of perfection in the "horizontal" section to follow. Such perfection for Jesus entails loving as God loves. 1 Corinthians 13 provides a beautiful account of what love entails on an interpersonal level. Such love is eternal. The ultimate hope for Christians entails the conviction that such love will be realized in our human experience. More will be said on what Christian love entails in the next section.

The ideal standard of perfection for the New Testament is found in the triune personal God, as expressed in the divine law of the Sermon on the Mount. In contrast, the ideal standard for discerning perfection and imperfection in Buddhism and in Aristotle is a natural form of law. For Buddhism, this law is karma. For Aristotle, it is natural law, which is a

---

[48]Leslie Stevenson, David L. Haberman, and Peter Matthews Wright, *Twelve Theories of Human Nature*, 6th ed. (New York: Oxford University Press, 2013), 113.

form of judgment that takes shape in concrete manifestations in political communities rather than a set of principles or standards that we apply unilaterally to every situation.[49]

Regarding the Buddhist conception of natural law or karma, leading Buddhist scholar Walpola Rahula claims the following:

> The theory of karma should not be confused with so-called "moral justice" or "reward and punishment." The idea of moral justice, or reward and punishment, arises out of the conception of a supreme being, a God, who sits in judgment, who is a law-giver and who decides what is right and wrong. The term "justice" is ambiguous and dangerous, and in its name more harm than good is done to humanity. The theory of karma is the theory of cause and effect, of action and reaction; it is a natural law, which has nothing to do with the idea of justice or reward and punishment. Every volitional action produces its effects or results.[50]

Rahula claims that ambiguity results from belief in a supreme being sitting in judgment. Some theists have also raised concern over God operating in an arbitrary manner and have proposed that God is subject to the moral laws of the universe. While I share the concern over any law being arbitrarily imposed, I maintain that God does not operate in an arbitrary manner. The moral laws of the universe flow from his character, which are on display in the life and work of Jesus Christ as disclosed in the Bible. There is nothing arbitrary about Jesus' life story. He is constant in all his ways, as the ultimate revelation of God, the incarnation of what Greek philosophy often referred to as the True, the Good, and the Beautiful.

Moreover, I take great comfort in the biblical conviction that the moral ground, grid, and goal of the universe is personal and relational. The Father grounds justice, the Son embodies it, and the Spirit completes or perfects it. There is nothing arbitrary about this personal God's love, in contrast to certain Buddhist critiques. It is centered in the reality of Jesus Christ as gracious and truthful. Contrary to impersonal karma, God's judgment is very personal though constant in

[49]Bernard Yack, "Natural Right and Aristotle's Understanding of Justice," *Political Theory* 18, no. 2 (May, 1990): 216-37.
[50]See Walpola Rahula, *What the Buddha Taught*, 2nd ed. (New York: Grove Press, 1974), 32.

keeping with his covenantal purposes revealed in Jesus. God's personal judgment signifies that we are personally responsible. We are not things. We have dignity. Contrary to the view that the Judeo-Christian tradition enslaves people, we find here the fundamental basis for personal and interpersonal freedom.

Various philosophers, theologians, and ethicists have eschatological visions. Plato taught that through the process of anamnesis or recollection, we reawaken and clearly perceive the eternal forms in which we participate. Our souls participate in the eternal forms of truth, goodness, and beauty beyond the cycle of reincarnation. Irenaeus wrote on the recapitulation or transformation of history through God's incarnate Son and the outpoured Spirit. Immanuel Kant presented the ideas of the existence of God, immortality of the soul, and coming judgment as postulates of reason in the effort to safeguard morality. Friedrich Nietzsche set forth the doctrine of eternal recurrence, whereby we will to live each moment of every day as if we will experience this same life forever. In our secular age, space exploration can serve as a contemporary, secular eschatology, as will be developed in the final chapter of this volume. The historical Buddha did not appear to hold to the idea of an afterlife, but rather an end to rebirth after life with the realization of nirvana. Similarly, Aristotle rejected the Platonic idea of reincarnation. The soul's existence ends with the termination of physical life. Perfection is the pursuit of a transcendent ideal in this life. Further to what was stated above in the case of Irenaeus's doctrine of recapitulation, Jesus' eschatological vision involved the inbreaking of God's kingdom in his life and ministry and the consummation of that perfect state with his return at the climax of history in the fullness of the Spirit. I will return to a comparison of Jesus, Buddha, and Aristotle under "horizontal" below to address their respective conceptions of teleological perfection. For now, we will unpack how Jesus' Beatitudes in the Sermon on the Mount present us with a view of "more" as eschatological perfection.

There are different views of perfection and what "more" entails. Sometimes we realize that the "more" is not what we had been looking or hungering and thirsting for in life. For Jesus, the more is "righteousness." Sometimes the "more" is less, as we find in the following Beatitudes:

"Blessed are the poor in spirit"; "Blessed are those who mourn"; "Blessed are the meek" (Matthew 5:3-5). The kingdom of the personal God whose name is disclosed in Jesus of Nazareth as Lord looks very different from the empire of nameless deity. Jesus' view of "more" entails a radically different conception of reality than what is found in the *Pax Romana*, or peace of Rome.[51]

Jesus inaugurates God's kingdom in the shadow of Rome's empire. In contrast to Rome's empire that blesses the rich in spirit, Jesus' kingdom blesses the poor in spirit (Matthew 5:3). In contrast to Rome's empire that blesses the comfortable, Jesus' kingdom blesses those who mourn (Matthew 5:4). In contrast to Rome's empire that blesses those displaying violent strength, Jesus' kingdom blesses the meek (Matthew 5:5). In contrast to Rome's empire that blesses those who are already satisfied and possess all that the world has to offer, Jesus' kingdom blesses those who hunger not for stuff, but for justice and righteousness (Matthew 5:6). In contrast to Rome's empire that blesses those who are merciless and retributive, Jesus' kingdom blesses those who are merciful (Matthew 5:7). In contrast to Rome's empire that blesses those who revel in lust, greed, and vengeance, Jesus' kingdom blesses the pure of heart (Matthew 5:8). In contrast to Rome's empire that blesses those who keep Rome's violent peace, Jesus' kingdom blesses those who make peace between warring factions (Matthew 5:9). In contrast to Rome's empire that blesses those who persecute the righteous, Jesus' kingdom blesses those who are persecuted for righteousness (Matthew 5:10).

Blessed are the poor in spirit. They don't see themselves as those who have arrived in terms of personhood. They need God's interpersonal intervention to attain perfection. Theirs is the kingdom of heaven. Blessed are those who mourn. They lament their instrumentalist inclination and the world system's preoccupation with impersonal forces of commodification and mechanization. They will be comforted. Blessed are the meek. They guard against exercising uncontrollable power to seize the earth and

---

[51]For discussions of Jesus' peace and the *Pax Romana*, see Douglas R. A. Hare, *Matthew*, Interpretation (Louisville, KY: Westminster John Knox, 1993), 42; Jürgen Moltmann, *The Crucified God: The Cross of Christ as the Foundation and Criticism of Christian Theology* (Minneapolis: Fortress, 1993), 136-45; and John Oakesmith, *The Religion of Plutarch: A Pagan Creed of Apostolic Times* (New York: Longmans, Green, 1902), 79-80.

its bounty and to divide and conquer. They will inherit the earth. Blessed are those who hunger and thirst for righteousness. They do not treat people and creation as impersonal means to their own self-satisfaction. They will be satisfied. Blessed are the merciful. They see their own need for mercy in the other needing their mercy. They will receive mercy. Blessed are the pure in heart. They do not conceive eye for an eye judgment and pursue retribution against their enemy. They do not "other" the other as less than their in-group but see everyone as interpersonally connected, including those whom they would otherwise destroy. They will see God. Blessed are the peacemakers. They reject efforts to keep the peace when it is indifferent, violent, and oppressive in nature. They pursue peace with those who are very different rather than discount and seek to destroy them. These peacemakers will be called sons and daughters of God. Blessed are those who are persecuted for righteousness—the kind of righteousness on display in the Beatitudes and Sermon on the Mount. They are willing to suffer personally for Jesus' personalist vision. Theirs is the kingdom of heaven here on earth.[52] They contend against what King calls a racialized, economically exploitative, and militarized world. They seek to move from a culture of things to a culture of persons as they follow Jesus, who is the decentered deity. He is decentered in that he turns everything inside out and upside down from his cross which is the scaffold that frames history. Perched on his shoulders on the cross, we see how we are made for more than what the impersonal, enslaving or commodifying, and mechanistic world system has to offer.

Notice how the first and last Beatitudes of "poor in spirit" and "persecuted for righteousness" bookend the others with "theirs is the kingdom of heaven." It is not that Jesus' followers bring about the kingdom through their actions. Rather, Jesus, who is their Lord, who reveals their spiritual poverty, and on account of whom they are persecuted for righteousness,

---

[52]See these and related themes at greater length in Paul Louis Metzger, *Beatitudes, Not Platitudes: Jesus' Invitation to the Good Life* (Eugene, OR: Cascade, 2018). For a definitive study on Matthew's Gospel, which includes detailed consideration of the Sermon on the Mount, see Frederick Dale Bruner, *Matthew: A Commentary*, vol. 1, *The Christbook, Matthew 1–12*, rev. and exp. ed. (Grand Rapids, MI: Eerdmans, 2007). For a leading text that seeks to approach major ethical issues from the vantage point of the Sermon on the Mount, see David P. Gushee and Glen H. Stassen, *Kingdom Ethics: Following Jesus in Contemporary Context*, 2nd ed. (Grand Rapids, MI: Eerdmans, 2017).

brings it about in their lives. As a result, they will be comforted as they mourn with him, inherit the earth as they are meek with him, be satisfied as they hunger and thirst for righteousness with him, receive mercy as they are merciful with him, see God as they are pure of heart with him, and be called children of God as they are peacemakers with him. Everything flows from his being with them—God with them, Immanuel (Matthew 1:23).

In view of him, there can be no sense of Aristotle's virtue of greatness of soul, which entails "being worthy of great things and being conscious of it." As one finds here:

> It is not universally agreed that greatness of soul is a virtue: the "beatitudes" in Jesus' Sermon on the Mount, "Blessed are the poor in spirit . . ." and "Blessed are the meek . . ." (Matthew 5:3-5), strongly suggest the contrary. Yet Nietzsche, in the late nineteenth century, fiercely rejected Christian humility and recommended something like Aristotelian greatsouledness instead.[53]

Nietzsche also rejected Christian love of neighbor, which Aristotle would also have found difficult to accept (unless that neighbor is of the noble, virtuous class), as we will note in the section to follow on embodied love.

MacIntyre acknowledges that Aristotle's account of the virtues differs substantially in content from the New Testament's depiction of what he terms virtues. He also claims that Aristotle "would certainly not have admired Jesus Christ and he would have been horrified by St. Paul." Still, MacIntyre maintains that the New Testament account of the virtues "has the same logical and conceptual structure as Aristotle's account." Such "parallelism," which entailed the attainment of the human telos through the exercise and internalization of virtues, made it possible for Saint Thomas Aquinas to set forth a synthesis of Aristotle and the New Testament.[54] I will briefly note this presumed parallelism at a later point in the "horizontal" section to which we now turn.

Horizontal. We mentioned at the outset of this section on hope that, as Dylan sang, we all want what belongs to God, presumably such

---

[53]Stevenson, Haberman, and Wright, *Twelve Theories of Human Nature*, 109.
[54]MacIntyre, *After Virtue*, 184.

qualities as righteousness and justice. Still, all we seem to find here on earth is corruption. Things are rather messed up here below. But that does not or should not deter us from pursuing perfection.

Consideration of advance, progress, and the pursuit of perfection drives the human spirit and imagination. Accounts of eschatology (that is, the theory of last things or the end times) and teleology (involving the end or telos for which something exists) capture human attention. Hope and the longing for freedom from senseless suffering and evil (natural or moral) account for many of these trajectories, whether they be theistic, atheistic, or nontheistic in scope.

It is worth noting here that Darwinian evolution teaches that humans developed from other, simpler life forms. In fact, all of life for Darwin has a common ancestry, possibly having emerged from some "warm little pond," as he wrote in a letter to J. D. Hooker in 1871. Still, given that life has developed in increasingly complex ways over the ages, evolution does not put humans on the same level with gnats or apes. Regardless of what one believes about evolution as a theory, the theory does not equate humanity—or place it on the same level—with other life forms. For all the possible connections, the differences are more than nominal. Evolution does not stand still. Rather, it proceeds generally toward greater complexity, *advancing* humanity beyond gnats and apes.[55]

While it is important to account for the origin and nature of the human species, such consideration should not be taken as determinative of how the human species ought to operate, as if human nature determined its ethical trajectory, that is, our species' moral telos. Christian Smith puts it well in his articulation of a teleological orientation to morality that accounts for naturalistic foundations: speaking of his own system, he writes, "As a normative system, this teleological approach is naturalistic in the sense that it expects to understand the *ought* as arising from the *is*, but it is not naturalistic in the sense of morality authorizing as ought that which is."[56] This caveat is quite instructive for our moral telos: just because we

---

[55]See Conor Cunningham, *Darwin's Pious Idea: Why the Ultra-Darwinists and Creationists Both Get It Wrong* (Grand Rapids, MI: William B. Eerdmans, 2010), 6-7. For works by Darwin, see Charles Darwin, *On the Origin of Species*, Penguin Classics (New York: Penguin, 2009); Charles Darwin, *The Descent of Man*, Penguin Classics (New York: Penguin, 2004).
[56]Smith, *What Is a Person?*, 486.

have a tendency to dehumanize those members of our species who appear to threaten those members we love, we ought not to dehumanize and exercise cruelty. The cognitive jump of friendliness or cooperation that equipped *Homo sapiens* to thrive, what Brian Hare and Vanessa Woods refer to as the "self-domestication theory," can easily go astray toward domination of those we deem dangerous outsiders.[57] Smith's account guards against intuitionism's misinterpretation of Hume to separate completely "is" from "ought," on the one hand,[58] and the move to frame natural process as the authoritative basis for ethical deliberations and practice, as often appears to be the case in evolutionary ethics, on the other hand.[59]

Darwin may have been divided in his own subjective judgment of whether there is progress in evolution.[60] But this should not come as too great a surprise. After all, progress does not always mean better—or better from every angle. For example, it is not always the smartest, or even the most virtuous people who win out according to evolution, but rather those who produce the most offspring that achieve adulthood and propagate.[61]

Darwin saw senseless waste and suffering in nature, which led him eventually to question God's providential involvement in what he took to be the evolutionary process. In addition to concerns over animals with useless appendages and those that experienced meaningless suffering, Darwin experienced the death of his eleven-year-old daughter as senseless.[62] It was not specifically Darwin's theory of evolution that led him to unbelief, but rather, the problem of evil, as he understood it. He

---

[57]Brian Hare and Vanessa Woods, *Survival of the Friendliest: Understanding Our Origins and Rediscovering Our Common Humanity* (New York: Penguin: 2020).

[58]See Smith's critique of G. E. Moore in *What Is a Person?*, 388-93.

[59]For examples of this move, see E. O. Wilson, *On Human Nature*, 2nd ed. (Cambridge, MA: Harvard University Press, 2004); *The Social Conquest of Earth* (New York: Liveright, 2012).

[60]See Cunningham, *Darwin's Pious Idea*, 138-39.

[61]Stevenson, Haberman, and Wright, *Twelve Theories of Human Nature*, 251.

[62]Darwin also questioned the doctrine of God's providential care in view of the doctrine of hell. Darwin could not imagine that his unbelieving father and brother as well as many friends, having died, would be banished to everlasting torment. See the following work for discussions of various contributing factors that shaped Darwin's views of God's relation to the world and eventual loss of faith: C. Michael Patton, "The Reason Darwin Left the Faith (And How We Can Learn Through His Pain)"; https://credohouse.org/blog/the-reason-darwin-left-the-faith; see also Karl W. Giberson, *How to Be a Christian and Believe in Evolution*, foreword by Francis Collins (New York: HarperCollins, 2008).

could not swallow something akin to Leibniz's "best of all possible worlds" theodicy.

It is not the place here to debate the possible merits of theodicy, but to account for different pursuits of the human telos in the face of imperfection, corruption, and suffering. Further to what was stated in the previous section, Buddhist lore chronicles that the young Indian prince Shakyamuni left his palatial confines to experience the world at large. He encountered great suffering and devoted his energies to liberate humanity from its plight, which resulted in the "Four Noble Truths" and "Noble Eightfold Path."[63] Heinrich Zimmer sets forth the following as the "Four Noble Truths" of Buddhism: first, "All li[f]e is sorrowful"; second, "the cause of suffering is ignorant craving"; third, "the suppression of suffering can be achieved"; and fourth, "the way is the Noble Eightfold Path." The Noble Eightfold Path involves "Right View, Right Aspiration, Right Speech, Right Conduct, Right Means of Livelihood, Right Endeavor, Right Mindfulness, and Right Contemplation."[64]

For evolution, "advance" is by way of natural selection. For Buddhism, at least for Shakyamuni, advance is by way of mental selection or meditation. For Aristotle, it is by way of moral, virtuous self-determination or habituation. One should not take from this assessment that there is no overlap. Emergence of one's person should account for how biological drives operate in tandem with mental and volitional activity. Moreover, intellectual and volitional operations can work in sync, as they do in Buddhist and Aristotelian systems. In other words, advance or progress or perfection should account for psychosomatic unity, though left to itself evolution on Darwin's account will not esteem mental acuity or virtue, only fertility.

Many of us realize that we have a long way to go to attain perfection. Buddhism's teaching of the Four Noble Truths and the eightfold path signifies one significant example of what perfection is and how to attain

---

[63]For a fascinating account of the Buddha's life, see Tenzin Chögyel, *The Life of the Buddha*, trans. with intro. and notes by Kurtis R. Schaeffer, Penguin Classics (Penguin Books, 2015).

[64]Heinrich Zimmer, "Buddhahood," in *The Ways of Religion: An Introduction to the Major Traditions*, ed. Roger Eastman, 3rd ed. (New York: Oxford University Press, 1999), 84. For a classic Buddhist text that presents the Four Noble Truths and Eightfold Path, see *Wisdom of the Buddha: The Unabridged Dhammapada*, trans. and ed. F. Max Müller (Mineola, NY: Dover, 2000).

it. Aristotle's *Nicomachean Ethics* provides an alternative. The Sermon on the Mount presents us with still another option. The list goes on. The positive form of comparison is that each paradigm pursues perfection teleologically on our historical or temporal plane that takes us beyond mere stuff and frivolity. However, we cannot go it alone. Jesus offers a personalist moral framework in which we participate in God's interpersonal operations, whereby we become more fully personal.

For all their differences from one another, the historical Buddha, Aristotle, and Jesus present ethical considerations of hoped-for realization or fulfillment in historical or this-worldly terms. While Jesus certainly envisions the realization of the kingdom of heaven, the kingdom breaks into history and culminates in history, not outside it. Each figure addresses those roadblocks that stand in the way of humanity realizing their telos. However, only Jesus accounts for the fundamental origin of our problem. Buddha focuses solely on the resulting problem. Each in their own way, Christianity and Buddhism deal with a problem in our condition and how to remedy it. For Jesus, according to historical orthodox theology, the problem centers on rebellion against God and the remedy entails repentance and obedient faith in Jesus' person and work along with reliance on the Spirit. For the historical Buddha, the problem entails grasping, which involves desire and ignorance of our ephemeral existence. The Buddha did not concern himself with questions of origins, but simply one's life situation.[65] The remedy entails a nongrasping approach to life found in mindfulness and right practices. The person of the Buddha serves humanity as a *Bodhisattva*, that is, as one who detains entrance into nirvana, which is not a "pure land" as in later Buddhist thought, but freedom from suffering and the cycle of rebirth associated with grasping. The Buddha's aim in detaining entrance into nirvana is compassionate, namely, to instruct and model for others the path to enlightenment. However, unlike Jesus, the historical Buddha did not

---

[65]A classic statement along these lines is Buddha's analogy of the poisoned arrow. Metaphysical questions do not address the fundamental problem of suffering that requires immediate attention. One must allow the surgeon to pull out the poisoned arrow rather than first seek to find out who shot it. Otherwise, the wounded party will die. See "*Cūlamālunkya Sutta*, The Shorter Discourse to Mālunkyāputta," in *The Middle Length Discourses of the Buddha*, trans., ed., and rev. Bhikkhu Bodhi, 4th ed. (Somerville, MS: Wisdom Publications, 2015), 533-36.

position himself as the object of salvation or the means through whom one attains nirvana. Aristotle, on the other hand, was far more positive: he focused on our end or telos for human fulfillment or flourishing (translations for the word *eudaimonia*) and how to achieve it through the formation of virtues, which are means between extremes, in contrast to vices.[66] The moral virtues are courage, moderation, liberality, magnificence, greatness of soul, ambition, gentleness, truthfulness, wittiness and tact, friendliness, and justice.[67] There is no iconic figure, as in the case of Jesus or the Buddha, who plays a fundamental, paradigmatic role in Aristotle's thought. His focus is simply on the formation of the virtuous person, whom he no doubt equates with certain members of the noble class in the Greek city-state.

What is the telos or ideal of such eschatological perfection? Is it beyond us? Is it personal? Impersonal? For the New Testament, the teleological or eschatological ideal is personal—Jesus of Nazareth and a community of people who participate in his virtuous life. He is the image of God and firstborn over all creation (Colossians 1:15). He has preeminence over all things as the firstborn from the dead (Colossians 1:18). He shares that image with his body the church (Colossians 1:18). The church is called to serve as a first fruits of all humanity and creation. Jesus declared, "Do not think that I have come to abolish the Law or the Prophets; I have not come to abolish them but to fulfill them" (Matthew 5:17). He also asserted, "Be perfect, therefore, as your heavenly Father is perfect," which is asserted in the context of enemy love and which he modeled supremely (Matthew 5:48). Jesus images his Father perfectly (Colossians 1:15; Hebrews 1:3). This personalist model of perfection looks quite different from Aristotle's noble class of people who model "greatness of soul."

When will we attain perfection? We cannot attain Jesus' level of perfection in the present. We must keep pursing him in community as the embodiment of the kingdom to the end. The canonical Gospels devote

---

[66]Look to the helpful "Overview of the Moral Virtues and Vices," in Aristotle's *Nicomachean Ethics*, trans. Robert C. Bartlett and Susan D. Collins (Chicago: The University of Chicago Press, 2011), 303-4. See also Stevenson, Haberman, and Wright, *Twelve Theories of Human Nature*, 105-6.
[67]See Aristotle's *Nicomachean Ethics*, book 2, chapter 7, 36-38.

a great deal of attention to eschatology by way of God's kingdom. Interestingly, the kingdom has a present tense and future tense aspect to it. The kingdom is now and not yet.[68] The New Testament presents Jesus' first coming as inaugurating the eschatological kingdom and his second coming at the end of the age as completing or realizing it. God intends for Jesus' community of faith in the present to serve as a concrete manifestation of the kingdom, but not to presume it has arrived in its fullness. The kingdom awaits consummation. There is eschatological remainder. To reference Zizioulas's notion again, human personhood awaits perfection in the eschatological future, at the culmination of our union with Jesus as the eschatological human at the end of history.

How will we attain this ideal? By human effort? Divine intervention? Both? Surely, we are to cultivate purity of heart if we would see God. But how can we ever attain purity without God making clear how impure of heart we are and surgically correcting our spiritual vision? God must intervene and repivot or redirect humanity in Jesus. Karl Barth argues along these lines in his critique of the Rule of Benedict. It is not obedience to a certain rule that "opens up" the kingdom of God, Barth says, contrary to what Benedict wrote. Rather, it is God's power "in the death of Jesus Christ" alone that empowers human beings to live obediently.[69]

Such perfection can only result from the Spirit's intervention in our lives. Following Barth and others in this tradition, including Dietrich Bonhoeffer and Helmut Thielicke, Donald Bloesch writes in his discussion of "Evangelical Contextualism" that "virtues indicate the unfolding of human potentialities, whereas graces are the manifestations of the work of the Holy Spirit within us." Bloesch adds, "It is not the

---

[68]For a discussion of the "now" and "not yet" aspects of the eschatological kingdom, see George Eldon Ladd, *The Gospel of the Kingdom: Scriptural Studies in the Kingdom of God* (Grand Rapids, MI: Eerdmans, 1959).

[69]Karl Barth, *Church Dogmatics*, IV/2, *The Doctrine of Reconciliation*, ed. G. W. Bromiley and T. F. Torrance (Edinburgh: T&T Clark, 1958), 18. While the following does not detract from our argument or Barth's own take about the proper order of faith and works, still Nicholas Healy's comment is instructive for students of Benedict's Rule: "Barth cites what he believed to be the last line of Benedict's Rule: *Facientibus haec regna patebunt superna* ("the heavenly kingdom will be opened up to those who follow this rule"). The argument has since been made that it was a somewhat later addition and does not reflect Benedict's own view." Nicholas M. Healy, "Thomas Aquinas and Karl Barth on the Christian Life: Similarity and Differences," *Scottish Journal of Theology* 69, no. 3 (August 2016): 261-62n15.

fulfillment of human powers but the transformation of the human heart that is the emphasis in an authentically evangelical ethics."[70]

While Bloesch does not specifically mention Luther, he certainly belongs to this tradition. For Luther, "We do not become righteous by doing righteous deeds but, having been made righteous, we do righteous deeds."[71] Luther's colleague Philip Melanchthon speaks of the same issue in this manner: "Internal affections are not in our power, for by experience and habit we find that the will (*voluntas*) cannot in itself control love, hate, or similar affections, but affection is overcome by affection."[72] Participation in Christ's life is the ground of the Christian life. As Luther scholar Heiko Oberman puts it, far from being an uncertain goal, union with Christ is a sure ground.[73] To return to the Beatitudes: the very first of the Beatitudes states that those who realize they are spiritually poor, empty, or bankrupt are blessed.[74] On this reading, they have no capacity to effect the qualities that follow in the remaining Beatitudes. Nor are they able to bring about the envisioned embodiment of grace on display in Jesus' teaching in the Sermon on the Mount. Who can love their enemies? As noted above, evolution wires our species to treat those we find threatening in cruel and inhumane terms, while preserving the filial bonds with members of our inner circle. But Jesus calls on us to love our enemies and pray for those who persecute us, showing ourselves to be children of our heavenly Father. This is what is entailed for those who would be perfect as our heavenly Father is perfect (see Matthew 5:43-48).

---

[70]Donald G. Bloesch, *Freedom for Obedience: Evangelical Ethics in Contemporary Times* (San Francisco: Harper & Row, Publishers, 1987), 191.

[71]Martin Luther, "Disputation Against Scholastic Theology," in *Martin Luther's Basic Theological Writings*, ed. Timothy F. Lull, foreword by Jaroslav Pelikan (Minneapolis: Fortress, 1989), 16.

[72]See Philipp Melanchthon's 1521 edition (in contrast to the 1543 edition) of the *Loci Communes Theologici* in *Melanchthon and Bucer*, ed. Wilhelm Pauck, The Library of Christian Classics: Ichthus Edition (Philadelphia: The Westminster Press, 1969), 27.

[73]Heiko A. Oberman, *The Dawn of the Reformation: Essays in Late Medieval and Early Reformation Thought* (Grand Rapids, MI: Eerdmans, 1992), 124.

[74]John R. W. Stott reasoned that "poor in spirit" conveys the idea of "spiritual bankruptcy" in *The Message of the Sermon on the Mount*, The Bible Speaks Today (Downers Grove, IL: InterVarsity Press, 1978), 39. It is worth noting at this juncture that Martin Luther King Jr.'s holistic spirituality was also formed through a prayer life that revolved around a daily recognition of being poor in spirit. Lewis V. Baldwin, "The Attuning Spirit: Martin Luther King Jr. and the Circle of Prayer," in *Revives My Soul Again: The Spirituality of Martin Luther King Jr.*, ed. Lewis V. Black and Victor Anderson (Minneapolis: Fortress, 2018), 135-68.

Given this envisioned state of perfection, we must rely completely on Jesus Christ, who models this reality in collaboration with the Spirit—through whom Jesus also lives—to produce these graces, or what others call biblical virtues, in our midst. That said, the Spirit works through natural processes and supernatural processes alike. Regarding the former, the Genesis account reflects on the Spirit hovering over the waters and God breathing the spirit of life into humanity (Genesis 1:2; 2:7). Grace grounds, transforms, and perfects nature. Thus, we need to go deeper than the materialists, who do not account for vitalism (that is, a vital principle or force beyond physiochemical factors that animates objects), but operate solely according to inert, mechanistic frames of reference. Acknowledging the Spirit's mysterious operations in the natural world, we should not be surprised when we find evidence of uncommon creaturely grace. Thus, we would be wise to acknowledge the possibility or reality of the Spirit's operations whenever we find evidence of compassion and sacrificial love in human society.

The preceding points demonstrate that the internalization of morals is key to the realization of our human end. But in keeping with what Bloesch and Barth maintain, humans cannot foster such internalization or make it happen. That is why we prefer the term *graces* to *virtues*, as Bloesch frames the terminology. We need God's supernatural aid or grace at all times. The Spirit is responsible for overseeing this process of internalization to completion. Such internalization will entail the pursuit of human flourishing for all people.

Smith's own naturalist personalist account involving virtues also entails the idea that "the proper, ultimate purpose of human life—its telos—is the thriving of personhood for all persons."[75] According to the New Testament, this telos of total thriving can only materialize here on earth when we love God with all our heart and our neighbors as ourselves. To the subject of embodied love, I now turn.

---

[75]Smith, *What Is a Person?*, 487.

THE TRIUNE LOVE AND EMBODIED ETHICS

The New Testament teaches that "God is love" (1 John 4:8). God is unconditionally and absolutely love as triune—three divine persons in eternal, loving communion. In Augustinian fashion, the heavenly Father is the one who initiates love within the divine life. The divine Son is the recipient or object of that love and responds in like manner. The Holy Spirit is the one who eternally bonds or unites the Father and Son in their communication of love. However, that bond is not a closed circle, which Colin Gunton sees as a Western theological tendency.[76] The Spirit does not close the divine circle but opens it to include the world in God's unconditional loving embrace. As triune, God does not need the world to be love, for God's eternally loving being is triune. True love always requires an "other." Authentic, unconditional love is never self-oriented. Unconditional love always turns outward toward another, not out of need or necessity, but from an overflow of abundance. The Father and Son reciprocate love one for another in and through the Spirit. There is a giving and receiving of love involving three divine persons in communion from all eternity so that God is love prior to loving the world. Therefore, God is free to create the world out of a superabundance of unconditional love. Just as the triune God does not need the world to be love, so God does not love the world and its inhabitants to serve as a mere means to some divine end, but as creaturely ends in themselves in communion with God.

If only we could love in this way. In our fallen condition, we do not love as God loves, or our neighbors as ourselves. Selfish love and narcissism all too easily gain the upper hand. Similarly, self-hatred often brings us down. Self-care is vitally important for a robust sense of personhood. How can we love and care for others as ourselves if we do not care for ourselves along with others? Affirming others' inviolable worth should never lead us to violate our own persons.

Paul Tillich puts the matter well in discussing "the moral imperative": "The moral imperative is the command to become what one potentially is, a *person* within a community of persons. Only man, in the limit of our

---

[76]Colin E. Gunton, *Act and Being: Towards a Theology of the Divine Attributes* (London: SCM Press, 2002), 146.

experience, can become a person, because only man is a completely centered self, having himself as a self in the face of a world to which he belongs and from which he is, at the same time, separated."[77] Belonging and separation marks one's identity in relation to others and the world at large. To act responsibly entails honoring one another's personal agency and taking seriously one's own self-determination as a moral agent. Again, to commandeer a line from Tillich, we must guard against those "disintegrating forces which tend to control the personal center and to destroy its unity" in our various relationships and society at large.[78]

Moral agency requires care for others' distinctive identity and our own as a community of individual persons before God. This is no easy task. The disintegrating forces that would destroy our individuality and communal well-being as persons wage war within our souls and in various structures round about us.

Knowing that we cannot fulfill the Great Commandments in our own strength, God enters the tired and weary world torn apart by indifference and hate. God transforms it from the inside out through his embodied or incarnate Son—the eternal Word—in the perfecting power of the Spirit who unites us to the Father and Son as God's indwelling personal presence (*vertical*). As Irenaeus writes, they serve as God's two divine hands.[79] The fact that the eternal Word is personal guards against a legalistic and impersonal rendition of absolute truth: God's love is relational. The fact that the personal Word is eternal—beyond creaturely time, space, and cultural flux—guards against relativism: God's love is transcendent and absolute. The fact that this eternal personal Word is embodied or incarnate guards against detachment and disengagement from the nitty gritty struggles of life: God's love is concrete. The fact that God's Word and Spirit work in perfect union signifies that the Spirit extends the import of the Word's action throughout the creaturely order in pursuit of eschatological perfection: God's love is perfecting. God transforms and perfects human life through the operations of the Son and

---

[77]Paul Tillich, *Morality and Beyond*, foreword by William Schweiker (Louisville, KY: Westminster John Knox Press, 1963), 19.

[78]Tillich, *Morality and Beyond*, 19.

[79]Irenaeus of Lyons, *Against Heresies*, 5.6, trans. William Rambaut and Alexander Roberts, in *Ante-Nicene Fathers*, vol. 1, ed. Alexander Roberts, James Donaldson, and A. Cleveland Coxe (Buffalo, NY: Christian Literature, 1880), 531.

Spirit. Such interpersonal mediation in time and space signifies the transformation of history and human hearts. This runs contrary to the hegemonic and oppressive imposition and control of a naked, impersonal divine will so often in play in the history of religion and philosophy. In view of our eschatological hope, we participate in the triune God's operations in the world as we love like God loves. We love God and neighbor not as a mere means to an end, but as ends in themselves. We love God with our whole being, not simply a part, or for some ulterior self-serving end. Similarly, we love our neighbor *as* ourselves, not for ourselves, and not to spite ourselves (*horizontal*). Kant's categorical imperative with its negative line of demarcation of not treating people as mere means rightly puts a check on using others.[80] However, we must go beyond merely negative safeguards. John Paul II's positive personalist construal goes beyond Kant's negative delimitation:

> This norm, in its negative aspect, states that the person is the kind of good which does not admit of use and cannot be treated as an object of use and as such the means to an end. In its positive form the personalist norm confirms this: the person is a good towards which the only proper and adequate attitude is love. This positive content of the personalist norm is precisely what the commandment to love teaches.[81]

We are made for more love. I bring the preceding reflections to bear on our entangled ethical deliberations in our pluralistic society.

Vertical. What is God like? According to Christian Scripture, the named God is self-sufficient. There is no need in God. Yet God is not numb to our sufferings. God cares. The God of the Bible stands in marked contrast to impersonal conceptions of deity. Referencing Étienne Gilson in his discussion of King's personalist conception of God, Rufus Burrow writes, "The God of the Bible is most assuredly a personal God who is immanent enough to care about what happens to persons in the world, unlike the god of Epicurus, Cicero, and Aristotle, who seemed to be so distant, impassive, and uncaring regarding human beings in the world."[82]

---

[80]Kant, *Groundwork of the Metaphysics of Morals*, 96.

[81]Karol Wojtyla, *Love & Responsibility*, rev. ed. (San Francisco: Ignatius Press, 1993), 41.

[82]Burrow, *God and Human Dignity*, 109. See also n72, which is a reference to Étienne Gilson's *God and Philosophy* (New Haven, CT: Yale University Press, 1941), chap. 1, "God and Greek Philosophy," especially 34-37.

I find a quintessential depiction of the God of the Bible in Exodus 3, 33, and 34. John's Gospel draws attention to Exodus 33 and 34 in John 1:14.[83] One may also find an allusion to Exodus 3 in John 8:58.[84] While God's revelation to Moses is certainly gracious, God's revelation in Jesus is the fullness of grace and truth (John 1:14). After all, he is the great I AM, who preexists Abraham (John 8:58). Further to what has already been argued, God reveals his personal and covenantal name to Moses at the burning bush (see Exodus 3:14-15). Moses and Aaron tell the elders of Israel and Pharaoh that the LORD has sent them (see Exodus 4:29-31; 5:1-3). The LORD declares that he will deliver his people from bondage (Exodus 3:7-10, 16-20). God later reveals his glory to Moses as his supreme goodness (Exodus 33:18-19; 34:5-7). First and foremost, God discloses himself to Moses as being merciful and compassionate in orientation. Even so, God will operate in keeping with the fullness of his identity as I AM, the self-defining God. Therefore, he is free to enact judgment on sin where he deems it necessary (see Exodus 33:18-19; 34:5-7).[85]

I find in these texts that God's perfections are relational, and that God leads with mercy and compassion. No wonder 1 John declares that "God is love" (1 John 4:8). Love goes to the very heart of God.

Now love requires expression. One cannot be loving if one does not love another. Love requires an object since love is active and relational.

---

[83]"'Full of grace and truth' echoes the Hebrew word pair 'steadfast love' and 'truth' (. . . *hesed* . . . and *emet*; e.g., Ex 34:6) that speaks of God's covenantal love and faithfulness." Gail R. O'Day, "The Gospel of John: Introduction, Commentary and Reflections," in *Luke–John*, The New Interpreter's Bible 9, ed. Leander E. Keck (Nashville: Abingdon, 1995), 522-23. "Glory" (*doxa*) is a key emphasis in John's Gospel and looks back to the Hebrew Scriptures' conception of glory as God's "manifest presence" that is now revealed in Jesus, who is the Word made flesh. A. T. Hanson also notes that this expression "full of grace and truth" hearkens back to Exodus 33 and 34. See Hanson, *Grace and Truth: A Study in the Doctrine of the Incarnation* (London: SPCK, 1975), 5. Refer also to F. F. Bruce's discussion of the connection here to the phraseology in Exodus 34 in *The Gospel of John: Introduction, Exposition and Notes* (Grand Rapids, MI: Eerdmans, 1983), 42.

[84]F. F. Bruce points out that "I am he" in John 8:58 also appears in John 8:24, 28. He also makes a connection to Isaiah 41:4's mention of "I am he": Jesus "echoes the language of the God of Israel, who remains the same from everlasting to everlasting. 'I, the LORD, the first, and with the last, I am He.'" Bruce, *Gospel of John*, 205.

[85]I am grateful to my colleague Karl Kutz for his exposition of Exodus 3, 33, and 34 set forth in the "Torah Scroll Dedication," Multnomah University, February 5th, 2015. One can find quotations taken from his lecture in my volume *Beatitudes, Not Platitudes: Jesus' Invitation to the Good Life* (Eugene, OR: Cascade Books, 2018), 56.

But if God exists in isolation from all eternity, then God would need to create the world to be loving. If that were so, then God's loving being is not self-sufficient and eternally secure. However, as the God who *is* love, God does not need to create the world to be loving, since God's triune being includes relational otherness.[86] There is a divine subject and object: God the Father eternally loves the Son in the Spirit. The Son responds to that love in the Spirit from all eternity.

God's love always turns outward within the divine life. God's eternal being is relational. Moreover, such love overflows and creates the world. Rather than close the divine circle, the triune God opens the circle to include us. God creates the world and becomes incarnate in the world to reveal and express God's love for us in tangible ways through the Spirit. The Father so loved the world that he gave his Son to flesh out that love among us and fill us with that love through the Spirit. The Son's loving presence is incarnate. The Spirit's loving presence is immediate.

Here I call to mind the doctrine of divine aseity, yet with a caveat. All too often, as Barth points out, this doctrine was taken to mean God's *independentia* or *infinitas* and later as "unconditioned" or "absolute." For Barth, and Gunton after him, aseity is not to be defined in terms of "opposition" (which is to be inferred from the prior terms), but sheer "otherness."[87]

God's own being involves relational otherness, which we find in the eternal communion of the distinct persons of the Father, Son, and Spirit. The very ground of God's being is fatherly, who relates to the world through the Son and Spirit. Regarding the Son and Spirit, Gunton argues,

> If the Son and the Spirit are in different ways focuses of God's movement outwards, to the other, God's aseity, the doctrine of his ontological integrity and completeness, will serve as the basis both of the creature's integrity, as truly itself by virtue of its being created in the Son and by the power of the Spirit, and of the utter gratuity and sovereignty of God's atoning love in Christ.[88]

---

[86]For another reflection on the necessity of the Trinity for the reality of divine love apart from the world, see Nicholas of Cusa, "Cribratio Alkorani," in *Nicholas of Cusa's De pace fidei and Cribratio Alkorani*, trans. Jasper Hopkins (Minneapolis: Banning, 1994), 108.

[87]Karl Barth, *Church Dogmatics*, vol. II/1, *The Doctrine of God*, G. W. Bromiley and T. F. Torrance (Edinburgh: T&T Clark, 1957–1975), 303. See also Gunton, *Act and Being*, 20.

[88]Gunton, *Act and Being*, 121.

For Gunton, the Spirit establishes God's aseity—God's self-sufficiency—and directs the love of the Father "outward" toward creation. He writes,

> The love of the Father, Son and Spirit is a form of love which does not remain content with its eternal self-sufficiency because that self-sufficiency is the basis of a movement outwards to create and perfect a world whose otherness from God—of being distinctly itself—is based in the otherness-in-relation of Father, Son and Spirit in eternity.[89]

Who does God love? While God loves the entire world, God gives preferential treatment to those so often discounted and oppressed by empires as "nonpersons." God is so free and secure in the divine love that God does not need those in positions of power, influence, and fame to esteem him, like we so often do. So, God is free to identify with the orphan, widow, and alien or sojourner in their distress (Deuteronomy 10:18; James 1:27) in sacrificial love. God intervenes in caring for the slave people Israel (Exodus 3). And God also loves the enemy. Only one who is truly free can love so unconditionally. God's triune being makes it possible for God to love in this way.

The LORD is so free that God loves those the rest of us ignore, neglect, and despise. As we will develop shortly, God's love creates attraction. Our attractiveness (or lack thereof) does not inspire or create God's love. God does not choose Israel and the church because of their presumed greatness and genius, but because of their seeming insignificance:

> For you are a people holy to the LORD your God. The LORD your God has chosen you out of all the peoples on the face of the earth to be his people, his treasured possession. The LORD did not set his affection on you and choose you because you were more numerous than other peoples, for you were the fewest of all peoples. But it was because the LORD loved you and kept the oath he swore to your ancestors that he brought you out with a mighty hand and redeemed you from the land of slavery, from the power of Pharaoh king of Egypt (Deuteronomy 7:6-8; see also 1 Corinthians 1:18-31).

God does not need us to be significant, for the triune God is secure and free in the greatness of the eternal communion of his liberating love. Moreover, God's significance and covenant faithfulness is all we need.

---

[89]Gunton, *Act and Being*, 146.

The LORD is so free that he loves even his enemy, and we are called to do the same. We find this emphasis in such texts as Romans 5:6-11 and 1 John 4:10. In fact, as Jesus claims in Matthew 5:43-48, we are to love in the same way (see also 1 John 4:11). Christian love is love of the enemy. This is easier said than done for all people, including Christians. We do not need to be perfect for God to love us. But such love perfects us or calls us to love perfectly like God does.

So, how do we come to love as God loves? It can appear to be an overwhelming and daunting task. The answer involves the personal presence of God's Spirit in our lives. Robert Jenson's discussion of Augustine on the personal presence of the Spirit in the believer's life is quite illuminating and helpful here.[90] Jenson quotes Augustine as saying, "The gift of the Holy Spirit is nothing other than the Holy Spirit."[91] Augustine follows in the tradition of earlier fathers of the church, including Basil the Great.[92] For Augustine, as well as Peter Lombard after him, the Holy Spirit is "'the mutual . . . love by which the Father and the Son love one another,' and it is this very love with which the Spirit fills also us."[93] Augustine wrote, "So the love which is from God and is God is distinctively the Holy Spirit; through him the charity of God is poured into our hearts, and through it the whole triad dwells in us."[94] Jenson adds that this "audacious doctrine" was "*too* audacious for subsequent theology," the result being that the Western church generally views the Spirit as only "the bond of love between Father and Son" and not also that "which binds us to God and one another." Of course, "there are rebels against the standard position." And Luther is one of them.[95]

Luther wrote that God's unconditional love revealed in Jesus and quickened by the Spirit serves as the basis for our attractiveness, which does not result from how spiritually or morally perfect we are. Luther's model resonates more with Plato and (the later) Augustine's model of

---

[90]Robert W. Jenson, *Systematic Theology*, vol. 1, *The Triune God* (New York: Oxford University Press, 1997), 149n20.

[91]Augustine, *De Trinitate*, trans. Edmund Hill (Hyde Park, NY: New City Press, 1991), 15.36:548.

[92]See Jenson, *Systematic Theology*, 1:148n15.

[93]Augustine, *De Trinitate*, 15.27; quoted in Jenson, *Systematic Theology*, 1:148.

[94]Augustine, *De Trinitate*, 15.32:544.

[95]Jenson, *Systematic Theology*, 1:148-49.

virtue rather than Aristotle and those Christian frameworks that reflect his inductive and teleological model. As Peter J. Paris describes it, "Building on the ideal Platonic virtues, Augustine claimed that God was the source of the virtues and their final end. . . . Ethics becomes deductive inquiry that begins with the being of God rather than the strivings of humans. From this line of Platonic thinking the Christian virtues were understood as supernatural and transcendent of human strivings."[96]

In keeping with Luther's framework, God's love creates attraction, not our state of perfection, moral, genetic, or otherwise. Luther writes of God's grace being extended to the degenerate in the Heidelberg Disputation: "The love of God does not find, but creates, that which is pleasing to it. The love of man comes into being through that which is pleasing to it." He goes on to argue,

> The love of God which lives in man loves sinners, evil persons, fools, and weaklings in order to make them righteous, good, wise, and strong. Rather than seeking its own good, the love of God flows forth and bestows good. There sinners are attractive because they are loved; they are not loved because they are attractive. . . . This is the love of the cross, born of the cross, which turns in the direction where it does not find good which it may enjoy, but where it may confer good upon the bad and needy person.[97]

Luther claims that our intellect is not able to grasp this way of being, for it can only acknowledge that which appears as true and good, not what exists simply and exclusively as a result of God's love—namely, "the poor and needy person" whom God makes good and true.[98]

The preceding discussion is not to suggest that people should continue to operate in a degenerate state. Rather, those who have understood experientially God's unconditional love live out God's grace in their regenerate state of being. Let's develop this framework. Jesus' love becomes

[96]Peter J. Paris, *Virtues and Values: The African and African American Experience*, Facet Series (Minneapolis: Fortress, 2004), 80. Paris draws a closer comparison with the Aristotelian framework in his analysis of African and African American virtue ethics, given the emphasis on cultural particularity in both African/African American and Aristotelian versions of virtue ethics.

[97]Martin Luther, "Heidelberg Disputation," in *Martin Luther's Basic Theological Writings*, ed. Timothy F. Lull (Minneapolis: Augsburg, 1989), 48.

[98]Luther, "Heidelberg Disputation," 48.

ours through faith, as we depend fully on God. This relationship is not based on presumed moral (or genetic) perfection. Contrary to that medieval monastic view of union with God whereby we become one with God through meritorious acts of love, we do so by faith, which is a response quickened by God's love poured out into our hearts through the Spirit.[99] On this view, the very love of God within us is not our own, but the presence of the Spirit "apart from our aid and volition."[100] The divine love quickens a response of faith, which leads to nonmeritorious acts of love toward God and neighbor.

On this view championed by Luther, we ascend to Jesus Christ by faith and descend to our neighbor in love quickened by the Spirit. The follower of Jesus does not live "in himself, but in Christ and in his neighbor. Otherwise he is not a Christian. He lives in Christ through faith, in his neighbor through love. By faith he is caught up beyond himself into God. By love he descends beneath himself into his neighbor. Yet he always remains in God and in his love."[101] To be precise, such love is the result of the Spirit's indwelling presence (Romans 5:5). Union with Jesus occurs through faith in God's act of love toward us. Such love is poured out into our hearts through the Spirit, creating faith that leads to a loving response toward God and others. Luther writes, "Therefore, if we recognize the great and precious things which are given us, as Paul says [Rom. 5:5], our hearts will be filled by the Holy Spirit with the love which makes us free, joyful, almighty workers and conquerors over all tribulations, servants of our neighbors, and yet lords of all."[102] Here Luther represents key

---

[99]In general, the medievals articulated three forms of love: *uncreated love*—otherwise known as the Holy Spirit, who is the reciprocal love of the Father and Son; *created love*—which is sacramental grace; and *acts of love*—which are meritorious acts. See Steven Ozment, *The Age of Reform, 1250–1550: An Intellectual and Religious History of Late Medieval and Reformation Europe* (New Haven, CT: Yale University Press, 1980), 242. Ozment relays the famed medieval spiritual theologian Gerson's views: "Our becoming like God [*similitudo*] is the cause of our union with him" (Ozment, 242). The principle of likeness was construed to be the basis for union between God and us. Since love was that which bound together the persons of the Trinity, God and the human soul, and human with human, love was considered to be the ground of union.

[100]Ozment, *The Age of Reform*, 31. The quotation from Ozment reflects Peter Lombard's position, which Ozment contrasts with Thomas Aquinas's cooperative model. Aquinas contended that Lombard failed to account for the merits of our actions (see 31-32).

[101]Martin Luther, "The Freedom of a Christian," in Lull, *Martin Luther's Basic Theological Writings*, 623.

[102]Luther, "The Freedom of a Christian," 619.

features of the later Augustinian tradition, which accounts for the personal presence and immediacy of the Spirit's work in and through Christ's followers.

Given this unilateral approach to love, how do we proceed? Where do we go from here? How do we engage other ethical systems, religious, naturalist, and the like, on the subject matter of love and related notions like altruism and empathy?

Horizontal. Altruism refers to those situations where people presumably pursue the well-being of others freely and selflessly. This notion flies in the face of those who believe natural selection and the survival of the fittest explain fully all human behavior in terms of strict competition.[103] On the latter view, purportedly selfless acts are at their source self-serving drives that benefit the individual and their kin or larger group's survival. This orientation looks at altruism as a dirty word.

E. O. Wilson, for example, argues that Mother Teresa's noble acts of charity for the poor and leprous were not ultimately selfless but the result of her hoped-for eternal reward or church's immortality.[104] Without knowing more about Mother Teresa's explicit aims, we will look to King. King asserted that his aim in loving his enemy who sought to harm and even kill him, his loved ones, and his people was to win his opponent over to friendship and inclusion in the beloved community of agape love. In a Christmas sermon just months before his death, King declared to those engaging in racial violence, "We will meet your physical force with soul force. Do to us what you will and we will still love you." And with daring hope, he concludes, "We will not only win freedom for ourselves; we will so appeal to your heart and conscience that we will win you in the process, and our victory will be a double victory."[105]

Richard Dawkins and Wilson debate the merits of kin versus group or multilevel selection theories of natural selection. And yet, both maintain that ultimately self-serving aims rather than altruism drive us, whether

[103]Richard Dawkins, *The Selfish Gene*, 40th anniv. ed. (Oxford: Oxford University Press, 2016).
[104]Wilson, *On Human Nature*, 164-65.
[105]Martin Luther King Jr., "A Christmas Sermon on Peace," in *A Testament of Hope: The Essential Writings and Speeches of Martin Luther King Jr.*, ed. James M. Washington (San Francisco: HarperCollins, 1986), 256-57.

for the self, kin, or larger group.[106] While I take issue with the notion that altruism is a dirty word and that it can be explained away by natural selection, as Dawkins and Wilson argue (in fact, Darwin himself urged that we need to consider cooperative tendencies alongside natural selection[107]), I don't have difficulty with the claim that altruism and cooperation may have a biological basis.[108]

It is worth noting here that recent studies have shown that cooperation and creativity explain human flourishing more adequately than competition between individuals and tribes. Take for example the recent work of Agustín Fuentes. He argues that in distinction from narratives that highlight the will to survive and reproduce, recent anthropology, paleontology, biology, and other disciplines have shown that the unique quality that characterizes humans is our ability for imaginative cooperation.[109]

It is also worth accounting for the import of oxytocin for discussions of empathy. A mother will produce oxytocin to care for her newly born offspring. There may be other occasions where oxytocin is produced organically, even synthetically. Certainly, oxytocin is a vitally important aspect of our humanity. It helps make the world go around.

---

[106]Chris Johnston, "Biological Warfare Flares Up Again Between E. O. Wilson and Richard Dawkins," *The Guardian*, November 6, 2014, www.theguardian.com/science/2014/nov/07/richard-dawkins -labelled-journalist-by-eo-wilson. Wilson writes of multilevel selection, "In a group, selfish individuals beat altruistic individuals. But, groups of altruistic individuals beat groups of selfish individuals." E. O. Wilson, "Evolution for the Good of the Group," *American Scientist* 96, no. 5 (2008): 380-89.

[107]See John Hedley Brooke, "'Ready to Aid One Another': Darwin on Nature, God, and Cooperation," in *Evolution, Games, and God: The Principle of Cooperation*, ed. Martin A. Nowak and Sarah Coakley (Cambridge, MA: Harvard University Press, 2013), 37-59.

[108]See the essays in Nowak and Coakley, which make this case from a variety of angles.

[109]Agustín Fuentes, *The Creative Spark: How Imagination Made Humans Exceptional* (New York: Random House, 2017). Refer also to Hare and Woods, *Survival of the Friendliest* and Joan B. Silk and Bailey R. House: "The Evolution of Altruistic Social Preferences in Human Groups," *Philosophical Transactions of the Royal Society B: Biological Sciences* 371, no. 1687 (2016); Adam Bear and David G. Rand, "Intuition, Deliberation, and the Evolution of Cooperation," *Proceedings of the National Academy of Sciences* 113, no. 4 (2016): 936-41; Kristian Ove R. Myrseth and Conny E. Wollbrant, "Models Inconsistent with Altruism Cannot Explain the Evolution of Human Cooperation," *Proceedings of the National Academy of Sciences* 113, no. 18 (2016): E2472. Without taking into account altruism, cooperation, and even imagination, we cannot understand the success of humanity. This is not identical to the group vs. kin selection argument, but it intersects with it. The major takeaway is that the "natural selection only" camp of Neo-Darwinism is in serious need of revision since they do not account for the myriad of other factors at play.

A biological basis is one thing. Biological reductionism is quite another. Consideration of oxytocin's merits does not ultimately suggest that we should be caring or even altruistic toward others, especially those beyond our kin or group. An ethical claim, David Hume reminds us, requires that we go beyond consideration of what is the case biologically to address what "should" be the case.[110] Ethics deals ultimately with prescriptions, not predictions of what humans or humanity will do based on biological emotive states (known as emotivism, which is a perspective championed by Wilson[111]).

To illustrate this point, let me briefly consider Patricia Churchland's fascination with oxytocin and its possible import for morality. Christopher Shea analyzes Churchland's position:

> Oxytocin's primary purpose appears to be in solidifying the bond between mother and infant, but Churchland argues—drawing on the work of biologists—that there are significant spillover effects: Bonds of empathy lubricated by oxytocin expand to include, first, more distant kin and then other members of one's in-group. . . . The biological picture contains other elements, of course, notably our large prefrontal cortexes, which help us to take stock of situations in ways that lower animals, driven by "fight or flight" impulses, cannot. But oxytocin and its cousin-compounds ground the human capacity for empathy. (When she learned of oxytocin's power, Churchland writes in *Braintrust*, she thought: "This, perhaps, Hume might accept as the germ of 'moral sentiment.'").[112]

In *Braintrust*, Churchland takes peptide oxytocin and associated neurochemicals into the realm of ethics.[113] Churchland's desire to see

---

[110]See for example the discussion of the distinction involving "is" and "ought" or natural and ethical in Stevenson, Haberman, and Wright, *Twelve Theories of Human Nature*, 254-55. See also David Hume, *A Treatise of Human Nature*, ed. Ernest C. Mossner, Penguin Classics (London: Penguin Books, 1969), 521.

[111]See Whitley Kaufman, "The Evolutionary Ethics of E. O. Wilson," *The New Atlantis: A Journal of Technology & Society* 38 (Winter/Spring 2013): 144-45.

[112]Christopher Shea, "Rulebreaker: When It Comes to Morality the Philosopher Patricia Churchland Refuses to Stand on Principle," *The Chronicle Review*, June 12, 2011, www.chronicle.com/article /The-Biology-of-Ethics/127789.

[113]Patricia S. Churchland, *Braintrust: What Neuroscience Tells Us About Morality* (Princeton, NJ: Princeton University Press, 2018). It is worth noting that for Hume, whom Churchland mentions in pondering whether oxytocin is the germ of moral sentiment, reason at its best can only direct the passions. Reason is not generative of moral positions. Only passions select ends, and intentional actions are the direct and immediate result of passions. Interpreters are divided as to what extent and in what way reason functions in Hume. Hume is often read as claiming that the

oxytocin as the foundation of morals does not actually answer the question about how we come to see this or that action or state of affairs *as* ethical or unethical. To be sure, oxytocin plays a role in reinforcing broader ethical considerations, but oxytocin cannot by itself explain why it is associated with certain situations and not others. In other words, Churchland has identified a chemical mechanism that helps reinforce moral norms and judgments, but not the source and authorization of moral norms and judgments themselves. To think otherwise would rather be like saying the meaning of Shakespeare can be divined from the chemical composition of the ink used, or the style of calligraphy used to shape the words. While not unrelated to the vehicles it uses for expression, the semantic content of Shakespeare has an integrity of its own not reducible to or deducible from its material forms.[114]

Beyond consideration of oxytocin, what is lost if altruism is a dirty word?[115] What is lost is a fuller explanation of what makes us tick rather than simply competitive notions of natural selection and the survival of the fittest. Moreover, human society and metaphysical frameworks provide feedback loops that bear on natural selection. Biology is certainly foundational, but it is not exhaustive of our humanity. It should

---

passions and actions arising from those passions are neither reasonable nor unreasonable, but the acts of judgment associated with them are. It is also worth noting that a few commentators read Hume in a purely emotivist direction where reason ultimately plays no role or is only a false justification for what is an otherwise contentless emotional choice. Rachel Cohon, "Hume's Moral Philosophy," *The Stanford Encyclopedia of Philosophy*, ed. Edward N. Zalta, fall 2018 edition, https://plato.stanford.edu/archives/fall2018/entries/hume-moral/. Churchland's position on ethics reflects a certain subjectivist trait that may signify a striking similarity to Hume. For a critique of Churchland's ethical framework, see Rabbi Eric H. Yoffie, "For Moral Guidance, Look to Religion—Not Neuroscience," *HuffPost*, July 21, 2011 (updated September 20, 2011), www.huffpost.com/entry/for-moral-guidance-look-t_b_904104.

[114]I am indebted to my colleague Derrick Peterson for his reflections on Churchland's position, including the Shakespeare analogy.

[115]Altruism is not a dirty word for evolutionary biologist and Distinguished Professor of Biological Sciences and Anthropology at Binghamton University David Sloan Wilson. He defines altruism as "a concern for the welfare of others." See this definition and the following explanation of altruism in *Does Altruism Exist? Culture, Genes and the Welfare of Others* (New Haven, CT: Yale University Press, 2015), 1. Wilson provides nuanced evolutionary arguments in support of the claim that humans engage altruistically, and in ways that go beyond kin bonding within family structures. Wilson is not a reductionist and models a positive view of religion. It is also worth noting that his earlier *Darwin's Cathedral: Evolution, Religion and the Nature of Society* (Chicago: University of Chicago Press, 2003) offered a compelling antidote to E. O. Wilson's sociobiology. I am grateful for the editorial input of Robert Lyman Potter in this section of the chapter.

not be taken to dictate human ideals since it cannot ground the better angels of our nature that lead us beyond kin and group or multilevel selection to Christian Scripture's celebration of agape and embrace of enemy love (which the quotation from King's Christmas sermon above illustrated so beautifully). Reductionism's only recourse is to try and explain away such ideals. Far from being a dirty word, altruism and agape as accounted for in Jesus' teaching are purifying and perfecting words that help us adjudicate between rival notions of love on a natural or societal level.

Here it is worth illustrating briefly the countercultural inbreaking of Christian love in human society. Islam promotes hospitality and love of neighbor. However, enemy love separates Christian love from Muslim love.[116] It often separates Jesus from Christians, too. We are often more Nietzschean, who looked at Christian love as weak and cowardly.[117] Aristotle has a beautiful treatment of friendship in his *Nicomachean Ethics*.[118] Like loves like. In contrast to Aristotle's definition, Christian love involves loving unlike. Christian love goes beyond fraternal allegiances among good and noble people.

The authors of *Twelve Theories of Human Nature* claim that, for Aristotle, love is limited (to one's friends) and conditional (based on the apparent merit and virtue of the other person) whereas for Christianity love is universal and unconditional. In a statement that bears critical import for kin and group or multilevel selection, they write of Christian Scripture's exposition of love:

> The ideal it puts before us is first that we should be loving or compassionate to *all* our fellow human beings, regardless of sex, race, class, ethnicity, or nationality. And, second, that our love or compassion should not depend on good behavior or individual talents, so that a change of heart and

---

[116]Miroslav Volf claims that although it is not accurate to assert that normative Christianity is a religion of love and official Islam is a religion of war, and while Muslims "insist" that we should be kind to all people—even those who mistreat us—"most reject the idea that [for Islam] the love of neighbor includes the love of enemy." Miroslav Volf, *Allah: A Christian Response* (New York: HarperOne, 2011), 183.

[117]One of the most penetrating and powerful sections of Barth's *Church Dogmatics* is his comparison of Jesus as the crucified, who is the "Neighbour," with Nietzsche's Dionysius-Zarathustra, who is the superman, or "humanity without the fellow-man." *Church Dogmatics*, III/2, 231-42.

[118]Aristotle, *Nicomachean Ethics*, books 8 and 9, 163-209.

forgiveness should always be seen as possible. This twin ideal is almost impossibly demanding on our frail human nature. But we may feel that there is something missing from an ethic that does not even set it before us.[119]

In view of what is missing without such an ideal, let us not treat altruism or agape as a dirty word. Rather, may such words refine our vocabulary and cause us to pursue elevating our humanity to involve them and radical empathy. The spirit is willing, though the flesh is weak. No doubt, we will need the Spirit of God to fill the gap between our biological drives and the lofty altruistic and empathic goal we seek to attain.

John E. Hare speaks of the need for God's intervention in filling the moral gap.[120] Such intervention is necessary in fulfilling the kind of love that King's Christmas sermon quoted from above idealizes. In his treatment of "Some African and African American Moral Virtues," Paris claims that King "represented African America's most prominent embodiment of the virtue of beneficence."[121]

King's beneficent spirit was expressed in his unrelenting commitment to the philosophy of nonviolent resistance, his strong belief in the redemptive power of unmerited suffering, his untiring devotion to the principle of loving one's enemies, his consistent view that nobody is beyond the pale of moral transformation, and his steadfast faith that love and justice will ultimately prevail over evil.[122]

It is worth noting that Paris's approach to African and African American virtue ethics sees greater commonality with the Aristotelian framework given his emphasis on the "cultural specificity of African and African American ethics."[123] Paris goes on to say, though, that beyond the "methodological similarities," there are significant differences.[124] It is also worth noting that Luther likely would have resonated with Paris at one point in his treatment of the virtues of love and forgiveness: "The way of

---

[119]Stevenson, Haberman, and Wright, *Twelve Theories of Human Nature*, 113-14.

[120]John Hare, *The Moral Gap: Kantian Ethics, Human Limits, and God's Assistance*, Oxford Studies in Theological Ethics (Oxford: Clarendon Press, 1997).

[121]Paris, *Virtues and Values*, 28.

[122]Paris, *Virtues and Values*, 29-30.

[123]Paris, *Virtues and Values*, 81.

[124]Paris, *Virtues and Values*, 81-82.

love and forgiveness is not, as often thought, the way of weakness but the way of strength, because it is not a natural response but rather a response that manifests a second nature."[125]

I find helpful Paris's particular concentration on African American virtues (which is in no way parasitic on Aristotle's system) and how his methodological account differs from the more Platonic deductive approach to ethical inquiry. On the whole, I favor the more Platonic and Augustinian approach, which entails "identifying God with the true end of human action." To repeat an earlier quotation, it "begins with the being of God rather than the strivings of humans. From this line of Platonic striving the Christian virtues were understood as supernatural and transcendent of human strivings."[126]

This preference is what led to framing this chapter's various sections first by way of the vertical dimension and then proceeding to the horizontal. While I espouse a form of teleological perfection, it follows from God's initiative: we are only able to perform virtuous acts as God's kingdom dawns in our midst. From the particular trinitarian perspective articulated in this volume, the virtues or graces are embodied in humans through participation in Jesus' life through the indwelling Spirit, who alone is able to fill what John Hare calls the moral gap. This moral gap entails the otherwise impossible call to love one's enemies as ourselves. In no way do Christians have a corner on the market on what sacrificial love entails,[127] as God's Spirit moves in mysterious ways beyond the confines of the church in service to Jesus, who is the image of the invisible God and firstborn of the entire creation.

Whether in and through the church or beyond its confines, through supernatural and natural means, God's Spirit makes possible the love of one's neighbors as oneself. God's Spirit provides secure attachment so that we can love freely from the heart. Martin Luther's conviction on how we ascend by faith in Christ to God who is love makes it possible for us to descend to our neighbors in love through the indwelling Spirit. Martin

[125]Paris, *Virtues and Values*, 56.
[126]Paris, *Virtues and Values*, 80.
[127]In fact, the church often fails to participate in God's sacrificial love, which manifests his kingdom reign. All too often, the fallen principalities and powers seduce the church so that it opposes God's redemptive operations in the world. See also Gushee and Stassen, *Kingdom Ethics*, xiv.

Luther King Jr's community's emphasis on God being "omnipotent-omnibenevolent,"[128] and his personal conviction that "a personal and loving God" who has created, sustains, and guides the universe accompanies us, leads God's people forward in the struggle for righteousness.[129] King's own nurturing, loving, and supportive home environment growing up led him to the conviction that there is a friendly, moral, objective order to the universe.[130] Only as we experience secure attachment with God and other people who serve as channels of God's love, are we free to love our enemies as ourselves and fight for righteousness and the beloved community. As King writes, "I am convinced that the universe is under the control of a loving purpose, and that in the struggle for righteousness man has cosmic companionship. Behind the harsh appearance of the world there is a benign power."[131]

POINTING THE WAY FORWARD ON THE ETHICAL JOURNEY

In what follows, I will attempt to engage a variety of themes and perspectives from a personalist vantage point. I will seek to show how a personalist moral vision serves as a helpful moral compass pointing the way forward to a life that is more than things. The three overarching motifs of entangled ethics of faith, eschatological ethics of hope, and embodied ethics of love will be with us throughout the journey.

Before heading out, it is important to load up the car with three questions. In each of the following chapters, I will be seeking to ask questions that H. Richard Niebuhr along with Harry Frankfurt raised in their own ethical deliberations. Niebuhr encouraged those engaged in ethical

---

[128]Burrow differs from Cone and others who maintain that King held unswervingly to the classical Christian view (along with the vast majority of African American Christianity) of God as "omnipotent-omnibenevolent" (Burrow, *God and Human Dignity*, 90). While King may not have held to the doctrine of divine omnipotence involving God doing "the impossible or the ridiculous" (89-90, 112), he did maintain that God is infinitely loving and matchless in power, and involves people in the struggle for justice. Burrow writes, "An infinitely loving God of 'matchless power' (not absolute or perfect power) would *want* and *need* the cooperation of free self-determining beings in the struggle to overcome injustice and to achieve (as nearly as possible) the beloved community" (113).

[129]Burrow, *God and Human Dignity*, 104.

[130]Burrow, *God and Human Dignity*, 184.

[131]Martin Luther King Jr., "Pilgrimage to Nonviolence," in *Strength to Love* (New York: Harper & Row, 1963), 141.

inquiry to ask at the outset, "What's going on here?" After providing an answer, he then encouraged others to answer the question, "What's the fitting or appropriate response?" For his part, Frankfurt asked the question, "What ought we to care about?" My colleague and mentor Robert Lyman Potter first introduced these questions in his articulation of medical ethics from a personalist vantage point. He inserts Frankfurt's question between the two questions posed by Niebuhr. Potter's order is "What's going on here?" "What should we care about?" and "What's the fitting response?" I will not raise these questions in an explicit manner in every chapter. However, they are embedded in the ethical deliberations of this book as we seek to account for a great variety of factors in every issue of ethics we address (i.e., what is the variety of issues and factors involved here to which we must give an account?), adjudicate between them in favor of what promotes a personalist moral vision (i.e., what should we care most about?), and by doing so provide an appropriate response to the ethical subject at hand (what's most fitting as a response?).

These questions are quite helpful in assessing and determining a path forward in ethical deliberations.[132] One may differ at points on various lines of inquiry and conclusions to ethical matters. However, this overarching trajectory is extremely beneficial for all those driving down the ethical highways and byways of life. It seeks to account for the full context of ethical factors to consider, the prioritization of empathic concern for what is most valuable from a personalist vantage point, and an appropriate response that is not fixed or static, but accounts for contextual variables in service to persons.

The first question, "What is going on here?" entails coming to terms with the various knotty and entangled ethical considerations and viewpoints on a given subject. It does so from a critical realist vantage point. No one sees with a God's eye point of view, though one works diligently to account for as many factors and perspectives as possible to get the lay of the land for one's winding road ethical journey from a personalist

---

[132]For the sources for this framework, see H. Richard Niebuhr, *The Responsible Self*, Library of Theological Ethics (Louisville, KY: Westminster John Knox, 1999); Harry G. Frankfurt, *The Importance of What We Care About* (Cambridge: Cambridge University Press, 1988).

vantage point. This is what the present book calls the entangled ethics of faith.

The second question, "What should I care about?" entails coming to terms with discerning the most important aspects to value in making ethical determinations. Given the personalist moral vision that drives this car or volume, I will seek to highlight the import of loving God with all our hearts and neighbors as ourselves as most important. This is the embodied ethics of love.

The third question, "What is the fitting response?" is the question of destination. What set of directions will get us to our designated telos or end of loving God with all our hearts and neighbors as ourselves on a given ethical subject? Answering this question of fitting response is all about what it will take to arrive home. This is what I call the eschatological ethics of hope. These three questions fit the overarching motifs of faith, hope, and love that serve the personalist moral compass for the journey.

PART TWO

FROM THE BEGINNING TO THE END OF LIFE

3

MORE THAN ABILITIES

Pro-Life for All in a Throwaway Culture

SUSTAINED ANALYSIS OF HUMAN PERSONHOOD should entail consideration of abilities or capacities. However, persons are not reducible to them, and we are made for more than them. This claim has a bearing on the topic of abortion. This present chapter will focus consideration on the sacredness of human life, no matter one's abilities and capacities. Special consideration will be given to Down syndrome and quality-of-life considerations.

ABORTION AND A THROWAWAY CULTURE
OF SUFFERING AND HAPPINESS

In a 2014 address, Pope Francis stated that although "human life is sacred and inviolable," we live within an "economy of exclusion and inequality." He continued, "This economy kills. Human beings are themselves considered consumer goods to be used and then discarded. We have created a 'throwaway' culture which is now spreading."[1] Pope Francis's reflections should make us pause to consider what, if anything, is truly sacred in a consumer capital society.

More recently, the pope remarked that the widespread move to abort fetuses with defects is similar to the Nazi ideology of trying to purify the race: "I say this with pain. In the last century the whole world was scandalized about what the Nazis did to purify the race. Today we do the

---

[1] Pope Francis, "Audience with Italian Movement for Life," *National Catholic Reporter*, April 11, 2014, www.ncronline.org/blogs/francis-chronicles/pope-s-quotes-throwaway-culture.

same, but now with white gloves."[2] Richard Dawkins reacted to the pope's statement: "And you thought Francis was the 'good Pope'? Abortion to avoid birth defects is not about eugenics. It's about the avoidance of individual human suffering."[3]

This was not the first time Dawkins engaged the subject of abortion and birth defects. In 2014, Dawkins created quite a stir when he responded to a tweet from a woman who told him she was not sure what to do if she were carrying a fetus with Down syndrome. According to Dawkins, aborting the fetus would be the morally superior response. His argument stems from his belief that giving birth to a child with Down syndrome neither "reduces suffering" nor "increases the sum of happiness." Though he assures the woman that the choice ultimately belongs to her, he still thinks the negative consequences outweigh the positive. "In any case," Dawkins writes, "you would probably be condemning yourself as a mother . . . to a lifetime of caring for an adult with the needs of a child. Your child would probably have a short life expectancy but, if she did outlive you, you would have the worry of who would care for her after you are gone." Thus, he concludes, "No wonder most people choose abortion when offered the choice."[4]

Dawkins did not realize his initial reply went out to his vast number of Twitter followers, as well as to the followers of his correspondent. He apologized for the stir and for his seemingly calloused response. However, he also took issue with those who accused him of "advocating a eugenic policy":

> That never entered my head, nor should it have. Down syndrome has almost zero heritability. That means that, although it is a congenital condition—a chromosomal abnormality that babies are born with— there is very little tendency for susceptibility to trisomy to be inherited genetically. If you were eugenically inclined, you'd be wasting your

---

[2]Hilary Clarke, Valentina DiDonato, and Carol Jordan, "Pope Francis Says Abortion to Avoid Birth Defects Is Similar to Nazi Crimes," *CNN*, June 17, 2018, www.cnn.com/2018/06/17/europe/pope -abortion-eugenics---intl/index.html.

[3]Richard Dawkins, "And you thought Francis was the 'good Pope'?," June 18, 2018, 3:15 a.m., https:// twitter.com/RichardDawkins/status/1008639227297435648.

[4]Richard Dawkins, "An Apology for Letting Slip the Dogs of Twitterwar," *Richard Dawkins Foundation for Reason and Science*, August 21, 2014, www.richarddawkins.net/2014/08/abortion-down -syndrome-an-apology-for-letting-slip-the-dogs-of-twitterwar/.

time screening for Down syndrome. You'd screen for genuinely heritable conditions where your screening would make a difference to future generations.[5]

Some will push back on Dawkins's claim that his stance does not lead to eugenics, or that there is "almost zero heritability." For the purposes of this chapter, I will focus primarily on his endorsement of a utilitarian form of ethics: "If your morality is based, as mine is, on a desire to increase the sum of happiness and reduce suffering, the decision to deliberately give birth to a Down baby, when you have the choice to abort it early in the pregnancy, might actually be immoral from the point of view of the child's own welfare."[6]

A utilitarian form of ethics is perhaps most often associated with John Stuart Mill. On Mill's account of utilitarianism, ethical determinations are made based on what actions bring about the greatest amount of happiness and least amount of pain for the greatest number of people. Here's Mill:

> The creed which accepts as the foundation of morals, Utility, or the Greatest Happiness Principle, holds that actions are right in proportion as they tend to promote happiness, wrong as they tend to produce the reverse of happiness. By happiness is intended pleasure, and the absence of pain; by unhappiness, pain, and the privation of pleasure.[7]

The focus is not on individual pleasure and suffering, but the majority's experience of pleasure and pain as far as it is possible to calculate.[8]

Whether Dawkins sees himself aligning with Mill's system at every turn is beyond the scope of this chapter. Dawkins seeks to promote happiness and reduce the suffering of individuals in question (not necessarily the majority population), such as the child with Down syndrome, as well as the parents, and anyone else tasked with caring for the individual if they outlive their parents.

---

[5] Dawkins, "An Apology."
[6] Dawkins, "An Apology."
[7] John Stuart Mill, *Utilitarianism* (New York: Barnes & Noble, 2005), 7.
[8] Mill, *Utilitarianism*, 17. It is important to note that a group does not experience pleasure or pain. Rather, only individual persons within a group experience pleasure or pain. It is unclear whether Mill recognized this distinction.

Attention now turns to analyze the merits of Dawkins's point on increasing happiness and decreasing suffering. Consideration will focus on quality-of-life indicators and the presumed merits of Dawkins's utilitarian framework.

QUALITY OF LIFE INDICATORS AND UTILITARIAN DEFICIENCIES

Disability paradoxes and advantages. Research analyzing the quality of life of those with disabilities suggests that contrary to popular opinion, many people with disabilities experience a very rich quality of life. Take for example the following study published in the *American Journal of Medical Genetics* titled "Self-Perceptions from People with Down Syndrome":

> Among those surveyed, nearly 99% of people with DS indicated that they were happy with their lives, 97% liked who they are, and 96% liked how they look. Nearly 99% people with DS expressed love for their families, and 97% liked their brothers and sisters. While 86% of people with DS felt they could make friends easily, those with difficulties mostly had isolating living situations. . . . They further encouraged healthcare professionals to value them, emphasizing that they share similar hopes and dreams as people without DS. Overall, the overwhelming majority of people with DS surveyed indicate they live happy and fulfilling lives.[9]

Further to this research, the journal *Social Science and Medicine* published an article titled "The Disability Paradox: High Quality of Life Against All Odds."[10] The authors, Gary L. Albrecht and Patrick J. Devlieger, ask about what they take to be "the disability paradox": "Why do many people with serious and persistent disabilities report that they experience a good or excellent quality of life when to most external observers these individuals seem to live an undesirable daily existence?"[11]

Using "a qualitative approach to develop an explanation of this paradox using semi-structured interviews with 153 persons with

---

[9]Brian G. Skotko, Susan P. Levine, and Richard Goldstein, "Self-Perceptions from People with Down Syndrome," *American Journal of Medical Genetics* 155 (September 9, 2011): 2360-69.

[10]Gary L. Albrecht and Patrick J. Devlieger, "The Disability Paradox: High Quality of Life Against All Odds," *Social Science & Medicine*, no. 48 (1999): 977-88.

[11]Albrecht and Devlieger, "Disability Paradox," 977.

disabilities," they found that "54.3% of the respondents with moderate to serious disabilities reported having an excellent or good quality of life confirming the existence of the disability paradox." Whether people reported a good quality of life or poor quality of life, it was found that "quality of life is dependent upon finding a balance between body, mind, and spirit in the self and on establishing and maintaining a harmonious set of relationships within the person's social context and external environment."[12]

Outside observers might presume that those with disabilities have "an undesirable daily existence."[13] However, based on an individualist-oriented utilitarian ethic, as is presumably in Dawkins's case, should that decision not be up to the person with the disability? Based on an individualistically oriented utilitarian ethic, like the one apparently espoused by Dawkins, one should not judge at the outset of life whether to terminate existence, but only after the person has lived a sufficient time period to make that call. Even then, one should ask, what is a sufficient time period? And what if, just around the bend in life's journey, a person with a disability were to find that their quality of life changed for the better based on experiencing a new balance involving spirit, mind, and body, as well as cultivating an enriching set of relationships? Given that they do not have omniscience, would it be wise to terminate their own lives based on such a quality-of-life calculus?

Going back to Pope Francis's claim about "throwaway culture," one wonders if Dawkins's stated compassionate stance toward those with disabilities is really a bias against them: "There is a decided negative bias in the attitudes and expectations of the public and health care workers toward persons with disabilities (Wright, 1988). At best, many people act with ambivalence toward or are non-supportive of persons with disabilities (Katz et al., 1988; Georges, 1997)."[14]

---

[12] Albrecht and Devlieger, "Disability Paradox," 977. The article also notes, "The domain of disability extends far beyond health related concerns to encompass the person's well-being, definition of self and social position (Grimby et al., 1988). As a holistic concept, quality of life goes beyond activities of daily living and disease categories because it directs attention to the more complete social, psychological and spiritual being" (979).

[13] Albrecht and Devlieger, "Disability Paradox," 977.

[14] Albrecht and Devlieger, "Disability Paradox," 978.

Dawkins appears to suffer from "ableism." Andrew Picard defines ableism:[15]

> Ableism is a term that emerged out of the disability rights movement to describe the "ideas, practices, institutions, and social relations that presume able-bodiedness, and by so doing, construct persons with disabilities as marginalized."[16] It highlights the prejudice and discrimination toward people who are classified as disabled, irrespective of their impairments.[17] Critics of ableism stress that it is society that disables through its physical and attitudinal barriers, rather than human impairment and difference. Ableism, and its cult of "normalcy," pathologizes forms of human impairment and difference and constructs them as loss.[18] Why is it that losing your hair is not considered a disability but losing your hearing is?[19]

How might ableism and disaffection for people classified as disabled shape the ethical decisions of utilitarians like Dawkins?

Of course, based on a utilitarian ethic, it is not only the individual with a disability that one must account for, but also those in their social network. As noted above, Dawkins rightly expresses concern for the individual's immediate relational network, such as the burden the parents bear in caring for an adult who has the needs of a child, as well as the weight of worrying about who will care for the child if they outlive their parents. Those are real issues that cannot be easily dismissed. Nor can we dismiss the role society plays in disabling people through what Picard calls "its physical and attitudinal barriers, rather than human impairment and difference."[20] We must seek to account for the full gamut of ethical issues in seeking to answer one of the three key questions set forth at the close of chapter two: "What is going on here?"

One must certainly account for the burden parents and other significant caregivers bear in supporting those with disabilities. But could not

---

[15]Paul Louis Metzger, "Beyond Ableism and Its Cult of 'Normalcy': An Interview with Andrew Picard," *Cultural Encounters: A Journal for the Theology of Culture* 16, no. 2 (Fall 2021): 63. Picard makes use of various sources in defining ableism (see notes in quote).

[16]Michelle R. Nario-Redmond, *Ableism: The Causes and Consequences of Disability Prejudice* (Hoboken, NJ: Wiley-Blackwell, 2020), 5.

[17]Nario-Redmond, *Ableism*, 6.

[18]Thomas E. Reynolds, *Vulnerable Communion: A Theology of Disability and Hospitality* (Grand Rapids, MI: Brazos, 2008), 18-21.

[19]Bill Hughes, *A Historical Sociology of Disability: Human Validity and Invalidity from Antiquity to Early Modernity* (New York: Routledge, 2020), 26.

[20]Metzger, "Beyond Ableism and Its Cult of 'Normalcy,'" 63.

these caregivers also experience something like "the disability paradox" highlighted above? Moreover, could they not make the necessary adjustments involving their spirit, mind, and body, as well as cultivate significant social networks as part of effective self-care?

Case in point. An opinion piece written in the *New York Times* challenges Dawkins's call for aborting a fetus bearing Down syndrome. The article highlights what is called the "Down syndrome advantage." Familial stress is often lower than for families with preschoolers suffering from autism and is sometimes comparable to families with nondisabled children. Divorce rates are lower for parents of children with Down syndrome than for parents of nondisabled children and those of children with other congenital disabilities. A very high percentage of siblings claim to be better people as a result of their Down syndrome family member. Moreover, Down syndrome individuals have much greater adaptive skills than their low IQ scores may convey.[21]

Genetic-intelligence reductions and the relational image of God. Dawkins appears to privilege biological abilities and capacities, which parallels his scientific focus on genes. What is lacking in Dawkins's overarching matrix is a sufficient account of how the individual with Down syndrome responds to their environment based on making sufficient adjustments, and how those in their social environment respond to them. This is where systems biologist Denis Noble's framework may prove more explanatorily advantageous than Dawkins's genetics outlook.

According to Noble, Dawkins's "gene centered view, the 'selfish gene' view, is a metaphorical polemic: the invention of a colourful metaphor to interpret scientific discovery in a particular way."[22] It rules his metaphysical outlook on life. Accounting for Dawkins's own confession in

---

[21]James Edgin and Fabian Fernandez, "The Truth About Down Syndrome," *New York Times*, August 28, 2014, www.nytimes.com/2014/08/29/opinion/the-truth-about-down-syndrome.html. There are some researchers who question the extent of the "Down syndrome advantage" as described in this article. One study that accounted for the variables of maternal age, socioeconomic status, and child adaptive behavior when comparing two diagnostic groups of Down syndrome families and families with other developmental disabilities found the "Down syndrome advantage" was significantly lessened when these factors were taken into account. April M. Corrice and Laraine Masters Glidden, "The Down Syndrome Advantage: Fact or Fiction?," *American Journal on Intellectual and Development Disabilities* 114, no. 4 (July 2009): 266.

[22]Denis Noble, *The Music of Life: Biology Beyond Genes* (Oxford: Oxford University Press, 2006), 11.

An Extended Phenotype[23] that there is no experiment that could prove his metaphorical claim of a gene-centered view of reality (that is, the selfish gene),[24] Noble goes on to offer an alternative reading of the biological domain.

Like Dawkins, Noble's metaphorical framework is also metaphysical. However, it provides more explanatory power for the scientific and philosophical domains in Noble's estimation. Noble claims that, contrary to Dawkins, in which genes swarm about in "gigantic lumbering robots" (i.e., humans), which genes have "created,"[25] humans are for Noble "highly intelligent beings" who imprison genes and are "the ultimate rationale for" genes' "existence."[26]

Dawkins's metaphorical account featuring genes appears to concentrate on what Christian Smith calls "upwardly emergent" human capacities.[27] By contrast, Noble's account seems to parallel Smith's more expansive framework. Noble believes Dawkins's gene-centered model provides insights into life, but it is not at all sufficient to describe life's fullness.[28] Noble also makes space for what Smith calls "upwardly emergent" capacities (bound up with genetics and other entities), but, like Smith, goes further than Dawkins. Noble awards primacy to human beings, not their genetic basis, mirroring what Smith refers to as the "downwardly dependent" "entities and processes" that higher-level phenomena can influence.[29]

It is worth noting at this point that Smith appears to apply standard notions of normalcy to people when classifying individuals as "disabled," yet without undercutting their dignity: "Radically damaged persons, to be clear, have not ceased to be persons. But they are damaged. And to deny the gap between the normal and the damaged is unhelpful."[30] And yet, Smith refuses to identify or equate human personhood or the dignity

---

[23]Richard Dawkins, *The Extended Phenotype: The Long Reach of the Gene*, afterword by Daniel Dennett (Oxford: Oxford University Press, 1999), 1.

[24]Noble, *Music of Life*, 13.

[25]Richard Dawkins, *The Selfish Gene* (Oxford: Oxford University Press, 1976), 21.

[26]Noble, *Music of Life*, 12.

[27]Christian Smith, *What Is a Person?* (Chicago: University of Chicago Press, 2010), 57, fig. 2.

[28]Noble, *Music of Life*, 11.

[29]Smith, *What Is a Person?*, 40-41, 57, fig. 2.

[30]Smith, *What Is a Person?*, 82; cf. 53.

of persons with capacities.[31] Personhood arises from properties and capacities but is not reducible to them. Dignity is itself a property of personhood. Smith writes, "Dignity, I suggest, is an emergent property of human personhood, not a quality of one or more of the specific capacities out of which personhood emerges."[32] Dignity is "ineliminable and irreducible."[33] It is inherent, though mysterious, like wetness to water. As with wetness and water, it is difficult to fathom "how dignity could characterize the emergent reality of personhood." Nonetheless, like water, it is real.[34]

Smith's belief in human dignity arises from theological convictions. However, he maintains that one must be able to engage those who do not believe in God or who demand evidence of dignity in human existence and experience.[35] Dogmatic claims, while some of them have merit, do not satisfy those who seek to identify dignity with capacities. If one were to claim that human dignity is dependent on God's existence, and if people do not believe in God's existence, what happens to dignity? How does one make a case for it in society at large?[36] On the other hand, capacity-based accounts have great difficulty explaining how those individuals who do not exercise certain capacities possess dignity.[37] That said, neither side proves convincing to the skeptic, who rejects the concept in its entirety and reframes the discussion, possibly in favor of utilitarian considerations.[38] A critical realist approach might not be able to provide an account absent of all mystery, or that is immune to criticism and debate. Still, mystery and ambiguity do not prove the skeptic right: "Difficulties in *explaining* real facts do not turn those facts into illusions. They mean we need to continue to work harder to better explain the facts."[39]

Speaking of skepticism, I am skeptical of utilitarian dismissals of human dignity as an inherent property of personhood. Let's consider

---

[31]Smith, *What Is a Person?*, 450, 454-55.
[32]Smith, *What Is a Person?*, 453.
[33]Smith, *What Is a Person?*, 446.
[34]Smith, *What Is a Person?*, 456, cf. 453.
[35]Smith, *What Is a Person?*, 452.
[36]Smith, *What Is a Person?*, 450.
[37]Smith, *What Is a Person?*, 448.
[38]Smith, *What Is a Person?*, 447.
[39]Smith, *What Is a Person?*, 451.

briefly Peter Singer's form of preference utilitarianism. Whereas Mill's brand of utilitarianism focused on happiness, Singer's brand focuses on preferences. One's behaviors must align with the preferences of those affected. Michael Specter writes,

> For Singer, killing is wrong because when you kill someone who wants to live you make it impossible for that person to fulfill his preferences. Obviously, if you kill somebody whose preferences don't have much chance of success–a severely disabled infant, for example, or somebody in an advanced stage of Alzheimer's disease–the moral equation becomes entirely different.[40]

Specter reports what Singer told him in an interview:

> "The notion that human life is sacred just because it's human life is medieval," he continued, talking about the treatment of the hopelessly ill. "The person that used to be there is gone. It doesn't matter how sad it makes us. All I am saying is that it's time to stop pretending that the world is not the way we know it to be."[41]

Singer argued in *Practical Ethics*, "It may still be objected that to replace either a fetus or a newborn infant is wrong because it suggests to disabled people living today that their lives are less worth living than the lives of people who are not disabled. Yet it is surely flying in the face of reality to deny that, on average, this is so."[42]

And yet, Singer could not help but "pretend" to operate like the majority of those whose loved ones suffer from a severe disability, or a disease like Alzheimer's. They cannot detach themselves emotionally from their loved ones, nor could Singer in the case of his mother suffering from Alzheimer's. While she herself had made very clear she did not wish to live in such a seemingly meaningless state, Singer provided state-of-the-art care for her. When pressed about the inconsistency between his ethical position and his care for his hopelessly ill parent, he said, "I think this has made me see how the issues of someone with these kinds of problems are really very difficult. . . .

---

[40]Michael Specter, "The Dangerous Philosopher," profile, *New Yorker*, September 6, 1999, 46.
[41]Specter, "Dangerous Philosopher," 46.
[42]Peter Singer, *Practical Ethics*, 2nd ed. (Cambridge: Cambridge University Press, 1993), 188.

Perhaps it is more difficult than I thought before, because it is different when it's your mother."[43]

The idea that one must align with the disinterested utilitarian calculus in favor of the greatest amount of happiness for the greatest number of people as in the case of Mill, or the preferences of the greatest number of people as in the case of Singer, may work in a lab, but not real life. It appears way too calculated, abstract, and unreal. When push comes to shove, and the loved ones of the most calculated, utilitarian skeptics are vulnerable, the skeptics might very well proceed as if the dignity of such vulnerable individuals is inherent. In espousing their ethical claims, they need to put themselves and their loved ones in vulnerable people's shoes to see how long they can walk about as skeptics of human dignity. The same goes for "pro-life" advocates, who condemn the choice of abortions, as we will discuss later. Only those reasoned ethical positions that embody the deeply personal struggles of life have the potential of being critically realistic.

This book's own critical realist account aims to engage a variety of traditions and life circumstances in pursuit of a compelling account of personalism and human dignity. While this moral vision is definitively theological in orientation, it is open to the findings of those who emphasize a capacity-based approach, or even a utilitarian framework, which is sometimes associated with certain skeptical trajectories, as has been done with consideration of the disability paradox at points. The starting point in all debate, though, is that people are not reduced to capacities and abilities, intellectual or otherwise. We are made for more than them. We are who we are in relation as constituted by the triune God in whose image we are made, as claimed in chapter two.

Our dignity results from God creating humans in his own image. It is not a capacity, intellectual or otherwise. Nor is it a character trait. Rather, it is a distinguishing mark of our imaging God in relational terms: we receive our dignity from God, who loves us and who places us in a web of relationships with other individual persons.[44] We cannot lose the

---

[43]Specter, "Dangerous Philosopher," 46.

[44]See Karl Barth's discussion of the image in covenantal relational terms in *Church Dogmatics*, III/1, *The Doctrine of Creation*, ed. G. W. Bromiley and T. F. Torrance (Edinburgh: T&T Clark, 1958), 200.

image through mental illness or an accident that impairs us in some manner, nor Down syndrome, since the image is not something we possess. Nor can society erase the image through prejudicing and marginalizing people based on classifying them as disabled.

As beings created in the image of God who is three persons in communion, we are human persons with all the accompanying dignity. Abilities and capacities help us flourish as humans, but they do not exhaust our persons. Nor should we equate them with our persons. No one experiences the fullness of all human abilities and capacities, but that does not take away from their personhood. We may not be able to express what is deemed the telos of our personhood, where all such capacities are functioning normally or optimally at any one point or throughout our lives. But given our fallen moral and fallible, frail psychosomatic condition, who can? Still, we may compensate for the lack with alternative functions. We may do so as individuals or in community. As those created and constituted in relation to God and one another, we exercise whatever abilities and capacities we do have relationally in the effort to experience the telos of the image: to love God with all our being and our neighbors as ourselves.

Questions of equality and relational intimacy. Quality-of-life indicators should not be limited to private mental and emotional states. They should also account for personal relationships involving various parties. In fact, well-being is enhanced among people with disabilities by caring for others. Often society presumes that people suffering from disabilities only wish to take and not give relationally. People suffering from disabilities can and often grow as persons as the disability transforms their values and perspectives. Such transformation includes increased care for others. Aborting fetuses with disabilities may very well undermine individual and communal growth. According to Albrecht and Devlieger's research on people with disabilities, "The experience of disability served to clarify and reorient the lives of numerous respondents. . . . Some people said that helping and giving to others improved their quality of life. Where it might be expected that people with disabilities should take from others, they also have a deep need to give to and help others."[45]

---

[45] Albrecht and Devlieger, "Disability Paradox," 983.

Many presumed "normal" people perceive that relational intimacy can only occur between equals, that is, with people of the same mental or material state. While this view has historical precedence, going back to Aristotle's prerequisites for friendship in the *Nicomachean Ethics*, it is often challenged philosophically today. According to the *Stanford Encyclopedia of Philosophy* entry on disability,

> Philosophers have often treated equality of some kind as a prerequisite of friendship. . . .
>
> Aristotle denied that parents and their children could ever be true friends, since the inequality between them could never be overcome no matter how much the child does for his parents. This position is rejected by English (1979) and Kristjansson (2006). Generally, contemporary accounts of friendship place less emphasis on equality or similarity of specific traits and more on equality of respect, investment, and commitment. Given the vast range of differences among close friends in talents, interests, and tangible contributions, it would not seem that disabilities pose any general barrier to intimacy.[46]

While it is certainly the case that a significant disability can weigh heavily on persons and relationships, it can also open us up to new vistas of enhanced relational intimacy and adaptive social skills.

Dawkins's biological fallacy and subjectivism. Now even if one were to grant Dawkins's particular utilitarian assertion that a fetus carrying Down syndrome should be aborted due to a lack of pleasure and increase in pain, is he not confusing an "is" statement with an "ought" statement, a distinction made famous by Hume? Just because one's biological condition leads to suffering, does that *require* one to terminate life? To refer back favorably to Smith's naturalistic teleological account, an *ought* arises from what *is* real, but it does not authorize "as ought that which is."[47] It is important not to reduce value to one's biological status involving pleasure and pain. Of course, pleasure and pain are part of what constitute our humanity. However, we are made for more than mere pleasure

---

[46]David Wasserman, Jeffrey Blustein, and Daniel Putnam, "Disability: Health, Well-Being, and Personal Relationships," in *Stanford Encyclopedia of Philosophy*, ed. Edward N. Zalta, winter 2016 ed., https://plato.stanford.edu/archives/win2016/entries/disability-health/.

[47]Smith, *What Is a Person?*, 486.

and pain. There are many other factors to which we must give account, including redemptive suffering, various kinds and degrees of pleasure and pain based on nonphysiological factors, and overarching values (beyond utilitarianism) that rank these various pleasures. The "disability paradox" exposes Dawkins's intellectualist biases that he mistakenly puts forth as indubitable.

It is worth noting that Darwin often safeguarded against making the same mistake on "is" and "ought" that Dawkins does. People often wrongly connect Darwin's doctrine of the survival of the biological fittest, including reproduction, with superiority in other spheres, such as morality, intellect, aesthetics, and spirituality. If anything, the moral to Darwin's biological framework is that people should have big families, where the children reach adulthood. What is termed Social Darwinism should probably be labeled Social Spencerism, following Herbert Spencer's social philosophy. Darwin did not fully accept Social Darwinism or "eugenics," which was coined by Darwin's cousin, Francis Galton.[48]

According to the account of *The Descent of Man* in *Twelve Theories of Human Nature*, Darwin held that society must care for its weaker members, and he did not allow his fear over the increase of inferior groups in society to overrule compassionate care for them. Here I call to mind the closing portion of the "General Summary" in *The Descent of Man*. Darwin claims that as important as natural selection is, other agencies are still more important for the cultivation of morality, namely, "the effects of habit, the reasoning powers, instruction, religion."[49] I believe Darwin's position bears on those with Down syndrome too (irrespective of Dawkins's claim that Down syndrome has "almost zero

---

[48]See the chapter on Darwinism in Leslie Stevenson, David L. Haberman, and Peter Matthews Wright, *Twelve Theories of Human Nature*, 6th ed. (New York: Oxford University Press, 2013), 251-52, 254-55, 257-58.

[49]Charles Darwin, *The Descent of Man*, Penguin Classics (New York: Penguin, 2004), 688-89. For a discussion of the debate over whether Darwin is a social evolutionist, see John C. Greene, "Darwin as a Social Evolutionist," in *Journal of the History of Biology* 10, no. 1 (Spring 1977): 1-27. See Agustín Fuentes's recent critique of *The Descent of Man*. He sees it as "often problematic, prejudiced, and injurious. Darwin thought he was relying on data, objectivity, and scientific thinking in describing human evolutionary outcomes. But for much of the book, he was not. 'Descent,' like so many of the scientific tomes of Darwin's day, offers a racist and sexist view of humanity." Agustín Fuentes, "The Descent of Man, 150 Years On," *Science* 372, no. 6544 (May 2021): 769.

heritability"). In view of Darwin, one could respond to the Social Darwinians as Stevenson, Haberman, and Wright do:

> Since our human evolution has given us both the sympathy to care for our fellow humans and the intelligence to institute laws and social programs to help them, shouldn't we use those mental capacities to try to steer human society in the direction of greater equality? Isn't that more "natural" to us than unflinching adherence to "the survival of the fittest"? It would be dangerous, however, to rest our case on the extremely slippery concept of what is "natural."[50]

Just as the Social Darwinian appeal to "nature" is dangerous, Dawkins's utilitarian appeal to the mere increase of "happiness" and the mere reduction of "suffering" as ultimate ideals is also problematic, even if most parents who abort such fetuses make the same or similar kinds of calculations. Broad-based support for a course of action does not make it inherently right and impacts the rights of others—namely, those who fall short on the pleasure calculus scale. What constitutes happiness and suffering? They are overly subjective terms that, for this topic under consideration (abortion), have life-changing bearing on the subjects in question—those with Down syndrome. What serves as the basis for authority to make judgments about what constitutes happiness and suffering and their bearing on whether to abort? Is not life worth suffering for in many cases, and is not pleasure sometimes worse than suffering? Many individuals whom Dawkins claims will not experience meaningful, pleasurable existence excel in happiness and find meaning in life, as already shown in the "disability paradox" discussion.

An unqualified emphasis on increasing happiness and reducing suffering begs the question. Is suffering always bad? What if the present suffering leads to greater happiness and pleasure down the road, challenging the presumed sense of omniscience in the moment that is all too often concomitant with utilitarianism? Here it is worth noting that on Mill's account of utilitarianism, sacrifice is not viewed as an inherent virtue. Rather, it is a good if and only if it leads toward the sum of happiness. "The utilitarian morality does recognize in human

---

[50]Stevenson, Haberman, and Wright, *Twelve Theories of Human Nature*, 254-55.

beings the power of sacrificing their own greatest good for the good
of others," writes Mill. "It only refuses to admit that the sacrifice is
itself a good."[51]

One can critique Dawkins on utilitarian grounds, if we talk about the
disability paradox in assessing quality of life articulated earlier or based
on Mill's overarching utilitarian model. Still, the utilitarian framework
does not provide a sufficient basis for making a proper judgment. Mill
himself reveals the inherent weakness in his particular utilitarian position when he talks about greater and lesser pleasures, contrasting
quality and quantity involving kinds of pleasure. What determines such
valuation? Mill appears to defer to proper instruction. But what constitutes proper instruction? There must be some ideals, even objective standards that would determine what is qualitatively superior or proper.
Though Mill will argue that his position puts utilitarianism "on higher
ground, with entire consistency," the only way it can be unshakable is on
an objective foundation, which runs contrary to utilitarianism. Still, one
could make a case for Mill's higher ground perspective safeguarding
against abortion of fetuses with disabilities based on the desire to cultivate more refined pleasures. In what follows, I will account for his
"higher though shaky ground" position before turning to a critique of
refined pleasures.

Higher though shaky ground utilitarianism. In writing on utilitarian
positions up to his time,[52] Mill claims that adherents of utilitarian positions evaluated various pleasures on the grounds of "circumstantial advantages rather than . . . their intrinsic nature."[53] While Mill maintains
that they argued their position satisfactorily, they could have made their
case on "higher ground, with entire consistency." He makes clear what
that higher ground would be:

> It is quite compatible with the principle of utility to recognize the fact, that
> some *kinds* of pleasure are more desirable and more valuable than others.
> It would be absurd that while, in estimating all other things, quality is

---

[51]Mill, *Utilitarianism*, 17.
[52]Mill's later refinement or nuancing of utilitarianism according to kinds of pleasure distinguished
him from his mentor Jeremy Bentham, who made no such distinction as to intrinsic vs. extrinsic.
[53]Mill, *Utilitarianism*, 8.

considered as well as quantity, the estimation of pleasures should be supposed to depend on quantity alone.[54]

Circumstantial evidences include "greater permanency, safety, un-
costliness, &c.," whereas the intrinsic framework favors "superiority in
quality." How does one determine such superiority involving differences
in quality? Mill answers: "Of two pleasures, if there be one to which all
or almost all who have experience of both give a decided preference, irrespective of any feeling or moral obligation to prefer it, that is the more
desirable pleasure." Even if there is "a greater amount of discontent" associated with it, they would still choose it over the other pleasure, no
matter the quantity of this other pleasure.[55]

Mill then makes his case for preferring pleasures associated with the
"higher faculties" over lower faculties. Those who are familiar with both
kinds of pleasures and able to experience generally agree that mental
pleasures are superior to bodily pleasures:[56]

> Few human creatures would consent to be changed into any of the lower
> animals, for a promise of the fullest allowance of a beast's pleasures; no
> intelligent human being would consent to be a fool, no instructed
> person would be an ignoramus, no person of feeling and conscience
> would be selfish and base, even though they should be persuaded that
> the fool, the dunce, or the rascal is better satisfied with his lot than they
> are with theirs.[57]

In sum, Mill compares and contrasts the "higher faculties" with the lower
faculties, higher pleasures with lower pleasures, "happiness" with con-
tentment or "content," and higher forms of rationality connected to the
higher faculties, pleasures, and happiness.[58]

Mill's talk of kinds of pleasures, including those of "intrinsic
superiority,"[59] begs the question: How are some pleasures intrinsically
superior, and how does one discern the qualitative differences between

---

54 Mill, *Utilitarianism*, 8.
55 Mill, *Utilitarianism*, 8-9.
56 Mill, *Utilitarianism*, 9.
57 Mill, *Utilitarianism*, 9.
58 Mill, *Utilitarianism*, 9-10.
59 Mill, *Utilitarianism*, 10.

pleasures? Pleasures do not have intrinsic properties. Discerning the presumed merits would require an appeal to some natural, rational, or religious system more basic than sensation. When Mill speaks of informed people's preference for higher over lower and says that "no instructed person would be an ignoramus," he is making value judgments that go beyond the pleasures themselves. Such supposed refined pleasures are the result of a certain kind of instruction that is bound up with a certain value system external to and independent of the pleasures. Mill's emphasis on the intrinsic superiority of certain pleasures places him on higher ground, but not a purely or truly utilitarian basis. In other words, he is inconsistent and operating parasitically on some other basis, whether religious, rational, or natural.[60]

Mill's distinction between higher and lower pleasures reveals the inadequacy of a utilitarian position as a foundational framework for ethics. On its own, it could never adjudicate between the presumed merits of different kinds of pleasure that should guide a populace. While accounting for pleasure and pain has its merit in making ethical determinations, utilitarianism cannot stand on its own. Mill, along with Bentham, leaves us hanging on how to determine which pleasure and which end we should pursue.

Alasdair MacIntyre pursues this critique, observing that "there are too many different kinds of enjoyable activity, too many different modes in which happiness is achieved." One is lost in prioritizing one of these modes from a utilitarian position. MacIntyre concludes, "If the prospect of his or her own future pleasure or happiness cannot for the reasons which I have suggested provide criteria for solving the problem of action in the case of each individual, it follows that the notion of the greatest happiness of the greatest number is a notion without any clear content at all."[61]

Such inconsistency leads us to seek firmer ethical ground on which to make judgments on such matters as abortion. Before looking for a higher

---

[60]See Alasdair MacIntyre's discussion of this dynamic in *After Virtue*, 3rd ed. (Notre Dame, IN: University of Notre Dame Press, 2007), 62-65.
[61]MacIntyre, *After Virtue*, 63-64.

or firmer ethical ground, let's consider one more facet—namely, Mill's consideration of suffering's import.

Refined sensibilities and greater suffering. Mill does not limit consideration to higher faculties and refined pleasures. He also accounts for the potential for greater suffering that ensues. A person with higher faculties and refined sensibilities faces the possibility of greater suffering because more is required to make them happy. Such happiness is harder to come by for them than for those who are satisfied with lesser pleasures: "A being of higher faculties requires more to make him happy, is capable probably of more acute suffering, and is certainly accessible to it at more points, than one of an inferior type; but in spite of these liabilities, he can never really wish to sink into what he feels to be a lower grade of existence."[62]

Though suffering has no intrinsic value that can serve as an end in itself from Mill's perspective, suffering can play a key role in increasing "the sum total of happiness."[63] So, what import might these statements about the probability of "more acute suffering" have for our present theme of people experiencing life with disabilities?

Would not the likelihood of greater suffering bound up with more refined pleasures suggest that those who are truly cultured take on a greater burden and care for those with disabilities rather than seek an abortion? Even if one were to consent that moral value is determined by the quality of life associated with pleasures involving the higher faculties of reason, how would that give rise to aborting someone who is deemed an "ignoramus" based on a mental disability? The focus is not on the individual with the disability but on the persons responsible for the well-being of the individual with the disability: not just the parents, but the entire society.

Contrary to Dawkins, one could argue based on Mill's higher-grade utilitarianism that higher reasoning and the pleasure associated with it would lead toward caring for the mentally disabled individual. If suffering is more acute for those with refined passions, they should not take the pain and sacrifice bound up with caring for the disabled person as a

---

[62]Mill, *Utilitarianism*, 9.
[63]Mill, *Utilitarianism*, 17.

sign that they are making a wrong determination. If anything, their more acute suffering in caring for the individual with the disability reveals how refined their pleasures are. In fact, to encourage the abortion might even be a sign of what Mill would call "a lower grade of existence."

The question arises, Is someone properly "instructed" who willingly terminates a fetus because it carries Down syndrome? A pleasure principle alone is not sufficient for providing an answer given the vast variety of competing pleasures. So, I must go in search of firmer ethical ground.

IN SEARCH OF FIRMER ETHICAL GROUND

The golden rule. Proper instruction in Mill's estimation would entail consideration of Jesus and the golden rule, which sums up utilitarianism's ethos. Mill writes, "In the golden rule of Jesus of Nazareth, we read the complete spirit of the ethics of utility. To do as one would be done by, and to love one's neighbor as oneself, constitute the ideal perfection of utilitarian morality."[64] How is this so? The "utilitarian standard" for Mill entails that the moral agent's concern is not their individual happiness, but the happiness of all persons involved. To do so, he must remain impartial and compassionate: "As between his own happiness and that of others, utilitarianism requires him to be as strictly impartial as a disinterested and benevolent spectator."[65] Surely, consideration of Jesus and the golden rule has a bearing on the subject of abortion in the case of a fetus carrying Down syndrome.

An entangled ethical framework in pursuit of firm ethical ground would also make room for other renditions of the golden rule, including Confucius's version and Immanuel Kant's comparable categorical imperative. Confucius was asked what one teaching could serve as the guide for conduct during one's lifetime. He responded, "Do not impose on others what you yourself do not desire."[66] Kant put forth the categorical imperative, which is often viewed as a refinement of the golden rule: "Act as if the maxim of your action were to become by your will a

---

[64]Mill, *Utilitarianism*, 17.

[65]Mill, *Utilitarianism*, 17.

[66]Confucius, *Analects*, trans. D. C. Lau, Penguin Classics (New York: Penguin Books, 1979), XV, no. 24, 135.

universal law of nature."[67] The categorical imperative treats the principled action as the point of reference rather than the individual's disinterested benevolence, as in the case of Mill's utilitarian paradigm.

If we were to apply Mill's presumed appropriation of the golden rule, namely disinterested benevolence for all parties, it would prove problematic and incoherent to call for the termination of the life of a fetus with Down syndrome given such factors as their perceived positive quality of life. Moreover, why should Dawkins or any other "able-minded" person be allowed to make the call to maintain or terminate the life of an individual fetus with Down syndrome? Those who make the call should be those bearing the same likeness, that is, Down syndrome, not the intellectual and cultural elite like Dawkins. Those with Down syndrome would be best able to grasp what it means "to do as one would be done by" in such cases, as Mill restates the golden rule.

In contrast to catering to the cultural elite, Jesus affirms childlike faith. So, a person that would ever remain a child in their mental processes does not constitute a negative quality in Jesus' mind. While he does not argue that we must become mentally impaired to inherit the kingdom of heaven, in an eschatological ethic based on Jesus' kingdom preaching, the inheritance of the kingdom is not bound up with intellectual prowess. Jesus affirms those who reflect a childlike state of being:

> At that time the disciples came to Jesus and asked, "Who, then, is the greatest in the kingdom of heaven?" He called a little child to him, and placed the child among them. And he said: "Truly I tell you, unless you change and become like little children, you will never enter the kingdom of heaven. Therefore, whoever takes the lowly position of this child is the greatest in the kingdom of heaven." (Matthew 18:1-4)

Then people brought little children to Jesus for him to place his hands on them and pray for them. But the disciples rebuked them. Jesus said, "Let the little children come to me, and do not hinder them, for the kingdom of heaven belongs to such as these" (Matthew 19:13-15).

---

[67]Immanuel Kant, *Groundwork of the Metaphysics of Morals*, rev. ed., trans. Mary Gregor and Jens Timmerman, Cambridge Texts in the History of Philosophy (Cambridge: Cambridge University Press, 2012), 4:421, 31.

Dawkins might wish to argue that the simple and uneducated can be content but not sufficiently happy. When coupled with Dawkins's logic involving those with disabilities, it might go something like this: Those with Down syndrome appear content, but that is only because they lack the ability to perceive how unhappy they really are and how great their suffering is. Those who are properly instructed and who have refined pleasures (those of "intrinsic superiority") must "compassionately" determine what's in their best interest, including the recommended termination of life in the case of fetuses carrying Down syndrome.

To be fair, Dawkins does not demand, but rather, when asked, encourages mothers carrying Down syndrome fetuses to abort them. And yet, what harm have they done to warrant Mill's "harm principle" that permits liberty except in the case where one person's liberty brings harm to others?[68] The fetus with a disability is not harming anyone. Dawkins's refined pleasure is not cultivated enough based on Mill's higher ground though inconsistent utilitarianism.

Of course, consideration of abortion must not be limited to the fetus. One must account for the well-being of the mother, as well as the relation of the fetus and mother to the community at large. A personalist approach seeks to account for all principal parties in formulating a moral stance. Religious traditions, including Judaism, Islam, and Christianity, have sought to do so in various ways. Let's consider them briefly in the effort to account for other perspectives beyond utilitarianism, including its appropriation of the golden rule.

Divine laws and religious traditions. I'll begin with consideration of Judaism. Rabbi D. Immanuel Jakobovits offers the following Orthodox Jewish perspective:

> In the Jewish view, the human conscience is meant to enforce laws, not to make them. Right and wrong, good and evil, are absolute values which transcend the capricious variations of time, place, and environment, just as they defy definition by relation to human intuition or expediency. These values, Judaism teaches, derive their validity from the Divine

---

[68]John Stuart Mill, *On Liberty*, Penguin Classics (New York: Penguin, 2007).

revelation at Mount Sinai, as expounded and developed by sages faithful to, and authorized by, its writ.[69]

He later quotes the Talmud: "He who saves one life is as if he saved an entire world; one human life is as precious as a million lives, for each is infinite in value."[70] Rabbi Jakobovits then adds, "For this reason, Jewish law forbids the surrender of a single life even if any number of other lives may thereby be saved."[71]

According to Fred Rosner, MD, the director of the Department of Medicine at Mount Sinai School of Medicine in New York, there is no explicit mention of intentional abortion in the Hebrew Scriptures, though there is discussion of "accidental abortion." According to Rosner, the fetus is not considered a person until it is born. Until that time, it is considered part of the mother.[72]

Rosner draws from the Hebrew Scriptures, the Talmud, and rabbinic writings in making his case. Rosner makes special note of Exodus 21:22-23, which he quotes: "When men fight and one of them pushes a pregnant woman and a miscarriage results, but no other misfortune ensues, the one responsible shall be fined as the woman's husband may exact from him, the payment to be based on judges' reckoning. But if other misfortune ensues, the penalty shall be life for life." Rosner points out that the great rabbinic scholar Rashi takes "no other misfortune" to mean the loss of the woman's life. Rosner also references Moses Maimonides, who claims, "If one assaults a woman, even unintentionally, and her child is born prematurely, he must pay the value of the child to the husband and the compensation for injury and pain to the woman." The Mishnah claims, "If a woman is having difficulty in giving birth [and her life is in danger], one cuts up the fetus within her womb and extracts it limb by limb, because her life takes precedence over that of the fetus. But if the greater part was already born, one may not touch it, for one

---

[69]Immanuel Jakobovits, "Jewish Views on Abortion," *Case Western Reserve Law Review* 17, no. 2 (1965): 482.

[70]See the Talmud, Sanhedrin 4:5; quoted in Jakobovits, "Jewish Views on Abortion," 492-93.

[71]Jakobovits, "Jewish Views on Abortion," 493n44.

[72]In no way should this claim be taken to justify that one can do anything with the fetus. Again, there is no explicit mention of intentional abortion, only accidental abortion. The fetus as part of the mother's life is sacred.

may not set aside one person's life for that of another." According to Rosner, Rabbi Yom Tov Lippman Heller comments on this passage that "the fetus is not considered a *nefesh* until it has egressed into the air of the world and, therefore, one is permitted to destroy it to save the mother's life." Rosner also argues that "similar reasoning is found in Rashi's commentary on the Talmudic discussion of this Mishnaic passage, where Rashi states that as long as the child has not come out into the world, it is not called a living being, i.e., *nefesh*. Once the head of the child has come out, the child may not be harmed because it is considered as fully born, and one life may not be taken to save another."[73]

Likewise, in the Muslim tradition, there is a rich and varied heritage of reflection on questions of abortion and the nature of human value. Looking to the Qur'an for guidance, while abortion is not specifically mentioned, general commands against killing are often studied to see if they have relevance to a given situation. In so doing, as Jonathan E. Brockopp points out, Muslims, too, run into the related question: Are fetuses to be considered "people"?[74] Much like Jewish Talmudic reflection, there is a lengthy tradition of Muslim commentary and reflection on the Qur'an, which provides "valuable sources for understanding the religious beliefs of Muslims through the centuries," even though there is "an uneasy relationship between the theoretical primacy of the sources and the application of this theory in the giving of ethical opinions."[75] In addition, there is the need to consult the hadith, or sayings of the Prophet Muhammad. Brockopp claims that "argument and disagreement are found even in the most authoritative collections

---

[73]Fred Rosner, "The Fetus in Jewish Law," My Jewish Learning, www.myjewishlearning.com/article /the-fetus-in-jewish-law/; taken from *Biomedical Ethics and Jewish Law* (Brooklyn, NY: Ktav Pub, 2001), 178-80. It should be noted, however, that like any tradition, Judaism has internal diversity. While Rosner represents Jewish opinions that go all the way back to Palestinian Judaism at least contemporary to Christ if not earlier, Jewish Alexandrian traditions more influenced by Aristotle's notion that at a certain point the fetus is "vivified" and receives what could be called the soul do argue for various points of "ensoulment" for the child during pregnancy. See O. M. Bakke, *When Children Became People: The Birth of Childhood in Early Christianity* (Minneapolis: Augsburg Fortress, 2005), 111-12.

[74]Jonathan E. Brockopp, "Taking Life and Saving Life: The Islamic Context," in *Islamic Ethics of Life: Abortion, War, and Euthanasia*, ed. Jonathan E. Brockopp (Columbia: University of South Carolina Press, 2003), 3.

[75]Brockopp, "Taking Life and Saving Life," 4.

of *hadith*," and so there is no one "Muslim" approach to abortion or other ethical issues.

In Islamic thought as a whole, there is a division of opinion regarding ethics and its relation to God's will: Is something good because God wills it, or is there a reason God wills what he does, a prior good or reason inherent to God that his will follows? This question is not unique to Islam but has also vexed Christian theologians, especially in the later Middle Ages. Far from being an esoteric question, it has ramifications for how Muslims discuss abortion. As Brockopp writes, a tendency to emphasize God's will leads many Muslim scholars to "reason from case, instead of principle."[76] The reason for this is that if God's will is absolute, and decides the good, one knows the good only from its instances and not from a general principle. This leads to decision-making on a case-by-case basis, but also distributes the ability to make ethical decisions across the whole community, as no single principle or authority is therefore in charge of interpretation on these matters.[77] In cases of euthanasia, for example, the decision is often left up to the family,[78] who are the only ones as a matter of course able to know the complexities of the situation.

Putting such emphasis on God's will also changes how decisions are made in terms of introducing "necessity" to the equation. "By describing difficult ethical situations (such as performing an abortion to save the life of the mother) as cases of necessity," writes Brockopp, "one preserves both the integrity of the transgressed command [not to take life] and also the unique characteristics of each ethical situation."[79] This same principle applies to limited cases in which the fetus has severe medical disorders and abortion would spare it from a life of great pain.[80] This principle of necessity, and sparing pain, is also why a fatwa (a ruling of Islamic law by a recognized authority) was given allowing Bosnian women who were raped by the Serbian army to abort the fetuses.[81] While they were strongly

---

[76]Brockopp, "Taking Life and Saving Life," 14.
[77]Brockopp, "Taking Life and Saving Life," 15.
[78]Brockopp, "Taking Life and Saving Life," 15.
[79]Brockopp, "Taking Life and Saving Life," 16.
[80]See "Sanctity of Life: Islamic Teachings on Abortion," British Broadcasting Corporation, September 9, 2009, www.bbc.co.uk/religion/religions/islam/islamethics/abortion_1.shtml.
[81]"Sanctity of Life: Islamic Teachings on Abortion."

urged not to seek an abortion, permission was still granted. However, any abortion performed in such exceptional cases should be done before 120 days, when in Islam the fetus is typically considered "ensouled" by God (though there is considerable debate on this point). These decisions come despite the fact that there are "strong presumptions against suicide and abortion" generally in Islam because of suras like Qur'ran 5:32: "Whoever has spared the life of a soul, it is as though he has spared the life of all people. Whoever has killed a soul, it is as though he has murdered all of mankind." The case-based nature of interpreting these commands "does not mean that the act itself is unimportant," concludes Brockopp, "but rather that by paying attention to the frame of the ethical situation they establish the intention of the Muslim actors to follow God's will in advance of both the action and its consequences."[82] This is why for Muslims, despite the case-based nature of ethical reasoning, instances of abortion or euthanasia are *never* considered the decisions of the individual.[83] Nor can abortion be done out of fear that the family will not be able to provide for the child, for they must trust Allah in these matters.[84] There is an entire array of community, conversation, and concern that needs to be taken into account. As such, instead of general principles, Muslims desire to stand in awe before God as a community in wrestling with difficult decisions and seeking to obey God's will.

In contrast to the Jewish and Muslim positions articulated here, the Christian tradition historically viewed the fetus's distinct human life beginning at conception. According to David Albert Jones, "The dominant view among Western Catholic Christians since the fifth century has been that the soul is immediately created by God and infused into the new human being that is formed in the womb. However, this has never been formally defined by the Church by a pope or an ecumenical council."[85]

While acknowledging the real differences between the Christian, Jewish, and Muslim positions, an entangled ethic recognizes common ethical ground, including the Jewish and Christian traditions' wariness

---

[82]Brockopp, "Taking Life and Saving Life," 16-17.
[83]Brockopp, "Taking Life and Saving Life," 17.
[84]"Sanctity of Life: Islamic Teachings on Abortion."
[85]David Albert Jones, *The Soul of the Embryo: An Enquiry into the Status of the Human Embryo in the Christian Tradition* (New York: Continuum International, 2004), 107.

of arguments favoring abortion based on reduced quality of life for the fetus.[86] Moreover, in the context of the Jewish and Christian scriptural heritage, it is important to guard against sweeping arguments favoring abortion on account of the mother's health. Rather, one must weigh each situation carefully to determine what kind and level of risk is present to the mother before possibly making an exception to the rule and permitting an abortion. However, there is no place for celebrating exceptions as a liberty. Nor is there sweeping or carte blanche support for aborting fetuses with severe disabilities. I now turn to consider exceptions to the rule and choosing to abort a fetus, on the one hand, and refusing to abort those deemed inferior on account of disabilities on the other hand.[87]

On abortion and exceptions to the rule. The Roman Catholic Church condemns the practice of "procured" or intended abortions in all cases. However, it does not assign culpability in cases where abortions were the unintended consequence of certain actions. Here is a definitive Catholic statement on procured abortions:

> The Magisterium has not expressly committed itself to an affirmation of a philosophical nature, but it constantly reaffirms the moral condemnation of any kind of procured abortion. This teaching has not been changed and is unchangeable.
>
> Thus the fruit of human generation, from the first moment of its existence, that is to say from the moment the zygote has formed, demands the unconditional respect that is morally due to the human being in his bodily and spiritual totality. The human being is to be respected and treated as a person from the moment of conception; and therefore from that same moment his rights as a person must be recognized, among which in the first place is the inviolable right of every innocent human being to life.[88]

While it is a contested claim, the United States Conference of Catholic Bishops maintains that the church has prohibited procured abortions since the first century.[89]

---

[86]For an exposition on this point and others, see Bakke, *When Children Became People*, 110-51.

[87]Jones, *Soul of the Embryo*, 57-74.

[88]*Donum Vitae* (Respect for Human Life), I/1; www.vatican.va/roman_curia/congregations/cfaith /documents/rc_con_cfaith_doc_19870222_respect-for-human-life_en.html.

[89]USCCB, "Respect for Unborn Human Life: The Church's Constant Teaching," www.usccb.org /issues-and-action/human-life-and-dignity/abortion/respect-for-unborn-human-life.

As noted at the outset of this section, the Catholic Church makes a distinction between direct and indirect abortions. The latter is when an abortion may result unintentionally from a medical procedure intended to save a pregnant woman's life. The abortion is indirect, that is, not intended.[90]

One finds parallels here with Aquinas's principle of double effect, which he developed in the context of permitting self-defense.[91] According to Aquinas, if you were to kill an assailant in self-defense, your action is permissible or justified so long as you did not intend to kill the other party: "Therefore, this act, since one's intention is to save one's own life, is not unlawful, seeing that it is natural to everything to keep itself in being as far as possible." Still, the permission is conditional, not categorical: "And yet, though proceeding from a good intention, an act may be rendered unlawful if it be out of proportion to the end. Wherefore, if a man in self-defense uses more than necessary violence, it will be unlawful, whereas, if he repel force with moderation, his defense will be lawful." Killing must never be the goal.

Here one must distinguish between *incidental* causation for the good end of preserving one's life from attack and *instrumental* causation for the good end of preserving one's life from attack. Killing cannot be the goal of one's actions, no matter the result, including the preservation of one's own life. In other words, the end does not justify the means. The goal of killing in self-defense involves a greater degree of vicious conduct than is merited for self-defense. Again, killing must be incidental, not instrumental.[92]

So, what does that mean in the case of determining whether to abort a fetus to save the life of the mother? Is that decision murder on this account? Certainly not from this vantage point in the case of uterine cancer in which the desired consequence is to remove the cancerous uterus to save the mother's life. If she dies during pregnancy, the baby dies, too. So, it is better to save the mother rather than lose both, even though that

[90]See for example Edwin F. Healy, SJ, *Medical Ethics* (Chicago: Loyola University Press, 1956), 213-30.

[91]Alison McIntyre, "Doctrine of Double Effect," in *Stanford Encyclopedia of Philosophy*, ed. Edward N. Zalta, winter 2014 ed., https://plato.stanford.edu/entries/double-effect/; refer also to Martha A. C. Newsome, "Abortion and Double Effect," *Catholic Answers*, September 1st, 2006; www.catholic .com/magazine/print-edition/abortion-and-double-effect.

[92]Thomas Aquinas, *Summa Theologica II-II*, q. 64, art. 7, "Of Killing," in *On Law, Morality, and Politics*, ed. William P. Baumgarth and Richard J. Regan, SJ (Indianapolis: Hackett, 1988), 226-27.

determination involves the undesired consequence of losing the fetus by removing the mother's diseased organ.[93]

It is also worth pointing out that there are laws still in place stipulating that those who kill a pregnant woman will be charged with double murder. It has nothing to do with whether the woman or fetus's life measures up to utilitarian quality-of-life indicators. The issue is not the presumed quality of this or that life, but the *inherent* value of all human life. This then requires us to ask, Is the fetus a human? Do utilitarian indicators of desirability shape the answer to the question about whether a fetus is a human? For many religious traditions, killing based on desirability or nondesirability would be perverse.

Many other faith traditions permit abortions in specific cases, whether it be the physical safety or the psychological safety of the mother. For example, Rabbi Jakobovits maintains that in Orthodox Judaism "present-day rabbis are unanimous in condemning abortion, feticide, or infanticide to eliminate a crippled being, before or after birth, as an unconscionable attack on the sanctity of life."[94] On the matter of exceptions, however, he maintains that

> Jewish law would consider a grave psychological hazard to the mother as no less weighty a reason for an abortion than a physical threat. . . . If it is genuinely feared that a continued pregnancy and eventual birth under these conditions might have such debilitating effects on the mother as to present a danger to her own life or the life of another by suicidal or violent tendencies, however remote this danger may be, a therapeutic abortion may be indicated with the same justification as for other medical reasons.[95]

Such fear for the mother would have to be well-grounded, Jakobovits maintains. Decisions about life and death must be carefully weighed.

On abortion and liberty. Although many religious communities permit abortions in certain cases, no tradition that champions the sanctity of all life celebrates abortion as a liberty. These traditions would

---

[93]See Newsome, "Abortion and Double Effect." For an article contending against the double effect doctrine in the case of abortion, see A. B. Shaw, "Two Challenges to the Double Effect Doctrine: Euthanasia and Abortion," *Journal of Medical Ethics* 28 (2002): 102-4.

[94]Jakobovits, "Jewish Views on Abortion," 488.

[95]Jakobovits, "Jewish Views on Abortion," 489.

take issue with a *New York Times* article that framed abortion in this way: "Abortion is not a fringe issue. Abortion is liberty."[96] A Libertarians for Life statement critiquing this basic mindset represents well many traditions' refusal to speak of abortion as liberty, or as the freedom to do whatever one wants:

> The essence of [liberty] is not the right to do whatever we choose. Instead it's the *negative* right to be free from aggression—the initiation of force or fraud. To be more exact, the essence is the negative obligation not to aggress. The non-aggression principle has an immediate consequence. Just as we may not initiate force, so we may not endanger the innocent without their consent. So, basic to [liberty] is the non-endangerment principle. Non-endangerment, also a negative obligation, is implicit in non-aggression.[97]

Buddhism features non-aggression as a cardinal value. It has a bearing on the subject of abortion. While there is no single view among Buddhist schools on abortion, Buddhists risk grave inconsistency if they view it as anything more than an unfortunate necessity. James Hughes writes, "Most Western and Japanese Buddhists come away believing in the permissibility of abortion, while many other Buddhists believe abortion to be murder."[98] Even so, he maintains that while many Western Buddhists perceive abortion as permissible, they do not celebrate it, but see it "as an unfortunate but necessary part of women's reproductive health care."[99]

The Dalai Lama permits abortion on a case-by-case basis, as with a mentally disabled fetus, or in the event of a birth creating "serious problems" for the mother. Nonetheless, he maintains that in Buddhism abortion "is an act of killing and is negative, generally speaking."[100] A Zen Buddhist priest, Kyogen Carlson, argued that he longed for the day when

[96]Lindy West, "Of Course Abortion Should Be a Litmus Test for Democrats," *New York Times*, August 2, 2017, www.nytimes.com/2017/08/02/opinion/trump-democrats-abortion-litmus-test.html.

[97]John Walker and Doris Gordon, "Abortion and Libertarianism's First Principles," Libertarians for Life ©1996, https://l4l.org/library/frstprnc.html.

[98]James Hughes, "Buddhism and Abortion: A Western Approach," in *Buddhism and Abortion*, ed. Damien Keown (Houndmills: Macmillan Press, 1998), 183.

[99]Hughes, "Buddhism and Abortion," 184.

[100]Claudia Dreifus, "The Dalai Lama," *New York Times*, November 28, 1993, www.nytimes.com/1993/11/28/magazine/the-dalai-lama.html.

there was no longer a need for abortions, since all life is sacred.[101] His Zen tradition acknowledges the emotional duress of the woman. Responding to those who have claimed that they were not upset about having an abortion, Zen teacher Robert Aitken maintains that "they were not sensitive to their own feelings at that particular time. . . . Surely self-awareness is never more important." He goes on to say,

> I get the impression that when a woman is sensitive to her feelings, she is conscious that abortion is killing a part of herself and terminating the ancient process, begun anew within herself, of bringing life into being. Thus she is likely to feel acutely miserable after making a decision to have an abortion. This is a time for compassion for the woman, and for her to be compassionate with herself and for her unborn child.[102]

Traditions pursuing a comprehensive sanctity of life model will guard against celebrating abortion as a liberty. They will also guard against turning a blind eye to mothers tempted to abort on account of such factors as poverty. Indifference to their plight for the sake of the majority's exercise and expansion of creative powers is not a form of liberty or virtuous happiness. True liberty involves serving those in need. According to the New Testament, biblical religion requires that we care for the marginalized, such as orphans and widows in their distress (James 1:27). The biblical tradition sees the need for social structures that serve as a safety net for persons in precarious situations, such as a vulnerable mother and child.[103]

Those who seek to restrict and ban abortions must do everything possible to put in place economic programs that help pregnant women and couples who face economic peril. A study in the *American Journal of Public Health* concluded that "women denied an abortion were more likely than were women who received an abortion to experience

---

[101]Paul Louis Metzger and Kyogen Carlson, "Politicians, Please Weigh Your Rhetoric—and Find Some Common Ground," *Oregonian*, April 22, 2012, www.oregonlive.com/opinion/index.ssf/2012/04/politicians_please_weigh_your.html.

[102]Robert Aitken, *The Mind of Clover: Essays in Zen Buddhist Ethics* (New York: North Point Press, 1984), 21. John Paul II also seeks to provide words of comfort and hope in the papal encyclical *Evangelium Vitae* to women who have had abortions. See thesis number 99: www.vatican.va/content/john-paul-ii/en/encyclicals/documents/hf_jp-ii_enc_25031995_evangelium-vitae.html.

[103]See Bakke, *When Children Became People*, 159.

economic hardship and insecurity lasting years. Laws that restrict access to abortion may result in worsened economic outcomes for women."[104] Regarding poverty, we must account for the following: "When women are asked why they want to end a pregnancy, the most common reasons are financial—in particular, not having enough money to raise a child or support another child."[105] Economic hardship may only intensify if the fetus has a significant disability. Combined economic hardship and the distress a woman or couple may experience in knowing that their fetus has a significant disability may lead many desperate persons to view abortion as the only tenable solution.

It is worth noting here that Mill, who also argued for sexual equality, wrote in *On Liberty* that an increase in happiness correlates with an increase in liberty or one's creative capabilities.[106] But as Mill's own distinction involving levels of happiness reveals, happiness is not a singular concept. We must discern between kinds of happiness and liberty with attention to their telos: Do happiness and liberty involve loving God with one's whole being and one's neighbor as oneself (Mark 12:30-31)?

Those who champion the sacredness of all life will seek to account and care first and foremost for the well-being of the fetus, with or without a disability, as well as the mother. We must love the fetus and mother as ourselves, as well as give special consideration to minority populations in making such ethical determinations.

Charles Marsh addresses the subject of a comprehensive model of the sanctity of life in his discussion of *Roe vs. Wade*. Regardless of the aims in formulating, supporting, or resisting *Roe vs. Wade*, neither dominant culture side (left or right) in the debate shared adequately the concerns of the civil rights movement in how the ruling disproportionately impacted the African American population. Marsh writes that Martin

---

[104]Diana Greene Foster et al., "Socioeconomic Outcomes of Women Who Receive and Women Who Are Denied Wanted Abortions in the United States," *American Journal of Public Health* 108, no. 3 (March 2018): 407. Refer here as well: Ronnie Cohen, "Denial of Abortion Leads to Economic Hardship for Low Income Women," *Reuters*, January 18, 2018, www.reuters.com/article/us-health -abortion-hardship/denial-of-abortion-leads-to-economic-hardship-for-low-income-women -idUSKBN1F731Z.

[105]Foster et al., "Socioeconomic Outcomes," 407.

[106]John Stuart Mill, *On Liberty* and *The Subjection of Women*, Penguin Classics (New York: Penguin, 2007).

Luther King Jr. "had spoken in judgment of the liberal establishment in his denunciations of Vietnam and the American culture of violence. His comprehensive devotion to the sacredness of life would have surely included the unborn, or risked grave inconsistency."[107] Thus, it would come as no surprise that fellow leaders in the civil rights movement reacted strongly to the Supreme Court's decision in *Roe vs. Wade* to legalize abortion. As Marsh chronicles, Fannie Lou Hamer ("forcibly sterilized in her twenties") protested the decision with these words, "Now they're starting to kill black babies."[108] Marsh goes on,

> The disproportionate number of aborted black babies to white in the South could be claimed by white liberals as a demonstration of social compassion only by mocking the civil rights movement's protection of society's most excluded and vulnerable. Reverend Ed King of the Mississippi Freedom Democratic Party had taken the Supreme Court decision as an expression of the "anti-poor policies of the Republican president, Richard Nixon," an insidious and now legal way of achieving massive cuts in welfare spending by "cutting down on black welfare babies."[109]

Social conservatives may try to use such claims as ammunition for their arguments against legalized abortion, but they should wait to hear Marsh out. Marsh goes on to assert:

> White conservative Christians could not share the civil rights movement's outrage at *Roe vs. Wade* because most white Christians had really never cared about black babies to begin with. Lacking a commitment to the poor and the excluded, conservative white opposition to abortion produced nothing so much as a generation of pious patriots; and, as it turned out, any action would be justified in waging war against abortion except support of precisely those social policies for the poor that would make abortion less desirable.[110]

Marsh's "pious patriots" reminds us of the scribes and Pharisees who sit on Moses' seat and whom Jesus rebuked in Matthew 23:4: "They tie

---

[107]Charles Marsh, *The Beloved Community: How Faith Shapes Social Justice, from the Civil Rights Movement to Today* (New York: Basic Books, 2005), 143.

[108]Marsh, *Beloved Community*, 143.

[109]Marsh, *Beloved Community*, 143.

[110]Marsh, *Beloved Community*, 143-44.

up heavy, cumbersome loads and put them on other people's shoulders, but they themselves are not willing to lift a finger to move them" (Matthew 23:4). The Pharisees failed to embody the care for others taught in the law, and instead made it a burden. We operate like these Pharisees of old when we tell the poor to pick themselves up by their own bootstraps, when they have no boots. King spoke to this issue: "It's all right to tell a man to lift himself by his own bootstraps, but it is a cruel jest to say to a bootless man that he ought to lift himself by his own bootstraps."[111]

If we wish to avoid Jesus' rebuke, we need an embodied ethic that gives pregnant impoverished women bootstraps so they can lift themselves out of poverty. Such freedom from poverty may liberate them to keep their young rather than choose to abort. We must guard against indifference and radical individuality. We must guard against blaming people victimized by life circumstances and take action in solidarity as a community to dismantle structures that create poverty and foster the emotional, psychological, and economic drive to abort.

Our free market society's reigning narrative is the radical individuality of humans: "The core assumption of standard economics is that humans are fundamentally individual rather than social animals. The theory holds that all economic choices are acts of authentic, unmediated selfhood."[112] Radical individuality and the mechanistic, Newtonian basis of free market economics blind many to the structural nature of poverty. Furthermore, economics becomes morally neutral. Cynthia Moe-Lobeda summarizes this well: "The laws governing economic life were considered as mechanistic, rational, universal, and irrefutable as those governing mathematics and physics. Economics became an explicitly neutral or value-free science, predicting outcomes, but not rendering moral judgments."[113] The natural conclusion based on a morally neutral,

[111]Martin Luther King Jr., "Remaining Awake Through a Great Revolution," *The Martin Luther King Jr. Research and Education Institute*, accessed on December 7, 2018, https://kinginstitute.stanford .edu/king-papers/documents/remaining-awake-through-great-revolution-address-morehouse -college.

[112]Gordon Bigelow, "Let There Be Markets," *Harper's Magazine*, May 2005, 35.

[113]Cynthia Moe-Lobeda, *Healing a Broken World: Globalization and God* (Minneapolis: Fortress, 2002), 64.

mechanistic view of economics is that individuals are the sole agents responsible for their economic plight: "All too often people assume that personal traits are the sole determinants of economic well-being."[114] This narrative fails to account for the vast social structures in place that perpetuate the cycle of poverty.[115]

What might it entail for us to move beyond pointing the finger and deference to the seemingly mechanistic invisible hand of the market to provide a helping hand to those in need? How badly do we wish to halt abortion in this country? Would it not entail fostering laws and policies that would make food stamps more available, as well as free access to safe and sound childcare for working mothers, greater incentives for providers and protections for those in foster care, increased opportunities for adoption by straight and gay couples, sex education that goes beyond mere abstinence strategies, and the transformation of the prison system so that mothers and fathers are not so readily removed from their families in need of them?

It is important that conservatives do not claim to stand on higher, firmer moral ground than liberals who would move for aborting a fetus based on a perceived lack of utilitarian quality-of-life indicators. Just as it is wrong to abandon a fetus to abortion simply because of a perceived lack of pleasure or happiness and greater amount of pain, it is also wrong to abandon a newborn and their parent to poverty for an indifferent majority population's happiness in a world of increasing pain.

This point calls to mind Ursula Le Guin's short story "The Ones Who Walk Away from Omelas," in which the happiness of the many in a utopian society depends on the horrible, unjust suffering of an innocent child who functions as a scapegoat.[116] Le Guin's story is often viewed as a critique of utilitarianism: the greatest amount of pleasure for the greatest number of people entails the vicarious suffering of an innocent

---

[114]John Iceland, *Poverty in America: A Handbook* (Berkeley: University of California Press, 2006), 96.

[115]Karen Seccombe, "Families in Poverty in the 1990s: Trends, Causes, Consequences, and Lessons Learned," *Journal of Marriage and Family* 62, no. 4 (2000): 1106-7; Daniel K. Finn, *Christian Economic Ethics: History and Implications* (Minneapolis: Fortress, 2013), 317-18; and Iceland, *Poverty in America*, 74.

[116]Ursula K. Le Guin, *The Ones Who Walk Away from Omelas* (Mankato, MN: Creative Education 1993). Refer also to David Brooks, "The Child in the Basement," *New York Times*, January 12, 2015, www.nytimes.com/2015/01/13/opinion/david-brooks-the-child-in-the-basement.html.

victim(s). Both sides on the abortion debate can easily blame one another, while ultimately scapegoating either the mother or fetus, or both mother and child brought into the world. One wonders if the scapegoat—either the grieving mother and aborted fetus or impoverished mother and child born into poverty—must pay the price so the liberal and conservative majority factions can live pleasurable and affluent lives.

Society must cultivate more refined pleasures in keeping with a comprehensive model of the sanctity of all human life. Such refined pleasures on this sure ground would involve enduring greater suffering bound up with sacrificing some of its own comforts for the sake of mother and child, including those with disabilities. A society that affirms higher or more refined pleasures or sensibilities in keeping with a comprehensive sanctity of life model would not pit the mother against the new life in her womb, whereby she is forced to decide whether to have an abortion to avoid poverty or face overwhelming psychological duress.

FROM DISPOSABLE TO INDISPENSABLE: BEYOND NORMALCY

We are made for more than our abilities. Abilities do not exhaust our personhood and do not constitute human dignity, contrary to certain forms of ableism. Besides, there are alternative abilities that people with disabilities, such as Down syndrome, generate and cultivate in keeping with their telos as humans. People with disabilities are indispensable to "normal" human flourishing in community. We must care for those with disabilities and their families. They are not alone.

In this chapter, I have sought to answer what is going on in our culture related to abortion, especially those fetuses with disabilities like Down syndrome, as well as the pressures pregnant women and couples face. I have accounted for a diversity of entangled ethical perspectives and have indicated that what we should care about is cultivating truly refined sensibilities, which involve love of our neighbors that society classifies as "disabled" as ourselves. The fitting response is that we will put in place conceptual perspectives and economic and relational structures that make it less desirable to abort and more compelling to keep the child, "normal" and "disabled" alike, supporting the fetus and mother, and viewing them as vital to community.

People with Down syndrome, which is classified as a disability, often enhance the dynamics of interpersonal relationships. They cultivate their inner persons and develop resilience, as well as a clear sense of purpose involving care of others in keeping with their telos as humans. Those persons with disabilities, like Down syndrome, also have inherent worth and inviolable dignity, created in the image of the triune God, just like the rest of us.

What if we were to look at people and fetuses often classified as "disabled," like those with Down syndrome, as being made for more than their respective capacities? Rather than view them as being less or suffering loss, let's consider how their personhood emerges in the face of disabilities. Let's not speak merely of "including" those with disabilities. Let's speak of belonging with them in community, where we lose out if they are not present. This is what is entailed by living in Jesus' eschatological community.

In keeping with Paul's first letter to the Corinthian church, this posture involves viewing those deemed weak and unimportant as "indispensable" (1 Corinthians 12:22). It guards against use of language and the development of those "refined sensibilities" that dismiss or ostracize people who are classified as having disabilities. With this point in mind, it is little wonder many minorities talk of refined sensibilities as code for discrimination: "People with disabilities have claimed minority status due to discrimination and vigorously reject being reduced solely to persons with poor health and diminished function."[117]

Those whose sensibilities are truly refined will take note that many people with disabilities celebrate and cherish them.[118] Many vulnerable persons look on their disabilities as inseparable from their persons and indispensable to their flourishing as humans. Their sense of refined sensibilities is quite different from the physical, mental, and cultural elite. They challenge the philosophy of ableism. It just goes to show that an emphasis on sensibilities requires consideration of other factors than mere pleasure and happiness for human flourishing.

---

[117]Albrecht and Devlieger, "Disability Paradox," 979.

[118]See Bethany McKinney Fox's discussion of this theme in *Disability and the Way of Jesus: Holistic Healing in the Gospels and the Church*, foreword by John Swinton (Downers Grove, IL: IVP Academic, 2019).

What would life look like if we viewed people with disabilities as indispensable to our own flourishing, celebrating their full participation in community? What would life look like if we were to see that we cannot be who we are without them? Our utilitarian throwaway culture is wrong precisely because it assumes one very limited and reductionistic picture of what quality of life and refined sensibilities entail. A relational or communal approach to disabilities reveals how vulnerable we all are. Those human fetuses and people with disabilities are not scapegoats but prophets who help us expand our outlook of what is entailed by being made for more. They point the way forward. They are priests who mediate to us relationally and imaginatively enriching ways of life otherwise inaccessible.

No one is fully operational. We all have strengths and weaknesses. People with disabilities learn to adapt. In fact, they are often master teachers on how to adapt in pursuit of their telos as persons. They can teach us how to learn to fire and rewire, compensating for our individual weaknesses by leaning into one another and ultimately the crucified and risen Jesus. He bears his glorious scars nobly in his community of faith as the lion of the tribe of Judah who is the lamb of God who had been slain (Revelation 5:5-6).

The Corinthian church struggled to come to terms with celebrating weakness, though Paul urged them to do so (see 1 Corinthians 1:26-31 and 2 Corinthians 12:9-11). The apostle Paul goes to great lengths in 1 Corinthians to articulate what is involved in belonging to the crucified and risen Jesus' upside-down eschatological kingdom community, in which God favors the weak and foolish, not those of noble status (1 Corinthians 1:18-31). Contrary to Aristotle's framework, which esteems friendship based on similarities, the New Testament's emphasis on cruciform, embodied love gives rise to a profound sense of belonging for people of all walks of life. No doubt, this orientation would include people with disabilities. Rather than being throwaways, the community at large cherishes and privileges them. Those who properly discern the body of Christ realize that Christ is wise and powerful in his cruciform and risen foolishness and weakness (1 Corinthians 1:18-25). He reorients his body to cherish those who are foolish and weak. Only together with those who are frail of limb and intellect are Christ's people truly wise and strong. Jesus makes possible full participation of all members of his body at the church family table (1 Corinthians 11:17-34).

The Spirit who forms the body of Christ determines and distributes gifts to its members for the common good (1 Corinthians 12:7, 11). The Spirit gives special consideration to those participants who are deemed inferior:

> Those parts of the body that seem to be weaker are indispensable, and the parts that we think are less honorable we treat with special honor. And the parts that are unpresentable are treated with special modesty, while our presentable parts need no special treatment. But God has put the body together, giving greater honor to the parts that lacked it, so that there should be no division in the body, but that its parts should have equal concern for each other. If one part suffers, every part suffers with it; if one part is honored, every part rejoices with it. (1 Corinthians 12:22-26)

The Spirit refines our sensibilities in keeping with God's determination to award greater honor to the parts that lack it, thereby guarding against divisions. Jesus' communal being values all members as vitally important. We can only experience the fullness of life as being made for more when we see those who are seemingly weaker as making us all stronger. They are indispensable.[119]

---

[119]For key works on disability theology, see Brian Brock, *Wondrously Wounded: Theology, Disability, and the Body of Christ*, Studies in Religion, Theology, and Disability (Waco, TX: Baylor University Press, 2019); John Swinton, *Becoming Friends of Time: Disability, Timefulness, and Gentle Discipleship*, Studies in Religion, Theology, and Disability (Waco, TX: Baylor University Press, 2018).

4

MORE THAN GENETIC PERFECTION

The Value of Imperfect Bodies

AS GENETIC RESEARCH OPENS new vistas of what is possible for humans to achieve, we must be sure to hold in tension what scientists can do and what they should or should not do. Scientific gains should never take precedence over people's welfare. Therefore, scientists must guard against posing unwarranted risks to people.[1] This point of tension is one key intersection where science meets religion and ethics. Drawing from diverse ethical traditions that affirm the sacredness of all life, this chapter focuses on genetic engineering and its import for the common good, while attempting to put in place appropriate ethical parameters and boundaries. The chapter will consider whether the pursuit of genetic enhancement is natural, virtuous, and hospitable. I will argue that no matter what genetic engineering can offer or promise, there is more to humanity than genetic enhancement and perfection. We are made for more.

GENETIC ENGINEERING AND THE GATTACAN FUTURE

It is important that we affirm science in its pursuit of the common good, including advances in genetic research. However, we must also account for ethical considerations that help us discern where such research goes beyond rightful bounds and manipulates human dignity. Take gene

---

[1] Janet D. Stemwedel, "Scientists' Powers and Ways They Shouldn't Use Them: Obligations of Scientists (part 2)," *Scientific American*, November 28, 2013, https://blogs.scientificamerican.com/doing-good-science/scientistse28099-powers-and-ways-they-shouldne28099t-use-them-obligations-of-scientists-part-2/. Refer also to Kristin Shrader-Frechette, *Ethics of Scientific Research* (Lanham, MD: Rowman & Littlefield, 1994).

engineering or manipulation, for example, including a new generation known as "gene editing."

What is genetic engineering? "Genetic engineering, sometimes called genetic modification, is the process of altering the DNA in an organism's genome."[2] It involves "techniques used to cut up and join different genetic material, especially DNA from different biological species, and to introduce the resulting hybrid DNA into an organism in order to form new combinations of heritable genetic material."[3] The Center for Genetics and Society has commented on the implications of gene editing, which involves "deliberately changing the genes passed on to children and future generations." They argue that while there is some "promise for helping people who are sick," there are also "grave safety, social, and ethical concerns." According to this statement, concerns "range from the prospect of irreversible harms to the health of future children and generations, to concerns about opening the door to new forms of social inequality, discrimination, and conflict."[4] In other words, the impact of such research and technologies can be colossally positive or negative—and perhaps both.

In reflecting on genetic engineering, some readers may call to mind science fiction tales of the distant future, or even "the not-too-distant future" as envisioned in the movie *Gattaca*.[5] Actually, the Gattacan future may already be upon us. A 2013 article in *Scientific American* drew attention to the movie in its discussion of "preimplantation genetic diagnosis" (PGD): "Are We Too Close to Making Gattaca a Reality?"[6] In view of a 2016 *Time* article titled "U.K. Approves First Studies of New Gene Editing Technique CRISPR on Human Embryos,"[7] the answer appears to be in capital letters, like DNA—YES.

---

[2]"What Is Genetic Engineering?" *Your Genome*, last updated Feb. 17, 2017, www.yourgenome.org /facts/what-is-genetic-engineering.

[3]See the abstract for Eugene Rosenberg, *It's in Your DNA: From Discovery to Structure, Function and Role in Evolution, Cancer and Aging* (London: Academic Press, 2017), at *Science Direct*, accessed on February 16, 2019, www.sciencedirect.com/topics/neuroscience/genetic-engineering.

[4]"About Human Germline Gene Editing," published by the Center for Genetics and Society, www .geneticsandsociety.org/internal-content/about-human-germline-gene-editing?id=8711.

[5]*Gattaca*, directed by Andrew Niccol (Los Angeles: Columbia Pictures, 1997).

[6]Ferris Jabr, "Are We Too Close to Making Gattaca a Reality?," *Scientific American*, October 28, 2013, https://blogs.scientificamerican.com/brainwaves/are-we-too-close-to-making-gattaca-a-reality.

[7]Alice Park, "UK Approves First Studies of New Gene Editing Technique CRISPR on Human Embryos," *Time*, February 1, 2016, http://time.com/4200695/crispr-new-gene-editing-on-human -embryos-approved/.

This matter is not one of abstract or fictional speculation. The parents of Vincent Freeman (played by Ethan Hawke) in *Gattaca* deal with pressing concerns related to assuring their children's happiness to the best of their abilities and opportunities. They witnessed their firstborn son Vincent's struggles given his genetic imperfections and did not want to see the same "mistakes" repeated in their next child. How many of us would not take the opportunity to improve our children's chances for success if we had the resources and means to do so? Of course, it all depends on how we define success and human flourishing, and what we would consider ethically appropriate to improve their chances of success.

Now what if we weren't talking simply about success, but survival? What if we knew that a baby to be born to us had a genetic predisposition for a life-altering or life-threatening disease? If it were plausible, would we seek a medical solution that entails editing or manipulating the DNA to eliminate the genetic predisposition? Many of us would seriously consider having this procedure performed if we were assured of its success. But what if there were unknown concerns pertaining to what the gene manipulation might do to other dimensions of the child's well-being, and society at large?

To return to resources and means for a moment, what if only those of significant financial means could afford a life-preserving, saving, or perfecting procedure? Would those with the financial means pursue genetic alterations if we knew it put other families of lesser means at a disadvantage? And what if there were no financial barriers to anyone? Would such financial freedom for some or for all remove all inhibitions? It is important that we all ask, "What should we do?" since the future of gene editing and manipulation is upon us.[8]

---

[8]See the following articles: Sarah Zhang, "Crispr Is Getting Better: Now It's Time to Ask the Hard Ethical Questions," *Wired*, December 1, 2015; David Cyranoski and Sara Reardon, "Embryo Editing Sparks Epic Debate," *Nature*, April 29, 2015; and Thomas Douglas and Julian Savulescu, "Destroying Unwanted Embryos in Research: Talking Point on Morality and Human Embryo Research," *EMBO Reports* 10, no. 4 (April 2009): 307-12. Elsewhere, Marcy Darnovsky, the executive director of the Center for Genetics and Society, writes, "In short, human gene editing for reproduction would be unsafe, is unneeded for medical purposes, and would be dangerously unacceptable on societal grounds. We need not and should not run those risks." Marcy Darnovsky, "The Perils of Human Gene Editing for Reproduction," *Washington Examiner*, March 9, 2016.

Fortunately, many scientists recognize they need assistance on making ethical and social determinations. A *Guardian* article recounting an international summit on human gene editing includes the following statement:

> Typically, discussions of new biomedical technologies that are organized by scientists focus on technical questions about safety and effectiveness. . . . The recognition that scientists alone can't decide whether to deploy this society-altering technology is perhaps the summit's most positive outcome. Already, more and more non-scientists are becoming aware of what's at stake for all of us and realizing that germline gene editing is a social and political matter, not just a scientific one.[9]

Michael Sandel, professor of government at Harvard University, also weighs in on the importance of considerations beyond the purely scientific—including theological concerns. Sandel suggests that the growing "powers of biotechnology" require deeper reflection because tools such as genetic engineering raise "questions about the moral status of nature, and about the proper stance of human beings toward the given world." These questions, Sandel says, "verge on theology." He points out four examples: "muscle enhancement, memory enhancement, growth-hormone treatment, and reproductive technologies that enable parents to choose the sex and some genetic traits of their children. In each case what began as an attempt to treat a disease or prevent a genetic disorder now beckons as an instrument of improvement and consumer choice."[10] The possibility of bioengineering beyond disease treatment opens the door to larger possibilities. Thus, in keeping with Sandel's point, this chapter will account for religious and theological reflections relevant to genetic engineering.

In exploring religious perspectives, we will first consider the ethical teachings of those close to the movie *Gattaca*'s lead actress, Uma

---

[9]Marcy Darnovsky, "Human Gene Editing Is a Social and Political Matter, Not Just a Scientific One," *Guardian*, December 4, 2015, www.theguardian.com/science/2015/dec/04/human-gene-editing-is -a-social-and-political-matter-not-just-a-scientific-one.

[10]Michael J. Sandel, "The Case Against Perfection: What's Wrong with Designer Children, Bionic Athletes, and Genetic Engineering," *Atlantic*, April 2004, www.theatlantic.com/magazine /archive/2004/04/the-case-against-perfection/302927/. For Sandel, "the moral quandary arises when people use such therapy not to cure a disease but to reach beyond health, to enhance their physical or cognitive capacities, to lift themselves above the norm."

Thurman (who plays Irene Cassini). Her father, Robert Thurman, is a distinguished Buddhist scholar and an ordained Tibetan Buddhist monk. We will consider the views on genetic engineering of the lead figure in his religious tradition, the Dalai Lama, who presided over Robert Thurman's ordination.

BUDDHIST DHARMA AND GENETIC GRASPING

One of the Dalai Lama's most admirable qualities is his profound compassionate care for all existence and supreme regard for humanity. Such compassionate care is on full display in his volume *The Universe in a Single Atom: The Convergence of Science and Spirituality*.[11] The chapter "Ethics and the New Genetics" assists us in navigating the issues surrounding recent discoveries in genetics.

By no means does the Dalai Lama come across as a reactionary in his engagement of genetic research. He affirms scientific progress that furthers the well-being of our planet. Nonetheless, he cautions scientists, business leaders, politicians, and society at large not to grasp and play God. This is quite noteworthy, given that Tibetan Buddhism hails the Dalai Lama as the rebirth of a line of divine or enlightened beings who are appearances of Avalokiteśvara, the bodhisattva of compassion.[12]

Here are some of the chapter highlights from "Ethics and the New Genetics" that bear on such subjects as PGD and CRISPR (Clustered Regularly Interspaced Short Palindromic Repeats).[13] They detail several

---

[11]Dalai Lama, *The Universe in a Single Atom: The Convergence of Science and Spirituality* (New York: Harmony Books, 2005).

[12]For the Dalai Lama's own view of compassion, see his article "Compassion and the Individual," accessed on February 16, 2019, www.dalailama.com/messages/compassion-and-human-values /compassion.

[13]The Broad Institute provides the following definition of CRISPR:

"CRISPR" (pronounced 'crisper') stands for Clustered Regularly Interspaced Short Palindromic Repeats, which are the hallmark of a bacterial defense system that forms the basis for CRISPR-Cas9 genome editing technology. In the field of genome engineering, the term "CRISPR" or "CRISPR-Cas9" is often used loosely to refer to the various CRISPR-Cas9 and -CPF1, (and other) systems that can be programmed to target specific stretches of genetic code and to edit DNA at precise locations, as well as for other purposes, such as for new diagnostic tools. With these systems, researchers can permanently modify genes in living cells and organisms and, in the future, may make it possible to correct mutations at precise locations in the human genome in order to treat genetic causes of disease. Other systems are now available, such as CRISPR-Cas13's, that target RNA provide alternate avenues for use, and with unique characteristics that have been leveraged for sensitive diagnostic tools, such as SHERLOCK.

concerns. I refer to the following four concerns as problems of pre-sumption, exploitation, bifurcation, and reduction.

First, knowledge of genetic predispositions of disease may lead one to abort a child whose disease will manifest itself in twenty years. Such knowledge of predisposition entails only a probability at best and does not account for the possibility that a cure may be found within ten years.[14] I refer to this matter as the problem of *presumption* or feigned omniscience.

Further to the Dalai Lama's point, we don't know the future. Yet we are playing God with making such determinations. We don't have the omniscience to back up our newfound omnipotence concerning the ter-mination or "creation" of life. It is important that as much as possible, we account for long-term consequences, not simply seemingly short-term gains. In all such affairs, we should tread very lightly and not rush in where angels and bodhisattvas fear to tread.

Take CRISPR for example. As the *Time* article referenced above notes, "If CRISPR can successfully change the genome of an embryo, it could forever alter the human gene pool—and diversity in the gene pool is an important part of keeping a species healthy. Intentionally manipulating that pool could have unpredictable consequences on our ability to fight disease, our life expectancy, and more—for good and for ill."[15]

Second, the Dalai Lama reasons that the cloning or breeding of "semi-human beings for spare parts" makes it difficult to guard against ma-nipulating "our fellow human beings whom the whims of society may deem deficient in some way."[16] Here we find the problem of *exploitation*. The *Scientific American* article noted earlier provides an example of what might be deemed exploitation:

> Couples have also created one child through IVF-PGD in order to save another. At least 30 fertility clinics in the U.S. will help parents conceive a "savior sibling"—a child whose umb[i]lical cord blood can be harvested as a source of stem cells to treat leukemia, Fanconi anemia or another terrible illness in his or her older sibling. . . .

"Questions And Answers About CRISPR," Broad Institute, www.broadinstitute.org/what-broad/areas-focus/project-spotlight/questions-and-answers-about-crispr.
[14]Dalai Lama, *Universe in a Single Atom*, 191.
[15]Park, "UK Approves First Studies."
[16]Dalai Lama, *Universe in a Single Atom*, 192.

Nominally, clinics agree to help parents in this way only if the couple had always intended to have several children. But some parents in this situation undoubtedly alter their original family plan out of desperation. So what happens if the treatment fails? How will the inevitable disappointment change the way parents feel about their second child? And how does learning that one's entire existence hinges on saving someone else's life warp the psychological development of a child or young adult?[17]

The personalist approach to life developed in this volume seeks to safeguard against a human being existing merely for someone else's benefit. Each person has inviolable worth and dignity that ensures that their various bodily parts and energies from which their persons emerge do not exist primarily as a means to someone else's end. They are ends in themselves.

Third, the Dalai Lama argues that the manipulation of genes for creating children with enhanced characteristic traits will lead us from "inequality of circumstance" to "inequality of nature." Given the costs involved with genetic technology, the rich will be in the position for the foreseeable future of benefiting from such technological opportunities to the detriment of the rest of society.[18] This economic restructuring of society at a genetic level intensifies the problem of *bifurcation* in our society.

For example, it will exasperate problems often associated with standardized testing. Anthony Carnevale, director of the Georgetown University Center on Education and the Workforce and coauthor of *The Merit Myth*, claims, "The SAT is basically a dodge. . . . It provides a shiny scientific cover for a system of inequality that guarantees that rich kids go to the most selective college. It makes all that sound like science when

---

[17]Jabr, "Are We Too Close?" Note also the following treatment of IVF-PGD: "Preimplantation genetic diagnosis (PGD) is a screening test used to determine if genetic or chromosomal disorders are present in embryos produced through in vitro fertilization (IVF). PGD screens embryos before they are transferred to the uterus so couples can make informed decisions about their next steps in the IVF process. Embryos unaffected by the genetic or chromosomal disorder can be selected for transfer to the uterus." "What Is Preimplantation Genetic Diagnosis?," Penn Medicine, www .pennmedicine.org/for-patients-and-visitors/find-a-program-or-service/penn-fertility-care /embryo-screening (accessed on 2/16/2019).

[18]Dalai Lama, *Universe in a Single Atom*, 194.

it's not."[19] If genetics enters the equation, such inequitable economic selectivity will actually be science.

The "inequality of nature" or bifurcation based on the economically determined manipulation of genes separates the righteous and the "de-gene-rate." The movie *Gattaca* also employs the term *de-gene-rate* to designate an individual who purchases someone's superior DNA. Contrary to genetic appearances, those whose parents pay for genetic enhancement are degenerate, like those who take steroids for competing in sports. Those with genetic enhancements will be wrongly deemed righteous based on their parents' ill-conceived labors to perfect them through economic advantage rather than on their own merit or native skill. As with Matthew 25, appearances can be deceiving. The goats (those with genetic enhancements) will think they are sheep. In stark contrast, the sheep—who do not belong to a special genetic class of people—will have no self-awareness of their own moral superiority. There are some things money can't buy. Even if it can buy genetic superiority, it cannot buy moral perfection or human value.[20]

This two-class system bound up with improving the genetic quality of certain members of a population gives rise to a democratic form of eugenics in which individuals and families pay for desirable inheritable traits to be passed on to their progeny. Interestingly, in addition to fostering inequality and inequity, it also has the unintended consequence of making the population more susceptible to sickness and destructive metamorphoses of human nature.

The *Scientific American* article noted above bears consideration for both concerns. It quotes a 2003 statement by Tania Simoncelli, then assistant director for forensic sciences in the White House Office of Science and Technology Policy: "Advances in PGD, together with cloning and genetic engineering, are tending towards a new era of eugenics. Unlike the state-sponsored eugenics of the Nazi era, this new eugenics is an

---

[19]Anthony P. Carnevale, Peter Schmidt, and Jeff Strohl, *The Merit Myth: How Our Colleges Favor the Rich and Divide America* (New York: The New Press, 2020). The quote is taken from Susan Adams, "How the SAT Failed America," *Forbes*, September 30, 2020; www.forbes.com/sites/susanadams /2020/09/30/the-forbes-investigation-how-the-sat-failed-america/?sh=38de865853b5.

[20]On market economics and morality, see Michael J. Sandel, *What Money Can't Buy: The Moral Limits of the Markets* (New York: Farrar, Straus, and Giroux, 2012).

individual, market-based eugenics, where children are increasingly re-garded as made-to order consumer products." Jabr then writes,

> An era of market-based eugenics would exterminate any lingering notions of meritocracy. Perseverance, adaptability, and self-improvement would become subordinate to what people would see as innate talent and near certain prosperity preordained by one's genes. Despite laws meant to prevent genetic discrimination, the world of *Gattaca* is a highly stratified one with two distinct classes: the valids—who have the right genes, the most prestigious jobs and the highest quality of life—and the in-valids, who were conceived in the typical fashion and are relegated to menial work and relative poverty.[21]

Fourth, the Dalai Lama claims that there is so much more to human beings than their genetic codes. Regardless of whether one has a dis-ability like Down syndrome or a genetic predisposition toward various diseases like "sickle-cell anemia, Hunting's chorea, or Alzheimer's," "all human beings have an equal value and an equal potential for goodness. To ground our appreciation of the value of a human being in genetic makeup is bound to impoverish humanity, because there is so much more to human beings than their genomes."[22] We refer to this as the problem of *reduction.*

The Dalai Lama is astutely challenging a reductionistic view of hu-manity bound up with genetics. For all the efforts at perfection, ge-netic engineering—at least when going beyond treating diseases and preventing genetic disorders—may be subtraction by multiplication, for we are far more than our genes. This calls to mind the discussion in chapter three of Denis Noble's response to Richard Dawkins's "selfish gene" framework in *The Music of Life: Biology Beyond Genes.* Rather than view all of life from the vantage point of genes, as Dawkins does, Noble approaches the gene from the perspective of the entire biological web.[23] A similar reductionistic account appears to be on

---

[21]Jabr, "Are We Too Close?"
[22]Dalai Lama, *Universe in a Single Atom,* 195.
[23]Denis Noble, *The Music of Life: Biology Beyond Genes* (Oxford: Oxford University Press, 2006); Richard Dawkins, *The Extended Phenotype: The Long Reach of the Gene,* afterword by Daniel Den-nett (Oxford: Oxford University Press, 1999).

display in 23andMe ads: it is as if one holds the keys to the universe and future if one can simply know one's DNA variables. In contrast to this popular orientation, we are more than our genotypes. We must account for the entire web of our "primary" and "secondary" qualities, as well as the vast network of creaturely and social relations we inhabit in our ecosystem.

It is so very easy to become reductionistic by focusing primarily or exclusively on genetics. Genetic engineering appears more tangible, quantifiable, and promising than attempting to shape and construct relational and social patterns of existence. However, due to various concerns, including those already raised, we must safeguard against moves that lead to grasping, objectifying, and separating genetics from the vast web of biological and social relations. As Christian Smith writes in a different context but with overarching import, "Reality is . . . significantly constituted through relationality, not merely composition."[24] Various religious and philosophical systems like Buddhism account for such diversity and view the various aspects of life in expansive rather than minimalist terms.

The Dalai Lama tends to soften the striking differences between various traditions' beliefs in search of a global ethic.[25] Rather than soften them, such differences can be constructive for the development of an entangled ethical framework that affirms human dignity and sacredness of life from diverse angles. Certainly, adherents of various religious traditions should guard against approaching ethics in a parochial and divisive manner that discounts possible parallels and rejects insights from other traditions. Rather, we should bring our differences to bear on ethical concerns to promote diverse strategies for addressing the various ethical quandaries we face.

For example, the Dalai Lama notes how from his Buddhist perspective it is difficult to justify people's cloning of themselves in the attempt to live longer. He writes, "From the Buddhist perspective, it may be an identical body, but there will be two different consciousnesses. They will still die."[26]

---

[24]Christian Smith, *What Is a Person?* (Chicago: The University of Chicago Press, 2010), 30.
[25]Dalai Lama, *Universe in a Single Atom*, 197-98.
[26]Dalai Lama, *Universe in a Single Atom*, 193.

An entangled ethic as developed in this volume does not minimize but maximizes this point. No doubt, there are keen differences in perceiving personhood by way of permanence (Christian) versus impermanence (Buddhism). Still, a Christian personalist perspective resonates with the Dalai Lama in the conviction that each individual soul is incommunicable in its worth, since emergent personhood is more than the sum of one's bodily parts and corporeal frames, no matter how similar the bodies are.[27]

GENETIC MASTERY AND ENSLAVEMENT
VERSUS AN ETHIC OF GIFTEDNESS

In addition to the Dalai Lama, Michael Sandel provides keen insight on the subject of genetic enhancement and invites religious traditions to address the topic in the public square. Born into a Jewish family, Sandel "rejects hardline secularism," welcoming "religious input in the political arena."[28] His ethical engagement of genetics is no exception to his appropriation of religious themes in public discourse and debate. In an *Atlantic* article (referenced earlier) that became the basis for his book on genetics titled *The Case Against Perfection*, Sandel writes,

> It is commonly said that genetic enhancements undermine our humanity by threatening our capacity to act freely, to succeed by our own efforts, and to consider ourselves responsible—worthy of praise or blame—for the things we do and for the way we are. It is one thing to hit seventy home runs as the result of disciplined training and effort, and something else, something less, to hit them with the help of steroids or genetically enhanced muscles. Of course, the roles of effort and enhancement will be a matter of degree. But as the role of enhancement increases, our admiration for the achievement fades—or, rather, our admiration for the achievement shifts from the player to his pharmacist. This suggests that our moral response to enhancement is a response to the diminished agency of the person whose achievement is enhanced.[29]

---

[27]Refer also to Smith's discussion of emergence and how the whole is more than the sum of its parts (in contrast to reductionism) on 31, 35, 37, and 53 of *What Is a Person?*

[28]Andrew Anthony, "Michael Sandel: Master of Life's Big Questions," *Guardian*, April 7, 2012.

[29]Sandel, "Case Against Perfection"; See also Michael J. Sandel, *The Case Against Perfection: Ethics in the Age of Genetic Engineering* (Cambridge, MA: Belknap Press, 2007).

Sandel sees value in this argument, as do I. It is quite difficult to affirm human dignity and moral goodness when we jettison responsibility. If the devil made me do something, why blame me? So, too, with genetics, albeit with success. If genetic enhancements led to someone's victory in a sporting contest, why applaud them? In fact, why shouldn't the medal be revoked?

That said, for Sandel, the ultimate problem is not the erosion of human agency, but what he refers to as "hyperagency": "a Promethean aspiration to remake nature, including human nature, to serve our purposes and satisfy desire." Thus, Sandel says, "The problem is not the drift to mechanism but the drive to mastery." The consequence of seeking genetic enhancement may be a loss of "appreciation of the gifted character of human powers and achievements."[30]

Sandel's reflection resonates with the Judeo-Christian doctrine of creation. Contrary to the Nietzsches of this world who maintain that life is something to be gained rather than given,[31] Sandel cautions against the Promethean drive for perfection. For Sandel, the appreciation for the giftedness of life and what it entails for humility involves "a religious sensibility. But its resonance reaches beyond religion."[32] After all, everyone—not simply religious people—celebrates athletic champions' natural prowess, not simply their hard work. They can take no credit for their natural giftedness, only their efforts to excel. In contrast, "enhancement can be seen as the ultimate expression of the ethic of effort and willfulness," which is now "arrayed against the claims of giftedness."[33]

---

[30]Sandel, "Case Against Perfection." See also the Pew Research Center, Religion and Public Life forum transcript, "The Pursuit of Perfection: A Conversation on the Ethics of Genetic Engineering," featuring Michael J. Sandel with Lee M. Silver responding, moderated by E. J. Dionne Jr., March 31, 2004; www.pewforum.org/2004/03/31/the-pursuit-of-perfection-a-conversation-on-the-ethics-of-genetic-engineering/.

[31]See Walter Kaufmann, "Friedrich Nietzsche," in *Encyclopedia of Philosophy*, ed. Paul Edwards (New York: Macmillan & The Free Press, 1967), for his discussion of the terms *gained* (*aufgegeben*) and *given* (*gegeben*). For Nietzsche, identity, meaning, and value are to be *gained* (*aufgegeben*) rather than *given* (*gegeben*). Edward Craig gives consideration to Nietzsche and the late modern move to reorient humanity from imitating God's thoughts and ways to creating life, meaning, and value. See Edward Craig, *The Mind of God and the Works of Man* (Oxford: Clarendon Press, 1987).

[32]Sandel, "Case Against Perfection."

[33]Sandel, "Case Against Perfection."

This point resonates with the theme of *presumption* highlighted in the account of the Dalai Lama's analysis of genetic engineering. We must guard against the Promethean complex to displace God and our gift-edness, which, in keeping with Sandel's article, ultimately impacts "humility, responsibility, and solidarity."[34]

Sandel reasons that one does not have to be religious to understand the importance of giftedness. "Humility, responsibility, and solidarity" are not inherently religious terms. Religious and secular people alike understand that "parenthood is a school for humility," since parents must remain "open to the unbidden."[35] In other words, no matter our demands or efforts at control, we cannot dictate what kind of children we will have or what they will grow up to be. Remove the gifted quality of our existence with genetic enhancement and we will endure the loss of humility and "explosion" rather than "erosion" of responsibility.[36] The propensity will emerge to become even more demanding and controlling. The more choices and control we have as parents the greater our moral responsibility,[37] which also entails culpability. In turn, the more control we have over our own destinies will make us less inclined to see ourselves as being in solidarity with the less fortunate. After all, "The more alive we are to the chanced nature of our lot, the more reason we have to share our fate with others."[38] Whether we believe in providence or fate, remove the sense of uncertainty about our own destiny given increased control over our well-being and that of our children and we will likely be less gracious and merciful to others. Rather than saying, "Except for the grace of God, there go I," we will resort to, "Except for my manipulation and control of the genetic lottery, there go I."

For Sandel, the ultimate problem is not mechanism but mastery. Sandel challenges the "autonomy argument" (which entails concern over mechanism) against human cloning and other types of genetic engineering, claiming that whether or not parents impose their choices on children's genetic makeup, children are still not free to choose for

---

[34]Sandel, "Case Against Perfection."
[35]Sandel, *The Case Against Perfection*, 86.
[36]Sandel, *The Case Against Perfection*, 87.
[37]Sandel, *The Case Against Perfection*, 89.
[38]Sandel, *The Case Against Perfection*, 89.

themselves: "The alternative to a cloned or genetically enhanced child is not one whose future is unbound by particular talents but one at the mercy of the genetic lottery."[39]

It is important to go beyond mere consideration of mechanism to account for the problem of mastery. That said, the two themes are related. Given the Judeo-Christian doctrine of the Creator and Sustainer as personal and free, impersonal mechanism results when we seek to displace God and attain mastery. We are only truly personal and free in relation to God and one another, never in isolation from relationship. The Great Commandments that call us to love God with all our being and our neighbor as ourselves are essential to true freedom and human flourishing (see Mark 12:30-31; Luke 10:25-37). Such relationality involves what Sandel refers to as "humility, responsibility, and solidarity" with God and neighbor.

Relationality goes to the heart of the matter. It puts a check on the penchant for mastery. The emphasis on the interpersonal, triune being of God supplements and safeguards Sandel's "ethic of giftedness." God is love, as Christian Scripture declares (1 John 4:8). As argued in chapter two, "God is love" entails the idea that God's eternal being is communal. Only a communal being could love the world freely since, on this view, God does not need the world to be loving. There is no need in God. God's love is utterly gracious. God gifts us freely so we can act from the vantage point of giftedness rather than willfulness, finding our identity in relational givenness rather than in what we might gain.

The triune God designed humanity to love freely in response. God has wired us to reject the drive that would seek mastery over others, including any penchant parents may have to gain mastery over their children's destinies pertaining to their skills and abilities. Such attempts at mastery appear to reveal a lack of grace, which may very well result from a lack of their own relational security. Rather than seek after perfection through children, those of us who are parents should seek to participate in the perfection of our relationally secure and unconditionally loving Creator, who liberates us not to master but serve others.

---

[39]Sandel, "Case Against Perfection."

Parents who seek after their own perfection through mastering their children's genetic codes love them conditionally. The world of their making fails to welcome the unexpected and uninvited. Nor does it promote humility and grace. As Sandel writes, "A *Gattaca*-like world in which parents became accustomed to specifying the sex and genetic traits of their children would be a world inhospitable to the unbidden, a gated community writ large. The awareness that our talents and abilities are not wholly our own doing restrains our tendency toward hubris."[40] Such "awareness" liberates us from enslavement to our Promethean complex of "hyperagency" that forces us "to remake nature, including human nature, to serve our purposes and satisfy our desires."[41]

DE-GENE-RATE PERFECTION AND REGENERATE ACTION

Sandel speaks of desires fueling the Promethean complex of hyperagency. What kind of desires shape us? What desires should satisfy us? Why is it that there is so much interest and longing for genetic enhancement and perfection for our progeny? It would appear that biological reductionism is often in play whereby we see humans as no more than their genes and other biological phenomena and operations, which in turn fuels the fire and ignites our Promethean master-craftsman impulses to re-create humanity.[42] Of course, genes play a causal role in shaping our humanity. However, while those biological conditions inform our humanity, they do not in any way exhaust it. Those who fall prey to biological reductionism fail to see that we are made for more than genetic enhancement and perfection. While personhood and social dimensions of life emerge

---

[40]Sandel, "Case Against Perfection."

[41]Sandel, "Case Against Perfection."

[42]Here is a helpful definition of "biological reductionism": "A theoretical approach that aims to explain all social or cultural phenomena in biological terms, denying them any causal autonomy. Twentieth-century incarnations of biological reductionism have relied to varying degrees on Darwin's theory of evolution and principles of natural selection. Within the human sciences, there have been attempts to explain observed differences in group behaviour—such as performance on intelligence tests, rates of mental illness, intergenerational poverty, male dominance or patriarchy, and propensity for crime—as being biologically determined, by claiming that groups have different biological capacities or evolutionary trajectories. The theories of Social Darwinism, eugenics, and sociobiology often involve biological reductionism. A recognition of the importance of biological conditions and human nature need not involve biological reductionism." See the entry "Biological Reductionism" in *A Dictionary of Sociology*, ed. John Scott and Gordon Marshall, 3rd ed. (Oxford: Oxford University Press, 2009), 43.

from this biological basis, they in turn causally impact lower-level entities, including genes.[43]

Here we return to the critique of Richard Dawkins's faulty genetic metaphorical framework noted in chapter three. Christian Smith writes that biological reductionism does not account for emergence. The biological cannot account for "the social and the personal" that emerge from it (and in turn shape it). Smith summarizes and critiques Dawkins and his biological reductionistic colleagues:

> What "really" moves and determines life are the natural physical operations of genes, neurons, and chemicals. This of course requires slipshod anthropomorphizing, as in the case of Dawkins's "selfish genes." The result is a hardcore anti-mentalist commitment that makes inconsequential people's ideas, beliefs, desires, feelings, values, aspirations, commitments, and intentions for understanding humanity. Those subjectivities are only being "used" by biology—the alleged true agents of human life—to accomplish the reproductive imperative, which is the single "will" of biology. Much that is phenomenologically real and important to human beings is pushed aside by the authoritative hand of biological reductionism.[44]

Such biological reductionism manifests itself in attributing moral failure to "bad genes." We must account for expansive accounts beyond what any one natural or social science can provide in explaining moral problems. As Smith says, "Most everything is interactive and responsive." So our analysis of problems and solutions must be expansive and multidisciplinary, as Smith seeks to demonstrate.[45]

For example, if we wish to understand and address the deeply destructive patterns of behavior among people, we should account for the lack of empathy. Empathy emerges from processes and capacities within the person and in relation to others.[46] Empathy not only arises from "temperamental personality" but also it emerges in the context of "loving

---

[43]See Christian Smith's diagram of upward emergence and downward causation on 33, fig. 1 of *What Is a Person?*

[44]Christian Smith, *To Flourish or Destruct: A Personalist Theory of Human Goods, Motivations, Failure, and Evil* (Chicago: The University of Chicago Press, 2015), 280n12.

[45]Smith, *To Flourish or Destruct*, 255.

[46]We must take into account biochemical interactions in reflecting on empathy. Empathy involves neurochemically induced relations. In other words, genetically coded structures and functions, not simply psychological properties, contribute greatly to empathy's development.

socialization" involving parents, other family members, and the extended relational network from a very young age.[47] As noted in various chapters in this volume, we must seek to cultivate empathic bonds in our various forms of interaction to foster healthy social behaviors.

We are far more than our genes. Therefore, placing our trust in genetic enhancement for moral uplift is an overly realized fool's gold eschatology. Fixing our genes will not solve our moral problems. Morals are so much more than having "good genes." Changing genes are not alone sufficient for changing our affections, wills, and behaviors. Regardless of what it can do for our intellect, intellect itself won't save us. It is hard to think of a more intellectually advanced nation than Germany at the time of WWI and WWII. Still, the German people gave way to the Kaiser's war effort and later Hitler's Nazi reign of terror.

The beloved community as an eschatological community welcomes the unbidden, the forgotten, the forlorn, those deemed weak and foolish. Its perfection that the Spirit makes possible is never reduced to genetic purity. Those Social Darwinians and social elitists who refuse the genetically unbidden entrance will never enter the kingdom of heaven.

Those who have only loved those deemed perfect in whatever way do not know or experience perfect love, which loves the unlovely and ignoble, the foolish and the weak. Perfect love, which characterizes heaven, loves the unlovely and perfects them through grace and gratitude for unmerited favor and divine gifting. They are the ones God calls and with whom God identifies as the crucified Lord who was unbidden and cast out, hanging outside the city gates. Moral perfection or perfectibility that accounts for the whole of our persons, including their capacities and properties, in the matrix of complex social relations rather than genetic enhancement should be our primary concern. Fixation on the latter is truly de-gene-rate and does not reflect the eschatological or beloved community.

Speaking of beloved community, the society at large today could learn or relearn a thing or two from those often treated with contempt and unbidden in its day, the civil rights movement, which was birthed in the

---

[47]Smith, *To Flourish or Destruct*, 255, 257.

African American church. Here I call to mind Martin Luther King Jr.'s protest registered on the steps of the Lincoln Memorial in our nation's capital in 1963. He longed for a future state when character rather than skin color would be the basis for judgment in the United States: "I have a dream . . . that my four little children will one day live in a nation where they will not be judged by the color of their skin but by the content of their character. . . . I have a dream today."[48] Perhaps, if he were alive today, Dr. King would edit the statement on skin color to read, "They will not be judged by the color of their skin *or genetic makeup* but by the content of their character." Which would you like for your children to be judged by? Their skin color, gender, abilities, disabilities, genetic codes, or character?

With this point in mind, we should ask, How might genetic enhancement impact morality and virtue? How might genetic enhancement impact those Promethean-made children negatively? Rather than help them overcome presumed disabilities and imperfections, we would remove those challenges, thereby shortchanging the cultivation of their character and resilience. Genetic engineering holds promise for curing diseases, but the perils bound up with presumption, exploitation, bifurcation, and reduction noted by the Dalai Lama, as well as mechanism and mastery (hyperagency) highlighted by Sandel, as well as moral struggle and perfectibility stated here, warrant against genetic enhancement.

To return to King, it is not only skin color and, with it, genetic makeup, that would serve as a faulty basis for making right judgments about people's value. Economic merit—which often makes available genetic advances—also serves as a faulty barometer for determining people's worth. When economic worth and genetic enhancement in pursuit of perfection rather than perfect love for people, especially those impoverished, drive us, we are focusing on things. As King argued in his "Beyond Vietnam" speech, America's fixation with things rather than persons inevitably leads to "the giant triplets of racism, extreme materialism, and

---

[48]Martin Luther King Jr., "I Have a Dream," in *A Call to Conscience: The Landmark Speeches of Dr. Martin Luther King, Jr.*, ed. Clayborne Carson and Kris Shepard (New York: Warner Brothers, 2001), 85.

militarism."[49] In King's mind, this was evident in the United States investing countless millions of dollars in killing brown people in Vietnam rather than caring for them in America's inner cities. As King observed in an article he wrote for the *Atlantic*, "It is estimated that we spend $322,000 for each enemy we kill, while we spend in the so-called war on poverty in America only about $53.00 for each person classified as 'poor.'" He concludes, "It challenges the imagination to contemplate what lives we could transform if we were to cease killing."[50]

King gives every indication of being a critical realist personalist. On the subject of moral perfection and perfectibility, Rufus Burrow writes that for King, "Neither the universe nor the world is perfect. Racism and injustice could not exist in a perfect world. And yet he believed in the ongoing perfectibility of the world when persons choose to cooperate with each other and God to make the world better than it is at any given moment."[51] Given King's personalist thrust, the pursuit of moral perfection involving character formation and virtue always express themselves in relational terms—namely, the cultivation of the beloved community.

Drawing from his African heritage as well as African American Christian tradition, King always pursued the community's well-being. Here, it is worth noting Peter Paris's claim in his account of King: "The preservation and promotion of community is the paramount goal of African peoples in all spheres of life. It is a practical goal deeply rooted in their cosmological thought and constitutive of all personal and public life. Thus, it is not only descriptive of public reality but also normative for every part of it."[52] Later, Paris writes that the African and African American ethical framework, which also shaped King and which he espoused, "is primarily concerned with the development of a certain kind of moral character, a character that reflects the basic values of their

---

[49]Martin Luther King Jr., "Beyond Vietnam," in Carson and Shepard, *Call to Conscience*, 157-58.

[50]This quote is taken from an *Atlantic* magazine excerpt of Martin Luther King Jr.'s speech delivered February 25, 1967, titled "The Casualties of the War in Vietnam," www.theatlantic.com/magazine /archive/2018/02/martin-luther-king-jr-vietnam/552521/.

[51]Rufus Burrow Jr., *God and Human Dignity: The Personalism, Theology, and Ethics of Martin Luther King, Jr.* (Notre Dame, IN: University of Notre Dame Press, 2006), 191.

[52]Peter J. Paris, *Virtues and Values: The African and African American Experience*, Facet Series (Minneapolis: Fortress, 2004), 5.

respective communities."[53] Virtues that King sought to embody, and are highly regarded by Africans and African Americans, are "beneficence,"[54] whose "converse is meanness"[55]; "forbearance,"[56] whose "converse" is "impatience or intolerance"[57]; "practical wisdom,"[58] whose "converse" is "natural instinct" involving "impulsive activities that are both unreasonable and uncontrolled"[59]; "improvisation,"[60] whose "converse" involves such dynamics as "rigidity"[61]; "forgiveness,"[62] whose "converse" is "the vice of hatred"[63]; and "justice," which for Paris is the supreme virtue and summation of the others in the African and African American context.[64] Given the presence of such virtues, there is no way that the beloved community is ever a "gated community writ large," to refer back to Sandel's discussion of genetic perfectionism. King, the civil rights movement, and Sandel share the conviction that the genetically "unbidden" are always welcome.

Moral goodness, which is not the same as genetic enhancement, is the pursuit of virtue in the individual person and entire community. One can never separate the one apart from the other. Since the whole of life is sacred, and since the moral virtue of individuals and that of the community are the same, African and African American ethics aims at enabling individual persons to become good so that they will also become good leaders in their respective communities. Africans and African Americans cannot conceive of the one apart from the other. Hence the goal of their ethics is the moral development of both the person and the community.[65] The individual exists for the community and the community seeks after the well-being of each individual member.

---

[53]Paris, *Virtues and Values*, 13.
[54]Paris, *Virtues and Values*, 20.
[55]Paris, *Virtues and Values*, 30.
[56]Paris, *Virtues and Values*, 31.
[57]Paris, *Virtues and Values*, 37.
[58]Paris, *Virtues and Values*, 38.
[59]Paris, *Virtues and Values*, 43.
[60]Paris, *Virtues and Values*, 43.
[61]Paris, *Virtues and Values*, 49.
[62]Paris, *Virtues and Values*, 50.
[63]Paris, *Virtues and Values*, 56.
[64]Paris, *Virtues and Values*, 59.
[65]Paris, *Virtues and Values*, 17-18.

A communal ethic involving beneficence and justice for all flows from communion with the divine. An ethic of giftedness that is truly gratuitous is grounded in God's unconditional agape love, which was a hallmark of King's philosophy of life.[66] The cooperation with God and others that King envisioned does not serve as the basis for our worth. Rather, our worth flows from our being constituted in relation to God and others. As human persons, we have inherent dignity as created by God, who unconditionally loves us. We are called to live in light of this reality. This relational constitution serves as the basis for human value, not economic and genetic advances. Human value is a given and the cultivation of character is an act of gratitude involving the affirmation of who we are as unconditionally loved by God. The cultivation of character in a spirit of gratitude reflects how well we realize that God loves us unconditionally.

King's namesake, Martin Luther, wrote of God's unconditional love serving as the basis for our attractiveness rather than resulting from how spiritually or morally perfect we are. This orientation has bearing on our conversation of community and genetic enhancement, as well as the cultivation of character. In keeping with Luther's framework, God's love creates the attraction, not our state of perfection, moral, genetic, or otherwise. As set forth in chapter two, Luther writes of God's grace being extended to the degenerate in the Heidelberg Disputation: "The love of God does not find, but creates, that which is pleasing to it. The love of man comes into being through that which is pleasing to it."[67]

God's love creates the attraction so that even the de-gene-rate and otherwise "unbidden" can be elect! This teaching inspires humility and wages war on hubris. It also gives rise to responsibility for others and solidarity with them. Sandel highlights all three in his account safeguarding against the pursuit of genetic perfectionism. Hopefully, we understand that except for the grace of God, we might be worse off than we are. So, we should be gracious toward others in need. The sheep (not

---

[66]Burrow, *God and Human Dignity*, 116.

[67]Martin Luther, "Heidelberg Disputation," in *Martin Luther's Basic Theological Writings*, ed. Timothy F. Lull (Minneapolis: Augsburg, 1989), 48.

simply cloned sheep like "Dolly"[68]) are different from the goats because they are humble and recognize their responsibility and solidarity with the poor, naked, and imprisoned—which includes Jesus (Matthew 25:31-46). It is not based on their merit that God accepts them into his kingdom. Rather, they sense their deep need for mercy as those who are spiritually bankrupt and mourn their moral state. It leads them to approach others mercifully (See Matthew 5:3-5). They realize that the degene-rate alone are elect!

True love is gracious and merciful. It is also genetically blind and holistic in its assessment. Here it is worth noting that even in the movie *Gattaca*, genetic perfection does not create and sustain the attraction between the young couple in love. After all, Vincent is genetically suspect whereas Irene is genetically advanced. Attraction to their persons—persons who emerge from their various capacities and energies but are not reducible to them—is what unites them.

FROM A GENETICALLY ENGINEERED TO A RELATIONALLY ENGENDERED COMMUNITY

Earlier in the chapter, Sandel was quoted as saying, "The moral quandary arises when people use such therapy not to cure a disease but to reach beyond health, to enhance their physical or cognitive capacities, to lift themselves above the norm."[69] One question that arises in this context is, What constitutes a disease? It is actually quite difficult in many cases to determine what constitutes a disease, or a disability for that matter, and even the difference between the two.[70] Moreover, even if one could adequately determine what constitutes a disability, is it appropriate to use gene therapy to remove the disability? There is a movement of people for whom their disabilities are not something they "have" and that can be separated from them. The disabilities are considered core to their identity and thus it would be wrong to remove them. Concerns arise in this

---

[68]See information on "Dolly the Sheep," the Roslin Institute, University of Edinburgh, accessed on February 16, 2019, www.ed.ac.uk/roslin/about/dolly.

[69]Sandel, "Case Against Perfection."

[70]See for example the discussion of this topic in an article published in a European Molecular Biology Organization periodical: Jackie Leach Scully, "What Is a Disease? Disease, Disability and Their Definitions," EMBO *Reports* 5, no. 7 (2004): 650-53.

context over presumed prejudice toward the disability community, as if they require biological "fixing."[71]

Another concern that arises in discerning what qualifies as a disability is the market's potential influence. "As the business literature shows, new clinical diagnoses are often welcomed primarily as opportunities for market growth." The example is given of FSD, that is, female sexual dysfunction. Against the backdrop of incredible market success for medical treatments addressing male erectile dysfunction, "drug companies were, to put it mildly, over-involved in the medical consensus meetings held between 1997 and 1999 that effectively drew up very inclusive clinical criteria for the definition of FSD."[72]

In the past, biomedical perspectives dominated society's thinking on how to define diseases and disabilities. Beyond the pressures posed by market forces, other concerns merit reflection, which put a check on a naive dependence on biomedical determinations as completely objective. While biomedical considerations certainly have their place, increasingly those considerations have had to make room for other factors. After all, what counts as a disease or disability is often culturally and socially construed.[73] Regarding disabilities from a "social model" point of view, Jackie Leach Scully writes,

> The social model's fundamental criticism of the medical model is that it wrongly locates "the problem" of disability in biological constraints, considering it only from the point of view of the individual and neglecting the social and systemic frameworks that contribute to it. The social model

---

[71]See Bethany McKinney Fox's helpful discussion of this and related themes in *Disability and the Way of Jesus: Holistic Healing in the Gospels and the Church* (Downers Grove, IL: IVP Academic, 2019), including 70, 72, 82, 90, 92. On 92, she writes, "A number of interpreters in the disability community note that bodily conformity seems to be the price of admission to the Christian community. This is decidedly unliberating for those who have come to see the locations of the problem in inaccessible cultural systems and not in their bodies. In response some refer to the healing narratives in the Gospels as 'biological engineering campaigns,'" where Jesus is viewed as approaching "disability simply as something to get rid of, an idea that many honoring a disability perspective critique." The quote within McKinney Fox's statement is taken from David Mitchell and Sharon Snyder, "Jesus Thrown Everything Off Balance: Disability and Redemption in Biblical Literature" in *This Abled Body: Rethinking Disabilities and Biblical Studies*, ed. Hector Avalos, Sarah J. Melcher, and Jeremy Schipper (Atlanta: Society of Biblical Literature, 2007), 182.
[72]Scully, "What Is a Disease?" 651.
[73]Scully, "What Is a Disease?" 650-51.

distinguishes between impairment (the biological substrate, such as impaired hearing) and the disabled experience.[74]

Impaired hearing or deafness is one thing, but a lack of accommodation such as subtitles on a television show or sign language interpreters for a public presentation is quite another.[75] "A social model does not ignore biology, but contends that societal, economic and environmental factors are at least as important in producing disability."[76]

If we are not careful, we can move increasingly from a culture of persons to things when we attempt to "fix" people biologically and think we have fully addressed their situation. Those who have genetic diseases and disabilities are not inherently virtuous, but those who are preoccupied with genetic enhancement fail to pursue moral perfectibility, especially when they exclude those with genetic imperfections. Physical cures have their place but given the prowess and success of the medical profession, we can easily move toward mistakenly presuming that by mastering the physical conditions of life, we master life in its totality.

Jesus always healed people in community. From the woman with the issue of blood (Luke 8:42-48) to Zacchaeus (Luke 19:1-10)—whose apparently extreme shortness was an impairment that was never cured[77]—Jesus made sure to operate socially. Jesus declared the woman clean (whose "issue of blood" stopped flowing upon touching Jesus' robe) by calling her "daughter" in the presence of Jairus, a synagogue ruler, and the crowds. Now that she was declared clean by Jesus, who would in turn raise Jairus's daughter from the dead, the woman could move about freely in Jewish social and religious life. Jesus also invited himself to the house of the chief tax collector Zacchaeus, whom the crowds and Pharisees despised as a Roman traitor and oppressor of his own people. Jesus later

---

[74]Scully, "What Is a Disease?" 651.

[75]Scully, "What Is a Disease?" 651.

[76]Scully, "What Is a Disease?" 651.

[77]On this point, see Mikeal C. Parsons, *Body and Character in Luke and Acts: The Subversion of Physiognomy in Early Christianity* (Waco, TX: Baylor University Press, 2011), 106-7; Amos Yong, *The Bible, Disability, and the Church: A New Vision of the People of God* (Grand Rapids, MI: Eerdmans, 2011), 67, 69. Their perspective provides a counter to the view implied by Robert F. Molsberry, *Blindsided by Grace: Entering the World of Disability* (Minneapolis: Augsburg Books, 2004), 92-93: "Can you think of even one who goes away content—secure in his or her relationship with God and with the community of the faithful—but without having been cured of the ailment?"

declared Zacchaeus a recipient of salvation upon hearing Zacchaeus's confession of repentance and determination to make things right with all those he had cheated.

Speaking of cheating, would we not be cheating our children if we were to specify their sex and various other genetic traits? Is not their sex core to who they are? Would we not be making them something they are not? Would we not be taking God's place in designing them? Remember Sandel's line: "A *Gattaca*-like world in which parents became accustomed to specifying the sex and genetic traits of their children would be a world inhospitable to the unbidden, a gated community writ large. The awareness that our talents and abilities are not wholly our own doing restrains our tendency toward hubris."[78]

Certainly, parents have a significant role to play in cultivating and nurturing their children's lives, but is not determining their natural constitution God's business alone? And if sexuality itself, and not simply sex, is part of who people are in terms of their natural condition, do we have any business trying to edit the genetic system that might bear on sexual proclivities, or sensory capacities like hearing for that matter? Take for example an evangelical couple in the US who wish they could have ensured that their son had not turned out to be gay if they could have paid for a medical service that could remove "the gay gene,"[79] or the lesbian couple in Australia who chose a sperm donor with a heritable form of deafness to increase the likelihood that their child would be deaf.[80]

[78]Sandel, "Case Against Perfection."

[79]On the subject of homosexuality and genetics, see Sarah Knapton, "Genes Linked to Homosexuality Discovered by Scientists," *Telegraph*, December 7, 2017, www.telegraph.co.uk/science/2017/12/07/genes-linked-homosexuality-discovered-scientists/. See also Anna Kosmynina, "Possible Genetic Links to Homosexuality Like 'Finding Needle in a Haystack,'" *Cosmos*, December 13, 2017, https://geneticliteracyproject.org/2017/12/13/possible-genetic-links-homosexuality-like-finding-needle-haystack/; Tina Saey, "'There Is No Gay Gene': But Study Suggests Genetics May Play Role in Choosing Same Sex Partner," *Science News*, October 26, 2018, https://geneticliteracyproject.org/2018/10/26/there-is-no-gay-gene-but-study-suggests-genetics-may-play-role-in-choosing-same-sex-partner/. See the following article documenting the blending of the hypothetical with the medical on the subject of the gay gene and the ensuing call for greater accountability on cross-disciplinary reporting: Kate O'Riordan, "The Life of the Gay Gene: From Hypothetical Genetic Marker to Social Reality," *Journal of Sex Research* 49, no.4 (2012): 362-68. For another article on this subject, see David Miller, "Introducing the 'Gay Gene': Media and Scientific Representations," *Sage Journals* 4, no. 3 (1995): 269-84.

[80]Liza Mundy, "A World of Their Own," *Washington Post Magazine*, March 31, 2002.

Of course, it could be reversed, where a gay couple might wish that they could help the genetic selection process along so that they could have a gay child, or a couple who has "normal" hearing wanting to safeguard against having a child who is hearing impaired by resorting to genetic engineering.

It is worth noting that the lesbian couple thought that having a deaf child would be "a special gift." Certainly, we can write up wish lists for gifts and ask our parents or other loved ones for certain presents (to be fair, the lesbian couple did not refuse to have a child with normal hearing; they simply sought to increase their chances of having a child who was deaf and decrease the chances of having a child who had normal hearing). But when we shape the variables that make it much more likely to acquire something or someone, it is no longer a gift.

Concerning the hypothetical or not-so hypothetical evangelical couple who wish they could go in search of "the gay gene" to remove it, should they not also go in search of a "greed gene" or "lust gene" to remove them, not only from their child but also from themselves and the rest of us? Otherwise, they are really saying that homosexual attraction (not even behavior) is a sin, in fact, the unforgiveable sin, which runs contrary to Christian Scripture's emphasis on the unforgiveable sin being blasphemy of the Holy Spirit (see Matthew 12:31-32). Besides, sin as well as salvation and sanctification from the vantage point of a relational trinitarian framework is to be construed in relational terms.

Our salvation is not based on the removal of a gene or genetic trajectory, or on the presence of a spiritual capacity either. Rather, salvation flows from the free, gracious gift of life through faith in Jesus, which in turn leads to righteous works of gratitude on the part of God's people (see Ephesians 2:8-10). Salvation is not a matter of natural selection or volition, but a divine call to communion (John 1:12-13).

Genetic engineering has its place in curing diseases, but not for creating a genetically enhanced society. A world in which genetic engineering triumphs over social engendering of unconditional love is far less perfect than the alternative. One's skin color and genetic makeup do not epitomize the height of perfection. Perfection entails affirming everyone's dignity, no matter their various features. Perfection involves modeling hospitality, dignified care, and empathy toward those lacking what is deemed the preferred gender, the right sexual attractional orientation, or perfect bodily constitution.

An ideal community practices an embodied ethic that reflects God's unchanging and perfecting grace and does not succumb to parental and societal whims that employ genetic enhancement in pursuit of hyperagency, which in turn can also diminish moral agency. The beloved community stands in stark contrast to a genetically engineered social order that conceives and values people only or primarily by way of their genetic traits and genetically enhanced potential. God's unconditional love and call on us to respond in kind creates confidence that while biological conditions are vitally important to our human identity, we are made for more than genetic enhancement and perfection.

5

MORE THAN SEXUAL PLEASURE
A Personalist Approach to Sex and Marriage

THERE IS NOTHING CASUAL about casual sex. Nor is sexual intimacy ever fully private. Sexual activity has a serious impact on us and our various relationships in one way or another. Sexual behavior treats people as either sacred or profane. This chapter clarifies the value of framing sexual intimacy in the context of monogamous marital relations and how that helps to foster the move from a culture of things to a culture of persons.

THE SEXUAL REVOLUTION REVISITED

Many liberal and secular-minded people viewed the sexual revolution of the 1960s as liberation from puritanical and prudish religious codes for full human flourishing. Those who celebrate the sexual revolution point out that women were empowered to pursue careers as equals in the workforce. Contraceptives were used to enhance relational intimacy through sexual activity rather than reduce sex to an instrument of reproduction. However, some liberal and secular-minded critics have called for a sexual counter-revolution in view of the scandals involving celebrities like Harvey Weinstein and Matt Lauer. These celebrities preyed on women, and even young men in some situations, as alleged in cases involving Kevin Spacey.[1]

Secular humanist Tom Krattenmaker wrote about this matter back in 2017 in an article titled "It's Time for a Sexual Counterrevolution."[2]

---

[1] Bindu Bansinath, "All of the Allegations Against Kevin Spacey," *The Cut*, updated November 16, 2022, www.thecut.com/article/all-of-the-allegations-against-actor-kevin-spacey.html.
[2] Tom Krattenmaker, "It's Time for a Sexual Counterrevolution," *Religion News Services*, December 14, 2017, https://religionnews.com/2017/12/14/its-time-for-a-sexual-counterrevolution/.

Krattenmaker celebrates the sexual revolution for a variety of reasons, but also wishes to counter certain abuses of it. Not wanting to return to the "more restrictive sex culture of old," he desires to get the revolution back on track. Here's Krattenmaker:

> We can credit the sexual revolution for honoring the joys of sex and cre-
> ating space for more people to enjoy it in more ways, provided that no one
> is forced or harmed. But in elevating the pleasures of sex, the revolution
> contributed to the development of a greedy fixation on it that now prevails
> among some men.
>
> One of the ways in which the sex revolution has gone sideways is that
> it's made sex too much a form of recreation, too much the spoils of power
> and wealth, too much a commodity that men clamor to get and have.
> Amid incessant messaging from media and the toxic sides of male culture,
> men have been sold the idea that good living means sex—lots of it, with
> lots of women, always on men's terms.
>
> When desire morphs into entitlement, as it can easily do, sex-pursuers
> distort the women whose bodies they want. In these men's sight and minds,
> a woman becomes less a full-fledged human person, with all the intelli-
> gence and emotional complexity that implies, and more of a one-dimen-
> sional object for sexual gratification. Her body is seen as not her own but,
> rather, something to which these predatory men have a rightful claim.
>
> This way of distorting women and trashing their humanity is light-
> years apart from the spirit of love and democratic values that we associate
> with the 1960s counterculture in which the sexual revolution took shape.
> And it's disgusting, contrary to all of our higher principles.[3]

Krattenmaker is an irenic secular humanist who sees the value of religious traditions in shaping a more humane treatment of others as sexual beings. In keeping with our entangled ethical framework, Christian ethicists should welcome the opportunity to dialogue with such humane and charitable secularist representatives. For Kratten-maker, the great monotheistic traditions of Judaism, Christianity, and Islam, contrary to the caricatures of oppression and prudishness, call on people to treat others as fully human, deserving our compassion and care. Sexual relations must never be viewed simply as a means for

---

[3]Krattenmaker, "Sexual Counterrevolution."

pleasure, or merely for reproduction. Ultimately, sexual intimacy is about relational intimacy.

Krattenmaker brings secular humanism into the discussion. What are the benefits of secular humanism for Krattenmaker's desired sexual counterrevolution?

> Humanism offers principles as transformative as they are simple: equality between the sexes, an embrace of the inevitability and benefits of sex, and acceptance of nontraditional sexualities, so long as sex is consensual and no one is hurt or abused.
>
> The sexual revolution proclaimed, "If it feels good, do it." The overdue counterrevolution rightly adds, "but only if it feels good for the other person, too."[4]

Krattenmaker's discussion of this theme is an important starting point for the present chapter. Although he does not explicitly say so, Krattenmaker goes in pursuit of the personalist ideal of pointing from a culture of things to a culture of persons. Krattenmaker's disgust with a culture of things is found in the line about sexual predation: "a woman becomes less a full-fledged human person." Just as the secular humanist Krattenmaker invites consideration of religious traditions in framing a sexual counterrevolution, so we wish to return the favor with our entangled ethic and invite consideration of nonreligious traditions, as well as non-Western spiritualities and ethical perspectives, in framing a sexual re-revolution.

I will not be dealing with the sexual revolution's import for everything sexual, such as what it meant for homosexual marriage and what Krattenmaker refers to as "acceptance of nontraditional sexualities," which I have dealt with elsewhere.[5] Here my task is to investigate monogamy (literally "one spouse") and fidelity in marriage.

The ensuing entangled ethical deliberations will proceed ecumenically and culminate with biblical and theological reflections at the chapter's close. While seeking to safeguard against the objectification of others and oneself for sexual self-fulfillment, consideration will also be given to Krattenmaker's statement: "The sexual revolution proclaimed, 'If it feels

---

[4]Krattenmaker, "Sexual Counterrevolution."
[5]See Paul Louis Metzger, *Connecting Christ: How to Discuss Jesus in a World of Diverse Paths* (Nashville: Thomas Nelson, 2012), 211-28.

good, do it.' The overdue counterrevolution rightly adds, 'but only if it feels good for the other person, too.'" Will that counteremphasis of "mutual feel good" do enough to safeguard against objectification and abuse? As I explore a variety of viewpoints, it will become apparent that to the contrary, it does not safeguard adequately against objectification and abuse. Also, it will be argued that humans can only realize their best sexual intuitions and appetites in monogamous marital relations for which a robust trinitarian, persons-oriented ethical framework provides the necessary moral conditions or foundations.

WHAT'S UP WITH MONOGAMY? MORALS IN FLUX

The year 2015 was revolutionary for defining, or redefining, marriage, when in a 5-4 ruling a divided Supreme Court decision ruled that same-sex couples nationwide could wed. It was even debated at the time as to whether legalizing same-sex marriage would open the door to legalizing polygamous marriages, among other unions.[6]

Is the move to affirm polygamy inevitable? Separately, will society become increasingly accepting of extramarital affairs? A Gallup poll taken in 2014 found that society largely frowned on extramarital affairs as well as polygamy.[7] However, a Gallup poll administered in 2020 revealed that the trend is moving toward greater acceptance of polygamy with a fourfold increase in approval rating in approximately fifteen years.[8]

[6]See for example the following articles: Stanley Kurtz, "Beyond Gay Marriage," *Weekly Standard*, August 4, 2003, www.washingtonexaminer.com/weekly-standard/beyond-gay-marriage; Fredrik Deboer, "It's Time to Legalize Polygamy: Why Group Marriage Is the Next Horizon of Social Liberalism," *Politico Magazine*, June 26, 2015, www.politico.com/magazine/story/2015/06/gay-marriage-decision-polygamy-119469; Conor Friedersdorf, "The Case Against Encouraging Polygamy: Why Civil Marriage Should Not Encompass Group Unions," *Atlantic*, July 9, 2015, www.theatlantic.com/politics/archive/2015/07/case-against-polygamy/397823/; and Cathy Young, "Polygamy Is Not Next," *Time*, June 30, 2015, https://time.com/3942139/polygamy-is-not-next/.
[7]Refer again to the article "Polygamy Is Not Next." According to a 2014 Gallop poll, a majority of Americans surveyed consider extramarital sex acceptable (66 percent of Americans surveyed said it was okay, while 58 percent said having a baby outside of marriage was okay). In contrast, the study asserts that polygamy and marital affairs are viewed as "highly unacceptable." Rebecca Riffkin, "New Record Highs in Moral Acceptability," Gallup, May 30, 2014, https://news.gallup.com/poll/170789/new-record-highs-moral-acceptability.aspx.
[8]Frank Newport, "Understanding the Increase in Moral Acceptability of Polygamy," Gallup, June 26, 2020, https://news.gallup.com/opinion/polling-matters/313112/understanding-increase-moral-acceptability-polygamy.aspx. Still, polygamy is seldom practiced today across the globe. See Stephanie Kramer, "Polygamy Is Rare Around the World and Mostly Confined to a Few Regions," Pew

However, extramarital affairs ranked as the least morally acceptable issue of those topics surveyed in 2020: only 9 percent favored it, 89 percent disapproved, and 2 percent were noncommittal.[9]

For those who buck the trend in favor of the growing acceptance of polygamy, why? And why do Americans still largely find extramarital affairs repugnant? Does the disfavor point perhaps to the lingering echo of an ancient divine decree? Vestiges of the essential nature of things, created or evolved?[10] Leftovers of classical or traditional reason, or a remaining fragment of human virtue? Mere cultural moorings that will evolve or dissolve in time based on changes to our response mechanisms to behaviors and those responses' neural impact on our psychological states?[11]

Regardless of our respective answers to these questions, philosopher and ethicist Ayn Rand went against the trend on extramarital affairs. She argued that reason properly framed provides warrant for extramarital sexual affairs in certain contexts. The chapter titled "The Sacred and the Profane" in her novel *Atlas Shrugged* illustrates her position.[12] Let's consider Rand's musings on the sacred and profane and its bearing on relationships.

Here are some questions to consider when pondering "sacred" and "profane." What makes someone or something sacred, that is, hallowed and revered? What makes someone or something profane, that is, defiled and dishonored? More specifically in our present context, what makes a marriage or extramarital affair sacred or profane? Is a marriage sacred if the union is sanctioned by God or the state? Are other unions sacred if

---

Research Center, December 7, 2020, www.pewresearch.org/fact-tank/2020/12/07/polygamy-is -rare-around-the-world-and-mostly-confined-to-a-few-regions/.

[9]Megan Brenan, "Record-Low 54% in U.S. Say Death Penalty Morally Acceptable," Gallup, June 23, 2020, https://news.gallup.com/poll/312929/record-low-say-death-penalty-morally-acceptable.aspx.

[10]Consider, for example, the debated topic of whether monogamy serves as the evolutionary foundation of cooperative societies, at least among insects: "Score One for Monogamy," *ScienceMag.org*, May 29, 2008, www.sciencemag.org/news/2008/05/score-one-monogamy. See also the following article on monogamy and evolution: Carl Zimmer, "Monogamy and Human Evolution," *New York Times*, August 2, 2013, www.nytimes.com/2013/08/02/science/monogamys-boost-to-human -evolution.html?referer=&_r=0.

[11]See Ernst Fehr and Colin F. Camerer, "Social Neuroeconomics: The Neural Circuitry of Social Preferences," *Trends in Cognitive Sciences* 11, no. 10 (Oct 2007): 419-27 and Luke J. Chang and Leonie Koban, "Modeling Emotion and Learning of Norms in Social Interactions," *Journal of Neuroscience* 33, no. 18 (May 2013): https://www.jneurosci.org/content/jneuro/33/18/7615 .full.pdf.

[12]Ayn Rand, *Atlas Shrugged*, 50th anniversary ed. (New York: Penguin Books, 1992), 237-73.

ratified by contract?[13] Moreover, is a marital union or extramarital affair good or bad based on the motives, reasons, and actions (all of which require defining)? These questions arise as I consider Rand's discussion of sexual relationships and industry.

In "The Sacred and the Profane," two principal characters, Hank Rearden and Dagny Taggart, have an affair. They are at the top of their game in the world of industry. Dagny delights in their sexual intimacy, which she takes to be merited by their mutual greatness. For her, it is sacred. However, Hank, a married man, is miserable, though his affair with Dagny continues. For him, their sexual relations are profane, not in the sense of simply being common or secular in contrast to sacred or holy. Rather, he sees their sexual intimacy, which he craves, as degrading. One commentator notes, "This is an overall sacred section, where Dagny and Rearden's relationship is put into words, but because of Rearden's (who is unable to free himself from the orthodox beliefs of sex and lust as sin) viewing their love as depraved, it is profane." Later, the same commentator writes, "What is the profane, and what is the sacred? There is the common belief that anything carnal is profane, despite the nature of the act. . . . Whereas, despite orthodox beliefs of original sin, what Dagny and Rearden share is sacred—the mutual giving of pleasure as an act of tribute for mutual greatness."[14] Their relationship stands in stark contrast to much of the world given to mediocrity, mere feeling, dishonesty, and waste. Such traits appear in Dagny's brother, James Taggart, who is not

---

[13]Refer to these articles on the government's role in marriages and the import of contracts: Rand Paul, "Rand Paul: Government Should Get Out of the Marriage Business Altogether," *Time*, June 29, 2015, https://time.com/3939374/rand-paul-gay-marriage-supreme-court/, and Jane Greenway Carr, "What It Means When Marriage Is a Contract," *Time*, July 8, 2015, https://time.com/3949457/gay-marriage-love-conquers-all/.

[14]The quotations are taken from commentary by Yosun Chang, "Chapter 9: The Sacred and the Profane," *Musings on Atlas Shrugged* (blog), August 9, 2005, http://atlasshruggednovel.blogspot.com/2005/08/chapter-9-sacred-and-profane.html. See also Fred Seddon, "Various Levels of Meaning in the Chapter Titles of Atlas Shrugged," in *Atlas Shrugged: A Philosophical and Literary Companion*, ed. Edward W. Younkins (New York: Routledge, 2007), 49. There Seddon writes, "Surely the most obvious meaning of this title is the respective attitudes expressed by Hank and Dagny on the nature of the sex they had the night before. Hank regards it as vile and degrading, but as something he wouldn't give up. It's profane, but he can't help needing and wanting it." In contrast, "Dagny regards the act as sacred. Since she doesn't hold any version of the soul-body dichotomy, she does not separate the values of her mind from the value of her body. She is sacred, as are work and her sexual activities."

great, but who delights in preserving his young acquaintance Cherryl Brooks's illusion that he is a heroic, industrious figure.

From Rand's vantage point, rational self-interest is the determining factor in any ethical quandary. For Rand, sacredness or virtue involves the pursuit and embodiment of excellence. It involves honesty in addition to rational self-interest.[15] Based on her philosophy of life, it appears that for Rand an extramarital affair can be either sacred or profane depending on whether it involves these traits.

Mere mutual consent is not sufficient for Rand. Valid mutual consent would require full transparency and knowledge of the respective merits and benefits for each party. There must be no dishonesty, lack of critical reflection, or capitulation to mere pleasurable desire. Rand was no Puritan, but she was no debauched hedonist either.

One may ask to what extent Rand considers the views of those most affected by the principal parties' decision to have affairs. How much consideration should be given to the views of spouses, as well as children? What if one's spouse does not approve of the affair? What if the affair scars children emotionally? And even if the spouse does consent, what are the factors that went into the decision? Are we ultimately autonomous and free individuals who enter and exit relationships, making and breaking contractual agreements as we wish?

It is worth noting that Rand engaged in extramarital relations with her young protégé Nathaniel Branden. While their respective spouses consented to the longstanding affair, one wonders if the force of Rand's presence in her community in addition to her skills of argumentation swayed their spouses' decision to support Rand's and Branden's wishes. What is evident is that the affair and its aftermath certainly left its mark on the couples as well as Rand's Collective. Among other things, after Rand's and Branden's affair started, her husband "began his self-destructive affair with alcohol."[16]

---

[15]For an account of Rand's Objectivist ethical framework, see Ayn Rand with Nathaniel Branden, *The Virtue of Selfishness* (New York: Signet, 1964).

[16]On Rand's extramarital relations with Branden and its impact on her husband, Branden, his wife, and the Collective, see Bruce E. Levine, "One Nation Under Galt: How Ayn Rand's Toxic Philosophy Permanently Transformed America," *Salon*, December 15, 2014, www.salon.com/control/2014/12/15/one _nation_under_galt_how_ayn_rands_toxic_philosophy_permanently_transformed_america_partner/;

Regardless of what one makes of Rand's chapter "The Sacred and the Profane," her book foreshadows, fosters, and illustrates a world where what we deem sacred and profane is very much in flux. Take for example the conversation a married man had with an acquaintance, who was known for flings with married and unmarried women alike. The man on the prowl said that someday he would enter a relationship again. The married man was surprised that his acquaintance saw value in being faithful to a sexual partner. He responded that he valued faithfulness, as long as it wasn't the monogamous kind. Perhaps if he comes to the point someday of ceasing to have extramarital affairs, and given his disregard of monogamy, he will consider polyamory a live option.[17]

Many Christians experience great consternation over the moral flux on marriage and the various live options for sexual expression today in our pluralistic society. But rather than pontificate and wage war against other positions, those Christians who are married should make a compelling case for their scruples with the depth of love they model in the care for their spouses. From the New Testament's vantage point, any form of nonmonogamous union is profane or depraved. However, not every instance of monogamy is thereby sacred. Perhaps nothing is more profane or degrading than looking down on others for their lifestyle choices while failing to live out one's own convictions. Consider the call to sacred care in Ephesians 5:21-33, with its emphasis on self-sacrificial, mutual love that cherishes one's spouse as a person,

Steve Chawkins, "Nathaniel Branden Dies at 84; Acolyte and Lover of Ayn Rand," *Los Angeles Times*, December 8, 2014, www.latimes.com/local/obituaries/la-me-nathaniel-branden-20141209-story.html; and William Yardley, "Nathaniel Branden, a Partner in Love and Business with Ayn Rand, Dies at 84," *New York Times*, December 8, 2014, www.nytimes.com/2014/12/09/us/nathaniel-branden-ayn-rands-collaborator-and-paramour-dies-at-84.html?referer. See also "Ayn Rand and the Brandens: A Chronology," Objectivism Reference Center, February 26, 2011.
[17]The following article appears to represent a Randian view on the subject: Sara Burrows, "Polyamory Is Next, and I'm One Reason Why," *The Federalist*, June 30, 2015, https://thefederalist.com/2015/06/30/polyamory-is-next-and-im-one-reason-why/. See also these articles on polyamory: Angi Becker Stevens, "My Two Husbands," *Salon*, August 5, 2013, www.salon.com/control/2013/08/05/my_two_husbands/; Jessica Bennett, "Polyamory: The Next Sexual Revolution?" *Newsweek*, July 28, 2009, www.newsweek.com/polyamory-next-sexual-revolution-82053; and Olga Khazan, "Multiple Lovers, Without Jealousy," *Atlantic*, July 31, 2014, www.theatlantic.com/health/archive/2014/07/multiple-lovers-no-jealousy/374697/.

and not a plaything. This is a high and worthy calling that is hard to put into practice.

In addition to the challenge of living out Scripture's high calling for marriage, it is also difficult to provide a compelling rational case for the merits of monogamous marriage to people who will not entertain biblical arguments. With this point in mind, it is worth reflecting on arguments that are intended to proceed only in accordance with reason.

MONOGAMOUS SEX AND CATEGORICAL IMPERATIVES

It is not just Christian Scripture with its divine decrees and stipulations that looks disapprovingly on extramarital sex. The Great Prussian philosopher Immanuel Kant would appear to make a compelling case against extramarital sex, albeit solely on an appeal to rational grounds. Kant always sought to frame discussion of ethics on rational terms rather than based on appeals to revelation claims or feeling. As will be developed below, it seems fair to assert that from a Kantian framework, extramarital sex could never prove virtuous. However, it should be noted that critics often claim there is a tension or contradiction in Kant's thought as to the appropriateness or virtue of sexual pleasure even in a marital context.

In an essay titled "Good Sex on Kantian Grounds, or a Reply to Alan Soble,"[18] Joshua Schulz lays bare Kant's removal of the intellectual dimension from sexual desire in his treatment of sexual ethics in his doctrine of right. A tension arises because elsewhere in the same doctrine, Kant argues that sexual desire in marriage includes both intellectual and sensual qualities. It is the intellectual dimension (bound up with human personhood) that safeguards against objectification.[19] Its removal from consideration leads to viewing sexual intimacy of whatever kind as morally problematic in Kant's ethical framework. Schulz seeks to

---

[18]See Joshua Schulz, "Good Sex on Kantian Grounds, or a Reply to Alan Soble," *Essays in Philosophy* 8, no. 2 (June 2007), https://commons.pacificu.edu/work/sc/72e5f24e-a5cb-4224-be8c-f0e 8abcd09e5.

[19]Kant claims that "rational nature exists as end in itself." Immanuel Kant, *Groundwork for the Metaphysics of Morals*, ed. and trans. Allen W. Wood (New Haven, CT: Yale University Press, 2002), Ak 4:429; 46.

resolve the seeming contradiction from the vantage point of Kant's overarching system.

Let's consider the possible moral dilemma posed by sexual pleasure. Kant maintains that a twofold objectification and degradation occurs when two (or more) individuals make their bodies instruments for one another's sexual pleasure: there is no sense of either (or any) party being an end in themselves. They are nothing more than a means to an end of one another's sexual gratification. Such dual objectification is morally repugnant or profane based on the second formulation of Kant's categorical imperative: one should always treat the other or oneself as an end, and never as a mere means. This formulation of the categorical imperative reads, "The practical imperative will thus be the following: *Act so that you use humanity, as much in your own person as in the person of every other, always at the same time as end and never merely as means.*"[20] If double degradation is inevitable, celibacy is not only inherently moral, but also a moral duty or necessity for everyone.[21]

This account of sexual intimacy as always morally deviant does not appear satisfactory based on Kant's overarching system. Beyond Schulz's own treatment, to which we shall return, we offer the following. How could celibacy as a moral duty, presumably imposed on all, advance life for the race? Would it not function in effect as the equivalent of collective suicide, that is, the collective determination to end human civilization? If so, this same determination would stand opposed to one of the formulations of Kant's categorical imperative: "Act as if the maxim of your action were to become through your will a universal law of nature."[22] If the aim is to cultivate virtue in the race, how would the equivalent of mass suicide in the form of universally binding celibacy foster virtue?[23] Universally binding celibacy would prove incoherent and unsatisfactory.

Schulz offers other reasons why celibacy is not a moral duty to which all people must adhere. In what follows, we will look briefly to Schulz's account of Kant's philosophy in the attempt to address further cases

---

[20]Kant, *Groundwork for the Metaphysics of Morals*, Ak 4:429; 46-47.
[21]Refer to Schulz's treatment of Kant, sex, and celibacy in "Good Sex on Kantian Grounds."
[22]Kant, *Groundwork for the Metaphysics of Morals*, Ak 4:421; 38.
[23]See a particular account of how suicide contends against the supreme principle of moral duty and virtue in Kant's *Groundwork for the Metaphysics of Morals*, Ak 4:421-22; 38-39.

where a couple can pursue sexual pleasure in a virtuous manner. Contrary to Rand's view, for Kant, one can never rightly view a relationship as virtuous if one looks at the other *simply* as a mere means to one's own self-cultivation—the just reward for one's own greatness, as in the case of Dagny Taggart and Hank Rearden in *Atlas Shrugged*. No matter how seemingly rational, this orientation lacks virtue, even if the other party operates with the same aim in mind. From a Kantian framework, there are certain conditions that help to ensure that happiness involving sexual intimacy is wed to virtue, which entails seeing the other party in a romantic, sexual relationship as an end in themselves, and not merely a means to one's own satisfaction.

According to Schulz's account, the following conditions make it possible for a couple to experience sexual pleasure in a virtuous manner from a Kantian framework. First, the couple only pursues sexual pleasure in a context that safeguards against moral degradation. A lifelong monogamous marriage, especially one that is legally sanctioned, can help to ensure virtuous sexual activity. It is worth pausing and pointing out here that according to Schulz, there may be other contexts beyond monogamy that can safeguard against concupiscence. Second, the union involving sexual intimacy features all the accompanying constraints, especially when they are preconditions for sexual intercourse, such as cohabitation and the mutual sharing of assets and joint care for a couple's offspring. Third, the monogamous sexual union entails the mutual beneficent care and cultivation of virtue in one's spouse. When practiced, these parameters make it possible for the two parties to pursue sexual intimacy in a morally virtuous manner.[24]

As cogent as this line of reasoning may appear, someone might still ask, Why should humans be considered ends in themselves based on intellectual capacities, or some other qualities, and not simply as mere means? Is this perspective ultimately a rational claim devoid of religious dogmatic underpinnings? Or did Kant unknowingly presuppose the biblical tradition with which he was very familiar? The biblical tradition includes such teachings as the image of God doctrine (Genesis 1:26-31),

---

[24]Refer again to Schulz, "Good Sex on Kantian Grounds."

which presents humanity as the pinnacle of creation (based on human-ity's ability to reason or on some other quality or condition), as well as the Great Commandments (Mark 12:30-31), which involve the tenet that we are to love our neighbors as ourselves in addition to loving God as the ultimate end.

Perhaps Kant would dismiss the idea that he presupposes the biblical tradition at one or more points in his presumed rationalist approach to ethics. What is beyond dispute, however, is that he would find abhorrent the notion that ethics is nothing more than mere cultural moorings that result from biological determinations, base instincts, and the herd men-tality. If that were the case, ethics, like sexual pleasure, would be equiv-alent to animal appetites. Whatever appeals to our natural appetites, or that benefits us biologically, would then be determinative of what's ethi-cally best for us. The problem with this outlook is that while the race would no doubt flourish, human dignity would appear to disappear. Let's consider further a biological approach to sexual expression and morality.

SEX, BIOLOGICAL DIVERSITY, AND BONDING

Are extramarital affairs inevitable because of biological "determinants" and benefits, increased external stimuli, and changing cultural moorings? And if inevitable, are such affairs thereby ethical? If so, what makes us different from animals and machines, and have we lost out on individual freedom, capitulating to the herd mentality?

Regardless of a biblical as well as Kantian concern over the apparent indignity of this approach, many find a biologically based approach to ethics appealing given the explanatory power of the natural sciences in our world today. A biological approach to sexual ethics would in-clude discussion of our being wired biologically toward marital fidelity or infidelity. Such a case would account for competing biological drives and accompanying biological benefits. For example, one might put forward such biologically related considerations in favor of marital fidelity: the increased protection and nurture of a couple's offspring. From the reverse angle, one might account for the following biology-based factors in favor of marital infidelity: the diversification of one's descendants and insurance against the inability to have descendants as the result of an infertile spouse or the untimely death of one's spouse. None of these reasons necessarily involve pleasure and the desire for intimacy.

Famed sociobiologist E. O. Wilson argues that the primary reason for sex is diversification: "Sex is not designed primarily for reproduction. . . . Nor is the primary function of sex the giving and receiving of pleasure. . . . The principal answer is that sex creates diversity."[25] After all, some biological specimens produce asexually. Sexual reproduction enhances diversification and makes a species more resilient and bountiful. Sexual pleasure, on the other hand, is unique to a few species. The main aim of sexual pleasure is bonding.[26] Wilson also points out that only a fourth of known cultures prize monogamy.[27] Perhaps the matter could be stated succinctly as follows: sexual bonding involving pleasure occurs for the sake of diversification in reproduction.

Interestingly, contrary to Charles Darwin,[28] Wilson mistakenly reduces or equates biological states with ethical considerations. What is the case leads automatically to what will be the case. If a certain biological state of affairs or wiring is the case and will be the case, it should be the case. On this evolutionary view, ethics involves predictions rather than prescriptions.[29]

Contrary to what many evolutionary ethicists maintain, there is a fine line between "what is the case" and "what should be the case" statements.[30] Even though we should account for biological states and propensities

---

[25]E. O. Wilson, *On Human Nature*, 2nd ed. (Cambridge, MA: Harvard University Press, 2004), 121-22.

[26]See Wilson, *On Human Nature*, 139, though the sentiment is peppered throughout the volume.

[27]Wilson, *On Human Nature*, 126.

[28]Leslie Stevenson, David L. Haberman, and Peter Matthews Wright, *Twelve Theories of Human Nature*, 6th ed. (New York: Oxford University Press, 2013), 250-55.

[29]See Whitley Kaufman, "The Evolutionary Ethics of E. O. Wilson," *New Atlantis: A Journal of Technology & Society* 38 (Winter/Spring 2013): 144-45.

[30]My colleague Derrick Peterson made a related point in distinguishing between "what was the case" and "what must be the case" statements. Evolutionary psychology often comes across as being mired in "just so" stories—we are the way we are today based on how our ancestors were formed while wandering the plains of Africa or Asia. Undoubtedly something like that plays a part, but as Conor Cunningham asserts in *Darwin's Pious Idea*, to accord too much weight to evolutionary psychology is anti-evolutionary. That is, it makes what happened ten, twenty, or thirty-plus years ago determinative rather than merely a component in a species' ongoing development. See Cunningham, *Darwin's Pious Idea: Why the Ultra-Darwinists and Creationists Both Get It Wrong* (Grand Rapids, MI: Eerdmans, 2010).

in ethical deliberations, it does not follow that we should automatically act out our biological drives.

Consider the following example. Perhaps early on in our species' development, a woman desired a mate to protect and provide for her and their offspring. After all, she carried the infant in her arms rather than on her back, as primates do. From this angle, once the child could walk about freely, the woman was free to use her arms to protect and provide for them. At that point, the woman's mate became dispensable. One finds here a striking correlation in contemporary society: most divorces today occur in a couple's fourth year of marriage, around the time a firstborn child would graduate from infancy. That said, there is no moral credence to terminate a marriage even if humans are predisposed biologically to bond only for the duration of their offspring's infancy years.[31] Morality does not authorize adherence to our biological drives and impulses.[32]

One of the important items to consider in evaluating ethical models is the weight they give to human dignity. Moral freedom and responsibility go hand in hand with the affirmation of human dignity. With this point in mind, it is as much a moral cop-out to say, "My genes (or societal forces) made me do it, so I am not responsible," as it is to say, "I had no choice, since the devil made me do it." Those who do not take moral responsibility for their actions fail to pay tribute to their human dignity.

Kant would share this concern. He wanted to safeguard moral freedom from the controlling mechanism of nature. Otherwise, what makes us distinctively human vanishes. Albeit from a different vantage point, Joseph Fletcher, the father of situation ethics, resonates with the position

---

[31]Here I call to mind biological anthropologist Helen Fisher's observations: "'Mono' means one, and 'gamy' means spouse. It does not mean sexual fidelity." In an interview with *Forbes*, Fisher claims, "Humans are among just 3% of mammals that form pair bonds. . . . Species like beetles, beavers and most birds share the instinct to partner up to rear their young. . . . It is a reproductive strategy, which Fisher posits evolved in humans because they walked upright. Unlike chimpanzees who carried their young on their backs, a human woman carried a child in her arms and thus likely desired a mate to protect and provide for her. Fisher notes that today, divorce commonly occurs in the fourth year of marriage, or about the length of human infancy. 'Maybe a woman needed a man to raise a child through infancy,' she speculates." Jenna Goudreau, "What's So Wrong with Monogamy?" *Forbes*, February 13, 2012, www.forbes.com/sites/jennagoudreau/2012/02/13/monogamy-sexual-fidelity-marriage-relationships/#2ff34277471d.

[32]Refer back to the discussion on this point in chapter two and Christian Smith, *What Is a Person?* (Chicago: University of Chicago Press, 2010), 486.

we take here. He sought to guard against the mindset that one is com-
pelled to obey one's desires. We will consider Fletcher's situational ethical
system in the next section. For Kant and Fletcher, adherence to a hedo-
nistic pleasure principle or fixation on a biological drive as morally determinative hurts intimacy with one's spouse and degrades the person
with whom one has extramarital sex. From a personalist vantage point,
such seeming laws of nature or pleasure principles make no room for
liberating love.

Moreover, sole focus on biological considerations does not help us in
differentiating between the better and lesser angels of our nature. From
a biological vantage point, it may be more socially advantageous to play
the field rather than remain faithful in marriage. According to biological
anthropologist Helen Fisher, "We've never found a species that's sexually
faithful." In fact, she believes humans developed a dual-reproductive
strategy, in which cheating had benefits too. It created more variety in
the woman's family line, doubled a man's potential offspring, and served
as an insurance policy against a spouse's death. "Through millions of
years of both strategies, what we have today is a tremendous drive for
social monogamy and also a drive to cheat."[33]

Based on these factors, one is hard pressed to discern whether it is
appropriate to remain faithful to one's spouse. To commandeer a line
from Shakespeare, "To cheat or not to cheat, that is the question!" We
must move beyond naturalistic reasoning to make a case for fidelity or
infidelity. For Fletcher, we must also go beyond general principles, as we
find in Kant, and account for the merits of a given situation to discern
whether having an extramarital affair is ever appropriate. To this subject,
I now turn.

SITUATIONAL ETHICS AND FAMILY AFFAIRS

It has been argued that a concealed affair can save one's marriage and that
an open sexual relationship may enhance one's marital union.[34] In his

---

[33]Jenna Goudreau, "What's So Wrong with Monogamy?"
[34]See for example Dan Savage, "Is It Ever Okay to Cheat?," video interview with Sanjay Gupta, and
   accompanying article by Mel Robbins, "What's Inside an Open Marriage?," CNN, June 9, 2015,
   www.cnn.com/2015/06/09/opinions/robbins-open-marriage/.

interview with Sanjay Gupta, Dan Savage offers the example of a marriage where one of the spouses is no longer willing or able to engage in sexual activity. What is the other spouse whose sexual desires are unfulfilled to do? One may contend that the spouse whose sexual advances in marriage are thwarted must remain true to their marital vows no matter what. But has not a spouse who is able to engage in sexual activity but who has rejected their partner's advances already compromised their union? After all, for most marriages, both parties understand that their marriage involves the expectation that they will seek to meet one another's sexual needs and desires.

It is important to pause here and add that some expectations are unfair. Moreover, no expectations should be imposed, which may constitute rape within marriage. Sexual intimacy requires mutual consent. Along similar lines, one should not use one's spouse as a plaything to fulfill one's sexual fantasies. Nor should one use sex as a tool or weapon to manipulate a spouse to do one's bidding outside the marriage bed. These qualifying remarks call to mind the earlier section where I reflected on Kant's claim that we should always engage one another not simply as means, but also as ends. We must guard against the objectification and degradation of one another as humans.

Now back to Savage. So, what is the spouse whose marriage partner constantly thwarts their sexual advances to do? Should he or she break off the marriage? Similarly, what should a spouse do if their mate is no longer able to engage in sexual activity because of a physical disability or impairment? While Savage does not take marital unfaithfulness lightly, he believes that such situations warrant the spouse with unmet sexual needs having a secret affair to satisfy those desires and thereby preserve the marriage. The only other option for the jilted spouse would be to seek a divorce.

So, let's say the concealed affair takes place. How long can the concealment last? What if a sexually transmitted disease is contracted? Savage addresses this question by encouraging caution in engaging in extramarital sexual activity. But let's say that one still contracts a sexual disease. Even if one is no longer having sexual relations with their spouse, the disease can still impact the marriage. A serious illness of whatever kind leaves an indelible impression on one's family circle. Moreover, sexual relations come with emotional and psychological ties. The affair may very well lead to the termination of the marriage anyway because the sexual bonds in the concealed affair can prove very strong and undo any remaining intimacy in the existing marriage. No course of action is fool proof and Savage may consider that the prospects for saving the marriage by way of the concealed affair outweigh the risks.

Let's consider another closely related option—an open marriage. Mel Robbins writes in "What's Inside an Open Marriage?" that the lover is welcomed into the family circle. Robbins shares how she and her husband entertained the idea of an open marriage, but then closed the door to the possibility after considering it more deeply. Here are the dynamics that alarmed them:

> When you step outside your marriage and into another person's bed you may say it's "just sex"—but in reality you just invited that person to step into your whole life, and they probably will. You'll be in your kitchen, with your spouse, when the texts appear on your phone. Are you free Saturday? You'll be driving in your car with your kids, when the song that reminds you of your lover plays. And suddenly, they are right there in the car with you.[35]

Indeed, an open sexual relationship gives the lover total access to one's life and family. While Robbins and her husband first thought an open marriage might add spice to their relationship, these alarm bells made them do a double take and reconsider.

Beyond the married couple, one needs to consider what a concealed affair or open marriage does to the person with whom one is having a sexual relationship. It is not just about one's marriage. One should again call to mind Kant's ethical concern noted above about not objectifying others. How does an individual's or couple's aim to save or spice up their marriage benefit the lover? The lover appears to be nothing more than a mere means to their own ends. The problem of mere means rather than ends does not go away if the lover or lovers are also engaged in the affair

---

[35]Robbins, "What's Inside an Open Marriage?"

to save or spice up their own marriages. The various lovers are using one another. Two or more wrongs do not make a right.

One also needs to account for the children, including their emotional states, especially if a concealed affair were to go public somehow, or if one takes part in an open marital relationship. And what about the children born out of wedlock? While not the focus of this section or chapter, matters become increasingly complex, it would seem, if one goes further and enters a polygamous marital arrangement, or a polyamorous one.[36] What about such matters as inheritance, or legal rights to healthcare through a spouse's policy, among other things? One needs to keep an open mind and consider all the variables. As one *TIME* magazine article titled "Polygamy Is Not Next" notes,

> The entire existing structure of modern marriage is designed for a dyad. DeBoer argues that there were similar practical objections to same-sex marriage—for instance, having to discard marriage license forms with the words "husband" and "wife" and replacing them with ones that list "Spouse 1" and "Spouse 2." But this onerous task hardly compares to the massive overhaul multi-partner marriage would require: including revising the rules on post-divorce property division or survivor benefits for three, five, or 10 people instead of two; adjusting child custody arrangement for multiple legal parents; and determining who has the legal authority to make decisions for an incapacitated spouse. . . .
>
> The bottom line is that as a practical matter, it's simply impossible for plural partners to have the same rights and benefits currently enjoyed by two spouses, gay or straight. It's likely that every group marriage would essentially have to be customized. This would remove what many advocates have always cited as a major advantage of marriage: a single, simple legal act that creates a standard set of privileges and obligations.[37]

As illustrated here, there are many ethical factors and practical items to consider in various situations.

Let's consider one more situation that further complicates the subject matter ethically. Fletcher addresses sex, including sexual relations outside

---

[36]Refer to Angi Becker Stevens, "Polyamorous Relationships Are About More Than Just Couples," *Huffington Post*, February 2, 2016, www.huffpost.com/entry/polyamorous-relationships_b _4370026.
[37]Young, "Polygamy Is Not Next."

of marriage, in his classic work *Situation Ethics.*[38] Situation ethics is not "antinomian" or antilaw. Nor is it "legalistic."[39] Situation ethics for Fletcher is never about "anything goes," or self-gratifying desire, which is an antinomian outlook. Nor does it entail adherence to external, legal codes as ends in themselves. Rather, situation ethics is attitudinal in the sense of the Christian rendering of love as agape. It always involves keeping unconditional concern for God and others firmly in mind.[40] Fletcher claims to follow Augustine's lead: "Love with care and *then* what you will, do," not the antinomian "Love with desire and do what you please."[41]

To drive home the point of situation ethics in relation to marriage and sexual relations, Fletcher shares the example of a German family torn apart by war at the close of WWII. The husband is a prisoner of war in a prison camp in Wales. While she is scavenging for food for her children on the streets back home in Germany, a Russian patrol picks up the wife and transports her to a prison camp in Ukraine, unbeknownst to her family. The children are scattered. After the husband is eventually released, he goes about finding the children, while also searching frantically for his missing wife. Someone gets word to her about her family's perilous state and that they are under great duress without her.

There are only two options for her at this time to be released from the prison camp in Ukraine. One option would be for her to become severely ill, where she would be released to a Soviet hospital for treatment that she could not receive in the camp. However, she still would not be able to return to Germany. The other opportunity for release would be for her to become pregnant while in captivity. In that case, she would be returned to Germany as "a liability." The woman chooses to explore the second option. She approaches a friendly prison guard and asks him to impregnate her so that she can be released and returned to Germany, where she could be reunited with her family. He obliges her request. She becomes pregnant and released to return home. Her family welcomes

---

[38]Joseph Fletcher, *Situation Ethics: The New Morality* (Philadelphia: Westminster, 1966). Reference his account of this theme within the framework of situation ethics on 13-14, 17, 79, 103-4, 117, 124, 126-27, 139, 146, and 163.

[39]Fletcher, *Situation Ethics*, 17.

[40]Fletcher, *Situation Ethics*, 79-80, 117.

[41]Fletcher, *Situation Ethics*, 79.

her with open arms, as well as the child born to her out of wedlock. In fact, they cherish him because his life is the reason for their reunion as a family.[42] What is one to make of this account, which Fletcher titles "Sacrificial Adultery"?[43]

From all that is known about the case in question, the woman's aim in pursuing sexual relations with the prison guard was not pleasure, but reunion with her family. But what was the guard's aim? Was his aim simply to help the woman get impregnated so that she could return to Germany? Regardless of whether it was for pleasure, there is still a form of objectification, in keeping with what Kant argues about regarding means and ends. Basically, the woman uses the guard to get impregnated and released. The guard may have used the woman for sexual pleasure, even while assisting her in getting home to be with her family. They become means to one another's own ends. That said, this example is not equivalent to having extramarital relations merely for the sake of sexual pleasure. At least in the wife and mother's case, she engaged in sexual activity outside marriage simply for the sake of her husband and children.

Is there a place for hierarchical ethics, wherein one makes allowances for the lesser of two evils, and for a relational good, namely in this case, reunion with one's family, which is barely surviving without the wife and mother? Here it is worth noting that in the Bible allowances appear to be made for polygamous relationships. While monogamy alone is ultimately affirmed, God does not normally require that men divorce additional wives. Here we must account for exceptions, like Ezra 9 and 10, where it appears that God requires the men of Israel to send away their foreign wives. While God encourages Abraham to account for Sarah's wish and send Hagar and Ishmael away, God promises to care for them and make Ishmael great (Genesis 21:8-21). God also makes allowances for divorce in Scripture, due to the people's hardness of heart, though Jesus allows for only one exception—marital unfaithfulness (Matthew 19:8-9). God's aim is to protect marital unions wherever possible, as well as safeguard against the exploitation of women.

---

[42]Fletcher, *Situation Ethics*, 164-65.
[43]Fletcher, *Situation Ethics*, 165.

Now one might argue from a biblical standpoint that if the German woman in the Ukrainian prison camp is a believer, she should pray for God to save her family from this crisis that does not involve her having to engage in extramarital sexual activity to get impregnated and released (see 1 Corinthians 10:13). God might not provide a way out of prison, but rather provide relief for her husband and children through extended family members or friends, who will come to her family's aid.

In the situation narrated here, we are told that the family, who knows about the circumstances involving her release, welcomes the woman and child with joy and open arms. But what happens if down the road, her husband and the children from their marital union change their view of the situation? Of course, the woman has no way of knowing what their short-term or long-term responses might be, when she resolves to act in prison. Nor does it seem fair to make her sort through all these possible scenarios as someone who is the victim of circumstances far beyond her control. No matter what one thinks about her determination, hopefully those aware of what occurred would not judge her but show empathy and compassion for the woman and her family's extreme duress.

SECURITY, SEXUAL INTIMACY, AND SPIRITUALITY

Throughout this chapter, I have focused consideration on the challenge to monogamy in our society and how it surfaces the overarching concern of this volume—the reduction of persons to things. In the future, monogamous sex may well be on the endangered sexual expression list. Monogamous sexual fidelity may be viewed simply as a cultural preference that is losing ground to more natural sociobiological drives and cultural moorings. Here I call to mind Wilson's placement of monogamy in a broader sociobiological context:

> We are, first of all, moderately polygynous [polygamy involving the marriage of one man to many women], with males initiating most of the changes in sexual partnership. About three-fourths of all human societies permit the taking of multiple wives, and most of them encourage the practice by law and custom. In contrast, marriage to multiple husbands is sanctioned in less than one percent of societies. The remaining monogamous societies usually fit that category in a legal sense only, with

concubinage and other extramarital stratagems being added to allow de facto polygyny.[44]

Wilson states that humans are "moderately polygynous." If correct, that might help to account for the fourfold increase over fifteen years of 20 percent of Americans now favoring polygamy, as noted earlier in this chapter.[45]

Regardless of the future prospects of monogamy, it is worth considering whether the increasing acceptance of polygamy, or more specifically, polygyny, will foster increasing objectification, that is, the reduction of persons to things in American society. It is important that we resist a hasty answer. Keep in mind that polygyny was a widespread practice in biblical times. Individuals like Jacob/Israel and David had multiple wives, and God permitted, if not sanctioned, polygamy. Only in the New Testament does one find that God esteems monogamy as the standard for his people (as in the Pastoral Epistles' emphasis on the overseer being the husband of one wife; 1 Timothy 3:2). Although not the ideal, polygamy was a means to safeguard against abuses of women who would otherwise be forced to fend for themselves.

It is not simply the Old Testament that was concerned for safeguarding against abuses of women through practices like polygamy. According to Karen Armstrong in *Muhammad: A Prophet for Our Time*, polygamy under Muhammad's influence actually promoted women's well-being. Armstrong acknowledges that polygamy is criticized in our day as a source of great anguish for Muslim women. Even so, she maintains that it was a social advance for women in Muhammad's time.[46] Armstrong argues, "The Qur'anic institution of polygamy was a piece of social legislation. It was designed not to gratify the male sexual appetite, but to correct the injustices done to widows, orphans, and other female dependents, who were especially vulnerable."[47] Polygamy, or better, polygyny, was preferable to polyandry, which was also

[44]Wilson, *On Human Nature*, 125-26.
[45]Frank Newport, "Understanding the Increase in Moral Acceptability of Polygamy," Gallup, June 26, 2020, https://news.gallup.com/opinion/polling-matters/313112/understanding-increase-moral-acceptability-polygamy.aspx.
[46]Karen Armstrong, *Muhammad: A Prophet for Our Time* (New York: HarperOne, 2006), 133-34.
[47]Armstrong, *Muhammad*, 135.

widespread in pre-Islamic society. According to Armstrong, polyandry functioned as "a form of licensed prostitution." Polyandrous societies determined that offspring belonged to the mothers. The fallout from this was that men did not bear responsibility for providing for women and children.[48]

The point of this discussion is not to promote polygamy as a live option for today, but to guard against anachronistic judgments of earlier civilizations. Against the ancient and premodern cultural backdrop, one can see that polygamy was an advance from polyandry in helping reduce abuses against women. One can also make a case that when looking at the Bible, the narrative and laws consider various complexities. God instilled gradual change leading toward monogamy so as not to cause undue societal disruption that would increase women's vulnerability in ancient societies. Some of those allowances would have been seen in their historical contexts as constructive developments.

Biblically speaking, monogamy is the ideal. Still, polygamy had relative and comparative merit in so far as it helped to correct injustices committed against vulnerable women. In contrast, polyandry, as well as polyamory (defined here as having many intimate loves outside marriage), would not provide adequate safeguards. Rather, such practices would increase the chances of women being treated as impersonal means to sexual ends.[49]

Kant's categorical imperative to treat others not simply as means but also as ends serves as a good challenge to reductionism in the context of sexual expression. It also resonates with different spiritual

---

[48]See Armstrong, *Muhammad*, 134-36. Note also her discussion of advances under Muhammad to promote greater gender equality and the Qur'an's affirmation of women's individual rights in such matters as inheriting and managing property.

[49]"Polyamory is one form of *consensual non-monogamy*. Consensual non-monogamy is an umbrella term for any relationship type in which people are not monogamous. Polyamory emphasizes emotional connection between or among more than two romantic partners who know about (and might even like) each other." Elisabeth Sheff, *When Someone You Love Is Polyamorous: Understanding Poly People and Relationships* (Portland, OR: Thorntree Press, 2016), 3. In contrast to other forms of consensual non-monogamy, like "swinging," polyamory involves greater relational complexity and emotional intimacy. Those who choose polyamory over these other forms often realize "they have to emphasize love over sex." (Sheff, 8). "People who identify as polyamorous . . . reject the idea that exclusivity is necessary for meaningful, sustainable relationships." Charlotte Nickerson, "What Is Polyamory?" *Simply Psychology*, March 23, 2022, www.simplypsychology.org/polyamory.html.

traditions' celebration of the sacred in sexual relations. Let's consider briefly Buddhism followed by Christianity. Zen Buddhist ethicist Robert Aitken claims,

> Sexual intercourse is misused when it is an addiction rather than the peak experience of love between a committed couple. All the Precepts point to addictive behaviour, stealing, lying, using alcohol or drugs, slandering, even killing. Addiction reveals a lack of confidence, a need for something from others, the interdependence of all things inverted for just one being. It is no good condemning promiscuity as immoral behaviour, for it is only a symptom of general immaturity. Like anybody else, the addict needs guidance to find a way to forget the self.[50]

Elsewhere Aitken claims that monogamous sexual intimacy expresses compassionate existence and a loss of self-centeredness. Having earlier claimed that "the practice of marriage is the lifetime cultivation of intimacy with an opposite," Aitken goes on to write,

> Very different is the argument that sex is fulfilling only when it breaks the established pattern—that human beings are not essentially monogamous. This is the view of people who cultivate power to attract others rather than a compassionate spirit in reaching out to them. Saving all beings is our practice, and in the home this can be just the simple act of doing the dishes or helping with homework—or it can be having a party when the kids are in bed. The dance of sex, the dance of life in all circumstances requires forgetting the self and giving over to the dance. Sexual intercourse is the dancing nucleus of our home, generating all being at climax, bringing rest and renewal.[51]

Although the metaphysical frameworks for Zen Buddhism and orthodox Christianity are strikingly different, Christian theologian Sarah Coakley's discussion of "commingling" resonates with Aitken's emphasis on the dance of sex.[52] Unlike Buddhists, Christians do not generally speak of the loss of self, but rather finding one's true self in harmonious

---

[50]Refer to Robert Aitken, "On the Ten Grave Precepts," thezensite, accessed on July 30, 2019, http://www.thezensite.com/ZenTeachings/Teishos/Ten_Grave_Precepts.htm.

[51]Robert Aitken, *The Mind of Clover: Essays in Zen Buddhist Ethics* (New York: North Point, 1984), 47.

[52]Sarah Coakley, *God, Sexuality, and the Self: An Essay "On the Trinity"* (Cambridge: Cambridge University Press, 2013), 284.

relation with others. Still, monogamous sex reflects the trajectory of both traditions' celebration of what Aitken calls "the interdependence of all things."

No doubt, Coakley would affirm Aitken's concern over the inversion of interdependence, and the objectification of others' bodies for the sake of an individual being's sexual fantasies. Such inversion is notoriously widespread today, as noted in Krattenmaker's article "It's Time for a Sexual Counterrevolution," featured in the introduction to this chapter. The addictive behavior appears to be spreading like an epidemic.

The solution is not to suppress sexual expression. How can we if, as Wilson writes, "human beings are connoisseurs of sexual pleasure"? Suppression is not the solution, but appropriate channels for expression. For Wilson, sexual pleasure "has little if anything to do with reproduction." Rather, "It has everything to do with bonding. . . . Most of the pleasures of human sex constitute primary reinforcers to facilitate bonding. Love and sex do indeed go together."[53]

Certainly, sex and love go together. So, too, do sexuality and spirituality. It is not that spirituality is ultimately about sex. Rather, sex and pleasure are ultimately about spirituality. The sexual re-revolution that this chapter envisions requires reconsideration of the life of God and union or "bonding" with God, to commandeer Wilson's term. This will require that spirituality or religion is no longer deemed to be a neurosis that involves the suppression of sex, as Freud argued, but as a cure to the neurosis that makes a god out of sex. Coakley puts the matter well: "Freud must be—as it were—turned on his head. It is not that physical 'sex' is basic and 'God' ephemeral; rather it is God who is basic, and 'desire' the precious clue that ever tugs at the heart, reminding the human soul—however dimly—of its created source."[54] She later writes, "Instead of 'God' language 'really' being about sex, sex is really about God—the potent reminder woven into our earthly existence of the divine 'unity,' 'alliance,' and 'commingling' that we seek."[55]

---

[53]Wilson, *On Human Nature*, 141.
[54]Coakley, *God, Sexuality, and the Self*, 10.
[55]Coakley, *God, Sexuality, and the Self*, 284.

Numerous theologians in the history of the church have taken up the biblical typology that refers to God's people as a bride.[56] Perhaps nowhere is that imagery more duly noted than in Paul's letter to the Ephesian church. In Ephesians 5, Paul exhorts the Ephesian Christians who were married to reflect Christ's eternal union with the church in their marital relations after speaking of mutual submission out of reverence for Christ (Ephesians 5:21-33).

Paul teaches an embodied ethic. Husbands are to love their wives, as Christ loved the church, laying down his rights for his bride. In response, wives are to honor their husbands. Paul's aim is not to fixate on husbands and wives. Their relationship is a type. The antitype is Christ and the church. The two shall become one flesh, Paul writes, not referring ultimately to husbands and wives, but Christ and the church. Our spiritual union with Christ, which Calvin calls "intercourse,"[57] is not something we can ultimately understand, but rather, feel. Calvin's discussion of intercourse and feeling suggests that sexual desire reminds us of our ultimate eschatological destination—affective union or bonding with God's Son through the divine Spirit of holy love.[58]

No stranger to sexual exploits in his youth, Saint Augustine, the father of Western theology, agonized over arriving late in his love of God.[59] Augustine opened his *Confessions* with a heart cry concerning the creative source and destination of his being: "Our hearts are restless until they find

---

[56]Martin Luther represents this tradition. See his essay, "The Freedom of a Christian," in *Martin Luther's Basic Theological Writings*, ed. Timothy F. Lull (Minneapolis: Fortress, 1989), 604.

[57]"Reason itself teaches how we ought to act in such matters; for whatever is supernatural is clearly beyond our own comprehension. Let us therefore *labour* more to feel Christ living in us, than to discover the nature of that *intercourse*." John Calvin, *Commentaries on the Epistles of Paul to the Galatians and Ephesians*, vol. 2, trans. William Pringle (Grand Rapids, MI: Baker, 1979), 324-25 (italics added).

[58]A further development of the themes of desire, union with Christ, and the symbolism of marriage is found in Sara Mannen's article, "Settling for Sex," *Cultural Encounters* 14, no. 2 (June 2019): 30-48.

[59]Here's Augustine: "Late have I loved Thee, O Beauty so ancient and so new; late have I loved Thee! For behold Thou wert within me, and I outside; and I sought Thee outside and in my unloveliness fell upon those lovely things that Thou hast made. Thou wert with me and I was not with Thee. I was kept from Thee by those things, yet had they not been in Thee, they would not have been at all. Thou didst call and cry to me and break open my deafness: and Thou didst send forth Thy beams and shine upon me and chase away my blindness: Thou didst breathe fragrance upon me, and I drew in my breath and do now pant for Thee: I tasted Thee, and now hunger and thirst for Thee: Thou didst touch me, and I have burned for Thy peace." *Confessions*, 2nd ed., trans. F. J. Sheed, ed. Michael P. Foley (Indianapolis: Hackett, 2006), X.27.38, 210.

their rest in God."[60] Only as our restless hearts find their rest in God will we be able to experience a sexual re-revolution. Only then can we move beyond the addictive behavior and neurosis bound up with making a god out of sex.

Although Augustine is often blamed for Christianity's uncomfortable relationship with sexuality, his own experience and theology resonate with the need for redemption for a sexual re-revolution. His negative assessment of sex beyond the need for procreation stems from his understanding of how sin affected sexual desire. Coakley summarizes his concerns: "What is really worrying to Augustine in the post-Fall condition, however, is the male loss of control in sex; the revolt of the body against the cooperative mental work of memory, understanding, and will—especially against the will. Thus what is nasty and 'shameful' about sex . . . is the independent revolt of the male phallus."[61]

Sin creates a disjunction, a loss of harmony, between the body and the soul. As a fitting punishment for the crime of disobedience, lust allows the body to revolt against the soul: "Man has been given over to himself because he abandoned God, while he sought to be self-satisfying; and disobeying God, he could not obey even himself."[62] Sexual desire and lust mirror humanity's sin of disobedience by reflecting the disordering of love and shattering of the harmony between man and God. John C. Cavadini aptly describes the significance of lust for Augustine: "Fallen sexual desire, that is, 'lust,' *is* a desire to turn away from God's embrace and be joined to the body of those who are turned away, toward incorporation into the world, the network of relations and identities configured by pride."[63] Only as we are pure of heart will we see God as participants in Jesus' kingdom reality (Matthew 5:7). Only as we are pure of heart and see God will we approach sexual expression in a healthy and holistic manner.

We are made for more than sexual encounters and pleasures. The aim of life is not for each of us to find sexual self-fulfillment. Nor is the aim

---

[60]Saint Augustine, *Confessions*, I.1.1, 3.

[61]Coakley, *God, Sexuality, and the Self,* 290.

[62]Augustine, *City of God,* XIV.24, *Nicene and Post-Nicene Fathers,* 1st series, vol. 2, ed. Philip Schaff (Buffalo, NY: Christian Literature Publishing Co., 1887), 281. Rev. and ed. for New Advent by Kevin Knight.

[63]John C. Cavadini, "The Sacramentality of Marriage in the Fathers," *Pro Ecclesia* 17, no. 4 (Fall 2008): 457-58. I am grateful to my colleague Sara Mannen for pointing out this aspect of Augustine's view of sex and sin set forth in this paragraph.

of sex ultimately to expand one's family line, or to expand a populace and advance the legacy of nation-states and empires.[64] Rather, sexually monogamous intimacy images Christ and union with his bride or kingdom community, which is history's aim, as the destruction of Babylon the whore (Rome) and the marriage supper of the Lamb reveals (see Revelation 18-19). Our eschatological ethic's great hope, as Jonathan Edwards put the matter, is that God will provide a bride for God's Son: "There was, [as] it were, an eternal society or family in the Godhead, in the Trinity of persons. It seems to be God's design to admit the church into the divine family as his son's wife. . . . Heaven and earth were created that the Son of God might be complete in a spouse."[65]

The biblical typology according to Edwards's historiography features the triune God's eternal love and interpersonal communion. This interpersonal God secures our identity permanently as human persons in the holy bond of desired "commingling that we seek" (Coakley) through our union with God's Son in the Spirit. Thus, we need not—indeed, we must not in our embodied ethic—subject our persons to the sexual compulsion that leads to addictive behavior in a society that would try to strip us of our eternal value as relational beings in holy communion and reduce us to nothing more than sexual instruments, techniques, and playthings. Our identity and relational security are not up for grabs before God. The triune God takes us in all our vulnerability as men and women, married and single, widows, widowers, and divorcées, and gives us a home and an eternal inheritance as a kingdom community with his Son. We are no longer alone. We belong to Jesus, the heavenly bridegroom.

---

[64]Here it is worth pointing to Peter Brown, *The Body and Society: Men, Women, and Sexual Renunciation in Early Christianity*, 2nd ed., Columbia Classics in Religion (New York: Columbia University Press, 2008). Brown makes the argument that often Christian sexual renunciation in early Christianity is greatly misunderstood. Far from demonizing sex, or the body (though this did occur), what was often occurring was a very specific cultural rebellion against Rome, which prodded its citizens to believe in the power of childbirth to further the legacy of empire in a time when "death fell savagely on the young" (6). Renouncing sexual activity was actually tenacious defiance of the might of earthly empires in favor of the God who breathes life into dust.

[65]Jonathan Edwards, *Miscellanies* (entry nos. a-z, aa-zz, 1-500), *The Works of Jonathan Edwards*, vol. 13, ed. Thomas A. Schafer (New Haven, CT: Yale University Press, 1994), 741.

6

MORE THAN THE BATTLE
OF THE SEXES

Gender, Patriarchy, and the Imperative for Equality

IN ONE WAY OR ANOTHER, the battle of the sexes flattens our humanity. Men all too often flatten women by negating their existence, quite literally in some cases,[1] as well as limiting opportunities for them to rise up the social ladder in society.[2] From the reverse angle, many men fear that contemporary culture flattens or emasculates them.[3] The way forward is not to disparage or flatten women or men, to discount their gendered humanity, or to provoke more battles between them, but to battle *for* the sexes.[4] This chapter will begin with a brief treatment of how

---

[1] "The War on Baby Girls Winds Down: How One of the World's Great Social Problems Is Solving Itself," *Economist*, January 21, 2017, www.economist.com/international/2017/01/21/the-war-on-baby-girls-winds-down. See also Elizabeth Gerhardt, *Gendercide: A Theological Response to Global Violence Against Women and Girls* (Downers Grove, IL: IVP Academic, 2014).

[2] Kim Elsesser, "Here's Why Glass Ceiling May Remain Intact Despite Female Leadership," *Forbes*, www.forbes.com/sites/kimelsesser/2020/12/14/heres-why-glass-ceiling-may-remain-intact-despite-female-leadership/?sh=3c56f69e5175.

[3] Former political adviser to President Donald Trump Steve Bannon expressed fear in early 2018 that the women's movement would emasculate men, according to David Remnick, "A Reckoning with Women Awaits Trump," *New Yorker*, February 11, 2018, www.newyorker.com/news/daily-comment/a-reckoning-with-women-awaits-trump.

[4] "Battle of the sexes" connotes the conflict between men and women. It is a battle involving gender identity and constructs. The "battle for the sexes" conveys an emphasis on collaboration involving people of different genders rather than degrading forms of competition. This chapter focuses on gender relations, not sex or sexual expression. For various treatments of gender, sex, sexuality, and related studies, refer to the following: C. E. Roselli, "Neurobiology of Gender Identity and Sexual Orientation," *Journal of Neuroendocrinology*, December 2017, www.ncbi.nlm.nih.gov/pmc/articles/PMC6677266/; Jennifer Tseng, "Sex, Gender, and Why the Differences Matter," *AMA Journal of Ethics*, July 2008, https://journalofethics.ama-assn.org/article/sex-gender-and-why-differences-matter/2008-07; Tim Newman, "Sex and Gender: What Is the Difference?" *Medical News Today*, May 11, 2021, www.medicalnewstoday.com/articles/232363#summary; Nan Zhu and Lei Chang,

important it is not to flatten or discount gender in an account of human persons. A full treatment of gender would need to include analysis of transgender, nonbinary, or gender neutral. Given insufficient space, this chapter will center discussion on relationships between men and women. After making clear the move to guard against discounting gender, consideration will then turn to how humanity has struggled from ancient times to the present in advancing biologically and socially. All too often, men have flattened or subjugated women. Patriarchy, as defined here, is a system of governance and organization that favors men and excludes women from positions of power and influence. Following this analysis, the discussion will shift to religion's critical role in nurturing or negating patriarchy through the ages. Rather than present a flat or unvarying, simplistic account of religion's relation to patriarchy, I will provide examples of how religion has both reinforced patriarchy and revolted against it. The chapter will conclude with an acknowledgment of how the battle for the sexes will not wind down anytime soon. We must continue to refine our motivations rather than fall prey to leveling our humanity. Such flattening could occur by giving in to our base instincts and negating the gendered other or by removing the problem associated with patriarchal wiring by genetic modification. I will address these reductionistic moves in this chapter.

EMBODIMENT, GENDER, AND HUMAN PERSONHOOD

Embodiment and gender are two key characteristic traits of human persons, as noted in chapter two. As those created in God's image, we are not simply individualistic, rationalistic entities, as was true of Enlightenment thinking generally. René Descartes summed up well this individualistic, rationalistic mindset with his maxim, "I think, therefore, I am."[5] In contrast, humans exist as embodied, gendered, rational souls or selves who are constituted in relation to God and one another.

"Evolved but Not Fixed: A Life History Account of Gender Roles and Gender Inequality," *Frontiers in Psychology* 10 (2019), www.ncbi.nlm.nih.gov/pmc/articles/PMC6664064/#!po=3.57143; and Catherine Driscoll, "Sociobiology," *Stanford Encyclopedia of Philosophy* (Spring 2018 Edition), ed. Edward N. Zalta, https://plato.stanford.edu/archives/spr2018/entries/sociobiology/.

[5]René Descartes, *Discourse on Method*, trans. Donald A. Cress, 3rd ed. (Indianapolis: Hackett, 1998), 18.

The Genesis 1 account of the image says nothing explicitly about reason as a property or feature of humanity, though it is implied as God speaks to them and gives them instructions (see Genesis 1:28-30). Nor does it focus on the individual man or woman. Together the man and woman image God. They are to work together, fill the earth, and exercise dominion throughout the creaturely order (Genesis 1:27-28). Human persons image God in their embodied and gendered particularity and relationality.

Christian Smith highlights the importance of embodiment and gender in discerning the traits of human personhood: "Persons embody particularity of many sorts, but including always the particularities of sex and gender. In this embodied definition of persons, we move helpfully away from the Enlightenment's notion of the person as emphasizing almost exclusively their rational minds."[6]

Further to what has been said, we must always consider human persons in terms of their embodied and gendered existence. Moreover, we must account for them not simply as individuals but also in relational terms. Rather than pit their gendered particularity against one another, a biblically framed account of human persons views people as gendered, embodied souls who are constituted in relation to one another as man and woman in "freedom and love."[7]

Unfortunately, freedom and love do not always or often come into play in consideration of the sexes. Biological and social forces often get in the way of battling *for* the sexes. To this subject, I now turn.

HYPERTROPHY AND PATRIARCHY

In his book *On Human Nature*, E. O. Wilson argues that hypertrophy is the "key to the emergence of civilization."[8] What is hypertrophy? It is "the extreme growth of pre-existing structures."[9] Wilson focuses consideration on hunter-gatherer cultures and how they "have metamorphosed from relatively modest environmental adaptions into unexpectedly

---

[6]Christian Smith, *What Is A Person?* (Chicago: University of Chicago Press, 2010), 72.
[7]Colin E. Gunton, *The Triune Creator: A Historical and Systematic Study*, New Studies in Constructive Theology (Grand Rapids, MI: Eerdmans, 1998), 210.
[8]E. O. Wilson, *On Human Nature*, 2nd ed. (Cambridge, MA: Harvard University Press, 2004), 89.
[9]Wilson, *On Human Nature*, 89.

elaborate, even monstrous forms in more advanced societies."[10] A few such monstrous forms of such hypertrophic modification are patriarchy, nationalism, and racism.[11] Let's consider patriarchy and its flattening of women.

Wilson draws attention to the "!Kung San" people of the Kalahari Desert in his analysis of hypertrophy and women's subordination. Although the adult members of the !Kung San "do not impose sex roles on their children," nonetheless differences appear and grow.[12] Wilson goes on to say,

> When societies grow still larger and more complex, women tend to be reduced in influence outside the home, and to be more constrained by custom, ritual, and formal law. As hypertrophy proceeds further, they can be turned literally into chattel, to be sold and traded, fought over, and ruled under a double morality. History has seen a few striking local reversals, but the great majority of societies have evolved toward sexual domination as though sliding along a rachet.[13]

Wilson reasons, "Most and perhaps all of the other prevailing characteristics of modern societies can be identified as hypertrophic modifications of the biologically meaningful institutions of hunter-gatherer bands and early tribal states." To justify hypertrophic moves, "civilizations have raised self-love to the rank of high culture, exalted themselves by divine sanction and diminished others with elaborately falsified written histories."[14]

So, what will reverse the trend and remove the curses of patriarchy, racism, and nationalism, as well as other negative instances of hypertrophic modification? Wilson's hope for greater equality among peoples and nations involves "pure knowledge." He claims it is "the ultimate emancipator."[15] And yet, even pure knowledge alone is not sufficient. It cannot overcome our biological trajectory from our ancient origins to the present time. While awareness of our biological wiring and

---

[10]Wilson, *On Human Nature*, 89.
[11]Wilson, *On Human Nature*, 91-92.
[12]Wilson, *On Human Nature*, 89, 91.
[13]Wilson, *On Human Nature*, 91-92.
[14]Wilson, *On Human Nature*, 92.
[15]Wilson, *On Human Nature*, 96.

emergence, including negative trajectories, is beneficial in mapping out a better course that leads to greater human flourishing, it is not sufficient. In Wilson's estimation, "we will not, however, eliminate the hard biological substructure until such time, many years from now, when our descendants may learn to change the genes themselves."[16]

Is the solution to patriarchy ultimately greater knowledge and genetic manipulation? According to the biblical account of humanity's fall into sin recorded in Genesis 3, fixation on the pursuit of knowledge led to patriarchy. Similarly, the solution does not appear to be biological first and foremost, but the personal intervention of the promised one who will deliver men and women from bondage to domination and subjugation. Contrary to that historiography that places blame for the subjugation of women at the feet of religion and specifically the biblical narrative, at various points Christian Scripture confronts patriarchal societies for presuming divine sanction for their hypertrophic moves. I will return to this discussion in due course.

Still, religion can and often does reinforce "the hard biological substructure." Moreover, as Wilson claims, it is incredibly difficult to trace the "gross transmutations" in spheres like religion "back to rudiments in the hunter-gatherers' repertory."[17] It is not that religious influences are absent. To the contrary, religion is enormously complex and exudes tremendous staying power: "The predisposition to religious belief is the most complex and powerful force in the human mind and in all probability an ineradicable part of human nature."[18]

Wilson presents a complex and conflicted view of religion. In one place, he indicates that he would never seek to eradicate religion in general or Christianity in particular, except for its creation and resurrection stories.[19] However, he also hopes that in the end scientific

---

[16]Wilson, *On Human Nature*, 96-97. Wilson asks elsewhere in the same volume, "Can the cultural evolution of higher ethical values gain a direction and momentum of its own and completely replace genetic evolution? I think not. The genes hold culture on a leash. The leash is very long, but inevitably values will be constrained in accordance with their effects on the human gene pool" (167).

[17]See Wilson, *On Human Nature*, 95-96.

[18]Wilson, *On Human Nature*, 169.

[19]See Wilson's *Spiegel* interview: Philip Bethge and Johann Grolle, "Interview with Edward O. Wilson: The Origin of Morals," *Spiegel Online*, February 26, 2013, www.spiegel.de/international /spiegel/spiegel-interview-with-edward-wilson-on-the-formation-of-morals-a-884767-2.html.

naturalism will gain the final upper hand by trying "to explain traditional religion, its chief competitor, as a wholly material phenomenon" and "divert the power of religion" to its own ends.[20]

In response, would it not be more beneficial to discern how religion can play a strategic part in contesting the hypertrophic drive to patriarchy than view it in flat, reductionistic, replaceable terms?[21] Religion has a biological basis.[22] It emerges from that basis and at times performs an invaluable reformist role in combating subjugating forces given religion's apparent indestructibility.[23]

Religion certainly has a checkered past and present. It serves as a conserver of patriarchy but also as a liberating force for human flourishing involving women as true equals to men. We neglect its potential for good and for ill to our peril. The following treatment of various classical religious and ethical traditions provide a multifaceted rather than flat account of religion's interface with patriarchy with an eye to the future for the sake of ongoing reform.

FROM REINFORCEMENT TO REFORM: RELIGION AND PATRIARCHY

In our entangled exploration, consideration will be given to several religious and ethical systems: Confucianism, Hinduism, Buddhism, Judaism, Islam, and Christianity. Now some might ask, If these ancient-contemporary systems present evidence of gender domination, why look to these classical frameworks for aid? To respond, one reason why classical frameworks are classic is because they have proven resilient in their universal explanatory power for life in the face of challenging and changing circumstances over the centuries. So, it makes

---

[20]Wilson, *On Human Nature*, 193.

[21]Wilson, *On Human Nature*, 192-93.

[22]For samples of a growing and relevant field of research, see the following articles on the cognitive science of religion: Justin L. Barrett, "Cognitive Science of Religion: What Is It and Why Is It?," *Philosophy Compass* 1, no. 6 (November 2007): 768-86. The abstract reads: "CSR is often associated with evolutionary science and anti-religious rhetoric but neither is intrinsic nor necessary to the field." See also Robert N. McCauley and Emma Cohen, "Cognitive Science and the Naturalness of Religion," *Philosophy Compass* 5, no. 9 (September 2010): 779-92.

[23]Wilson acknowledges reformist religious movements' past contributions—namely, Buddhism's and Jainism's confrontation of caste systems and their call for the humane treatment of animals. See *On Human Nature*, 95.

sense to take a closer look at these traditions for how they hinder and foster gender equity.

Confucianism and patriarchy. According to one report referenced at the outset of this chapter, gendercide is waning worldwide, including China. However, other reports suggest that China is becoming more patriarchal in recent years. Confucianism is returning to prominence and gaining import not simply nationally but also internationally.[24] Confucianism's reemergence is proving alarming to many when it comes to matters of gender discrimination.[25]

Concerned parties often criticize Confucianism as inherently sexist and patriarchal.[26] Take for example the following statement by Confucius recorded in the *Analects*: "The Master said, 'In one's household, it is the women and the small men that are difficult to deal with. If you let them get too close, they become insolent. If you keep them at a distance, they complain.'"[27] Someone trying to defend Confucianism from the charge of sexism might argue that women alone are not singled out. After all, Confucius criticizes "small men." Even so, at least at face value, a class of men, not all men, are singled out, whereas all women appear to be targeted. Could it be simply low-ranking women and low-ranking men Master Confucius has in mind? It could be the case that the statement reveals how many of them failed to observe appropriate social dealings with their superiors. Confucius appears to want to aid them but is frustrated with their sense of entitlement and presumption at every

---

[24]Evan Osnos, "Confucius Comes Home: Move Over, Mao," *New Yorker*, January 5, 2014, www .newyorker.com/magazine/2014/01/13/confucius-comes-home.

[25]Eileen Otis, "Inequality in China and the Impact on Women's Rights," *Conversation*, March 19, 2015, https://theconversation.com/inequality-in-china-and-the-impact-on-womens-rights-38744.

[26]There are a few passages in the *Analects* of Confucius that are reserved for special critique. See 6:28; 8:20; 9:18; 16:7; 16:14; and 17:25. For a critical assessment, see Robin R. Wang, "Analects of Confucius," in *Images of Women in Chinese Thought and Culture: Writings from the Pre-Qin Period Through the Song Dynasty* (Indianapolis: Hackett, 2003), 62-66. For more favorable assessments of Confucius and Confucianism, see Anne Behnke Kinney, "Women in the *Analects*," in *A Concise Companion to Confucius*, ed. Paul R. Godin, Blackwell Companions to Philosophy (Oxford: John Wiley & Sons, 2017), 148-63, especially 161-62. Li-Hsiang Lisa Rosenlee has argued that Confucianism is not inherently biased against women in *Confucianism and Women: A Philosophical Interpretation*, SUNY Series in Chinese Philosophy and Culture (Albany: State University of New York Press, 2006).

[27]Confucius, *The Analects*, trans. D. C. Lau, Penguin Classics (London: Penguin Books, 1979), 17:25, 148.

turn. According to Anne Behnke Kinney, the Confucius of the *Analects* did not show bias based on students' social class, parentage, or age. She further argues,

> Low-ranking women did not have access to education or enjoy the same freedom of movement as their male counterparts (as limited as these opportunities may have been for low-ranking men). Moreover, the ethic of *Analects* 17.25 and the paternalistic ethos of many passages in the *Analects* suggest that both men and women of the lower orders should be content with their positions in the hierarchy and yield to the superior judgment of their social and moral betters (*Analects* 1.4 . . .). But *Analects* 17.25 nevertheless reveals a sense of reciprocity, specifically, Confucius' (or whoever the intended agent is) awareness of an obligation to his inferiors, as slight, ill-defined, and botched as their effort might be, and not just a desire for their unquestioning subservience. He wants to draw near but his efforts are met with presumptuous demands. What may divide these lowly people from the disadvantaged students that Confucius welcomed is, perhaps, their resistance to or rejection of the Master's instruction and ideals in favor of more worldly goals. . . . It is the grasping and manipulative behavior on the part of both men and women, the refusal to observe the limitations of one's hierarchical position in society, and not gender alone that prompted Confucius' comments in *Analects* 17.25.[28]

Kinney's reflection draws attention to how many women did not have opportunities for formal education during Confucius's era, unlike their "male counterparts." The same was true for many women in the Roman Empire at the time of Saint Paul. That is the likely reason why Paul urges women to ask their husbands at home about questions they had at church for the sake of orderly worship (1 Corinthians 14:35). The point here is not intended to excuse patriarchy, but to situate patriarchy in its surrounding context. Moreover, one finds an emphasis in Confucius on character rather than parentage, class, age, or prior legal standing. From this vantage point, Confucius's teaching was prophetic in its egalitarian import.

Many present-day readers will struggle with Confucius's paternalistic sentiment and expectation that people be content in their social rank.

---

[28]Kinney, "Women in the *Analects*," 151-52.

While Confucius was willing to educate people no matter their background and rank so long as they approached the Master with virtuous intent, his instruction was not intended to challenge social hierarchies. One finds in Confucius's vision for society a lack of sufficient *latitude* and liberty that moves civilization beyond paternalism and authoritarianism. As with many dominant ethical systems through the ages, Confucianism's liberating emphases compete with perhaps equally strong conserving dynamics.

The *Analects* also draws attention to a controversial episode involving Confucius and the morally suspect Nan Zi, wife of the marquis of Wey.[29] Kinney writes, "Confucius felt that honoring the rituals of Wey, or taking the opportunity to engage with and morally influence Nan Zi (and by extension, the marquis of Wey), was more important than maintaining strict rules concerning sexual segregation or avoiding contact with unsavory characters."[30]

As with Jesus centuries later, Confucius appears to prize engagement of controversial persons for the sake of honoring cherished, sacred tradition. Instruction of such persons in virtue challenges preoccupation with legalistic, depersonalizing forms of ceremonial purity. It calls to mind Jesus praising a woman of ill-repute, who kisses and washes his feet with expensive perfume and dries his feet with her hair at Simon the Pharisee's home. Aware of Simon's pharisaical consternation and scorn, Jesus commends the woman for her dignifying honor and rebukes Simon for disregarding the cherished tradition of hospitality for his guest. Simon had not given Jesus a customary kiss, poured olive oil on his head, or provided water for his feet (Luke 7:36-49).

It is not just China and Confucianism that have been criticized over the years for promoting patriarchy and men's domination of women. India has also received criticism. Fortunately, advocacy efforts for women and girls in India are challenging patriarchy.[31] Similarly, grassroots initiatives such as the Women's March and #MeToo are speaking truth to power across the globe and may be gaining the upper hand. Referencing the 2017 Golden Globes where Oprah Winfrey and other women gained

---

[29]Refer to Confucius, the *Analects*, 6:28; 85n9.
[30]Kinney, "Women in the Analects," 161.
[31]"War on Baby Girls Winds Down."

widespread acclaim for their defiance of abuse of women, Steve Bannon exclaimed, "It's a Cromwell moment! . . . It's even more powerful than populism. It's deeper. It's primal. It's elemental. The long black dresses and all that—this is the Puritans. It's anti-patriarchy."[32]

Hinduism and patriarchy. To turn to India, let's consider briefly sacred texts that have a bearing on developments and trends in one direction or another. It has been argued that other sacred literature in the vast and manifold Hindu tradition is exclusionary and elitist.[33] That view is not universal. For example, the Hindu American Foundation points out that texts such as the Upaniṣads "see no difference in gender" since they claim that "the eternal soul wears no gender." Further, "absolute divinity" itself "gives light to an array of manifestations that include feminine deities," such as Parvarti, Saraswati, and Lakshmi. The article states that "in pure essence, absolute divinity in Hinduism takes no form or gender because it simply is a celestial amalgamation of both."[34]

Similarly, one finds in the *Brihad Aranyaka Upaniṣads* the following claim: "The world was just a single body (*ātman*) shaped like a man" that split itself into two—forming a husband and a wife. The resulting man had sexual relations with the woman. As a result of "their union human beings were born." So, too, were the rest of creaturely pairs, albeit through the first couple's ongoing metamorphosis into various life forms and succeeding cycle of copulation.[35]

---

[32]Remnick, "A Reckoning with Women Awaits Trump."

[33]Consider the following: "Although women participate actively in the metaphysical discussions of the *Brihad Aranyaka Upaniṣads*, and although there is no textual evidence to suggest they were in any way excluded from the higher goals expressed in that text, women are excluded from Shankara's order of renouncers and are never allowed to serve as temple priests in Ramanuja's tradition of Shri Vaishnavism. Although Ramanuja opened his tradition to women and the lower classes, Vendanta philosophy in general, and Shankara's school in particular, tend to be very elitist. It requires a knowledgeable religious practitioner who is well educated in scripture, at least in its expectations for the highest realization. In classical Indian society, this deters all but those who occupy the upper classes. Those denied such preparation by birth are likewise often denied the opportunity for the highest achievement—at least in this lifetime." David L. Haberman, "Upanishadic Hinduism: Quest for Ultimate Knowledge," in *Twelve Theories of Human Nature*, ed. Leslie Stevenson, David L. Haberman and Peter Matthews Wright, 6th ed. (Oxford: Oxford University Press, 2013), 53.

[34]Pooja Deopura, "On Faith: Gender Discrimination a Cultural Bias, Not Religious Truth," Hindu American Foundation, April 14, 2010.

[35]See the *Upaniṣads*, trans. Patrick Olivelle, Oxford World's Classics (Oxford: Oxford University Press, 1996), 1.4.3, pages 13-14. 1.4.8 on page 15 of the same text refers to the *ātman* as the "innermost thing," the "self."

Here it is worth pointing out a similarity with Islam. The Qur'an teaches that God created all humanity from "a single soul": "People, be mindful of your Lord, who created you from a single soul, and from it created its mate, and from the pair of them spread countless men and women far and wide." The likely meaning and import of the statement is that we are all connected and so we should be very careful how we treat one another.[36] While the Bible speaks of the fundamental unity and equality of man and woman, the view is expressed differently than in these texts. Humanity does not come forth from a single soul or self. The Bible takes for granted that all people are distinct souls created by God and individually embodied.

It is also worth pointing out that one finds women engaging in conversations on ultimate reality in the *Brihadaranyaka Upaniṣads*. For example, at one point, we find a man discussing theology with his wife, specifically the importance and nature of the self (*ātman*). We are told that she often shared her own thoughts in these conversations.[37] A discussion between a man and his wife on this theological or metaphysical topic would be deemed most noteworthy in ancient times.

In theory, one could make a theoretical case for women being greatly honored traditionally in Hindu India, but such esteem often had a difficult time making it into social reality. As one analysis puts the matter, "Historically, the status of women in India was ambiguous. In theory, she had many privileges and enjoyed an exalted status as an aspect of goddess. But in practice, most women led miserable lives as servants to their husbands."[38]

Perhaps the most famous and controversial example of this ambiguous state of affairs is found in *suttee* or *satī* (translated as "chaste wife, virtuous woman"), which is taken to refer to the practice often translated as "widow burning." Debated features include whether the practice is sanctioned by the Hindu Scriptures and traditions and why the now forbidden (but still occasionally occurring) custom was

---

[36]See the beginning of the section titled "Women" in the *Qur'an*, trans. M.A.S. Abdel Haleem, Oxford World's Classics (Oxford: Oxford University Press, 2010), 50.

[37]See *Upaniṣads*, 4.5, 69-71.

[38]Jayaram V, "Traditional Status of Women in Hinduism," Hinduwebsite.com, accessed July 31, 2019, www.hinduwebsite.com/hinduism/h_women.asp.

promulgated. Given the constraints of space, we will consider these matters very briefly.

Inspiration for the rite is sometimes traced to the goddess Sati, who contested her father's dishonoring of her husband, the god Shiva, by burning herself to death.[39] It should be noted that the story in question is not an incident of *sati*, since the husband (Shiva) is alive and avenges his wife by destroying her father. A text that is often used as an official prohibition of widow burning is found in the *Rig Veda* 10.18.8. Here the preceding verse (10.18.7) is included. The verses appear to suggest that the widow of the deceased is first to go to her dead husband as his lifeless body rests on the funeral pyre. Presumably, she is to wish him goodbye and then leave the pyre and remain in the land of the living rather than be burned alongside the corpse:

> [7]Let these unwidowed dames with noble husbands adorn themselves with fragrant balm and unguent.
>
> Decked with fair jewels, tearless, free from sorrow, first let the dames go up to where he lieth.
>
> [8]Rise, come unto the world of life, O woman: come, he is lifeless by whose side thou liest.
>
> Wifehood with this thy husband was thy portion, who took thy hand and wooed thee as a lover.[40]

By no means uniformly and unconditionally affirmed as a practice, nonetheless, it does appear that sanction grew in certain circles in premodern times. Seeking to account for what he considers to be the oft-neglected theological and ethical engagement of the practice, David Brick argues that "the broader Brahmanical community gradually shifted its outlook toward *sati* over time from widespread rejection to unqualified acceptance."[41]

---

[39]Wendy Doniger, "Suttee," in *Encyclopedia Britannica Online*, last accessed on July 31, 2019, www .britannica.com/topic/suttee.

[40]Vedas, *Rig-Veda*, trans. Ralph T.H. Griffith, X. 8, accessed on July 31, 2019, www.sacred-texts.com /hin/rigveda/rv10018.htm.

[41]David Brick, "The Dharmaśāstric Debate on Widow-Burning," *Journal of the American Oriental Society* 30, no. 2 (April–June 2010): 203-23.

In *Sati—Widow Burning in India*, Sakuntal Narasimhan argues that the Hindu Scriptures' endorsement of *satī* is ambiguous. Still, Narasimhan also maintains that the practice was and is part and parcel of the long-standing denigration of women. Narasimhan seeks to show how a culture that affirms compassion as well as nonviolence can still make room for such a controversial rite due to religious and economic dynamics, lack of education, and sexism.[42]

A key element relates to lineage, particularly the economic factor of widows' right to inheritance. One of the reasons cited for women performing *satī* was the pressure they received from the family of the deceased to terminate their own lives so the family could receive the dead man's inheritance. As Wendy Doniger claims, "The larger incidence of suttee among the Brahmans of Bengal was indirectly due to the *Dayabhaga* system of law (*c.* 1100), which prevailed in Bengal and which gave inheritance to widows; such women were encouraged to commit suttee in order to make their inheritance available to other relatives."[43] Even if a woman had the right to her husband's inheritance, it did not safeguard against abuse. Still, the fact that Hindu women in India sometimes had rights to a share in their deceased husbands' property is noteworthy when set in the context of patriarchy.

Islam and patriarchy. Let's transition at this point to consider the subject of inheritance in a Muslim context. As Karen Armstrong argues, Muhammad also sought to safeguard women's right to shares in their family's inheritance. This was a radical advance most everywhere in Muhammad's cultural context. In fact, Armstrong indicates that it was not until the nineteenth century that most women in the West obtained inheritance rights.[44] In Armstrong's estimation, polygamy, at least in the social context in which Islam emerged, was an

---

[42]Sakuntal Narasimhan, *Sati—Widow Burning in India* (New York: Penguin Books India, 1990). It has also been claimed (without seeking to affirm the practice) that those who honor the memory of these women who sacrificed themselves on their husbands' funeral pyres are not promoting or endorsing violence against women, but veneration of saints. Refer here to Paul Louis Metzger, "Widow Burning: An Interview with Dr. Mrinalini Sebastian and Dr. J. Jaykiran Sebastian," *Cultural Encounters* 9, no. 2 (2013): 86.

[43]Doniger, "Suttee."

[44]Karen Armstrong, *Islam: A Short History* (New York: Modern Library, 2002), 16. See also Armstrong, *Muhammad: A Prophet for Our Time* (New York: HarperOne, 2006), 134-35.

advance from the pre-Islamic period, and helped to safeguard a woman's inheritance:

> All too often, unscrupulous people seized everything and left the weaker members of the family with nothing. They were often sexually abused by their male guardians or converted into a financial asset by being sold into slavery. . . . The Qur'an bluntly refutes this behavior and takes it for granted that a woman has an inalienable right to her inheritance. Polygamy was designed to ensure that unprotected women would be decently married, and to abolish the old loose, irresponsible liaisons; men could have *only* four wives and must treat them equitably; it was an unjustifiably wicked act to devour their property.[45]

It is also worth noting that, according to Armstrong, Muhammad empowered women to be actively engaged in various matters, including political affairs, even though this egalitarian spirit of collaboration put Muhammad at even greater odds with his adversaries, who sought to dishonor him as a result.[46] "The Prophet did not regard his women as chattel. They were his 'companions'—just like the men."[47]

It is important to pause and nuance the discussion. Elizabeth L. Young and Fatma Müge Göçek ponder how much significance should be awarded to Muslim women's rights and restrictions generally based on Muhammad's wives' lives. To put the matter as a question, How much do the Qur'anic and hadith materials pertain specifically to Muhammad's wives, and how much do they bear on Muslim women generally? For example, the Prophet's wives were awarded special status (see the Qur'an, 33:32). Moreover, certain

---

[45]Armstrong, *Muhammad*, 135. Refer also to "Women," the *Qur'an*, 50-66. No doubt, modern readers will not find sufficient what is written here, including such matters as "a son should have the equivalent share of two daughters" (*Qur'an*, 51). However, if Armstrong is right, this is still an advance given that daughters/women could inherit property in Islam over against much of the surrounding world at the time of the Prophet. To qualify matters, it is worth noting that according to *The Oxford Encyclopedia of Islam and Women*, "In reality, polygamy was prohibited since the Qur'ân only permitted it contingent on a husband's equal treatment of all his wives (4:3, 3:4), a situation that Abduh and Ali argued was impossible." Elizabeth L. Young and Fatma Müge Göçek, "Gender Equality," in *The Oxford Encyclopedia of Islam and Women*, ed. Natana J. Delong-Bas, vol. 1 (Oxford: Oxford University Press, 2013), 362. For a view that accounts for women's engagement of the Qur'an, see Amina Wadud, *Qur'an and Woman: Rereading the Sacred Text from a Woman's Perspective* (Oxford: Oxford University Press, 1999).

[46]Armstrong, *Muhammad*, 136-37.

[47]Armstrong, *Muhammad*, 136. See also Young and Göçek, "Gender Equality," 361 for a discussion of Muhammad's wives and how many of them were actively involved in Muslim affairs.

restrictions were placed on them, such as not being able to remarry after Muhammad's death (33:52). Did this apply universally to other Muslim women? The same goes for veiling. Were all Muslim women required to be veiled, or only the Prophet's wives?[48] Regardless of the answers to these questions, still it is clear that when placed in historical context, Islam advanced the status of women in comparison with pre-Islamic society, where "women were treated as nothing but chattel. Married women were treated as heritable property, to be inherited by the heirs of a husband."[49]

Consideration of the various classical traditions under review must guard against anachronism. From the vantage point of modernity, we may find all these traditions suspect in terms of challenging patriarchy. An ethical approach concerning engagement of the past involves asking whether a tradition, or movement within a given tradition, serves as an advance in its historical setting, capitulation to the status quo, or a regression. The same question appears when dealing with Buddhism in its historical context. Buddhism is very complex with seemingly countless trajectories. I will account briefly for just two texts representing different vantage points, the Pali canon and *Lotus Sutra* respectively.

Buddhism and patriarchy. The sister of the Buddha's mother approached the Buddha three times to leave behind household life and begin a monastic life and become a Buddhist priestess. Three times the Buddha told her no. Similarly, three times the Buddha told a close disciple named Ānanda no when Ānanda entreated the Buddha on her behalf. Finally, the Buddha's disciple asked,

> Are women competent, Reverend Sir, if they retire from household life to the houseless one, under the Doctrine and Discipline announced by The

[48]Young and Göçek, "Gender Equality," 361. See also 360 for treatment of Adam and Eve, their respective responsibilities, and the roles and rights of their posterity, including possible contrasting positions on women's equality in the Qur'an and hadith material. For the claim that Qur'an and hadith literature present contrasting positions, see Fatima Mernissi, *The Veil and the Male Elite: A Feminist Interpretation of Women's Rights in Islam*, trans. Mary Jo Lakeland (Reading, MA: Addison-Wesley, 1991). For a treatment of modernist, conservative, and fundamentalist Muslim assessments of women in the Qur'an in keeping with their respective worldviews and sociopolitical agendas, see Barbara Freyer Stowasser, *Women in the Qur'an, Traditions, and Interpretation* (Oxford: Oxford University Press, 1994). In apparent tension with Mernissi's work, Mohammad Ali Syed maintains continuity between the Qur'an and the hadith. See *The Position of Women in Islam* (Albany: State University of New York Press, 2004).
[49]Syed, *Position of Women in Islam*, 1.

Tathâgata, to attain to the fruit of conversion, to attain to the fruit of once returning, to attain to the fruit of never returning, to attain to saintship?

The Buddha responds,

Women are competent, Ânanda, if they retire from household life to the houseless one, under the Doctrine and Discipline announced by The Tathâgata, to attain to the fruit of conversion, to attain to the fruit of once returning, to attain to the fruit of never returning, to attain to saintship.[50]

Given her key role in helping to raise the Buddha as a child, it is hard to imagine the Buddha's strong, initial, and consistent dismissal of these requests. It is perhaps equally difficult to comprehend that the Buddha then allowed her entrance to the monastic way of life after his initial rejection, albeit with qualifications that still placed her and other priestesses under men. It is possibly even more shocking that the Buddha added a closing remark that "the Good Doctrine" or Buddhist dharma would "abide" only five hundred years instead of one thousand because of what he takes to be women's lesser qualities. He claims that a religion with a few men is like a house with only a few men. The household is "easily overcome by burglars."[51]

It is important to keep note of the fact that such a negative example does not undermine Buddhism, since it is not ultimately about segregation and denunciation by way of gender. For the evident patriarchy in many Buddhist texts, the *Lotus Sutra* offers a more positive view. Women partake of Buddha nature just like men, as well as the potential to attain enlightenment. "A Teacher of the Law," chapter ten of the *Lotus Sutra*, expresses this outlook. There we are informed by the Buddha that both "good sons and good daughters" who adhere to the way of the Buddha "will become buddhas in future worlds."[52] We find a similar statement in "Devadatta," chapter twelve of the *Lotus Sutra*.[53]

---

[50]Henry Clarke Warren, *Buddhism in Translations*, vol. 3, Harvard Oriental Series (Cambridge, MA: Harvard University Press, 1896), 443-44.

[51]Warren, *Buddhism in Translations*, 447.

[52]"A Teacher of the Law," in *The Threefold Lotus Sutra: The Sutra of Innumerable Meanings, the Sutra of the Lotus Flower of the Wonderful Law, and the Sutra of Meditation on the Bodhisattva Universal Virtue*, trans. Bunno Kato, Yoshiro Tamura, and Kojiro Miyasaka, rev. W. E. Soothill, Wilhelm Schiffer, and Pier P. Del Campana (New York: Weatherhill, 1975), 187.

[53]"Devadatta," in *The Threefold Lotus Sutra*, 210.

Perhaps most striking is the account in "Devadatta" of the dragon king's daughter, who attained enlightenment or Buddhahood at the age of eight.[54] The Buddhist teacher Nichiren (1222–1282), who was devoted to the *Lotus Sutra*, referenced this account in support of his position of the fundamental equality of women. Nichiren writes, "The fact that the dragon king's daughter attained Buddhahood does not mean that she alone did so. It means that all women can attain Buddhahood." Nichiren contrasts this story with other texts. "In other Mahayana sutras apart from the *Lotus Sutra*, it seems that women can attain Buddhahood or be reborn in the Pure Land. Yet they may only do so after they have been reborn as men." In the *Lotus Sutra*, women as women can attain Buddhahood. Thus, writes Nichiren, "when the dragon king's daughter attained Buddhahood, it opened the way for all women to attain Buddhahood eternally."[55]

If it weren't for the *Lotus Sutra*, Nichiren could not imagine life as a woman. He writes in *Shijō Kingo-dono nyōbō gohenji*, "When I, Nichiren, read sutras other than the *Lotus Sutra*, I have absolutely no desire to become a woman."[56] According to one interpreter, Nichiren wrote with a clear sense of his times, but we must not assume his context today would prescribe the same—no, he would remove the hierarchy, having already envisioned its removal. Ichiu Mori states, "Nichiren wrote of women in terms of the realities of feudal society, and his view of women accords with the prevalent view of the time. Yet he never clung to such notions as 'women must behave in a certain way simply because they are women.'" From within the feudal context, Mori says, "Nichiren clearly envisaged the elimination of the secular, hierarchical relationship between men and women."[57]

While I certainly appreciate Mori's engagement of Nichiren and the desire to affirm women's equality, still it appears that the story of the

---

[54]"Devadatta," 213.

[55]Nichiren, *Showa teihon Nichiren Shonin ibun* 昭和定本日蓮聖人遺文, vols. 1-2, ed. Rissho Daigaku Nichiren Kyogaku Kenkyujo (Minobu: Minobu-san Kuon-ji, 1988), 1:589-90; quoted in Ichiu Mori, "Nichiren's View of Women," *Japanese Journal of Religious Studies* 30, nos. 3-4 (2003): 282.

[56]Nichiren, STN 1:856; quoted in Mori, "Nichiren's View of Women," 283.

[57]Ichiu, "Nichiren's View of Women," 284-85.

dragon king's daughter favors a patriarchal view of the eternal state. To be precise, why does the dragon king's daughter become a man after having attained enlightenment? The text reads, "She was suddenly transformed into a male."[58] This text does not seem to support the following account of the story:

> Shakyamuni Buddha then proclaimed, "In the same manner, all living beings throughout the Ten Worlds can attain Buddhahood, *without having to change or alter themselves* nor repeat lifetime upon lifetime of lengthy Buddhist austerities. This is the benefit of the Lotus Sutra." Nichiren Daishonin stated in the "Opening of the Eyes" (Kaimoku Sho), "The significance of the enlightenment of the Dragon King's daughter is not that a single woman was able to attain Buddhahood. This parable signifies the enlightenment of all women which was an impossibility in the teachings before the Lotus Sutra. Until the teachings of the Lotus Sutra there had been discrimination against evil people, women and others. . . . However, within the correct teachings of the Buddha, it is preached that all living beings, no matter what form of the Ten Worlds their lives take, inherently possess the seed of Buddhahood and are able to attain enlightenment through correct faith."[59]

The quotation attributed to the Buddha (in italics) mentions there is no need "to change or alter themselves" to attain enlightenment. Perhaps the quotation and mention of the dragon king's daughter's transformation into a man can be harmonized in this way: The daughter of the dragon king had already attained enlightenment, and then was transformed into a man. So, becoming a man in a future state was not required to attain Buddhahood. Still, it is plausible to take from this account that manhood was still more highly esteemed given her metamorphosis into a man.

One should not be surprised to find such apparent tensions in ancient sacred writings given the times in which they were written. After all, they are not atemporal documents, but enculturated texts, yet which as classics have lives beyond their original settings. Any spiritual

---

[58]"Devadatta," 213.
[59]Nichiren Shoshu Temple, "The Dragon King's Daughter," *Nichiren Shoshu Temple* 1995, accessed on August 2, 2019. Emphasis added.

community must seek to be true to the heritage yet move forward in ways that are appropriate in the current cultural milieu. This is not simply true of Buddhism or other traditions already noted. It is also true of Judaism and Christianity. While there are fundamental differences between adherents of various sects of any given faith tradition, they are all seeking to locate the right balance between faithful commitment to an ancient text and the community's contemporary context. This is no easy task and can easily lead to extremes.

How does this matter bear on gender specifically? There are two extremes when accounting for gender. Mori accounts for the first: entrenchment of patriarchy. Male Buddhist scholars and priests in Nichiren's school seek to use Nichiren to entrench patriarchal notions of the past. Li-Hsiang Lisa Rosenlee accounts for the second: the importation and imposition of alien egalitarian or feminist constructs that fail to account for cultural particularity.

Rosenlee argues that while gender as a concept has been keenly engaged in feminist scholarship, the same cannot be said for consideration of cultural context. This failure poses difficulties in application to other cultures and traditions, as in the case of Confucianism, including its historical context in ancient China: "The lack of attention to the element of 'culture' in feminist writings constitutes an obstacle to a genuine understanding of the gender system in an alien culture, where gender is encoded in the context of a whole different set of background assumptions."[60] It is important not to foist constructs belonging to antiquated cultural contexts (such as premodern views of gender in Japan) on the present, or impose alien cultural contexts (such as postmodern views of gender from the West) on the past. There must be an ethic of cultural sensitivity in engaging ancient texts and contemporary contexts across the globe. As noted earlier, what should be an abiding question when approaching such subjects as gender in ancient ethical systems is, Did the ethical system in question simply reinforce prevailing models of patriarchy at the time, especially in ways that demeaned women in their historical settings, regress from what was

---

[60]Rosenlee, *Confucianism and Women*, 2.

already in place, or challenge and amend such patriarchal models in support of women's value and flourishing?

Let's consider Rosenlee's account of foot binding. Many Westerners are quick to assume that foot binding conveyed nothing more than "the imposition of male sexual desires projected onto the passive female body or the victimization of women by the patriarchal system." However, as Rosenlee notes, "it expressed, among other things, women's gender identity, the Han civility, and ethnic identity." Women were not simply passive entities, but active agents who found ways to express themselves as gendered beings in the limited space available to them. Just as we should fight against the victimization of women, we should also fight against the victimization of the East by the West, where Western scholars fail to account for the historical and cultural contexts in which gender is addressed in various ethical systems. As Lee writes, "For without such an understanding, women in third world countries remain frozen in time as mere passive victims of their 'sexist' traditions whose liberation can only be justified by Western ethical theories that supposedly rise above parochial, 'cultural' moralities."[61]

Flat readings of sacred texts and their communities of interpreters that make sweeping judgments rather than account for on-the-ground historical and cultural particulars are unethical, as are views of women that demean and dehumanize them. I have attempted to guard against broad, white-washing judgments in assessing Confucianism, Hinduism, Islam, and Buddhism. We will now attempt to analyze the Judeo-Christian tradition in the same spirit.

---

[61] Rosenlee, *Confucianism and Women*, 11. Rosenlee's cautionary rebuke of Western feminist critiques is important. It is always important to guard against sweeping generalizations in view of a foreign construct such as gender applied to a very different cultural context. However, the opposite mistake should also not be made—silencing critique simply to safeguard against promoting new forms of colonialism. As Ibtissam Bouachrine writes in *Women and Islam*, "Silencing the critique of Islamic societies out of fear of assisting imperialism or promoting a negative image of Islam has led some feminist scholars to what Lebanese intellectual Mai Ghoussoub calls an 'accommodation of obscurantism.'" Ibtissam Bouachrine, *Women and Islam: Myths, Apologies, and the Limits of Feminist Critique* (Plymouth, UK: Lexington Books, 2014), xii. In the end, what appears most beneficial is to foster sustained feminist dialogue involving the various parties of East and West, moving beyond "us vs. them" false binaries, while still accounting for the distinctive cultural contexts and histories of a given region. It is important to raise open questions, challenging sweeping generalizations bound up with a neocolonialist posture and mindset, while at the same time championing human dignity and confronting oppression along with obscurantism wherever they are found.

Judaism and patriarchy. An excellent example of sound exegetical engagement along feminist lines is Talmudic scholar Judith Hauptman's work *Rereading the Rabbis: A Woman's Voice.*[62] She refers to her own model as "contextualized feminism"[63] and categorizes the rabbis as presenting a "benevolent patriarchy."[64] Rather than plucking and splicing together different texts to make up the rabbinic view, Hauptman provides deep dives into rabbinic treatments of women in legal discussions and case by case shows how the rabbis gradually put in place interpretations of Jewish law favorable to women. Instead of viewing patriarchy in the Jewish world of Scripture and tradition as being made of one seamless cloth, there was a dynamism that moved in the direction of higher regard and more rights for women over time. The rabbis, writes Hauptman, "began to introduce numerous, significant, and occasionally bold corrective measures to ameliorate the lot of women." She continues, "In some cases they eliminated abusive behaviors that had developed over time. In others, they broke new ground, granting women the benefits that they never had before, evet at men's expense."[65]

Whether they did it independently or borrowed from the neighboring cultures or from those who proceeded them, the rabbis made these moves freely.[66] Hauptman also references Ilana Pardes, among others, that "countervoices," albeit "suppressed" remnant perspectives, actually appear in the biblical text and challenge the patriarchy found in Scripture.[67]

Closer to my home base within evangelical Christianity, Carolyn Custis James demonstrates how such Old Testament figures as Ruth and

---

[62]Judith Hauptman, *Rereading the Rabbis: A Woman's Voice, Radical Traditions* (Boulder, CO: Westview, 1998).

[63]Hauptman, *Rereading the Rabbis*, 11.

[64]Hauptman, *Rereading the Rabbis*, 5.

[65]Hauptman, *Rereading the Rabbis*, 4.

[66]Hauptman, *Rereading the Rabbis*, 4.

[67]See Hauptman, *Rereading the Rabbis*, 11, 14. See also Ilana Pardes, *Countertraditions in the Bible: A Feminist Approach* (Cambridge, MA: Harvard University Press). Also, consider the following accounts of Esther as a complex figure challenging patriarchy in her day: Michael V. Fox, "The Women in Esther," TheTorah.com, 2015, www.thetorah.com/article/the-women-in-esther; Michael V. Fox, *Character and Ideology in the Book of Esther*, 2nd ed. (1991; repr., Eugene, OR: Wipf and Stock, 2010); Sidnie Ann White, "Esther: A Feminist Model for Jewish Diaspora," in *Gender and Difference in Ancient Israel*, ed. Peggy Day (Minneapolis: Fortress, 2000), 161-77; Sidnie White Crawford, "Esther: Bible," in *Jewish Women: A Comprehensive Historical Encyclopedia*, Jewish Women's Archive, https://jwa.org/encyclopedia/article/esther-bible.

the book that bears her name challenge the dominant assumptions and disregard of women in Israel during that time period. What is perhaps even more striking is how Ruth is a foreign woman (from Moab) whom God honors in Israel, just as Scripture accords honorific space to Esther, a Jewish woman, living in captivity under Persian rule in a foreign land. Ruth is honored as an ancestress of David and the Messiah, Jesus of Nazareth, according to Matthew 1. So, too, Jesus' ancestral line includes Rahab the righteous Gentile who was a prostitute, as well as Tamar, who is more honorable than her father-in-law Judah (from whose tribe David and Jesus come) and his sons. Carolyn Custis James argues that in the biblical world, God created woman as a warrior (*ezer*), which is a better rendition than "helpmate," given its contemporary associations. Women as warriors serve in battle alongside men, not against men. God intended men and women to work together. They were to wage war together rather than against one another. However, the fall account in Genesis 3 reveals how the serpent undermined their solidarity. Rather than the narrative reflecting the battle for the sexes, we find the battle of the sexes. We fall prey to the same devices today to the detriment of human flourishing whenever we pit the one against the other.[68]

Let's pause at this point to reflect more fully on the story of Adam and Eve in Genesis 1–3. The creation-fall account chronicles their initial state of innocence followed by their temptation and deception, which involves rebellion against God. The aftermath of their separation from God includes men's subjugation of women. Genesis 3:16 records God telling the woman her fate:

> To the woman he said,
> "I will make your pains in childbearing very severe;
>   with painful labor you will give birth to children.
> Your desire will be for your husband,
>   and he will rule over you." (Genesis 3:16)

---

[68]For representative examples of Carolyn Custis James's work, see the following: *The Gospel of Ruth: Loving God Enough to Break the Rules* (Grand Rapids, MI: Zondervan, 2008); *Half the Church: Recapturing God's Global Vision For Women* (Grand Rapids, MI: Zondervan, 2011); *Malestrom: Manhood Swept into the Currents of a Changing World* (Grand Rapids, MI: Zondervan, 2015); *Lost Women of the Bible: The Women We Thought We Knew* (Grand Rapids, MI: Zondervan, 2005).

Whereas they had been given the authority to reign over all creation together side by side, hip to hip, now man in his own fallen, broken, and enslaved state will rule over the woman head to foot. Such rule is not God's intent, but the result of our hardness of heart. Still, there is hope. Unlike the man who failed to stand in solidarity with his wife but let his guard down as the serpent made its advance in the garden, the seed of the woman, which Paul identifies as Jesus (Galatians 3:15-16), goes to battle for her as well as the man and their progeny. This seed or offspring inflicts a fatal blow to the serpent, crushing its head, while being wounded in the process. Instead of manipulating the genome, as E. O. Wilson appears to favor (which I alluded to earlier in this chapter), Jesus destroys the power of sin through the crucible of sacrificial love and calls us to follow in his footsteps. God declares to the serpent,

> And I will put enmity
> between you and the woman,
> and between your offspring and hers;
> he will crush your head,
> and you will strike his heel. (Genesis 3:15)

The ultimate human person or "the great humanizer,"[69] as my secularist friend Tom Krattenmaker calls Jesus, lays down his life for humanity through his bride, the church. He does not dominate her but serves her sacrificially. If only Adam had cared for Eve in the same way as the Lord cared for his bride: "Husbands, love your wives, just as Christ loved the church and gave himself up for her" (Ephesians 5:25). Let's consider further Christianity's engagement of patriarchy.

Christianity and patriarchy. It is worth noting that in at least one place, the father of Western theology, Saint Augustine, argues that Adam is ultimately responsible for the fall's consequences. After all, for Augustine, Adam is deemed the true source of original sin, not Eve. Moreover, Augustine's writings may suggest that Adam is ultimately responsible for the fall into sin itself because, on Augustine's view, Adam did not exercise proper rule over Eve in a manner that parallels reason

---

[69]Tom Krattenmaker, *Confessions of a Secular Jesus Follower: Finding Answers in Jesus for Those Who Don't Believe* (New York: Convergent, 2016), 78.

ruling over the passions.[70] However unflattering this account may be toward women, it strikingly places blame primarily on Adam's shoulders, not Eve's, contrary to the judgment of many.

One analysis of Augustine's work goes so far as to compare Adam's failure and Christ's victory in terms of how the former did not show Eve mercy and sacrifice himself for his spouse, whereas Christ did. Moreover, Adam blamed Eve, whereas Christ accepted responsibility for his spouse, which is the church. Though innocent of all wrongdoing and blame, nonetheless, he sacrificed himself on behalf of the church of the new humanity, cleansing her through his sacrifice on her behalf. John Cavadini writes,

> It is true that Adam preferred to enter a fellowship of sin rather than to abandon Eve, but, in fact, these were not the only alternatives available to him. This is the way Adam, already a self-pleaser, constructed them. Adam already has the lack of imagination, and, thus, the carelessness, that afflicts all of the complacent and proud. What does not occur to Adam, who has learned to lift up his heart to himself instead of to God, is that, in some way, he could sacrifice himself for his wife in order to save her from the devil who had obviously fooled her (albeit through her own pride), instead of letting her stay in his thrall, thus sacrificing their companionship to Adam's own pride. He should have had mercy on her. Sacrifice is mercy, and, in *ciu.*, mercy is the true worship of God, though this worship is precisely what is refused by those who deny their heart to God.
>
> That Adam had some alternative is clear from the contrasting story of the second Adam. Christ did not abandon us, and, though he joined us sinners, he did not enter into a fellowship of sin with us. He was prepared, in mercy, to sacrifice his own life for Eve, now in the person of the church, the new Eve (which presumably includes the old Eve). Adam had the chance, it would seem, to somehow "save" Eve by his own compassionate mercy, but he preferred to take advantage of Eve, committing himself to the complacent truncation of the imagination, the "myth" of the false alternatives.[71]

---

[70]See Felecia McDuffie, "Augustine's Rhetoric of the Feminine in the *Confessions*: Woman as Mother, Woman as Other," in *Feminist Interpretations of Augustine*, ed. Judith Chelius Stark (University Park: Pennsylvania State University Press, 2007), 104-6.

[71]John C. Cavadini, "Spousal Vision: A Study of Text and History in the Theology of Saint Augustine," *Augustinian Studies* 43, nos. 1/2 (2012): 135-36.

Whatever one makes of the other details in this brief account of Augustine, it is important to highlight the pressing point for our present purposes that domination does not spell true manhood, or humanity for that matter. Rather, self-denial, mercy, and sacrificial love for the other characterizes true manhood and womanhood. Those who are meek inherit the earth (Matthew 5:5). Those who are merciful will experience divine mercy (Matthew 5:7). This is the way of Jesus' kingdom, not empire. Such qualities are distinguishing marks of human dignity.

One must guard against a flat reading of Augustine, as well as Christian Scripture. Here it is worth asking if the "countervoices" mentioned earlier in the discussion of Hauptman and Pardes that could be used to describe Ruth and Esther, among others, prove as canonical directives and correctives to prevailing cultural thought forms accounted for in the Bible and within which the fallen patriarchal system expands and dominates, contrary to God's designs. Surely, from a Christian perspective, the ultimate biblical countervoice is Jesus, who, according to Matthew's genealogy, is the climax of Ruth's, Tamar's, and Rahab's ancestral line.

Jesus was born into a Jewish patriarchal culture. Even his genealogy at the outset of Matthew's Gospel reflects this patriarchal backdrop. The genealogy comes through the men, not the women. Only five women are mentioned, four of them by name: Tamar, Rahab, Ruth, Uriah's wife (Bathsheba), and Mary, Jesus' mother. It is striking that Matthew refers to Bathsheba as the wife of Uriah (rather than David's), whom David had killed after he violated and impregnated Bathsheba.[72] God judged David

---

[72]See David E. Garland and Diana R. Garland, "Bathsheba's Story: Surviving Abuse and Loss," in *Flawed Families in the Bible: How God's Grace Works Through Imperfect Relationships* (Grand Rapids, MI: Brazos, 2007), www.baylor.edu/content/services/document.php/145462.pdf. "In Jewish tradition Tamar, Rahab, and Ruth were regarded as heroines, and it is David rather than Bathsheba who is stigmatized for their adultery." R. T. France, *The Gospel of Matthew*, New International Commentary of the New Testament (Grand Rapids, MI: Eerdmans, 2007), 37. Another source reframes the discussion to ask if those using language of rape to describe this incident are imposing a modern-day notion on the biblical world's presentation of rape. At the same time, it challenges the view that Bathsheba seduced David in any way. See Alexander Izuchukwu Abasili, "What Is Rape? The David and Bathsheba Pericope Re-examined," *Vetus Testamentum* 61, no. 1 (January 2011): 1-15, http://booksandjournals.brillonline.com/content/journals/10.1163/1568533 11x548596; Antony F. Campbell, SJ, *2 Samuel*, The Forms of the Old Testament Literature, vol. 8 (Grand Rapids, MI: Eerdmans, 2005), 104. Campbell thinks the recorded incident may warrant the use of the word *rape* today in scholarly discussion in view of how often Bathsheba has been blamed for the incident. However, in light of its ancient context and the ambivalence in the text,

but also had mercy on Bathsheba. She became the mother of Solomon, who would later reign as king and extend the messianic line.

The mention of Uriah here signifies how seriously God takes the sin of adultery (in this case, David's heinous act). Jesus reflects this supreme regard for marriage when he remarks that the only ground for a man seeking divorce is marital unfaithfulness (Matthew 19:9). While some in our day might take this text to lack redemptive merit, the whole point is that it safeguarded women from being willy-nilly abandoned by their husbands with no recourse to their protection outside of marriage in this patriarchal culture.[73] In other words, Jesus' stringent declaration is radical in its defense of women.

Similarly, women were not permitted to divorce their husbands on account of adultery.[74] The most they could do was ask the courts to convince their husbands to divorce them due to neglect.[75] While women were not viewed as chattel in the Hebrew Bible and Jewish culture, a "technical inequality" appears to have existed here, as well as elsewhere.[76] With this point in mind, Jesus protects a woman accused of adultery from being stoned (see John 8:1-11). The incident signifies a gross injustice from an Old Testament perspective, as the woman's accusers did not bring forth the man with whom she had supposedly committed

---

he settles for the "violation of Bathsheba" as perhaps "the least unsatisfactory terminology." He certainly prefers it to the term *adultery*, as do I.

[73]Wolfgang Schrage, *The Ethics of the New Testament*, trans. David E. Green (Philadelphia: Fortress, 1988), 95, 97. See also Walter Rauschenbusch, *The Social Principles of Jesus* (New York: Association Press, 1916), 85.

[74]The following statement is quite helpful in framing the rabbinic teaching on divorce and adultery: "Although a man could divorce his wife for adultery, a woman could not divorce her husband for adultery because the law allowing polygamy made it technically impossible for a man to be sexually unfaithful to his wife. The fact that a husband could have more than one wife meant that he did not have to promise to be faithful to his wife when he married. This did not mean that a man could not be guilty of adultery, but if he committed adultery it was an offense against the other woman's husband, and not against his own wife. If he committed fornication with an unmarried woman, the offense was against the woman's father with whom he had failed to make a contract. This did not mean that women were chattels to be bought and sold, because a woman could not be married against her will, but a technical inequality very definitely existed in this area." David Instone-Brewer, *Divorce and Remarriage in the Bible: The Social and Literary Context* (Grand Rapids, MI: Eerdmans, 2002), 98.

[75]Instone-Brewer, *Divorce and Remarriage in the Bible*, 132.

[76]Refer to Instone-Brewer's discussion of "technical inequality" in *Divorce and Remarriage in the Bible*, 98.

adultery.[77] Both of them should have been stoned, according to Old Testament law (see Leviticus 20:10; Deuteronomy 22:22). Jesus defended her, likely to his own eventual demise, as the religious leaders who brought her forth did so to test Jesus on the basis of a technical inequality in order to bring a charge against him (John 8:6).

The Gospels include stories of Jesus elevating women beyond their cultural status and various situations in his day. Mary was allowed into the inner circle to receive Jesus' rabbinic teaching (Luke 10:38-42), even though only men were designated as the first apostles in keeping with the patriarchs and the twelve tribes of Israel descending from Jacob's sons in this patriarchal society. We find Jesus speaking to a Samaritan woman (John 4:1-45), protecting the woman caught in adultery who was wrongfully charged (John 8:1-11), as noted earlier, and healing the daughter of a Gentile woman who actually instructs Jesus, to his amazing delight (Matthew 15:21-28).[78] Jesus' supreme regard for the woman with the issue of blood who touched him also stands out, especially in that particular setting: he was in the presence of Jairus, the synagogue ruler who begged him to come to his house and heal his own daughter. Jesus calls the woman whom he heals of the issue of blood "daughter." Why would he allow this woman to touch him, call her to make public profession of her former state and miraculous healing, and then announce her clean? To affirm her dignity (see Luke 8:41-48). In addition, we must account for the resurrected Jesus' appearance to Mary Magdalene at the empty tomb. She was the first witness to his victory and bore this good news to the apostolic community of men (John 20:11-18).

People debate the presence of patriarchy and gender equality through Western history, including the church,[79] though there are signposts that

---

[77]Jesus did not permit divorce for any other reason than that which was stipulated in Scripture. In Jesus' day, a woman could be divorced for "encouraging" adultery, even if she did not engage in sexual activity: "A woman could also be divorced for encouraging adultery, even though no adultery took place. Encouragement could involve as little as going out of the house with her hair loose or her arms bare." Instone-Brewer, *Divorce and Remarriage in the Bible*, 98.

[78]I suppose, though, that if the woman's accusers were operating simply according to rabbinic law, as noted in the previous footnote, no man would need to be condemned alongside her, that is, if she had simply gone out of the house with loose hair or bare arms. That alone might have been grounds for condemnation in their minds, since such an action would be taken to be "encouraging" adultery.

[79]For example, Michael Novak quipped that "feminists believe that Christianity established patriarchy in the West, whereas Nietzsche believed it feminized the West." Michael Novak, *Unmeltable*

point the way toward greater inclusion and equality among men and women in the Christian era.[80] Certainly, Paul's Epistles include texts that may be taken to signify that men are over women, but there are other texts in his corpus that point in the direction of equality across the board. Galatians 3:28 is one such text that points in the direction of equality, not simply in terms of standing before God by faith, but also standing before one another in our exercise of faith and spiritual gifting.[81] The eschatological hope of Christ's kingdom is partially realized now in the church as an equal reality for both men and women. Perhaps it could be argued to some degree that as in the case of slavery which Paul could not abolish under imperial Roman rule, Paul was ministering in various patriarchal cultures of differing degrees in the Roman Empire,[82] and could not have made significant gains toward gender inclusion and equality within one generation. However, I maintain that the kernel of wheat is evident in Jesus' own practice and certain passages of the New Testament (such as Galatians 3:28, as pointed out by F. F. Bruce referenced in n82), and could and should be taken forward in our own day in advocating for women's rights and a rightful view of women as fully human and as men's equals in all spheres of leadership and responsibility.

Some might consider Christian proponents of women's rights in our day examples of "Johnny-come-latelies." Regardless of what one is to

---

Ethnics: Politics & Culture in American Life (New Brunswick, NJ: Transaction Publishers, 1996), xiv.

[80]See for example Elisabeth Schüssler Fiorenza, *In Memory of Her: A Feminist Theological Reconstruction of Christian Origins* (London: SCM, 1995).

[81]F. F. Bruce puts the matter this way: "No more restriction is implied in Paul's equalizing of the status of male and female in Christ than in his equalizing of the status of Jew and Gentile, or of slave and free person. If in ordinary life existence in Christ is manifested openly in church fellowship, then, if a Gentile may exercise spiritual leadership in church as freely as a Jew, or a slave as freely as a citizen, why not a woman as freely as a man?" F. F. Bruce, *The Epistle to the Galatians*, New International Greek Testament Commentary (Grand Rapids, MI: Eerdmans, 1982), 190.

[82]On patriarchy in first century Roman society, see "Women," *The Roman Empire in the First Century*, PBS, http://www.pbs.org/empires/romans/empire/women.html. It has been argued elsewhere that Rome underwent significant changes in regard to women, from widespread patriarchy to greater inclusion. See Eva Cantarella, "Women and Patriarchy in Roman Law," in *The Oxford Handbook of Roman Law and Society*, ed. Paul J. du Plessis, Clifford Ando, and Kaius Tuori (Oxford: Oxford University Press, 2016), 419-32. See Jacques Ellul's critique of Christianity as antifeminist, including his challenge to the view of "constant progress" that portrays earlier centuries as regressive on women's rights, and his rebuttal to the claim that the Christian community was passive in response to patriarchy in the early period. Jacques Ellul, *The Subversion of Christianity*, trans. Geoffrey W. Bromiley (Grand Rapids, MI: Eerdmans, 1986), 73-75.

make of that notion, Jesus was far ahead of his time. Rather than come lately, Jesus came early. It is important that we embody Jesus' example in our day and fan the flames of gender equality in all spheres of power and influence.

GENETIC MODIFICATION, PERSONAL MOTIVATIONS, AND EQUALITY

How will such equality come about? Through genetic modification, a transformation of our motivations and affections, or something else? As noted earlier in the chapter, E. O. Wilson proceeds by way of genetic modification, whereas I proceed by way of motivations and affections.

Wilson longs for the day when science can harness religion's strengths to its own ends. In the concluding chapter of *On Human Nature* titled "Hope," which follows his chapter on religion, Wilson speaks with great confidence in science given its success in resolving so many of the universe's riddles. The combination of biology and the social sciences provides a new mythology, which replaces the "seemingly fatal deterioration of the myths of traditional religion and its secular equivalents."[83] Science also addresses the crisis or loss of a "moral consensus," which entails "a greater sense of helplessness about the human condition and a shrinking of concern back toward the self and the immediate future."[84] Wilson envisions a "biology of ethics," which will reorient the social sciences and "provide a more deeply understood and enduring code of moral values."[85]

Wilson's confidence in science's ability to replace religion as a reigning "ethos" is bound up with science's "repeated triumphs in explaining and controlling the physical world," "its self-correcting nature" that is open to peer evaluation, its willingness to leave no stone unturned in its quest for knowledge, whether the subject matter is deemed "sacred" or "profane," and lastly, "now the possibility of explaining traditional religion by the mechanistic models of evolutionary biology."[86] Science will be able to address "the third and perhaps final spiritual dilemma,"

---

[83]Wilson, *On Human Nature*, 195.
[84]Wilson, *On Human Nature*, 195.
[85]Wilson, *On Human Nature*, 196.
[86]Wilson, *On Human Nature*, 201.

which involves genetics' increasing ability to change our humanity: "the human species can change its own nature," "the very essence of humanity." What will we choose? Will we alter our genetics to resemble "the more nearly perfect nuclear family of the white-handed gibbon or the harmonious sisterhoods of the honeybees"? Or "perhaps there is something already present in our nature that will prevent us from ever making such changes. In any case, and fortunately, the third dilemma belongs to later generations."[87]

So much for hope given Wilson's sense of relief that "fortunately" we can leave the decisions to a future generation in view of his apprehension that science will have to do the heavy lifting and determine whether to change human nature. This is not the only time Wilson has kicked the can down the street for posterity to make the necessary choices. He makes the same move at the very end of *Sociobiology*, when in the closing line he assures his reader that we still have one hundred years before we have to make the hard mechanistic decisions. Playing off the word *fortunate* here as well, he pays tribute to a "foreboding insight of Camus." Camus claims it is incredibly painful to live in a "universe divested of illusions and lights," which turns humanity into an "alien." "His exile is without remedy since he is deprived of the memory of a lost home or the hope of a promised land."[88] As Wilson confesses on the closing page, we might find "hard to accept" our ability to explain ourselves solely in the "mechanistic terms" at the foundational level of "the neuron and gene." Playing off the word *fortunate* again, Wilson writes, "Unfortunately," Camus is right. But at least, we can enjoy for now what science is able to accomplish, since "we still have another hundred years."[89]

For someone so hopeful about science's accomplishments, including replacing religion as the reigning ethos, Wilson becomes extremely reticent when it comes to making the decisive turn to mechanism, and for good reason. What happens to human dignity if, and when, we do? Does Wilson's new mythology have the kind of staying power that is needed

---

[87]Wilson, *On Human Nature*, 208.
[88]Wilson, *Sociobiology*, 575.
[89]Wilson, *Sociobiology*, 575.

to supplant religion once it has explained religion solely in scientific and biological terms?[90] Based on what he writes here and in *Sociobiology*, one wonders.

It's not that we should settle for what Camus (and Wilson) would call "a world that can be explained even with bad reasons" since at least "it is a familiar world."[91] Rather, Wilson's own reasoning proves questionable. He does not go far enough when he goes "right down to the levels of the neuron and gene."[92] We are made for more than genetic determinism and reductionism, made for more than our neurons and genes, made for more than "the more nearly perfect nuclear family of the white-handed gibbon." Wilson can boast all he wants that the Genesis account of origins pales in comparison to the Big Bang account proposed by scientists,[93] but Wilson's preferred interpretation robs us of our sense of wonder in human identity and dignity.

The discussion of Wilson calls to mind Christian Smith's brief consideration of B. F. Skinner's behavioralist model. Smith finds it "deeply misguided" and welcomes Skinner's frank confession that he conceives humanity as "beyond freedom and dignity." Smith also contends against those scientific models (like Wilson's) that do not see humans as motivated actors but "determined by their genes or neural systems." In contrast, Smith gives sustained attention to motivations in advocating for "a robust humanism."[94] One will not find in Smith an appreciation for the way in which Wilson seeks to put in place the proper neurobiological, ethological, and sociobiological "foundation" so that the "discontinuity" between the natural sciences and social sciences along with the humanities can "be erased."[95] The sociologist Smith rejects sociobiologist Wilson's totalizing and reductionistic approach. His rejection of this paradigm parallels his affirmation of emergence, noted in prior chapters. In Smith's estimation, Wilson and his counterparts view humanity as

---

[90]Wilson, *On Human Nature*, 192-93.

[91]Wilson, *Sociobiology*, 575.

[92]Wilson, *Sociobiology*, 575.

[93]Wilson, *On Human Nature*, 202.

[94]Christian Smith, *To Flourish or Destruct: A Personalist Theory of Human Goods, Motivations, Failure, and Evil* (Chicago: University of Chicago Press, 2015), 3.

[95]Wilson, *On Human Nature*, 195.

"nothing more than biological organisms that happen to embody more highly evolved (that is, more complex and capable) functions compared to other biological organisms."[96]

To be fair, the urbane Wilson embodies humane instincts in seeking to bring an end to patriarchy. However, his proposed solution involving genetic modification undermines what makes us most human—our motivations. Certainly, the Big Bang would be marvelous to behold. But the Genesis creation narrative, which Wilson thinks pales in comparison, is breathtaking in its beautiful affirmation of human freedom and agency. We are not cogs in the mechanistic machine of genetic reductionism's design. The same God who breathes his Spirit into humanity grants freedom to men and women to love or despise the Creator. Only when there is freedom to love does humanity flourish. A genetically modified being that controls the motivations quenches the Spirit and erodes moral freedom.

Eschatological hope is not based on genetic modification, but the Spirit's alignment of our affections and motivations with the God who became human and who laid down his life for his bride. Rather than settle for "Blessed are the genetically modified," Jesus says, "Blessed are the merciful."

Wilson keenly sees the problem of patriarchy and rightly cares to overcome it. However, his proposed course of action involving genetic modification is not a fitting response. It does not fit the situation adequately. Wilson does not go deep enough to what ultimately makes us humans tick or what we care about. As fundamentally important as our genes are, our loves or motivations drive our reason and complete our humanity. All such dignified qualities involving human emotions, human values, and motivations might be lost if the determination is made to alter the human genome, as Wilson recommends in confronting hypertrophy's negative influence. We are made for more.

One need not be alarmed by the search for a biological basis for religion. The same holds true for genetic factors for that matter, contrary to what "extreme environmentalism" claims. According to anthropologist Anthony Leeds, "extreme environmentalism" in sociological and

---

[96]Smith, *To Flourish or Destruct*, 7. Smith mentions Wilson by name as a representative of this framework.

anthropological studies maintains that no significant behavior results from biological or genetic sources.[97] Only humans' environmental or cultural constructs and institutional derivatives shape us. This stands in stark contrast to Wilson's genetic determinism and certain forms of evolutionary psychology, which espouse genetic essentialism. Genetic essentialism does not account for environmental, non-genetic forces that shape humanity.[98] Extreme environmentalism and genetic essentialism fail to account for the merits of the other position.

To return to the biological basis of religion, there is no dualism involving primary and secondary causes. God uses secondary causes to achieve his will. Similarly, from an anthropological vantage point, there is no dualism between mind and body.[99] Even so, any truly evolutionary search must not simply go back to analyze the past but also move forward toward the future. In other words, this search must account for humanity and religion's own growth and development, not simply its origins or its missteps along the way. While religion might be an emergent property of our human constitution, its subject matter should not be reduced to an evolutionary psychological state. Nor should religion be rejected out of hand as forever keeping humanity submerged in a primordial soup of monstrous biological urges. Given religion's complexity, power, and resilience, as Wilson acknowledges, it behooves us to look for religious contributions in trying to contend against the biological pull toward domination and subjugation. It makes good sense to account for religion's reflexive import for emancipating women—and men—from patriarchy.

Leeds maintains that Wilson's genetic reductionistic trajectory fails to account for reflexivity in humans. Reflexivity allows us to reflect on ourselves and break rules that arise from our genetic and biological constitution.[100] For example, Leeds maintains that sexual dimorphism, which

[97]Anthony Leeds, "Sociobiology, Anti-sociobiology, and Human Nature," *The Wilson Quarterly,* vol. 1, no. 4 (Summer 1977): 131.

[98]See the critique of genetic essentialism in Nan Zhu and Lei Chang, "Evolved but Not Fixed: A Life History Account of Gender Roles and Gender Inequality," *Frontiers in Psychology* 10 (2019), www.ncbi.nlm.nih.gov/pmc/articles/PMC6664064/#!po=3.57143. See also D. C. Geary, "Sexual Selection and Human Life History," in *Advances in Child Development and Behavior,* ed. Robert Kail, vol. 30 (Cambridge, MA: Academic Press, 2002), 41-101.

[99]Leeds, "Sociobiology, Anti-sociobiology, and Human Nature," 130.

[100]Leeds, "Sociobiology, Anti-sociobiology, and Human Nature," 134-35.

entails differences in structure, size, color, and shape of males and fe-
males of a given species, collates with pregnancy and childbirth, as well
as the hunter-gatherer differentiation involving men and women, whom
Leeds calls the "Baby-Producer."[101] Leeds finds in this dynamic a genetic
and biological basis that is nearly universal across societies. While men
and women have tended to follow the normative pattern bound up with
genes in various societies across the world, still human reflexivity allows
the rules, or better, tendencies, as Leeds calls them, to be broken so that
we can transcend or dismantle the divide.[102] Women can and do defy the
regulative pattern and hunt while men can gather.[103] Moreover, men and
women can and should challenge the subjugation of women to men.

Rather than reduce people to biological drives that all too often lead
to the subjugation of women, we need to expand our thinking. Subjugation is not inevitable, nor is genetic manipulation the ultimate source
of liberation. Classical religious and ethical traditions provide reflexive
and reform-oriented glimmers of hope and inspiration that help to
reform our values in constructing gender roles that do not justify or reinforce patriarchy. Jesus is "the ultimate emancipator," not knowledge
derived from a narrow and naive view of reason, as is the case for
Wilson,[104] which he uncritically opposes to emotion.[105] Nor is the ultimate emancipator genetic modification and mechanism, which replace
motivations like love and compassion, which make us truly human.

Through the Spirit of Jesus, we can and must cultivate compassionate
forms of engagement. Compassion as a motivating emotion or affection
shapes reason in its reflexive response to Jesus' own confrontation of
patriarchy. Jesus invites us to engage reflexively and break the rules of
hypertrophic extremes that denigrate women. Jesus as the second Adam
invites the sons of Adam to embody mercy and sacrificial love so that
together with the daughters of Eve we can move from the battle *of* the
sexes to the battle *for* the sexes. We were made to be one.

---

[101]Leeds, "Sociobiology, Anti-sociobiology, and Human Nature," 138.
[102]Leeds, "Sociobiology, Anti-sociobiology, and Human Nature," 138.
[103]Leeds, "Sociobiology, Anti-sociobiology, and Human Nature," 138.
[104]Wilson, *On Human Nature*, 96.
[105]Leeds, "Sociobiology, Anti-sociobiology, and Human Nature," 128-30.

7

MORE THAN THE MERE END OR EXTENSION OF LIFE

On Physician-Assisted Suicide

FITTING CONSIDERATION OF HUMAN PERSONHOOD entails reflection on the beginning, continuation, and end of life. From the personalist perspective set forth in this volume, once someone is a person, they are always a person. One's worth and dignity is always inherent and so one never loses it, no matter the circumstances along life's journey. Moreover, proper attention to our telos or end as human persons involves learning how to flourish in living well and in dying well. A person's life should never merely end or extend indefinitely. Too much is at stake for human dignity and worth. A personalist may not resonate with his stoicism or his determination to commit suicide, but the Roman philosopher Seneca was right on target when he wrote, "A whole lifetime is needed to learn how to live, and—perhaps you'll find this more surprising—a whole lifetime is needed to learn how to die."[1] One should never merely live or merely die. Great care in thought and action should be given to how to live and die well. This chapter will focus on dying well and the moral prospects of physician-assisted suicide.

PHYSICIAN-ASSISTED SUICIDE: PROMINENCE, PROPER DELINEATION, AND PARAMETERS

Physician-assisted suicide is by no means the only topic to address when dealing with the ethics of end-of-life care. Still, it is not a minor issue. In

---

[1]Seneca, quoted in James S. Room, "Introduction" to Seneca, *How to Die: An Ancient Guide to the End of Life*, ed. James S. Room (Princeton, NJ: Princeton University Press, 2018), xx.

fact, it has gained increasing prominence in the US. For example, physician-assisted suicide was a controversial discussion point during Neal Gorsuch's confirmation hearing for US Supreme Court justice. Gorsuch wrote a book on the subject in which he contested the practice. Physician-assisted suicide has been viewed with increasing favor in the US since the famous case of Brittany Maynard, who chose to die with the legal aid of a physician after enduring terminal illness caused by brain cancer. After her death, a national poll revealed that 68 percent of respondents were now in favor and 28 percent were against the practice. This was a dramatic upsurge in favor of physician-assisted death.[2] No matter where people stand on the issue, high-profile and celebrity suicide cases will only increase the visibility, scrutiny, and controversy surrounding the possible merits of physician-assisted death.[3]

It is important to point out that some who favor physician assistance in death oppose the use of the term *suicide*. They claim the word invokes fear and social stigma with the intent of undermining support for the practice.[4] Alternative language includes phrases like *death with dignity*, which refers to the laws governing the practice in certain US states. Many proponents prefer phrases like *physician-assisted death* or *physician aid-in-dying* in place of suicide. This chapter will present the three terms interchangeably to account for the complexity.

One 2018 *Medical News Today* article defines euthanasia and physician-assisted suicide as "deliberate action taken with the intention of ending a life, in order to relieve persistent suffering."[5] There are various

---

[2]"Physician-Assisted Suicide Fast Facts," CNN, January 3, 2019, www.cnn.com/2014/11/26/us/physician-assisted-suicide-fast-facts/index.html. It is worth noting that against the backdrop of growing public support, the American College of Physicians claimed as recently as October 2017 that the arguments prohibiting physician-assisted suicide are the most persuasive. Lois Snyder Sulmasy and Paul S. Mueller, "Ethics and the Legalization of Physician-Assisted Suicide: An American College of Physicians Position Paper," *Annals of Internal Medicine* 167, no. 8 (October 2017): 576-78.
[3]Kirsten Powers, "Americans Are Depressed and Suicidal Because Something Is Wrong with Our Culture," *USA TODAY*, June 9, 2018, updated June 13, 2018, www.usatoday.com/story/opinion/2018/06/09/kate-spade-suicide-anthony-bourdain-depression-culture-success-column/68738002/?utm_sq=fsa30oxpls.
[4]"Terminology of Assisted Dying," *Death with Dignity*; https://deathwithdignity.org/resources/assisted-dying-glossary/. See also https://deathwithdignity.org/resources/assisted-dying-glossary/#:~:text=Assisted%20Death,ending%20medications%20from%20their%20physician.
[5]Christian Nordqvist, "What Are Euthanasia and Assisted Suicide?," *Medical News Today*, December 17, 2018; www.medicalnewstoday.com/articles/182951.php.

and sometimes conflicting presentations on what differentiates euthanasia and physician-assisted death. The article differentiates them in the following manner:

> Euthanasia: A doctor is allowed by law to end a person's life by a painless means, as long as the patient and their family agree.

> Assisted suicide: A doctor assists a patient to commit suicide if they request it.[6]

The article also differentiates between voluntary, nonvoluntary, and involuntary forms of euthanasia. Voluntary euthanasia involves patient assent. Nonvoluntary euthanasia involves ending a person's life "who is unable to consent due to their current health condition. In this scenario the decision is made by another appropriate person, on behalf of the patient, based on their quality of life and suffering." Involuntary euthanasia is "when euthanasia is performed on a person *who would be able* to provide informed consent, but does not, either because they do not want to die, or because they were not asked. This is called murder, as it's often against the person's will."[7]

Lastly, the *Medical News Today* piece distinguishes between passive and active forms of euthanasia. "Passive euthanasia is when life-sustaining treatments are withheld," whereas active euthanasia "is when someone uses lethal substances or forces to end a patient's life, whether by the patient or somebody else."[8]

Currently, most countries prohibit euthanasia. In the United States, most states presently forbid physician-assisted suicide. Those states and jurisdictions where physician-assisted dying/suicide is legal restrict the practice to terminally ill persons who are legal adults and who are deemed mentally competent. Those who support physician-assisted suicide emphasize that the patient (rather than the attending physician) must initiate and oversee the entire process. Moreover, they must operate with full knowledge and keen awareness of the various matters, while also remaining free from compulsion. The physician who agrees to

---

[6]Nordqvist, "What Are Euthanasia and Assisted Suicide?"
[7]Nordqvist, "What Are Euthanasia and Assisted Suicide?" Italics added.
[8]Nordqvist, "What Are Euthanasia and Assisted Suicide?"

consider a patient's request for physician-assisted death/suicide must account for the following three factors in the evaluation process. The physician must

- ensure that the patient is making the decision while fully informed about the law, procedure, and consequences of ingesting the chemical mixture;
- ensure that the patient is not making the decision because of the influence of depression or organic mental disorders; and
- ensure that the patient is not making the decision because of any outside pressures, including those posed by family, friends, or the medical and insurance industries.

One finds here various safeguards against the careless and high-handed exercise of physician-assisted death. Critics should at least affirm that a good death includes keen awareness and knowledge of the various relevant factors, freedom from emotional and mental dynamics that cloud sound decisions, and freedom from abuse and manipulation. Physician-assisted suicide seeks to account for all three factors.

One other stipulation appears in Oregon's Death with Dignity Act.[9] It sets forth very specific requirements that patients must meet to participate. A patient must be:

- 18 years of age or older;
- a resident of Oregon (as of March 22, 2022, the courts made the decision to remove residency in Oregon as a requirement; the legislature has not yet changed the law);
- capable of making and communicating health care decisions for himself/herself; and
- diagnosed with a terminal illness that will lead to death within six months.

It is the last stipulation that is noteworthy. Only those with a terminal illness leading to death in a relatively short period of time may seek death with a physician's assistance. This requirement helps guard against a

---

[9]"Death with Dignity Act," *Oregon Health Authority*, accessed on August 5, 2019, www.oregon.gov /oha/ph/providerpartnerresources/evaluationresearch/deathwithdignityact/pages/index.aspx.

slippery slope move where anyone with a sickness or struggle could seek a physician's aid-in-dying.

SLIPPERY SLOPE CONCERNS IN PHYSICIAN-ASSISTED SUICIDE

All people experience vulnerability at the end of their lives. Mortality with its accompanying vulnerability is no respecter of persons. And yet, while everyone is vulnerable, that vulnerability often increases exponentially for members of minority populations. Thus, there must be serious safeguards put in place to protect against abuse of minorities. Moreover, with increased vulnerability comes increased wariness in many contexts. And so, it will also be important to consider minority populations' level of trust for the medical community and how their moral and spiritual convictions (often not shared by the medical establishment) factor into their decision-making process on end-of-life care.

Slippery slope arguments are not always fallacies. A slippery slope fallacy jumps from an action to a series of actions with no proof of causal connection. A legitimate form of slippery slope argument only makes causal claims when there is proof. Alternatively, it will suggest possible rather than claim necessary or actual connections. Proper slippery slope arguments will also caution against hasty determinations in view of possible negative outcomes.

That said, slippery slope concerns have arisen in discussions of physician-assisted death. Further to what was stated above, a good death could never involve manipulation or abuse, including and especially the most vulnerable members of society. Consideration of outside pressures in physician-assisted death must include attentiveness to potential abuse of vulnerable populations such as the poor, the uninsured, the disabled, and ethnic minorities.

The *Journal of Medical Ethics* published an article in 2007 titled "Legal Physician-Assisted Dying in Oregon and the Netherlands: Evidence Concerning the Impact on Patients in 'Vulnerable' Groups."[10] The article highlights debates over slippery slope dynamics that lead to abusing

---

[10]Margaret P. Battin et al., "Legal Physician-Assisted Dying in Oregon and the Netherlands: Evidence Concerning the Impact on Patients in 'Vulnerable' Groups," *Journal of Medical Ethics*, vol. 33/10 (October 2007): 591-97.

individuals representing vulnerable populations.[11] As the title suggests, the research focused on Oregon and the Netherlands, which were at the time "the two principal jurisdictions in which physician-assisted dying is legal and data have been collected over a substantial period."[12] The results of the study showed the only vulnerable "group with a heightened risk was people with AIDS." Thus, the study concludes that "where assisted dying is already legal, there is no current evidence for the claim that legalized PAS or euthanasia will have disproportionate impact on patients in vulnerable groups."[13]

Certainly, various parties will continue to debate the results of the research. In any event, key points from this study to consider are the "heightened risk" to "people with AIDS" and "no current evidence." Whether one supports physician-assisted death, the responsible parties in jurisdictions where it is practiced should remain vigilant in accounting for possible disparities involving outside pressures on vulnerable populations, including people with AIDS. The conviction that all human persons have inalienable human value and dignity signifies that every effort should be made to eradicate abuses.

In 2009, another study of the Dutch system was conducted. It sought to determine the merits of the enduring slippery slope argument that physician aid-in-dying inevitably leads to the termination of the patients' lives against their wills. Based on qualitative research, it was found that usually there are "extensive deliberations, the majority of which do not end" in physician-assisted death. The extensive deliberations or "talk" involves at minimum two consequences: such deliberations put "the onus on patients to continue discussions towards a euthanasia death" and foster "a socio-therapeutic component, which tends to affirm social bonds and social life." The study concludes that "while this qualitative evidence cannot disprove existence of abuse, it suggests that euthanasia practices have evolved in such a way

---

[11]See for example the various statements voicing slippery slope concerns over vulnerable populations by US, Canadian, and British legal and medical authorities in box 1, titled "'Slippery-slope' concerns about vulnerable patients in health policy statements on physician-assisted dying" in Battin et al., "Legal Physician-Assisted Dying in Oregon and the Netherlands," 592.

[12]Battin et al., "Legal Physician-Assisted Dying in Oregon and the Netherlands," 591-92.

[13]Battin et al., "Legal Physician-Assisted Dying in Oregon and the Netherlands," 591-92.

that patients are more likely to talk about euthanasia than to die a euthanasia death."[14]

A publication in 2015 notes rising concern in the Netherlands over a slippery slope involving the normalization of medically assisted death that will eventually cross boundaries presently considered "taboo." Many doctors challenge the slippery slope argument based on the very limited number of prosecutions, with zero convictions of euthanasia and physician-assisted suicides in the Netherlands. Still, the article claims,

> What is inarguable, however, is that the number of euthanasia procedures carried out has risen considerably in 13 years. Initially the annual total hovered at around 1,900, but since 2006 it has increased by an average of 15% a year. In 2013 the number of euthanasia and assisted suicide cases stood at 4,829, nearly three times the 2002 figure.[15]

Ethicist Theo Boer claims that the stipulations in the Netherlands are too broad: "It doesn't make any mention of terminal illness, or illness at all. You could have a situation in the Netherlands where somebody goes bankrupt and, knowing he will never get back up to the same level financially, argues he is suffering unbearably and puts in a request for euthanasia." Boer also claims that in the Netherlands, euthanasia "was originally introduced to protect doctors." However, it "quickly came to be regarded as a patient's right. 'The debate has changed. Euthanasia is no longer a last resort. It was originally seen as a law that gave doctors rights rather than patients. But we very frequently hear it discussed in terms of a patient's right to euthanasia.'" Boer has also criticized "phenomena such as 'duo-euthanasia,' where the partner of a terminally ill patient asks to die with them because he or she cannot face life alone."[16]

How does one safeguard against lessening restrictions on euthanasia and physician-assisted suicide prior to the six-month window for those

---

[14]Frances Norwood, Gerrit Kimsma, and Margaret P. Battin, "Vulnerability and the 'Slippery Slope' at the End-of-Life: A Qualitative Study of Euthanasia, General Practice and Home Death in the Netherlands," *Family Practice* 26, no. 6 (December 1, 2009): 472-80; https://pubmed.ncbi.nlm.nih.gov/19828573/.

[15]Gordon Darroch, "Rise in Euthanasia Requests Sparks Concern as Criteria for Help Widen," DutchNews.nl, July 3, 2015, www.dutchnews.nl/features/2015/07/rise-in-euthanasia-requests-sparks-concern-as-criteria-for-help-widen/.

[16]Darroch, "Rise in Euthanasia Requests Sparks Concern as Criteria for Help Widen."

who are terminally ill, or to aid those who are not terminally ill, but who no longer wish to live? For example, Belgium allows nonterminally ill patients and children to request euthanasia.[17] Children as young as nine have utilized this law and ended their lives.[18]

Another perhaps related slippery slope concern involves the romanticization of suicide. What structures must be put in place to safeguard against suicide being romanticized and made increasingly popular, or that physician-assisted suicide raises rather than reduces the number of violent forms of suicide? It has been claimed that favorable media coverage inspires "imitative suicidal behaviors."[19] One study concluded that legalizing assisted suicide does not reduce or substitute for more "violent" suicides but increases total suicides.[20]

The last slippery slope worth mentioning involves trust. American and British medical authorities have raised concerns that physician-assisted death has the potential to undermine trust between the patient and physician.[21] These dynamics are perhaps even more important when engaging minority populations. Increased vulnerability involves increased wariness in many contexts. And so, it will also be important to consider minority populations' level of trust for the medical community and how their moral and spiritual convictions (often not shared by the medical establishment) factor into their decision-making process on end-of-life care.

In addressing end-of-life care decisions including physician-assisted suicide, one must account for levels of trust or distrust of vulnerable

---

[17]See PBS News Hour, "The Right to Die in Belgium: An Inside Look at the World's Most Liberal Euthanasia Law," PBS, January 15, 2015, www.pbs.org/newshour/show/right-die-belgium-inside -worlds-liberal-euthanasia-laws.

[18]Charles Lane, "Children Are Being Euthanized in Belgium," *Washington Post*, August 6, 2018, www .washingtonpost.com/opinions/children-are-being-euthanized-in-belgium/2018/08/06/9473bac2 -9988-11e8-b60b-1c897f17e185_story.html?noredirect=on.

[19]World Health Organization, *Preventing Suicide: A Resource for Media Professionals* (WHO: Geneva 2008): 6, 7, 8.

[20]See D. Jones and D. Paton, "How Does Legalization of Physician-Assisted Suicide Affect Rates of Suicide?" *Southern Medical Journal* 108 (2015): 599-604. For more information along these and similar lines, see Richard Doerflinger, "The Effect of Legalizing Assisted Suicide on Palliative Care and Suicide Rates: A Response to Compassion and Choices," *On Point* 13 (March 2017): 1-7; https://lozierinstitute.org/wp-content/uploads/2017/03/The-Effect-of-Legalization-of-Assisted -Suicide.pdf.

[21]See again box 1, "'Slippery-slope' concerns about vulnerable patients," in Battin et al., "Legal Physician-Assisted Dying in Oregon and the Netherlands," 592.

populations toward the medical community and how vulnerable groups often approach the subject based on their spiritual and moral values. Here it is important to highlight the article titled "Racial Differences in Attitudes Toward Euthanasia."[22] According to this research, many studies have argued that suspicion of medicine is a key factor in why African Americans have "less favorable attitudes toward euthanasia."[23] However, no quantitative assessment has demonstrated this claim. This article offers a different rationale for the basis for African American suspicion of euthanasia: "Results indicate that while African Americans exhibit higher levels of distrust of medicine, this is not related to attitudes toward euthanasia, which seem predominantly to be a spiritual matter."[24] "Religious or spiritual beliefs" play a "dominant role."[25] "Ultimately, this research shows that while race is relevant to one's attitude toward medicine, euthanasia is largely seen as an abstract moral and spiritual issue, unrelated to both individual and cultural experience with medicine."[26] Now one might find the phrase "euthanasia is largely seen as an abstract moral and spiritual issue" to be abstract and negatively biased, since for people of faith there is nothing "abstract" about religious and spiritual convictions. In any event, those medical practitioners or physicians who wish to build trust over end-of-life care issues with their African American patients of religious or spiritual aptitude will need to show appropriate concern for the role of faith and spirituality in medical determinations. Their aim should not be to persuade their patients in one direction or the other, but to assist them in coming to their own self-determined and settled conclusions on end-of-life matters. Any historical bias in medicine bordering on "there ain't no sin and there ain't no virtue. There's just stuff people do"[27] simply will not do.

---

[22]Jason Wasserman, Jeffrey Michael Clair, and Ferris J. Ritchey, "Racial Differences in Attitudes Toward Euthanasia," *OMEGA—Journal of Death and Dying* 52, no. 3 (September 2005): 263-87.

[23]Wasserman et al., "Racial Differences in Attitudes Toward Euthanasia," 263.

[24]Wasserman et al., "Racial Differences in Attitudes Toward Euthanasia," 263.

[25]Wasserman et al., "Racial Differences in Attitudes Toward Euthanasia," 283.

[26]Wasserman et al., "Racial Differences in Attitudes Toward Euthanasia," 284.

[27]This line is followed by "It's all part of the same thing. And some of the things folks do is nice, and some ain't nice, but that's as far as any man got a right to say." John Steinbeck, *The Grapes of Wrath* (New York: Penguin Books, 2002), 23.

We need to account for a constructive engagement of spirituality and its incorporation into end-of-life care and medical ethics. Fortunately, there is headway being made in this domain. Take for example *Making Health Care Whole: Integrating Spirituality into Patient Care* by Christina Puchalski and Betty Ferrell.[28] The rights of vulnerable groups must include respect for their spiritual and ethical convictions, as well as others. People are more than matter. In sum, one must account for patients' spiritual and ethical convictions, which are themselves vulnerable in certain medical and scientific circles where suspicion of religion and its moral values reign. Otherwise, there will be no opportunity to build trust with many ethnic minorities—and other people of robust faith regardless of their ethnic background—in addressing important end-of-life care concerns.

If one wishes to guard against slipping into careless consideration of what is fitting by way of end-of-life determinations, one must account not simply for legal and medical considerations, or potential abuses, as important as they are, but a wide array of spiritual and ethical vantage points to know what is at stake. A good life and a good death require careful self-examination. After all, the personalist account of human beings offered in this volume accounts for our reflexive nature.

In chapter two, we quoted Christian Smith's definition of person, which indicates that a "person" is "conscious, reflexive."[29] Humanity is likely the only species that engages in self-conscious or self-examining activity. For example, dogs and cats do not reflect on their lives and decide to kill themselves due to circumspection involving existential despair. Anthropologist Anthony Leeds asserts that suicide is a distinctively human act bound up with "reflexivity and the breakdown of postulation that humans arrive at suicide." It is a "philosophical, not a biological problem."[30]

Whether his suicide involved a breakdown of postulation, Socrates, who committed suicide, asserted that an unexamined life is not worth

---

[28]Christina M. Puchalski, and Betty Ferrell, with a foreword by Rachel Namoi Remen, *Making Health Care Whole: Integrating Spirituality into Patient Care* (West Conshohocken, PA: Templeton, 2010).

[29]Christian Smith, *What Is a Person?* (Chicago: University of Chicago Press, 2010), 61.

[30]Anthony Leeds, "Sociobiology, Anti-sociobiology, and Human Nature," *The Wilson Quarterly* 1, no. 4 (Summer 1977): 135.

living. It just won't do to limit analysis to what is legally and medically at issue. More is needed than ensuring that the patient is fully informed about the law, procedure, and consequences of ingesting the chemical mixture. The patient should also reflect carefully on possible moral sanctions and prohibitions. A distinctively human, personalist account of what is entailed by a good life and a good death, including the relative merits of a physician-assisted death, must include critical, reflexive consideration of what is at stake morally. To this subject, we now turn.

THE RIGHT TO IN-DEPTH ETHICAL REFLECTION AT LIFE'S END

All too often, debates over end-of-life care, including the subject of physician-assisted death, become so politicized and contentious that it is difficult to consider the various factors openly and in depth. While a single chapter dedicated to end-of-life care in a book on ethics cannot do justice to all the facets, at the very least, it should point the way forward in ethical deliberations. Too much is at stake not to reflect carefully on end-of-life matters. We should all prepare ourselves well ethically for this inevitable journey.

Medical professionals and hospice chaplains, among others, often operate from the mindset that the stakeholder's convictions that merit their greatest consideration on end-of-life care decisions are those of the dying person. From a personalist perspective, this is only right, as the individual person's identity is inviolable. No outside pressures, no matter the stakeholder, should predominate. Keen care for the patient's decision-making process should include respect for their moral and religious perspectives, as was noted in the prior section. Unfortunately, well-meaning parties—whether they be doctors, chaplains, family members, or friends—can easily forget the power imbalance and impose their own convictions on the dying person. It is extremely difficult for the dying person to put up a great fight. After all, they are a captive audience in many ways.

There is a real temptation to impose one's views given so many variables in play, including sheer love of the dying person, financial challenges, and one's own spiritual and ethical values. One must remain vigilant to guard against overstepping appropriate bounds in conversation with the dying person. Still, some may argue that it is not appropriate to allow the dying party alone to determine the course of action, since they fear the terminally ill person's determination may overstep others' boundaries and impact them negatively with singular decisions. For example, precious loved ones would likely experience intense loss and grief if the person near the end of life chooses to die by requesting the removal of life-supporting systems and aids of various kinds. Others may point to the financial drain on the family, health care industry, and society at large, if the person near death chooses artificial means for staying alive indefinitely.

No matter the challenges and pressures others face, given that the terminally ill person has the most at stake to lose—namely, their lives— they should have final say about whether to pursue life-sustaining measures or be taken off life support. To those who would challenge the position that the dying person's wishes are of primary import, we offer a form of the Golden Rule: "Do unto others as you would have them do unto you." Would we like it if we were dying, and others of various perspectives sought to impose their convictions on us?

Let us say you are an evangelical Christian; and a Muslim doctor, Hindu chaplain, atheist friend, or your children of conflicting convictions sought—perhaps repeatedly tried—to convince you to change course on your end-of-life care convictions based on their own metaphysical and ethical outlook and without you requesting their input. How would you feel? Would it not be adding insult to the injury you are already experiencing with impending death? So, in caring for someone else nearing life's end, would it not be better for those of us who have strong religious convictions, who believe in God's providential direction, to pray for wisdom for the dying person and ask that we be good companions who empathize well with them, asking God for discernment if asked for our perspectives, so that we might speak compassionately, truthfully, and graciously?

All well and good, by and large, but what if the dying person wishes to commit suicide and asks a physician to assist them with ending their cruel suffering? Should we support their wishes? Is it sufficient to give assent to their wishes based merely on the dictates of the law of a given state or land? No, it is far from sufficient to commend a position, no matter what it is, as moral or immoral based on its legal status. There are positions that are moral even if outlawed, and positions that are immoral, even if they are legal. In other words, there are higher laws or better outcomes or more virtuous stances to which one must give an account. How might such laws, outcomes, and stances, whatever they may be, bear on determining whether to support physician-assisted death?

We will not come to a definitive and universally affirmed and satisfying resolution on the ethical viability of physician-assisted suicide that accounts for all possible scenarios in any one chapter. Even so, our entangled ethic will at least account for different ethical approaches bearing on physician-assisted death. Consideration in the next section will begin with Immanuel Kant and deontological ethics, followed by Joseph Fletcher and situation ethics, which is a form of consequentialism, and then Aristotle and virtue ethics. After that, the effort will be made to account for various religious perspectives on physician aid-in-dying.

Immanuel Kant, the highest good, and suicide. Kant engages the subject of suicide at a few places in his philosophical corpus.[31] The *Journal of Medical Ethics* has published articles on Kant's philosophical and ethical consideration of suicide. Take for example the following helpful essay by Gerard Vong: "In Defence of Kant's Moral Prohibition on Suicide Solely to Avoid Suffering."[32]

As the title of the article suggests, Vong argues that for Kant, suicide is immoral if one simply seeks to avoid suffering: "When the suicidal individual is motivated by some contingent end, such as happiness (or avoiding suffering), to commit suicide, they are treating the rational will, the very source of value and thereby obligation, as a means to obtain a conditionally valuable end (Ak 4:429)."[33] For Kant, this is true whether or not the rational will is intentionally treated this way.[34] Later Vong

---

[31]See for example Immanuel Kant, *Grounding for the Metaphysics of Morals* (Indianapolis: Hackett, 1993), Ak IV, 422.

[32]Gerard Vong: "In Defence of Kant's Moral Prohibition on Suicide Solely to Avoid Suffering," *Journal of Medical Ethics* 34, no. 9 (September 2008): 655-57. Vong's article is a critique of a prior article in the same journal: Ian Brassington, "Killing People: What Kant Could Have Said About Suicide and Euthanasia but Did Not," *Journal of Medical Ethics* 32, no. 10 (October 2006): 571-74.

[33]Vong, "In Defence of Kant's Moral Prohibition," 656.

[34]Vong, "In Defence of Kant's Moral Prohibition," 656.

writes, "In Kant's normative system, the suffering of one individual is only of contingent value and is therefore outweighed by the highest good of all, a moral agent's good will. It then follows that suicide solely to avoid suffering is immoral in Kant's ethical system."[35]

For Kant, moral deliberation is essential to human value, rather than mere sensation. Thus, one could not be morally justified in ending one's life based solely or primarily on the desire to end one's individual suffering. This may prove difficult to comprehend in our society today, which is so often framed by experience including emotions of joy and sorrow and pleasure and pain. Perhaps it could be said that instead of humanity being the wise or thinking creature, as was true for Aristotle and Kant, humanity is now viewed as the supremely feeling creature.

According to Vong, in Kant's philosophy,

> the only unconditional, fundamental value is good will directed by pure reason. . . . By good will, Kant refers to the agent's intention to uphold moral duties motivated by rationally valid, universal rules that are created by the agent's applications of the categorical imperative. All moral value is derived from the good will directed by reason. On this account, happiness is only contingently morally good if the action that produces it can be recommended by a sound application of the categorical imperative. Happiness (or preventing suffering) itself is not necessarily good—the happiness a sadist receives by engaging in wanton torture is immoral.[36]

Vong also argues,

> According to Kant's moral philosophy, rationality is the necessary condition and source of all moral value: without it, we are unable to deliberate over actions and apply the categorical imperative. Rationality, as a unique feature of humanity, is what gives humans dignity (Würde) and makes them invaluable.[37]

In addition to arguing that suicide is immoral because it treats "the rational will, the very source of value and thereby obligation, as a means to obtain a conditionally valuable end,"[38] it is also morally wrong because

---

[35]Vong, "In Defence of Kant's Moral Prohibition," 657.
[36]Vong, "In Defence of Kant's Moral Prohibition," 656.
[37]Vong, "In Defence of Kant's Moral Prohibition," 656.
[38]Vong, "In Defence of Kant's Moral Prohibition," 656.

it intentionally removes the "essential physical conditions required for" the "unconditionally morally valuable function" of the rational will's employment of the categorical imperative.[39]

However, according to Vong, there are two exceptions. The only times when suicide could be justified on Kant's view is in a scenario like the advanced stages of Alzheimer's, where the reason is irrevocably impaired beyond use, or in a situation like rabies where a person commits suicide to keep from harming others in a state of wild derangement.[40] It should be underlined that although Kant allows for such exceptions, these allowances are framed in terms of his overarching system, including the categorical imperative, rather than proving self-contradictory.[41]

Before we turn from Kant to consider other ethical perspectives, it is important to note that one must account for the totality of an ethical system in making judgments on that system's conclusions on a particular ethical issue. Regardless of whether one agrees with Kant's position, Kant's approach to suicide makes perfect sense within his overarching philosophy, which prizes moral reason involving the categorical imperative as fundamental and ultimate to human identity. Regardless of one's ethical stance, philosophical and theological anthropology certainly comes into play. For those who operate from a utilitarian framework, pleasure or happiness is prized over duty to a moral law. In a situational ethical framework, which like utilitarianism is consequentialist or outcomes based, love or compassion framed in terms of quality of life replaces adherence to a law that prizes sanctity of life. An emphasis on sanctity of life often if not always entails deontology or moral duty, as in Kantian ethics, which maintains that people are more than mere means, but rather ends in themselves. It also

---

[39]Vong, "In Defence of Kant's Moral Prohibition," 657.

[40]Vong, "In Defence of Kant's Moral Prohibition," 657.

[41]The *Encyclopedia Britannica* provides a very good summary of Kant's categorical imperative: "A moral law that is unconditional or absolute for all agents, the validity or claim of which does not depend on any ulterior motive or end. 'Thou shalt not steal,' for example, is categorical as distinct from the hypothetical imperatives associated with desire, such as 'Do not steal if you want to be popular.'" *Encyclopedia Britannica Online*, s.v. "categorical imperative," www.britannica.com/topic/categorical-imperative. See also the discussion of Kant's categorical imperative, including its various formulations, in Robert Johnson and Adam Cureton, "Kant's Moral Philosophy," in *Stanford Encyclopedia of Philosophy*, ed. Edward N. Zalta, Spring 2018 Edition, https://plato.stanford.edu/archives/spr2018/entries/kant-moral/.

includes divine decree models, as in the Judeo-Christian tradition with its doctrine of humanity as created in God's image and the divine command not to kill.

Joseph Fletcher, the situated good end, and suicide. Having alluded to situation ethics at the close of the last subsection, it would be beneficial to account for this model in greater detail. The chapter on monogamy gave attention to situation ethics' chief architect, Joseph Fletcher.

Fletcher was a passionate proponent of active euthanasia in end-of-life medical care. Before accounting for his ethical deliberations on active euthanasia, it would be good to recount briefly Fletcher's overarching model. In his volume *Situation Ethics*, Fletcher claims to approach ethical concerns in view of love, mediating between the extremes of lawlessness and legalism. From this vantage point, the person approaches a given moral problem "armed with the ethical maxims of his community and its heritage, and he treats them with respect as illuminators of his problems. Just the same, he is prepared . . . to compromise them or set them aside *in the situation* if love seems better served by doing so."[42] From what Fletcher argues here, it appears that he would approach any patient pondering end-of-life decisions respecting not only the moral principles of the person's community and heritage but their own as well. In the end, however, he may push beyond those convictions of this or that heritage in view of his understanding of the principle of love.

Fletcher accounts for community and heritage, noting how there are all kinds of foundational ideological and traditional dynamics already in play. There is no such thing as an ethical vacuum. People come morality laden, regardless of whether they are aware of this dynamic. Unfortunately, all too often people enter difficult situations, such as at a patient's bedside in a hospital room, facing head on end-of-life decisions without realizing the various ethical perspectives that the various stakeholders (and shareholders) in the hospital complex bring with them. It is all too easy, especially under stress, to operate as if one alone is thinking ethically and everyone else is functioning without a moral compass. This

---

[42]Joseph Fletcher, *Situation Ethics* (Philadelphia: Westminster, 1966), 26.

myopic perspective is due in part to our inability much of the time to account for the various philosophical and theological convictions and opinions that shape our ethical stances and moral sentiments.

In an article titled "Ethics and Euthanasia," Fletcher draws attention to the various metaethical issues that are hovering overhead, including at the hospital bedside and boardroom: "There are many pre-ethical or 'metaethical' issues that are often overlooked in ethical discussions. People of equally good reasoning powers and a high respect for the rules of inference will still puzzle and even infuriate each other. This is because they fail to see that their moral judgments proceed from significantly different values, ideals, and starting points."[43]

Those who operate based on the maxim that God's will prohibits any human initiative in the stages of death, or that physiological life must be cherished and preserved no matter what, will reject outright any form of euthanasia. However, according to Fletcher, if "the highest good is personal integrity and human well-being, then euthanasia . . . could or might be the right thing to do, depending on the situation."[44]

Fletcher champions personal integrity and human well-being as the highest good and love as his guiding light in any given situation. The dying patient's situation frames the discussion and evaluation process rather than a transcendent and divine person or secular universal ideal. Fletcher writes,

> It is harder morally to justify letting somebody die a slow and ugly death, dehumanized, than it is to justify helping him to escape from such misery. This is the case at least in any code of ethics which is humanistic or personalistic, i.e., in any code of ethics which has a value system that puts humanness and personal integrity above biological life and function. . . . What counts *ethically* is whether human needs come first—not whether the ultimate sanction is transcendental or secular.[45]

Fletcher distinguishes between quality of life and sanctity of life, favoring the former over the latter. While Kant's framework has been labeled

---

[43]Joseph Fletcher, "Ethics and Euthanasia," *The American Journal of Nursing* 73, no. 4 (April 1973): 671.

[44]Fletcher, "Ethics and Euthanasia," 671.

[45]Fletcher, "Ethics and Euthanasia," 670.

personalist in orientation,[46] Fletcher argues that his quality-of-life orientation reflects a personalist framework that prizes rationality over mere physiology. It just goes to show that personalism itself does not predict the ethical determination and conclusion in any given case. Fletcher describes his view this way:

> One way of putting this is to say that the traditional ethics based on the sanctity of life—which was the classical doctrine of medical idealism in its prescientific phases—must give way to a code of ethics of the *quality* of life. This comes about for humane reasons. It is a result of modern medicine's successes, not failures. . . . This conclusion is of great philosophical and religious interest because it reaffirms the ancient Christian-European belief that the core of humanness, of the *humanum*, lies in the *ratio*—man's rational faculty. It is not the loss of brain function in general but of cerebral function (the synthesizing "mind") in particular that establishes that death has ensued.[47]

An emphasis on sanctity of life is often associated with a traditional notion of deity where God as Creator determines ethical value as well as when life begins and when it can end. Fletcher challenges this view of God and offers an immediate and forceful rejoinder to those who level the charge that modern medical care involves a great amount of playing God: "'Yes, we are playing God.' But the real question is: Which or whose God are we playing?"[48] Here Fletcher reflects on different concepts of deity: a God who has a monopoly over creation and death versus a God who is the creative principle. The former operates alone whereas the latter operates in tandem with us as cocreators. Fletcher rejects out of hand the former as primitive, outdated, and obsolete, unable to deal with the modern world of advanced scientific and medical advances. Fletcher puts it this way:

> We must rid ourselves of that obsolete theodicy according to which God is not only the cause but also the builder of nature and its works, and not

---

[46]Thomas D. Williams and Jan Olof Bengtsson, "Personalism," *Stanford Encyclopedia of Philosophy* ed. Edward N. Zalta, Spring 2020 Edition, https://plato.stanford.edu/archives/spr2020/entries /personalism/.

[47]Fletcher, "Ethics and Euthanasia," 672.

[48]Fletcher, "Ethics and Euthanasia," 672.

only the builder but even the manager. On this archaic basis it would be God himself who is the efficient as well as the final cause of earthquake and fire, of life and death, and by logical inference any "interference with nature" (which is exactly what medicine is) is "playing God." That God, seriously speaking, is dead.[49]

I will return shortly to Fletcher's rejection of the traditional notion of deity and how that bears on end-of-life decisions. For now, however, let's make sure to highlight the main issue that is at stake from Fletcher's perspective: "What, then, is the real issue? In a few words, it is whether we can morally justify taking it into our own hands to hasten death for ourselves (suicide) or for others (mercy killing) out of reasons of compassion."[50]

The law of love—not what he takes to be legalism bound up with strict adherence to natural and scriptural law or unprincipled lawlessness ("antinomian unprincipledness")—drives Fletcher.[51] The law of love is to be prized over legalism of whatever kind—whether divine or human. Fletcher affirms natural law's emphasis on "reason as the instrument of moral judgment, while rejecting the notion that the good is 'given' in the nature of things, objectively." Moreover, his situation ethics model "goes part of the way with Scriptural law by accepting revelation as the source of the norm while rejecting all 'revealed' norms or laws but the one command—to love God in the neighbor."[52] Whether accounting for claims involving natural or scriptural law, the focus is not on an objective truth claim, but the situation of the person in need: "The situationist follows a moral law or violates it according to love's need."[53]

While the traditional theist and Christian ethicist will no doubt take issue with Fletcher's framework, perhaps one area where they overlap is in contending against the legalism associated with market ideology: humanity was made for the market, not the market for humanity. Fletcher would likely contend against market ideology and legalism because it discounts the person in need as the primary focus of ethical deliberation.

---

[49]Fletcher, "Ethics and Euthanasia," 672.
[50]Fletcher, "Ethics and Euthanasia," 673.
[51]Fletcher, *Situation Ethics*, 26.
[52]Fletcher, *Situation Ethics*, 26.
[53]Fletcher, *Situation Ethics*, 26.

For Fletcher and traditionalists alike, the following probably holds true: the market was made for humanity, including the person in need, not humanity for the market. From this vantage point, economic and market pressures to terminate a life would be deemed immoral. While it is beyond the scope of our present inquiry, it would be interesting to consider how market pressures involving limited financial resources to care for those in desperate need of medical care would influence Fletcher and traditionalists, for that matter, on what to do in individual patient care involving those who would rather die. To put it as a question, How could a responsible party allocate limited resources for medical treatment to someone who wishes to die rather than invest those same resources in caring for someone who wishes to live?

Now let's compare Fletcher and Kant, albeit briefly. Both figures locate human worth in reason. Fletcher also claims that the traditional Christian-European worldview prizes reason as the essential feature of humanity. However, it should be noted that the image of God motif set forth in Christian Scripture, with which reason is often associated, accounts for other possibilities. In addition to reason, theologians have put forth dominion, moral attribution, and relation as constitutive of human nature and what the image of God entails.[54]

In addition to Kant and Fletcher prizing reason's import for human value, they both take issue with the traditional Christian notion of deity. However, unlike Fletcher, who moves in a pantheistic direction, Kant operates largely from a deistic point of view: God functions as a distant and removed moral postulate of reason. One key difference in framing the import of human reason in Kant's and Fletcher's ethical systems is that rational, dutiful adherence to the moral law is Kant's focus irrespective of a situation that for Fletcher warrants compassionate release from suffering. For Fletcher, compassion is the focus. Reason plays an instrumental role in promoting love in every given situation.

So, what does this discussion entail for the subject of physician-assisted suicide? Let's assume that Kant's stance on suicide, including

---

[54]See Karl Barth's discussion of the image of God in relational terms in dialogue with these other perspectives in *Church Dogmatics*, vol. III/1, *The Doctrine of Creation*, ed. G. W. Bromiley and T. F. Torrance (Edinburgh: T&T Clark, 1958), 191-206.

exceptions to the rule, bears relevance for the subject of physician-assisted death. In Kant's view, as outlined by Vong, it would be immoral for a physician to assist a dying patient in taking their lives. Those who are endowed with sound reasoning powers must always act in accordance with the categorical imperative. Only those who no longer possess such rational powers and who try to commit suicide or assist one in doing so are spared moral censor. However, as noted earlier in this chapter, in the US, physicians can only assist patients where the patient is deemed rationally fit to make determinations related to the termination of life.

Fletcher's stance takes him in a different direction than Kant. Fletcher argues for the moral viability of active euthanasia to end the life of someone who is severely mentally disabled or who suffers from incapacitating brain damage. Based on his system of thought, it follows that he would also affirm physician-assisted suicide when a well-reasoning patient requests it based on the desire to end their suffering. This stance follows from his novel take on a person-centered approach. Regarding this valuation, Fletcher writes,

> Many of us look upon living and dying as we do upon health and medical care, as person-centered. This is not a solely or basically biological understanding of what it means to be "alive" and to be "dead." It asserts that a so-called "vegetable," the brain-damaged victim of an auto accident or a microcephalic newborn or a case of massive neurologic deficit and lost cerebral capacity, who nevertheless goes on breathing and whose midbrain or brain stem continues to support spontaneous organ functions, is in such a situation no longer a human being, no longer a person, no longer really alive. It is personal function that counts, not biological function.[55]

Based on his emphasis on love and compassion, and further to what was stated above, Fletcher would not limit euthanasia to these scenarios involving the rationally incapacitated. The physician would also assist patients requesting their help in ending their own lives: "If the end sought is the patient's death as a release from pointless misery and dehumanization, then the requisite or appropriate means is justified."[56]

---

[55]Fletcher, "Ethics and Euthanasia," 671.
[56]Fletcher, "Ethics and Euthanasia," 674.

In *Situation Ethics*, Fletcher references H. Richard Niebuhr's emphasis on "fitting" response.[57] Fletcher argues that what matters is "contextual appropriateness," not the question of what is the "good" or "right," but what is "*fitting*."[58] It is worth referencing Niebuhr's other methodological factor that he brought to ethical situations and adding to them an intermediate item. We mentioned these methodological considerations in chapter two. Before seeking to discern the fitting response, Niebuhr asks, What is going on in the particular situation?[59] As noted in chapter two, medical ethicist Robert Lyman Potter inserts an intermediate question: "What ought we to care about?" which he derived from Harry Frankfurt.[60] In order, the questions read, "What is going on here? Describe the situation"; then, "What ought we to care about? Empathically encounter the patient"; and finally, "What is the fitting response to what is going on? Make the decision, and then take action. Ethics is having good reasons for action."[61] Ultimately, concern for what the terminally ill patient wants must take precedence over other parties' convictions. From Potter's vantage point, they are the most important person in the given situation since it is their life and death which is at stake. We ought to care most for their desires and aims in ethical determinations.

In Potter's treatment, the emphasis is on the *value* of the person who is dying. It is also worth accounting for the *virtue* or kind of person who is tending to the dying patient. At this juncture, let's turn to Aristotle, as there is a possible connection between his position and Frankfurt's "What ought we to care about?" as well as Niebuhr's emphasis on "What is the fitting response?"

---

[57]See H. Richard Niebuhr, *The Responsible Self*, Library of Theological Ethics (1963; repr., Louisville, KY: Westminster John Knox Press, 1999), 60-61.

[58]Fletcher, *Situation Ethics*, 27-28.

[59]Niebuhr, *The Responsible Self*, 59-68. Over against deontological and teleological ethics, Niebuhr presents a cathecontic approach, which emphasizes "an ethic of appropriateness or fitting response." See the foreword by Schweiker to Niebuhr, *The Responsible Self*, xi.

[60]Harry G. Frankfurt, "The Importance of What We Care About," in *The Importance of What We Care About* (Cambridge: Cambridge University Press, 1998).

[61]Robert Lyman Potter, quoted in Paul Louis Metzger, "At the Crossroads: Medicine, Ethics and Religion, Part 1," *Uncommon God, Common Good*, Patheos, April 24, 2017, www.patheos.com /blogs/uncommongodcommongood/2017/04/at-the-crossroads-medicine-ethics-and-religion -part-1/.

Aristotle, the good person, and suicide. In caring empathically for the patient, we need to care for what they care about. While Fletcher acknowledges the need to account for religious and ethical traditions, his article "Ethics and Euthanasia" does not convey respect for ethical and end-of-life care positions that differ from his own. How unfortunate this posture and attitude would be if a physician who is influenced by Fletcher brought it to bear on interaction with a dying patient who views life from a traditional Judeo-Christian perspective, or from a Buddhist framework. More on this shortly.

It is not alone sufficient to get it right when it comes to discerning between such systems as Kantian deontological ethics and consequentialist ethics, including Fletcher's model,[62] which seeks to determine the best result. One must also account for the ethical posture or disposition, attitude, and character of the medical professional, as they engage a dying patient in end-of-life care scenarios. Frankfurt's point on care, as Potter presents it, as well as concern for fitting response, reflects the *kind of person* required. Some might refer to it as "bedside manner." But there is more involved. Not only should we be concerned for the quality of life and quality of care physically speaking, but also we must be concerned for the quality or virtuous conduct of the person making medical-ethical determinations in end-of-life scenarios.

This framework resonates with Aristotle's ethical paradigm. Aristotle connected virtue with the cultivation and embodiment of noble character. For Aristotle, virtue is a settled rational disposition that mediates between extremes of excess and deficiency.[63] As applied to medical ethics,

---

[62]Fletcher acknowledges in the following statement that his position on euthanasia is consequentialist in orientation: "This position comes down to the belief that our moral acts, including suicide and mercy killing, are right or wrong depending on the consequences aimed at . . . and that the consequences are good or evil according to whether and how much they serve humane values. In the language of ethics this is called a 'consequential' method of moral judgment." Fletcher, "Ethics and Euthanasia," 674.

[63]See Aristotle, *Aristotle's Nicomachean Ethics*, trans. Robert C. Bartlett and Susan D. Collins (Chicago: University of Chicago Press, 2011), book two, 27-41. There are three forms of virtue ethics in the modern period: Eudaimonism, agency, and care. Eudaimonism bases virtues on human flourishing, where flourishing is equated with performing well humanity's distinctive function or vocation of rational deliberation. An agent-based model favors common-sense intuitions, i.e., those quality attributes we esteem in others. An ethical framework of care extends ethical consideration beyond deliberations of justice and autonomy alone. "Caring and nurturing" are indispensable.

right conduct includes virtues such as compassion (empathy for the patient's situation), benevolence (philanthropic conduct that helpfully addresses the patient's needs), and respectfulness (honorable regard for the patient as a person). Liezl van Zyl applies virtue ethics involving the qualities mentioned here to end-of-life care and makes allowances for euthanasia as a last resort.[64]

In commenting on Liezl van Zyl's virtue ethics approach to euthanasia in *Death and Compassion*, Richard Huxtable offers the following summary:

> The virtue of compassion encourages an empathetic identification, and hence engagement, with the patient and his or her suffering. Benevolence encourages truly beneficent, helpful actions, which will result from this fuller understanding of the patient's predicament. Finally, respectfulness encourages full respect for the patient as a self-realising individual. A dialogue conducted in accordance with this virtue will result in shared decision making, as opposed to the doctor or patient-directed approaches presumed by, respectively, paternalistic and autonomy-based models.[65]

One of the ways that virtuous conduct is demonstrated toward patients at the end of life is honoring their metaethical positions, regardless of whether they are fully formulated or emotive and intuited. Such respect is lacking in Fletcher's dismissal of the traditional notion of a transcendent Creator God who determines the beginning and end of life as

---

See Nafsika Athanassoulis, "Virtue Ethics," *Internet Encyclopedia of Philosophy*, accessed on August 12, 2019, www.iep.utm.edu/virtue/.

[64]Liezl van Zyl, *Death and Compassion: A Virtue-Based Approach to Euthanasia* (Farnham, Surrey, UK: Ashgate, 2000). For a paper surveying utilitarian consequentialism, Kantian deontology, and virtue ethics focusing on physician-assisted suicide and contending against the practice based on a virtue-ethics position, see Madeline Jordan, "The Ethical Considerations of Physician-Assisted Suicide," *Dialogue & Nexus* 4 (Fall 2016–Spring 2017): 1-7. Lynn A. Jansen argues for virtue ethics having a limited role in medicine, subordinating it to other ethical frameworks emphasizing moral principles and rules. Lynn A. Jansen, "The Virtues in Their Place: Virtue Ethics in Medicine," *Theoretical Medicine and Bioethics* 21, no. 3 (June 2000): 261-75, https://link.springer.com/article/10.1023/A:1009988003614. See also the following article by van Zyl contending from an Aristotelian stance on law and governance against legislation pertaining to euthanasia being based on moral and religious beliefs, including Aristotelian virtue ethics. Liezl van Zyl, "Euthanasia, Virtue Ethics and the Law," *New Zealand Bioethics Journal* 3, no. 1 (February 2002): 18-27, www.ncbi.nlm .nih.gov/pubmed/15587484.

[65]Richard Huxtable, review of "Death and Compassion: A Virtue-Based Approach to Euthanasia," *Journal of Medical Ethics* 28, no. 4 (August 2002): 278.

"a primitive 'God of the gaps'—a mysterious and awesome deity who filled the gaps of our knowledge."[66] Many individuals belonging to traditional faith communities cherish this framework (as do many leading ethicists of various religious and philosophical persuasions). It simply will not do to exhort medical professionals, as Fletcher does here, to dismiss this or any other concept of deity in end-of-life situations. An entangled ethic that takes seriously other belief systems and ways of life will embody or model respectful and genuine interest in a patient's convictions as they make end-of-life decisions. The caregiver who aims to provide a fitting response will honor the thoughts, beliefs, and convictions of the terminally ill patient.

Fletcher's conviction that the transcendent God "seriously speaking, is dead,"[67] if imposed on the terminally ill patient of a traditional religious bent, will harm trust in the medical professional who is overseeing care, as already noted in this chapter.[68] While it is important for an attending physician to have metaethical and ethical reasons for the medical actions they take, their actions must be performed with respect for the concerns and values of the entire community. Rather than standing over against the patient, they must work in harmony with the patient. As William Schweiker writes of Niebuhr's cathecontic model, "We answer to and with others," responding "'fittingly' within ongoing patterns and communities of interaction."[69]

Moreover, Fletcher's attempt to separate quality of life from sacredness of life emphases and choice of the former over the latter flies in the face of various religious traditions. The distinction is problematic. From a religious tradition's vantage point, it is a distinction without a difference. One need not abandon consideration of sacredness of life to account for quality-of-life concerns. One's beliefs play a key role in framing one's sense of quality of life, including how one approaches suffering. For now, however, it is worth drawing attention to some of the religious traditions that stand in opposition to Fletcher's orientation.

---

[66]Fletcher, "Ethics and Euthanasia," 672.

[67]Fletcher, "Ethics and Euthanasia," 672.

[68]Refer back to the discussion surrounding Wasserman et al., "Racial Differences in Attitudes Toward Euthanasia," 263-87.

[69]Schweiker, "Foreword" to Niebuhr, The Responsible Self, xi.

Select religious traditions, the sacred, and suicide. The official Roman Catholic teaching opposes physician-assisted suicide. Such opposition is based on the Roman Catholic conviction that all life comes from God. Even so, the Roman Catholic Church permits a terminally ill person to refuse extraordinary medical care that will only minimally prolong life.[70]

It is worth noting here that in Christian Scripture, there are several instances of suicide mentioned: Abimelech (Judges 9:50-55); Samson (Judges 16:25-30); Saul (1 Samuel 31:3-5); Saul's armor-bearer (1 Samuel 31:5); Ahithophel (2 Samuel 17:23); Zimri (1 Kings 16:15-20); and Judas (Matthew 27:3-4). While Scripture condemns murder in sweeping terms, it neither explicitly condones nor condemns these specific suicidal acts referenced here. The various texts suggest that each suicide was in some manner the consequence of the dead person's and others' failure to follow God's ways at key moments or during momentous seasons in life. That said, those who view suicide as an/the unforgiveable sin are making a severe stretch of the biblical corpus. For example, there is no mention of suicide as an "unforgiveable sin" in Matthew 12, where Jesus accuses his opponents of committing this gravest of acts. The context indicates that his adversaries claim that he performs his miraculous acts by the power of Satan, not the Holy Spirit.

Regardless, though, it is important to keep in mind that questions of physician-assisted suicide or the indefinite prolongation of one's life and related themes would not have entered the biblical authors' moral deliberations. This is due in part to radical differences in medical care from the ancient biblical world to contemporary society. Such differences include modern-day progress in medical technology in the effort to prolong life or hasten death. On this point, Pope John Paul II writes,

> It would be anachronistic to expect biblical revelation to make express reference to present-day issues concerning respect for elderly and sick persons, or to condemn explicitly attempts to hasten their end by force. The cultural and religious context of the Bible is in no way touched by such temptations; indeed, in that context the wisdom and experience of the

---

[70]See United States Conference of Catholic Bishops, "Assisted Suicide and Euthanasia: Beyond Terminal Illness," USCB.org, accessed on August 5, 2019, www.usccb.org/issues-and-action/human -life-and-dignity/assisted-suicide/to-live-each-day/upload/SuicideNonterminal2018.pdf.

elderly are recognized as a unique source of enrichment for the family and for society.[71]

The pope also claims that while life here on earth in the present is "not an absolute good for the believer," one must account for the fundamental truth that "no one, however, can arbitrarily choose whether to live or die; the absolute master of such a decision is the Creator alone, in whom 'we live and move and have our being' (Acts 17:28)."[72] Later, the pope defines euthanasia as the intention to cause death either by "an action or omission" with the aim of "eliminating all suffering." John Paul rejects euthanasia while also distinguishing it "from the decision to forego so-called 'aggressive medical treatment.' . . . It needs to be determined whether the means of treatment available are objectively proportionate to the prospects for improvement. To forego extraordinary or disproportionate means is not the equivalent of suicide or euthanasia; it rather expresses acceptance of the human condition in the face of death."[73]

Let's move from consideration of official Roman Catholic teaching to non-Christian traditions. The general consensus among Buddhists is that physician-assisted suicide and euthanasia are wrong.[74] While there is no official Hindu teaching on physician-assisted suicide and euthanasia, it is argued that to circumvent suffering in this life (which is assumed to be based on misdeeds committed in a prior existence) will only increase bad karma in the ensuing reincarnate state.[75] Islam claims that taking a life is a sin, since God is the author of life. Thus, physician-assisted suicide and euthanasia would appear to be prohibited.[76]

---

[71]John Paul II, *Evangelium Vitae* (Rome: Libreria Editrice Vaticana, 1995), section 46; http://w2.vatican.va/content/john-paul-ii/en/encyclicals/documents/hf_jp-ii_enc_25031995_evangelium-vitae.html.

[72]John Paul II, *Evangelium Vitae*, section 47.

[73]John Paul II, *Evangelium Vitae*, section 65.

[74]See "Religious Groups' Views on End-of-Life Issues," Pew Research Center, November 21, 2013, www.pewforum.org/2013/11/21/religious-groups-views-on-end-of-life-issues/. See also Damien Keown, "End of Life: The Buddhist View," *Lancet* 366 (2005): 952-55.

[75]See Pew Research Center, "Religious Groups' Views on End-of-Life Issues." See also Namita Nimbalkar, "Euthanasia: The Hindu Perspective," National Seminar on BIO ETHICS, January 24–25, 2007, Joshi-Bedekar College, Thane; https://www.vpmthane.org/Publications/Bio-Ethics/Namita%20Nimbalkar.pdf.

[76]See Pew Research Center, "Religious Groups' Views on End-of-Life Issues." See also Kiarash Aramesh and Heydar Shadi, "Euthanasia: An Islamic Ethical Perspective," *Iranian Journal of Allergy, Asthma and Immunology* 6, no. 5 (2007): 35-38. Even within Islam's focus on God as the author of

Judaism's three major branches forbid physician-assisted suicide and euthanasia. According to Rabbi Leonard Sharzer, "All three major Jewish movements in the United States—Orthodox, Conservative and Reform—prohibit suicide and assisted suicide, even in cases of painful, terminal illnesses. 'There are some minority views—that suicide might be permissible in rare, certain circumstances—but the majority view among all [movements] is that it's not permissible to take one's own life under any circumstances.'"[77]

Fletcher's dismissive attitude and antagonism of traditional religious models of the sacredness of life is especially disconcerting given his aim to convince medical professionals of the rightness of his stance. Would not those who look to Fletcher as a model for their practice dismiss out of hand in thought and action those patients as persons who adhere to traditional notions of God and the sanctity of life? Apart from the presumed merits of his arguments favoring physician-assisted death, Fletcher's rhetorical conduct and disposition does not reflect the necessary virtuous character traits of compassion, benevolence, and respectfulness required of the medical community. It is important that medical professionals, no matter their personal ethical convictions, enter respectful dialogue with their patients, especially given their vulnerable condition as they face the end of their lives.

Having drawn attention to Fletcher's problematic posture, it is also important that those who reject euthanasia policies do not portray their opponents, like Fletcher for example, as proponents of Nazi eugenics. Contrary to how Fletcher's critics might portray him, Fletcher rejects Nazi experimental and extermination policies. He describes

---

life, it is important to note that Islam's theological voluntarism leads to "locating ethical knowledge in the mind of God." This limits the role of humans and religious councils in establishing ethical norms, and "many significant ethical acts are left up to individual conscience, effectively establishing a limited right to privacy" (15). Jonathan E. Brockopp, "Taking Life and Saving Life: The Islamic Context," in *Islamic Ethics of Life: Abortion, War, and Euthanasia*, ed. Jonathan E. Brockopp (Columbia: University of South Carolina Press, 2003), 15.

[77]For the quote and a succinct account of the Jewish perspective, as well as other traditions, see Pew Research Center, "Religious Groups' Views on End-of-Life Issues," www.pewresearch.org /religion/2013/11/21/religious-groups-views-on-end-of-life-issues/. For more on Judaism's engagement of this theme, see the following brief account: Fred Rosner, "Euthanasia and Assisted Suicide: Some Biblical and Rabbinic Sources," https://www.myjewishlearning.com/article/euthanasia -jewish-biblical-and-rabbinic-sources/.

what the Nazis did as "merciless killing, either genocidal or for ruthless experimental purposes," rather than engaging in euthanasia within proper parameters.[78]

Moreover, one should not take the high moral ground against proponents of active euthanasia by insisting that by refusing to do anything to hasten a person's death, they are not responsible in some manner for their demise. As Fletcher writes, "It is naive and superficial to suppose that because we don't 'do anything positively' to hasten a patient's death we have thereby avoided complicity in his death. Not doing anything is doing something; it is a decision to act every bit as much as deciding for any other deed."[79]

The question is not whether one is responsible, but whether a person is irresponsible in what one chooses to do or not do. The medical professionals and various other stakeholders at the bedside of the dying patient need to account as keenly as possible for what is going on, what they should care about, and what the fitting response is to the situation at hand. It will do them no good to kick the can of decision-making down the hospital or care facility corridor to another party.

On the subject of responsible action and kicking the moral can down the corridor, Aristotle would instruct us that only someone who is free from compulsion can act virtuously on an ethical matter. Thus, a preprogrammed moral machine in a hospital setting could never act virtuously. Only persons can. Speaking of machines, prejudices and racial biases come into play there just as they do in other contexts involving medical decisions being made related to vulnerable communities. Like us, machines are far from operating in an objective manner. They reflect the biases of their creators.[80] If society ever gets to the point of claiming that a machine should make the decision for us, it would be morally irresponsible. Moreover, doing so would only lead us further down the road from a culture of persons to things.

[78]Fletcher, "Ethics and Euthanasia," 671.
[79]Fletcher, "Ethics and Euthanasia," 675.
[80]Consider the following article's claim that artificial intelligence is becoming racialized: Stephen Buranyi, "Rise of the Racist Robots—How AI Is Learning All Our Worst Impulses," *Guardian*, August 8, 2017, www.theguardian.com/inequality/2017/aug/08/rise-of-the-racist-robots-how-ai-is-learning-all-our-worst-impulses.

Decisions on end-of-life care involving a conscious and mentally stable patient who wishes to die is one of the most challenging issues a medical professional will face. Regardless of where we stand, empathy is required of all parties in the decision-making process.[81] The issue before us is perhaps even more difficult to process than the subject of abortion given that the fetus cannot engage in rational deliberations. Empathy is required for engaging the patient, as well as the various other stakeholders, as they suffer through exceedingly difficult and painful end-of-life care decisions.

Speaking of empathy, the Christian takes comfort from knowing that God is not distant and indifferent but enters our suffering. The Christian is called to enter others' suffering in view of God's intimate care. I now turn to address this subject.

CRUCIFORM SUFFERING, RADICAL EMPATHY, AND THE ULTIMATE END OF LIFE

Roman Catholic ethicist John Di Camillo contends that suicide often results from such challenges as "poor pain management, despair and loneliness, or the feeling of being a burden on family and others. These conditions, he believes, can be addressed with better palliative and psychological care." Di Camillo adds that terminally ill people often receive insufficient care due to our own fears and inability to come to terms with death.[82] It is important that people of all walks of life take to heart these vital issues since death will come to us all. Moreover, the Christian community must be vigilant and address these matters in view of Jesus' cruciform identity, which shapes the church's existence. It is one thing to be critical of suicide. It is quite another to address some of the medical, emotional, and psychological challenges so that people will be less prone to take their own lives.

Here Henri Nouwen's insights prove invaluable. In *The Wounded Healer*, Nouwen writes, "A minister is not a doctor whose primary task

---

[81]Note, for example, the agonizing account found here: Catherine Sonquist Forest, "I'm a Doctor. Here's What It's Like Helping Terminally Ill Patients End Their Lives," *Vox*, September 21, 2017, www.vox.com/first-person/2017/9/21/16335534/aid-in-dying-california-legal-end-of-life.

[82]See Pew Research Center, "Religious Groups' Views on End-of-Life Issues."

is to take away pain. Rather, he deepens the pain to a level where it can be shared."[83] This statement bears on the Christian life in two ways. First, Jesus is the ultimate wounded healer. Second, he makes possible the minister's ability to engage severe pain in a deeply meaningful and abiding way. Those who do not understand why people take their lives have not endured such pain. We need to share life with those who are struggling. We must connect with them rather than condemn them. Solidarity is key.

Jesus fosters a community of fellow sufferers. An embodied ethic that features Jesus as the wounded healer deepens a person's pain in community rather than isolates the wounded party and their grief. Those who embrace this embodied ethic take pain to the level where others share in it. Jesus cultivates a community of faith that accounts for his passion and glorious scars. This fellowship of believers identifies empathically with one another and a suffering world in view of Jesus.

This emphasis on solidarity calls to mind Dietrich Bonhoeffer's account of Jesus as the man for others and the church as the community for others in *Letters and Papers from Prison*.[84] Bonhoeffer speaks against a "God of the gaps" theology and writes in the affirmative about God's death. Bonhoeffer's use of this terminology differs from Fletcher's account noted earlier. Fletcher's framework bears similarities to the "God is dead" movement's conception. While the "God is dead" proponents pay tribute to Bonhoeffer, they distort his paradigm.

Bonhoeffer writes about God's death and the need to move beyond the God who fills gaps: "God consents to be pushed out of the world and onto the cross: God is weak and powerless in the world and in precisely this way, and only so, is at our side and helps us." It is only the suffering God who helps us, according to Bonhoeffer.[85] While Bonhoeffer appears to place suffering and omnipotence in opposition to one another here, the apostle Paul's articulation of Jesus' suffering and

---

[83]Henri J. M. Nouwen, *The Wounded Healer: Ministry in Contemporary Society* (New York: Image, 1979), 92-93.

[84]Dietrich Bonhoeffer, *Letters and Papers from Prison*, ed. John W. de Gruchy, Dietrich Bonhoeffer Works, vol. 8 (Minneapolis: Fortress, 2010), 501, 503.

[85]Bonhoeffer, *Letters and Papers from Prison*, 479. On God of the gaps or deus ex machina, see *Letters and Papers from Prison*, 366 and 450.

weakness in 1 Corinthians 1 does not negate divine power but frames it in terms of the weakness of the cross. God revealed in Jesus enters powerfully into our struggle in a weak, vulnerable, and healing manner. The church must follow suit and become a community of fellow sufferers through which relational healing occurs. This theological paradigm is critically important for fostering better palliative and psychological care for dying patients.

Fletcher fails to account for Jesus' decisive dynamic of being incarnate as God in the gallows of human grief and pain. Jesus bears the sickness unto death. He does not stand over and above us but enters this world to provide relational healing as he participates in our suffering. He goes so far as to refuse to drink the wine mixed with myrrh to dull the pain of the crucifixion (Mark 15:23), bearing our sickness as the wounded healer, and redeeming us in view of our future hope at his return. Moreover, through the Spirit of Jesus, the community of faith is called to participate in Jesus' deep empathic dive into the dying person's struggle. The dying person is not left to die in isolation, or to be reduced to a pathetic caricature of their former self. God's love embodied through the community of faith creates and preserves the affection for the terminally ill person, not the other way around. The aim is not to end life, but to pursue their ultimate *end* or destiny together in the community of the wounded healer.

This point on "end" leads us to make the following point about quality-of-life concerns. Fletcher, and Niebuhr before him, raised the important question: What is the fitting response to a given situation? Seeking to discern what one's fitting response should be apart from accounting for one's telos would be impossible from a historical Christian perspective, as well as Aristotelian framework. The same is true of "quality of life" considerations. From a historical Christian vantage point, "quality of life" is too subjective a category and must be framed in view of the sacredness of life. Such subjectivity fails to account for the objective grounding of humanity in Jesus who is God's image.

Here it is worth drawing attention to Alasdair MacIntyre's treatment of subjectivism in *After Virtue*. MacIntyre argues that emotivism on the one hand and consequentialism/utilitarianism on the other hand are two sides of the same genealogical coin.[86] Together they constitute the aftermath of the disintegration of the original virtuous whole bound up with traditional theism, most notably the Christian faith. While for virtue ethics, humanity is presently in a deficient state proceeding toward a future ideal state, emotivism fosters good wishes for the future, yet without clear ethical content or direction. Moral statements have no ontological basis, but merely "emote" or express the preferences of the individual or group desiring them. On the other side, utilitarianism is a kind of immanentized teleology, where the pursuit of an ideal future or eschatological state of being is the greatest amount of pleasure or happiness for the majority. On this view, all means become subordinate to happiness without any real consideration of the need to move from a deficient, fallen, or corrupt state of affairs to one that is inherently and objectively virtuous. All these ethical systems have different forms of "eschatology," which drive the guiding principles for ethical decisions.

For MacIntyre, emotivism and consequentialism operate in a piecemeal way. According to his genealogy of morals, these systems were originally united as elements of virtue but were then separated out and forced to fend for themselves. Both emotivism and utilitarianism suffer because the resources originally available in the traditioned whole are now expected to be compensated for by happiness defined by way of pleasure rather than virtue.[87] Something similar could be said of situation ethics given its subjective emphasis on quality of life, love, and suffering.

The Christian past and its eschatological vision would not separate virtue from love or even suffering. Suffering can play a critical role in the formation of virtue. Even Jesus learned obedience through his

---

[86]Alasdair MacIntyre, *After Virtue: A Study in Moral Theory*, 3rd ed. (Notre Dame, IN: University of Notre Dame Press, 2007), 51-79.

[87]I do not intend the discussion above to take away from consideration of all utilitarian forms of argumentation in rejecting physician-assisted death. For example, from a utilitarian vantage point, could one not argue that increasing support for vastly improving palliative care drugs to minimize pain would reduce suicides? Furthermore, would not prohibition take pressure off doctors from various parties, minimize the risk of abuse, and diminish the appeal of suicide in other domains? One of the weaknesses of utilitarianism, beyond what MacIntyre argues above, is that it presumes omniscience. One does not know the outcome. What if a miracle drug were to emerge within weeks that would advance life and even effect a cure for the patient pondering suicide?

suffering: "During the days of Jesus' life on earth, he offered up prayers and petitions with fervent cries and tears to the one who could save him from death, and he was heard because of his reverent submission. Son though he was, he learned obedience from what he suffered and, once made perfect, he became the source of eternal salvation for all who obey him" (Hebrews 5:7-9). Jesus pleaded with God to remove the cup of passion that he was prepared to drink. Still, Jesus submitted and entrusted his life and future to God (Luke 22:42). He did not take matters into his own hands.

Redemptive suffering is not isolated to the Christian tradition. In Islam, suffering is viewed as a form of purification: "In the Islamic tradition, end-of-life suffering is seen as a way to purify previous sins so that by the time you meet God, you do so in a [more pure] state."[88] The point here in this section is not that suffering has inherent value, or that one should not ever use medicines to alleviate or reduce pain, but rather that bringing an end to suffering is not ever the ultimate good or end. We should not use medical technology to prolong the inevitable. Nor should we hasten or precipitate the inescapable or probable either.[89] We need to approach suffering, pain relief, and healing from the standpoint of our ultimate end as humans before God and others (Mark 12:30-31).

While we should not treat the life given to us as an idol but rather worship the Giver of Life, still, we should cherish life, not death. Given the intrinsic value of humans, we should seek to preserve and cultivate life as long as and as fittingly as possible, using only those treatments that, as John Paul II wrote, "are objectively proportionate to the prospects for improvement," foregoing only "extraordinary or disproportionate means." There should be no intended "action or omission" to end a life to eliminate "all suffering."[90]

Similarly, US Supreme Court Justice Neil Gorsuch writes, "All human beings are intrinsically valuable and the intentional taking of human life

---

[88]See Pew Research Center, "Religious Groups' Views on End-of-Life Issues."

[89]Regarding "probable," there are situations where a patient is misdiagnosed and recovers. Moreover, one should be alert to the possibility of new medications or procedures in the works and under review that could lead to a cure or healing.

[90]John Paul II, *Evangelium Vitae*, section 65.

by private persons is always wrong."[91] Later in his book he argues based not on "abstract logical constructs (or religious beliefs)," but on the basis of "practical human experience," in keeping with what he finds Aristotle doing in the *Nicomachean Ethics*:[92]

> We seek to protect and preserve life for life's own sake in everything from our most fundamental laws of homicide to our road traffic regulations to our largest governmental programs for health and social security. We have all witnessed, as well, family, friends, or medical workers who have chosen to provide years of loving care to persons who may suffer from Alzheimer's or other debilitating illnesses precisely because they are human persons, not because doing so instrumentally advances some other hidden objective. This is not to say that all persons would always make a similar choice, but the fact that some people have made such a choice is some evidence that life itself is a basic good.[93]

During the US Senate confirmation hearings for his nomination to the US Supreme Court, Gorsuch spoke of the import of powerful drugs used to alleviate pain in palliative care: "Anything necessary to alleviate pain would be appropriate and acceptable, even if it caused death, not intentionally, but knowingly."[94] Traditional hospice care resonates with this overarching framework: "We do not hasten death or prolong life. We provide compassionate care up to the patient's final day of life."[95]

---

[91]Neil M. Gorsuch, *The Future of Assisted Suicide and Euthanasia* (Princeton, NJ: Princeton University Press, 2006), 4-5.

[92]Gorsuch, *The Future of Assisted Suicide and Euthanasia*, 158. Gorsuch's appeal to "practical human experience" resonates with his affirmation of natural law. Natural law operates according to reason apart from the dictates of a divine authority. Regarding such freedom for natural moral reasoning, a Roman Catholic theologian claims that "the autonomous nature of moral reasoning protects the moral law from being imposed heteronomously by even a divine authority." Thomas R. Kopfensteiner, "Death with Dignity: A Roman Catholic Perspective," *Linacre Quarterly* 63, no. 4 (November 1996): 65. Following the orientation of Aquinas, for whom grace does not destroy but completes nature, scriptural revelation complements and enriches natural law, but does not overturn or impose itself upon it. See also the following account of a secular natural law ethical perspective on the subject of euthanasia and physician-assisted suicide: Craig Paterson, *Assisted Suicide and Euthanasia: A Natural Law Ethics Approach*, Live Questions in Ethics and Moral Philosophy (New York: Routledge, 2017).

[93]Gorsuch, *Future of Assisted Suicide and Euthanasia*, 158-59.

[94]See the video that includes Gorsuch's Supreme Court Justice confirmation hearing at "Physician-Assisted Suicide Fast Facts," CNN, January 3, 2019, www.cnn.com/2014/11/26/us/physician-assisted-suicide-fast-facts/index.html.

[95]"Common Hospice Concerns," Providence Health & Services Washington, accessed on August 7, 2019, https://www.providence.org/locations/wa/hospice-of-seattle/frequently-asked-questions#tabcontent-1-pane-2.

It is worth noting that according to *Modern Healthcare*, concerns have been raised that the debate over physician-assisted suicide has distracted from the need to continue improving palliative and hospice care treatment, as well as confusing hospice care with "medical aid in dying." Regarding the point of confusion, *Modern Healthcare* quotes Warren Fong, MD, president of the Medical Oncology Association of Southern California: "There's a really big misconception about what hospice is, and this whole suicide debate has worsened that misconception." "When people go on hospice, they think, 'I'm giving up, I'm failing my family. I'm committing suicide.' It's not that, it's just acceptance that we're humans."[96] Regarding the concern over distraction, it is claimed that those states where physician-assisted suicide is prohibited see marked improvements in palliative care involving powerful drugs intended to reduce or manage pain.[97]

All these issues are important. Even so, it is even more important that we do not get distracted from accounting for the ultimate concern: one's quality of life must be framed in terms of the sanctity of life grounded in the reality of the triune God who unconditionally, lovingly affirms and confirms the dying person's dignity in communal terms.

LOVE AS THE END OF LIFE

In closing, I return to Seneca's statement quoted at the beginning of the chapter: "A whole lifetime is needed to learn how to live, and—perhaps you'll find this more surprising—a whole lifetime is needed to learn how to die."[98] What does a good death entail? No external pressure. No romanticized ideal. No desire to escape life's challenges, however severe, or

---

[96]Lisa Schencker, "Assisted-Suicide Debate Focuses Attention on Palliative, Hospice Care," *Modern Healthcare*, May 16, 2015, www.modernhealthcare.com/article/20150516/MAGAZINE/305169982.

[97]A Johns Hopkins University School of Medicine palliative care expert claimed that "in Maryland as well as in every state that had passed such legislation [prohibiting physician-assisted suicide], there was an increase in the legitimate prescription of opioids and other strong medications used for pain control. Indeed, physicians universally expressed a mixture of relief and elation on knowing that, for the first time, such protective legislation existed." See F. Michael Gloth, III, ed., *Handbook of Pain Relief in Older Adults: An Evidence-Based Approach* (New York: Humana Press, 2004), 193. Regarding initial findings concerning the prescribed usage of opioids in Oregon in comparison with the nation since Oregon's Death with Dignity Act's enactment in 1997, see Susan Tolle et al., "Trends in Opioid Use over Time: 1997 to 1999," *Journal of Palliative Medicine* 7, no. 1 (2004): 39-45.

[98]Seneca, *How to Die*, xx.

to alleviate suffering as the ultimate end. A willingness to suffer for a noble cause.[99] What does a good life entail? The extension of life in a merely quantitative manner will not do, nor senseless suffering. The one who lives a good life struggles and suffers and may very well die for noble ideals in service to God and humanity.

The preceding reflections call to mind the life of Socrates. Socrates was found guilty of corrupting youth, preaching strange gods, and undermining Athenian democracy. Having been found guilty, he was required by Athenian law to serve as his own executioner and commit suicide by drinking hemlock.[100] Most likely, he could have avoided this fate if he had requested exile. Given that he did not request exile, he could have been forced to swallow the poison if he had resisted. The person who administered the hemlock instructed Socrates on what to do upon drinking it. Every indication suggests that Socrates knowingly and willingly chose to consume the full contents of the poisonous cup that would kill him, the consequence of living in keeping with his ideals.[101] A life for which nothing is worth dying is a life not worth living. If ever suicide is considered a noble death, this was it.

While Jesus did not kill himself, he could have avoided death by hiding himself as he had done in the past (John 8:59), or by calling on a vast multitude of angels to deliver him (Matthew 26:53). He voluntarily laid down his life for his followers and for the world. He had authority to lay it down and take it up again, but he did not kill himself. Others killed him (see John 10:15-18). Each in their own way, Socrates and Jesus gave themselves for their ideals and followers so that they could truly live freely, while they entrusted themselves to heaven and in hopes of a better life to come.

Learning how to live and how to die involves learning how to love well. Jesus told his followers: "Greater love has no one than this: to lay down

[99]Here it is worth noting that the Japanese samurai code of Bushido entailed ritual suicide known as "seppuku." Seppuku was intended to demonstrate loyalty and honor, as well as a sign of protest. It did not entail a desire to alleviate suffering. It was a painfully slow and agonizing form of suicide. Michael Ray et al., "Seppuku," *Encyclopedia Britannica*, www.britannica.com/topic/seppuku.

[100]See Plato, *The Last Days of Socrates: Euthyphro, The Apology, Crito, Phaedo*, trans. Hugh Tredennick (New York: Penguin Books, 1959); Charles Freeman, *The Greek Achievement: The Foundation of the Western World*, 1st ed. (New York: Penguin Putnam, 1999); I. F. Stone, *The Trial of Socrates* (New York: Anchor Books, 1989).

[101]R.G. Frey, "Did Socrates Commit Suicide?" *Philosophy* 53, no. 203 (January 1978): 106-8.

one's life for one's friends" (John 15:13). Moreover, God gave his Son to the world that is terminally ill from sin in a spirit of unconditional, sacrificial love (John 3:16). The God who comes to us in Jesus through the Spirit is the Master Physician who astutely and empathically tends to us and ministers healing to our persons in holistic love (see Matthew 12:9-21; Luke 5:31-32).

Learning to love patients well is one of the best forms of preventive medicine. While it is important in medicine to "Do no harm," as professional medical ethics requires, it is equally important or even more important to "try to prevent it," as Geoffrey Hughes writes in the *Emergency Medical Journal*.[102] One key area of prevention involves changing attitudes and behaviors of A&E staff (emergency department personnel) toward patients who have harmed themselves. According to the Royal College of Psychiatrists, a survey showed that "in a nutshell, patients are better able to cope after discharge from A&E if staff are respectful, positive and nonjudgmental. The significant minority who are told that they are wasting hospital time and resources, often coupled with an undercurrent of hostility, can and do self-discharge to self-harm again almost immediately."[103]

This point is not simply for emergency department staff to ponder, or for those prone to self-inflicted harm. We should all take to heart the importance of love as preventive medicine, as we are all caregivers and patients in one way or another in times of crisis. We will not all agree on physician-assisted suicide. However, hopefully we will all agree on how important it is to treat every patient with respect, being nonjudgmental, and positively affirming their dignity and worth. It makes an incredible difference when such constructive attitudes and behaviors are evident. We should cultivate that same mindset in our treatment of others at home, at the workplace, and in the market.

Kant was right: we should never treat people as mere means to ends. Even so, as with the Hippocratic Oath, more is needed than a negative formulation. Preventive medicine finds a fitting companion in the

---

[102]Geoffrey Hughes, "First Do No Harm; Then Try to Prevent It," *Emergency Medical Journal* 24, no. 5 (May 2007): 314, www.ncbi.nlm.nih.gov/pmc/articles/PMC2658469/.
[103]Hughes, "First Do No Harm," 314.

positive form of personalist ethics: "The person is a good towards which the only proper and adequate attitude is love."[104]

The global pandemic has waged war on our psyches and our lungs and has left an indelible impact physically and socially. It is critically important that we learn how to love each person before us. As someone who lost his elderly mother just before Covid-19 hit, and whose adult son was at first in a coma and now in a minimally conscious state following a traumatic brain injury in 2021, I am learning how to live and love my neighbor better.

I have witnessed cruelty, indifference, negligence, and incompetence by those responsible for tending to patients and engaging family members. I have also witnessed exceptional empathy, keen attentiveness, courage, and excellence in patient and family care. What have those responsible for caring for my son witnessed in me?

We are all on life support in one way or another, including the much-needed loving support of others. Secure attachments help us cope, hope, and increase in resilience. We need to learn how to care well for others, whether they are medical personnel, patients, family members, or friends. It is important that we treat one another as persons, each of whom is a good worthy of love. Patients and caregivers alike are loved by God and have invaluable worth, which no insurance company can quantify, or inheritance can match. We are all made for more than the mere end of life, or a hospital and care facility stay. We are made for love, which is life's ultimate end.

A good life and a good death do not involve prolonging the inevitable,[105] or intentionally hastening death. Both efforts—prolonging the inevitable or hastening death—wage war against our inherent dignity.[106] The New

---

[104]Karol Wojtyla, *Love & Responsibility*, rev. ed. (San Francisco: Ignatius Press, 1993), 41.

[105]This notion appears to conflict with the findings of Andrea C. Phelps, Paul K. Maciejewski, Matthew Nilsson et al., "Religious Coping and Use of Intensive Life-Prolonging Care Near Death in Patients with Advanced Cancer," *Journal of American Medical Association* 301, no. 11 (March 18, 2009): 1140-47, https://jamanetwork.com/journals/jama/fullarticle/183578. The counterintuitive conclusion of the study reads, "Positive religious coping in patients with advanced cancer is associated with receipt of intensive life-prolonging medical care near death. Further research is needed to determine the mechanisms for this association."

[106]For concern over how to die well and affirm or preserve human dignity, see Lydia S. Dugdale, *The Lost Art of Dying: Reviving Forgotten Wisdom* (New York: HarperOne, 2020).

Testament makes clear that humanity's ultimate comfort and hope are not found in extending this life quantitatively, nor by way of avoiding suffering and trying to escape death, or quickening life's end. Human personhood is inviolable in this life and beyond. Jesus encourages his followers that though they mourn now, they will be comforted (Matthew 5:4). They who are meek will inherit the earth (Matthew 5:5). Though they experience suffering and even persecution, the kingdom of heaven belongs to them (Matthew 5:10). Christians' ultimate comfort and eschatological hope is that they belong to the Wounded Healer who loves them, who suffered beyond comprehension in spirit and in body for their sake, and who now lives an indestructible life as the resurrected, ascended, and returning one. Blessed are those who cling to the divine name Jesus shares with the Father and the Spirit. Jesus will be with them always, every day throughout the age (Matthew 28:18-20), in all matters of life and death.

If you or someone you know is thinking of suicide, call the 988 Suicide and Crisis Lifeline for support and resources.

PART THREE

FROM CLOSE TO HOME AND ACROSS THE GLOBE TO OUTER SPACE

8

MORE THAN RACIAL DIVISIONS

Race, Power, and the Beloved Community

DEEP DIVISIONS ALONG RACIAL LINES characterize our society today. This chapter seeks to move beyond in-group dynamics where we are prone to dehumanize other racial groups to maintain our sense of security and self-worth. Our sense of self-worth should *not* come *at the expense of* the other *but in solidarity with* one another as human persons. People are more than the evolving social and psychological racial constructs that we impose and that we often wrongly label as units of biology. Such moves turn racial inequities into self-fulfilling prophecies. Our battle is not with one another and different racial groups, but with indifference, disgust, and hate. These disturbing emotions and affections fuel power imbalances as well as feed off them. They foster arbitrary and irrational racial divisions. We must break down walls of racial division and private affection through benevolent regard for all people. Private affection makes no space for love of those who do not belong to our nuclear families and sociodemographic affinity groups. We need to cultivate benevolent regard for *all* people.

The argument will proceed as follows: first, I will attend to the way racial constructs shift and reinforce power imbalances; second, I will go in search of moral laws and spiritual values that do not change based on shifts in ideological constructs and inequitable power dynamics; and third, I will highlight the need for virtuous and coercive love to dismantle impersonal and inequitable structures and build what Dr. King called the beloved community.

ON RACE: DEEP BENEATH THE COLOR OF ONE'S SKIN

E. O. Wilson writes in *The Social Conquest of Earth*, "To form groups, drawing visceral comfort and pride from familiar fellowship, and to defend the group enthusiastically against rival groups—these are among the absolute universals of human nature and hence of culture."[1] A few pages later, Wilson writes, "The elementary drive to form and take deep pleasure from in-group membership easily translates at a higher level into tribalism. People are prone to ethnocentrism. It is an uncomfortable fact that even when given a guilt-free choice, individuals prefer the company of others of the same race, nation, clan, and religion."[2] Wilson turns from "tribalism" to war. While "tribalism" is "a fundamental human trait," war is viewed "as humanity's hereditary curse." Upon discussing the conflict leading to genocide involving the Hutus and Tutsis in Rwanda, Wilson remarks, "Once a group has been split off and sufficiently dehumanized, any brutality can be justified, at any level, and at any size of the victimized group up to and including race and nation."[3] The lines of demarcation between groups can be physical, ethnic, national, political, religious, and so on. Wilson notes that they can even be arbitrarily assigned.[4] The disturbing desire for mastery over others leads to concocting and projecting racial lines of separation. In short, it is one more way in which we are prone to divide and conquer.

An *Independent* article argues that the conflict between the Hutus and Tutsis was not tribal or ethnic. John Lichfield writes, "By all the most common definitions, Hutus and Tutsis are the same people, which makes their violent history even more tragically incomprehensible to outsiders."[5] While the genocide is incomprehensible on one level, Wilson maintains that the immediate cause was political and social. He goes further and claims that ultimately the source of the conflict was overcrowding.[6]

---

[1]Edward O. Wilson, *The Social Conquest of Earth* (New York: Liveright, 2012), 57.
[2]Wilson, *Social Conquest of Earth*, 60.
[3]Wilson, *Social Conquest of Earth*, 63.
[4]Wilson, *Social Conquest of Earth*, 59.
[5]John Lichfield, "Guide to the Zaire Crisis: The Difference Between a Hutu and a Tutsi," *Independent*, November 16, 1996, www.independent.co.uk/news/world/guide-to-the-zaire-crisis-the-difference-between-a-hutu-and-a-tutsi-1352558.html.
[6]Wilson, *Social Conquest of Earth*, 63. In response to Wilson, if overcrowding were the ultimate issue, why doesn't tribal differentiation and genocide happen more often under crowded conditions? The

What Wilson describes as the emergence of "tribalism" and "ethnocentrism" from "the elementary drive to form and take deep pleasure from in-group membership" is not simply a problem in African countries such as Rwanda and Burundi. We find the same problematic dynamic at work in the United States of America. So, let's shift our attention to the United States where the lines of separation and subjugation are often physical, as in skin color, but not always so.

Take, for example, the fact that Americans first viewed the Irish as "Negroes." Members of the surrounding community sometimes called the Irish "Negroes turned inside out" and African Americans "smoked Irish." However, when it came to the abolition of slavery, the Irish did not support African Americans because of Irish people's desire to climb the social ladder in the United States.[7]

In the South, prior to the Civil War, skin color was not the determinative line of demarcation between the "deserving" and "undeserving." Here we see how subjective skin color is as a separator between people and between those who rule and those who are ruled. The line of demarcation between the two classes of people prior to the Civil War was whether someone was a slave owner or a slave, not whether they were Black or White. Consider the following claim in an article titled "The Invisible Line Between Black and White":

> Before the Civil War, the most important dividing line in the South was not between black and white, but between slave and free. Those categories track each other, but not perfectly, and what really mattered above all to most people when they had to make a choice was that slavery as an institution had to be preserved. But by the 19th century, there were enough people with some African ancestry who were living as respectable white people—people who owned slaves or supported slavery—that to insist on racial purity would actually disrupt the slaveholding South.[8]

---

ultimate cause was likely that the colonial manipulation of the Tutsi elite to rule over the Hutus created a huge animosity that broke free when the Hutus gained power.

[7]See Ciara Kenny, "When the Irish Became White: Immigrants in Mid-19th Century US," *Irish Times*, February 12, 2013.

[8]T. A. Frail, "The Invisible Line Between Black and White," Smithsonian.com, February 18, 2011, www.smithsonianmag.com/history/the-invisible-line-between-black-and-white-335353/#SXpSDKJ5PJtO5okI.99.

It was not simply the antebellum South where people of different racial ancestry were living as "respectable white people." The same kind of adaptability manifests itself today. Contrary to all the talk that white supremacy will cease to exist with the browning of America, John Blake maintains that white supremacy will continue unabated, albeit with a "tan." White supremacy, which Blake claims emerged on the scene about five hundred years ago in Europe "to justify slavery and colonialism," will not go quietly or quickly into the night. The pull and impulse to adapt and identify as White remains quite strong at the present time. The article states, "Whiteness isn't a fixed identity; it's like taffy—it expands to accommodate new members, if they have the right look." As with Irish, Italians, and Jews in the past, who were able to make the switch to being considered "fully" White in the United States,[9] Blake wonders how the growing Hispanic or Latino population will seek to present itself. Blake notes, "The enhanced status and socio-economic benefits that come from identifying as White will be too tempting for many to ignore."[10]

The ever-evolving dynamics of racial separation and disparity are surprising to many people and blind them to how racialized our country continues to be. We do not live in a postracialized society. We must account for what Michael Emerson and Christian Smith argue in *Divided by Faith*: racialization operates by evolving variables, not constants.[11] It continues to manifest itself in different ways. We have moved from slavery to segregation to post–civil rights era status structures with accompanying "benefits."

---

[9]David R. Roediger, *Working Toward Whiteness: How America's Immigrants Became White—The Strange Journey from Ellis Island to the Suburbs*, updated ed. (New York: Basic Books, 2018); Noel Ignatiev, *How the Irish Became White* (New York: Routledge Classics, 2009). More broadly, whiteness has dominated popular culture globally for a considerable period of time, as reflected in the massive popularity of skin lighteners. See Lynn M. Thomas, *Beneath the Surface: A Transnational History of Skin Lighteners* (Durham, NC: Duke University Press, 2020).

[10]John Blake, "White Supremacy, with a Tan," CNN, September 4, 2021, www.cnn.com/2021/09/04/us/census-browning-of-america-myth-blake/index.html. Refer also to this Pew study: Mark Hugo Lopez, Ana Gonzalez-Barrera, and Gustavo López, "Hispanic Identity Fades Across Generations as Immigrant Connections Fall Away," Pew Research Center, December 20, 2017, www.pewresearch.org/hispanic/2017/12/20/hispanic-identity-fades-across-generations-as-immigrant-connections-fall-away/.

[11]Michael O. Emerson and Christian Smith, *Divided by Faith: Evangelical Religion and the Problem of Race in America* (New York: Oxford University Press, 2000), 8.

Speaking of the ever-evolving dynamics of race, race is a social rather than biological reality. In other words, "'Race' was, and is, something we created."[12] Race is real. However, it is not biological, but psychological, according to anthropologist Agustín Fuentes. Racial dynamics are deep beneath the color of one's skin in the mind, as well as in the social structures we create. Thus, its impact is not simply in the head. It frames analysis of society in such a way that we tend to excuse disparities between communities as natural phenomenon. As Fuentes writes, all humans belong to the same biological race. Yet "societies, like the U.S., construct racial classifications, not as units of biology, but as ways to lump together groups of people with varying historical, linguistic, ethnic, religious, or other backgrounds. These categories are not static; they change over time as societies grow, diversify, and alter their social, political and historical makeups." Thus, to view race through a biological lens rather than through its function in society is to commit what Fuentes calls "the biologized racial fallacy."[13]

This biological fallacy is extremely treacherous and destructive, as Fuentes shows. When we construe racial dynamics in biological terms, we tend to look at social disproportions and inequities as unavoidable and inevitable forces of nature. While not natural or biological in origin, such social dynamics and constructs can still negatively impact us biologically, as Fuentes reasons. Social configurations along racialized lines affect minorities in a variety of ways, including their access to good health care and their "racialized self-image." In turn, such limited access and distorted self-imaging impact their biological development and immune systems.[14] We end up blaming the victims of racialization: for example, the faulty line of reasoning is that Blacks are more prone to

---

[12]David P. Gushee and Glen H. Stassen, *Kingdom Ethics: Following Jesus in Contemporary Context*, 2nd ed. (Grand Rapids, MI: Eerdmans, 2017), 407. Refer to their discussion of critical race theory and White privilege on 397, 406-9.

[13]Agustín Fuentes, "Race Is Real, But Not in the Way Many People Think—Busting the Myth of Biological Race," *Psychology Today*, April 9, 2012, www.psychologytoday.com/us/blog/busting-myths -about-human-nature/201204/race-is-real-not-in-the-way-many-people-think.

[14]Fuentes, "Race Is Real." See also Troy Duster, "Race and Reification in Science," *Science* 307 (2005): 1050-51; Nina G. Jablonski, *Skin: A Natural History* (Berkeley: University of California Press, 2013), 117-18; Clarence C. Gravlee, "How Race Becomes Biology: Embodiment of Social Inequality," *American Journal of Physical Anthropology* 139 (2009): 47-57.

poor health in certain cases (not to mention poverty and imprisonment) because they are not White.

We need to reconfigure our understanding of race and view it as psychological, not biological in origin. After all, all people are *Homo sapiens sapiens*. Still, the propensity to objectify and reduce others and promote one's own group based on one's skin color or other features and traits is a perennial problem.

As already noted, Blake reasons that Europeans concocted the racial hierarchy that serves as the underpinning of white supremacy five hundred years ago "to justify slavery and colonialism."[15] However, the historical and cultural forces go back even further. They also manifest themselves in the East and Middle East apart from and prior to European sources, including the interpretation of Holy Scripture.

Malcolm X argued that Muslims in the Arab world had been guilty of enslaving Black Africans, just as was true of European Christians. He made this claim while a member of the Nation of Islam to push back at orthodox Muslims who charged his movement with inspiring racial hostility.[16] Malcolm X was right. In fact, the move to associate servitude with skin color can be traced back several centuries prior to the rise of colonialism in Christian Europe and even appears in Christian, Muslim, and Jewish readings of sacred literature.

The factors and reasons that lead people to biologize skin color are no doubt varied. Sometimes the psychological and social constructs surface in the pursuit of military conquest and wealth. As noted above, such factors influence how many have read the Bible and sacred literature over the centuries. Let's consider briefly this subject of sacred texts and skin color.

According to David Goldenberg, there was a "gradual introduction of blackness into the retelling of the biblical story" of Noah's curse of slavery

---

[15]Blake, "White Supremacy, with a Tan."

[16]Bruce Perry, *Malcolm: The Life of a Man Who Changed Black America* (Barrytown, NY: Station Hill, 1991), 268. Malcolm X's views on race evolved. Early on, he was a principal architect in championing a form of Islam that privileged Blacks (Perry, *Malcolm*, 195-96). He was a forceful proponent of Black separatism (187). Later, Malcolm X's views on separatism became more ambiguous (273). His views on Whites evolved, helped by his trip to Mecca, as he worshiped alongside white-faced and blue-eyed Muslims from around the world (268, 271-72). Malcolm X's perspective on Islam, including Black Islam, also changed. Islam was not only for Blacks (206, 268, 271-72).

on Canaan. The story "was originally colorless." However, that perspective changed beginning in the fourth century AD.

Beginning with the fourth-century Syriac Christian *Cave of Treasures*, a biblical tradition that saw Canaan as cursed with slavery now included a statement informing the reader or listener that Canaan was the ancestor of dark-skinned people. The link of blackness and slavery in the various versions of this work is clear, though implicit, while an explicit link, in the form of a dual curse of both blackness and slavery, begins to appear in seventh-century Islamic texts. This exegetical innovation coincides with the seventh-century Muslim conquests in Africa, which brought an increasing influx of Black African slaves to the Near East. From this time onward, the curse of Ham, that is, the exegetical tie between blackness and servitude, is commonly found in works composed in the Near East, whether in Arabic by Muslims or in Syriac by Christians.

It is also worth noting what Goldenberg states about the shift from skin color signifying personal complexion to ethnicity:

> Where skin color in Arabic literature previously described personal complexion, it is now used to designate ethnic groups, with "black" referring to the dark-skinned peoples. The same phenomenon occurred in sixteenth-century England. After England's encounter with black Africans, white and black became the terminology for "self" and "other." . . . This new way of categorizing humanity by skin color was also mapped onto the biblical grid. Beginning in the seventh century, it is found in Jewish, Christian, and Muslim biblical interpretations that see Noah's sons as representing the three human skin colors of the world's population.[17]

---

[17]David M. Goldenberg, *The Curse of Ham: Race and Slavery in Early Judaism, Christianity, and Islam* (Princeton, NJ: Princeton University Press, 2005), 197. According to Dale Eickelman, "The Qur'an states that humankind has been separated into nations and tribes to 'know one another' (49:13) and to 'compete in goodness' (5:48). Muslims insist that commitment to Islam supplants ties of ethnicity, that is, the ways in which individuals and groups characterize themselves on the basis of shared language, culture, descent, place of origin, history—and today many would add gender. Yet from the first Muslim conquests in seventh-century Arabia, as Muslim armies spread out from the Arabian Peninsula to encounter peoples who neither spoke Arabic nor could claim Arab descent, ethnic concerns frequently surfaced." Dale F. Eickelman, "Ethnicity," in *The Oxford Encyclopedia of Islam and Women*, ed. Abish Khatun bint Sad II-Mut'ah (Oxford: Oxford University Press, 2013), 1:272.

Closer to home in space and time, Mark Noll points out that support for the practice of slavery from Scripture failed to answer why human servitude was "black only" in the United States.[18] All too often, psychological and sociological forces frame our interpretation of Scripture to justify human greed and oppression, as in the case of the sugar industry, which was a major force in the formation and continuation of the slave trade.[19] In our current cultural context, it is not always the reinterpretation of Scripture by Whites but often the acceptance of the fundamentalist Christian charge of the African American community's biblical illiteracy that undermines and displaces their distinctive and vital role in the church in confronting White dominance.[20]

Servitude and segregation bound up with skin color also surfaced in South Africa as well as in India, where Christian colonizing forces failed to account for Scripture's import. As is well documented, Mahatma Gandhi, who impacted Martin Luther King Jr., was enamored with Jesus and the Sermon on the Mount.[21] However, he was quite critical of Christianity based on Christians in the West failing to adhere to the sermon's teachings[22] as well as his experiences with the apartheid system in South Africa, which used the Bible to defend its system of separation, social hierarchy, and exploitation based on skin color.[23]

While Gandhi espoused racist views of blacks when he was younger, his views on race evolved over the course of his life. One writer states, "Much debate surrounds Gandhi's views on black Africans, as a portion

---

[18]Mark A. Noll, *The Civil War: A Theological Crisis* (Chapel Hill: University of North Carolina Press, 2006), 51. Refer also to Julie Zauzmer Weil, "The Bible Was Used to Justify Slavery. Then Africans Made it Their Path to Freedom," *Washington Post*, April 30, 2019, www.washingtonpost.com/local/the-bible-was-used-to-justify-slavery-then-africans-made-it-their-path-to-freedom/2019/04/29/34699e8e-6512-11e9-82ba-fcfeff232e8f_story.html.

[19]For a discussion of the sugar industry and slave trade, see Khalil Gibran Muhammad, "The Barbaric History of Sugar in America," *New York Times*, August 14, 2019, www.nytimes.com/interactive/2019/08/14/magazine/sugar-slave-trade-slavery.html.

[20]Vincent L. Wimbush, *The Bible and African Americans: A Brief History* (Minneapolis: Fortress, 2003), 72-73.

[21]Mahatma Gandhi, *The Collected Works of Mahatma Gandhi* (New Delhi: Publication Division, Ministry of Broadcasting, Government of India, 1956–1994), 48:438.

[22]Gandhi, *Collected Works of Mahatma Gandhi* 48:421. See also Gandhi, *Collected Works of Mahatma*, 35:248, 328.

[23]See for example Elelwani B Farisani, "Interpreting the Bible in the Context of Apartheid and Beyond: An African Perspective," *Studia Historiae Ecclesiasticae* 40, no. 2 (December 2014): 207-25.

of his writings suggest an attachment to the ideas that Indians are actually 'Aryans' and therefore in the same category as Europeans. But many of these kinds of writings come from earlier in his career."[24] Later, Gandhi's position on race underwent change. B. R. Nanda argues that "no one did more than Gandhi to undermine the centuries-old caste system and to remove the blot of untouchability from Hinduism."[25]

Perhaps Gandhi's own negative treatment at the hands of White South Africans impacted him in his move from earlier racist views. Moreover, the waning of "pseudo-scientific racism" at the time likely left its mark on his thinking. This account of race has been defined as follows: "The paradigm classified humans according to physical characteristics of skin colour, body hair, hair texture, cranial measurements, and so forth. Those with similar physical features were then grouped to create a race identity. Thus were created Mongoloids, Caucasians, Blacks and so on." Gandhi came to terms with Jean Finot's volume *Race Prejudice* around 1907. It severely undermined the association of physical features with racial identity "by demonstrating that human physical characteristics were partly products of the milieu. He insisted that race was an invented fiction because it cannot survive impartial scientific scrutiny."[26] In the end, Gandhi's affirmation of Jesus and the Sermon on the Mount, critique of Western Christianity, rejection of racism, deflation and undermining of the caste system, and nonviolent confrontation of British imperialism were no doubt connected. I will turn to

---

[24]Paul Harvey, "Civil Rights Movements and Religion in America," in *Oxford Research Encyclopedia of Religion*, August 2016, http://religion.oxfordre.com/view/10.1093/acrefore/978019934 0378.001.0001/acrefore-9780199340378-e-492 (accessed on April 16, 2019). Consider also the discussion on racial and caste tensions in Gandhi's thought and practice in Joseph Lelyveld, *Great Soul: Mahatma Gandhi and His Struggle with India* (New York: Alfred A. Knopf, 2011), 57, 60.

[25]B. R. Nanda, *Gandhi and His Critics* (Delhi: Oxford University Press, 1985), 18. For further reading on the subject of race and caste in Indian thought, consider the following discussion on caste and color: Constance A. Jones and James D. Ryan, "Caste," *Encyclopedia of Hinduism* (New York: Facts on File, 2007), 100; see also the entry for "Varna" (color), 478-79. Refer as well to the entry "Caste" in *Society, Religious Specialists, Religious Traditions, Philosophy*, vol. 3, of *Brill's Encyclopedia of Hinduism*, ed. Knut A. Jacobsen (Boston: Brill, 2011), 25-37.

[26]Krishna Akhil Kumar Adavi, Swaha Das, and Hari Nair, "Was Gandhi a Racist?," *The Hindu*, December 3, 2016, www.thehindu.com/news/international/Was-Gandhi-a-racist/article16754773.ece. For a recent treatment against the validity of racial categories as biologically fixed and natural, see Guy P. Harrison, *Race and Reality: What Everyone Should Know About Our Biological Diversity* (Amherst, NY: Prometheus Books, 2010).

Gandhi later in consideration of King and his approach to confronting racism and segregation.

Caste systems of racial hierarchy manifest themselves in a variety of contexts globally. Isabel Wilkerson writes that "caste and race are neither synonymous nor mutually exclusive. They can and do coexist in the same culture, and serve to reinforce each other. Caste is the bones, race the skin. Race is what we can see, the physical traits that have been given arbitrary meaning and become shorthand for who a person is. Caste is the powerful infrastructure that holds each group in its place."[27] In the effort to contend against this powerful infrastructure involving psychological moves and arbitrary impositions, including the ways we interpret sacred literature that objectify and exploit people based on the color of their skin, we will go in search of natural and supernatural supports in pursuit of equity and justice. We will begin with consideration of natural law. Then we will turn our attention to biblical and theological resources.

NATURAL, ETERNAL, AND INCARNATE LAW: HIGH ABOVE SERVITUDE AND SEGREGATION LAWS

One cannot find natural grounds for a caste system of any kind based on the color of one's skin. As stated previously, we are all *Homo sapiens sapiens*. That said, humans are ingenious at concocting hierarchies of various kinds, including skin color, that make possible moves to dehumanize others.

Some might view Aristotle's distinction between people who are slaves by nature and slaves by law or societal norm and custom as a move to dehumanize sectors of humanity. Aristotle has come under criticism for his claim in book one of *The Politics* that some people are better off as slaves based on their natural constitution: "Those who are as different [from other men] as the soul from the body or man from beast—and they are in this state if their work is the use of the body, and if this is the best that can come from them—are slaves by nature. For

---

[27]Isabel Wilkerson, "America's 'Untouchables': The Silent Power of the Caste System," *Guardian*, July 28, 2020, www.theguardian.com/world/2020/jul/28/untouchables-caste-system-us-race-martin-luther-king-india. See also Isabel Wilkerson, *Caste: The Origins of Our Discontents* (New York: Random House, 2020).

them it is better to be ruled in accordance with this sort of rule, if such is the case for the other things mentioned."[28] Efforts have been made to reconcile Aristotle's teaching on slavery with his overarching view of nature, which might make him more palatable to modern readers. Here it has been argued that since for Aristotle nature is alterable, natural slavery is, too.[29] And while it has been claimed that Aristotle is a natural law theorist,[30] one may go a different route in advancing a natural law argument against slavery.

Saint Thomas Aquinas is a principal proponent of natural law. According to Aquinas, "natural law is a participation in the eternal law." The eternal law serves as the "rational plan" for ordering creation and serves as the basis for natural law. Again, for Aquinas, "natural law constitutes the basic principles of practical rationality for human beings, and has this status by nature." This position suggests that "the precepts of the natural law are universally binding by nature . . . and that the precepts of the natural law are universally knowable by nature."[31] It appears to follow naturally and logically that since we are created in God's image, and since scientifically speaking all people are *Homo sapiens sapiens*, we could not justify or tolerate servitude, segregation, and inequity of any kind.[32]

It all sounds good on paper. However, like other ethical models, natural law is not foolproof. Similar to the interpretation of Scripture, natural law can easily be abused to justify oppression or even conveniently neglected at times to advocate for slavery, segregation, and various forms of inequity. The problem of neglect may very well have been the case for John Locke, who is often hailed as the spokesperson of

---

[28]Aristotle, *The Politics*, trans. and intro. Carnes Lord (Chicago: University of Chicago Press, 1984), book 1, chapter 5, 41. For a critical account of Aristotle, see Darrell Dobbs, "Natural Right and the Problem of Aristotle's Defense of Slavery," *Journal of Politics* 56, no. 1 (1994): 69-94.

[29]See Philippe-André Rodriguez, "L'impérialisme institutionnel et la question de la race chez Aristote," *European Review of History* 23, no. 4 (2016): 751-67.

[30]Tony Burns, *Aristotle and Natural Law* (New York: Bloomsbury, 2011).

[31]Mark Murphy, "The Natural Law Tradition in Ethics," in *The Stanford Encyclopedia of Philosophy*, ed. Edward N. Zalta, Summer 2019 ed., https://plato.stanford.edu/archives/sum2019/entries/natural -law-ethics/.

[32]For an article on Aquinas, the image of God, and natural law, see Craig A Boyd, "Participation Metaphysics, The 'Imago Dei,' and the Natural Law in Aquinas' Ethics," *New Blackfriars* 88, no. 1015 (May 2007): 274-87. For an argument for how the image of God bears on notions of equality in legal considerations, see George P. Fletcher, "In God's Image: The Religious Imperative of Equality Under Law," *Columbia Law Review* 99, no. 6 (October 2000): 1608-29.

liberty. Locke generally advanced a form of natural law in supporting a just war account of slavery (see Locke's *Second Treatise of Government*), though he did not extend its import to the American colonies. Moreover, while Locke did not propose a racial doctrine justifying slavery, nonetheless, he advanced colonialism and supported human servitude. His positive reception among Southern defenders of the African slave industry certainly complicates Locke's reputation as a defender of freedom from tyranny.[33]

In view of arguments put forth over "slaves by nature" and inconsistencies over the employment of natural law, it is little wonder, then, that African American natural law looks quite different in orientation. For one, it does not articulate a precise notion of human nature. According to Vincent W. Lloyd, Black natural law perceives human nature as "unrepresentable," "paradoxical," and "inexpressible." As such, one can never locate or fix its content. Such "locating" or "fixing" the content of human nature has historically and presently led to abuses of African Americans in the forms of slavery, segregation, and mass incarceration.[34]

Moreover, contrary to other forms of natural law that claim all humans are correspondingly able to discriminate what natural law is, "the black natural law tradition" that Martin Luther King Jr. also represents recognizes the "epistemic privilege" of the downtrodden, whose suffering attunes them to justice.[35] Black natural law focuses its attention on the inherent though inexpressible rights of the marginalized, excluded, and oppressed.[36]

Last, for our purposes, it is important to note that as Lloyd points out, King often asserts in later publications and addresses "that there is a hierarchy of law, beginning with the local, ascending to the national (the Supreme Court), and finally rising to the highest form of law, the law of

---

[33]James Farr, "Locke, Natural Law, and New World Slavery," *Political Theory* 36, no. 4 (May 2008): 495-522.

[34]Vincent W. Lloyd, *Black Natural Law* (Oxford: Oxford University Press, 2016), ix, 159.

[35]Lloyd, *Black Natural Law*, ix. As Lloyd remarks on King and others in the Black natural theological tradition, Blacks have "epistemic privilege" due to their redemptive suffering. See ix and 150 for the use of "epistemic privilege." See also 97 and 99 for related items. Lloyd highlights the emphasis in this tradition that Whites will be saved by Blacks, who are closer to God through their unwarranted suffering.

[36]Lloyd, *Black Natural Law*, 162.

God as embodied in a perfect individual, Jesus."[37] We must account not only for natural law but also the incarnation of God's eternal law—the Word made flesh, Jesus Christ. King's emphasis on Jesus was by no means a private sentiment. King conceived of Jesus as central to his prophetic work in the public square. In his sermon on the Vietnam War, King declares, "We shall overcome because James Russell Lowell is right: 'Truth forever on the scaffold, wrong forever on the throne. Yet, that scaffold sways the future.'"[38] The scaffold or cross of Christ frames history's direction and telos.

It is not simply alleged natural law advocates such as King who emphasize the public import of Jesus' cross. Trinitarian theologian T. F. Torrance makes a similar point: Jesus' "cross has the effect of emptying the power-structures that the world loves so much, of their vaunted force."[39] For Torrance, the work of Christ issues forth from his person. The Bible depicts one humanity and one mediator between God and humanity—namely, God, who became human as the Jewish man Jesus of Nazareth, who since the incarnation forever remains a Jew while also existing eternally as the Son of God.[40] He represents Israel and the rest of humankind in their differentiated identity. Given that there is one humanity and one mediator between God and humankind, the racial lines of separation that we find in society are not intrinsic or essential. They have no theological or biological grounding but are psychological and sociological patterns of thought. The significance of the centrality of the cross is that it upends oppressive power structures and patterns of thought and makes possible equitable restoration of relationships.

In this context, it is worth noting the import of Israel in the history of salvation. God chooses to bless Israel and make it a blessing to the nations, although the nations refuse to obey God and acknowledge Israel's

---

[37]Lloyd, *Black Natural Law*, 94.

[38]"Martin Luther King Jr., 'Why I am Opposed to the War in Vietnam,'" YouTube video, 22:48, Non-Corporate News, January 11, 2007, www.youtube.com/watch?v=b80Bsw0UG-U. This is an audio recording of Martin Luther King Jr.'s speech given at Ebenezer Baptist Church, Atlanta, April 30, 1967.

[39]Thomas. F. Torrance, *The Mediation of Christ* (Colorado Springs, CO: Helmers & Howard, 1992), 31.

[40]Thomas F. Torrance, *Incarnation: The Person and Life of Christ*, ed. Robert T. Walker (Downers Grove, IL: IVP Academic, 2008), 43.

unique status as God's chosen people throughout much of its history. Torrance highlights Israel's "vicarious role"[41] in the history of humanity's redemption. He resists any move to discount Israel's central placement in God's redemptive purposes. As he writes elsewhere,

> Rebellion against the reconciling purpose of God being worked out through Israel cannot but bring fragmentation among the peoples and nations of [hu]mankind, for it detaches them from their creative centre in God's providential activity in history, when they are thrown back upon their separated existences and cultures as national entities. Nationalism of this kind can only take the form of group-egoism or ethnic sin, which is the poisonous root of all racism.[42]

Israel has certainly borne the brunt of various forms of nationalism and xenophobia. Just as other nations must guard against nationalism and nativism, so, too, Israel must be diligent to guard against such parochial patterns of thought and behavior. To this end, Israel must preserve its emphasis on being a people, not simply a nation. This nuance will help safeguard against Jewish forms of nationalism.

Torrance asserts that Israel is not only a nation but a people: "Unlike any other nation Israel is not just a nation, an *ethnos*, but a people of God, a *laos*."[43] Israel is primarily God's covenant partner and must therefore safeguard against cultivating a completely nationalistic outlook. Israel has a perennial role to play in God's work of mediation in and through Jesus of Nazareth. In other words, "Israel cannot completely nationalize its own existence without detaching itself from the very covenant with God which constitutes it the people that it always has been and is."[44]

Even though Israel has a "vicarious role" to play, it remains subordinate to Jesus' own vicarious humanity[45] when confronting white nationalism and racism.[46] Jesus Christ, not Israel, is "the controlling centre

---

[41]Torrance, *Mediation of Christ*, 34-36.

[42]Thomas F. Torrance, "The Divine Vocation and Destiny of Israel in World History," in *The Witness of the Jews to God*, ed. David W. Torrance (Edinburgh: Handsel, 1982), 87.

[43]Torrance, *Mediation of Christ*, 14.

[44]Torrance, *Mediation of Christ*, 14.

[45]On Jesus' vicarious humanity, see Torrance, *Mediation of Christ*, 93.

[46]For a discussion of White Christian nationalism, see Joseph O. Baker, Samuel L. Perry, and Andrew L. Whitehead, "Keep America Christian (and White): Christian Nationalism, Fear of

of the mediation of divine revelation in and through Israel" given his identity as "the personal self-revelation of God to man, the eternal Word of God made flesh once and for all." Jesus "constitutes the reality and substance of God's self-revelation, but Jesus Christ in Israel and not apart from Israel."[47]

Torrance calls out the Gentiles' perpetual antagonism and renunciation of Israel in its obedience to God. He argues that the nations transfer their resistance against God onto Israel: "While our real quarrel is with the searching light of divine revelation reflected by Israel, it is against Israel itself that we vent our resentment. There we have, I believe, the root of anti-semitism."[48]

Similarly, Torrance takes issue with those in the church who refuse to live into the new humanity inclusive of Jews and Gentiles, which Jesus inaugurates with the new covenant. At one point, he calls out the evangelical community in South Africa during the apartheid era in view of the church's calling as one people made up of Jews and Gentiles in Jesus. In her analysis of Torrance on race, Jacquelynn Price-Linnartz quotes Torrance and summarizes his view of the needed Christian response to apartheid as follows:

Torrance is "ashamed of many so-called 'evangelicals' in [South Africa] who live and act in such a way as to condone apartheid, keeping their Christian witness apart from any resolve to actualise in the flesh and blood of human existence reconciliation in Christ with one another." Too many missionaries in South Africa, he judges, had detached Christianity from Christ, removed Christ from the center, rejected Christ's "sole mediatorship," and imposed "European Church divisions upon African people." He issues a call to action, that the churches should "combat and

Ethnoracial Outsiders, and Intention to Vote for Donald Trump in the 2020 Presidential Election," *Sociology of Religion* 81, no. 3 (Autumn 2020): 272-93.

[47]Torrance, *Mediation of Christ*, 22-23. J. Kameron Carter also emphasizes the Jewishness of Jesus. According to Carter, the Enlightenment project Hellenizes him, taking away his Jewish particularity bound up with Israel as an elect community (rather than a race). This bears on colonialist and imperialist trajectories abroad: the West (with its Hellenized Christ principle) is always better than the rest. J. Kameron Carter, *Race: A Theological Account* (New York: Oxford University Press, 2008). See also Willie Jennings, *The Christian Imagination: Theology and the Origins of Race* (New Haven, CT: Yale University Press, 2010), for a discussion of the theological importance of Israel in addressing race.

[48]Torrance, *Mediation of Christ*, 11.

eliminate obstructions to the Gospel of reconciliation through divisive policies enacted in the name of a Christian State and with the backing of a Christian Church." If the churches did not unite ecumenically to overcome the divisions of apartheid, then they were living a lie.[49]

While Torrance focuses his attention on Gentile moves to discount Israel, F. F. Bruce reflects on Jewish moves to discount Gentiles, as reflected in the New Testament community. Both trajectories involving Gentiles and Jews are wrong-headed. What we find in both Torrance and Bruce is an emphasis not on biology but on sociality. Both writers discuss Ephesians 2:11-22.[50] Bruce refers to the division between Jews and Gentiles as a "psychological barrier, the antipathy aroused by the separateness of the Jews." But, he argues, this antipathy "has been abolished by Christ 'in his flesh'—that is, by his death. . . . How? Because by his death he has done away with that which separated the Jews from the Gentile, 'the law of commandments, ordinances and all.'"[51]

Further to Bruce's reflection, there is no hint of race or skin color being an issue for Jews and Gentiles as recorded in Ephesians 2:11-22. Anyone could become a Jew through circumcision. What made someone a Jew was covenantal faith involving circumcision and adherence to the law. Now Jesus, who is the peace between Jews and Gentiles, has destroyed the dividing wall of hostility between them (Ephesians 2:14) "by setting aside in his flesh the law with its commands and regulations. His purpose was to create in himself one new humanity out of the two, thus making peace" (Ephesians 2:15).

Just to be clear, it was the application of the Mosaic law that was problematic and divisive, not the law itself. Remember that, as noted earlier in this section, the highest form of law is embodied in the person of Jesus Christ, God's living Word. According to Jesus, he did not come to abolish Moses' law but to complete or fulfill it (Matthew 5:17). A sense of Jewish

---

[49]Jacquelynn Price-Linnartz, "Christ the Mediator and the Idol of Whiteness: Christological Anthropology in T. F. Torrance, Dietrich Bonhoeffer, and Willie Jennings" (ThD diss., Divinity School of Duke University, 2016), 83, quoting T. F. Torrance, "Strategy for Mission," in Thomas F. Torrance Manuscript Collection (Special Collections, Princeton Theological Seminary Library, 1976), 1, 2.

[50]See for example Torrance, *Mediation of Christ*, 103-5.

[51]F. F. Bruce, *The Epistles to the Colossians, to Philemon, and to the Ephesians*, 2nd rev. ed., New International Commentary on the New Testament (Grand Rapids, MI: Eerdmans, 1984), 298.

separation and superiority based on a problematic reading of the law proved deeply destructive. Similarly, it needs to be said that elsewhere in the New Testament we find that a faulty sense of superiority bound up with Gentiles' liberty from circumcision and dietary laws could prove equally devastating to unity and peace. In Christ Jesus, there could be no sense of separation and superiority given that only together in Christ Jews and Gentiles are the new humanity.

The apostle Paul frames the discussion of Jews and Gentiles in the church in view of the triune God. Jesus has removed the dividing wall of hostility between Jews and Gentiles through the cross (Ephesians 2:16). Together they make up God's household, the church (Ephesians 2:19). Jesus is the chief cornerstone of God's temple (Ephesians 2:20-21), in which God lives by the Spirit (Ephesians 2:22).

Speaking of the Spirit, in addition to Israel and Jesus playing vicarious roles in the drama of salvation, Torrance argues that the Spirit of God "intervenes in vicarious intercession on our behalf and pours out the love of God into our hearts."[52] Bruce writes that the needed transformation for reconciliation between Jews and Gentiles occurs through Jesus' high priestly sacrifice and the empowerment of the Spirit in our inner persons:

> It is not the law as a revelation of the character and will of God that has been done away with in Christ. . . . The righteousness required by the law of God is realized more fully by the inward enabling of the Spirit—in Jew and Gentile alike—than was possible under the old covenant. But the law as a written code, threatening death instead of imparting life, is done away with in Christ.[53]

Those who sense their poverty of spirit (Matthew 5:3) and rely on the Spirit, who pours out God's love into human hearts (Romans 5:5), are free to put aside hostilities involving formerly divided peoples and live into the reality of the new humanity in Jesus (Ephesians 2:15).

The old humanity that divides people dehumanizes and depersonalizes others based on arbitrary fixation with certain traits such as skin color. Jesus, who according to Torrance is the humanizing human and

---

[52]Torrance, *Mediation of Christ*, 109-10.
[53]Bruce, *Epistles to the Colossians, to Philemon, and to the Ephesians*, 298.

personalizing person,[54] makes it possible for us to break through psychological and social barriers that we invent for societal advantage. Jesus liberates us so that we no longer see other humans from a "worldly point of view" (2 Corinthians 5:16). God gives people the mind of Christ (1 Corinthians 2:16) so that we view others as persons, not as "other" or as things. Such gracious transformation in Christ comes about through God's Spirit.

This emphasis on grace and the Spirit does not negate consideration of nature and biology. If there is one place that biology can bear relevance, it is in consideration of secure attachments and their import for racial divisions. Further to what was stated in chapter two, a mother produces oxytocin in caring for her newborn child. It secures or solidifies bonds between parent and child. Oxytocin is a vitally important aspect of our humanity. Beyond mother and child, communities can help to foster secure attachments and empathy.

Even so, while vital for understanding what makes us tick as humans in relation to one another, consideration of oxytocin's merits does not ultimately suggest that we *should be* caring or even altruistic toward others, especially those beyond our kin or group. We need a moral compass that informs us of the need to increase our sphere of secure attachments. God does not limit the divine affection to the realm of family and friends and those of our own skin color or subculture. The Spirit, who pours God's love into our hearts, makes possible secure attachments that break through these walls of division. As the Spirit of Jesus floods our hearts with divine love, we are moved to expand our private circles of affection in pursuit of equity for all. To this subject we now turn.

VIRTUOUS LOVE: FAR BEYOND PRIVATE AFFECTION

True virtue involves concern for the other as equivalent to one's own concerns. There can be no such thing as virtuous self-love existing in isolation from God and neighbor, as in Ayn Rand's system, which champions "the virtue of selfishness" (the title of her book). Contrary to Rand's

---

[54]Torrance, *Mediation of Christ*, 47-49, 67-72. See also Paul Louis Metzger, "The Import of Thomas F. Torrance's Theological Anthropology for Addressing Racialization in Contemporary Society," *Participatio* 9 (2021): 129-56.

conception, which we will reflect on in this section,[55] Jonathan Edwards presents a communal or relational notion of virtue in his volume *The Nature of True Virtue*. The intratrinitarian mutual love "between the several persons of the Godhead" extends outward toward the creation.[56]

We cannot love as we ought in isolation from God. Edwards argues that participation in the life of the triune Godhead, whose love is inherently communal, is the fount of true virtue. Participation in the triune God's gracious love is the essence of morality. William Danaher puts the matter this way: "The moral life is one of gracious participation in the triune love of God."[57]

For Edwards, love for being in general is the fount of virtue. Being in general is the triune God and, by extension, all being. Since love for being in general or the triune God is the fount of virtue, God's love must first be for God's triune self and then extend outward, "flowing out to particular beings."[58] Private or particular affection does not convey true virtue, which, as just noted, involves a general benevolence toward all and flows from being in general, which is the triune God. Edwards writes,

> No affection limited to any private system, not dependent on, nor subordinate to Being in general can be of the nature of true virtue; and this, whatever the private system be, let it be more or less extensive, consisting of a greater or smaller number of individuals, so long as it contains an infinitely little part of universal existence, and so bears no

---

[55]Some may disagree that Ayn Rand is a figure worth considering in academic circles. While she may not currently be favored among many academics (though this is debatable and no doubt depends on which academics we are talking about), Rand's views are still very common today especially outside academia. She has influenced leading political and economic figures. Moreover, statistics from 2008 indicated that that year alone the combined sales of *Atlas Shrugged, The Fountainhead, We the Living*, and *Anthem* topped eight hundred thousand copies. See Jennifer Burns, *Goddess of the Market: Ayn Rand and the American Right* (Oxford: Oxford University Press, 2009), 1-2. In large part, there was a resurgence in Rand's popularity after the 2008 financial meltdown, as a counterreaction to rising anticapitalist sentiments. Rand and her ideas are not going away any time soon.

[56]For reflection on the love of God's triune self preceding and extending to the love of creation (trinitarian overflow), see Jonathan Edwards, *The Nature of True Virtue*, in *Ethical Writings*, ed. Paul Ramsey, *The Works of Jonathan Edwards* (New Haven, CT: Yale University Press, 1989), 8:557.

[57]William J. Danaher Jr., *The Trinitarian Ethics of Jonathan Edwards*, Columbia Series in Reformed Theology (Louisville, KY: Westminster John Knox, 2004), 178.

[58]Edwards, *Nature of True Virtue*, 557.

proportion to the great all-comprehending system. And consequently, that no affection whatsoever to any creature, or any system of created beings, which is not dependent on, nor subordinate to a propensity or union of the heart to God, the supreme and infinite Being, can be of the nature of true virtue.[59]

Grievously, Edwards did not extend the radical implications of his thought to seeking the immediate abolition of slavery in colonial America. Given his claim that "consent, propensity and union of heart to Being in general" is "*immediately* exercised in a general good will,"[60] he should have called for an *immediate* rather than gradual response to abolishing slavery and other racialized forms of oppression. There is a gross inconsistency and irregularity in Edwards at this point.[61] However, certain first-generation disciples of Edwards did not follow him in his hesitation and failure to make such connections. Rather, they called for the *immediate* emancipation as well as racial integration of slaves in the American colonies.[62]

This tension in Edwards's thought reflects a tension in all humanity. We need to account for the better and lesser angels of our nature, while longing, as Abraham Lincoln did, that the better angels will prevail, including for him in the conflict between North and South involving slavery,[63] segregation, status, and beyond. Without wishing to discount inconsistencies in Edwards's thought, it is important to emphasize his system's strengths. Private affection or a propensity of love limited to groups of individuals, or solitary love of self, does not reflect or participate in God's captivating love. Such captivating love flows from the

---

[59]Edwards, *Nature of True Virtue*, 556-57. See also 554-55.

[60]Edwards, *Nature of True Virtue*, 540. Italics added.

[61]See the treatment of the Spirit's immediate work in the believer not simply at conversion but throughout life in Jonathan Edwards, "Discourse on the Trinity," in *Writings on the Trinity, Grace and Faith*, ed. Sang Hyun Lee, *The Works of Jonathan Edwards* (New Haven, CT: Yale University Press, 2003), 21:53, 196. For an editorial reflection on an apparent difficulty in Edwards's theology in discerning distinctions involving the immediate work of the Spirit in conversion, the ongoing life of the believer, the common life of all people—Christian and non-Christian alike—and all creaturely reality, see 53.

[62]Kenneth P. Minkema and Harry S. Stout, "The Edwardsean Tradition and the Antislavery Debate, 1740-1865," *Journal of American History* 92 (June 2005): 48.

[63]Abraham Lincoln, *Lincoln Speeches*, ed. and intro. Allen C. Guelzo, Penguin Civic Classics (New York: Penguin Books, 2012), 117.

Godhead's "infinitely strong propensity" of the "divine persons one to another,"[64] which is being in general and which arouses a general benevolence, or love for *all* people.

Edwards espoused a human ontology or theory of what it means to be human. Edwards's conception of human identity involves the themes of interdependence and freedom/human agency, which followed from his overarching trinitarian theology. While humanity entails individual persons finding their identity in communion with others, they are not coerced in their interconnection but interact freely. Ideally, humans will engage lovingly out of concern for one another and not simply self-concern. On the import of trinitarian thought forms for human ontology in Edwards, Danaher writes,

> God's self-love is not merely a force of unity motivated by a love for what is best, but is generative, comprehensive, and properly social. Thus, self-love in God is as much an act of self-transcendence as it is an act of self-esteem. Likewise, compounded self-love yields a love that desires the union with, and the well-being of, another. Self-love, in short, has not only a positive connotation in Edwards, but his definition of compounded self-love derives from his conception of God's love as a dynamic and relational state of communion between the persons of the Trinity.[65]

In contrast to Edwards, Rand views self-concern as of the utmost importance.[66] Self-concern or self-love in Edwards involves "self-transcendence,"[67] which flows from his trinitarian ontology. "Simple mere self-love" and "love to God are entirely distinct, and don't enter into the nature of the other at all." However, self-love does not end there for Edwards in terms of his overarching framework: "Compounded self-love" "also arises from a principle uniting him to another being, whereby the good of that other being does in a sort become his own. This second sort of self-love is not entirely distinct from love to God, but enters into its

---

[64]Edwards, *Nature of True Virtue*, 557.

[65]Danaher, *Trinitarian Ethics of Jonathan Edwards*, 60.

[66]Ayn Rand, *The Virtue of Selfishness: A New Concept of Egoism*, with additional articles by Nathaniel Branden (New York: A Signet Book, 1964).

[67]Danaher uses these categories of "self-esteem" and "self-transcendence" in his discussion of self-love and compounded self-love: "Self-love in God is as much an act of self-transcendence as it is an act of self-esteem." Danaher, *Trinitarian Ethics of Jonathan Edwards*, 60.

nature."[68] For Edwards, natural love is good, when it is simple self-love. It is essential to our self-preservation and happiness. However, simple self-love without the mediation of God's Spirit, through which compounded self-love comes to us, leads to ruin. Here's Edwards: "This natural and necessary inclination to ourselves, without that governor and guide, will certainly without anything else produce, or rather will become, all those sinful inclinations which are in the corrupted nature of man."[69]

God's love is truly social for Edwards as well as for Martin Luther King Jr. Both Edwards and King balanced consideration of the importance of the autonomous or free individual and community. For Edwards, it flows from his trinitarian theology, which involves such themes as God's compounded self-love, which goes beyond mere self-love, involving both "self-transcendence" and "self-esteem." Excellence involves "consent" toward others. The word *consent* is taken to convey the idea that one "actively desires their welfare."[70]

At this point, it is worth drawing attention to the logical connection Edwards makes between consent and the Trinity. Now, it would be extremely odd to consider God lacking in excellence. But how could God be excellent if God existed in eternal isolation, which would make it impossible for God to consent to others' well-being in eternity, actively desiring their welfare? Edwards resolves the matter by saying, "One alone cannot be excellent, inasmuch as, in such case, there can be no consent. Therefore, if God is excellent, there must be a plurality in God; otherwise, there can be no consent in him."[71]

For Edwards, "love of benevolence" concerning any person is *consent* to their well-being or "an inclination to their good." But there is more: "Evermore equal to the inclination or desire anyone has of another's good,

---

[68]Jonathan Edwards, "Love to God. Self-Love," in *The "Miscellanies," 501–832*, ed. Ava Chamberlain, *The Works of Jonathan Edwards* (New Haven, CT: Yale University Press, 2000), no. 530, 18:74-75.

[69]Jonathan Edwards, "Sin and Original Sin," in *The "Miscellanies,"* ed. Thomas A. Schafer, *The Works of Jonathan Edwards* (New Haven, CT: Yale University Press, 1994), no. 301, 13:387.

[70]See subsection "3.2 Aesthetics" of William Wainwright, "Jonathan Edwards," in *The Stanford Encyclopedia of Philosophy*, ed. Edward N. Zalta, Winter 2016, https://plato.stanford.edu/archives/win2016/entries/edwards/.

[71]Jonathan Edwards, "Trinity," in Schafer, *The "Miscellanies,"* no. 117, 13:284.

is the delight he has in that other's good if it be obtained, and the uneasiness if it be not obtained."[72] It would seem that this notion of delighting in another obtaining the good they desire involves Edwards's notion of *complacence*, which is the feeling of satisfaction, delight, and pleasure in another being.[73] Here one finds an aesthetic quality to Edwards's ethical framework.

Edwards's prizing of "interdependence and free will," as noted above, appears to follow from his trinitarian ontology, which includes elements of consent and complacence. It is not clear whether King ever envisioned the individual and community in view of his understanding of the Trinity, but he did hold the two elements—individual and community—together. As Rufus Burrow says, "King always held in tension the value of the autonomous individual and that of the community."[74] Burrow also notes, "Following the lead of Paul Tillich, King held that freedom constituted the essence of personhood, and that to be a person is to be free, and vice versa."[75] And finally,

> His staunch conviction that a person cannot be all that he can be in isolation was consistent with both the personalistic principle of the unity of humanity and the Afrikan traditional view of the primacy of community. We are not persons in isolation. Human beings are, rather, persons-in-community. . . . A person cannot be a person without interaction with other persons.[76]

---

[72]Edwards, "Love to God. Self-Love," no. 530, 18:74.

[73]Here is what the *Stanford Encyclopedia of Philosophy's* entry for Jonathan Edwards has to say about benevolence and complacence in his thought: "True virtue aims at the good of being in general and therefore also prizes the disposition that promotes it. Truly virtuous people thus love two things—being and benevolence. They not only value benevolence because it promotes the general good, however; they also 'relish' or delight in it for its own sake. Hence, while virtue 'most essentially consists in benevolence to being' (*True Virtue*, 1765; Edwards 1957, vol. 8, 540), in a wider sense it includes not only benevolence but also 'complacence' in benevolence's intrinsic excellence or beauty." See subsection "3.1 Ethics" of Wainwright, "Jonathan Edwards." Moreover, the entry on Edwards has this to say about benevolence and consent: "One who loves others, for instance, or actively desires their welfare, 'agrees' with them or 'consents' to them. Love's scope can be narrower or wider, however. Agreement or consent is 'comprehensive' or 'universal' only when directed towards being in general. Only true benevolence, therefore, is truly beautiful." Wainwright, "3.2 Aesthetics."

[74]Rufus Burrow Jr., "Some Reflections on King, Personalism, and Sexism," *Encounter* 65, no. 1 (Winter 2004): 37.

[75]Burrow, "Some Reflections on King," 35.

[76]Burrow, "Some Reflections on King," 36-37.

Human love that reflects or images God's love will always entail affirmation of the individual as well as the community for King, as well as
for Edwards. As such, it stands in stark contrast to Rand's vision of
love which involves only self-esteem. There is no role or place for self-
transcendence in her system.

Rand's rugged individualism has a bearing on her analysis of racism.
Rand was critical of racism on the one hand and the civil rights movement
on the other hand. Rand rejected altruism and interdependence in favor
of rational self-interest as developed in her ethical system of objectivism.

In her 1963 essay titled "Racism," Rand claims that the Civil Rights Bill
puts forth a reverse form of racism. To set the matter in context, Rand
wrote this essay at the time the Civil Rights Bill was working its way
through Congress toward enactment the following year (1964). Rand
opposed directives that would automatically award employment to a
racial minority over a White applicant when the two candidates were
equally qualified. Individuals should be held responsible for their own
actions, not those of other people past and present. While Rand was
against discrimination in areas of public and governmental programs,
she supported granting the freedom to individuals to operate private
businesses along racist lines, however abhorrent she found such practices. It is important to note that Rand also affirmed opposition to those
individuals engaged in racist practices, albeit "only by private means"
through such endeavors as "economic boycott or social ostracism."[77] So,
while Rand opposed legal coercion or imposition, she favored coercion
in a private capacity.

Now, it should be noted that in addition to attacking the Civil Rights
Bill based on her supreme regard for individual freedoms, including
property rights, Rand also fervently attacked racism. "The overwhelming
majority of racists are men who have earned no sense of personal identity,
who can claim no individual achievement or distinction, and who seek
the illusion of a 'tribal self-esteem' by alleging the inferiority of some
other tribe," writes Rand. She illustrates the point by asserting that
"racism is much more prevalent among the poor white trash than among

---

[77]Ayn Rand, "Racism," in *Virtue of Selfishness*, 156.

their intellectual betters."[78] Rand goes on to blame collectivism for racism. "Historically, racism has always risen or fallen with the rise or fall of collectivism. Collectivism holds that the individual has no rights, that his life and work belong to the group . . . and that the group may sacrifice him at its own whim to its own interests."[79]

Rand presented the individual as the focal point of ethical deliberations. Moreover, she espoused a high confidence in the power of reason and exhorted all persons to cultivate this feature of their humanity. Last, she championed free-market capitalism apart from any governmental restraints as key to human flourishing. In fact, in addition to the philosophy of individualism, Rand proclaimed,

> There is only one antidote to racism: the philosophy of individualism and its politico-economic corollary, laissez-faire capitalism. . . . It is capitalism that gave mankind its first steps toward freedom and a rational way of life. It is capitalism that broke through national and racial barriers, by means of free trade. It is capitalism that abolished serfdom and slavery in all the civilized countries of the world. It is the capitalist North that destroyed the slavery of the agrarian-feudal South in the United States.[80]

While Rand's antipathy to racism is noteworthy, she did not show appreciation for the structural power dynamics bound up with racialization, including economics. It is a gross error to claim that free-market economics is the solution to abolishing slavery and serfdom. New England's wealth depended in many respects on the slave industry. The North often claimed moral superiority, and yet Wall Street was built on the backs of slaves in the South.[81] Moreover, notions of reverse racism fall flat since

[78]Rand, "Racism," 149. Nancy Isenberg seriously challenges the notion that uneducated "poor white trash" are more prone to racism. For a history of "white trash" and class in America, see Nancy Isenberg, *White Trash: The 400-Year Untold History of Class in America* (New York: Penguin Books, 2016).

[79]Rand, "Racism," 149.

[80]Rand, "Racism," 150-51.

[81]David Von Drehle, "150 Years After Fort Sumter: Why We're Still Fighting the Civil War," *TIME*, April 7, 2011, https://content.time.com/time/magazine/article/0,9171,2063869,00.html. See also Maurie D. McInnis, "How the Slave Trade Built America," *New York Times*, April 3, 2015, https://opinionator.blogs.nytimes.com/2015/04/03/how-the-slave-trade-built-america/; Dina Gerdeman, "The Clear Connection Between Slavery and American Capitalism," *Forbes*, May 3, 2017, www.forbes.com/sites/hbsworkingknowledge/2017/05/03/the-clear-connection-between-slavery-and-american-capitalism/#6de032c67bd3; Sven Beckert and Seth Rockman, eds., *Slavery's Capitalism:*

equity is absent. While there can be racial prejudice working both ways, racism, as defined in this chapter, involves prejudice entailing power imbalances favoring the dominant culture. In fact, the racialized society that Rand wished to locate in the past is still with us. One must account for present-day power imbalances, as well as the historical impact on present-day situations.

POWER DYNAMICS, LOVE, AND HOPE

In contrast, Reinhold Niebuhr, who was a contemporary of Rand and King, had a firm grasp of negative structural dynamics and how the dominant culture would not pursue equity for all if it were not forced to do so. In Niebuhr's mind, society's structures often escalate and perpetuate individual sins, giving them life long after the sins have been committed or the sinner has died. We must account for power dynamics that enforce, reinforce, and expand various iniquities, including those pertaining to our racialized system.

By way of a reminder, this is not the first time we have accounted for the development and expansion of abusive power dynamics in this volume. Recall here the chapter on gender. There we referenced E. O. Wilson's discussion of the problematic biological feature known as hypertrophy and how it surfaces in such areas as patriarchy, racism, and nationalism.[82] Hypertrophy concerns "the extreme growth of pre-existing structures"[83] that "have metamorphosed from relatively modest environmental adaptions into unexpectedly elaborate, even monstrous forms in more advanced societies."[84]

King prized Niebuhr's realist critique of power dynamics, including those forces bearing on African Americans and segregation. It was almost as if King took a page or two out of Niebuhr's volume *Moral Man, Immoral Society* in his civil rights campaign. Moreover, he refers to Niebuhr in making his case in his "Letter from Birmingham Jail":

A New History of American Economic Development, Early American Studies (Philadelphia: University of Pennsylvania Press, 2016).

[82]E. O. Wilson, *On Human Nature* (Cambridge, MA: Harvard University Press, 1978, 2004), 91-92.
[83]Wilson, *On Human Nature*, 89.
[84]Wilson, *On Human Nature*, 89.

My friends, I must say to you that we have not made a single gain in civil
rights without determined legal and nonviolent pressure. Lamentably, it
is an historical fact that privileged groups seldom give up their privileges
voluntarily. Individuals may see the moral light and voluntarily give up
their unjust posture; but, as Reinhold Niebuhr has reminded us, groups
tend to be more immoral than individuals.[85]

Niebuhrian realism accounts for the affections' distorting reason and the
import of dominant culture structural dynamics at the corporate level
that undermine moral self-determination. Niebuhr writes of group
power undercurrents and the need to address them in order to foster
justice and equity for all people in a given society or group. Coercion is
necessary for cooperation: "All social co-operation on a larger scale than
the most intimate social group requires a measure of coercion."[86] Nations
and other social groupings do not achieve some form of consensus
without coercion.[87]

   When a minority group believes it has some form of advantage, is intent
on gaining equity, or is desperate enough to do so, it will not succumb to
the dominant culture's dictates but resist.[88] The only way that African
Americans would be able to gain equity in America would be through
nonviolent means. It would not come naturally through the good will of
the dominant culture: "It is hopeless for the Negro to expect complete
emancipation from the menial social and economic position into which
the white man has forced him, merely by trusting in the moral sense of
the white race. It is equally hopeless to attempt emancipation through
violent rebellion."[89]

   For Niebuhr, the problem is not primarily an individual matter but a
group structural reality: "However large the number of individual white
men who do and who will identify themselves completely with the
Negro cause, the white race in America will not admit the Negro to equal

---

[85]Martin Luther King Jr., "Letter from Birmingham Jail," in *The Autobiography of Martin Luther King, Jr.*, ed. Clayborne Carson (New York: Warner Books, 1998), 191.

[86]Reinhold Niebuhr, *Moral Man, Immoral Society: A Study in Ethics and Politics* (Louisville, KY: Westminster John Knox, 1960), 3.

[87]Niebuhr, *Moral Man, Immoral Society*, 6.

[88]Niebuhr, *Moral Man, Immoral Society*, 4.

[89]Niebuhr, *Moral Man, Immoral Society*, 252.

rights if it is not forced to do so."[90] Niebuhr recommends boycotts of financial institutions that do not practice equity in loans, businesses that benefit from African American consumption but that do not employ them, public-service institutions that discriminate against African Americans, and refusal to pay taxes to states that spend a fraction of the amount on the education of African American youth that is spent on their White peers.[91]

King applied these strategies to the civil rights movement. King and Niebuhr's critical assessment and strategic approach calls to mind Lloyd's analysis of Black natural law. Rather than focus on "absolute principles" as guides to "political engagement," Black natural law centers attention on "strategic political organizing against laws that favor the interests of the few."[92]

The powerful few fail to see and hear. They need to see through the eyes and hear through the ears of the marginalized masses. However, apart from rare exceptions, the powerful will not willingly do so. Power and greed readily blind and deafen those in control. Still, while they have legal and economic privilege, they do not have "epistemic privilege." As Lloyd argues, "epistemic privilege" goes to those who endure redemptive suffering, who are more attuned to justice and equity.[93]

Black natural law finds a parallel in divine law, as the Sermon on the Mount highlights the need to be poor in spirit. Such poverty of spirit and the mourning that accompanies it provides epistemic access and entry points to God's upside-down kingdom. The Sermon on the Mount in Matthew's Gospel and the Sermon on the Plain in Luke's Gospel are two distinct dimensions of Jesus' eschatological kingdom reality and community. God blesses the poor and curses the rich. God blesses the meek and curses the oppressor. Jesus certainly gives preferential treatment to the dispossessed: the poor in spirit *and* the poor (compare Matthew 5:3 and Luke 6:20), those who mourn now, the meek, those who hunger and thirst for righteousness *and* those who are hungry (compare Matthew 5:6

---

[90]Niebuhr, *Moral Man, Immoral Society*, 253.
[91]Niebuhr, *Moral Man, Immoral Society*, 254.
[92]Lloyd, *Black Natural Law*, ix.
[93]Lloyd, *Black Natural Law*, ix, 150.

and Luke 6:21), the merciful, the pure of heart, the peacemakers, and those who are persecuted for righteousness and excluded on Jesus' account. They are blessed as they identify with Jesus and participate in his kingdom mission.

There is something in these texts to offend all those in power, whether conservative or liberal. Gordon Fee and Douglas Stuart put the matter well:

> In Matthew the poor are "the poor in spirit"; in Luke they are simply "you poor" in contrast to "you that are rich" (6:24). On such points most people tend to have only half a canon. Traditional evangelicals tend to read only "the poor in spirit"; social activists tend to read only "you poor." We insist that *both* are canonical. In a truly profound sense the real poor are those who recognize themselves as impoverished before God. But the God of the Bible, who became incarnate in Jesus of Nazareth, is a God who pleads the cause of the oppressed and the disenfranchised. One can scarcely read Luke's gospel without recognizing his interest in this aspect of the divine revelation (see 14:12–14; cf. 12:33–34 with the Matthean parallel, 6:19–21).[94]

These reflections on the Sermon on the Mount and Sermon on the Plain call to mind Gandhi, who was one of the principal influences on King's civil rights work and philosophy of nonviolent civil disobedience. Gandhi saw the Sermon on the Mount as pivotal for addressing corrupt power structures through nonviolent resistance. The Sermon on the Mount shaped Gandhi's philosophy of *satyāgraha*.[95] Gandhi sought to live according to Jesus' example and teaching set forth in this sermon, along with the *Bhagavad Gita* (ultimately, he saw no difference between them).[96]

---

[94]Gordon Fee and Douglas Stuart, *How to Read the Bible for All Its Worth*, 2nd ed. (Grand Rapids, MI: Zondervan), 125.

[95]According to P. T. Subrahmanyan, "Gandhi's philosophy of *Satydgraha* has been influenced by the Sermon on the Mount, as the concept of *Satydgraha* appeared to become a nonviolent path for truth in line with the teachings of the Sermon on the Mount." See his article, "Mahatma Gandhi and the Sermon on the Mount," *Gandhi Marg* 39, no. 1 (April–June 2017), www.mkgandhi.org /articles/mahatma-gandhi-and-sermon-on-the-mount.html. See also James D. Hunt, *Gandhi and Nonconformists Encounters in South Africa* (New Delhi: Promilla, 1986), 146.

[96]John Dear, "Gandhi's Daily Scripture Readings for Peace," *National Catholic Reporter*, August 20, 2013, www.ncronline.org/blogs/road-peace/gandhis-daily-scripture-readings-peace.

Consideration of Gandhi must include his affirmation of the Hindu concept of detachment from worldly pleasures and the Buddhist and Jain concept of nonharm. Gandhi's notion of *ahimsa* entails an active love that does no harm to others and acts to shield them from injury. For Gandhi, such active love entails a forceful grasping or coercion (*agraha*, part of *satyāgraha*, meaning "firmness" or "forcefully grasping") to keep others from doing harm.[97] These themes resonate with King's view of agape.

King's whole ministry was framed by way of the powerful love of God revealed in Jesus. Contrary to Nietzsche and his kind, whom King mentions in his Vietnam War address, love is not "weak and cowardly."[98] It is quite strong and courageous. In the face of human resistance to emancipation, civil rights, and full integration, such love might even express itself in nonviolent coercion and civil disobedience. David Cortright presents King's position in the following terms:

> King . . . retained a strong commitment to nonviolence, but this was tempered by a realization of the limitations of human nature. It is utopian to believe that ethical appeals alone can bring justice. Social power must be applied in addition to moral reasoning if real political change is to occur. Ethical appeals remain important, King wrote, but these "must be undergirded by some form of constructive coercive power." Power and love are usually considered polar opposites, King wrote. Love is identified with a resignation of power and power with a denial of love.[99]

For King, love and power must come together for the sake of justice. King integrated love and power beautifully: "What is needed is a realization that power without love is reckless and abusive, and that love without power is sentimental and anemic. . . . Power at its best is love . . . implementing the demands of justice, and justice at its best is love correcting everything that stands against love."[100] The agape love of an embodied

---

[97]David Cortright, *Peace: A History of Movements and Ideas* (Cambridge: Cambridge University Press, 2008), 213-14, 216, 218.

[98]Martin Luther King Jr., "Beyond Vietnam," in *A Call to Conscience: The Landmark Speeches of Dr. Martin Luther King, Jr.*, ed. Clayborne Carson and Kris Shepard (New York: Warner Books, 2001), 161.

[99]Cortright, *Peace*, 219.

[100]Martin Luther King Jr., "Where Do We Go from Here?," in *Call to Conscience*, 186.

ethical framework actively works to establish God's kingdom justice in the present. Agape is never ethereal, weak, or passive.

Having noted Edwards's emphasis on virtuous love earlier in this section, it is worth noting here that King would have challenged Edwards's version of love as applied to the slavery issue as abstract, "sentimental and anemic."[101] Similar to the White moderates who opposed King in Birmingham, King would not have been able to tolerate Edwards's hierarchical orientation (that is, adherence to established authority structures) and gradualism (which resisted calls for immediate emancipation) that appeared in Edwards and many of his followers, though not those first-generation Edwardseans such as Edwards's son and Samuel Hopkins.[102] King took issue with the White moderates insisting on honoring the laws of the land and proposing gradualism on addressing segregation laws. For those moderates who, like Edwards, would take issue with coercion and coercive love, they as well as Edwards needed to come to terms with the fact that they themselves were supporting coercive practices against Black people in failing to stand up to segregation laws in Birmingham and to slavery in colonial America.[103] For King, the only way forward involved coercive love. Even if such coercion entailed civil disobedience, it was warranted in view of the overriding and foundational natural laws established by God. As King

---

[101]King, "Where Do We Go from Here?," 186.

[102]For a selection of Hopkins's work, see the excerpts taken from Samuel Hopkins's *A Dialogue, Concerning the Slavery of the Africans; Shewing It to Be the Duty and Interest of the American Colonies to Emancipate All Their African Slaves (1776)* titled "Practical Disinterested Benevolence," in *Early Evangelicalism: A Reader*, ed. Jonathan M. Yeager (Oxford: Oxford University Press, 2013), 283-90. Hopkins found his mentor Edwards's *Nature of True Virtue* abstract and sentimental where aesthetics replaced ethics. Moreover, Hopkins maintained that Edwards gave too much autonomy to nature in relation to divine grace and wrongly promoted self-love in place of selfless love. For Hopkins, there is no place for self-love. True love is always disinterested. Hopkins was also critical of gradualism on slavery. See Minkema and Stout, "Edwardsean Tradition and Anti-slavery," 47, 54, 55.

[103]Leigh-Anne Walker writes that Edwards "defined will as an act of the mind that enabled it to choose, and freedom of the will as freedom from impediment. Activities that coerced or otherwise deprived another of free will violated the injunction to love one's neighbor as oneself by violating an essential part of what constituted humanity." Moreover, for Edwards, economic transactions must benefit the whole of society rather than harm it. See Leigh-Anne Walker, "Economic Thought," in *The Jonathan Edwards Encyclopedia*, ed. Harry S. Stout (Grand Rapids, MI: Eerdmans, 2017), 173. If this is so for Edwards, he should have taken to heart that the financial transactions involving slavery harmed the general populace, both those enslaved and those buying and selling slaves, and taken action to dissolve the institution of slavery.

says in his "Letter from Birmingham Jail" to the White clergy who were troubled by his civil disobedience,

> One may well ask: "How can you advocate breaking some laws and obeying others?" The answer lies in the fact that there are two types of laws: just and unjust. I would be the first to advocate obeying just laws. One has not only a legal but a moral responsibility to obey just laws. Conversely, one has a moral responsibility to disobey unjust laws. I would agree with St. Augustine that "an unjust law is no law at all."[104]

It is important to note that for King, such coercion could never be applied for the sake of private interests, only for the sake of the beloved community's realization among all people.

Speaking of the beloved community, realism must always guard against pessimism. Here it is worth noting that while King found Niebuhr's realism critically important for addressing corrupt power structures, he claimed that Niebuhr "overemphasized the corruption of human nature." While Niebuhr was astute in diagnosing what ails human nature, he did not situate the problem in relation to divine nature and "the cure" found in God's grace.[105] King maintained that effective social change could at least be partially realized in this age in the beloved community.[106]

King went beyond Niebuhrian equilibrium involving a balance of power to an expansion of God's powerful love breaking in on the racialized human stage. In King, one senses a spirit of optimism or hope based on his eschatological concept of the beloved community's inbreaking. It helped King guard against total disillusionment and despair in the face of so much opposition.

White supremacists, Black nationalists, and White moderates all stood in the way of the beloved community's actualization. No doubt, King struggled at times with bewilderment and bitterness. And yet, he held firmly to hope—not in human ability, but in God's miraculous grace that not only transforms individual hearts but also social structures. King did

---

[104]King, "Letter from Birmingham Jail," 193.

[105]King, *Autobiography of Martin Luther King*, 31.

[106]Burrow, *God and Human Dignity*, 167-70. Lloyd offers a different perspective on the beloved community: it may perhaps be "simply rhetoric that encourages us to interrogate worldly laws that deface the infinite worth of the human being and struggle together to change them." *Black Natural Law*, 117.

not give up hope in the face of countless obstacles and overwhelming ordeals: "I have not lost faith. I'm not in despair, because I know that there is a moral order. I haven't lost faith, because the arc of the moral universe is long, but it bends toward justice," as he declared in a post–Riverside Church address on the Vietnam War at Ebenezer Baptist Church, on April 30, 1967.[107] King knew that Good Friday came before Easter and was confident that the ultimate Easter was still ahead. His vision of God's eschatological kingdom and arrival of the beloved community kept him going. As he envisions in his Christmas sermon just months before his assassination, the beloved community's actions of tenacious and coercive love will not only win rights for marginalized and oppressed minorities but also win over their oppressors, thereby ensuring a "double victory." After King reflects on the violence his community endures at the hands of white oppressors, he concludes:

> Send your propaganda agents around the country, and make it appear that we are not fit, culturally and otherwise, for integration, and we'll still love you. But be assured that we'll wear you down by our capacity to suffer, and one day we will win our freedom. We will not only win freedom for ourselves; we will so appeal to your heart and conscience that we will win you in the process, and our victory will be a double victory.[97]

King's words involving coercive, redemptive love mixed with hope call to mind N. T. Wright's reflection on Jesus' response to dehumanizing violence in the Sermon on the Mount, including turning the other cheek to one who strikes Jesus' followers (Matthew 5:38-39). Turning the other cheek forces the oppressor to look the violated party in the eye and see them as an equal, as a human, since as N. T. Wright points out, "To be struck on the right cheek, in that world, almost certainly meant being hit with the back of the right hand." Being backhanded "implies that you're an inferior, perhaps a slave, a child, or . . . a woman." Thus Wright asks, "What's the answer? Hitting back only keeps the evil in circulation. Offering the other check implies: hit me again if you like, but now as an equal, not an inferior."[108]

---

[107]"Martin Luther King, 'Why I Am Opposed to the War in Vietnam.'"

[108]N. T. Wright, *Matthew for Everyone, Part I: Chapters 1–15* (Louisville, KY: Westminster John Knox, 2004), 51-52.

This new and promising way of being human can win over the oppressor rather than keep the cycle of vengeance going. Jesus opens the
door to this new order of being in his person as God with us, as Wright
argues,[109] and as King and the civil rights movement sought to embody.
King's nonviolent, civilly disobedient protest flowed from Jesus' call to
love our enemies and pray for those who persecute us (Matthew 5:44).
No wonder John R. W. Stott calls King the greatest example of Jesus' ethic
disclosed in this passage in modern times.[110]

God's powerful, cruciform love, inaugurated and revealed in Jesus'
upside-down kingdom, is at work in society. Everyone has some potential
for good—even the most racist person—to advance the beloved community (the kingdom of God). King was ever mindful of this reality and
this possibility. As Cortright claims, pessimism does not overshadow
hope in King:

> Although King was a Niebuhrian realist, he was not completely pessi-
> mistic about human nature. King shared Gandhi's view that "no human
> being is so bad as to be beyond redemption." He believed that even the
> most ardent segregationist had some potential for goodness and could be
> reached through the power of love. Like the force of magnetism, love has
> a unique power to attract. . . . Love is the strongest form of human energy
> and has transformative power both personally and socially.[111]

Similarly, the idea of divine blessing disclosed in the Sermon on the
Mount and the Sermon on the Plain signifies that the temptation to despair must bow before eschatological hope that is not passive but active.
As highlighted in chapter two, eschatological hope is both now and
future. The kingdom is present and future, and the community of hope
is a concrete manifestation of the eschatological kingdom. We bring the
future into the present through embodying Jesus' teaching in the here
and now. As a result of union with Jesus and participating in his kingdom
mission, we are blessed now and in the future.[112]

---

[109]Wright, Matthew for Everyone, 51-52.

[110]John R. W. Stott, The Message of the Sermon on the Mount (Matthew 5-7): Christian Counter-
Culture, The Bible Speaks Today (Downers Grove, IL: InterVarsity Press, 1978), 113.

[111]Cortright, Peace, 220.

[112]See the discussion of eschatology and hope in Brad Harper and Paul Louis Metzger, Exploring
Ecclesiology: An Evangelical and Ecumenical Perspective (Grand Rapids, MI: Brazos, 2009).

No moral vision for society should minimize either human depravity or hope. According to Danaher, Niebuhr maintained that a social ethic that is worthy of consideration will give serious attention to human depravity and how it masquerades in noble dress.[113] Just as no social ethic is worthy of consideration if it does not account for the human proclivity to put forth selfish agendas under the guise of presumably philanthropic ideals, as Niebuhr maintained, so no presumably Christian social ethic is worthy of sustained consideration and implementation that does not account for the divine drive of general benevolence to move in people's hearts and lives to effect change for the good of the whole rather than promote selfish ambitions from whatever quarter of society. A discerning moral vision will wisely account for evil but will not settle for a presumed equilibrium between the good and the bad. Rather, those who embrace the hope of God's intervention through Jesus in the Spirit will pray to participate fully in the divine life and embody the coming kingdom for the sake of all and with anyone who will join them in this mission, as in the inspirational work of Gandhi, who sought to live out the Sermon on the Mount.

King was not alone in his assessment of Niebuhr's pessimism. Those inspired by Edwards would also take issue with Niebuhr's realism on this point. As Danaher writes, "From Edwards's perspective, Niebuhr's account of communal unity is unduly narrow. While Niebuhr believes that communities are essential for human flourishing he acknowledges that communities invariably represent the basest drives of individuals, and that coercion is therefore 'an inevitable part of the process of social cohesion.'"[114] The solution for Niebuhr is to put in place a balance of power to achieve some sort of equilibrium. Certainly, checks and balances are important to an extent. But as Edwards contends, equilibrium is not satisfactory as a final solution:

> Edwards would argue that Niebuhr's "realism" neglects the positive point that all communities reflect the paradigm of community established by the triune God, whose victorious love brings the church into a communion of perfect unity, individuality, and friendship. Where Niebuhr's

---

[113]Danaher, *Trinitarian Ethics of Jonathan Edwards*, 178.
[114]Danaher, *Trinitarian Ethics of Jonathan Edwards*, 179.

doctrine of original sin provides a vision for how pluralistic and frag-
mented societies can maintain a fragile sense of equilibrium, Edwards's
doctrine of original sin provides a vision for the church's unique confidence and hope in Christ.[115]

How does all this talk of equilibrium, optimism, and virtuous, coercive love bear on society presently? For one, Gandhi and King confronted caste systems of different kinds and would no doubt contend
against what Michelle Alexander calls the new caste system in the United
States. The racial caste system has not been terminated, only "redesigned."[116]
Young African American men "are part of a growing undercaste, permanently locked up and locked out of mainstream society" based on legalized discrimination bound up with the drug war.[117]

This is a subject that concerns all Americans and requires all Americans to get involved. But will we seek to work with others to solve this
ongoing problem of social segregation? An entangled ethic recognizes
that we need others' help if we are to experience the beloved community,
Christians and non-Christians alike. The call for solidarity in the fight
against racial oppression extends to all people of all faith traditions and
walks of life.

Psychological walls of division and social barriers from the States to
South Africa and India, including the prison system here in the United
States, which gives pride of place to African American men, are self-
fulfilling prophecies that harm and enslave individuals, communities,
and society at large. We must not let down our guard but must dismantle
the ideological structures that suggest that those of a darker skin color
are naturally inferior and by default predisposed or predetermined to be
drug dealers, rapists, and murderers. Their skin color does not signify
they are made for less. Like the rest of humanity, they are created in God's
image. As *Homo sapiens sapiens*, they are made for far more. We must
ensure them the lifelong opportunities and inroads for success that we
in the dominant culture prize.

---

[115]Danaher, *Trinitarian Ethics of Jonathan Edwards*, 179.
[116]Michelle Alexander, *The New Jim Crow: Mass Incarceration in the Age of Colorblindness*, with a
   new foreword by Cornel West (New York: New Press, 2012), 2.
[117]Alexander, *New Jim Crow*, 7.

The pursuit of racial equality, equity, and inclusion does not negate natural affections such as love of family members and one's town and nation, which entail self-preservation and happiness, and which for Edwards is never divorced from self-transcendence. They possess something of "the general nature of virtue."[118] King himself made clear to his fellow Americans on various occasions that his prophetic challenges and civil disobedience work were manifestations of his natural love for his country. But one cannot love one's country if one only loves one tribe or people group within that country to the detriment of all.

Where does all this lead us in the end? God's self-transcending love and the immediacy of God's Spirit signify that the dominant culture must transcend itself and move beyond private interests and tribalism to overcome segregation and status structures in its various forms with immediate steps of action. Such overcoming will sometimes take the form of coercion to effect equity, though always out of love, knowing that injustice impacts all tribes and people groups negatively. As King declared in his "Letter from Birmingham Jail," "Injustice anywhere is a threat to justice everywhere. We are caught in an inescapable network of mutuality, tied in a single garment of destiny. Whatever affects one directly, affects all indirectly."[119] But may we not simply be drawn to overcoming injustices. May we also be drawn to the beauty of authentic integration and diversity. With King, "Let us be dissatisfied until integration is not seen as a problem but as an opportunity to participate in the beauty of diversity."[120] And with Edwards, let us be transformed as a people by the glorious vision of heaven's manifold unity, most noticeably the triune God, who is "the supreme harmony of all."[121]

---

[118]Edwards, *Nature of True Virtue*, 609. See also 617.
[119]King, "Letter from Birmingham Jail," 189.
[120]King, "Where Do We Go from Here?," 196.
[121]Jonathan Edwards, "Heaven," in Schafer, *The "Miscellanies,"* no. 182, 13:329.

9

MORE THAN IMPORT MARKET VALUE

Immigration Reform Beyond Meritocracy

THIS CHAPTER ADDRESSES the subject of immigration reform in the United States, primarily the emphasis on merit-based rubrics. I will argue that a personalist approach to morality frames consideration of immigration reform based on meeting needs and honoring preexisting relationships rather than catering to merit-based models. We are made for more than what the market values.

I will begin by analyzing market- or merit-based immigration reform and then turn to an emphasis on moral influence over affluence to address migrants and refugees' needs. Then I will consider how preexisting relationships with other people groups and nations long abandoned and conveniently forgotten foster various disquieting migration patterns. I will take it one step further and highlight "disaster capitalism's" role in fostering regional and international social upheaval. Contrary to popular opinion in some circles, disaster capitalism is a far cry from Adam Smith's free-market economic system and his concept of the invisible hand. I will conclude the chapter by reflecting on the visible hand of the Son of Man, who will judge the nations based on how they treat the stranger in their midst.

MARKET-BASED IMMIGRATION REFORM

US President Donald Trump called for an immigration policy based on merit. Trump claimed that this involves accepting only those people with good intentions. In his estimation, a vast number of people wanting to immigrate do not have good intentions. They do not intend to build up the US but exploit it for their own benefit or tear it down. He also made clear that immigration based on merit means accepting only those people with good or great IQs and desirable skills for the marketplace.[1]

Trump's merit-based approach to immigration is not without precedent. It is reminiscent of Gary Becker's proposal in 1987 to determine who gets to immigrate based on market relations and financial transactions. Instead of America's complex rubric that determines who can immigrate, Becker proposed that those who could front $50,000 or higher would be given the right of passage to the United States.[2] Julian L. Simon proposed a similar solution involving an auction of visas to those who outbid others. If they did not have the money at the time, they could pay it back through income tax over several years.[3] In 1990, Congress passed legislation that allowed applicants and their families to enter and stay in the United States for two years if they paid $500,000. After two years, they could gain permanent visas if they showed proof of having created ten jobs during their initial tenure.[4] Still another proposal came to the foreground. Peter Schuck argued for implementing an international quota system according to which countries take responsibility for welcoming a certain number of refugees per year in proportion to national wealth in order to address the global refugee crisis. Countries could decline admittance by paying an equivalent sum to another country to admit them.[5]

The United States government has gone back and forth through American history on giving pride of place to economic factors being a driving force in immigration policies. Take for example the following historical reflection. Chen Huan-Chang compares Confucius's model with those of Europe and the United States prior to the 1911 revolution

---

[1]David Nakamura, "What Trump Means by 'Merit-Based Immigration System,'" *Washington Post*, February 1, 2018, www.washingtonpost.com/video/politics/what-trump-means-by-merit-based -immigration-system/2018/02/01/9f0c976c-07be-11e8-aa61-f3391373867e_video.html.

[2]Gary S. Becker, "Why Not Let Immigrants Pay for Speedy Entry?," in *The Economics of Life*, ed. Gary S. Becker and Guity Nashat Becker (New York: McGraw Hill, 1997), 58-60. It was originally published in *Business Week*, March 2, 1987.

[3]Julian L. Simon, "Auction the Right to Be an Immigrant," *New York Times*, January 28, 1986.

[4]See Nick Timiraos, "Foreigners' Sweetener: Buy House, Get a Visa," *Wall Street Journal*, October 20, 2011.

[5]Peter H. Schuck, "Share the Refugees," *New York Times*, August 13, 1994.

in China that replaced the imperial system and Qing dynasty with the
Republic of China:

> The Confucian theory is exactly the opposite of actual conditions in
> America and European countries. While the restriction and the exclusion
> of immigrants in the United States is based mainly on the economic
> struggle—that is, the laborers want to get more money—the theory of
> Confucius is based on politics, ethics and religion. Indeed, his theory
> tends to make a universal empire, a universal religion, a universal con-
> ception, a universal law, a universal custom, a universal route, a universal
> language, a universal calendar, *etc.* These ideas can be summed up in a
> single word—universalism. Confucius says: "When there is the teaching,
> there shall be no distinction between the races, nor between the sexes, nor
> between the classes." From such a point of view it is necessary to en-
> courage immigration in order to realize universalism.[6]

I will return to discuss Confucianism in this chapter. At present, I only
wish to highlight that economic merit versus moral merit appears to be
a recurring struggle in US history.

Here is how the United States Conference of Catholic Bishops define
merit-based immigration:

> Merit-based immigration (also known as a "point-based system"), gives
> favorable consideration or "points" to prospective immigrants who have
> specific employment-related characteristics that are found to be desirable
> for high-skill employment, such as: education, specialized work skill sets,
> employment experience, English language proficiency, and age.[7]

In contrast to the merit-based model, the Roman Catholic Church advocates for the continuation of a family-based immigration system, which
they maintain has been the foundation of US policy on immigration,
albeit informally until the adoption of the Immigration and Nationality
Act in 1965. The family-based model, which the act formally established,
is the primary (not only) method to immigrate legally since the nation's

[6]Chen Huan-Chang, *The Economic Principles of Confucius and His School* (New York: Columbia
University, Longmans, Green & Company, Agents, 1911), 314-15.
[7]United States Conference of Catholic Bishops, "The Importance of Maintaining a Family-Based
Immigration System," Justice for Immigrants, https://justiceforimmigrants.org/wp-content/uploads
/2020/12/Family-Unity-Backgrounder.pdf.

beginning.[8] The US Conference of Roman Catholic Bishops' definition of the merit-based immigration model makes no mention of financial transactions in which people pay for the right to immigrate to the United States. For our purposes, I am including the point system and financial transactions under the heading of a market- and merit-based approach.

What are we to make of such market- and merit-based systems from the personalist perspective championed in this volume? I will argue that a personalist perspective gives points or better pride of place to a host country's moral influence in meeting needs rather than catering to affluence. Moreover, a personalist orientation on immigration reform prizes the need to honor a history of relational commitments rather than favor intellectual capacities, educational aptitude, skilled labor prowess and potential, or economic resources. Human worth does not rise and fall with market value. In addressing this subject, I will draw attention to various ethical figures and their value systems.

MORAL INFLUENCE VERSUS AFFLUENCE

In his volume *What Money Can't Buy: The Moral Limits of Markets*, Michael Sandel accounts for various merit-based models of immigration reform. Sandel voices his sustained concern over the move from a market-based economy to a market-oriented society. For Sandel, it is deeply disturbing to conceive all human relationships as market transactions. For example, the move to outsource refugees cultivates patterns whereby we "think of refugees as burdens to be unloaded or as revenue sources, rather than as human beings in peril."[9] The merit-based model is affluence oriented, whereas Sandel's model aims at limiting the reach of market ideology and expanding moral influence to meet needs.

I should add at this juncture that one could make a case for market ideology fostering a form of morality that caters to supply-and-demand thinking and the fear of scarcity. From this perspective, it is best to conserve compassion rather than extend it because it is a rare commodity.

---

[8]United States Conference of Catholic Bishops, "Importance of Maintaining a Family-Based Immigration System."

[9]Michael J. Sandel, *What Money Can't Buy: The Moral Limits of Markets* (New York: Farrar, Straus, and Giroux, 2012), 64.

Contrary to this way of thinking, like a muscle, if we do not use compassion, we will lose it.

Those who lack compassion are perhaps in even greater need than those seeking to immigrate. It is not only the immigrants and refugees who are in peril. Any society that views them as financial burdens or revenue sources is also in peril. We lose a sense of human dignity as inherent and invaluable when we view people as commodities. We become what we value. So, if we view other humans as commodities, we reduce ourselves to commodities, too. We were made for more than viewing other persons as economic burdens or goods to exchange. We need to extend moral influence through concrete acts of compassion and welcome the stranger in need rather than conserve compassion and quantify and commodify human worth.

Contrary to those who think markets are only mechanisms of wealth distribution, Sandel contends that markets can easily influence how we evaluate life and distort our value systems: "Markets are not mere mechanisms. They embody certain norms. They presuppose—and promote—certain ways of valuing the goods being exchanged."[10] Sandel goes on to assert, "Economists often assume that markets do not touch or taint the goods they regulate. But this is untrue. Markets leave their mark on social norms. Often, market incentives erode or crowd out nonmarket incentives."[11]

Economic value often stands in the way of moral value, not just in our market-driven society but throughout the centuries. Mention was made of Confucius in the previous section. Confucius is a striking figure in that he stands in stark contrast to dominant patterns of American and Chinese governmental policy involving the role of ethics in economics.[12] His ethical system also merits consideration in view of historical and recent policies of exclusion of Chinese from the United States.[13]

---

[10]Sandel, *What Money Can't Buy*, 64.
[11]Sandel, *What Money Can't Buy*, 64.
[12]Martha A. Starr, ed., *Consequences of Economic Downturn: Beyond the Usual Economics*, Perspectives from Social Economics (New York Palgrave Macmillan, 2011); Di Shang, Guanchu Liu, and Shixiong Cao, "Why Are Chinese Ethics Declining?," *Time and Society* 28, no. 1 (2019): 438-53.
[13]Yuning Wu, "Chinese Exclusion Act, United States [1882]," *Britannica*, www.britannica.com/topic/Chinese-Exclusion-Act; Stuart Anderson, "Inside Trump's Immigration Order to Restrict Chinese

Confucius would have taken issue with a market-based society, including a market-based approach to immigration and exclusion. Instead of *affluence* or profit serving as the basis for crafting immigration policies, Confucius approached the subject of immigration from the vantage point of extending *moral influence*. That is, the opportunity to influence would-be immigrants and the world at large in terms of the virtues of good or moral rule was critically important to Confucius.

Central to Confucianism is the conflict involving morality and profit. In *The Analects*, Confucius states, "The gentleman understands what is moral. The small man understands what is profitable."[14] Morality—regard for the well-being of society—should serve as the guide for one's various pursuits. Profit through labor is by no means bad, but the means through which one gains profit and the aim in making profit is of the utmost importance.

Rather than worry about people wishing to immigrate, Confucius maintained that the influx of immigrants is a sign of good governance. People will seek to immigrate based on virtuous rule and will emulate their sovereigns. As is written in *The Analects*, "When those above love the rites, none of the common people will dare be irreverent; when they love what is right, none of the common people will dare be insubordinate; when they love trustworthiness, none of the common people will dare be insincere." Then "the common people from the four quarters will come with their children strapped on their backs."[15] Confucius also asserted that those in leadership should "ensure that those who are near are pleased and those who are far away are attracted."[16]

In view of this quotation, Confucius would no doubt affirm President Trump's rightful concern that would-be immigrants should have good intentions in wishing to live in America. However, Confucius would put the onus on those in government to cultivate good intentions and love

---

Students," *Forbes*, June 1, 2020, www.forbes.com/sites/stuartanderson/2020/06/01/inside-trumps-immigration-order-to-restrict-chinese-students/?sh=71b569bc3bec.

[14]Confucius, *The Analects*, trans. and intro. D. C. Lau, Penguin Classics (London: Penguin Books, 1979), book IV, no. 16; 74. See also this discussion pertaining to virtue and politics: Jeffrey Riegel, "Confucius," in *Stanford Encyclopedia of Philosophy*, ed. Edward N. Zalta, Summer 2013, http://plato.stanford.edu/entries/confucius/#ConPol.

[15]Confucius, *Analects*, 119.

[16]Confucius, *Analects*, 121.

what is good and virtuous, including the well-being of all people. By and large, from Confucius's viewpoint, if the intentions of those in leadership are good, those who immigrate will be good. We attract those who share our values. If our intentions are bad, we will attract those who are bad.

With this point in mind, it is worth noting how Trump referred to those supposedly coming to the United States with bad intentions. "When Mexico sends its people, they're not sending their best," declared Trump on the 2015 campaign trail. "They're sending people that have a lot of problems, and they're bringing those problems with us. They're bringing drugs. They're bringing crime. They're rapists."[17]

Confucius would likely wonder about the kind of leadership and citizens that characterize the United States if the people flocking to the United States fit the former president's description. To reiterate a prior point, if a country and ruler are good, people like them will come. If the rulers are bad, they will attract those who are bad.

Beyond the examples Trump gives, if fixation on accumulating money shapes the United States, then would-be immigrants will likely pursue material profit as their ultimate goal. What then will happen to this country? A government and populace that increasingly fixate on commodities will objectify all of life and jettison virtue. They will ultimately foster a moral vacuum. If, however, the aim is to cultivate virtue involving faithfulness in relationships and care for the downtrodden and marginalized, they will expand their moral value and influence.

Like Confucius, Aristotle invested much thought in consideration of virtuous conduct. A virtuous act is one not performed for popularity or profit, or based on compulsion, but involves the pursuit of perfection. Perfection involves the cultivation of noble or virtuous character. For Aristotle, one becomes good by exercising good: "By doing just things we become just."[18] The pursuit of goodness requires practice or habituation.

---

[17]Michelle Mark, "Trump Just Referred to One of His Most Infamous Campaign Comments: Calling Mexicans 'Rapists,'" *Business Insider*, April 5, 2018, www.businessinsider.com/trump-mexicans -rapists-remark-reference-2018-4.

[18]Aristotle, *Nicomachean Ethics*, trans. Robert C. Bartlett and Susan D. Collins (Chicago: University of Chicago Press, 2011), 27 (1103b).

Virtuous people do not make their primary ambition in life the accumulation of wealth but cultivation of virtuous friendships. Aristotle's view of virtue involves consideration of friendship and love. They are exceptionally important to him. As he declares at the outset of his discussion of friendship in the *Nicomachean Ethics*, "Without friends, no one would choose to live, even if he possessed all other goods."[19] Humans pursue friendships for many reasons. But true friendship, what Aristotle calls "complete friendship," involves companionship between noble people of good character. Aristotle argues,

> But complete friendship is the friendship of those who are good and alike in point of virtue. For such people wish in similar fashion for the good things for each other insofar as they are good, and they are good in themselves. But those who wish for the good things for their friends, for their friends' sake, are friends most of all, since they are disposed in this way in themselves and not incidentally.[20]

> Given that these are the forms into which friendship has been divided, base people will be friends on account of what is pleasant or useful to them, since it is in this respect that they are alike, whereas the good will be friends on account of who they themselves are, in that they are good. The latter, then, are friends simply, whereas the former are friends incidentally and only by resembling the latter.[21]

It is worth noting here the similarity with Confucius that *like attracts like*. For Confucius, a good government will attract good people. For Aristotle, virtuous people attract others who are virtuous or noble. Aristotle maintains that those who are virtuous cultivate friendships with those who are good by nature, like themselves. In contrast, "base people" cultivate friendships with those they find "pleasant or useful."

To shift momentarily to our contemporary context, in a market-driven society in which markets shape incentives, individuals often favor friendships based on utility. What Aristotle refers to as "complete friendship" based on constancy and stability of virtue would never be the goal where the markets shape values. A market-driven society could only cultivate

---

[19] Aristotle, *Nicomachean Ethics*, book VIII, chapter 3, 163.
[20] Aristotle, *Nicomachean Ethics*, 168.
[21] Aristotle, *Nicomachean Ethics*, 170.

base people who pursue friendships with those they find pleasing or convenient. Like the markets with their supply-and-demand mercurial loyalty, friendships are expedient. This value system will in turn impact the kind of immigrants the society attracts and forms as citizens.

It is worth noting that for Aristotle friendship with foreigners does not rise to the level of "complete friendship." Aristotle mentions friendship with foreigners in his treatment of the friendship of utility, which involves the pursuit of personal advantage:

> And such people do not frequently live with each other either, for sometimes they are not even pleasant to each other. They therefore have no additional need of this sort of association if they supply no benefit to the other, for they are pleasant to each other only insofar as they foster hopes of obtaining something good from the other. It is also among these sorts of friendship that people place the kind connected with foreigners.[22]

The editors of the English edition of Aristotle's *Nicomachean Ethics* comment on this statement regarding "foreigners": "*Xenikos* (from *xenia*), that is, the friendship between host and guest," was "an important relationship in ancient Greece, which carried obligations of hospitality and the protection of Zeus. It also had a political dimension, in the hosting of and giving gifts to foreign guests or ambassadors."[23]

As is clear, hospitality toward foreigners was important in ancient Greece. But, at least for Aristotle, it appears that such care was provided for personal or societal benefit. Given Aristotle's framework, what "benefit" might there be with undocumented people and refugees? After all, they are not quite "foreign guests or ambassadors." In the case of the undocumented, would it be that they provide labor that no one else can perform for the sake of the economy? In the case of refugees who are permitted safe passage, is it because they might have expertise in fields of employment and research where such skill is in short supply? And what if there is no perceived benefit or pleasure? Would we send them back to where they came from no matter how great their need?

---

[22]Aristotle, *Nicomachean Ethics*, 167.
[23]Aristotle, *Nicomachean Ethics*, 167n18.

What does it say about the level or quality of virtue of a given society if we approach "foreigners" simply from the vantage point of benefit and utility? What if there is no place for unconditional love that views others based on their need rather than personal or national benefit and utility? How would we like it if the tables were turned and we were the ones in need of compassionate care and unconditional love? Those who reject welcoming "foreigners" or immigrants and refugees apart from apparent benefit or advantage are in great moral need. They may be in far greater need than those denied entry. A moral compass that sees the need to move from a culture of things to persons is missing.

Leslie Stevenson and his colleagues reveal what's missing on friendship and love from Aristotle's paradigm by way of comparison with the Bible. They account not only for friendship and love but also competing concepts of the divine and their import for human relationships:

> Aristotle's gods are purely intellectual beings, and if they care at all about human affairs, he represents them as caring only that we (or the cleverest of us) should emulate their intellectual insight. But the Hebrew God was a God of love as well as knowledge, who is represented as caring about His people collectively and individually, and in particular as caring about social justice (e.g., about the fate of the poor and the orphaned) and as capable of forgiveness. All this carries over to the Christian conception of a God of Love.[24]

Now on the issue of friendship and love, Stevenson and his coauthors argue:

> Aristotle is far from ignorant of the importance of human love; indeed, he devotes two whole books (NE VIII and IX) to the topic of friendship. . . . And he notes that there is a sense in which one should love oneself, namely wishing for the very best for oneself (1168b30). But friendship (*philia*) is, on Aristotle's conception, only possible with a few people; moreover, it can really exist only between good people. In contrast, the New Testament conception of love (*agape*, formerly translated as "charity") is supposed to be universal and unconditional. It involves more, I take it, than Aristotle's "good will" (NE1166b30). The ideal it puts before us is first that we should

---

[24]Leslie Stevenson, David L. Haberman, and Peter Matthews Wright, *Twelve Theories of Human Nature*, 6th ed. (New York: Oxford University Press, 2013), 113.

be loving or compassionate to *all* our fellow human beings, regardless of sex, race, class, ethnicity, or nationality. And, second, that our love or compassion should not depend on good behavior or individual talents, so that a change of heart and forgiveness should always be seen as possible.[25]

Aristotle and Jesus would voice concern over a market-based system of merit. However, the Aristotelian and biblical views of friendship and love are markedly different. Aristotle makes space for friendship with foreigners for advantage and affirms complete friendship between those who are virtuous. But the God of the Bible does not love us based on our merit or usefulness or seeming virtue. God's love is unconditional. Otherwise, we would never experience God's hospitality and love. As Stevenson and his associates conclude, something is missing from any ethic that does not account for loving those unlike us, the unlovely, and seemingly unlovable. When we fail to love the needy, we demonstrate that something is missing in our own lives—unconditional, gracious love. Those who love unconditionally are truly virtuous according to the Bible.

Biblical religion involves loving and caring for the orphan, widow, and alien in their distress (Deuteronomy 10:18; James 1:27). Not only that, but God loves his enemies. In fact, when we were God's enemies, Jesus died for us to reconcile us to God (Romans 5:8). Virtuous love in Christianity looks very different than it does in Aristotle's thought. Jesus puts it best in the Sermon on the Mount when he calls for enemy love:

> You have heard that it was said, "Love your neighbor and hate your enemy." But I tell you, love your enemies and pray for those who persecute you, that you may be children of your Father in heaven. He causes his sun to rise on the evil and the good and sends rain on the righteous and the unrighteous. If you love those who love you, what reward will you get? Are not even the tax collectors doing that? And if you greet only your own people, what are you doing more than others? Do not even pagans do that? Be perfect, therefore, as your heavenly Father is perfect. (Matthew 5:43-48)

According to Jesus, if we only love those who are like us and who like and love us, we are no different from base people, namely, the tax collectors.

---

[25]Stevenson, Haberman, and Wright, *Twelve Theories of Human Nature*, 113-14.

Jesus calls us in the Sermon on the Mount to live on higher moral ground through enemy love.

As already noted in this section, how we engage those in need reveals to us our own level of need and poverty. But what if we do not have eyes to see our own need? If we who are Americans have never sensed how dependent we are on others' beneficent care at times, will we be willing to admit that our ancestors who immigrated to America's shores may have been in great need at the time of arrival and reliant on others' good will and mercy? Just like Israel, many Americans today appear to have difficulty recalling that most of our ancestors were immigrants. Moreover, many did not come from noble stock. Some people's ancestors and many recent immigrants fled religious and political persecution or faced the threat of ethnic cleansing in other countries.

The biblical prophets and apostles reminded Israel and the church that God did not choose them based on their inherent greatness but God's grace and unconditional love, as well as their depths of need. Just as God cared for them and delivered them from slavery in Egypt and led them to the Promised Land, they, too, should care for orphans, widows, and aliens in their distress. Here are three texts that reflect the theme of need and grace, as well as the need to care for others like God cared for his people when they were in desperate need:

> The LORD did not set his affection on you and choose you because you were more numerous than other peoples, for you were the fewest of all peoples. But it was because the LORD loved you and kept the oath he swore to your ancestors that he brought you out with a mighty hand and redeemed you from the land of slavery, from the power of Pharaoh king of Egypt. (Deuteronomy 7:7-8)

> For the LORD your God is God of gods and Lord of lords, the great God, mighty and awesome, who shows no partiality and accepts no bribes. He defends the cause of the fatherless and the widow, and loves the foreigner residing among you, giving them food and clothing. And you are to love those who are foreigners, for you yourselves were foreigners in Egypt. (Deuteronomy 10:17-19)

> Brothers and sisters, think of what you were when you were called. Not many of you were wise by human standards; not many were influential; not many were of noble birth. But God chose the foolish things of the

world to shame the wise; God chose the weak things of the world to shame the strong. God chose the lowly things of this world and the despised things—and the things that are not—to nullify the things that are, so that no one may boast before him. It is because of him that you are in Christ Jesus, who has become for us wisdom from God—that is, our right-eousness, holiness and redemption. Therefore, as it is written: "Let the one who boasts boast in the Lord." (1 Corinthians 1:26-31)

We are all in need of God's mercy. Based on God's merciful, faithful, covenantal care for us during times of need, we should be sure to care for others such as foreigners in their distress.

Contrary to a personalist framework, market-driven approaches don't value people based on inherent worth and dignity and therefore dis-regard preexisting relationships, contracts, and covenants in times of need. Rather, in a market-driven society, value depends on economic merit and utility. Market-driven approaches do not account for safe-guarding relationships and communities. Rather, they readily destroy virtuous communities, as I will illustrate.

As noted in this section, we should engage people when they are in need, noting our own need and what is lost for our persons if we do not meet the needs of others in times of crisis. People are not made for the market. The market is made for people. We lose our way when we reduce people and people groups to their economic value as solitary individuals or commodities in isolation. We must come to see them as persons and nations made up of human communities in indispensable relation. Such loss of direction entails honoring relationships with other peoples or na-tions for however long they profit us, conveniently forgetting the treaties and covenants we have made with them and blaming those who cry out for help and come to our borders in search of aid based on what we as a society have taken from them in foreign investment, trade, and transfer of resources and profits. Given the long-standing relationships with such diverse people and countries, we should see their own citizens as native born. Rather than discounting and disregarding them, we should take to heart God's exhortation to Israel: "The foreigner residing among you must be treated as your native-born. Love them as yourself, for you were foreigners in Egypt. I am the LORD your God" (Leviticus 19:34). To this subject of amnesia and how important it is that we should call to mind and honor long-standing relationships with other peoples, we now turn.

AMNESIA AND AFFLUENZA

There were certainly competing visions of what Israel and the church were created to be: an invulnerable people versus a people for the vulnerable, the home of the great, mighty, and wise who despise the sick versus a haven of rest and a hospital for those struggling to survive. The same competition between opposing visions has taken place throughout American history in terms of what this nation is called to be.

Take for example the debate that surfaced around Emma Lazarus's poem "The New Colossus," which is emblazoned on a bronze plaque at the base of the Statue of Liberty. The proceeds of the sale of her poem were designated for building the base for the statue, which the United States had recently received as a gift from France. Lazarus's vision of America did not award entrance based on noble birth, great riches, or high achievement. Rather, her America welcomed those without significant status or resources and who longed for a new home as a haven of rest. Lazarus's poem includes the following lines:

> Not like the brazen giant of Greek fame,
> With conquering limbs astride from land to land;
> Here at our sea-washed, sunset gates shall stand
> A mighty woman with a torch, whose flame
> Is the imprisoned lightning, and her name
> Mother of Exiles. From her beacon-hand
> Glows world-wide welcome; her mild eyes command
> The air-bridged harbor that twin cities frame.
> "Keep, ancient lands, your storied pomp!" cries she
> With silent lips. "Give me your tired, your poor,
> Your huddled masses yearning to breathe free,
> The wretched refuse of your teeming shore.
> Send these, the homeless, tempest-tost to me,
> I lift my lamp beside the golden door!"[26]

---

[26]Emma Lazarus, "The New Colossus," in *Nineteenth-Century American Women Poets: An Anthology*, ed. Paula Bernat Bennett (Oxford: Blackwell, 1998), 287.

Given that the poem is immortalized at the foot of the Statue of Liberty, one might mistakenly believe Lazarus's vision of America was the dominant ideal in the late nineteenth century. Here it is worth pointing out a *Washington Post* article on Lazarus's poem in historical context.[27] Her poem was commissioned at a time (1883) when US immigration policies bore a striking resemblance to those of the Trump administration:

> Lazarus's poem was itself an act of defiance against anti-immigrant policies. She drafted it at a time during which both U.S. immigration policy and foreign policy were flagrantly antagonistic to ideals like freedom, liberty, sovereignty and sanctuary. . . . Lazarus recognized what those who quote her poem today see: allowing racism to shape migration policy fatally short-circuits freedom of movement and political autonomy—two hallmarks of open societies.[28]

The same article claims that the poem has never accurately reflected America's historical view of immigration, contrary to those who would use it to rewrite history. Rather, as already claimed, the poem serves as "an act of defiance,"[29] not only in our nation's past but also in recent times. The preceding block quotation also points out that US immigration policy and foreign policy often go together. Whereas the United States claims to be an open society that champions freedom and autonomy, our policies have often shipwrecked people's access to the land of the free, while also exacting a heavy toll on their countries of origin or where we have taken up residence.

As a young, developing empire, the United States displaced the host people whose land we invaded. However, just as people can rewrite the history of immigration policy in view of Lazarus's poem, others rewrite American history and discount the grave injustices committed against native peoples or those of other lands.

---

[27]Christopher Petrella, "What We Get Wrong About the 'Poor Huddled Masses': We Can't Fix Our Immigration Policy Without Understanding Its History," *Washington Post*, December 18, 2018, https://www.washingtonpost.com/outlook/2018/12/18/what-we-get-wrong-about-poor-huddled -masses/; see also Theresa Vargas, "Trump Adviser Stephen Miller Was Right About the Statue of Liberty's Famous Inscription," *Washington Post*, August 2, 2017, https://www.washingtonpost.com /news/retropolis/wp/2017/08/02/a-trump-adviser-was-right-about-the-history-of-the-statue-of -libertys-famous-inscription/.
[28]Petrella, "What We Get Wrong."
[29]Petrella, "What We Get Wrong."

The United States has broken scores of treaties with the indigenous peoples of the land.[30] And yet, we have the audacity to sing the national anthem with words such as "the land of the free and home of the brave." The late Lakota Sioux Christian leader Richard Twiss once remarked in my presence, "The reason why they call it the land of the free is because they never paid us for it." One is left to wonder whether God will judge this country for its past sins that have present bearing on the plight of First Nations or Native American peoples, just as God judged Israel under David for what transpired when Saul slaughtered the Gibeonites, with whom Joshua had made an irrevocable covenant in the Promised Land (2 Samuel 21:1-14).

Even if we who are Christians acknowledge the gross injustices committed against indigenous people in this country, we may fail or refuse to admit or conveniently forget that those engaged in atrocious acts of violence against the people whose resources and land we took were Christian. Whether we are talking of extraction policies in the Americas or on the African continent, Western empires, including the United States, enslaved and removed people and precious materials and other resources from lands as well as colonized entire countries in the name of God and country.

The Christian faith and *Pax Americana* have been used to justify the oppression of other peoples, including the indigenous people of what we now call the United States. The mantra of manifest destiny was "Kill the Indian, and save the man."[31] Christianizing attempts have led one Native theologian, Vine Deloria Jr., to write, "Where the cross goes, there is never life more abundantly—only death, destruction, and ultimately betrayal."[32]

---

[30]See US Senator Daniel K. Inouye's foreword to *Documents of American Indian Diplomacy* (ix). Senator Inouye claims that our nation broke or failed to ratify many treaties made with indigenous peoples over the course of US history (ix). Vine Deloria and Raymond J. DeMallie, *Documents of American Indian Diplomacy: Treaties, Agreements, and Conventions, 1775–1979*, 2 vols., Legal History of North America 4 (Norman: University of Oklahoma Press, 1999). See chap. 13 of volume 2 for a list of treaties that the government failed to ratify. Consider also Karl Menninger's treatment of our nation's inexplicable and despicable treatment of Native Americans in *Whatever Became of Sin?* (New York: Hawthorn Books, 1973), 128-32.

[31]Ward Churchill, *Kill the Indian, Save the Man: The Genocidal Impact of American Indian Residential Schools* (San Francisco: City Lights, 2004).

[32]Vine Deloria Jr., *God Is Red: A Native View of Religion* (Golden, CO: Fulcrum, 1994), 261.

It is easy for Christians today to remark flippantly that those colonizing and dehumanizing leaders were not real Christians, as if that liberates us from any responsibility or culpability. It is like saying the Protestant Reformation leader Martin Luther wasn't a real Christian given what he wrote against the Jewish people in 1543, which served as fuel for the Nazis' Holocaust gas chambers centuries later.[33] Deloria challenges the claim of those who would seek to put a wedge between leaders who committed atrocious acts against Native Americans and the Christian religion, even though Christendom esteemed them as Christian heroes. "They really were Christians. In their day they enjoyed all the benefits and prestige Christendom could confer," writes Delora. "They were cheered as heroes of the faith, enduring hardships that a Christian society might be built on the ruins of pagan villages. They were featured in Sunday school lessons as saints of the Christian church. Cities, rivers, mountains, and seas were named after them."[34]

Some of those engaged in heinous extraction policies no doubt operated solely from materialist versions of manifest destiny. However, others justified their activities through recourse to the biblical narrative of Israel's conquest of the Promised Land. What such positions failed to consider was that, whereas Israel was promised the land of Palestine, as recorded in Old Testament Scripture, the Bible never makes such promises regarding Africa or the Americas. Moreover, Israel was a slave people, while Portugal, Spain, England, France, Germany, and the United States were and/or are global powers similar to the empires that conquered and enslaved Israel.

---

[33] According to Rabbi Joseph Telushkin, Hitler made horrific use of Luther's most heinous piece, "On the Jews and Their Lies," in advancing his policies of extermination of the Jewish people and viewed Luther as a forerunner. Telushkin also points out that Nazi propagandist Julius Streicher claimed in his defense at the Nuremberg trials that everything he said against the Jews Luther had already said. Telushkin refers to Luther as "the most extreme example in history of a Jew lover who turned into a Jew-hater when the Jews refused to convert to his ideology." Rabbi Joseph Telushkin, "Martin Luther and the Protestant Reformation," in *Jewish Literacy: The Most Important Things to Know About the Jewish Religion, Its People, and Its History*, rev. ed. (New York: William Morrow, 2008), 210-11.

[34] Deloria, *God Is Red*, 261-62. An example of such Christian involvement in genocide against Native Americans can be found in the words and actions of Methodist minister and US Colonel John Chivington. Chivington was responsible for the 1864 Sand Creek Massacre. Chivington asserted, "I believe it is right and honorable to use any means under God's heaven to kill Indians." Quoted in Russell Means with Marvin J. Wolf, *Where White Men Fear to Tread: The Autobiography of Russell Means* (New York: St. Martin's, 1995), 518.

It is quite likely that we conveniently forget such stark realities on our nation's shores. We have a hard time recollecting the distant and recent past immigration policies that Lazarus would have found repugnant. Perhaps it is fair to say that it is very difficult to recall the past correctly when we have invested so much and gained a great deal from trade and investment/extraction policies in the distant and recent eras. One of the crippling effects of affluenza is how it distorts our memories and frames our narratives regarding "us" and "them," such as between US nationals and foreign migrants. Affluenza easily gives rise to amnesia.

Remember that Lazarus's poem was commissioned in 1883. In 1882, the United States signed into law the Chinese Exclusion Act, which was basically in effect until 1943. In 1884, the United States participated in a "Conference on Africa" in Berlin, Germany, that represented what might be termed an *extraction* act. The *Washington Post* article noted above includes the following lines:

> As historian G. Macharia Munene writes, the United States was "fully aware" that the conference endeavored "to agree on the doctrine of free trade and navigation in rivers Congo and Niger and to define methods of annexing territories that had 'not yet been subjected to the flag of any civilized state.'" In so doing, the United States put its political weight behind the invasion, occupation, colonization and annexation of Africa— the full eradication of African political autonomy—by European powers.[35]

The subtitle to the *Washington Post* article makes clear the need for gaining a rightful understanding of US history on immigration if we are to make humane changes to our immigration policies. It reads, "We can't fix our immigration policy without understanding its history." Indeed, we will never make things right with our approach to immigration until we understand our complicated and conflicted history involving xenophobia pertaining to immigration and foreign policy, including our perceptions of Chinese, Japanese, Africans, and Central and South Americans, among others.

---

[35]Petrella, "What We Get Wrong." Here is the reference for the article mentioned by Petrella: G. Macharia Munene, "The United States and the Berlin Conference on the Partition of Africa, 1884–1885," *Transafrican Journal of History* 19 (1990): 73-79.

Here it is worth considering whether one of the greatest European philosophers fostered or simply followed his predecessors in cultivating colonialist and xenophobic ideological patterns of thought. What complicates matters is that the philosopher in question, Immanuel Kant, argued that people should not be treated as mere means but as ends in themselves.[36] He did not go far enough in his personalist orientation, for he viewed European men alone as rational and as ends in themselves, not mere means.[37] What might that entail for Africans, Arabs, and Mexicans, especially given his notion of a good will, which is properly delimited in accordance with the canons of Kantian reason?[38]

In our attempt to get history right, we need to account for the historical forces that shaped such faulty ideological patterns of thought. We must also account for relationships in the past, as well as those in the present, that bridge borders and connect us with other countries in subtle and overt ways. Here we call to mind Tisha M. Rajendra's work *Migrants and Citizens: Justice and Responsibility in the Ethics of Immigration*.[39] In an interview, Rajendra states that "we need a new account of justice that can respond to relationships that cross international borders. I call this account of justice 'justice as responsibility to relationships.'"[40] Rajendra goes on to claim,

[36]Immanuel Kant, *Groundwork for the Metaphysics of Morals*, ed. and trans. Allen W. Wood (New Haven, CT: Yale University Press, 2002), 4:429; 46-47.

[37]See Thomas E. Hill Jr. and Bernard Boxill, "Kant and Race," in *Race and Racism*, ed. Bernard Boxill, Oxford Readings in Philosophy Series (Oxford: Oxford University Press, 2001), chap. 18. One can find a PDF of the chapter here: http://www.faculty.umb.edu/lawrence_blum/courses/465_11/readings/Race_and_Racism.pdf.

[38]Kant starts off his *Groundwork of the Metaphysics of Morals* by stating, "Nothing can possibly be conceived in the world, or even out of it, which can be called good without qualification, except a *good will*." *First Philosophy: Fundamental Problems and Readings in Philosophy*, 2nd ed., ed. Andrew Bailey with Robert M. Martin (Ontario: Broadview, 2011), 647. Furthermore, "a good will is good not because of what it accomplishes or effects, not by its aptness for the attainment of some proposed end, but simply by virtue of the volition—that is, it is good in itself" (648).

[39]Tisha M. Rajendra, *Migrants and Citizens: Justice and Responsibility in the Ethics of Immigration* (Grand Rapids, MI: Eerdmans, 2017).

[40]Paul Louis Metzger, "Reforming Our Understanding of Migrants and Approach to Immigration Reform: An Interview with Dr. Tisha M. Rajendra," *Uncommon God, Common Good*, Patheos, September 27, 2017, www.patheos.com/blogs/uncommongodcommongood/2017/09/reforming-our-understanding-of-migrants-and-approach-to-immigration-reform-an-interview-with-dr-tisha-m-rajendra/.

The dominant narrative of migration is that immigrants come "here"—or to wealthy liberal democracies seeking "a better life." While this is true in some ways, migration theorists posit that mass migration always occurs in the context of pre-existing relationships initiated by host countries. Most often, these relationships are not morally neutral. Colonialism, guest worker programs and economic interventions are asymmetrical relationships that benefit host countries at the expense of citizens of receiving countries. Often, these interventions start "migration flows" into host countries. But citizens of host countries often think that migrants are strangers—poor people who arrive unbidden, clamoring for a share in our social goods. Nothing could be further from the truth! If we knew our own history—of colonialism in the Philippines, of military intervention in Central America, of the ways that economic intervention didn't just take jobs away from our factory workers—it destabilized parts of rural Mexico—we would not consider migrants strangers.[41]

Rajendra's relational model stands in stark contrast to the merit-based model that readily breaks and forgets covenantal relations. It finds a compatible emphasis in the family-based model of immigration that reunites families, which was noted earlier and which the United States Conference of Roman Catholic Bishops favors. While not literal families, these nations have long-standing relational ties with the United States based on our investments and extractions from their native lands. As Rajendra reasons, we need to remember and honor these regional and international relationships rather than conveniently forget them. We must not allow our affluence resulting from those relationships to foster amnesia. The opportunities and benefits for our respective countries should be comparable. But all too often there is great disparity, though not in these other nations' favor. If we follow the flow of activity from the United States' initiation of relationships, investments, and withdrawal of profits, we will understand why so many people from other countries to the

---

[41]Metzger, "Reforming Our Understanding." For additional reflections on immigration, and the biblical concepts of hospitality, justice, and compassion, see M. Daniel Carroll R., *Christians at the Border: Immigration, the Church, and the Bible*, 2nd ed. (Grand Rapids, MI: Brazos, 2013); Matthew Kaemingk, *Christian Hospitality and Muslim Immigration in an Age of Fear* (Grand Rapids, MI: Eerdmans, 2018); and Matthew Soerens and Jenny Yang, *Welcoming the Stranger: Justice, Compassion & Truth in the Immigration Debate*, rev. ed. (Downers Grove, IL: InterVarsity Press, 2018).

south of us seek to migrate here. They are going in search of regaining what we have taken from them.

As we continue to debate the merits of a wall on our southern border, we as a nation should account for our intrusions not as refugees but as capitalists who invest enormous financial resources in various continents, only to extract the capital whenever convenient and advantageous to ourselves with no concern for the people of the land. Martin Luther King Jr. addresses this matter in his Vietnam War sermon, proclaiming that "a true revolution of values will soon look uneasily on the glaring contrast of poverty and wealth." This revolution is global in scope; it "will look across the seas and see individual capitalists of the West investing huge sums of money in Asia, Africa, and South America, only to take the profits with no concern for the social betterment of the countries," and it will criticize this as an injustice. "The Western arrogance of feeling that it has everything to teach others and nothing to learn from them is not just," King states.[42]

King's critique of the Vietnam War did not sway the Johnson administration to pull out from Vietnam. Nor did the reminder of King's rebuke of American incursions in Asia, Africa, and South America lead the Nixon administration to withdraw troops from Vietnam or to refrain from sponsoring Pinochet's coup in Chile in 1973. For all our emphasis on promoting democratic freedom and free trade, we are often guilty of intruding on the sovereignty of diverse peoples and countries. Given our tendency to forget this tendency and our proclivity for such intrusions, we must put in place safeguards against moral deregulations that promote laissez-faire or permissive policies favoring the political and economic elites that all too often crush individual persons and vulnerable populations.

DISASTER CAPITALISM AND THE MIGRATION OF HUMAN VALUE

Mention was made of the Nixon administration and Chile, where political pressures gave rise to economic pressures, similar to what King chronicled in his Vietnam War sermon. Naomi Klein's 2007 *New York*

---

[42]Martin Luther King Jr., "Beyond Vietnam," in *A Call to Conscience: The Landmark Speeches of Dr. Martin Luther King, Jr.*, ed. Clayborne Carson and Kris Shepard (New York: Warner Books, 2001), 158.

Times bestseller, *The Shock Doctrine: The Rise of Disaster Capitalism*, addresses this subject.[43] According to Klein, Milton Friedman and his associates exploited dramatic social upheaval and disasters in various countries to instill drastic or severe free-market economic policies. Hence the term *disaster capitalism*. Contrary to the mythical claim that Friedman's free-market economic revolution gained power peacefully on the global scene, she argues that they used economic forms of "shock treatment" to force sudden corporate makeovers in various countries. Disaster capitalism involves utilizing catastrophic trials in various societies to put in place structures of extreme privatization combined with the privatization of the accompanying disaster response.

Klein documents how Friedman and his associates destabilized Chile's infrastructure to bring about a free-market economic system when Augusto Pinochet came to power with the backing of the United States during the Nixon era. Prior to Pinochet's takeover, the United States had imposed a debilitating financial embargo on the democratically elected socialist regime in Chile.

In Klein's estimation, Friedman's style of capitalism was promoted as a miraculous turnaround of Chile's economy, when in fact it was a massive disintegration of their public infrastructure, which was turned over to private control. Pinochet came to power in "a bloody US-backed coup" of "the democratically elected socialist president," Salvador Allende. Friedman and his "Chicago Boys" were brought in to enact a "shock" to reformulate the Chilean economy into a free-market system. Friedman's policy was essentially "never let a good crisis go to waste." Crises prime societies to be pliable to radical and immediate reforms, which Friedman uses to enact free market-based strategies that from one angle are lucrative but from another angle are completely destructive.[44]

---

[43]Naomi Klein, *The Shock Doctrine: The Rise of Disaster Capitalism* (New York: Picador, 2007).

[44]Klein offers a window into her book in her account of Milton Friedman and his Chicago Boys and what transpired in Chile under Pinochet in "Milton Friedman Did Not Save Chile," *Guardian*, March 3, 2010, www.theguardian.com/commentisfree/cifamerica/2010/mar/03/chile-earthquake. The subtitle reads, "To say the late economist deserves credit for the country's building codes shows a lack of knowledge of pre-coup Chile." Here is another article addressing similar dynamics and concerns: Orlando Letelier, "The 'Chicago Boys' in Chile: Economic Freedom's Awful Toll," *Nation*, September 21, 2016, https://www.thenation.com/article/archive/the-chicago-boys-in-chile -economic-freedoms-awful-toll/. The subtitle reads: "Repression for the majorities and 'economic

Klein challenges the claim that Pinochet's regime with Friedman's economic oversight was responsible for the building code that gave rise to
houses of brick in Chile, which in turn spared it from incredible earthquake devastation in 2010. The building code responsible for the brick
houses was crafted in 1972, during "a crippling economic embargo,"
which was imposed by the United States and intended by Nixon to "make
the economy scream." It was only later that Pinochet seized power and
Friedman's economic policies were free to roam.

It is also worth noting that according to Klein, Friedman was wary of
building codes based on the limits they impose on free-market capitalism. The building code was not updated again until the 1990s, long
after Friedman's Chicago Boys were removed from positions of power.
Additionally, Klein claims that "the Chile of the 1960s had the best health
and education systems on the continent, as well as a vibrant industrial
sector and a rapidly expanding middle class. Chileans believed in their
state, which is why they elected Allende to take the project even further."[45]

According to Cynthia Moe-Lobeda, the laissez-faire neoclassical
economic orientation associated with Friedman affirms eliminating "economic 'discrimination' against dictatorships."[46] Friedman writes, "An
impersonal market separates economic activities from political views
and protects men from being discriminated against."[47] But what about
dictators' as well as economic empire elites' impersonal or very personal
discrimination against others?

A few pages later, Moe-Lobeda comments that Friedman is "a foundational theorist of laissez-faire liberalism or the laissez-faire pole of
neo-classical economic theory as developed in the University of Chicago
school of economics."[48] She references Carol Johnston's summary of

---

freedom' for small, privileged groups are two sides of the same coin." For a US government account
of Allende's presidency, American opposition to Allende, and the end of forty-six years of democratic rule in Chile with Pinochet's military coup, see "The Allende Years and the Pinochet Coup,
1969–1973," *Office of the Historian*, Foreign Service Institute, United States Department of State,
https://history.state.gov/milestones/1969-1976/allende.

[45]Klein, "Milton Friedman Did Not Save Chile." See also Cynthia D. Moe-Lobeda, *Healing a Broken
World: Globalization and God* (Minneapolis: Fortress, 2002), 51-52, 62, 64, 196, including her engagement of Friedman on 192, 197.

[46]Moe-Lobeda, *Healing a Broken World*, 192.

[47]Milton Friedman, *Capitalism and Freedom* (Chicago: University of Chicago Press, 1962), 21.

[48]Moe-Lobeda, *Healing a Broken World*, 197.

Friedman's model of freedom.[49] According to Johnston, freedom is associated with economics, and freedom is "the ultimate goal and the individual" is "the ultimate entity in the society." Friedman frames freedom in "purely individualistic terms."[50] For Friedman, "freedom" is "liberty from control by others."[51] Friedman is often associated with removing government interventions and regulations in the market. The one apparent exception is his approval of governmental interventions to bring about greater autonomy, though not "equity."[52] Here's Friedman: "We do not wish to conserve the state interventions that have interfered so greatly with our freedom, though, of course, we do wish to conserve those that have promoted it."[53]

This model stands in stark contrast to King's personalism that affirms individual autonomy or freedom, but never in isolation from one's fellow humans of all walks of life. For King, every individual has infinite worth and value that involves individual autonomy or freedom. But such freedom does not exist in a vacuum but in voluntary and mutual terms of communal association.[54]

King's emphasis on moral freedom involving the individual in harmonious relationship with the community and universe made by the hand of a benevolent personal God pits him against ideological migrations that favor or "dictate" viewing the market as a force of nature.[55] For all the talk of individual autonomy, political and economic forces favoring market ideology such as Friedman's plan overwhelm vulnerable individuals and communities in situations such as Chile and destroy human agency. All too often, those in control view such forces serving the ideological interests of liberal democracies and their economies as inevitable.

---

[49]Carol Johnston, *The Health or Wealth of Nations: Transforming Capitalism from Within* (Cleveland: Pilgrim, 1998), 101-9.

[50]Johnston, *Health or Wealth of Nations*, 101.

[51]Moe-Lobeda, *Healing a Broken World*, 197.

[52]Johnston, *Health or Wealth of Nations*, 101; Moe-Lobeda, *Healing a Broken World*, 197.

[53]Friedman, *Capitalism and Freedom*, 6. See also 8 and 9.

[54]See here Rufus Burrow Jr., "Some Reflections on King, Personalism, and Sexism," *Encounter* 65, no. 1 (Winter 2004): 36-37.

[55]See Rufus Burrow Jr., *God and Human Dignity: The Personalism, Theology, and Ethics of Martin Luther King, Jr.* (Notre Dame, IN: University of Notre Dame Press, 2006), 184, for an account of King's doctrine of the moral ground of the universe being personal and benevolent.

They claim that the invisible hand of the market, whether supernatural or natural in origin, is responsible.[56]

Such political and economic forces can easily confuse Adam Smith's doctrine of self-interest with selfish desires and justify the latter as carrying out the inevitable will of the invisible hand. However, Smith, who is the originator of the phrase *invisible hand* and author of *The Wealth of Nations*, which is considered the "bible of capitalism" and "the first system of political economy,"[57] did not equate self-interest with selfishness. Rather, self-interest simply means care for one's own interests as well as one's immediate circle in the economic domain, not society as a whole. When coupled with Smith's emphases on sympathy and justice, self-interest (not selfish, greedy desires) serves the invisible hand that paves the way for a well-ordered society and economic system that brings about the greatest good for everyone.[58]

Smith was quite wary of those who would operate from greed and intentionally harm others to benefit themselves economically. According to Lauren Hall,

> Rather than defending active vice as something that leads to virtue, Smith is critical of vicious behavior and argues in both *Wealth of Nations* and *The Theory of Moral Sentiments* that benevolent and virtuous behaviors are both necessary and desirable for stable social orders. Far from providing rationale for selfish material pursuits, Smith's self-interest, properly understood, encourages a kind of virtue that protects both individuals and their communities.[59]

---

[56]See the following treatment of Adam Smith's metaphor, arguing that we find here a notion of general providence that does not make space for special providence. Rather, in Smith we find "'immanentized' providentialism" and "providential deism." Cornelis van der Kooi and Jordan J. Ballor, "Providence, Divine Power, and the 'Invisible Hand' in Adam Smith," *Journal of Economics, Theology and Religion* 1, no. 1 (2021): 25-44, https://j-etr.org/2020/10/27/providence-divine-power -and-the-invisible-hand-in-adam-smith/.

[57]"Adam Smith Biography," Biography.com, April 2, 2014; updated April 15, 2021, www.biography .com/scholar/adam-smith.

[58]Lauren Hall writes, "Fortunately, our desire for the approbation of our fellow humans binds self-interest to keep it consistent with the demands of sympathy and justice. Self-interest is therefore consistent with justice and propriety. Selfishness, the desire to better oneself without regard to even the demands of justice, is not." Lauren Hall, "Self-Interest Rightly Understood," AdamSmithWorks, www.adamsmithworks.org/documents/self-interest-rightly-understood.

[59]Hall, "Self-Interest Rightly Understood."

How is what occurred in Chile evidence of Smith's invisible hand? The economic embargo and disaster-capitalist incursion all too visibly revealed the US's hand.

Moreover, contrary to a free-market society, where only that which has economic merit is valuable, Smith did not see economic self-interest as the focus and summation of all human ventures. Nor did he think self-interest was the height of human qualities, but rather, that those traits that flow from self-interest rank low on the chart of human virtues.[60]

A personalist ethical system that does not equate human value with economic value is critically important. It will require putting in place safeguards against the all-too-visible hand of military and economic powerhouses wreaking havoc on vulnerable populations whose degree of dignity does not depend on economic merit or equation with revenue sources and market shares. Without such safeguards, vulnerable populations may be displaced and migrate to the country or countries responsible for shocking their economic systems, creating need and dependency and displacing them.

A personalist moral vision benefits greatly from an understanding of God's identification with the oppressed and alien in their distress and call for his people to rescue them from the oppressor's hand: "This is what the LORD says: Do what is just and right. Rescue from the hand of the oppressor the one who has been robbed. Do no wrong or violence to the foreigner, the fatherless or the widow, and do not shed innocent blood in this place" (Jeremiah 22:3). As with Confucius and his universal vision, the personalist moral vision for immigration reform sketched in this chapter does not focus on the economic struggle between the employer

---

[60]Refer to the following accounts of self-interest vs. selfishness in Smith's thought: Hall, "Self-Interest Rightly Understood"; Stephen Miller, "What Did Adam Smith Really Believe?," *Washington Examiner*, February 13, 2017, www.washingtonexaminer.com/weekly-standard/what-did-adam-smith-really-believe. See also Gavin Kennedy, "Adam Smith Never Believed That 'Greed Is Good' and Economics Students Who Act as If They Should Be Greedy Are Woefully Misled by Their Tutors," Adam Smith's Lost Legacy, October 28, 2013, https://adamsmithslostlegacy.blogspot .com/2013/10/adam-smith-never-believed-that-greed-is.html. The reader is encouraged to read the relevant passages in Smith's works, *The Theory of Moral Sentiments* (Erie, PA: Gutenberg, 2011), especially part IV, chapter 1, and *An Inquiry into the Nature and Causes of the Wealth of Nations*, ed. Edwin Cannan (Chicago: University of Chicago Press, 1976), especially book IV, chapter 2.

and worker. Rather, it features ethics and religion as well as political theory, which in turn should impact economic policies.

Moreover, a personalist ethic does not reduce persons to their economic self-interests that discount human agency. Economics are not inevitable and impersonal natural forces but human forces. This personalist orientation runs contrary to the dominant narrative in many circles.

On the subject of natural forces Francis Fukuyama writes, "The logic of modern natural science would seem to dictate a universal evolution in the direction of capitalism."[61] He argues further "that liberal democracy may constitute 'the end point of mankind's ideological evolution,' and 'the final form of human government,' and the 'end of history.'"[62] Fukuyama's comments on evolution and capitalism call to mind Gordon Bigelow's reflections on the faulty viewpoint that markets are "phenomena of nature":

> Economics, as channeled by its popular avatars in media and politics, is the cosmology and the theodicy of our contemporary culture. More than religion itself, more than literature, more than cable television, it is economics that offers the dominant creation narrative of our society, depicting the relation of each of us to the universe we inhabit, the relation of human beings to God. And the story it tells is a marvelous one. In it an enormous multitude of strangers, all individuals, all striving alone, are nevertheless all bound together in a beautiful and natural pattern of existence: the market. This understanding of markets—not as artifacts of human civilization but as phenomena of nature—now serves as the unquestioned foundation of nearly all political and social debate.[63]

The placement of markets in nature's domain deregulates them and makes them impenetrable to moral scrutiny in a post-Kantian world that divides nature and moral freedom. When the only bridge between them is artistic genius subjectively construed, there is no ultimate safeguard against abuse of the individual human subject. The end result is commodification, which is exactly what is on display in a free-market society

---

[61]Francis Fukuyama, *The End of History and the Last Man* (New York: Free Press, 2006), xv.

[62]Fukuyama, *End of History*, xi.

[63]Gordon Bigelow, "Let There Be Markets: The Evangelical Roots of Economics," *Harper's* (May 2005): 33.

brought to bear on those migrating from place to place in a state of limbo. They are not at home on land or on the high seas. Here we call to mind Simon Critchley's reflection on the Kantian divide and its problematic import for human value:

> How is freedom to be instantiated or to take effect in the world of nature, if the latter is governed by causality and mechanistically determined by the laws of nature? How is the causality of the natural world reconcilable with what Kant calls "the causality of freedom"? How, to allude to Emerson alluding to the language of Kant's Third Critique, is genius to be transformed into practical power? Doesn't Kant leave human beings in what Hegel and the young Marx might have called the *amphibious* position of being both freely subject to the moral law and determined by an objective world of nature that has been stripped of any value and which stands over against human beings as a world of alienation? Isn't individual freedom reduced to an abstraction in the face of an indifferent world of objects that are available to one—at a price—as commodities?[64]

The increasing commodification of life, not simply goods in the marketplace, is a real threat to human existence and personhood. While we debate the supposed threat of migrants at our national borders, we are often unaware of the hazard posed within our borders and our value system: freedom and human existence are themselves treated as commodities. If we won't regulate markets based on concerns over abuses to vulnerable populations abroad, what's to keep us from deregulating market intrusions into our views of human value generally? Human personhood is then in a state of limbo as it migrates from one transaction to another, where we are no more than commodified means to impersonal, capitalistic ends.

Moe-Lobeda draws attention to Larry Rasmussen's view that capitalism "is not just an economic form but a way of being," or "way of life."[65] For Rasmussen, the transition from an economic form to a way of being involves the transitional element "that the moral order and culture are organized on the same principles as the economic and share its ethos."[66]

[64]Simon Critchley, "What Is to Be Done? How to Respond to Nihilism," in *Continental Philosophy: A Very Short Introduction* (Oxford: Oxford University Press, 2001), 76.
[65]Moe-Lobeda, *Healing a Broken World*, 62.
[66]Larry Rasmussen, *Moral Fragments and Moral Community: A Proposal for Church in Society* (Minneapolis: Fortress, 2000), 48.

"Rational self-interest" is the defining economic and ethical factor. Becker, a Nobel laureate from the Chicago school of economics, illustrates this point: "The economic approach is a comprehensive one that is applicable to all human behavior."[67] No doubt, this orientation shapes his merit-based model of immigration reform referenced at the outset of this chapter.

Moe-Lobeda and Rasmussen draw attention to Adam Smith's paradigm, which would appear to run counter to a market-based ethical paradigm. Their interpretation of Smith calls to mind Sandel's distinction on the market economy versus market society. Sandel has no difficulty with a free-market economy. However, he takes issue with a free-market society.[68] Those who favor a free-market economy but not a free-market society champion a noncapitalist morality involving mutual love of neighbor and delight in their well-being along with proportionate support of government in keeping with one's means. This framework is foundational to an economic system that would lead to equitable human flourishing.[69]

In Moe-Lobeda's view, it is wrong to invoke Smith's name in support of deregulating global markets. Such appeals fail to account for Smith's overarching economic framework. First, his system presupposes rooting capital in domestic contexts. "His discussion of the 'invisible hand' is located in his assertion that capital invested *domestically* creates more wealth for individuals and nations."[70] Second, his economic system presupposes competition between buyers and sellers apart from the intrusive behavior of oligarchic monopolies that dramatically affect the

---

[67]Gary S. Becker, *The Economic Approach to Human Behavior* (Chicago: University of Chicago Press, 1978), 8.

[68]Sandel, *What Money Can't Buy*, 5-6.

[69]Moe-Lobeda, *Healing a Broken World*, 199n67.

[70]Moe-Lobeda, *Healing a Broken World*, 51. In this vein, Eugene Heath argues, "In Part IV, chapter 1, of *The Theory of Moral Sentiments* (1759)," Adam Smith "explains that, as wealthy individuals pursue their own interests, employing others to labour for them, they 'are led by an invisible hand' to distribute the necessities that all would have received had there been an equal division of the earth. In Book IV, chapter 2, of *An Inquiry into the Nature and Causes of the Wealth of Nations* (1776), arguing against import restrictions and explaining how individuals prefer domestic over foreign investments, Smith uses the phrase to summarize how self-interested actions are so coordinated that they advance the public interest. In those two instances, a complex and beneficial structure is explained by invoking basic principles of human nature and economic interaction." Eugene Heath, "Invisible Hand," *Britannica*, www.britannica.com/topic/invisible-hand.

market valuation of products. Third, Smith's model involves the conviction that the hourly increase in productivity would give rise to the parallel increase of wages. Fourth, the market system he proposes champions the accompanying sufficiency of wages to sustain laborers and their families.[71]

As already noted, by no means would Smith's affirmation of economic self-interest or his famed invisible hand applaud making another country's economy scream for one's own nation's security or for greedy gain. While Smith would not include those who are unknown migrants in one's family or inner circle of self-interest requiring parental or patron care, he would champion sympathy and justice. Given such nuance, it seems correct to deduce that those who would claim to be Smith's progeny in free-market capitalism should extend their aspirations for economic well-being and prosperity to include the well-being of those on our nation's doorsteps who have been exploited by our economic policies for financial gain.

The purpose of this discussion is not to focus consideration on free-market economics per se but to address the need for regulations that safeguard against abuses in global markets, which in turn impacts dramatically immigration and migration patterns. To the extent the United States deems it necessary to increase focus on securing national borders from undocumented immigrants, it needs to increase scrutiny on securing international borders from undocumented or unregulated market intrusions by transnational companies that exploit developing nations' vulnerabilities.

One is left to wonder how often what King declared and Klein documents has occurred in various regional and global settings involving the US government and US business enterprises. We must account for these and other stories of international interference. We must also change the dominant narrative, which is American exceptionalism and its erroneous claim that this country is unique in virtue and worthy of the international community's undying adulation. Reminiscent of King's critique of American exceptionalism in his Vietnam War address, Stephen Walt states,

---

[71]Moe-Lobeda, *Healing a Broken World*, 51-52.

"The idea that the United States is uniquely virtuous may be comforting to Americans. Too bad it's not true."[72] While it is great in many ways, including foreign aid, strategies such as disaster capitalism are by no means virtuous. Nor are our colonialist strategies, coupled with free-market ideology, which limits loyalty to other countries based merely on national self-interest and economic benefits. Until we change the narrative, we will not be able to account for these stories and make necessary changes. Moreover, if we do indeed want the world's adulation based on virtues of equity and empathy, we must honor our relationships with other countries. If we do not account for our own unwelcome economic and political migrations as intrusions in other countries, and what we need to do at this hour to bring stability and rebuild infrastructure that helps these countries flourish, perhaps any wall we build on our southern border should be constructed to keep the United States locked inside our borders to do no more harm to Central and South American nations rather than to keep them out.

THE HEAVENLY HOST AND DIVINE STRANGER AT HISTORY'S END

The end of history will look very different from Fukuyama's *End of History and the Last Man*, if the parable of the sheep and the goats in Matthew 25 has any lasting merit. For over thirty years, many Western intellectuals have celebrated the widespread success of liberal democracy and free-market capitalism with the symbolic import of the Berlin Wall's fall in 1989. They have affirmed Fukuyama's claim that no other movement of thought would presume to take the high moral ground universally, not that history would literally end or that every society would conform to the Western democratic and capitalistic paradigm.

In his landmark article titled "The End of History?" Fukuyama argues, "It is not necessary that all societies become successful liberal societies, merely that they end their ideological pretensions of representing different and higher forms of human society."[73] In the book that followed,

---

[72]Stephen M. Walt, "The Myth of American Exceptionalism," *Foreign Policy*, October 11, 2011, https://foreignpolicy.com/2011/10/11/the-myth-of-american-exceptionalism/.

[73]Francis Fukuyama, "The End of History?," *The National Interest* 16 (Summer 1989): 13, www.jstor.org/stable/24027184?seq=16#metadata_info_tab_contents.

The End of History and the Last Man, Fukuyama reasons, "For a very large part of the world, there is now no ideology with pretensions to universality that is in a position to challenge liberal democracy."[74] That said, in the past few years, Fukuyama has had second thoughts about liberal democracy's staying power.[75]

Regardless of whether liberal democracy and free-market capitalism are on the wane, Christian Scripture bears witness that "the last man," who looks very different from Fukuyama's representative human, claims universality and without pretense. He is Jesus of Nazareth. Fukuyama was right in warning that nationalism and religion would not disappear and that they could come back to "bite" humanity.[76] Nationalism and nativism are part of our nation's current problem, as is nationalistic religious piety. However, Jesus of Nazareth as Lord over all nations, not to be identified with any one of them, calls to account such nationalistic religious piety.

Jesus is no respecter of persons or nation and will separate the sheep and the goats, placing the sheep on his right hand and the goats on his left hand. He is the heavenly host who invites all those who have honored him in history as divine stranger and guest into his kingdom (Matthew 25:31-33). His very visible right hand welcomes them as sheep. The last man who is "the King will say to those on his right, 'Come, you who are blessed by my Father; take your inheritance, the kingdom prepared for

---

[74]Fukuyama, *End of History and the Last Man*, 45.

[75]Ishaan Tharoor, "The Man Who Declared the 'End of History' Fears for Democracy's Future," *Washington Post*, February 9, 2017, www.washingtonpost.com/news/worldviews/wp/2017/02/09/the-man-who-declared-the-end-of-history-fears-for-democracys-future/; Louis Menand, "Francis Fukuyama Postpones the End of History," *New Yorker*, August 27, 2018, www.newyorker.com/magazine/2018/09/03/francis-fukuyama-postpones-the-end-of-history.

[76]In a recent interview, Fukuyama writes that "the whole 'Last Man' section is about what could go wrong with democracy in the future. One of the issues is that if you simply have a society that's stable, prosperous, and peaceful, people don't have anything to aspire to. That aspiration—what I call megalothymia, the desire to be recognized as greater than other people—doesn't get satisfied. You have to have outlets for this, and if you can't struggle for justice, as in prior history, then you'll struggle for injustice." Later, he writes, "Part of my book's point was that there are plenty of sources of discontent other than serious insecurity or serious material privation, which really have to do with people's feelings of dignity. People will not be satisfied with endless consumerism and buying the new iPhone every 18 months, because they actually want to be recognized for something. I do think that critics failed to recognize how I said that nationalism and religion would not disappear from the world, and could come back to bite us." See Francis Fukuyama, Charles Davidson, and Jeffrey Gedmin, "The Last Man and the Future of History," *American Interest*, May 3, 2019, www.the-american-interest.com/2019/05/03/the-last-man-and-the-future-of-history/.

you since the creation of the world. For I was hungry and you gave me something to eat, I was thirsty and you gave me something to drink, I was a stranger and you invited me in, I needed clothes and you clothed me, I was sick and you looked after me, I was in prison and you came to visit me'" (Matthew 25:34-36). The heavenly host grants kingdom citizenship papers to all those who have welcomed him as a stranger, when his divinity was invisible to them. Even so, Jesus is by no means an invisible hand. He entered history with the Holy Spirit as God's two hands, to allude to Irenaeus's claim in chapter two. Jesus is God's visible demonstration of his aims and calling for our lives.

Christian Scripture does not provide us with an in-depth analysis of free-market systems and what they signify for immigration reform. However, the Bible does tell us how to treat our neighbors—to love them as ourselves. How we wish to be treated serves as a barometer: if we do not wish for people to reduce us to our economic import or export merit or worth, we should not do that to them either. Just as the Sabbath was made for people and not people for the Sabbath, the market was made for people, not people for the market.

In addition, Christian Scripture appears to account for various levels of moral sentiment in the discussion, to allude to Adam Smith's language, or to what social psychologist Jonathan Haidt calls various moral foundations. Haidt has observed and classified what he takes to be six moral foundations ("sources of intuitions and emotions") that register in people's minds: harm/care, fairness/reciprocity, in-group/loyalty, authority/respect, purity/sanctity, and liberty. Haidt argues that we must account for these "foundations" when seeking to address society's moral concerns.

Yes, there is a place for what Adam Smith might refer to as "self-interest" beyond the economic sphere, as both the sheep and the goats express concern over their eternal status as they stand before the last man. Moreover, the text reflects on what Smith categorizes as moral sentiments of sympathy and justice, or what Haidt classifies as the moral intuitions of care and fairness or equity.[77] After all, the sheep shower compassion on the stranger,

---

[77]See the homepage of Moral Foundations, http://moralfoundations.org/. Haidt wrote a book in this domain titled *The Righteous Mind: Why Good People Are Divided by Politics and Religion* (New York: Pantheon Books, 2012). See also http://righteousmind.com/.

among others. The last man or "Son of Man" who "comes in his glory" (Matthew 25:31) judges fairly or justly. He commends those who cared for others in need. In doing so, they cared for him: "The King will reply, 'Truly I tell you, whatever you did for one of the least of these brothers and sisters of mine, you did for me'" (Matthew 25:40). He also condemned those who ignored or discounted those in need, including him:

> Then he will say to those on his left, "Depart from me, you who are cursed, into the eternal fire prepared for the devil and his angels. For I was hungry and you gave me nothing to eat, I was thirsty and you gave me nothing to drink, I was a stranger and you did not invite me in, I needed clothes and you did not clothe me, I was sick and in prison and you did not look after me."
>
> They also will answer, "Lord, when did we see you hungry or thirsty or a stranger or needing clothes or sick or in prison, and did not help you?"
>
> He will reply, "Truly I tell you, whatever you did not do for one of the least of these, you did not do for me." (Matthew 25:41-45)

Moreover, we find here in Jesus' parable an emphasis on Smith's and Haidt's valuation of liberty in that the sheep and the goats were permitted to act freely in keeping with their level of self-interest and interest in the well-being of others, including those outside their immediate circles of responsibility. However, liberty apart from loyalty is problematic. Smith and Haidt esteem the moral sentiment or intuition of loyalty, or caring for one's own. The sheep do so in tending to the Son of Man, but the goats appear to care only for themselves. As we find in the Samaritan of sacrificial love in Luke 10, whoever we find on our path in need is our neighbor. God calls us to love our neighbor as ourselves (Luke 10:25-37).

Haidt's moral intuitions of authority and purity come into play. The Son of Man is the final court of appeal. He is the highest law in any land as he passes judgment while sitting on "his glorious throne" (Matthew 25:31). Moreover, the Son of Man welcomes the sheep into his kingdom, which is the heavenly host country, given their pure devotion to the Son of Man in caring for those in need. In contrast, the goats, who lack such pure devotion, remain on the other side of the wall and are destined for eternal punishment (Matthew 25:46).

The parable of the sheep and the goats says nothing about secure national boundaries, whether one should honor human-made laws at every

turn, or ensure fairness to those who pay taxes, and keep families together rather than separate them. That is not to say that these issues lack
importance. Certainly, each government is awarded authority to protect
their citizens from harm by those with bad intentions; make laws regarding admittance of immigrants in keeping with their corporate self-
interest; safeguard against sluggards who take advantage of others' good
intentions, thereby jeopardizing the common good; and foster solid,
secure familial relationships and relational networks that will benefit the
society at large.[78] If the church and society at large are to account for
Jesus' teaching on caring for the stranger and the rightful interests of
nation-states, it is important to consider and preserve the well-being of
outsiders (immigrants) and insiders (citizens) respectively.

One example of a bipartisan attempt at immigration reform that appears to account for outsiders and insiders and many, if not all, of Haidt's
moral foundations is set forth at the Evangelical Immigration Table. The
statement "I was a stranger" found in the parable of the sheep and the
goats leaps out on the homepage of their website. The Evangelical Immigration Table brings together evangelical Christian perspectives from
across the political and ideological (moral intuition?) spectrum. The ar-
chitects of the statement claim that a "bipartisan solution on immigration" accounts for these six values: "Respects the God-given dignity
of every person"; "Protects the unity of the immediate family"; "Respects
the rule of law"; "Guarantees secure national borders"; "Ensures fairness
to taxpayers"; and "Establishes a path toward legal status and/or citizenship for those who qualify and who wish to become permanent resi-
dents." One finds here care for one's in-group as well as outgroups.

The parable of the sheep and goats in Matthew 25 indicates that our
care must extend beyond our nuclear families and relational networks to
address the well-being of immigrants regardless of outsiders' economic
merit. The hungry and thirsty individual, the stranger, the person
needing clothing, the one who is sick or in prison, is in need of our help.
The Son of Man, in contrast to Aristotle's gods noted earlier in this
chapter, does not look for the brightest in our midst to emulate his

---

[78]Evangelical Immigration Table, http://evangelicalimmigrationtable.com/.

intellectual prowess but for the pure of heart who will do his will, which involves compassion for people regardless of their level or lack of virtue and merit. We may belong to colonialist nations that have divided continents and annexed property belonging to those we do not consider civilized.[79] We may choose to commodify all of life, not just items subject to trade in the free market. We may even determine to bring harm to others for the sake of gaining greater affluence. But one thing we should not do: try to justify and excuse our actions as the inevitable outworking of the invisible hand of the market before the last man, who will judge our "ideological pretensions" of universal scope that claim to represent the last and highest form of "human society." The last man, who is Jesus of Nazareth, will have the final say. His kingdom will have universal appeal and sway. He will draw people from every nation in pursuit of virtuous care for the stranger to enter his kingdom's gates.

---

[79]Regarding the deeply problematic division of continents and annexation of property according to those who are deemed civilized, it is worth considering treatments of John Locke's model of appropriation of land in John Douglas Bishop, "Locke's Theory of Original Appropriation and the Right of Settlement in Iroquois Territory," *Canadian Journal of Philosophy* 27, no. 3 (September 1997): 311-37. See also James Tully, "Rediscovering America: The Two Treatises and Aboriginal Rights," in *Locke's Philosophy: Content and Context*, ed. G. A. J. Rogers (Oxford: Clarendon Press, 1994), 165-96; Barbara Arneil, "Trade, Plantations, and Property: John Locke and the Economic Defense of Colonialism," *Journal of the History of Ideas* 54 (1994): 591-609.

10

MORE THAN JUST WAR

Human Value and Drone Warfare

DRONE STRIKES APPEAL to civilized and technologically advanced societies for their reputed surgical efficiency and reduction of troop and civilian casualties. This chapter will seek to sensitize readers to the moral challenges facing drone warfare. It will include consideration of various factors, such as claims of drones' accuracy and reduction of casualties. I do not presume to provide a definitive answer about the merits and perils of drone warfare that will satisfy all parties. My aim is more modest. In short, I will deliberate on the actual tenets of just war theory and the fallibility and various vulnerabilities of drone technology in the effort to caution and chasten readers against simplistic mention of "just war" and drones' infallibility to justify rash use of drone strikes to resolve our various international conflicts. Concomitantly, I will call for undying support for the long-suffering work of diplomacy.

Along the way, I will analyze Kant's principle of publicity in warfare, as well as just war doctrinal tenets of necessity, discrimination, and proportionality. Attention will also be given to whether the United States operates justly in its fight against terror or fans the flames of a war of terror, especially in the Muslim world. I will also analyze Christian and Muslim views of engaging conflict in pursuit of understanding and diplomacy to cultivate peace. In the conclusion, I will argue that a personalist perspective requires that we go beyond "drone essentialism" in affirming the essential teaching that humanity is made for far more than drone warfare.

STRIKING OUT JUSTICE: EMPERORS AND
PIRATES, PRESIDENTS AND TERRORISTS

What is the difference between a pirate and an emperor if an emperor does not operate in a just manner? What is the difference between a terrorist and a democratically elected president if the latter strikes justice out of their foreign policy? Augustine reflects on this theme in the *City of God*. He suggests that kingdoms without justice are "but gangs of criminals on a large scale," that is, "a group of men under the command of a leader, bound by a compact of association, in which plunder is divided according to an agreed convention." Augustine continues:

> If this villainy wins so many recruits from the ranks of the demoralized that it acquires territory, establishes a base, captures cities and subdues peoples, it then openly arrogates to itself the title of kingdom, which is conferred on it in the eyes of the world, not by renouncing of aggression but by the attainment of impunity. For it is a witty and truthful rejoinder which was given by a captured pirate to Alexander the Great. The king asked the fellow, "What is your idea, in infesting the sea?" And the pirate answered, with uninhibited insolence, "The same as yours, in infesting the earth! But because I do it with a tiny craft, I'm called a pirate: because you have a mighty navy, you're called an emperor."[1]

Is there a parallel between the pirate with his tiny craft and the terrorist with his comparatively small arsenal of bombs? Is there a similarity between the emperor with his mighty navy and the democratically elected president with his military-industrial complex filled with state-of-the-art drone warfare technology?

President Obama came into office seeking to pull troops out of war zones. In seeking to keep his campaign promise to remove troops and his reticence over putting troops in harm's way in various trouble spots, Obama turned increasingly to drones when dealing with terrorist threats. In fact, he relied on drone strikes ten times more than President Bush during their respective terms in office. Jessica Purkiss and Jack Serle note that "a total of 563 strikes, largely by drones, targeted Pakistan, Somalia

---

[1]Saint Augustine, *City of God*, trans. Henry Bettenson, Penguin Classics (New York: Penguin Books, 2003), IV.4; 139.

and Yemen during Obama's two terms." Obama argued that drone warfare safeguarded against the loss of ground forces and civilian life. But is that true? Purkiss and Serle continue, "Between 384 and 807 civilians were killed in those countries, according to reports logged by the Bureau."[2] So does drone warfare, like warfare generally, increase hostilities or subdue them?

The US drone program has drawn criticism, but what about the scores of citizens and political leaders, including Obama and his presidential successors, who support and champion our increasing reliance on drone strikes? Could it be that those souls and minds who are not critical of the drone program but who embrace it wholeheartedly and unreservedly have been "so totally poisoned," to use Martin Luther King Jr.'s phrase,[3] that they leave no room for nonviolent options as alternatives? Are drone strikes viewed as the only viable alternative to ground troops, even if it is determined that contrary to those who preach drones' surgical efficiency, scores of innocent civilians' lives are lost in the process? One political commentator who reflected on the comparisons made between Obama and King quipped that instead of King's "I have a dream" speech, Obama's second inaugural address could have been titled "I have a drone." It is not hard to imagine that the civil rights leader and principal proponent of nonviolent engagement, whom Obama idealized, would have severely criticized his drone warfare policy.[4]

Questions and concerns did not decrease but increased when President Obama left office. President Trump sought to remove some of the limits on drone strikes that were present during the Obama administration and

---

[2]Jessica Purkiss and Jack Serle, "Obama's Covert Drone War in Numbers: Ten Times More Strikes Than Bush," Bureau of Investigate Journalism, January 17, 2017, www.thebureauinvestigates.com /stories/2017-01-17/obamas-covert-drone-war-in-numbers-ten-times-more-strikes-than-bush. See also Conor Friedersdorf, "Obama's Weak Defense of His Record on Drone Killings," Atlantic, December 23, 2016, www.theatlantic.com/politics/archive/2016/12/president-obamas-weak-defense -of-his-record-on-drone-strikes/511454/.
[3]Martin Luther King Jr., "Beyond Vietnam," in A Call to Conscience: The Landmark Speeches of Dr. Martin Luther King, Jr., ed. Clayborne Carson and Kris Shepard (New York: Warner Books, 2001), 144.
[4]For reflections on these points, see Glenn Greenwald, "MLK's Vehement Condemnations of US Militarism Are More Relevant Than Ever," Guardian, January 21, 2013, www.theguardian.com /commentisfree/2013/jan/21/king-obama-drones-militarism-sanctions-iran.

dramatically increased using drones in warfare.[5] President Biden also intends to rely on drones in such theaters as Afghanistan.[6] Regardless of the political party and politician in power, the temptation to employ drones will only become more alluring given the increasing sophistication of the weapon technology, finger-tip access and convenience, and decreased threat of political collateral damage that secretive drone warfare makes possible.

If might makes right, then perhaps the United States has nothing to fear. However, if justice matters, and democratically elected officials desire to safeguard against the possibility that they are simply terrorists with more weapons and more advanced technology, then we must analyze whether drone warfare is just and to what extent.

JUST A WAR VERSUS A JUST WAR

Augustine is known as a principal architect of just war doctrine. Later in the *City of God*, he reflects on the consternation and grief that this subject should cause us:

> But the wise man, they say, will wage just wars. Surely, if he remembers that he is a human being, he will rather lament the fact that he is faced with the necessity of waging just wars; for if they were not just, he would not have to engage in them, and consequently there would be no wars for a wise man. For it is the injustice of the opposing side that lays on the wise man the duty of waging wars; and this injustice is assuredly to be deplored by a human being, since it is the injustice of human beings, even though no necessity of war should arise from it.[7]

---

[5]Charlie Savage and Eric Schmitt, "Trump Poised to Drop Some Limits on Drone Strikes and Commando Raids," *New York Times*, September 21, 2017, www.nytimes.com/2017/09/21/us/politics /trump-drone-strikes-commando-raids-rules.html; Rachel Blevins, "Trump Has Killed More Civilians with Illegal Drone Strikes in 9 Months Than Obama Did in 8 Years," Ron Paul Liberty Report, October 18, 2017, www.ronpaullibertyreport.com/archives/trump-has-killed-more-civilians-with -illegal-drone-strikes-in-9-months-than-obama-did-in-8-years; Conor Friedersdorf, "Giving the Deep State More Leeway to Kill with Drones," *Atlantic*, September 22, 2017, www.theatlantic.com /politics/archive/2017/09/giving-the-deep-state-more-leeway-to-kill-with-drones/540777/.

[6]"President Biden Is Weighing How Extensively to Use Drones: More Civilian Casualties Abroad Seem the Likeliest Outcome," *Economist*, October 7, 2021, www.economist.com/united -states/2021/10/07/president-biden-is-weighing-how-extensively-to-use-drones. Audrey Kurth Cronin, "The Future of America's Drone Campaign: Time for a Clean Break with a Failed Approach," *Foreign Affairs*, October 14, 2021, www.foreignaffairs.com/articles/afghanistan/2021-10-14 /future-americas-drone-campaign.

[7]Saint Augustine, *City of God* XIX.7; 862. For contemporary treatments of the theory, see for example Richard Norman, *Ethics, Killing, and War* (Cambridge: Cambridge University Press, 1995);

We rarely find that those who claim to wage just wars do so with consternation and "heartfelt grief," as Augustine describes. Rather, an overbearing confidence and bravado often fills the airwaves. Have the political and military figures leading the way into conflict remembered that they are human, to allude to Augustine's reflection, or have they lost sight of their humanity? Also, have they carefully and wisely deliberated on the relative merits of their cause being just? If Augustine is right, the wise and humane will "lament the fact" that they are "faced with the necessity of waging just wars."

Over the centuries, those in power have claimed to ascribe to just war theory in their military campaigns, even though most do not honor the canons of just war theory. Michael Walzer writes, "The rulers of this world embraced the theory, and did not fight a single war without describing it, or hiring intellectuals to describe it, as a war for peace and justice. Most often, of course, this description was hypocritical: the tribute that vice pays to virtue."[8] Some go even further and claim they are engaged in a holy crusade, called by God to destroy the powers of evil.[9] Those who carefully account for just war doctrine will bridle at such overbearing confidence and will be extremely wary of the widespread use of drone strikes.

Many Americans maintain that a war is just if we wage it. When this mindset is in place, there will be little patience for building on Augustine's account of the pirate captain and Alexander the Great by comparing the American government with a terrorist organization. Perhaps hubris makes it difficult for us to see the relative merits of the evaluation. A November 2012 *Economist* article titled "Bombing Kant's Test—Obama's Drone

Brian Orend, *War and International Justice: A Kantian Perspective* (Waterloo: Wilfrid Laurier University Press, 2000); Barrie Paskins and Michael Dockrill, *The Ethics of War* (London: Duckworth, 1979); Michael Walzer, *Just and Unjust Wars: A Moral Argument with Historical Illustrations*, 5th ed. (New York: Basic Books, 2015); and Brian Orend, *Michael Walzer on War and Justice* (Montreal: McGill-Queen's University Press, 2001). See also articles by Thomas Nagel, "War and Massacre," *Philosophy & Public Affairs* 1, no. 2 (Winter 1972): 123-44; and G. E. M. Anscombe, "War and Murder," in *Nuclear Weapons: A Catholic Response*, ed. Walter Stein (New York, 1961), 44-52.

[8]Michael Walzer, "The Triumph of Just War Theory (and the Dangers of Success)," *Social Research* 69, no. 4, International Justice, War Crimes, and Terrorism: The U.S. Record (Winter 2002): 926.

[9]Rupert Cornwell, "Bush: God Told Me to Invade Iraq," *Independent*, November 15, 2011, www.independent.co.uk/news/world/americas/bush-god-told-me-invade-iraq-6262644.html. BBC Editors, "US Is 'Battling Satan' Says General," BBC News, October 17, 2003, http://news.bbc.co.uk/2/hi/americas/3199212.stm.

Guidelines" claims that "we Americans are inclined to think of ourselves as a morally upstanding lot who act according only to the highest ideals in our violent escapades abroad." But that is only *our* self-image. "Much of the rest of the world is inclined to view us rather differently, as smugly unwitting Thrasymacheans who cannot see the difference between what is right and what America, in its unmatched might, gets away with."[10]

The same *Economist* article also claims that Obama sought to provide stipulations on the limits of drone strikes only when it was feared he might lose his bid for reelection. One wonders whether those in power, like Americans generally, suffer from hubris, thinking themselves far more astute than their successors or predecessors in discerning the appropriate use of drones in warfare.

During his presidency, Obama claimed that he was operating in accordance with just war standards in his use of drone strikes. In a 2013 address at the National Defense University, he stated that "this is a just war—a war waged proportionally, in last resort, and in self-defense." He argued, "We were attacked on 9/11," so "under domestic law, and international law, the United States is at war with al-Qaeda, the Taliban, and their associated forces." Drone strikes are not "strikes to punish individuals," Obama claimed. "And before any strike is taken, there must be near-certainty that no civilians will be killed or injured—the highest standard we can set."[11]

An April 2016 *Salon* article from which this quotation is taken begs to differ with the president's assertions based on the testimonies of his remote-control pilots who pushed the drone strike buttons. The title of the piece says it all: "We're Not the 'Good Guys': American Drone Warfare Is Terrorizing the Middle East." The article states, "The Obama administration clings to Hollywood fantasy about the war on terror, even as its whistleblowers call foul."[12]

[10]W. W. Houston, "Bombing Kant's Test—Obama's Drone Guidelines," *Economist*, November 30, 2012, www.economist.com/democracy-in-america/2012/11/30/bombing-kants-test.

[11]The White House, Office of the Press Secretary, "Remarks by the President at the National Defense University," May 23, 2013, https://obamawhitehouse.archives.gov/the-press-office/2013/05/23/remarks-president-national-defense-university.

[12]Pratap Chatterjee, "We're Not the Good Guys: American Drone Warfare Is Terrorizing the Middle East," *Salon*, April 24, 2016, www.salon.com/2016/04/23/were_not_the_good_guys_partner/.

In what follows, more detailed consideration will be given to just war theory, which Obama and other US presidents claim to champion. While just war theory maintains that for a war to be just it must be waged by a recognized government, not every recognized government's determinations in war are just, even if it sees itself as the leader of the free world. As Augustine argued, apart from justice shaping an empire's pursuits, there is no difference between a pirate and an emperor. Other factors must come to bear on the matter, such as the just war tenets of necessity, discrimination, and proportionality previously mentioned and to which President Obama alluded in his address at the National Defense University.

No leader or country is foolproof. There is always a need to develop guidelines that can be applied universally or generally and that involve accountability, thereby safeguarding against individual or national self-serving determinations. Certainly, one should appreciate the dilemma a government faces in needing to act with urgency to protect a nation's citizens and their interests. One cannot take terror threats lying down as a sitting president. Still, haste, overconfidence, and secrecy can also cause further waste and destruction, as well as foment increasingly hostile reactions. The international response to the United States' preemptive use of drones for military campaigns was one of rising fury. Although there are many times when prompt responses are required, universal or general principles that are intended to hold us all accountable would help mitigate haste, waste, and relational fallout and reactions on the world stage. Not only would such overarching principles help safeguard against increasing frustration and anger from the international community, but they also would put a check on a president or country's whims.

It is also worth noting here that in contrast to the international community's negative reactions, drone strikes have been quite popular with the American public. Take, for example, the following analysis: "According to a national survey conducted by the Pew Research Center" in 2015, "a majority of the U.S. public supports U.S drones strikes. A higher proportion of Republican respondents, about 74%, support U.S. drone strikes, while about 52% of Democrats approve of the strikes. These statistics are largely mirrored in the primary candidate field."[13]

Now, just because a stance is popular does not make it just or right. Moreover, popularity for a stance, when coupled with hubris, makes the situation even more tenuous. To the extent that hubris plays a part in public opinion where national opinion discounts or minimizes global opinion, the appeal to national opinion polls becomes even more troubling, since drone strikes take place on foreign soil.

In what follows, consideration will focus on Immanuel Kant's principle of "publicity," as well as just war principles of necessity, discrimination, and proportionality. For Kant, publicity does not privilege a policy's popularity, but rather awareness and accountability. Kant's deontological orientation, which seeks to account for the rightness of a stance, does not depend ultimately on the popularity of a position but reason, as he frames it. If popularity were definitive, there would be no need for ethical inquiry. Consideration of Kant on publicity as well as analysis of the just war principles of necessity, discrimination, and proportionality will assist us in safeguarding against mere opinion and hubris.

Popularity and publicity. For Kant, a person in power should only pursue a policy that would be advisable not simply for that administration but for any succeeding administration, and not based merely on popularity. In the second appendix to his treatise "Perpetual Peace," Kant establishes the principle of publicity: "All actions affecting the rights of other human beings are wrong if their maxim is not compatible with their being made public."[14] There would be no exception in matters of warfare, including drone warfare.

This point on "publicity" may have more merit than the principle or element of universality, which is expressed in Kant's categorical imperative. Before reflecting further on Kant's principle of publicity, let's consider why the categorical imperative framework alone might not prove

[13]Arthur Holland Michel, "The Presidential Candidates on Drones," Center for the Study of the Drone at Bard College, October 16, 2015, https://dronecenter.bard.edu/presidential-candidates-on-drones/. See also "Public Continues to Back U.S. Drone Attacks," Pew Research Center, May 28, 2015, www.people-press.org/2015/05/28/public-continues-to-back-u-s-drone-attacks/.
[14]Immanuel Kant, "Perpetual Peace," in *Kant's Political Writings*, ed. Hans Reiss, trans. H. B. Nisbet (Cambridge: Cambridge University Press, 1970), 126.

advantageous for considering the merits of drone warfare. Universality signifies that one is to act only in a way that all other parties could act. But what do you do as a ruler of a country if your nation is at war with another nation? Given that Kant considered himself a realist, he maintained that war, though evil, appeared inevitable at times. He would also understand that in the heat of battle, nations will not apply the universality argument. In the case of war, the universality argument might read: only use a weapon if all other nations, including the one(s) you fight, use that weapon. From a realist perspective, all nations understandably seek to gain an advantage in combat. Thus, they would seek to develop and use weapons/weapon technologies (perhaps including drones) not used by their adversaries to put themselves in an advantageous situation to win and end the war.

Moreover, one might also argue that Kant's universality argument does not apply when engaging terrorist groups. Why? As already noted, just war theory maintains that for a war to be just it must be waged by a recognized government, which excludes terrorist organizations. Thus, it might be argued that the governing rules and conventions of warfare do not apply when combating terrorist organizations. I am not advocating for this line of reasoning but only seeking to provide parameters for what might constitute merits for engaging in drone warfare from a Kantian perspective. One will have to account for other factors than the universality argument associated with the categorical imperative to make a well-rounded case.

It is also difficult to employ the "ends and means" principle associated with the categorical imperative in the case of waging war. Recall that, for Kant, the ends-and-means version of the categorical imperative involves treating others not simply as means but also as ends in themselves. Now, what's so difficult about applying this version of the categorical imperative in the context of warfare? For just war theorists and "realists" such as Kant, war is inevitable in some instances. If so, the loss of human life is an inevitable result of war. Killing one's enemy is a means to the end of victory. All wars involve such loss of life among enemy combatants, though ideally not civilians. The same "realist" mindset would apply in the use of drones in warfare.

There is one more complexity in trying to employ Kant's categorical imperative to determine whether a nation should wage war. It has been argued that, for Kant, the categorical imperative in its various forms does not apply to sovereign states but to individual ethical determinations. Given the various complexities noted here related to the categorical imperative, it is advantageous to look to Kant's argument in "Perpetual Peace" with its emphasis on publicity, as it most certainly applies to sovereign states and international affairs.

Steven Mazie considers the publicity argument in Kant's thought in reflecting on drone warfare.[15] In appendix two of "Perpetual Peace," which has as its heading, "On the Agreement Between Politics and Morality According to the Transcendental Concept of Public Right," Kant addresses the subject of secrecy and how to address it ethically:

> A maxim which I cannot declare openly without thereby frustrating my own intention, or which must at all costs be kept secret if it is to succeed, or which I cannot publicly acknowledge without thereby inevitably arousing the resistance of everyone to my plans can only have stirred up this necessary and general (hence *a priori* foreseeable) opposition against me because it is itself unjust and thus constitutes a threat to everyone.[16]

In the same context, Kant writes, "All actions affecting the rights of other human beings are wrong if their maxim is not compatible with their being made public."[17]

In reflecting on Kant's argument, Mazie maintains that as with warfare generally, there may be instances where secrecy is required for "covert" operations. However, there would be no justification for a systematic, widespread use or "crusade" of drone-strike operations veiled in total secrecy. That position would be incongruous with Kant's discussion of warfare in "Perpetual Peace."[18] As Mazie reasons, "While specific covert measures may be necessary at times militarily, operating a campaign of remotely piloted aircraft under complete cover of secrecy is incompatible

---

[15]Steven Mazie, "Reorienting the Kantian Attack on Drones," Big Think, December 6, 2012, http://bigthink.com/praxis/rethinking-the-kantian-attack-on-drones.

[16]Kant, "Perpetual Peace," 126.

[17]Kant, "Perpetual Peace," 126.

[18]One wonders whether Kant would make the allowances Mazie does. Kant's line of reasoning would appear to disallow even occasional use of drones/cover operations.

with Kant's publicity requirement and clears a path for Obama and future presidents to send missiles anywhere in the world without explanation or accountability."[19]

The publicity argument, while important, may not be so popular to many. After all, the horrific attack on American soil on 9/11 has been claimed as justification for carrying out drone strikes, often operated by intelligence agencies in secrecy and trespassing on other nations' territories to strike at targets when there is no recognized war zone. That said, while likely unpopular in many circles, there is a need for independent inquiries into each account of targeted killings to make sure nations engaged in drone strikes in non–war zones are operating in accordance with international law. Certainly, this same accountability structure must apply to the United States. Otherwise, the leader of the free world may become synonymous with the leader of the free and uninhibited use of drone strikes anywhere in the world.

In addressing his concern over secrecy and the need for publicity, Mazie refers his readers to Omar Bashir's reflection on the Obama administration and its stance on drone warfare. Bashir calls for a panel providing independent oversight that could assure the public at home and abroad that the military use of drones honors and fulfills "the requirements of necessity, discrimination, and proportionality" that are found in just war theory.[20]

Seumas Miller argues that the three principles of discrimination, necessity, and proportionality are "logically interdependent."[21] Miller argues that the principle of discrimination prohibits targeting innocent civilians and placing their lives at unnecessary risk when such peril was foreseen and could have been avoided. The principle of necessity forbids a needless or unnecessary show of force to accomplish the

---

[19]Mazie, "Reorienting the Kantian Attack on Drones."

[20]See Omar S. Bashir's argument in "How to Improve the Drones Debate," Monkey Cage, November 15, 2012, https://themonkeycage.org/2012/11/how-to-improve-the-drones-debate/. See also "Who Watches the Drones? The Case for Independent Oversight," *Foreign Affairs*, September 24, 2012, www.foreignaffairs.com/articles/united-states/2012-09-24/who-watches-drones.

[21]Seumas Miller, "Collective Responsibility for the Robopocalypse," in *Super Soldiers: The Ethical, Legal and Social Implications*, ed. Jai Galliott and Mianna Lotz, Emerging Technologies, Ethics and International Affairs (Surrey, UK: Ashgate, 2015), 157; see also Alexander Moseley, "Just War," in Internet Encyclopedia of Philosophy, accessed September 5, 2019, www.iep.utm.edu/justwar/.

military objective. Proportionality requires the other two principles. The risk to civilians' lives must be proportionate to what is necessary to fulfill the military objective and what is morally permissible or justifiable.[22] It will be important to unpack these principles in order to discern whether the use of drones complies with just war theory or whether the war *on* terror is really a war *of* terror. These three checks complement the Kantian principle of "publicity" (in contrast to secrecy). Here they are in question form:

> The principle of necessity: Is this use of force necessary, indeed, the only or best way that one can ultimately bring an end to the hostility? Has one exhausted all other options?

> The principle of discrimination: Does the use of force discriminate between military targets and civilians, or are civilians targeted, too?[23]

> The principle of proportionality: Is the devastation of the strike in question in proportion to the threat posed by the enemy, or is it excessive?

I will consider each of these in turn.

Just war and the principle of necessity. The principle of necessity seeks to determine whether the use of force is the only or best way to bring an end to hostilities. It seeks to ensure that all other options have been exhausted.

Under just war theory, if there are no diplomatic solutions, one needs to discern which military option would be necessary and morally permissible to bring about an end to the conflict. Certainly, limiting casualties to troops and airmen is of great import, and drone strikes would seem to make most sense in this regard. Moreover, in dealing with terrorist organizations or cells located in other countries with which one's nation is not formerly at war, it would be far more problematic to send in ground troops. While those nations might not be able to root out the terrorist organizations in question due to a lack of military capabilities and the sophistication of the terror networks (among other factors), sending in ground troops would be viewed by those countries and their

---

[22]Miller, "Collective Responsibility," 157.

[23]Steve Coll, "The Unblinking Stare: The Drone War in Pakistan," *New Yorker*, November 17, 2014, www.newyorker.com/magazine/2014/11/24/unblinking-stare.

allies as a very visible provocation constituting an act of war. Special forces operating undercover and aerial bombardments may be options, but the determination to use them poses threats to the military personnel, as has already been noted. Thus, drones may be determined to be the best military option.

This decision would not necessarily remove moral culpability for various reasons to be accounted for under just war doctrine's appeals to discrimination and proportionality. In addition, the action would likely give rise to international rebuke. Initiating drone strikes without obtaining the permission of the foreign governments in question, especially those not providing haven to terrorist groups operating under cover there, would violate international laws honoring the sovereignty of nations concerning their own territories. Even so, if the person or cell is deemed an imminent threat to the country in question, such as the United States, drone strikes may still be viewed as the best of all possible options.

But will the option bring an end to the hostilities? The principle of necessity requires closure. Does war ever truly bring an end to violence, or does it simply keep the cycle of vengeance going? Here I call to mind G. E. Caird's assertion: "Evil is defeated only if the injured person absorbs the evil and refuses to allow it to go any further."[24]

Regardless of whether evil generates more evil in each instance, some argue that drone strikes inadvertently generate more violence by creating more terrorists. Take for example the testimonies of several former drone operators.

The former drone operators argue that the strategy is self-defeating, as the high number of civilian casualties and the callousness of drone killings merely propagate anti-US hatred. "Right now it seems politically expedient," said Cian Westmoreland. "But in the long term the bad side of a Hellfire missile and drones buzzing overhead is the only thing that a lot of these people know of the United States or Britain."[25]

---

[24]G. B. Caird, *Principalities and Powers: A Study in Pauline Theology* (1956; repr., Eugene, OR: Wipf & Stock, 2003), 98.

[25]Ed Pilkington and Ewen MacAskill, "Obama's Drone War a 'Recruitment Tool' for Isis, Say US Air Force Whistleblowers," *Guardian*, November 18, 2015, www.theguardian.com/world/2015/nov/18/obama-drone-war-isis-recruitment-tool-air-force-whistleblowers.

A man who is on the West's kill list also reasons that drone warfare is counterproductive and only makes matters worse by multiplying terrorist cells. He criticizes the terrorizing of innocent bystanders and speaks of the need for further diplomatic work, including the unthinkable—negotiating with terrorists. "The mantra that the West should not negotiate with 'terrorists' is naive," writes Malik Jalal. "It is always better to talk than to kill." Jalal shows this in his own life: "I have travelled halfway across the world because I want to resolve this dispute the way you teach: by using the law and the courts, not guns and explosives."[26]

A 2013 *Atlantic* article also reflects on the negative fallout of drone strikes, noting that the problem is not just that they lead to civilian deaths. Rather, it is their "inherently secret nature," which "creates a persistent feeling of fear in the areas where drones hover in the sky, and the hopelessness of communities that are on the receiving end of strikes causes severe backlash."[27]

In addition to the possibility that drone strikes radicalize Muslim populations, US drone strikes may very well lead other nations to follow suit and resort to drone strikes for targeted killings, which would further threaten and weaken long-established international law.[28] Rather than serve as a deterrent to war and bring an end to hostilities, there is a good likelihood that drone strikes fan war's flame by radicalizing populations and increasing the popularity of drone combat.

It is important to pause and recognize that not everyone agrees drone strikes create more terrorists. An article in *International Security* claims that it is not drone strikes that radicalize Muslim populations but rather economic and political factors, repressive governments in their homelands, forced conscription of youth by terror groups, online exposure to jihadist groups, and "a transnational Islamic identity's appeal to young immigrants

---

[26]Malik Jalal, "I'm on the Kill List. This Is What It Feels Like to Be Hunted by Drones," *Independent*, April 12, 2016, www.independent.co.uk/voices/i-am-on-the-us-kill-list-this-is-what-it-feels-like-to-be-hunted-by-drones-a6980141.html.

[27]Hassan Abbas, "How Drones Create More Terrorists," *Atlantic*, August 23, 2013, www.theatlantic.com/international/archive/2013/08/how-drones-create-more-terrorists/278743/.

[28]See Owen Bowcott, "Drone Strikes Threaten 50 Years of International Law, Says UN Rapporteur: US Policy of Using Drone Strikes to Carry Out Targeted Killings 'May Encourage Other States to Flout International Law,'" *Guardian*, June 21, 2012, www.theguardian.com/world/2012/jun/21/drone-strikes-international-law-un.

with conflicted identities," as well as "state immigration and integration policies that marginalize Muslim communities," among other factors.[29]

Regardless of whether drone strikes play a significant role in radicalization, they do not help to foster good relations. In the end, it is important to develop better relationships between the West and Muslim world, including on immigration reform, integration into Western societies, and international diplomacy. Let us now turn to reflect on the second principle of just war theory, that is, discrimination.

Just war and the principle of discrimination. The principle of discrimination prohibits indiscriminate killing. A government has the moral responsibility to identify and determine enemy combatants. Along with such determinations, there must be no targeting of civilian populations. The case is often made that the use of drone strikes is more conducive to discriminating between enemy combatants and civilians. For one, it is argued that robots are more precise. In other words, to err is human, not robotic. For another, robots are deemed more "objective," that is, not swayed by erratic human emotions in the heat of battle.

Others do not find the use of drones a comforting thought.[30] For example, some fear that the increasing and possibly indiscriminate use of drones will lead to a Terminator-like reality of countless killing machines. While emotions can prove erratic, an emotionless being or machine lacks empathy. Moreover, a machine could malfunction and go on an emotionless killing spree before its programmers could correct the problem or shut the machine down. So, do drone strikes truly advance the discussion, providing increased care and protection of civilian populations?

Speaking of the *Terminator*, science fiction often gives us a sense of the future, as a *Complex* article claims.[31] It is worth pointing out that

---

[29]Aqil Shah, "Do U.S. Drone Strikes Cause Blowback? Evidence from Pakistan and Beyond," *International Security* 42, no. 4 (2018): 47-84.

[30]Refer to the Human Rights Watch's "Losing Humanity: The Case Against Killer Robots," Human Rights Watch, November 19, 2012, www.hrw.org/report/2012/11/19/losing-humanity/case-against -killer-robots#page; see also the report to the United Nations, Humans Right Council, "Report of the Special Rapporteur on Extrajudicial, Summary or Arbitrary Executions," United Nations General Assembly, April 9, 2013, https://documents-dds-ny.un.org/doc/UNDOC/GEN/N22/452/71 /PDF/N2245271.pdf?OpenElement.

[31]Brenden Gallagher, "25 Ways Sci-Fi Movies Have Accurately Predicted the Future," Complex, November 2, 2013, www.complex.com/pop-culture/2013/11/sci-fi-movies-predicted-the-future/.

Britain's Ministry of Defence alluded to science fiction's *Terminator* in its discussion of drone warfare back in 2011, according to the UK's *Guardian*.

> The report warns of the dangers of an "incremental and involuntary journey towards a Terminator-like reality," referring to James Cameron's 1984 movie, in which humans are hunted by robotic killing machines. . . . "It is essential that before unmanned systems become ubiquitous (if it is not already too late) . . . we ensure that, by removing some of the horror, or at least keeping it at a distance, we do not risk losing our controlling humanity and make war more likely."

The report is titled "The UK Approach to Unmanned Aircraft Systems."[32]

An interesting article on the Cartoon Network's *Clone Wars* argues that the use of clones in warfare appears to lower the threshold for lethal violence not only among the Jedi knights but also among programmers and viewers of the animated version.[33]

Science fiction often raises key ethical issues about the future, whether *Her* or *Gattaca*, as noted in previous chapters, or *Terminator* and *Star Wars* noted here, as does one's response to it. It is not simply a matter for consideration in a "galaxy far, far away," whether in the distant past or future. We must come to terms with the real possibility that the use of drones in combat will desensitize individuals and nations to violence and increase warfare and indiscriminate killing of civilians in the here and now.[34] Like Goethe's "Sorcerer's Apprentice" or Mary Shelley's *Frankenstein*, sometimes humans' creations can get the better of us and undo our humanity.

Not everyone appreciates the appeal to science fiction in discerning how best to proceed on the drone warfare front. In "The Science Fiction of Dronephobia," Joshua Foust argues, "Many opponents of autonomous robots in warfare appeal to science fiction to make their case. This is not only lazy thinking, it distracts from the bigger questions about regulation

---

[32]Richard Norton-Taylor and Robe Evans, "The Terminators: Drone Strikes Prompt MoD to Ponder Ethics of Killer Robots," *Guardian*, April 17, 2011, www.theguardian.com/world/2011/apr/17/terminators-drone-strikes-mod-ethics.

[33]Matthew Belinkie, "The Bioethics of the Clone Wars," Overthinking It, August 4, 2011, www.overthinkingit.com/2011/08/04/bioethics-of-clone-wars/.

[34]Brianna Lee, "5 Things You Need to Know About. . . . ," *PBS*, September 13, 2012.

and ethical uses."[35] He takes special aim at the International Committee for Robot Arms Control.[36] Foust does not believe autonomous robots will spawn apocalyptic horrors, as science fiction may at times project.

Among other things, Foust argues that robots can undergo total systems upgrades when errors occur in combat. Humans do not have such ability for systems upgrades and can break down beyond repair psychologically under extreme duress in combat. Moreover, he rejects the claim that a proper combatant must be human since humans alone experience emotional connections. He points out that the development of robots with the ability to form emotional bonds with humans is already underway.[37] While some critics of the use of drones in warfare will discount such emotional bonds as sheer simulation, from the vantage point of the robots, these emotional connections are real. Foust seeks to turn the appeal to science fiction in pursuit of a ban on the use of robots in combat on its head. He notes that in *Terminator 2*, Schwarzenegger's character T-101 was reprogrammed so that he might come to "understand and defend humanity." Robots developed to operate autonomously "to follow the same Rules of Engagement" and "with the same base-level emotional desire not to wantonly kill other humans" can serve to limit the number of human casualties, including innocent civilians.

Regardless of what one makes of science fiction's role in helping us assess the merits of drone warfare, according to just war theory, the direct and intentional attack of civilians is never legitimate. From this standpoint, there is never justification to target deliberately a civilian population for the purposes of bringing about a speedier end to a war and thereby limiting further casualties, chiefly to one's own troops.

This being the case, the United States' dropping of atomic bombs on the civilian populations of Hiroshima and Nagasaki in Japan during World War II was a total abandonment of the just war principle of

---

[35]Joshua Foust, "The Science Fiction of Dronephobia," accessed September 10, 2019, https://joshua foust.com/writing/essays/the-science-fiction-of-dronephobia/. Refer to his exchange with members of this committee. A link to the discourse is embedded in his article.

[36]See the website of the International Committee for Robot Arms Control for more information on their position, www.icrac.net.

[37]See for example Alok Jha, "First Robot Able to Develop and Show Emotions Unveiled," *Guardian*, August 8, 2010, www.theguardian.com/technology/2010/aug/09/nao-robot-develop-display -emotions.

discrimination. The attacks were direct and intentional. The atomic bombings were purportedly based on the egregious rationale that this overwhelming, violent show of force against the civilian populations of these two cities would force the Japanese government to surrender, thereby bringing about a quicker close to the war and sparing US forces of more casualties.[38]

Justice is blind to playing favorites, but no country, especially one like the United States that claims to operate according to just laws of combat, can turn a blind eye to civilian casualties. It is worth pointing out that in Christian Scripture, the hypocrites (who in Jesus' stinging rebuke in Matthew 23 are religious leaders in power) are those whose actions are incongruent with their public show of righteousness. Moreover, Scripture holds those who know better to greater account for their actions. One of the deeply disturbing twists of history is that a country that claims to be the champion of justice is the only country ever to drop nuclear bombs on another, indeed, its civilian population. Moreover, this same country often presents itself as the policeman of the whole world, a point Dr. King made in his Vietnam War address: "And don't let anybody make you think that God chose America as his divine, messianic force to be a sort of policeman of the whole world. God has a way of standing before the nations with judgment, and it seems that I can hear God saying to America, 'You're too arrogant!'"[39]

Noam Chomsky employed the term *military humanism* to critique the United States for fighting in Kosovo. The leaders of our liberal democracy presented their decision to wage war in humane terms—for the sake of democracy and international well-being, yet apart from the canons of international law and without a United Nations directive. The United States often operates from the view that given our presumed exceptional status, we are forced to bear the unwanted messianic burden of restoring

---

[38]For critical analysis of President Truman and the US's rationale and actions, refer here: "The Decision to Drop the Bomb," U.S. History, www.ushistory.org/us/51g.asp; Alonzo L. Hamby, "The Decision to Use the Atomic Bomb," *Britannica*, www.britannica.com/topic/Trumans-decision-to-use-the-bomb-712569/End-game.

[39]Martin Luther King Jr., "Why I Am Opposed to the War in Vietnam," YouTube video, 22:48, Non-Corporate News, January 11, 2007, www.youtube.com/watch?v=b80Bsw0UG-U. This is an audio recording of Martin Luther King Jr.'s speech given at Ebenezer Baptist Church, Atlanta, on April 30, 1967.

order to a dysfunctional and chaotic world, and if necessary, through use of force. From Chomsky's perspective, our supposed concern for human rights violations and well-being of civilians masks our insatiable and cruel craving for gaining greater geopolitical and military advantage and entrée to new markets and resources.[40]

This messianic burden or impulse extends to our presumed right to determine whether other nations can possess nuclear technology and bombs. Given this habitual messianic impulse and posture related to nuclear weapons, our use of them on civilian populations, and our failure to acknowledge our moral wrongdoing, it is very doubtful that the United States would operate differently as to the merits of drone strikes. The only (faulty) justification we could offer for our presumed right to determine whether another nation could use drones in warfare and on whom is American power and prestige. But might never makes right.

It won't work to try to justify our actions and deflect responsibility by claiming that in all situations the United States has good intentions. After all, as the old saying goes, "The road to hell is paved with good intentions," not bad ones. In the effort to immunize the nation from criticism, we might easily try to deflect responsibility to machines and blame robotic malfunction. But robots lack moral freedom and cannot be judged for their actions or intentions. This is a real concern, as we often find instances in our society where government bureaucrats will say that a problem resulted from a computer glitch and could not be helped. But robots and machines require human agency at some point along the assembly and operation line to function. Thus, the drone operators are responsible and accountable. So, too, are the military and government officials who ultimately hand down the decisions on drone strikes. Moreover, a society governed in whole or in part by the will of the people is responsible. No matter how far removed from the battle-field we may think we are, no matter whether we determined to take out a specific person or group of people in a particular drone strike, and regardless of whether a machine that did our bidding malfunctions and goes on a killing spree, such factors do not decrease our responsibility.

---

[40]Noam Chomsky, *The New Military Humanism: Lessons from Kosovo* (London: Pluto, 1999).

In fact, the degree of responsibility and culpability may in fact increase regardless of intent.

Here I call to mind Hannah Arendt's oft-cited account of the Israeli court's judgment in the case of Adolf Eichmann, who was one of the principal organizers of the Holocaust: "In general *the degree of responsibility increases as we draw further away from the man who uses the fatal instrument with his own hands.*"[41] One of the interesting points that arose from the case of Eichmann was that while it was determined that he never intended to exterminate Jewish people, he was still involved in various determinations that led to their extermination and so was found guilty.[42] If the same consideration is given to drone warfare, one cannot justly say, "The drone killed the civilians. I didn't intend to kill anyone in particular. In fact, my superiors did not even let me know the identity of the target I was commanded to take out." Nor can one assert rightly, "The operator killed the person. I only gave orders to take out the imminent threat," or "I only invented the drone," or "I only voted for the politician in question who determined to go to war with drones." In this situation, I believe the political and military leadership is most responsible. Culpability increases the further up the chain the determination to employ drone strikes goes, even when a drone malfunctions and kills "unintended" targets. These sobering factors should increase our sense of alarm and make us more diligent to consider the presumed ethical merit and import of drone strikes.

Those who would blame the machine for their actions, or those down the line in the chain of command who accuse others, discount their own human worth. When those in control refuse to take responsibility for their actions, they minimize their own dignity as persons. As Marguerite Shuster wrote in *The Fall and Sin*, "Loss of the category of sin at the individual level more surely robs us of dignity and of hope than does the most punishing 'miserable sinner' theology of another age."[43]

---

[41]Hannah Arendt, *Eichmann in Jerusalem: A Report on the Banality of Evil*, rev. ed. (New York: Penguin Books, 1977), 247 (italics original).

[42]Refer to Iris Marion Young's helpful discussion of the Eichmann trial and Arendt's account in *Responsibility for Justice* (New York: Oxford University Press, 2011), chapter three.

[43]Marguerite Shuster, *The Fall and Sin: What We Have Become as Sinners* (Grand Rapids, MI: Eerdmans, 2004), 101.

Add to this the impersonal, indirect, mild language, sometimes called euphemisms, that political and military leaders often use in discussing human fatalities, such as "targeted killings." One source argues,

> Euphemisms are also used frequently by governmental institutions—especially by the military—to hide unpleasant or disturbing ideas. These euphemisms play down the degree of violence, objectivize the enemy as well as the means of warfare and can lead to social double-thinking by forming a kind of code that distorts reality.
>
> Thus, an invasion becomes an "intervention," a "liberation" or an "incursion." A coup is a "regime change." Protracted war becomes "overseas contingency operations," and drone assassinations are "targeted killings."[44]

The refusal to take responsibility as well as the use of euphemistic language increases the depersonalization and minimization of human life and dignity that is already an issue in warfare.

The principle of discrimination requires incredible care to adjudicate rightly between enemy combatants and innocent bystanders. The secrecy of drone warfare, the stealth nature of drones, the transfer of responsibility to machines or those down the command line (or up the command line, as the case may be), the veiled identities of those often targeted, and the use of euphemisms and impersonal language besiege the principle of discrimination and do not permit quick resolutions.

The ambiguities and impersonal dynamics also pose challenges for honoring the just war doctrine's principle of proportionality. Whereas the principle of discrimination deals with intended harm to civilians, the principle of proportionality deals with the unintended though foreseen and anticipated consequences. One must analyze all three principles of necessity, discrimination, and proportionality in conjunction with one another. Even if one does not intend to do harm to civilians, harm is still done in a number of ways, including psychological trauma and dread resulting from the "eye" flying overhead in the skies. Thus, one must account for anticipated collateral damage to civilian populations, as the tenet of proportionality requires.

---

[44]Stephen J. Thorne, "Euphemisms, Acronyms and Outright Lies: The Language of War," *Legion: Canada's Military History Magazine*, June 19, 2019, https://legionmagazine.com/en/2019/06/euphemisms-acronyms-and-outright-lies-the-language-of-war/.

Just war and the principle of proportionality. An article in the *New Atlantis* helpfully develops the relation and distinction of the principles of discrimination and proportionality:

> The criterion of *discrimination* prohibits direct and intentional attacks on noncombatants, although neither international law nor the just war tradition that has morally informed it requires that a legitimate military target must be spared from attack simply because its destruction may unintentionally injure or kill noncombatants or damage civilian property and infrastructure. International law and just war theory only insist that the anticipated collateral damage—the "merely foreseen" secondary effects—must be "proportionate" to the military advantage sought in attacking the legitimate military target. This sense of *proportionality* . . . has to do almost entirely with the foreseen but unintended harm done to noncombatants and to noncombatant infrastructure.[45]

Paul Ramsey, the great twentieth-century ethicist, summarized the meaning and relation of these two criteria in his book *The Just War* (1968):

> One does not calculate a prudent number of babies to be murdered (directly killed) for the sake of any good consequences (such as getting at the government); but one may and must calculate the prudent number that will and may be killed as an unavoidable side or collateral effect of military operations targeted upon the force to be repelled and whose goal and other consequence is expected to be the saving of many more from slaughter or from an oppressive tyranny, or in order to preserve in the international system accepted patterns in the actions of states on which grave consequences depend.[46]

The argument for use of drones in combat often involves the claim that drones remove casualties to US forces as well as reduce civilian casualties. Regarding the latter, the assertion is made that drones are extremely precise and thereby fulfill the stipulation of "proportionality," since there is far less collateral damage than with conventional weaponry. However, this claim is not without its detractors. According to an article in

---

[45]Keith Pavilschek, "Proportionality in Warfare," *New Atlantis*, no. 21 (Spring 2010): 21.
[46]Paul Ramsey, *The Just War: Force and Political Responsibility* (Lanham, MD: Rowman & Littlefield, 2002), 348 (italics added).

Scientific American, "Numerous reports of civilian casualties, however, indicate that these robotic aircraft are precise only to a certain degree." And though "the CIA and White House have been quick to point out they have found no evidence of collateral deaths from U.S. counterterrorism operations outside of Afghanistan or Iraq," this claim has been disputed by "British and Pakistani journalists."[47]

Consideration also needs to be given to the meaning of casualties here under proportionality. Does physical death or severe injury resulting from a drone strike alone count as a casualty, or can the extreme emotional trauma that fearful populations experience as a result of the ever-present threat of drone strikes count too? Similar forms of trauma are experienced by those pushing the buttons of the unmanned drones thousands of miles away.[48]

Regarding civilians, a study produced by Stanford University and New York University considered the mental-health impact of drone strikes and their seeming omnipresence.

> Community members, mental health professionals, and journalists interviewed for this report described how the constant presence of US drones overhead leads to substantial levels of fear and stress in the civilian communities below. . . . Interviewees described the experience of living under constant surveillance as harrowing. In the words of one interviewee: "God knows whether they'll strike us again or not. But they're always surveying us, they're always over us, and you never know when they're going to strike and attack." Another interviewee who lost both his legs in a drone attack said that "everyone is scared all the time. When we're sitting together to have a meeting, we're scared there might be a strike. When you

---

[47]Larry Greenemeier, "The Drone Wars: 9/11-Inspired Combat Leans Heavily on Robot Aircraft," *Scientific American,* September 2, 2011, www.scientificamerican.com/article/post-911-military-tech-drones/.

[48]The following articles document the rise in trauma and posttraumatic stress disorder in drone pilots. "And it's not just what they see, but the weight of decisions they have to make, he says. Airmen often have to discern whether they're looking at a group of women and children or a group of combatants." Sarah McCammon, "The Warfare May Be Remote but the Trauma Is Real," NPR, April 24, 2017, www.npr.org/2017/04/24/525413427/for-drone-pilots-warfare-may-be-remote-but-the-trauma-is-real. See also Pratap Chatterjee, "A Chilling New Post-traumatic Stress Disorder: Why Drone Pilots Are Quitting in Record Numbers," *Salon,* March 7, 2015, www.salon.com/2015/03/06/a_chilling_new_post_traumatic_stress_disorder_why_drone_pilots_are_quitting_in_record_numbers_partner/.

can hear the drone circling in the sky, you think it might strike you. We're always scared. We always have this fear in our head."[49]

Other considerations pertaining to proportionality that are reflected in the Stanford and New York University report include the impact on the education of children in the region. Many children are removed from school due to fears over drone strikes, or to restore income lost resulting from a family member killed or badly injured by a drone strike. Weighty evidence exists that civilians also fall victim to "double-tap" strikes where follow-up strikes take out rescuers. Many survivors will not even gather in public for the victims' funerals out of fear of further strikes. All these factors signify that drone bombings may not be the surgical and efficient solutions to terrorism that we may have been led to believe.

Another factor to consider when dealing with proportionality is standards of identification. *Business Insider* reports on the claim that different standards are applied in the case of drones than in the case of soldiers on the field of combat: "Drones do not need to confirm positive identification of a target before firing, a vastly different approach from what a soldier would need before firing on a threat in Afghanistan, for example."[50] The article goes on to highlight another report found in the *New York Times*:

> Some State Department officials have complained to the White House that the criteria used by the C.I.A. for identifying a terrorist "signature" were too lax. The joke was that when the C.I.A. sees "three guys doing jumping jacks," the agency thinks it is a terrorist training camp, said one senior official. Men loading a truck with fertilizer could be bomb makers—but they might also be farmers, skeptics argued.[51]

The claim that drone warfare greatly minimizes civilian casualties should be subject to great scrutiny. Such scrutiny should ultimately take the

[49]International Human Rights and Conflict Resolution Clinic (Stanford University) and Global Justice Clinic (NYU School of Law), "Living Under Drones: Death, Injury, and Trauma to Civilians from US Drone Practices in Pakistan," September 2012, 80-81, https://law.stanford.edu/wp-content/uploads/sites/default/files/publication/313671/doc/slspublic/Stanford_NYU_LIVING_UNDER_DRONES.pdf.
[50]Paul Szoldra, "Obama's First Drone Strike in Yemen Proved the Strategy Is All Wrong," *Business Insider*, March 7, 2013, www.businessinsider.com/drones-are-losing-war-on-terror-2013-3.
[51]Jo Becker and Scott Shane, "Secret 'Kill List' Proves a Test of Obama's Principles and Will," *New York Times*, May 29, 2012, www.nytimes.com/2012/05/29/world/obamas-leadership-in-war-on-al-qaeda.html.

form of an impartial, international tribunal noted earlier under the Kantian call for publicity. In a world where efficiency—which often involves machines—is prized above all or nearly all other factors, consideration of human impact in the form of proportionality must be taken most seriously.

Speaking of efficiency, we live at a time when what is viewed as fitting or appropriate is framed by way of market growth and productivity. Efficient machines, not virtuous people engaging other humans with complex, humane variables to consider, easily take precedence. The mechanistic age in which we live replaces the sanctity of life with the efficiency of life. Only that which is efficient has sanctity.[52] Only that which is financially expedient is deemed valuable. We need to hit the pause button rather than the drone-strike button and account for the fact that not everything deemed efficient is effective for cultivating human flourishing and well-being. Our increased reliance on machines to do our dirty work can easily lead us to blur lines and lose sight of the needed humaneness of ethical considerations.

The emphasis on efficiency and the use of machines reflects a certain eschatological vision. In the end, only those who are efficient will be saved by the all-seeing but unseen eye in the sky, or so we think. To the contrary, and as it concerns proportionality, to the extent that we have been expedient and efficient in our moral deliberations and judgments but not judicious and wise, to that proportion it will be measured to us. As Jesus makes clear in the Sermon on the Mount, "Do not judge, or you too will be judged. For in the same way you judge others, you will be judged, and with the measure you use, it will be measured to you" (Matthew 7:1-2).

Speaking of judgment, let's return briefly to consider Augustine's story of Alexander the Great and the pirate noted at the outset of the chapter. What's the difference between a nation-state that employs drone strikes and a terrorist operation? Both operate in secret. From the vantage point of those populations terrorized by drones, surely the necessary diplomacy work was never done to broker peace, since they are innocent

---

[52]Jacques Ellul writes of the mechanization of life, where efficiency in the guise of technique frames value. See Jacques Ellul, *The Technological Society* (Toronto: Vintage Books, 1964), 6, 12, 21.

bystanders who often feel targeted for a crime they did not commit. If taken out by strikes, they are unintended collateral damage. In the end, what's the real difference between drone strikes and terrorist attacks? The mere fact that the Western powers do not intend to take out civilians, only terrorists, is little comfort to the civilian victims of drone strikes and their loved ones. After all, as noted previously, the road to hell is paved with good intentions.

 Mention was made of the Western powers' intent. It is worth highlighting that a great many drone operations target Muslim extremists. Why is that? Is it due to a negative view of Muslims? Earlier in the chapter, I noted how one must account for how the West marginalizes Muslim populations, including in the areas of immigration and integration in society. Couple that with the challenges the West faces with understanding and engaging Muslim nations well diplomatically. Perhaps the long-standing battle between Christendom and Islam carries over into the secularized liberal democratic tradition's engagement with Islam. In what follows, we will seek to remove misunderstandings for the sake of cultivating more peaceable relations.

DRONES AND DEITIES, THE CROSS AND CRESCENT

Much of the United States' war on terror has involved use of drone strikes in predominantly Muslim countries. Many Muslims have a difficult time disconnecting religion and politics. Given our increasing secularity as Americans, it is very difficult for us to see why many Muslims would make such connections. That said, we should ask what our increasing use of drone strikes might say to the watching Muslim world about America and its God, which is often associated with Christianity.

We secularized Americans also fail to recognize that there is a connection between our past deities and present concepts of the state in the West. As Carl Schmitt writes,

> All significant concepts of the modern theory of the state are secularized theological concepts not only because of their historical development—in which they were transferred from theology to the theory of the state, whereby, for example, the omnipotent god became the omnipotent lawgiver—but also because of their systematic structure, the

recognition of which is necessary for a sociological consideration of these concepts.[53]

If our concepts of the state are secularized theological concepts, and if the state's use of drones for warfare follows from our secularized theologies, what might we learn from our increasing dependence on drones about the "deity" or "deities" that our secularized society worships and esteems? Might this god(s) be a nameless, impersonal, invisible deity who operates in secret, whose ways are inscrutable, unpredictable, irrational, unstable, and violent? If so, how does that shape our approach to resolving conflicts?

It seems that the drone deity reflects all these qualities. It is reminiscent of Kafka's *Trial*, where a pervasive and featureless or faceless bureaucratic system accuses, condemns, and executes an innocent man named Joseph K. for committing an unidentified crime. He eventually believes he is guilty and that his execution is just.[54] Similarly, a young Pakistani man named Faheem Qureshi and his family were the innocent victims of a drone strike. Qureshi "was 14 when a drone attack on his home left him with horrific injuries, several family members dead and his dreams for the future in tatters." He wondered what he and his family had done to be the recipients of bombs dropped by drones: "Qureshi remembered thinking to himself in his hospital bed during the anxiety of his month-long blindness: 'What did I do for which I was punished so badly? What did my family do? Why did it happen to me?'"[55] To this point, as far as I know, unlike the protagonist in Kafka's *Trial*, Qureshi has not accepted blame for the unspecified crime and judgment, nor has the nameless and faceless bureaucratic system come out into the open and accepted responsibility. Just as Qureshi was blinded by the drone strike, so the drone pilot operators are largely in the dark concerning their victims: "Worryingly, the drone pilots . . . say they often had little idea who was being killed—a view echoed by CIA

---

[53]Carl Schmitt, *Political Theology: Four Chapters on the Concept of Sovereignty* (1922; repr., Chicago: University of Chicago Press, 2006), 36. For more on latent theologies in political thought in the modern period, see William T. Cavanaugh's work *Field Hospital: The Church's Engagement with a Wounded World* (Grand Rapids, MI: Eerdmans, 2016).

[54]Franz Kafka, *The Trial* (New York: Tribeca Books, 2011).

[55]Spencer Ackerman, "Victim of Obama's First Drone Strike," *Guardian*, January 23, 2016.

documents leaked to McClatchy, which found hundreds of the dead recorded simply as 'other.'"[56]

What we need is statecraft representing "deities" that are not impersonal, indifferent, inscrutable, erratic, and violent, but rather personal, visible, and engaged, reaching out, listening empathically to others' cries, and sharing life with people of all walks of life.

In addition to the possible parallel between secular concepts of deity and drones, there may also be a parallel between them and our engagement with people in those theaters abroad where we employ drone strikes. We engage Muslim nations from thirty thousand feet above human life. The secular West's god or deities, and those created in these gods' images, will wreak havoc and distrust in the minds and imaginations of those who are always in range of the eye in the sky as objects of suspicion and derision. The only way forward to resolving deep-seated conflict is not through hovering and striking but hanging with Muslims in solidarity amid human suffering and sharing life with them, as reflected in the way of Jesus and the cross.

The West has always found Islam a deeply problematic religion. In fact, apart from Genghis Khan,[57] perhaps no other Eastern figure has been viewed with as much suspicion and scorn in the Western world as Muhammad. Islam has often posed a threat to Western security and ambitions. All we need do is consider the Ottoman Empire's expansion into parts of Europe in the distant past, the Ayatollah's deposing of the Shah of Iran, and Osama Bin Laden and al-Qaeda's assaults of the Twin Towers and Pentagon on 9/11.

One of the reasons for the presumed Islamic threat is its refusal to separate religion and politics. According to William Cavanaugh, the secular state claims to wage war against Muslim nations for what the West takes to be rational over against religious or irrational reasons.[58] In

---

[56]Alice Ross, "Drones May Predate Obama, but His Resolute Use of Them Is Unmatched," *Guardian*, November 18, 2015, www.theguardian.com/world/2015/nov/18/us-military-drones-obama -afghanistan-yemen-isis.

[57]See Jack Weatherford, *Genghis Khan and the Making of the Modern World* (New York: Three Rivers, 2004).

[58]See Cavanaugh on the theme of secularity, Islam, and rationality pertaining to war in *The Myth of Religious Violence: Secular Ideology and the Roots of Modern Conflict* (Oxford: Oxford University Press, 2009), 13.

contrast, the Muslim reaction to the West today involves suspicion of Western colonialist ambitions that have carved up non-Western nations through a privatized view of religion and set up governments that have catered to Western political and economic interests.[59]

Given that many Muslims tend to view the United States as a Christian nation, since Islam tends to unite religion and state, the church in the United States must be even more emphatic in distinguishing itself as a prophetic witness whose ultimate allegiance is to Jesus' upside-down kingdom rather than to the state and market. It does so by safeguarding against capitulating to greed and the abuse of power, including violence, and against viewing the state as the harbinger of the common good.

Here it is important to pause and account for Cavanaugh's analysis of the nation-state's claim that it is the champion of the common good.[60] Cavanaugh challenges the notion that the state is "natural," a "product of society," and that it plays only a "limited part of society." In his assessment, the state is not the natural but "artificial" maker or architect of society. It also "absorbs society into itself."[61] It is not that the state always fails to advance and defend the common good, or that the state is absent civic virtue, or that any form of collaboration with the government lacks merit. Rather, the state is "simply not in the common good business." The realization that the state is not the guardian of the common good should hardly trouble us, though. What should trouble us, according to Cavanaugh, is that the state presents itself as "the keeper of the common good and repository of sacred values that demands sacrifice on its behalf."[62] This marketing of the state is so pervasive that the state replaces or eclipses the church in claiming to provide enlightening communion and guard against disunion. Also problematic is how the church fails to seize the opportunity to encourage the "formation of alternative social bodies." Instead, the church views the state as responsible for resolving all social

---

[59]See for example Cavanaugh, *Myth of Religious Violence*, 91, 97-98.
[60]See Cavanaugh, "Killing for the Telephone Company: Why the Nation-State Is Not the Keeper of the Common Good," *Modern Theology* 20, no. 2 (April 2004): 243-74.
[61]Cavanaugh, "Killing for the Telephone Company," 245, 250, 255.
[62]Cavanaugh, "Killing for the Telephone Company," 266.

dilemmas.[63] The Christian community needs "to demystify the nation-state and to treat it like the telephone company."[64] Moreover, the Christian community must be alert and work hard to "complexify" or "promote the creation of spaces in which alternative economies and authorities flourish."[65] Two of the avenues available to the church to complexify space are to foster and promote authentic common spaces where the rich and poor dwell together, and to reclaim the moral authority to discern when Christians can participate in war and kill.[66]

The Christian church must also seek to cultivate understanding and pursue peace with Islam. Diplomacy is key. Such efforts will put a check on the hermeneutic of suspicion propagated by Western powers. Along with caring for the poor and denouncing greed and oppression as well as adjudicating whether and when Christians should be involved in war, it is important that Christians foster understanding of Muhammad's own values and concerns in these domains.

Muhammad opposed Mecca because of Mecca's deterioration of piety and disregard of the defenseless and poor.[67] Moreover, contrary to popular opinion, Muhammad did not default to violence at every turn to bring an end to conflicts. For example, in 628, Muhammad determined to do everything within his power to bring about a cessation of hostilities through nonviolent means. It was not only surprising to his bitter and resentful enemies but also counterintuitive and disturbing to his followers. Even later, in 630, when he captured Mecca in response to his opponents' failure to abide by the treaty they had made with him, Muhammad did so without shedding a drop of his enemies' blood.[68]

As with most if not all religious movements, Islam's history is complex.[69] Here it is worth pointing out that, according to Karen Armstrong,

[63]Cavanaugh, "Killing for the Telephone Company," 267-68.
[64]Cavanaugh, "Killing for the Telephone Company," 266.
[65]Cavanaugh, "Killing for the Telephone Company," 267.
[66]Cavanaugh, "Killing for the Telephone Company," 268.
[67]On Muhammad's surrounding context, see the chapter titled "Mecca" in Karen Armstrong, *Muhammad: A Prophet for Our Time* (New York: HarperOne, 2006), 9-39.
[68]Karen Armstrong, *Islam: A Short History* (New York: Modern Library, 2002), 22-23.
[69]The following statement related to Islam's historical complexities, specifically the differences involving the Meccan and Medinan periods, is instructive: "Through most of the Medina period, the Muslim community was in mortal danger and surviving in a defensive mode. Between 624 and

Muhammad demonstrated restraint in many cases when conquering his adversaries. The Qur'an also highlights the need for restraint in various situations and promotes its own version of a just war: one of self-defense for preservation of life that is honorable. It rejects wanton killing and destruction. "The Quran does not sanctify warfare."[70]

That said, Armstrong also acknowledges that Muhammad and his Muslim forces destroyed all men of the Jewish tribe of Qurayzah and enslaved all their women and children. The Jewish tribal people had rebelled and sided with Mecca against the Muslims. Armstrong argues that Muhammad was not antisemitic. Hatred of Jewish people occurred only with the creation of Israel as a Jewish state in 1948 and the eventual loss of "Arab Palestine." Armstrong also notes that the Qur'an is not hostile toward Jewish people but honors their prophets and calls for respecting people of the book. While she admits that the destruction of the Qurayzah was a horrific incident, she encourages the reader to place the event in its historical context rather than view it through modernity's lens.

I would add that the same or similar kind of contextualization is required of the Jewish conquest of Palestine recorded in the Old Testament. The Muslims had barely escaped being exterminated themselves, just like the Jews in ancient Palestine. All warring parties understood battles were often fights to the death of all losing forces. Moreover, in that day, given the cycle of retribution, those who would have been allowed to escape would have regrouped and called for reinforcements in the effort to retaliate and completely destroy their enemies.[71] Armstrong also reasons that "Arabia was a

---

627 especially, the Muslim community was often quite literally fighting for its life. It is no accident that the concepts of jihad and martyrdom were developed at this time." The analysis continues:

> Though the Qur'an takes on more temporal issues in the Medinan Period, it does not abandon the notions of spiritual striving and God consciousness that were hallmarks of the Meccan Period. Even the concept of defensive warfare is placed within the larger concept of jihad as striving for what is right. Though jihad might involve bloodshed, it has the broader meaning of exerting an effort for improvement, not only in the political or military realm, but also in the moral, spiritual, and intellectual realms. Muhammad is often cited in Islamic tradition for calling the militant aspect of jihad the "minor" or "little" jihad, while referring to the improvement of one's self as the "greater" jihad.

"Muhammad and Violence and Jihad," in *Muhammad: Legacy of a Prophet*, www.pbs.org/muhammad/ma_violence.shtml.

[70]Armstrong, *Islam*, 30; Armstrong refers the reader to the Qur'an: 2:194, 252; 5:65; 22:40-42.

[71]Armstrong, *Islam*, 21.

chronically violent society, and the ummah [community] had to fight its way to peace. Major social change of the type Muhammad was attempting in the peninsula is rarely achieved without bloodshed."[72] After the Battle of the Trench, where this horror occurred, Muhammad embarked on his "peace offensive" involving the hajj to bring about lasting victory in a peaceful manner.[73] Again, the Jewish people found themselves in a similar context in ancient Palestine with the conquest of the Promised Land, when kings such as David and Solomon made alliances with rulers of other kingdoms.

Speaking of peaceful efforts in the spread of Islam, Lamin Sanneh details the emergence and evolution of a pacifist tradition in the African Muslim context. He argues that contrary to the widespread though distorted narrative, Islam did not always spread by the sword. A great many Africans accepted Islam apart from the threat of military power and coercion on account of diverse forms of accommodation and adaptation.[74]

Ronald Choong, who pursued a graduate degree under Professor Sanneh's supervision at Yale University, remarked that it is important to ask not simply whether a tradition is violent, but whether it is more violent, or less violent, than what preceded it. This view accounts for historical context and guards against imposing contemporary notions of what is virtuous on prior societies and movements.[75] Later, Choong added in correspondence that "Homo sapiens are competitive mammals sharing habitats in which we alone migrate to all habitable continents. Our populations increase geometrically in tandem with our capacities to resist disease and overcome the natural weaknesses of our anatomy. As a result, population encounters are inevitable and to survive extinction or competitive loss, violence became an endemic trait of humanity."[76]

Even if such dynamics are part of human evolution, including the problematic dynamics of hypertrophy noted earlier in this volume, the New

---

[72]Armstrong, *Islam*, 22.

[73]Armstrong, *Islam*, 22.

[74]Lamin Sanneh, *Beyond Jihad: The Pacifist Tradition in West African Islam* (Oxford: Oxford University Press, 2016). For those interested in an assessment of jihad in West Africa in the modern period, see John Ralph Willis, "Jihād Fī Sabīl Allāh—Its Doctrinal Basis in Islam and Some Aspects of Its Evolution in Nineteenth-Century West Africa," *Journal of African History* 8, no. 3 (1967): 395-415.

[75]Ronald Choong, in discussion with the author, February 4, 2018.

[76]Ronald Choong, email message to author, November 22, 2019.

Testament calls the church to a higher form of engagement. Contrary to Islam and Judaism, which were associated with nationhood and the acquisition of land at a very early stage, the New Testament views the church as a holy nation and not belonging to a given nation(s) (1 Peter 2:9). It is a distinctive polis formed by Jesus' upside-down kingdom mission. Its upside-down kingdom mission involves moving forward with an embodied ethic involving redemptive suffering and sacrificial love.

Various scholars have pointed out the fundamental difference in mission between Jesus and Muhammad. Christianity prizes cruciform and redemptive suffering, while Islam prizes success. Kenneth Cragg puts the matter this way for Muslims: Jesus makes "no triumphal entry into a capitulating Mecca," as was true of Muhammad. This being the case, "Muhammad's more 'effective' destiny is further seen as indicating his 'finality' as 'the seal of the prophets.'"[77] From a Muslim perspective, Muhammad was successful in conquering Mecca as the final prophet, whereas the prophet Jesus would have died a humiliating death on the cross had God not delivered him. As great as Jesus was as a prophet, Muhammad was greater still, according to Islam, given his successful entry into Mecca.

Daniel W. Brown makes the following comparison:

> The cross remains the point at which Islam and Christian theology clash not just because the Qur'an denies the crucifixion (a disputed point), or because Muslims reject its historicity (some do not), but because the cross, viewed as the ultimate self-manifestation of God, demands a response of faith—Jesus is Lord—that the Muslim reserves for the revelation of the Qur'an. Ultimately, Muslims and Christians are divided over whether the character of God is most clearly revealed in a perfect life culminating in redemptive death or in a perfect book giving rise to a perfect life.[78]

Armstrong frames the distinction between the two faiths in the following terms: "Where Christians discerned God's hand in apparent failure and

---

[77]Kenneth Cragg, *Muhammad and the Christian: A Question of Response* (Maryknoll, NY: Orbis Books, 1984), 45.

[78]Daniel W. Brown, "Clash of Cultures or Clash of Theologies? A Critique of Some Contemporary Evangelical Responses to Islam," *Cultural Encounters: A Journal for the Theology of Culture* 1, no. 1 (Winter 2004): 84.

defeat, when Jesus died on the cross, Muslims experienced political success as sacramental and as a revelation of the divine presence in their lives."[79] However, Armstrong cautions against reading Islam as a violent, militaristic, and coercive faith: "Western people often assume that Islam is a violent, militaristic faith which imposed itself on its subject peoples at sword-point. This is an inaccurate interpretation of the Muslim wars of expansion." The wars of expansion were purely "pragmatic" in nature. Muslims went in search of "plunder" and a common cause or occupation that would cultivate solidarity in their community.[80]

Reuven Firestone sheds light on the historical genesis of the concept of holy war in Islam: "The point is that what began as traditional Arabian raiding forays (albeit against one's own kin) came to be considered divinely sanctioned because of historical circumstances. This typifies the transition process from mundane to holy war."[81] Jihad is commonly misunderstood as primarily focused on the non-Muslim and war. To the contrary, the greatest jihad pertains to one's own heart. It is directed against one's sinful inclinations.[82]

Christianity has no holy war with Islam, only those powers that destroy piety and oppress the poor. Islam and Christianity pursue equity and charity, honoring God and those of humble estate, but through different avenues. Christians are called to die to the old order of being and live according to Jesus, who died on the cross and rose from the dead to bring about a new order of life in service to all humanity, viewing everyone on our path as our neighbors, including those least like us and whom we least like, as Jesus' parable of the Samaritan of incredible mercy makes clear (Luke 10:25-37).

Jesus died on the cross as the demonstration of God's love of his enemies. In the Sermon on the Mount, Jesus exhorts his followers to be perfect as God is perfect and love as God loves. Unlike so much of the world, who only love their own people, Jesus' disciples are to love their enemies and pray for those who persecute them (Matthew 5:43-48). Paul

---

[79] Armstrong, *Islam*, 29.

[80] Armstrong, *Islam*, 29-30.

[81] Reuven Firestone, *Jihād: The Origin of Holy War in Islam* (New York: Oxford University Press, 1999), 132.

[82] Firestone, *Jihād*, 16-18.

picks up on the enemy theme in Romans: while we were still God's enemies, Christ died for us (Romans 5:10). John writes that we did not first love God. Rather, God first loved us and sent his Son to die as an atoning sacrifice for our sins (1 John 4:10). Enemy love is distinctive of the Christian faith. Miroslav Volf claims that "though Muslims insist that we should be kind to all, including those who do us harm, most reject the idea that the love of neighbor includes the love of enemy." In contrast, "Christians affirm unequivocally that God commands people to love even their enemies."[83]

How does the preceding discussion bear on drone warfare? Get to know your enemy. Don't hover above them and strike them down but hang with them and share life with them. King embraced and modeled a cruciform ethic and the need for empathic listening, not droning on about the need to get even. King spoke of the need for diplomacy in his address on the Vietnam War, centering it on his commitment as a follower of Jesus Christ. In view of Jesus, who did not threaten his enemies with death but laid down his life for them, King states, "Can I threaten them with death, or must I not share with them my life?" In view of his conviction to share his life with them, he adds, "It is clear to me that there will be no meaningful solution there until some attempt is made to know them and hear their broken cries."[84] Later in the same message, King reasons,

> Here is the true meaning and value of compassion and nonviolence, when it helps us to see the enemy's point of view, to hear his questions, to know his assessment of ourselves. For from his view we may indeed see the basic weaknesses of our own condition, and if we are mature, we may learn and grow and profit from the wisdom of the brothers who are called the opposition.[85]

But how can we ever get to know them and hear them out if we let machines do our work for us? If we don't get to know them, they will view us increasingly with suspicion and as their ultimate enemies, just as we do them. The end result in places such as the Middle East and North Africa

---

[83]Miroslav Volf, *Allah: A Christian Response* (New York: HarperOne, 2011), 183.
[84]King, "Beyond Vietnam," 145-46.
[85]King, "Beyond Vietnam," 151.

will be similar to what occurred in Vietnam: "Now they languish under our bombs and consider us, not their fellow Vietnamese, the real enemy."[86]

King wrote of the need to move from "sectional" to "ecumenical" loyalties. He argued that "every nation must now develop an overriding loyalty to mankind as a whole in order to preserve the best in their individual societies." King continues, "This call for a worldwide fellowship that lifts neighborly concern beyond one's tribe, race, class, and nation is in reality a call for an all-embracing and unconditional love for all men."[87]

An entangled ethic requires that we seek to understand those of a different religious tradition, way of life, or opposing side of a pressing conflict. We need to listen empathically to their perspective rather than dismiss them outright. An embodied ethic requires that we hang and share life with people of different places rather than hover and strike. An eschatological ethic requires that we do not place our hope in drones to navigate conflicts and bring an efficient end to warfare and broker peace, but rather in Jesus and his manner of engaging people. Our eschatology must parallel an embodied ethic that promotes persons over things. Speaking of eschatology, I will close this chapter out with consideration of drone essentialism and what is called "Over the Horizon."

"OVER THE HORIZON": BEYOND DRONE ESSENTIALISM

Our technological society presupposes that drone technology dictates or determines its application. Such "drone essentialism," as it is called, fails to account for the human element and the untold collateral damage to civilian populations. In addition to evaluating the technology, we have to look "at the targeting protocols, the operational cultures of the agencies that deploy them, and the enculturated instincts, assumptions, and practices of the operators whose thumbs hover over the red button." Rather than cast blame only on drone operators, we need to account for the pervasive milieu and ethos, which so easily diminishes targeting procedures and leads to "ethical slippage" involving civilian populations.[88]

---

[86]King, "Beyond Vietnam," 148.
[87]King, "Beyond Vietnam," 160-61.
[88]Hugh Gusterson, "Drone Warfare in Waziristan and the New Military Humanism," *Current Anthropology* 60, no. 19 (February 2019): S79.

Such ethical slippage results from our "thing-oriented society," as King referred to it. We cannot conquer militarism "when machines and computers, profit motives and property rights, are considered more important than people."[89]

Couple these factors with the US "over-the-horizon" (OTH) strategy, which President Biden hails as the way forward, and the results can be quite disturbing. Biden celebrates the OTH plan in the following statement: "We have what's called over-the-horizon capabilities, which means we can strike terrorists and targets without American boots on the ground."[90] Easier said than done. It sounds good on paper or from thirty thousand feet in the air. But what are circumstances like closer to the ground? At the close of US operations in Afghanistan, US forces launched a drone strike in response to a terrorist attack that took the lives of thirteen American military staff. Rather than kill the terrorists, the drone strike killed ten innocent civilians, among them children.

Ironically, perhaps, successful drone operations that safeguard against human tragedies such as the situation in Afghanistan require "relational" resources: proximate bases from which to operate in the region and local partners who will assist in operations. When one or both are lacking, the results can be devastating to civilian populations. According to Sarah Kreps and Paul Lushenko,

> These seemingly easy drone strikes require an elaborate array of bases from which to launch, recover, refit, and extend the loitering potential of armed drones; synchronize intelligence to identify targets; and manage cooperation with allies and partners, especially to corroborate intelligence, which is decisive in targeting high-value terrorists.[91]

The "intuitive appeal" of OTH bound up with drone essentialism gives rise to a false hope, Kreps and Lushenko argue. Technological

[89]King, "Beyond Vietnam," 157-58.
[90]Benjamin Schwartz, "The Human Cost of 'Over the Horizon': The Lack of Americans on the Ground Makes Drone Strikes Likelier to Go Wrong," *Wall Street Journal*, September 27, 2021, www.wsj.com/articles/over-the-horizon-afghanistan-ground-drone-strike-kids-children-killed-civilian-casualties-11632776009.
[91]Sarah Kreps and Paul Lushenko, "US Faces Immense Obstacles to Continued Drone War in Afghanistan," TechStream, October 19, 2021, www.brookings.edu/techstream/us-faces-immense-obstacles-to-continued-drone-war-in-afghanistan/.

sophistication never removes the need for consideration of the human element. To err may be human, but to consider drones in abstraction from the human, relational component is also erroneous. Drones can't live with humans or without them. OTH is neither effective nor expedient. When the relational resources of "proximate bases" and "regionally coordinated counterterrorism strategy" with allies are absent, the threat to civilians will rise dramatically.[92]

The threat of terror is certainly an urgent matter to address, and drones may play a limited role in addressing the grave danger. Here we find ourselves in no-man's land, that is, the uninhabited area between two warring parties—casual just war theorists and principled pacifists. All too often, proponents of a conflict glibly and hypocritically declare that their call to arms is just, as Michael Walzer points out.[93] Such casual and distorted endorsement of just war theory does not do justice to the views of principled pacifists. However, those who argue that there is never a case for going to war may inadvertently cause more carnage by choosing not to resist with arms.

With the latter point in mind, King's principled pacifism and nonviolent philosophy of life[94] works well in a democratic society. It also has prophetic import for safeguarding against aggressors and oppressors in a conflict claiming the high moral ground. Still, it may not prove satisfactory in dealing with the brutal contempt for human life found in ISIL or al-Qaeda. While addressing different contexts, Peter Paris's comparison of King, Mahatma Gandhi, and Nelson Mandela may shed light on the matter: "King's practice of nonviolent resistance was practical because he could rely on such structures through the actions of the Supreme Court and the National Guard." In contrast, after decades of effort the African National Congress concluded that nonviolence "was no longer workable because of the lack of such structures of justice for restraining violence" in their context. Paris continues, "Neither Mahatma

---

[92]Kreps and Lushenko, "US Faces Immense Obstacles."

[93]Walzer, "Triumph of Just War Theory," 926.

[94]The King Center, "The King Philosophy," accessed May 3, 2019, https://thekingcenter.org/about -tkc/the-king-philosophy/. These principles are found in King's book *Stride Toward Freedom: The Montgomery Story*, ed. and intro. Clayborne Carson, The King Legacy (Boston: Beacon, 2010).

Gandhi nor Martin Luther King Jr. faced such ruthless disregard for human life as did Mandela and his African National Congress. Neither Gandhi nor King and their respective movements were banned from civil society."[95]

Certainly, King, Gandhi, and Mandela were not the leaders of powerful nation-states fearing terrorist threats (nations that also may have inadvertently provoked such threats through their own violent actions). Rather, they and their communities were oppressed parties in conflicts. Still, there is a difference between powers such as the United States that apart from serious breaches or "ethical slippage" seek to limit civilian casualties and forces such as ISIL or al-Qaeda that intentionally target civilian populations. That said, King's undying pursuit of diplomacy must take precedence over other options such as ground forces and drone strikes. Undying efforts must be made to resolve conflicts by peaceful means wherever and whenever possible.

We must not allow the technological society that fosters a culture of things to win out over the horizon, according to which we place our hopes in drones to do our bidding, as if they can do no wrong. Contrary to drone essentialism, there is nothing "constitutively inherent" to drone warfare that will spare civilians.[96] If we fall prey to such drone-essentialist miscalculations and become prone to more ethical slippage in the face of increasing threats and tactical nightmares, our "emperors" will be nothing more than "pirates" with "more ships." That is, our presidents will be nothing more than terrorists with more abundant sophisticated weapons technology.

Having official policy guidelines that promote just war tenets such as "discrimination" and "proportionality" regarding civilian casualties is one thing. Acting out those just war tenets and policies rather than falling prey to "ethical slippage" in Hiroshima, Nagasaki, and other places in Japan during World War II,[97] My Lai and other locales during the

---

[95]Peter J. Paris, *Virtues and Values: The African and African American Experience*, Facets (Minneapolis: Fortress, 2004), 57-59.

[96]Gusterson, "Drone Warfare in Waziristan," S79.

[97]James Carroll, *House of War: The Pentagon and the Disastrous Rise of American Power* (Boston: Houghton Mifflin Harcourt, 2006), chap. 2.

Vietnam War,[98] and Waziristan in Pakistan during the war on terror is quite another. Better yet is making every diplomatic effort imaginable to resolve conflicts by peaceful means. We were made for more than living according to an illusory hope that drones can solve our current conflicts. Left to themselves, they will only create new ones.

---

[98]Nick Turse, *Kill Anything That Moves: The Real American War in Vietnam* (New York: Picador/ Macmillan, 2013).

$$\boxed{11}$$

MORE THAN DOMINATION
OF THE EARTH

Humane Care for Creation

THE CHRISTIAN DOCTRINE OF CREATION celebrates rather than denigrates the natural world. God creates everything good and will heal and perfect creation in all its materiality through the incarnate Son and Spirit. There is no place for pessimism or contempt of the creaturely order in its current state of upheaval and decay in view of the biblical hope. Moreover, the biblical mandate in Genesis 1 to subdue the earth and have dominion over it (Genesis 1:26, 28) does not entail domination but tending, ordering, and stewarding it well for the glory of God. Those trajectories of denigration and domination destabilize the nonhuman sphere as well as human life. Human persons do not exist in isolation but in intimate connection with the rest of creation. When we mistreat the creation, we operate in an inhumane manner that degrades our own personal dignity as well as those we would displace and discount in the pursuit of expansion and world domination. We do not flourish as humans apart from good governance in the nonhuman sphere. This chapter will seek to counter this distortion of our human vocation in the creation by addressing three problematic constructs: the polarities of spirit over matter (gnosticism), humanity (especially men) over the nonhuman realm (anthropocentrism), and the West over the rest (imperialism and colonialism). One of the key takeaways of this chapter will be the realization that being made for more entails guarding against inordinate desires and cultivating refined appetites that want less.

SPIRIT OVER MATTER: THE GNOSTIC CHALLENGE

The Christian faith calls for cherishing the material world, while opposing materialism on the one hand and gnosticism on the other hand. Let's turn our attention to gnosticism. Gnosticism prizes spirit over matter. It devalues material reality. The gnostic mindset appears in countless ways and can be traced back to ancient times. Contrary to the casual observer, Christian orthodoxy does not discount but celebrates material reality and contends against gnostic ways of thinking.

Paul opposed gnostic influences creeping into the Christian community in his letter to the Colossian church. For example, Paul resisted those ascetic practices shaped by protognostic influences that affirmed the abuse of the body (Colossians 2:20-23). Downstream from Platonism, which viewed the material universe as a shadow of the immaterial, transcendent realm, the protognostic teaching Paul was contending against viewed materiality in any form as subject to the whims of repressive spiritual forces at work in the world. Against this backdrop, it is very difficult to value the body. On this view, materiality is evil, or at least deficient. If this is so, one can treat the human body with disdain, as with extreme ascetic practices. If this is the case for humanity, just think what one can do to the earth.

Christian ethical deliberations regarding the environment must account for the significance of Jesus Christ. He is the eternal Word who became flesh and blood in space and time. The eternal Word became material. Such theological considerations should guide Christians not simply in their deliberations of Jesus' identity, but also in their reflections on the creation. All too often, Christians affirm orthodox theology but operate as gnostics in their engagement of material reality, including the environment.

The most challenging issue for Christian orthodoxy in its fight with gnosticism centered on Jesus' identity, surfacing in the heretical teaching of docetism (i.e., the teaching that Jesus only appeared to be human). Docetism rejects the idea that Jesus was incarnate as a human being. Moreover, docetism rejects the idea that Jesus was raised from the dead in an embodied manner.

Paul stood opposed to gnostic and docetic tenets in highlighting Jesus' incarnate or embodied reality. Jesus is the firstborn of the new creation

(Colossians 1:15). All God's fullness appears in bodily form (Colossians 2:9). Similarly, John argues that the Word became flesh (John 1:14). First John asserts that anyone who denies that Jesus has come in the flesh is not from God. The denial of Jesus' embodiment is the spirit of the antichrist (1 John 4:3).

Christian orthodoxy teaches that Jesus was glorified in a bodily state. It also claims that Jesus' resurrected body is the same body as that which was crucified. In fact, as the New Testament reveals, Jesus' resurrected and glorified body bears the nail and spear marks of his passion (John 20:26-28; Revelation 5:6). Now, it would appear to follow that if Jesus' resurrected and glorified body bears the marks of his earthly existence, and if we are raised bodily and glorified in the same way as the Lord, then the earth on which we have always dwelled will not be annihilated but purified and transformed. In fact, second-century theologian Irenaeus of Lyons with his radical critique of gnosticism believed that 2 Peter 3:10 describes a process of transformation or purification rather than the annihilation of the planet in the apocalypse.[1]

Christology has a bearing on cosmology. A christological-cosmological framework unites Jesus' transfiguration and humanity's future reality and the transfiguration of the whole world and universe. Here it is worth noting that Byzantine theologian Maximus the Confessor speaks not simply of the transfiguration of humanity but of the entire cosmos through Christ. Maximus presents a christocentric-cosmological framework.[2] From an orthodox Christian standpoint, the incarnation is the ultimate affirmation and demonstration of the material creation's goodness. Matter matters to God, for God became material: the Word became flesh (John 1:14). As a result, we should celebrate and honor the material universe.

Such honor does not in any way entail the worship of the creation, but only worship of the one who became part of the creaturely order. John of Damascus puts it this way: "I do not worship matter, I worship the

---

[1]See for example Carsten Peter Thiede, "A Pagan Reader of 2 Peter: Cosmic Conflagration in 2 Peter 3 and the Octavius of Minucius Felix," *Journal for the Study of the New Testament* 26 (1986): 79-86.
[2]See Saint Maximus the Confessor, *On the Cosmic Mystery of Jesus Christ: Selected Writings from St. Maximus the Confessor*, trans. Paul M. Blowers and Robert Louis Wilken, Popular Patristics Series (Crestwood, NY: St. Vladimir's Seminary Press, 2003), 38, 100n2, 100n4.

God of matter, who became matter for my sake and deigned to inhabit matter, who worked out my salvation through matter. I will not cease from honoring that matter which works for my salvation. I venerate it, though not as God."[3]

Christians do not worship matter but the one who became material. As a result, we must honor and cherish the material universe. The creation in all its physicality is not evil. Indeed, it is good, as God declares in Genesis 1. God's declaration and Jesus' incarnation—as well as Jesus' bodily resurrection and glorification—assure us that the creation is not inherently evil. The fall did not destroy the creation, nor undermine our hope. The incarnation assures us that God will bring light out of darkness and order out of chaos. Moreover, God works through the Spirit, who hovered over the face of the waters when the earth was formless and void and the deep was covered in darkness (Genesis 1:2) to transform the creation.

Irenaeus speaks of this transformation in terms of the triune God's recapitulation of the creaturely order.[4] In developing the doctrine of recapitulation in his refutation of gnosticism, Irenaeus refers figuratively to the Son and Spirit in corporeal terms as God's two hands. God redeems all creation from the inside out rather than from the outside in, working through the material world rather than over against it. God enters the world and clothes himself in "tired and soiled matter" through his Son in the Spirit to reestablish his sovereign order of life on behalf of his creation.[5]

Irenaeus argues that God works to create the world through Jesus and the Spirit, who are also God, and not through angelic mediation. Irenaeus rejects the gnostic teaching that God needed angelic agents to

---

[3]John of Damascus, *Three Treatises on the Divine Image*, trans. Andrew Louth (New York: St. Vladimir's Seminary Press, 2003), 8.

[4]Irenaeus writes on the theme of recapitulation here: "The Word of God, Jesus Christ our Lord, who because of his surpassing love became what we are so that he might equip us to become that which he is." Irenaeus, *Adversus Haeresus* V, in Alexander Roberts and James Donaldson, *The Ante-Nicene Fathers*, vol. 1, *The Apostolic Fathers, Justin Martyr, Irenaeus* (1885; repr., Peabody, MA: Hendrikson, 1994), prologue, 524.

[5]See Colin Gunton's christological and pneumatological articulation of the transformation of the creation in an Irenaean vein in *The Christian Faith: An Introduction to Christian Doctrine* (Oxford: Blackwell, 2002), 32.

create the world. Rather, God creates all things through his two hands, the Son and Spirit:

> As regards His greatness, therefore, it is not possible to know God, for it is impossible that the Father can be measured; but as regards His love (for this it is which leads us to God by His Word), when we obey Him, we do always learn that there is so great a God, and that it is He who by Himself has established, and selected, and adorned, and contains all things; and among the all things, both ourselves and this our world. We also then were made, along with those things which are contained by Him. And this is He of whom the Scripture says, *"And God formed man, taking clay of the earth, and breathed into his face the breath of life"* (Genesis 2:7). . . . With Him were always present the Word and Wisdom, the Son and the Spirit, by whom and in whom, freely and spontaneously, He made all things, to whom also He speaks, saying, *"Let Us make man after Our image and likeness"* (Genesis 1:26); He taking from Himself the substance of the creatures [formed], and the pattern of things made, and the type of all the adornments in the world.[6]

God does not simply create the world through his "two hands." God also sustains and perfects the world through the Son and Spirit. The Father does nothing apart from the Son and Spirit, nor do the Son and Spirit operate independently of the Father or from one another. Their triune work of recapitulation or transformation involves their perichoretic union of mutual indwelling as the one God.

For Irenaeus, Christ sums up and heals the whole creation, including animals and plants.[7] Irenaeus speaks of Christ summing up all things in himself and offering the whole creation back to God. In his rebuttal of the gnostic teaching that would separate Jesus from Christ, Irenaeus claims that the Word of God

> who is always present with the human race, united to and mingled with
> His own creation, according to the Father's pleasure, and who became

---

[6]Irenaeus, *Against Heresies* IV. 20.1 (*ANF* 487-88). The *Ante-Nicene Fathers* volumes are hereafter abbreviated *ANF*.
[7]Refer here for his discussion in *Against Heresies* V. 33.4 (*ANF* 562-63), where Irenaeus refers to the kingdom of God by noting that "when also the creation, having been renovated and set free, shall fructify with an abundance of all kinds of food from the dew of heaven, and from the fertility of the earth."

flesh, is Himself Jesus Christ our Lord, who did also suffer for us, and rose
again on our behalf, and who will come again in the glory of His Father,
to raise up all flesh, and for the manifestation of salvation, and to apply
the rule of just judgment to all who were made by Him. There is therefore,
as I have pointed out, one God the Father, and one Christ Jesus, who came
by means of the whole dispensational arrangements [connected with
Him], and gathered together all things in Himself (Ephesians 1:10). But in
every respect, too, He is man, the formation of God; and thus He took up
man into Himself, the invisible becoming visible, the incomprehensible
being made comprehensible, the impassible becoming capable of suffering, and the Word being made man, thus summing up all things in
Himself: so that as in super-celestial, spiritual, and invisible things, the
Word of God is supreme, so also in things visible and corporeal He might
possess the supremacy, and, taking to Himself the pre-eminence, as well
as constituting Himself Head of the Church, He might draw all things to
Himself at the proper time.[8]

The trinitarian emphasis presented in this section signifies that the orthodox Christian faith espouses a form of spirituality that is embodied and
celebrates the material realm. As noted above, according to the biblical
revelation, in contrast to gnosticism, which denies the incarnation, the
divine Word becomes matter. Again, the Christian tradition does not
champion spirit over matter, but spirit through and in indissoluble relation
to matter. The Spirit of God indwells the embodied Jesus—the cosmic
Redeemer—and his body the church as well as operates within the cosmos
to bring about the transformation and perfection of all things. The Spirit
and the bride, the church, welcome us to drink our fill of the water of
eternal life (Revelation 22:17). This holistic and hope-filled orientation that
contends against gnosticism has import for contending against harming
the environment since material reality matters to God. Far from undermining or discounting the natural order, Christian orthodoxy provides the
resources for a robust theology of creation and environmental stewardship.

The Christian doctrine of creation goes so far as to provide a more
constructive framework for affirming the natural order than modern

---

[8]Refer here to *Against Heresies* III. 16.6 (*ANF*, 442-43), from which the quote from Irenaeus is taken;
see also *Against Heresies* V. 18.2-3 (*ANF*, 546) for a discussion of Christ and the Spirit's work.

natural science in all its wondrous accomplishments. There is nothing inherent to modern science of the ultra-Darwinian vantage point that would enable it to account for purposiveness and teleology.[9] So, it is not so difficult to imagine how someone such as Richard Dawkins could celebrate natural science and at the same time approach the natural order in pessimistic terms. As Dawkins writes, science has the capacity to invoke "awed wonder," which he describes as "one of the highest experiences of which the human psyche is capable."[10] But this wonder is immediately confronted by Dawkins's pessimism:

> The total amount of suffering per year in the natural world is beyond all decent contemplation. During the minute that it takes me to compose this sentence, thousands of animals are being eaten alive, many others are running for their lives, whimpering with fear, others are slowly being devoured from within by rasping parasites, thousands of all kinds are dying of starvation, thirst, and disease. It must be so. If there ever is a time of plenty, this very fact will automatically lead to an increase in the population until the natural state of starvation and misery is restored. In a universe of electrons and selfish genes, blind physical forces and genetic replication, some people are going to get hurt, other people are going to get lucky, and you won't find any rhyme or reason in it, nor any justice. The universe that we observe has precisely the properties we should expect if there is, at bottom, no design, no purpose, no evil, no good, nothing but pitiless indifference.[11]

Counter to this nihilistic, materialistic account of physical reality, the historical Christian doctrine of creation, which provided invaluable resources for the formation and development of modern science,[12] affirms exploration and preservation of the natural sphere. It resonates with Jane Bennett's point that "the problem of meaninglessness arises only if 'matter' is conceived as inert, only as long as science deploys materialism

[9]See Conor Cunningham, *Darwin's Pious Idea: Why the Ultra-Darwinists and Creationists Both Get It Wrong* (Grand Rapids, MI: Eerdmans, 2010), 6-7.
[10]Richard Dawkins, *Unweaving the Rainbow: Science, Delusion, and the Appetite for Wonder* (New York: Mariner Books, 1998), x.
[11]Richard Dawkins, *River Out of Eden: A Darwinian View of Life* (New York: Basic Books, 1995), 155.
[12]See for example Michael B. Foster, "The Christian Doctrine of Creation and the Rise of Modern Natural Science," *Mind* 43, no. 172 (October 1934): 446-68; R. G. Collingwood, *The Idea of Nature* (Oxford: Clarendon, 1945).

whose physics is basically Newtonian."[13] Matter is "enchanted," as Bennett claims. That is, "matter has a liveliness, resilience, unpredictability, or recalcitrance that is itself a source of wonder for us."[14]

Here we find one attempt to counter what Max Weber called the "progressive disenchantment of the world" with the rise of scientific progress that at the time discounted mystery and demanded explanations of all forms of life in rationalistic, predictable, and mundane terms.[15] Weber's "disenchanted materialism" involves the opposition of spirit and matter, where matter is viewed as "lifeless stuff."[16] Other efforts are underway today to reenchant the universe in keeping with secular reason.[17]

Christian theology also has much to offer. All of material life, including the human image of God as an embodied soul, is what Colin Gunton calls a "project." It is not inert or motionless but moving toward a destination.[18] God is in the process of shaping, healing, and perfecting the whole of creaturely life in a purposeful manner. Speaking of the whole creation, human persons only find their fulfillment in what Christian Smith calls "loving relationships with other personal selves and with the nonpersonal world,"[19] from which they emerge and in turn impact.[20] A Christian doctrine of creation and personalist account of reality contends against a pessimistic, materialistic view of life, as well as gnostic trajectories that also discount material reality. Moreover, it challenges those anthropocentric forms of thought that entail domination and abuse of the natural order. I now turn to consider how the Christian doctrine of creation does not pit humanity against the rest of creation but views humanity with the rest of creation as an integrated whole.

---

[13]Jane Bennett, *The Enchantment of Modern Life: Attachments, Crossings, and Ethics* (Princeton, NJ: Princeton University Press, 2001), 64.

[14]Bennett, *Enchantment of Modern Life*, 64.

[15]Refer here for consideration of this theme: Eu Jin Chua, "Disenchantment," *Encyclopedia Britannica*, www.britannica.com/topic/disenchantment-sociology.

[16]Bennett, *Enchantment of Modern Life*, 64.

[17]See Joshua Landy and Michael Saler, eds., *The Re-enchantment of the World: Secular Magic in a Rational Age* (Stanford, CA: Stanford University Press, 2009).

[18]For his treatment of the creation as a project, see Colin E. Gunton, *The Triune Creator: A Historical and Systematic Study*, New Studies in Constructive Theology (Grand Rapids, MI: Eerdmans, 1998), 209.

[19]Christian Smith, *What Is a Person?* (Chicago: University of Chicago Press, 2010), 61.

[20]Smith, *What Is a Person?*, 33, fig. 1; cf. 57, fig. 2.

HUMANITY OVER NATURE: THE
ANTHROPOCENTRIC CHALLENGE

Orthodox Christian theology is personalist in orientation. There is indeed a sense in which one could call Christian theology anthropocentric, but not in a manner that orients the human person against the nonhuman. Orthodox Christian theology is anthropocentric simply in the sense that human persons alone are created in God's image as the highest life form, which emerges from and in turn influences the rest of creation for the sake of cosmic flourishing.

Consideration of cosmic flourishing must account for the realization of an organic and relational connection between humanity and the rest of creation. There is a harmonious and interdependent symbiosis between human health, animal health, and the health of our planet. While humanity is the crown of creation, the entire cosmos has sacred value as a palace and temple that serves as God's dwelling in our midst.

Here I find a creative tension between the Judeo-Christian doctrine of creation and Eastern thought forms that do not award special status to humanity. For example, "The human being has no special status as the crown of creation in Shinto or Buddhism. In Shinto the human being is simply a harmonious part of nature."[21] That said, Christian theology resonates from one angle with the Shinto and Buddhist reverence for nature as sacred, apart from Shinto's animistic traits or Buddhism's vision that mountains, rivers, and trees become manifestations of Buddha nature.[22] From a Christian perspective, all creaturely life has spiritual and transcendent value as God's habitation. Moreover, one finds a parallel between Christian theology and the Chinese concept of differentiation in unity, while also maintaining distance from the Chinese notion that human identity as a species is not permanent:

> Presumably, from the cosmic vantage point, nothing is totally fixed. It need not be forever the identity it now assumes. . . . We can also talk about degrees of spirituality in the entire chain of being. Rocks, trees, animals,

[21]Masakazu Hara, "Shinto," in *Encyclopedia of Science and Religion*, ed. Wentzel Van Huyssteen et al. (New York: Macmillan Reference, 2003).
[22]Motohisa Yamakage, *The Essence of Shinto: Japan's Spiritual Heart* (New York: Kodansha, 2012), 29-31.

humans, and gods represent different levels of spirituality based on the varying compositions of *ch'i*. However, despite the principle of differentiation, all modalities of being are organically connected. They are integral parts of a continuous process of cosmic transformation. It is in this metaphysical sense that "all things are my companions."[23]

For all its differences from Eastern religious thought, orthodox Christian theology views all life as sacred. Thus, it contends against what I refer to as "the anthropocentric challenge," which wrongly conceives the earth's value merely in instrumentalist terms: the earth and its various life forms only have value to the extent that humans find them useful and desirable. Unfortunately, many Christians espouse this form of anthropocentrism, which does not reflect orthodox Christian theology.[24]

Many environmentalists wrongly assume that Christian orthodoxy is the culprit in opposing humanity to the rest of creation and fostering a utilitarian and domineering approach to the natural order. For example, Lynn White famously proposed that the conceptual source for the current ecological crisis is "the orthodox Christian arrogance toward nature." According to White, the Christian doctrine of creation arising from the opening chapters of Genesis separates humanity from nature, promotes humanity's domination of nature, and suggests that nature only exists for our benefit and use.[25]

Certainly, multitudes of Christians reflect such biases, and numerous critics claim that it proves, reflects, or supports White's thesis about Christianity on the environment. They find it difficult to see the connection between water pollution, air pollution, pesticides, and people's health; how the endangering of other species endangers ecosystems; and how renewable energies lead to flourishing of the planet, including

---

[23]Tu Wei-Ming, *Confucian Thought: Selfhood as Creative Transformation*, SUNY Series in Philosophy (Albany, NY: SUNY Press, 1985), 43-44.

[24]Refer to the helpful discussion of various approaches to an ethic of creation care as well as the rejection of an exploitive reading of Genesis 1:1–2:3, specifically an "anthropocentric-utilitarian human domination of creation," in David P. Gushee and Glen H. Stassen, *Kingdom Ethics: Following Jesus in Contemporary Context*, 2nd ed. (Grand Rapids, MI: Eerdmans, 2017), 385-92. They write, "The 'dominion' given to humans in Genesis 1:26-29 does imply a human preeminence, a theme echoed in such passages as Psalm 8, but it opposes a theology of domination (Brueggemann, *Genesis*, 73ff.)" (390). The full listing for the work in parentheses is Walter Brueggemann, *Genesis* (Atlanta: John Knox, 1982).

[25]Lynn White Jr., "The Historical Roots of Our Ecological Crisis," *Science* 155 (1967): 1203-7.

human civilizations. Although the following statement by Brian Palmer does not go so far as to defend White's thesis, the reflection is suggestive:

> A large number of evangelicals, arguably the most powerful voting bloc in America, barely ever think about the environment. And when they do, the framework they are working through suggests that they might be committing a venial sin by putting trees above people.
>
> Thirty-seven years ago, in a discussion of conservation, Interior Secretary James G. Watt mused to Congress, "I do not know how many future generations we can count on before the Lord returns." You can draw a straight line backward from Scott Pruitt's scripture-based support for oil exploration, through Watt's wait-for-Jesus stewardship philosophy, to evangelical ambivalence for the environmental movement of the early 1970s. And if Lynn White Jr. is correct, you can keep drawing that line backward 2,000 years.[26]

Palmer indicates that there is widespread resonance among conservative evangelical Christians with the stance White critiques, including those with political power and influence such as past US Secretaries of the Interior Pruitt and Watt. Does their particular conservative stance reflect orthodox Christianity, and does White's argument that orthodox Christianity arrogantly demeans creation stand the historical test of time?

White's thesis is not without its detractors. However, as already suggested, it continues to influence environmentalist critiques of the traditional Christian doctrine of creation. Rarely if ever do the rebuttals to White's thesis address the historical backdrop. Esteemed historian Peter Harrison has provided such an assessment, finding White's argument and historiography of the traditional Christian doctrine of creation flawed on several counts.[27]

Harrison presents four historical corrections to White. First, it is only in the early modern period that the connection is made between "the exploitation of nature and the Genesis creation narratives," not earlier, as

---

[26]Brian Palmer, "God's EPA Administrator: Did the Politics and History of Evangelical Christianity Create Scott Pruitt?," *Slate*, June 8, 2018, https://slate.com/technology/2018/06/evangelicals-lack-of-environmentalism-explains-scott-pruitt.html.
[27]Peter Harrison, "Subduing the Earth: Genesis 1, Early Modern Science, and the Exploitation of Nature," *The Journal of Religion* (January 1999): 86-109.

White claims.[28] It is this new connection of exploitation with the Genesis narrative combined with early modern science that leads to the violent forms of domination in certain quarters in the modern period.

Second, anthropocentrism is not in itself a fundamental driving force in the exploitation of nature. Rather, modern intellectuals distorted the Copernican revolution to signify a loss of human worth and dignity. Ironically, perhaps, this sense of loss fueled domination and exploitation: "For the moderns, it was precisely the loss of this centrality that motivated the quest to conquer an obstinate and uncooperative earth."[29] This is one key reason why Harrison takes issue with White's association of anthropocentrism and environmental degradation: "It is by no means clear that anthropocentrism inevitably leads to an aggressive violation of the integrity of nature."[30] It is the loss of humanity as the center or pinnacle of nature, or anthropocentrism, as Harrison carefully construes it, that leads to the modern notion that humankind is over and above and against nature. It is this negative and abusive form of anthropocentrism that I critique in this chapter. In keeping with Harrison's argument, man resorts to exerting mastery over nature when he no longer sees himself as the center or pinnacle of creation. It is this adverse form of anthropocentrism that arises in the modern period.

Third, contrary to popular assessments, the early modern approach to nature did not divorce dominion from stewardship. Even though they differed on their understanding of the natural condition, these early moderns and contemporary environmentalists share a vision for restoring the creation to its natural state.[31]

Fourth, building on the last assertion, one could develop "an ecologically sensitive theology" based on the early modern approach to the creation and fall accounts in Genesis. This stands in stark contrast to many ecotheological treatments that perceive the traditional doctrine of

---

[28]Harrison, "Subduing the Earth," 107.
[29]Harrison, "Subduing the Earth," 107. Dennis Danielson explains, "But a trick of this supposed dethronement is that, while purportedly rendering 'Man' less cosmically and metaphysically important, it actually enthrones us modern 'scientific' humans in all our enlightened superiority." Dennis R. Danielson, "Myth 6: That Copernicanism Demoted Humans from the Center of the Cosmos," in *Galileo Goes to Jail: And Other Myths About Science and Religion*, ed. Ronald Numbers (Cambridge, MA: Harvard University Press, 2009), 57.
[30]Harrison, "Subduing the Earth," 104.
[31]Harrison, "Subduing the Earth," 107-8.

creation as problematic and in need of revision.[32] Here's Harrison's concluding assessment:

> While it is tempting to speculate about simple connections between such ideas as divine transcendence or human dominion on the one hand, and attitudes of arrogance toward the natural order on the other, and while such links may seem to have a prima facie plausibility, history bears out the fact that the real situation is rather more complex. . . . However ecologically naive our seventeenth-century forebears might now appear, and however misguided their efforts to "improve" the natural world, their program of retrieving a nature that had fallen into ruin on account of human transgressions seems not entirely inappropriate for the late twentieth century.[33]

Harrison does not claim that the conquest of the earth only begins in the modern period, but that such conquest is pragmatically rather than ideologically driven until that time: "Undeniably, the conquest of nature is well in evidence during the Middle Ages, but for the most part this is to be attributed to pragmatic rather than ideological concerns."[34]

Harrison points out that historical revisionism leads to theological revisionism in the case of ecotheology. While Harrison acknowledges differences of view over what the "natural condition" of the creaturely order is, he maintains that "early modern advocates of dominion and contemporary environmentalists share a common concern—to preserve or restore the natural condition of the earth, with the crucial difference between them residing in their respective views of what that 'natural condition' is believed to be."[35] In Harrison's view, early modern conceptions of the creation and fall accounts in Genesis provide "the resources for an ecologically sensitive theology." Thus, he finds it "intriguing" that "so many advocates of ecotheology (such as Thomas Berry, Sally McFague and Matthew Fox) have tended to regard traditional theology as the problem rather than the solution."[36]

---

[32]Harrison, "Subduing the Earth," 108.

[33]Harrison, "Subduing the Earth," 109.

[34]Harrison, "Subduing the Earth," 96.

[35]Harrison, "Subduing the Earth," 108.

[36]Harrison, "Subduing the Earth," 108-9. For a critical assessment of White's thesis from a scholar within the ecotheology ranks, see Willis Jenkins's essay, "After Lynn White: Religious Ethics and Environmental Problems," *Journal of Religious Ethics* 37, no. 2 (2009): 283-309.

Apart from differences of view regarding the characteristic trait of dominion in the early modern period, the question must still be asked, What led to the new readings of dominion? There are many factors according to Harrison. One factor is the move from dominion or control in the human mind to control over the natural world. Another factor is the loss of vitalism or a vital force unique to living organisms that explains their nature and operations and the rise of mechanism. Still another factor is the demise of symbolic representation and a sacramental outlook on the whole of creaturely reality. One more factor entails Protestantism's world-oriented spirituality, the accompanying "Protestant work ethic," hermeneutical literalism, and voluntarism. Harrison writes,

> While the themes of moral and intellectual dominion have not entirely disappeared in the seventeenth century, "dominion over the earth" is now read by most commentators as having to do with the exercise of control not in the mind, but in the natural world. A variety of interrelated factors can be suggested to account for this shift: the demise of the rich, arcane conception of the microcosm in which features of the natural world had been mapped onto the human psyche; the "death of nature," which saw the replacement of Aristotelian vitalism with a mechanical world view; the collapse of the "symbolist mentality" of the Middle Ages and the radical contraction of sacramentalism, which resulted in a denial of the transcendental significance of the things of nature; the appearance on the religious landscape of this-worldly Protestantism with its attendant work ethic; and finally, the new hermeneutics of modernity, which looks to the literal sense as the true meaning of a text. It is this last factor in particular which brings about new readings of the biblical imperative "have dominion."[37]

As noted above, theological voluntarism is also a factor for Harrison:

> The rise of theological voluntarism is also a relevant consideration here. If the laws of nature rested upon the divine will, rather than the divine reason, the basis of the regularities of nature could only be discovered through empirical investigation and not merely through the exercise of human reason alone.[38]

---

[37]Harrison, "Subduing the Earth," 96-97.
[38]Harrison, "Subduing the Earth," 106n72.

Similarly, Jürgen Moltmann contends that voluntarism's adjoining notion, nominalism (i.e., universals are names without accompanying reality; only particular things or entities are real), as well as the Renaissance, are to blame for the rise of human domination of the natural world, and not the Judeo-Christian tradition. Moltmann challenges the supposed "anthropocentric" view projected onto the Jewish and Christian Scriptures and instead places the blame squarely on the will to power over nature bound up with modern thought forms:

> God is almighty, and *potentia absoluta* is the pre-eminent attribute of his divinity. Consequently God's image on earth, the human being (which in actual practice meant the man) had to strive for power and domination so that he might acquire *his* divinity. Power became the foremost predicate of the deity, not goodness and truth. But how can the human being acquire power, so that he may resemble his God? Through science and technology. . . . The goal of the scientific knowledge of natural laws is over nature, and with that the restoration of the human being's resemblance to God and his hegemony.[39]

Moltmann goes on to argue that the biblical tradition's emphasis on human rule in the creaturely realm has nothing whatsoever to do with lordship over life and death: "Because human beings and animals are to live from the fruits of the earth, the rule of human beings over the animals can only be a rule of peace, without any 'power over life and death.' The role which human beings are meant to play is the role of a 'justice of the peace.'"[40] Rather than claiming humanity is the center of the universe and the crown of creation, which resonates with the particular or distinctive "modern anthropocentric view of the world," Moltmann argues for a theocentric perspective with the Sabbath as creation's crown.[41]

Harrison would take issue with Moltmann's handling of historical developments. Harrison maintains that humanity was viewed as the center and crown of creation in the medieval period. Regardless of the historical veracity of Moltmann's account, one can still benefit from

[39]Jürgen Moltmann, *God in Creation: A New Theology of Creation and the Spirit of God* (San Francisco: Harper & Row, 1985), 26-27.
[40]Moltmann, *God in Creation*, 30.
[41]Moltmann, *God in Creation*, 31.

Moltmann's theological prescription for viewing humanity's relation to the creation today.

Moltmann does not end consideration of the subject with arguing for a theocentric orientation. Ultimately, he centers God's rule in Jesus Christ. In this vein, Moltmann writes of the "imago Christi" as "the messianic calling of human beings."[42] Christ Jesus is the true image of God.[43] Here's Moltmann:

> In the messianic light of the gospel, the appointment to rule over animals and the earth also appears as the "ruling with Christ" of believers. For it is to Christ, the true and visible image of the invisible God on earth, that "all authority is given in heaven and on earth" (Matt. 28.18). His liberating and healing rule also embraces the fulfilment of the *dominium terrae*— the promise given to human beings at creation. Under the conditions of history and in the circumstances of sin and death, the sovereignty of the crucified and risen Messiah Jesus is the only true *dominium terrae*. It is to "the Lamb" that rule over the world belongs. It would be wrong to seek for the *dominium terrae*, not in the lordship of Christ, but in other principalities and powers—in the power of the state or the power of science and technology.[44]

One cannot avoid the sense in Genesis 1 that humanity bears the image of God in a unique and qualitatively different sense from any other life form and as a result is given the responsibility of having dominion in the creation. Ultimately, Christ bears that responsibility. While this christocentric thrust is correct, one must make clear the meaning of the terms *dominion* and *subdue* in this context. It is also important to specify how this context relates to the Christian Scriptures in their entirety, including their christocentric rather than merely anthropocentric orientation.

So, what do "have dominion" and "subdue" mean? Do these terms mean ruling over other life forms? Yes. Do they entail using the creation in whatever way one deems fit? No. James Barr argues that the word *rada* for "have dominion" is used to refer to the peaceful rule of King Solomon. The word *kabash* for "subdue" conveys "the 'working' or 'tilling' of the

---

[42]Moltmann, *God in Creation*, 225.
[43]Moltmann, *God in Creation*, 225.
[44]Moltmann, *God in Creation*, 227-28.

ground in the J story."[45] If we wish to see what peaceful rule ultimately entails, we should look to King Jesus, the one who is greater than Solomon (Matthew 12:42), the High Priest over the whole creation, and to the Spirit of God, through whom Jesus operates in the creaturely realm.

Jesus' lordship as king, which hails from the tribe of Judah, is never separate from his priestly office. In fact, consider how Hebrews develops Psalm 110, which portrays the Messiah as king and as high priest in the order of Melchizedek (Hebrews 7:13-17). Just as Jesus' lordship is defined by his peaceful rule and servanthood, so his lordship complements his priestly and cleansing work of healing and restoring. Jesus does not wreak havoc and destroy the earth. As Moltmann reasons, Jesus' rule is "liberating and healing."[46] It is also important to highlight that as the ultimate and only high priest in the final order of Melchizedek, which surpasses the Aaronic priesthood, Jesus offers himself as the lamb of sacrifice. He is once for all delivered for the sins of the world, bringing an end to animal sacrifices (Hebrews 10:1-18; see also John 1:29).

The more seriously we take Jesus' humane and once-for-all holy sacrifice, the more seriously we will take the humane treatment of animals.[47] Moreover, the Hebrew Scriptures serve as a fitting backdrop for Jesus' sacrifice, and in a variety of ways. God commanded the humane treatment of animals, including those prepared for sacrifice. Indeed, holiness requires their humane treatment.[48] Holiness is holistic and comprehensive, with import not simply for one's interior state of the soul but also for the larger context of our creaturely estate, including dominion in the creation.

The claim that holiness involves the humane treatment of animals is not a politically correct statement, but a biblically correct one. Note for example the prohibition against boiling a young goat in its mother's milk

---

[45]James Barr, "The Ecological Controversy and the Old Testament," *Bulletin of the John Rylands Library* 55 (1972): 9-32. Note in particular 22.

[46]Moltmann, *God in Creation*, 227-28.

[47]I wish to express thanks to my student Jonah Carpenter for his keen observation of a related point. In the Hebrew Scriptures, animal sacrifice places the animal in an important position as the means of mediation between God and humans. Animals destined for sacrifice are placed in a dignified position and are deserving of honor.

[48]Refer to David Sears, *The Vision of Eden: Animal Welfare and Vegetarianism in Jewish Law and Mysticism* (Spring Valley, NY: OROT, 2003).

in Exodus 23:19; 34:26; and Deuteronomy 14:21. The latter passage reads, "Do not eat anything you find already dead. You may give it to the foreigner residing in any of your towns, and they may eat it, or you may sell it to any other foreigner. But you are a people holy to the LORD your God. Do not cook a young goat in its mother's milk."

One might be tempted to think this prohibition comes out of nowhere. That assessment would be mistaken. The prohibition to boil a young goat in its mother's milk is bound up with God's abiding concern to distinguish his people from the surrounding nations. As with the prohibition to eat anything that has died naturally, this prohibition is connected to Israel being "a people holy to the LORD your God" (Deuteronomy 14:21).

It has been argued that some of the foreign nations sought their gods' blessing and aid through the practice of boiling a young goat in its mother's milk for greater agricultural yields and the increased fertility of their flocks. God and his people are very different from those gods and nations engaged in such practices. God demonstrates his uniqueness and holiness in prohibiting his holy people from copying such customs and practices.

Holiness is not prudish and irrelevant to creation's and society's well-being. The practice of boiling a young goat in its mother's milk was deemed cruel and inhumane. When humans treat animals in a cruel manner, it degrades our humanity as well as the animals themselves. It also dishonors God, who created them and us. A society that cherishes life as sacred will treat animals respectfully. It follows from a personalist account of human identity and dignity.

The Jewish Scriptures forbid cruelty and promote minimal suffering of animals slaughtered for ritual purposes and for food. Rabbi David Sears's work, *The Vision of Eden: Animal Welfare and Vegetarianism in Jewish Law and Mysticism*, includes the following reflection:

> The act of slaughter must be sanctified in a unique manner—"as I have commanded you"—with a minimum of pain to the animal. Thus, the person will take to heart the fact that he is not involved with a random object that moves about like an automaton, but with a living, feeling creature. He must become attuned to its senses, even to its emotions, to the feeling it has for the life of its family members, and to its compassion

for its own offspring. Thus, it is biblically forbidden to kill the mother bird with her children on the same day, or to slaughter a calf before it is eight days old; and it is a positive precept to send away the mother bird before taking her young (Rabbi Avraham Yitzchak Kook, Chazon HaTzim-chonut V'HaShalom, sec. 14).[49]

It is also worth pointing out the claim that "Israel was only given the laws of ritual slaughter to refine their moral sensitivities (*Midrash Tanchuma, Shemini*, 7)."[50] In addition to the needless harming of animals, those who coarsen rather than refine their moral sensitivities in this way hurt their own humanity. In addition, those who treat animals harshly may very well harden themselves toward compassionate care for their fellow humans. To the degree one lacks compassion for animals and one's fellows, one lacks humaneness and holiness. This trajectory runs counter to a Christian personalist account of human flourishing.

Could there be a correlation between a society's treatment of animals and its treatment of the most vulnerable human communities and individuals? Both animals and the poor, disabled, and elderly are dependent on the good will of the affluent and able-bodied among us. How we treat the one often bears on how we will treat the other. For all their differences as human and nonhuman, they are both at-risk populations. A humane society will treat the human and nonhuman in a respectful and dignified manner. An "advanced" society that does not cherish these at-risk communities is advanced in technology and material capital only.

Jesus is not domineering. He is the decentered God-human, whose rule involves his self-sacrifice, as Hebrews 2 reconfigures Psalm 8. He has dominion over all creation through his incarnate state of suffering unto death and through the renewal of all reality through his resurrection, ascension, and return. The triune God makes all things new through the

---

[49]Sears, *Vision of Eden*, 93. My student Cody Sibley noted how C. S. Lewis reflects a biblical approach to the humane treatment of animals in his Chronicles of Narnia series. For Lewis, animals are not mere things or the equivalent of automatons. For more on Lewis, refer to Doris T. Myers, "Hrossa, Pigs, and Teddy Bears: The Animal Kingdom According to C. S. Lewis; Guest of Honor Address at the 1996 Mythopoeic Conference," *Mythlore* 22, no. 2 (84), C. S. Lewis Centenary Special Issue (Summer 1998): 4-9. See also Michael J. Gilmour, *Animals in the Writings of C. S. Lewis*, Palgrave Macmillan Animal Ethics Series (London: Palgrave Macmillan, 2017).
[50]Sears, *Vision of Eden*, 94.

transformative process of recapitulation. Recapitulation and transformation of the creation serve as powerful prophetic anecdotes to the doctrines of annihilation and eradication that manifest themselves in statements such as "Why polish the brass on a sinking ship?" and "It's all going to burn up in the end anyway (so why bother preserving and cherishing the creation?)."

Jesus gives himself as the firstfruits of God's harvest and in place of animal sacrifices, recapitulating all creaturely life through himself as signified by the bread and wine. While we may still eat meat, may we raise animals and prepare food in a humane way. As stewards of creation, may we be mindful of Jesus' care for the creation and his sacrifice on behalf of all creation as its Lord.

As the image of the invisible God, firstborn over all creation and firstborn from the dead, through whom God reconciles all things to himself on earth and in heaven, making peace through his blood that was shed on the cross (Colossians 1:15-20), Jesus is creation's chief steward and source of healing. He frames our vocation and envisions for us what human rule in the creation entails. Jesus' dominion involves his own personal sacrifice on behalf of the whole creation. Rather than promoting a generic anthropocentric orientation or generic theocentric orientation, both divine and human vocations come together in this christocentric framework revealed in Jesus.

The Eastern Orthodox approach the subject in a most helpful manner. For the Orthodox, humanity is the "microcosm" of the world, and as such the "mediator," reconciling and harmonizing "the noetic and the material realms."[51] This point brings us back to Harrison, who speaks of the loss in early modernity of humanity as a microcosm that orders and rules the world in the mind, not physically in nature.

Moreover, as Harrison indicated, the rise of modernity also spelled the loss of a sacramental view of creaturely life. While this perspective has been largely lost in Protestant circles, Orthodoxy construes the image-of-God thesis to include consideration of humanity as "priest and king of the creation." Humanity is not simply a logical creature but

---

[51]Kallistos Ware, *The Orthodox Way*, rev. ed. (Crestwood, NY: St. Vladimir's Seminary Press, 1998), 50.

ultimately a "eucharistic" creature, who sees the world as a divine gift and sacrament and offers "the world back to God in thanksgiving."[52] Ultimately, given the christocentric framing of creation and humanity in Orthodox thought, it is appropriate to claim that Christ as the archetypal human is the priestly king and mediator who serves God and creation as the ultimate eucharistic creature.

Concern for God is vitally connected to concern for humanity, the land, and sea. The disconnect between them can be fueled by or give rise to fixation on economic profit as primary with all that this emphasis entails. Concern over this disconnect calls to mind the following statement by Moltmann:

> The natural environment of human beings cannot be understood apart from the social environment. The processes which intervene destructively in the natural environment originate in the economic and the social processes. So if the destruction of nature is to be halted, the economic and social conditions of human society must be changed. Societies which are primarily out to develop production, and increase the efficiency of human labour, and make further strides in already existing technologies, can neither restrict nor overcome the progressive destruction of the environment which they are causing.[53]

Primary or exclusive emphasis on production and human labor efficiency in the social, economic, and technological spheres will no doubt only serve to negate attempts at protecting the natural environment. Thus, it is important to reorient our values so that we do not place the former over the latter but see them as vitally connected. I will return to this point in the conclusion. To adapt a line from Scripture, what does it profit a man or society to gain economic wealth if he harms the long-term physical health of his children and the planet on which they live by pollution and the inhumane treatment of animals? Shortsighted consideration of economic growth will lead to long-term negative, even catastrophic, consequences. Consideration of sustainability is an important value to embrace not simply for the environment and

---

[52]Ware, *Orthodox Way*, 50, 53, 54.
[53]Moltmann, *God in Creation*, 23-24.

economics, but also for one's relational, social assets and future generations of people.

So far, discussion has focused on gnosticism and anthropocentrism.
Consideration now turns to imperialism, which includes colonialist
and expansionist perspectives. Gnosticism, anthropocentrism, and imperialism are interconnected and together lead to the destruction of the
creation. If all that matters are human prowess, technological advance,
pleasure, and profit, humanity can do anything it wishes with the nonhuman creation. This distorted approach to life has even manifested
itself in evangelism and mission worldwide. Converts to Christianity in
other lands are inclined to renounce their rights to the land in view of
an otherworldly spirituality that benefits the imperialists and colonizers. The converts end up receiving their "eternal inheritance" in exchange for "real estate" and various worldly "commodities."[54] However,
Jesus' kingdom is not otherworldly and ethereal, but earthly. In telling
Pilate at his trial that his kingdom is not of this world, Jesus does not
convey that his kingdom discounts the world, ignores the worldly
powers, or has no bearing on creaturely life. Rather, he asserts that his
kingdom originates elsewhere and that he does not do business Pilate's
and Rome's way (see John 18:36). In fulfillment of God's promise to
Abraham and his descendants, Jesus' kingdom confronts imperialist
and colonialist conquests.

THE WEST OVER THE REST: THE IMPERIALISTIC CHALLENGE

As shown in Harrison's as well as Moltmann's reflections, it is important
to guard against the sweeping accusation that the traditional doctrine of
creation and dominion is the ideological basis for the current environmental crisis. At the same time, it is important to come to terms with
how a problematic form of anthropocentrism involving distorted notions of dominion furthered imperialistic and colonialist expansion
along with violent domination of the earth and its inhabitants.

---

[54]I am reminded here of Willie Jennings's statement: "In the age of discovery and conquest supersessionist thinking burrowed deeply inside the logic of evangelism and emerged joined to whiteness
in a new, more sophisticated, concealed form." Willie James Jennings, *The Christian Imagination:
Theology and the Origins of Race* (New Haven, CT: Yale University Press, 2010), 36.

It would be good to pause to gain clarity on the meaning of such terms as *imperialism* and *colonialism*. One article acknowledges the difficulty in distinguishing between colonialism and imperialism in a consistent manner. The article uses "colonialism as a broad concept that refers to the project of European political domination from the sixteenth to the twentieth centuries that ended with the national liberation movements of the 1960s. Post-colonialism" describes "the political and theoretical struggles of societies that experienced the transition from political dependence to sovereignty." The article also refers to "imperialism as a broad term that refers to economic, military, political domination that is achieved without significant permanent European settlement."[55] Imperialism precedes and continues long after European settlements are gone.

Having briefly provided working definitions, we now seek after an answer to the following question: What was the ideological backdrop to colonialism? At least part of the answer can be found in the modern scientific worldview that is sown in European ideological soil. Harrison writes,

> In the seventeenth century we find practitioners of the new sciences, preachers of the virtues of agriculture and husbandry, advocates of colonization, and even gardeners explicitly legitimating their engagement with nature by appeals to the text of Genesis. The rise of modern science, the mastery of the world that it enabled, and the catastrophic consequences for the natural environment that ensued, were intimately related to new readings of the seminal Genesis text, "Have dominion."[56]

According to Harrison, the reading of dominion in the Genesis creation narratives in the early modern period does not entail violence. Dominion aims at removing the moral fall's imprint and scars on the creation: "Dominion, then, was not exercised so that humanity could leave its mark on the earth. On the contrary, it was to erase those scars that embodied the physical legacy of a moral fall. These measures were intended to

---

[55]Margaret Kohn and Kavita Reddy, "Colonialism," in *Stanford Encyclopedia of Philosophy*, Fall 2017 ed., ed. Edward N. Zalta, https://plato.stanford.edu/entries/colonialism/.
[56]Harrison, "Subduing the Earth," 96.

improve the earth, to reinstate a paradise on earth, and provide an anticipation of heaven."[57]

Harrison writes that the understanding of the biblical mandate to dominion in the seventeenth century shifted from control by the mind to "control in the natural world." As specified previously, Harrison argues that the shift resulted from several factors, including these: "the 'death of nature,' which saw the replacement of Aristotelian vitalism with a mechanical world view; the collapse of the 'symbolist mentality' of the Middle Ages and the radical contraction of sacramentalism, which resulted in a denial of the transcendental significance of the things of nature."[58] It would seem that this shift involving desacramentalism that led to the eventual domination of the planet gave rise to the displacement of people who refused to control and subordinate the earth. Harrison contends,

> A final incentive for this energetic engagement with the material world came with the linkage of the imperative "have dominion" to justifications of property ownership and colonization. In his *Second Treatise of Government* (1689), John Locke set out the view that in the state of nature, all land had been common. Land became private property when it was improved by clearing, planting, cultivation, or stocking with animals. The justification for this influential understanding of the basis of property ownership came from the biblical story of creation: for inasmuch as "God and his reason commanded him to subdue the earth, i.e. improve it for . . . the benefit of life. . . . He that in obedience to this command of God, subdued, tilled, and sowed any part of, thereby annexed to it something that was his property." Logically, it followed that those who occupied lands, yet had done nothing to bring them under control, could legitimately be dispossessed of them. Such notions were to play an important role in the justification of overseas plantations and colonies.[59]

Harrison adds, "Developing conceptions of private property, along with commercial incentives for colonization, thus played their role in the modern conquest of nature, and these factors, too, found their

---

[57]Harrison, "Subduing the Earth," 104.
[58]Harrison, "Subduing the Earth," 96.
[59]Harrison, "Subduing the Earth," 100-101.

ideological justification in seventeenth- and eighteenth-century readings of Genesis."[60] Again, critiquing White, Harrison writes,

> In the rhetoric of seventeenth-century scientists and exegetes, then, we encounter new and momentous applications of the biblical imperatives "subdue" and "have dominion." It is difficult to escape the conclusion that the Genesis creation narratives provided the program for not only the investigation of nature but its exploitation as well. Stripped of their allegorical and moral connotations, these passages were taken to refer unambiguously to the physical world and its living occupants. Whatever the ecological practices of medieval societies had been, at no time in the West prior to this do we encounter so explicit an ideology of the subordination of nature. White was correct to assign an important role to the creation story in the development of modern science and technology but mistaken in locating that effect earlier than the seventeenth century.[61]

Stripping the text of these various literary and moral associations, the creation narratives could be put to very different use, as could the accounts of the conquest of Canaan. It could lead to efforts to strip people of their land, following Locke's reading of Genesis. It could also lead to attempts of stripping the people of these colonized lands of their human worth and dignity.

Certainly, the objectification and commodification of life preceded the seventeenth century, even if the interpretation of the creation narratives did not undergo change prior to that time. People became commodities, just like land. Willie Jennings reflects back on the time when European nations' slave ships sailed the world. As Africans were transported in the bowels of these vessels, they shared space with "other cargo," "commodities," such as rum, muskets, horses, and plants. If one were to read the ship cargo lists, one would find humans grouped together with other "things." The Black body was property, and as such a symbolic representation of the commodification of all reality at the hands of White colonizers and expansionists.[62] Jennings goes on to argue that whatever could be transported would be listed along with slaves as

---

[60]Harrison, "Subduing the Earth," 101.
[61]Harrison, "Subduing the Earth," 101-2.
[62]Jennings, *Christian Imagination*, 188.

commodities or property. Such accounts were very apparent beginning with colonialism.[63]

We find here the beginning stages of a capitalistic way of viewing all life. Capitalism attributes value to "things" based on supply and demand. Supply and demand impose value on someone as something, along with other "things," such as animals and plants, and uproot them from their relational and spatial settings. Jennings puts the matter this way. Capitalism does not require place in the same way as was true of the precolonial period. Taken from their relational orbit and exported globally, produce from the land, people, and animals are brought together in close proximity, as in the bowels of the slave ship. Their association is not communal or relational but as accumulated commodities that are used and abused and then discarded.[64]

The modern Western world views property owners as alone sacred. On this view, it appears that the more property one owns, the more sacred one is. In contrast, from a biblical and theological vantage point, humans are landed creatures, but we are not necessarily private property owners who cultivate land for economic gain. Thus, property owners are not more sacred than others. All people are sacred as created in God's image. We must not treat "Black" or "dark-skinned" people, or those with less property, as property or commodities to be exploited or enjoyed for personal gain.

Perhaps no graver commodification occurred than with Black women, who were often systematically displaced, exported, raped, or forced into sexual relationships for the sake of reproduction as if they were chattel. Melanie Harris brings home this connection from the conquest of Africa to the present, focusing on the objectification of Black women's bodies: "Noting the paradoxical historical relationship that African American women have had with the earth (i.e., being named as property the same as the earth, and devalued in similar ways as the earth) in the midst of surviving a white supremacist society, ecowomanism pays attention to the complex subjectivity of African American

---

[63]Jennings, *Christian Imagination*, 188.
[64]For a description of the commodification that happened on slave ships, see Jennings, *Christian Imagination*, 176.

382 PART THREE: FROM CLOSE TO HOME . . .

women."[65] Harris defines ecowomanism in the following terms: "Eco-womanism is critical reflection and contemplation on environmental justice from [a] womanist perspective and more specifically from the perspectives of African and Indigenous women. It links a social justice agenda to environmental justice and recognizes the similar logic of domination at work in parallel oppressions suffered by women and the earth."[66]

Harris pays tribute to Delores S. Williams's essay, "Sin, Nature and Black Women's Bodies" (1993). It serves as a primary catalyst for eco-womanism and "argues that there is a connection between the logic of domination present in white supremacy, colonial Christianity, and sexist ideology that sanctioned the objectification of Black enslaved women's bodies during slavery (and since)."[67] Williams writes on the connection of degradation between Black women's bodies and nature, "Put simply, the assault upon the natural environment today is but an extension of the assault upon black women's bodies in the nineteenth century" under slavery.[68]

To overturn this imperialist and colonialist orientation, we must return to the biblical narrative and see the creation as bound up with Israel and the Jewish Messiah, who is the servant king fulfilling the promise to Israel as a liberated slave people in the Promised Land of Canaan, rather than a gnostic and Aryan superhuman master. Even so, Jesus does not rule only on behalf of Israel but on behalf of all people who together benefit from the creation being wed to God's covenant people Israel and the church.

Similarly, Jennings argues against extracting Israel from creation. Creation belongs to Israel from Genesis 1 onward. When we divorce the two

---

[65]Melanie L. Harris, "African Diaspora: African American Environmental Religious Ethics and Eco-womanism," in *Routledge Handbook of Religion and Ecology*, ed. Willis Jenkins, Mary Evelyn Tucker, and John Grim (New York: Routledge, 2016), 204.

[66]Harris, "African Diaspora," 203. The term *womanist* comes from Alice Walker, *In Search of Our Mothers' Gardens*. See Delores Williams, "Womanist Theology: Black Women's Voices," in *Learning to Breathe Free: Liberation Theologies in the United States*, ed. Mar Peter-Raoul, Linda Rennie Forcey, and Robert Frederick Hunters (Maryknoll, NY: Orbis, 1990), 62.

[67]Harris, "African Diaspora," 203.

[68]Delores S. Williams, "Sin, Nature, and Black Women's Bodies," in *Ecofeminism and the Sacred*, ed. Carol J. Adams (New York: Continuum, 1993), 24-25.

(as in the colonialist quest's linkage of the biblical drama with manifest destiny), it gives rise to the displacement of people groups from their places in creation. Instead of place demarcating us, race or rather color (White bodies) demarcate us. Displacement from the land led to a transference to the White body and with it the commodification of the Black body. As Jennings writes, "Whiteness replaced the earth as the signifier of identities."[69] Displacement preceded the racialized world and gave rise to it: "Before this agency would yield the 'idea of race,' 'the scientific concept of race,' the 'social principle of race,' or even a fully formed 'racial optic' on the world, it was a theological form—an inverted, distorted vision of creation that reduced theological anthropology to the commodified body."[70]

White Euro-Americans roamed wild, removing non-Whites from their land, not seeing them as identified with their land. They raped the land and the women of the land while transporting them thousands of miles away to a new land. The point of reference was not the land from which they were taken or the land to which they went, but the White bodies that replaced their sense of place. This move was bound up with the supersessionist orientation that replaced Israel. As Jennings claims, "Indeed, supersessionist thinking is the womb in which whiteness will mature."[71]

The White Euro-American man is the one who is internally displaced, restless, formless, void, roaming aimlessly. Not only does this have a bearing on the peoples and lands he subjugates, but also it has a bearing on him. Jennings references Vine Deloria Jr., who writes,

> The white man, when viewed in this context, appears as a perennial adolescent. He is continually moving about, and his restless nature cannot seem to find peace. Yet he does not listen to the land and so cannot find a place for himself. He has few relatives and seems to believe that the domestic animals that have always relied upon him constitute his only link with the other peoples of the universe. Yet he does not treat these animals as friends but only as objects to be exploited.[72]

---

[69]Jennings, *Christian Imagination*, 58.
[70]Jennings, *Christian Imagination*, 58.
[71]Jennings, *Christian Imagination*, 36.
[72]Vine Deloria Jr., *For This Land: Writings on Religion in America* (New York: Routledge, 1999), 241.

In Jennings's view, it is critically important to contend against the theological displacement of Israel from the land and the Messiah from Israel.[73] This position should not be taken to confer on Israel a mandate today to exterminate people groups in the land—and if Israel is not given such a mandate, neither is any other people group with manifest destiny aims. While God worked out his covenant aims through violence and death in the conquest of Canaan, God brought an end to violence and death through the violent death of Jesus. God alone has power over life and death. God shrinks down the use of violence and death through Israel in the conquest of Canaan. The termination point is the body of Jesus. From that point on, God's people must not enact violence.[74] Just as Jesus brings an end to animal sacrifices, so Jesus brings an end to violence and death through his slain body on the tree.

Further to the last idea on the theological displacement of Israel from the land and the Messiah from Israel, it is also of great import to safeguard against translating or transferring the point of reference to White bodies who serve in Christ's stead on earth to fulfill the Great Commission. Whereas whiteness was a status to be acquired or conferred on light-skinned and darker-skinned people alike by White-bodied elites such as Columbus,[75] Abraham and his descendants become Jews by faith in God's promise. God alone reckons to them this righteousness, which comes by faith, not acquired status as found in imperialists' conferring of whiteness.

It is also vitally important that we reenvision the world as sacred and not as mere matter. The desacralized world is a key factor for the roaming, conquering, raping, and displacement of people and land. Whiteness followed on from the total desacralization of the world, in which whiteness and its manifest destiny aims emerge from the void left by the loss of the sacred. Jennings puts the matter in this way: "It would be a mistake to see this replacement as a discursive practice fully controlled by

---

[73]Jennings, *Christian Imagination*, 36.

[74]Willie Jennings in an interview with the author, April 30, 2018.

[75]Consider Jennings's discussion of Christopher Columbus, who confers whiteness on native peoples in various lands based on what he takes to be their elevated status. Whiteness is more than a skin color. It is a status acquired and conferred. Jennings, *Christian Imagination*, 29-31.

Europeans. It *is* a discursive practice, but one that presented itself as the only real option given the aggressive desacralization of the world."[76]

So where does this lead us today? We must move beyond exploitation and the subordination of land and the people on it, especially the most vulnerable populations.[77] This will entail a rejection of a mechanistic outlook and a return to a sacramental view of life in all its forms, including the human non-White population and nonhuman domain as well. All of life has transcendent significance. Thus, the value of various life forms must not be reduced to their presumed efficiency, productivity, and marketability. That said, the sacramental view of life presented here does not deny but affirms that environmental well-being will have a positive bearing on economic health and vitality. This holistic perspective entails that we must not pit human well-being against itself or against other life forms, or environmental health against economic health and technological advancement. Rather, we must view life in all its manifestations and domains as interconnected for the sake of the whole. We must come to see all life as a sacred ecosystem, which should lead us to favor restraint in our various pursuits to guard against imbalances. To this subject we now turn.

LIFE AS SACRED ECOSYSTEM: THE INESCAPABLE
NETWORK OF MUTUALITY

The personalist orientation envisioned in this book seeks to safeguard against reducing people to disembodied individuals who exist autonomously from God, other humans, and the nonhuman world. Human persons are permanently who they are in relation to God, the rest of humanity, and creation in their embodied state. This framework resonates with what Martin Luther King Jr. writes of the "inescapable network of mutuality" of life and destiny in his "Letter from a Birmingham Jail":

> In a real sense all life is inter-related. All men are caught in an inescapable network of mutuality, tied in a single garment of destiny. Whatever affects one directly, affects all indirectly. I can never be what I ought to be

---

[76]Jennings, *Christian Imagination*, 58.

[77]Pope Francis's encyclical *Laudato Si* puts forth a theology of life that brings together concerns over global climate change and vulnerable human communities. Pope Francis, *Laudato Si*, encyclical letter, May 24, 2015, http://w2.vatican.va/content/francesco/en/encyclicals/documents/papa-francesco_20150524_enciclica-laudato-si.html.

until you are what you ought to be, and you can never be what you ought
to be until I am what I ought to be. . . . This is the inter-related structure
of reality.[78]

I find resonance between King and Harris with her ecowomanist perspective and its challenge to hierarchal notions of reality of any kind
bound up with African cosmology, which she embraces: "African cosmology connects the realms of spirit, nature, and humanity into one
flowing web of life. That is, instead of a hierarchal or dualistic structure,
African cosmology functions in a circular manner emphasizing interconnectedness and, in the words of Thich Nhat Hahn (1988), 'interbeing.'"[79]

We are all interconnected. Black lives matter. Green life matters. All
life matters. No community or individual must be left behind. No habitat
should undergo travail. To guard against such abandonment and abuse,
we must leave behind the insatiable hunger to satisfy our carnal appetites,
which leads us to devalue life in whatever form. As Mahatma Gandhi
wisely remarked, "The world has enough for everyone's need, but not
enough for everyone's greed."[80] Being made for more entails craving less.

It is vital that we conceive humanity in relation to the whole creation.
Thus, it follows that if one abuses the natural order, one abuses the human
order. How we treat the land and the rest of creation reflects on how
we treat others. Moreover, how we treat the rest of creation reflects how we
treat ourselves: we reduce our humanity when we minimize creation and
one another's well-being.

Further to what was stated in chapter one, life is a sacred ecosystem
of inseparable particles and waves with transcendent value rather than a
flat, mechanistic sphere of replaceable parts like cogs in a machine where
evaluations are based on mundane market gains and losses. The value of
all life comes from beyond us and is never reduced to supply and demand
and human appetite. A sacramental framework as articulated here will
entail the following. Humanity flourishes when we see all human life as

---

[78]Martin Luther King Jr., "Letter from Birmingham Jail," in *The Autobiography of Martin Luther King, Jr.*, ed. Clayborne Carson (New York: Warner Books, 1998), 189.

[79]Harris, "African Diaspora," 202.

[80]Oliver Balch, "The Relevance of Gandhi in the Capitalism Debate," *Guardian*, January 28, 2013, www.theguardian.com/sustainable-business/blog/relevance-gandhi-capitalism-debate-rajni -bakshi.

sacred, including those not given to ownership of property (i.e., "non-Whites"). Moreover, humanity flourishes when we see the whole of creation as sacred and not mere property to use and consume. Furthermore, humanity flourishes when we view human health and environmental health as well as economic health as interconnected components in "the inescapable network of mutuality."

Human well-being and environmental well-being are mutually constitutive. Humanity requires clean air, clean water, and healthy land to flourish. How can it be otherwise when, as the Bible reveals, God took humanity from the soil and breathed life into us (Genesis 2:7)? From dust we come and to dust we return (Genesis 3:19; Ecclesiastes 3:20). Unfortunately, issues involving human health and environmental health are often tackled separately.

One significant example is the partitioning of the work of the US Department of Health and Human Services (HHS) and the US Environmental Protection Agency (EPA). Pollutants that are regulated by the Environmental Protection Agency (such as lead in drinking water and polycyclic aromatic hydrocarbons and ozone in the air) are serious health hazards. The problem is only exacerbated for the poor, since the rich can usually make adjustments by purchasing clean water and healthy foods and reducing exposure to unclean air. It is important to oversee and find ways to protect environmental health and human health together.

Take pesticides for example. Types of pesticides cause developmental damage when exposure occurs during pregnancy. The mother passes along infected material across the placenta to her unborn child. Thus, environmental exposure leads directly to in utero exposure. Why, then, are they not addressed together? The EPA regulates exposure to pesticides under the Clean Water Act and Safe Drinking Water Act. The EPA also oversees the registration of new pesticides. However, the Food and Drug Administration (part of HHS) regulates exposures through the Food Safety Modernization Act, as well as the Food Quality Protection Act, which monitors children's health. To this point, there is no joint oversight.[81]

---

[81]Here I am indebted to environmental scientist Steve Kolmes: "Clearing Up the Smog: An Interview with an Environmental Scientist on Comprehensive Health," Uncommon God, Common Good,

Environmental well-being, human well-being, and economic well-being are mutually beneficial. Economic valuation should favor human flourishing in community rather than prize individual profit margins that ignore and even violate the most vulnerable populations. If it is the case that we view human flourishing through the lens of an ethical ecosystem where all life forms are required and cherished, then we realize that an imbalance favoring economics to the neglect of everything else pollutes society. Thus, employment opportunities that bring increased risks to children are by no means satisfactory.

Government and industry must work together for the good of workers, children, and the planet. One positive example that benefits all parties is the wind-power industry, which not only benefits the environment but is also growing jobs.[82] One poor example is the coal-mining industry. It cannot compete economically with the growing supply of inexpensive natural gas. The problem is not air-quality regulations but economic viability. An analysis by the Institute for Energy Economics and Financial Analysis[83] has demonstrated that there will be increased reductions in the labor force in the coal industry as a result of the increase in use of natural gas and wind power. Thus, it is important to create new industries that will increase jobs and benefit the environment. Moreover, it is also vital that structures are put in place to help communities transition from outdated industries to commerce involving new energy sources so that no community is left behind.

In closing, there is one more area of balance to which to attend. In addition to balancing and collating environmental and human health,

---

Patheos, March 31, 2017, www.patheos.com/blogs/uncommongodcommongood/2017/03/clearing-smog-interview-environmental-scientist-comprehensive-health/.

[82]See Silvio Marcacci, "Renewable Energy Job Boom Creates Economic Opportunity as Coal Industry Slumps," *Forbes*, April 22, 2019, www.forbes.com/sites/energyinnovation/2019/04/22/renewable-energy-job-boom-creating-economic-opportunity-as-coal-industry-slumps/#8f4dea736654; Elka Torpey, "Green Growth: Employment Projections in Environmentally Focused Occupations," Career Outlook, US Bureau of Labor Statistics, April 2018, www.bls.gov/careeroutlook/2018/data-on-display/green-growth.htm?view_full.

[83]For this analysis, see Tom Sanzillo and David Schlissel, "IEEFA 2017 U.S. Coal Outlook: Short-Term Gains Will be Muted by Prevailing Weaknesses in Fundamentals," Institute for Energy Economics and Financial Analysis, January 19, 2017, http://ieefa.org/wp-content/uploads/2017/01/IEEFA-2017-US-Coal-Outlook-ShortTerm-Gains-Will-Be-Muted-by-Prevailing-Weaknesses-in-Fundamentals_JAN-2017.pdf.

along with economic health, the "inescapable network of mutuality" requires that we pursue a balance between the biological and technological domains. Wendell Berry helps us here.

We enlightened Westerners have much to learn from indigenous and African cosmologies, which perceive how everything is connected for good or for ill and how we must treat humanity and creation as a whole with sacred regard.[84] An entangled ethical framework entails that we technologically sophisticated moderns can also learn a thing or two from the Amish, whom Wendell Berry esteems in his account of the needed moral injunction of restraint.

One does not have to be Amish to practice a theology of restraint. A restrained eschatology that accounts for finiteness, limitations, and embodiment is key. We are not infinite or immortal. We cannot transcend our creaturely limitations no matter how much we try. Technology is not our savior. In fact, our fixation on technology to solve our problems is part of the problem. It reflects a gnostic or disembodied metaphysic and outlook on life, which discounts morality. As Berry writes, the energy crisis is not technological but moral. What we need to cultivate is a moral argument of "restraint."[85] We have yet to develop "mechanical restraint."

In our insatiable and restless craving for immortality and infinity, we have turned to the machine for deliverance from our finitude. Berry cautions us to restrain these impulses and trajectory: "Much as we long for infinities of power and duration, we have no evidence that these lie within our reach, much less within our responsibility. It is more likely that we will have either to live within our limits, within the human definition, or not live at all." Berry concludes, "The knowledge of these limits and of how to live within them is the most comely and graceful knowledge that we have, the most healing and the most whole."[86]

---

[84]Regarding an African cosmology, Melanie Harris claims that the African American quest for earth justice goes back further than "the origins of African American environmentalism at the start of black agrarianism, during the height of the transatlantic slave trade, or in the midst of Jim and Jane Crow." Rather, "a disciplinary lens from religion suggests that the origins of African American environmentalism lie in a history much deeper than that: in the heart of African cosmology." Harris, "African Diaspora," 202.

[85]Wendell Berry, *The Unsettling of America: Culture & Agriculture* (Berkeley, CA: Counterpoint, 1996), 94-95.

[86]Berry, *Unsettling of America*, 94.

Perhaps Deloria's point on the White man's adolescent state of relentless restlessness and Jennings's analysis of the idealized construct of
whiteness manifesting itself in the White man's wraithlike body and the
bowels of the slave ship displacing land as the signifier of identity come
into play here as well. While overwhelmingly White, the Amish do not
cater to these gnostic impulses that discount finitude and situatedness in
favor of transcendence through the machine. The rest of us must follow
suit and place restraints on technology so that just because we can
transport Black bodies and other marginalized people in the bowels of
ships with "other cargo," we dare not do so. Just because we can transport
the wealthy, wise, and strong to other planets and leave the rest behind
to endure a coming environmental apocalypse, we dare not do so.

Longing for infinity or leaving for outer space to escape planet Earth
through advanced forms of technology involves a faulty eschatology. We
are created as finite beings who are earth dwellers and who must learn
to steward our planet well. If we cannot steward well this planet, how will
we ever learn to live well on some other sphere? We need to come to an
understanding of our limits as embodied creatures. Eschatology does not
entail the removal of limits, but abiding meekly and peaceably within
those limits, and hungering and thirsting for righteousness (Matthew 5:5-6,
9) in the Promised Land. This eschatological hope spells the end of
craving rapaciously for more stuff as we aimlessly roam the earth or the
heavens. Being made for more involves craving less. Building on these
points, we now turn to the subject of outer space, which serves as the
final ethical frontier.

$$12$$

MORE THAN SPACE EXPLORATION

The Ethics of the Final Frontier

IT IS FITTING THAT this book closes with a chapter on space exploration as the final ethical frontier. As with space travel, where astronauts go into orbit and eventually circle back to earth, space exploration raises ethical issues that stretch the boundaries of our experience before returning and landing close to home. Sometimes the return to earth is more like a crash landing! With space exploration, we are forced to deal—perhaps abruptly—with long-standing though easily ignored ethical issues in unique ways. Such subjects include race and slavery, disabilities, national borders, human identity, and more.

I will circle back to several ethical issues addressed in this volume. While these are matters that may await future materialization or realization in space, they are very real here below and yet are often taken for granted. If we do not learn to put our own house and globe in order before we populate another planet, we will only repeat the same cataclysmic mistakes twice, thrice, or more. After all, as Ray Bradbury writes in *The Martian Chronicles*, "We earth men have a talent for ruining big, beautiful things."[1] We cannot postpone forever facing and dealing with the consequences of our actions here on earth. Escaping to a distant galaxy will not leave humanity's faulty condition behind.

For many secular-minded people, space exploration can function as an alternative soteriology and eschatology—"don't get left behind"—as the human race pursues deliverance and glorification on another planet far, far away. We are destined to face judgment even in a secular

---

[1]Ray Bradbury, *The Martian Chronicles* (New York: Simon & Schuster, 1977), 71.

eschatology, where outer space becomes our eternal estate of heaven or hell. After all, as with orbiting planets, so with ethical actions and their import—what goes around comes around.

A personalist account of human value and dignity requires that we take responsibility for our actions for deeds done in the body here and in outer space. So, how do we get our house in order here on earth before taking up residence in outer space? It requires decentering our concept of deity, humanity, and world. It is only as we prize the human person in relation to God and the universe that we will finally come to a place of existential rest whereby we no longer need to be on center stage to conquer and consume. Instead, we flourish by restraint.

DECENTERED DEITY AND SPACE EXPLORATION

Our deities make the world go around. They also make us go around worlds in outer space. In one way or another, such exploration is bound up with our quest for deification, whether we seek to become like God or one with God, as with Christian humanism and the Orthodox notion of *theosis* respectively, or replace God, as with forms of secular humanism.[2] This section calls for embracing and promoting decentered notions of deity, where God does not make everything revolve around himself as a glory-grabbing deity. What we see in Christian Scripture is that God in Christ empties or pours himself out in humility to heal and bring honor to humanity and the whole of the creation. *Kenosis* (self-emptying) is *theosis* (becoming like God). We are most like God in Christ, the decentered deity, when we pour ourselves out for others.[3]

---

[2]For an invigorating discussion of "Christian humanism," refer to David Brooks's interview with Luke Bretherton, "Christian Humanism: A Truer Story," *Comment: Public Theology for the Common Good*, https://comment.org/christian-humanism/.

[3]Michael J. Gorman writes, "*Kenosis* is *theosis*," in *Inhabiting the Cruciform God: Kenosis, Justification, and Theosis in Paul's Narrative Soteriology* (Grand Rapids, MI: Eerdmans, 2009), 37. Ron Cole-Turner reflects on Gorman's claim in an article on human-enhancement technologies. Regardless of how people view such technologies' import for space exploration, they should keep in mind the following point, which relates to our overarching emphasis on decentered deities and humanity: "The difference between Christian faith and enhancement culture is not based on using or refusing specific technologies. It is based instead on how we see the goal of human transformation. Is it to become more secure and powerful in our individual human existence by expanding and enhancing ourselves, or to become more like the God we know in Christ?" Cole-Turner goes on to write, "The contrast comes down to an irreconcilable difference between self-expansion and self-emptying, between enhancing ourselves for our own sake or glorifying God for our neighbor's sake." Ron

It is not just religious types who employ religious and theological categories in approaching space exploration, or who frame consideration of the gods and space in benevolent and malevolent terms. An interview in the *Atlantic* on cosmism, which is "the new religion of space exploration," includes the tagline, "Carl Sagan and Neil deGrasse Tyson are high priests, astronauts are like saints that ascend into heaven, and extraterrestrials are as gods—benevolent, wise, and capable of manipulating space and time."[4] Ross Anderson interviews the late Albert A. Harrison, a professor of psychology at the University of California, Davis and pioneer in astrosociology: "In what ways does Cosmism resemble a religion?" Here's Harrison's response:

> In the modern era, Cosmism is generally thought to have originated with early twentieth century Russians. There are a couple different ways that you see the religious aspects of Cosmism. One place you see it is in the tremendous faith that both Russians and Americans have in technology; specifically, the idea that technology can solve the problems of humanity, and that we need to leave Earth to create a better society, to find, in some sense, perfection in space. You see this idea over and over when space exploration is discussed, the idea that we can leave behind the problems that plague society here on Earth and we create these wonderful new societies in space. There's a general resemblance in this thinking to religious views of heaven, and in particular notions of salvation.[5]

It is worth noting the connection Harrison makes between Russian cosmism and Russian Orthodox theology: "Russian Cosmism actually preceded the Bolshevik Revolution, which meant that the first instances of it were culturally intermingled with the Russian Orthodox Church, which may have lent it some of these religious overtones. You see this kind of messianic approach to space flight, with people touting this deliverance that awaits man in the cosmos."[6]

Cole-Turner, "A Christian View of Human Enhancement Technologies," *Cultural Encounters: A Journal for the Theology of Culture* 17, no. 2 (2022): 15.

[4]Ross Anderson, "The Holy Cosmos: The New Religion of Space Exploration," *Atlantic*, March 29, 2012, www.theatlantic.com/technology/archive/2012/03/the-holy-cosmos-the-new-religion-of-space-exploration/255136/.

[5]Harrison, quoted in Anderson, "Holy Cosmos."

[6]Harrison, quoted in Anderson, "Holy Cosmos." Refer also to Albert A. Harrison, "Russian and American Cosmism: Religion, National Psyche, and Spaceflight," *International Journal of Space Politics & Policy* 11, nos. 1-2 (2013): 25-44.

One way or another, whether Russian, American, Christian, or secularist, space exploration tells us a lot about our "deities." It also tells us a lot about ourselves. Similarly, just as space exploration tells us a great deal about our deities and ourselves, so space exploration tells us a great deal about pressing ethical issues here below that take us beyond ourselves, as was noted in the introduction to this chapter. I will touch on various pressing ethical issues in this chapter. For now, it will be helpful to consider the theological import of space exploration.

Saint Augustine and Ludwig Feuerbach write of how we often pay homage to the gods we image or who image us. Sometimes, to reference Feuerbach, they are one and the same. Mary-Jane Rubenstein writes on the topic of worship and the close connection between our conceptions of divine and human sovereignty: "If, as thinkers as varied as Augustine and Ludwig Feuerbach have argued, there is a reciprocal relationship between human beings and their visions of the divine—if, to put it crudely, people worship gods who look like them—then the Atomists' refusal of divine sovereignty should have profound consequences for human sovereignty as well."[7] The import of the atomists' "refusal of divine sovereignty" was not lost on Alexander the Great. He was filled with grief over the atomist teaching that there is an infinity of worlds: "Is it not worthy of tears that, when there are infinitely many *kosmoi*, we are not yet masters of one?"[8] The aim of the atomists' teaching on an infinity of worlds was to combat the notion of divine hegemony or oppressive control and, it would seem, the human drive to conquer everything.

Considering the preceding reflections, it is worth asking, What kinds of deities do we worship? Those who subdue and abuse all that come across their path, including other planets, or those who decenter themselves, that is, care for and serve creation, steward life and foster it so that we might flourish? As the old saying goes, "Like father, like son"; similarly, "Like deity, like humanity."

Now, let's consider "Like deity, like planet." This statement refers to that trajectory past and present to project our religious and superhuman

---

[7]Mary-Jane Rubenstein, *Worlds Without End: The Many Lives of the Multiverse* (New York: Columbia University Press, 2014), 52.
[8]Rubenstein, *Worlds Without End*, 52.

ideals onto outer space. Such projections surface in what Harrison states in his *Atlantic* interview: "The polytheistic gods of yesteryear lent their names to planets." Indeed, it is striking that some creative and aspiring minds of ancient and modern times named all the planets except Earth after Greek and Roman deities.[9] Take Mars, for example. The "red planet," as it is often called, was named after the Greek god of war, Ares, whose Roman name was Mars. Its reddish color is said to resemble blood, which is appropriate for the war god. It is worth noting that not only Mars but also Mars's satellites have been associated with the Greek god of war. According to the Gazetteer of Planetary Nomenclature, which is maintained by the Planetary Geomatics Group of the USGS Astrogeology Science Center and supported by NASA, Mars is "named by the Romans for their god of war because of its red, bloodlike color." Mars I, Phobos, is the "inner satellite of Mars. Named for one of the horses that drew Mars' chariot; also called an 'attendant' or 'son' of Mars. . . . This Greek word means 'flight.'" Mars II (Deimos) is the "outer Martian satellite" and "was named for one of the horses that drew Mars' chariot; also called an 'attendant' or 'son' of Mars. . . . Deimos means 'fear' in Greek."[10] Elsewhere, NASA provides a slightly different account as to the meaning of the moons' names: "Mars has two small moons: Phobos and Deimos. Phobos (fear) and Deimos (panic) were named after the horses that pulled the chariot of the Greek war god Ares, the counterpart to the Roman war god Mars."[11]

"War," "flight," "fear," and "panic" might give us cause to pause before considering whether humans should seek to take up residence on Mars. I find that same ominous quality in Bradbury's *Martian Chronicles*, where humans travel from Earth to colonize Mars, only to be killed in mass numbers by Martian forces until the Martians themselves die off because of humans having transmitted chicken pox (as also happened to Native

---

[9]See the nomenclature for the various planets at Gazetteer of Planetary Nomenclature, USGS Astrogeology Science Center, accessed October 4, 2019, https://planetarynames.wr.usgs.gov/Page /Planets; refer also to Elizabeth Nix, "Who Named the Planets?," History.com, August 28, 2015, updated August 22, 2018, www.history.com/news/who-named-the-planets.
[10]Gazetteer of Planetary Nomenclature.
[11]"Martian Moons," Mars Exploration Program, NASA, https://mars.nasa.gov/all-about-mars /moons/summary/.

Americans with the arrival of the Europeans[12]). Humans eventually return from Mars to Earth, where they bring about their own destruction through an apocalyptic war. Humans are responsible for the destruction of Mars as well as Earth. Regarding the latter, Bradbury writes, Earth "strangled itself with its own hands."[13] Given how often humanity pursues war rather than peace, perhaps our prized deity resides in the heavens after all, albeit on the red planet.

In keeping with the previous reflections, including on atomism, divine sovereignty, the number of worlds, and human rulers such as Alexander the Great, space exploration helps us explore our deities and ourselves. It also illumines ethical questions and problems here below. One of the most important ethical considerations to which we must attend is how to put a check on hegemony bound up with certain notions of the divine, whether religious or secular in origin. As noted above, the atomists sought to place a check on hegemony bound up with notions of divine, and human sovereignty through their theory of an infinity of worlds.

Does the best way to put a check on hegemony or domination today entail calling into question divine and human sovereignty, or does it involve getting clear on which notions of divine and human sovereignty safeguard against hegemony and which fan the flames of conquest, affirming the former and jettisoning the latter? Perhaps the problem and solution are not sovereignty and an infinite number of worlds respectively. Perhaps the solution to hegemony is a concept of deity that is characterized by infinite humility and mercy, as well as sovereign love. Karl Barth gets at this latter concept of deity when he writes of the God revealed in Jesus Christ:

> God shows Himself to be the great and true God in the fact that He can and will let His grace bear this cost, that He is capable and willing and

---

[12]Peter Reuell, "New World Devastation," *Harvard Gazette*, January 28, 2016, https://news.harvard.edu/gazette/story/2016/01/study-captures-ferocity-of-new-world-depopulation/; Cheyenne Mac-Donald, "Native Americans Were Wiped Out by Plagues Brought to Their Homes by European Missionaries," *Daily Mail*, January 25, 2016, http://www.dailymail.co.uk/sciencetech/article-3416402/Native-Americans-wiped-PLAGUES-brought-homes-European-missionaries.html.

[13]Bradbury, *Martian Chronicles*, 240. See also Bryan Curtis, "Mars: Can *John Carter* Make the Red Planet Cool Again?," *Slate*, March 8, 2012, http://www.slate.com/articles/arts/the_middlebrow/2012/03/john_carter_whatever_happened_to_the_mars_of_h_g_wells_and_ray_bradbury_.html.

ready for this condescension, this act of extravagance, this far journey. What marks out God above all false gods is that they are not capable and ready for this. In their otherworldliness and supernaturalness and otherness, etc., the gods are a reflection of the human pride which will not unbend, which will not stoop to that which is beneath it. God is not proud. In His high majesty He is humble. It is in this high humility that He speaks and acts as the God who reconciles the world to Himself.[14]

If Christendom had operated according to this decentered notion of divine sovereignty involving humility rather than hegemony, or oppressive control, there would have been no seemingly Christian impulse to colonialism on various shores across the world. God in Christ does not come to earth to conquer and control, but to construct and connect with humanity and the world.

In keeping with the entangled ethical framework set forth in this volume, Christian theologians and ethicists should also welcome other articulations of the divine that contend against hegemony, or oppressive control, rather than seek to dismiss and conquer them. Otherwise, we are not operating in keeping with the majesty of God who is truly high in humility. With this point in mind, it is worth drawing attention to Lao Tzu's work *Tao Te Ching—The Book of the Way*.

Lao Tzu reflects on "the Way," which is the mother or source of all existence and guiding principle of life. Humility characterizes the Way. Thus, the wise person and wise ruler who live according to this guiding counsel will be humble, too. Like father or mother, like child. Like deity, like human. They do not live for themselves but for others. Here is Lao Tzu:

Heaven is eternal, and earth is lasting.
The reason heaven and earth are eternal and lasting
is because they do not live for themselves.
That is why they will ever endure.
Therefore the wise man humbles himself—
and because of humility,
he is worthy of praise.

---

[14]Karl Barth, *Church Dogmatics*, vol. IV/1, *The Doctrine of Reconciliation*, ed. G. W. Bromiley and T. F. Torrance (Edinburgh: T&T Clark, 1956), 159.

He puts others first,
and so becomes great.
He is not focused on outcomes or achievements;
therefore he always succeeds.[15]

While orthodox Christianity does not see the heavens and earth as existing eternally, nonetheless, those who take to heart Barth's emphasis on divine glory in humility would resonate with Lao Tzu's trajectory. Also, if humans created in God's image would follow suit, we would not be prone to destroy Earth and Mars, as Bradbury fears.

All too often, colonialism in religious and secular form is a distorted attempt at divinization, whereby we become like the gods of war and conquest we so often emulate. We need to be grounded in our hearts and thoughts on Earth even as we explore outer space. After all, *Earth* derives from words associated with the phrases "on the ground" and "piece of land."[16] None of its associations are bound up with Greek or Roman deities. The gravitational pull of humility is essential to human flourishing no matter the planet we visit or on which we reside. Humility guards against restlessness and fosters restraint in keeping with shalom. As Lao Tzu makes clear, peace, freedom, and good governance come with "restraint," not "greed."[17]

If our deities are restless, so are we. We need a decentered concept of deity that is at rest in the universe and who affirms grounded existence and restraint. Lao Tzu provides us with one such model. As Huston Smith writes, it is "a testament to humanity's at-home-ness in the universe."[18] We find true humanity's "at-home-ness" in humility. Lao Tzu wisely reasons: great rulers identify with the lowly and find their roots among them. They never wander from them.[19] Like the Great Tao, they are found among the weak, not the strong.[20]

---

[15]Lao Tzu, "Humility," *Tao Te Ching—The Book of the Way*, rev. and ed. Sam Torode (n.p.: Ancient Renewal, 2009), 7.

[16]Gazetteer of Planetary Nomenclature.

[17]Lao Tzu, *Tao Te Ching*, 3, 57.

[18]Refer to the back-cover endorsement of Lao Tzu, *Tao Te Ching*.

[19]Lao Tzu, *Tao Te Ching*, 39.

[20]See the back-cover depiction of Lao Tzu's *Tao Te Ching*. The Great Tao is always in close proximity to the weak, not the strong.

Closer to home in Christian circles, the triune God stays grounded even in Christ's ascent. Humanity is at rest in Jesus' ascent, the Spirit's descent, and Jesus' return at the end of the age. The Christian concept of *theosis* (divinization) orbits the incarnation and exaltation of the crucified, risen, ascended, and returning Jesus. Jesus' exalted state does not discount or eradicate his humanity but cherishes and completes it. In his high humility, restraint, and compassionate care for us as the decentered deity, he became what we are so that we might become what he is, as Irenaeus and Athanasius exclaim. Irenaeus writes, "Our Lord Jesus Christ, who did, through his transcendent love, become what we are, that He might bring us to be even what He is Himself."[21] Athanasius reflects in the same vein: "He became man that we might be made God."[22] There is no suggestion here of disowning our estate but raising, elevating, and exalting it in all its cruciform earthenness and humaneness.

May we discover the drives that propel us into orbit. Hopefully, they are self-sacrificial drives and predilections of divine love that cause life here on Earth and life forms on other planets to flourish. Such predilections are far superior to those propensities that decimate the various planets through the gods of militarism, racism, and economic exploitation. Having reflected on a decentered view of divinity, let's turn to consider what is entailed by a decentered view of humanity.

DECENTERED HUMANITY AND SPACE EXPLORATION

It is often claimed that the Copernican revolution demoted the cosmos and humanity's value in the universe. Sigmund Freud was a brilliant writer and polemicist[23] whose historiographical account of Copernicus makes this very point. Just as Freud argued persuasively to many that history is progressively overcoming religious illusion and repression

---

[21]Irenaeus, *Against Heresies*, book V, preface, trans. Alexander Roberts and William Rambaut, in *Ante-Nicene Fathers*, vol. 1., ed. Alexander Roberts, James Donaldson, and A. Cleveland Coxe (Buffalo, NY: Christian Literature, 1885), 526.

[22]Athanasius, *On the Incarnation* 54.3, in *Nicene and Post-Nicene Fathers*, second series, vol. 4, ed. Philip Schaff and Henry Wace, trans. Archibald Robertson (Grand Rapids, MI: Eerdmans, 1891), 65.

[23]Regarding Freud, refer here to Harold Bloom's own assessment: "Freud, the Greatest Modern Writer," *New York Times*, March 23, 1986, www.nytimes.com/1986/03/23/books/freud-the-greatest-modern-writer.html.

through the liberating advance of science whereby God is dethroned and banished to oblivion, Freud also sought to dethrone humanity. Just as God is useless and irrelevant, so, too, is humanity.

Such conceptions of deity and humanity as useless are deeply problematic. This section of the chapter will account for divine and human insecurity bound up with such idle notions. It will also address the need to provide a more secure understanding of humanity that flows from an understanding of God as so secure in being God that he lavishes his affection on humans and thereby dignifies those who otherwise are so small and finite against the backdrop of an awe-inspiring and possibly intimidating universe. God's affection provides all the security we need. If God does not control us but seeks to connect to construct the world and outer space in healthy ways, so, too, should we.

While Freudianism is hardly credible today among many psychologists, the idea that humans are little more than products of unconscious forces, or that God is merely a projection of desire, still looms large both in the academy and at a popular level. Freud is certainly a pivotal figure in framing the narrative that God and the traditional view of humanity retreated with the advance of science. That narrative depicts God as unnecessary and irrelevant for making sense of the world, since science has all the answers. There are no more gaps for God to fill in history given human progress.[24] Nor is there a place left for humanity as sacred.

For Freud, the Copernican revolution, Darwin's theory of evolution, and ultimately—and, according to one author, narcissistically[25]—Freud's own work on consciousness unraveled the traditional "naive self-love" view of humanity. Here's Freud in his own words:

> Humanity has in the course of time had to endure from the hands of science two great outrages upon its naive self-love. The first was when it realized that our earth was not the center of the universe, but only a tiny speck in a world-system of a magnitude hardly conceivable; this is associated in our minds with the name of Copernicus, although Alexandrian

---

[24]See Lonnie D. Kliever, *The Shattered Spectrum: A Survey of Contemporary Theology* (Atlanta: John Knox, 1981), 1-19.

[25]See John Horgan, "Copernicus, Darwin and Freud: A Tale of Science and Narcissism," *Scientific American*, September 1, 2015, https://blogs.scientificamerican.com/cross-check/copernicus -darwin-and-freud-a-tale-of-science-and-narcissism/.

doctrines taught something very similar. The second was when biological research robbed man of his peculiar privilege of having been specially created, and relegated him to a descent from the animal world, implying an ineradicable animal nature in him: this transvaluation has been accomplished in our own time upon the instigation of Charles Darwin, Wallace, and their predecessors, and not without the most violent opposition from their contemporaries. But man's craving for grandiosity is now suffering the third and most bitter blow from present-day psychological research which is endeavoring to prove to the ego of each one of us that he is not even master in his own house, but that he must remain content with the veriest scraps of information about what is going on unconsciously in his own mind.[26]

Humanity is not master in the universe, in this world, or even in its own head. If anything, this loss of control fosters a neurosis of a collective consciousness of a controlling personality for humanity, which spelled destruction. To refer back to Peter Harrison's observation in the last chapter, "for the moderns, it was precisely the loss of this centrality that motivated the quest to conquer an obstinate and uncooperative earth." Harrison adds, "Doubts about the cosmic status of human beings motivated the investigation of nature in the search for hitherto hidden utilities. Such considerations furthered the cause of the scientific enterprise and indirectly contributed to environmental degradation."[27] The only ones who presume to have the intellectual basis for self-worth are the scientific elite. Dennis Danielson explains, "But a trick of this supposed dethronement is that, while purportedly rendering 'Man' less cosmically and metaphysically important, it actually enthrones us modern 'scientific' humans in all our enlightened superiority."[28]

Some might ask why we are dealing with older, historical figures such as Freud and not contemporaries. It is because their polemics have staying power. They even surface in pop culture, including the movie

---

[26]Sigmund Freud, *Introductory Lectures on Psychoanalysis*, ed. Angela Richards, trans. James Strachey (London: Penguin Books, 1991), 109.
[27]Peter Harrison, "Subduing the Earth: Genesis 1, Early Modern Science, and the Exploitation of Nature," *Journal of Religion* (January 1999): 107.
[28]Dennis R. Danielson, "Myth 6: That Copernicanism Demoted Humans from the Center of the Cosmos," in *Galileo Goes to Jail: And Other Myths About Science and Religion*, ed. Ronald Numbers (Cambridge, MA: Harvard University Press, 2009), 57.

Batman v Superman. Freud might have been elated and devastated at the same time if he had been able to watch Neil deGrasse Tyson's historiographical deconstruction in the film of "our own sense of priority in the universe" as humans resulting from the appearance of Copernicus, Darwin, and most recently Superman—not Freud![29] Perhaps that shift would even cause Freud some anxiety of not being at home in his own historiography. While "Darwinism" might be outdated referencing the current ins and outs of, say, evolutionary developmental biology, "Darwinism" as an idea indicating a completely naturalistic, random, and vicious process of selection that pushed God out of the picture has not gone away. The same might be said of Freud.

Freud's historiography that moved us from persons to things construed the Copernican revolution as conceiving a universe that was inhospitable to humanity. The destructive nature of Freud's historiography is not lost on Bradbury in the *Martian Chronicles*:

> They knew how to live with nature and get along with nature. They didn't try too hard to be all men and no animal. That's the mistake we made when Darwin showed up. We embraced him and Huxley and Freud, all smiles. And then we discovered that Darwin and our religions didn't mix. Or at least we didn't think they did. We were fools. We tried to budge Darwin and Huxley and Freud. They wouldn't move very well. So, like idiots, we tried knocking down religion. We succeeded pretty well. We lost our faith and went around wondering what life was for. If art was no more than a frustrated outflinging of desire, if religion was no more than self-delusion, what good was life? Faith had always given us answer to all things. But it all went down the drain with Freud and Darwin. We were and still are lost people.[30]

Bradbury's trenchant diagnosis of humanity's problematic condition in the modern period certainly bears troubling import for space exploration. Further to what Harrison claimed about our modernist insecurity leading to a degrading of the earth, it is only a matter of time before we extend that exponentially to outer space.

---

[29]Neil deGrasse Tyson, comment on *Batman v Superman: Dawn of Justice* (2016), https://www.imdb .com/title/tt2975590/characters/nm1183205.
[30]Bradbury, *Martian Chronicles*, 86-87.

It is important to pause at this point and challenge Freud's historiography as it relates to Darwin. Shortly, we will turn to critique Freud's historiographical account of Copernicus. A case could be made for Darwin not moving in Freud's pessimistic direction. For one, Darwin did not engage in historiographical and ideological flurries, like Freud. It is worth noting here that Darwin never intended his views on nature to denounce religion or supersede or replace ethics, although he did intend to replace Paley's particular-design arguments, which should not be equated with the breadth of Christianity itself. In fact, Darwin believed one must bring the Bible or other religious and philosophical sources to bear on developing ethics. In the "General Summary" in *The Descent of Man*, Darwin claims that as important as natural selection is, other resources are still more important, such as "reasoning powers," "instruction," and "religion," for the cultivation of morality.[31] And yet, Freud makes use of Darwin as well as Copernicus, as already noted, to foster a sense of insecurity in the universe, across the earth, and in our own heads.

Now, no matter our worldview, we still must come to terms with the incomprehensible vastness of reality and our finitude. How should we respond—in fear and dread? Here I call to mind Blaise Pascal in the *Pensées*: "Man is only a reed, the weakest in nature, but he is a thinking reed. There is no need for the whole universe to take up arms to crush him: a vapour, a drop of water is enough to kill him. . . . Thus all of our dignity consists in thought. It is on thought that we must depend for our recovery, not on space and time, which we could never fill. . . . The eternal silences of these infinite spaces fill me with dread."[32] I am never one to discount or dismiss Pascal, whose honest struggle is always quite refreshing; nonetheless, it is not, as Pascal suggests, our thinking or "thought" that ultimately preserves or makes possible the "recovery" of our human dignity, but God's gracious disposition and thoughtfulness toward us in Jesus Christ (a point I believe Pascal would quite readily affirm).

---

[31]See Charles Darwin, *The Origin of Species by Means of Natural Selection or the Presentation of Favored Races in the Struggle for Life* & *The Descent of Man and Selection in Relation to Sex*, 6th ed. (New York: Modern Library, 1872), 909-20.
[32]Blaise Pascal, *Pensées*, ed. and trans. Roger Ariew (Indianapolis: Hackett, 2005), 64.

Here it is worth pointing to Psalm 8, which declares that while we are infinitesimally or microscopically small in comparison with the universe, we are telescopically large due to God's favor. In other words, it is not our thoughts that serve as the basis for our preservation but God's thoughts and care for us:

> When I consider your heavens,
> the work of your fingers,
> the moon and the stars,
> which you have set in place,
> what is mankind *that you are mindful of them,*
> human beings *that you care for them*? (Psalm 8:3-4; emphasis added)

Ultimately, this psalm's question and exploration finds its answer and destination in Jesus, as Hebrews 2:5-9 conveys. Hebrews 2 highlights the christocentric telos of biblical anthropology, which has a profound bearing on ethical deliberations. Certainly, it matters where we fix our gaze and thoughts: on our pitiful smallness against the seemingly endless void of the universe or on the largeness of our significance in the eyes of God, who is overflowing in the fecundity of peace, joy, and unbounded love. To be sure, the biblical vision of God's ever-mindful attentiveness toward us and this world secures our destiny and should fill us with eschatological wonder and hope rather than dread.

Ironically, the Copernican move from a geocentric to heliocentric universe may have dethroned Aristotle's view of earth's centrality, but not humanity and the world's importance. Aristotle and others following him did not see centrality in the universe as necessarily positive. Danielson shows how the geocentric universe did not paint the world in the most endearing light, neither for Aristotle nor for Aristotle's great Christian sympathizer, Thomas Aquinas. Centrality meant heaviness and grossness, not greatness. The very center of the universe was earth's center point—the lowest pit of hell in Dante's *Inferno.*[33]

Danielson argues that the accompanying claim that the Copernican revolution demoted the biblical view of humanity is equally fallacious. Just as *center* does not always mean "best," so smallness does not always

---

[33]Danielson, "Myth 6," 52-53.

signify least prized. Humanity is the "object of divine blessing despite" our "conspicuous finitude and smallness relative to the world at large."[34] The decentered deity is found among the weak, not the strong, the humble, not the haughty, according to Christian Scripture. After all, as Paul writes that God's grace "is made perfect in weakness" (2 Corinthians 12:9). Freud's historiographical flurry falls far short of its intended mark. Human finitude and frailty are the center point of divine and cosmic favor. We need to regain our sense of decentered balance in view of God's abundant care for the weak and humble before we go too far into space. Only a decentered deity and humanity bodes well for space exploration. Pride bound up with an all-consuming colonialist insecurity goes before a fall.

So why does the claim that Copernicus's revolution demoted humanity persist? In addition to a confusion of categories such as "the center is always best," there is also the unfortunate reality that if a myth gets repeated enough times, it must be right. What generated the myth in the first place? Further to what was stated earlier, Danielson hints at one of the factors: "enlightened" moderns who demoted humanity[35] promoted themselves in all their seemingly scientific grandeur.[36] Such moves hurt not only humanity but also the view of science as a friend of the common good. That said, sound scientific exploration fosters intellectual humility. Like the Copernican revolution, it is a friend to the Christian faith and the common good.

The moral to the story is that human insecurity leads to hypersecurity and with it a fear of scarcity that leads us to conquer and exploit the universe. We need a concept of divinity and humanity that moves us in the opposite direction. As divine and human, Jesus opens the way to a new order of being in his others-centered life. He provides the secure attachment for us to operate in a decentered way.

Dietrich Bonhoeffer is one theologian and ethicist who develops this decentered motif. He argues that the only God who exists with and for

---

[34]Danielson, "Myth 6," 52.
[35]Danielson references Bernard le Bouvier de Fontenelle in his *Discourse of the Plurality of Worlds*, 1686. See Danielson, "Myth 6," 57.
[36]See Danielson, "Myth 6," 57-58.

us today is the God-forsaken God on the cross.[37] "God consents to be pushed out of the world and onto the cross: God is weak and powerless in the world and in precisely this way, and only so, is at our side and helps us." It is only the suffering God who helps.[38] Jesus reveals the God who is with and for others in weakness. He is also the paradigmatic human, who exists for others. Bonhoeffer writes, "Encounter with Jesus Christ. Experience that here there is a reversal of all human existence, in the very fact that Jesus only 'is there for others.' Jesus's 'being-for-others' is the experience of transcendence!"[39] Similarly, the church is a community for others: "The church is church only when it is there for others. As first step it must give away all its property to those in need."[40] On a related note, James Gustafson also calls for decentering humanity, where God pursues the well-being of the entire cosmos, not just humanity.[41] We will return to these points.

How would the notion of Jesus' decentered existence bear on the discussion of multiverse? Is Jesus concerned only for the well-being of this universe, or would he be "for others," as in life forms on other planets in other universal domains? If the multiverse existed, to Alexander the Great's chagrin noted at the outset of this chapter, Jesus may well have become incarnate on all these planets to atone for sin. In that sense, we would not have a corner on God's compassion in contrast to extraterrestrials. Or perhaps, Jesus would choose not to become incarnate elsewhere because there is no need—that is, if earthlings alone require salvation. Extraterrestrial life may be angelic or exist in a state of innocence.

On this view, reminiscent of Maximus the Confessor's perspective, Jesus became incarnate in this world as the cosmic Redeemer to save humans as a microcosm of his gracious love for the entire universe/all universes. Maximus's emphasis on Christ as cosmic Redeemer and humanity as a microcosm of the universe does not suggest an anthropocentric orientation

---

[37]Dietrich Bonhoeffer, *Letters and Papers from Prison*, ed. John W. de Gruchy, Dietrich Bonhoeffer Works 8 (Minneapolis: Fortress, 2010), 478-79.

[38]Bonhoeffer, *Letters and Papers from Prison*, 479.

[39]Bonhoeffer, *Letters and Papers from Prison*, 501.

[40]Bonhoeffer, *Letters and Papers from Prison*, 503.

[41]See for example James M. Gustafson, *Ethics from a Theocentric Perspective*, 2 vols. (Chicago: University of Chicago Press, 1981–1984). For his framing of environmental ethics from a theocentric perspective, see *A Sense of the Divine* (Cleveland: Pilgrim, 1994).

that devalues the rest of creaturely reality. Rather, one could argue that Christ became incarnate to transform humanity from being a cancer in the cosmos to make it a healing force for the entire universe. Apart from him, humanity would be the cancer of the universe(s). Only in him would we be a healing presence.[42] Only then could we travel to distant planets, not to conquer but to connect. On this view, Jesus made the weakest link—humanity—the strongest link in the universal/multiversal chain. He did so by replacing our old humanity with himself, thereby making us a point of connection that holds everything together. Now we must live to connect, not to conquer, in view of what Jesus intends for us.

The preceding reflection gives rise to the ethical implication that until we get our own house in order, we had better be careful about leaving Earth to live on other planets. Otherwise, we might be the malevolent aliens we dread. Instead of being colonized, we might be driven by the desire to colonize other planets!

Ours might be the "silent planet," as C. S. Lewis penned, known to the entire universe for its tragic state of existence bent toward evil, including the attempted subjugation of other forms of life in the universe at large.[43] In countering this deeply disturbing predisposition, Jesus invites us to experience a new order of being that involves subjugating our carnal passions rather than other planets through his cosmic passion unto death. Jesus' necessary decentered and others-centered existence is the all-sufficient ground that makes it possible for us to die to ourselves and resist seeking out other planets to conquer.

Rather than seek to have a corner on the religious market in the universe at large, Christians should welcome the knowledge that the Christian faith is not alone in calling for a decentered view of humanity. Take, for example, the Buddhist teaching of the bodhisattva vow, which

---

[42]For Maximus's conception of Christ's significance for humanity as cosmic Redeemer and our role as a microcosm of the universe (apart from consideration of extraterrestrial life), see Maximus the Confessor, *On the Cosmic Mystery of Jesus Christ*, ed. and trans. Paul M. Blowers and Robert Louis Wilkin (New York: St. Vladimir's Seminary Press, 2003).

[43]See C. S. Lewis, *Out of the Silent Planet* (New York: Scribner, 1938). Lewis depicts the human impulse to subjugate those on other planets in his *Space Trilogy* (New York: Scribner Book Company, 1986).

involves "promising publicly to achieve Buddhahood in order to liberate all beings from *saṃsāra*," which means the cycle of wandering or drifting aimlessly.[44] While compassion and enlightenment are framed differently in Buddhism and Christianity, still one finds here a striking account of profound care for the well-being of others. Consider the following excerpt from the bodhisattva vow:

> In a world without protection, without refuge, without a home, without friends and without a haven, I will be a protector, a refuge, a home, a friend and a haven. I will free all those sentient beings who have not crossed the ocean of existence. I will take completely beyond sorrow those who have not passed completely beyond sorrow by leading them beyond sorrow to the unobstructed *dharmadhātu*. I will quell the suffering of those whose suffering has not been quelled.[45]

Such decentered views of liberation help to secure humanity from having to grasp and clutch and conquer.

We must bring a decentered conception of humanity to bear on our current state. A faulty view of human being has virtually undone us and our world. Consider what Pope Francis writes about "a misguided anthropocentrism" in *Laudato Si'* 122:

> A misguided anthropocentrism leads to a misguided lifestyle. . . . When human beings place themselves at the centre, they give absolute priority to immediate convenience and all else becomes relative. Hence we should not be surprised to find, in conjunction with the omnipresent technocratic paradigm and the cult of unlimited human power, the rise of a relativism which sees everything as irrelevant unless it serves one's own immediate interests.[46]

Such misguided anthropocentrism skews our values so that we see unlimited human ambition and our own immediate interests as divinely ordained rather than demonic. In contrast, the God who inconvenienced himself by becoming incarnate in a lowly human state challenges us to

---

[44]See "The Bodhisattva Vow," in *Buddhist Scriptures*, ed. Donald S. Lopez Jr. (London: Penguin Classics, 2004), 389.

[45]"Bodhisattva Vow," 392.

[46]Pope Francis, *Laudato Si'* encyclical letter, May 24, 2015, http://w2.vatican.va/content/francesco/en/encyclicals/documents/papa-francesco_20150524_enciclica-laudato-si.html, 122.

approach one another, our world, and the universe(s) at large with humility rather than with arrogance and pride. In view of this decentered deity and humanity, we can live securely. Such secure attachments foster an embodied ethic of others-centered love. Such others-centered love will lead us to foster such qualities as frail human emotions and compassion rather than harden ourselves toward others. Compassionate love will also lead us to extinguish and replace the fallen passion to conquer creation, reducing it to mere property to be used as commodities, with the life-giving desire to connect and cultivate creation for the sake of building community. In what immediately follows, we will consider the import of emotions and then more specifically empathy or compassion for the needed decentering of humanity. After that, we will turn to consider what is entailed by a decentered earth bearing on the themes of property and our overarching priorities in relation to the universe at large.

Space exploration and emotions. One of the ethical considerations to account for in space travel is the incredible psychological and physiological challenges humans will face if we are to abandon Earth for space to survive, as Stephen Hawking predicts. An article titled "How Will Living on Mars Affect Our Human Body?" addresses some of these subjects.[47] Humans have always developed to adjust to their environment. Such adaptations or transformations would be necessary to survive on a place such as Mars.

The movie *The Martian* reveals some of the technologies that NASA is developing to help humans make the journey to Mars in the 2030s.[48] Movies such as *The Martian* and *Interstellar* reflect how difficult space travel can be for astronauts. Just think of the sense of isolation Matt Damon's characters experience in the two movies: in *Interstellar*, the sense of isolation leads him—Dr. Mann ("Mann" as the representative human?)—to

---

[47]Nikita Marwaha, "How Will Living on Mars Affect Our Human Body?," *Space Safety Magazine,* accessed October 9, 2019, http://www.spacesafetymagazine.com/space-exploration/mars-mission/earthlings-martians-living-red-planet-affect-human-bodies/.

[48]Steve Fox, ed., "Nine Real NASA Technologies in 'The Martian,'" NASA.gov, August 6, 2017, www.nasa.gov/feature/nine-real-nasa-technologies-in-the-martian; Carl Zimmer, "Living on Mars: How to Survive the Red Planet," *Popular Mechanics,* October 1, 2009, www.popularmechanics.com/space/moon-mars/a2116/4221805/.

madness. One question that follows from this concern is, Would it do us good to adapt or change the human species to limit or remove many if not all emotions for the sake of survival on isolated spheres?

Here it is worth drawing attention to an interview in *Spiegel* with famed sociobiologist E. O. Wilson. Wilson engages questions about what makes us distinctive as humans. He entertains a thought experiment about what organisms would stand out to aliens traveling to earth ten million years ago. Not surprisingly, given his passion for insects, Wilson says insects rather than our ancestors would have caught their attention. Wilson also discusses religion and Mary's ascent to heaven, as well as whether we should change or extract many of our emotions. Here is a portion of the interview:

SPIEGEL: "Humans," the saying goes, "have Paleolithic emotions" . . .

Wilson: "Medieval institutions and god-like technology." That's our situation, yeah. And we really have to handle that.

SPIEGEL: How?

Wilson: So often it happens that we don't know how, also in situations of public policy and governance, because we don't have enough understanding of human nature. We simply haven't looked at human nature in the best way that science might provide. I think what we need is a new Enlightenment. During the eighteenth century, when the original Enlightenment took place, science wasn't up to the job. But I think science is now up to the job. We need to be harnessing our scientific knowledge now to get a better, science-based self-understanding.

SPIEGEL: It seems that, in this process, you would like to throw religions overboard altogether?

Wilson: No. That's a misunderstanding. I don't want to see the Catholic Church with all of its magnificent art and rituals and music disappear. I just want to have them give up their creation stories, including especially the resurrection of Christ.

SPIEGEL: That might well be a futile endeavor . . .

Wilson: There was this American physiologist who was asked if Mary's bodily ascent from Earth to Heaven was possible. He said, "I wasn't there; therefore, I'm not positive that it happened or didn't happen; but of one thing I'm certain: She passed out at 10,000 meters." That's where science comes in. Seriously, I think we're better off with no creation stories.

SPIEGEL: With this new Enlightenment, will we reach a higher state of humanity?

Wilson: Do we really want to improve ourselves? Humans are a very young species, in geologic terms, and that's probably why we're such a mess. We're still living with all this aggression and ability to go to war. But do we really want to change ourselves? We're right on the edge of an era of being able to actually alter the human genome. But do we want that? Do we want to create a race that's more rational and free of many of these emotions? My response is no, because the only thing that distinguishes us from super-intelligent robots are our imperfect, sloppy, maybe even dangerous emotions. They are what makes us human.[49]

Wilson has toyed with the idea of changing our genome and manipulating emotions in other contexts, as noted previously in this volume. Here he is more cautious. I share Wilson's wariness here, and not (simply) because of Wilson's claim that emotions are "the only thing that distinguishes us from super-intelligent robots." The removal or manipulation of our emotions could lead us to treat those around us and our world in less humane or inhumane ways.

It would be a mistake to assume that what we mean by decentering humanity entails defanging humans of many or all of our emotions. We should not radically transform ourselves or move toward a posthuman state of robotics for superhuman feats, including space travel. Contrary to Wilson's move to discount creation stories, our ultimate point of reference is our Creator, who situates us within certain creaturely confines, which are only relatively adaptable.[50] The resurrection of Jesus Christ, which Wilson also rejects as superfluous to the church's existence, is critical not only to the church but to all creaturely existence. The transformation Jesus brings about in his glorified state is

---

[49]Philip Bethge and Johann Grolle, "Interview with Edward O. Wilson: The Origin of Morals," *Spiegel*, February 26, 2013, www.spiegel.de/international/spiegel/spiegel-interview-with-edward -wilson-on-the-formation-of-morals-a-884767.html.

[50]Robin Lovin makes a similar point about the need to move forward with caution on adaptations to humanity in light of the doctrine of creation at the John W. Kluge Center at the Library of Congress in an event titled, "Astrobiology and Theology: A Discussion," June 18, 2014, www .youtube.com/watch?v=rzUXbcoCv5Q&feature=youtu.be. The entire discussion offers a fascinating account of the technological possibilities and ethical merits and concerns over pursuing posthuman and transhuman life for space travel, among other things.

not the removal of creaturely limits but our perfection within those limits. As it relates to the emotions, the fruit of the Spirit of Jesus Christ replaces the fruit of the flesh, whereby love eclipses concupiscence (Galatians 5:19, 22).

We will turn shortly to discuss the emotion of love involving empathy and how important that is to space travel. However, before doing so, it is appropriate to pause and give brief attention to transhumanism, which involves consideration of editing and enhancing emotional capabilities.

Why discuss transhumanism in a chapter on space exploration? Here's the answer: "Transhumanists envision that human enhancement is a precondition for travel and expansion into the cosmos." They maintain that "'unmodified' tourists may thus be deemed comparatively unfit for space travel, particularly to far away destinations. While government space agencies and the private spaceflight industry continue to refer to the 'opening' of outer space to everyone, transhumanist ideas indicate that this democratisation of space tourism might not occur."[51] Thus, it is important to make note of transhumanism and ethical considerations, albeit briefly, in a chapter on space exploration.

According to *Britannica*, transhumanism is defined as the "social and philosophical movement devoted to promoting the research and development of robust human-enhancement technologies. Such technologies would augment or increase human sensory reception, emotive ability, or cognitive capacity as well as radically improve human health and extend human life spans."[52] Religiously minded people debate whether the move toward transhumanism complements or competes with religious notions such as resurrection, ascension, reincarnation, and exaltation. Consider the Church of Jesus Christ of Latter-day Saints's metaphysical views of divine and human progression and theory of exaltation. Might it affirm transhumanism in various ways?[53] From another angle, consider

---

[51]Erik Cohen and Samuel Spector, "Transhumanism and Cosmic Travel," *Tourism Recreation Research* 45, no. 2 (October 2019): 1-9.

[52]Sean A. Hays, "Transhumanism: Social and Philosophical Movement," *Britannica*, www.britannica.com/topic/transhumanism.

[53]Refer to "Mormonism Mandates Transhumanism," YouTube Video, 2:17, Mormon Transhumanist Association, July 6, 2014, http://youtu.be/VePRByRNIAc. It also appears at their website: http://transfigurism.org.

Orthodox Christianity's doctrine of *theosis*. Could Orthodoxy affirm transhumanism on account of its doctrine of *theosis*? According to Jon Robertson, an Eastern Orthodox Christian and patristics scholar, "True humanity is not a limitation for the Orthodox, but a realization."[54] So, does this understanding of true humanity involving the notion of *theosis* serve as possible grounds for transhuman explorations, a cautionary note, or an outright rejection of it?

The Vatican has taken issue with transhumanism. According to an article in *Business Insider*,

> In 2002, the Vatican issued a statement called *Communion and Stewardship: Human Persons Created in the Image of God*, in which it is stated that "Changing the genetic identity of man as a human person through the production of an infrahuman being is radically immoral." The same statement also argued that the creation of a superhuman or spiritually superior being is "unthinkable," since true improvement can come only through religious experience.[55]

The Vatican is not alone in its concerns. According to the same article, left-leaning intellectuals, including Francis Fukuyama and Jürgen Habermas, maintain that transhumanism would impact negatively human identity. They argue that transhumanism would erode our egalitarian, democratic, and social ideals. Outside forces would end up governing our identity at the very core of our being.[56]

---

[54]Jon M. Robertson, *Christ as Mediator: A Study of the Theologies of Eusebius of Caesarea, Marcellus of Ancyra, and Athanasius of Alexandria* (Oxford: Oxford University Press, 2007).

[55]Preetam Kaushik, "Transhumanism in India: Between Faith and Modernity," *Business Insider India*, February 26, 2015, www.businessinsider.in/Transhumanism-in-India-Between-faith-and -modernity/articleshow/46383180.cms. You can find the Vatican document here: International Theological Commission, *Communion and Stewardship: Human Persons Created in the Image of God*, encyclical letter, accessed October 10, 2019, http://www.vatican.va/roman_curia /congregations/cfaith/cti_documents/rc_con_cfaith_doc_20040723_communion-stewardship _en.html.

[56]For other articles weighing in on transhumanism, including definitions and ethical considerations, see "Beyond Human: Exploring Transhumanism," Kelsey Wharton, *ASU News*, November 19, 2014, https:// news.asu.edu/content/beyond-human-exploring-transhumanism; Dirk Bruere, "Transhumanism —The Final Religion?," Institute for Ethics and Emerging Technologies, July 16, 2015, https:// archive.ieet.org/articles/bruere20150715.html; Andre Evans, "2045 'Immortality' Transhumanism Program Threatens Humanity's Integrity," Natural Society, August 2, 2012, https://naturalsociety .com/2045-immortality-transhumanism-program-threaten-humanity-integrity/. In addition, refer to the "Transhumanist Declaration," Humanity, accessed December 5, 2022, www.humanity plus.org/the-transhumanist-declaration.

As for religious responses, not all those adhering to forms of the Christian tradition are opposed to transhumanism.[57] Still, those belonging to Eastern religious thought forms are perhaps more readily able to affirm transhumanism. Take Hinduism for example. Depending on the employment of Hindu methods and resources, its open-source orientation, practice of yoga, and doctrine of reincarnation may encourage transhumanist pursuits.[58]

Without wishing to provide a definitive response to transhumanism, it is important to express concern over it from the personalist position set forth in this volume. There is an insoluble connection between the soul and body, along with emotions as well as reason, in constituting the human person. For this reason, I take seriously the alarm sounded in the following article in *Natural Society*. According to Andre Evans, transhumanism threatens humanity's integrity:

> Being advocates of natural health and believing the human body has its own intricate design, an attempt to become a synthetic avatar would potentially erase all of the aspects of humanity that define our character and being.
>
> This technology at its fruition would also attempt to delve into realms of reality no scientist has ever been able to grasp within a natural, human viewpoint of comprehension. Theoretical physicists are beginning to admit that our universe is a shadow of a larger reality, and the natural man can scarcely understand it with his own devices. Like it or not, this universe is far more complex than what we have observed.[59]

Having briefly engaged transhumanism, let's return to consider the importance of emotions for space travel. Emotions or passions are

---

[57]See the diverse religious engagement of the subject, including Christian faith, in Calvin Mercer and Tracy J. Trothen, eds., *Religion and Transhumanism: The Unknown Future of Human Enhancement* (Santa Barbara, CA: Praeger, 2014); see also the Christian Transhumanist Association: http://www.christiantranshumanism.org/.

[58]See again the discussion of this topic in Kaushik, "Transhumanism in India." For more on Hinduism, see Christopher Key Chapple, "Hinduism: Many Paths, Many Births," in *Transhumanism and the Body: The World Religions Speak*, ed. Calvin Mercer and Derek F. Maher (New York: Palgrave Macmillan, 2014), 51-65. While the author does not appear to put forth reincarnation as encouraging transhumanism, I wonder whether the doctrine's claim that our souls are not wed to the same bodies in various cycles of life makes possible a religious basis for the move to transport consciousness and memory to artificial intelligence. One can also find treatments of other religions and their engagement of transhumanism in the volume.

[59]Evans, "2045 'Immortality' Transhumanism Program."

MORE THAN SPACE EXPLORATION   415

essential to our relational engagement. All too often, we define humanity in terms of our capacities and abilities to perform certain tasks, including greater efficiency in our technological society,[60] and not in terms of our relational interactions. While technology certainly assists us in connecting with others in a variety of ways, it can also impair our various relationships.

Klaus Schwab, the founder of the World Economic Forum, claims that the digital revolution requires leadership that is more human. He asserts that the fourth industrial revolution is a "system revolution," not a "product revolution," like the previous three. He maintains that "no one" is considering the "long-term consequences" of the breakthroughs in technology, such as with "robots, drones, intelligent cities, artificial intelligence, brain research." Schwab also weighs in on questions of what makes humanity distinct from robots:

> If you think about what a human being is, we exist because of brains, soul, heart. What we can replicate in a robot is a brain. But you never will replicate the heart, which is passion, compassion. And the soul, which enables us to believe. The robot will never have the ability to believe in something. So perhaps we will have at the end of this revolution—possibly, possibly—a basis for a new human renaissance.[61]

Hopefully, Wilson's envisioned new scientific enlightenment will pair with Schwab's new human renaissance. But I do not think we can get there without empathic care for humans and the heavens and earth, as reflected in the Judeo-Christian tradition among others. What good will space exploration be if all we do is restlessly and fruitlessly seek to conquer "the eternal silences of" those "infinite spaces"? Only the meek will inherit the earth—and the heavenlies. The only way we can fill the black hole of dread that Pascal experienced is through love and compassion.

Here it is worth pointing back to *Interstellar*. The movie portrays love as being a most powerful force, like gravity. David Brooks picks up on this theme in his review of the film, titled "Love and Gravity," in the *New*

---

[60]Here I have in mind Jacques Ellul's concern in *The Technological Society* (Toronto: Vintage Books, 1964).

[61]See Michael Duffy, "Seven Questions with Klaus Schwab," *TIME*, January 25, 2016, 28.

York Times. I quoted from Brooks's review earlier in this volume. The following lines bear repeating. Brooks maintains that *Interstellar* is "something of a cultural event." As he goes on to say, "In the era of Quantum entanglement and relativity, everything looks emergent and interconnected. Life looks less like a machine and more like endlessly complex patterns of waves and particles." Where "vast social engineering projects look less promising, because of the complexity, . . . webs of loving and meaningful relationships can do amazing good."[62]

Let's take up the subject of love and compassion or empathy as it relates to space exploration. We will seek to answer the question: In view of the race to space to survive, who gets left behind? How might "webs of loving and meaningful relationships" that "do amazing good" shape our response?

Space exploration and empathy. Some might consider the question, "Who gets left behind if we must abandon Earth as a species for space?" and its answer as a secularized version of Tim LaHaye and Jerry Jenkins's Left Behind drama. One way or another, the question about who gets left behind if we abandon earth for the heavenlies is by no means an abstract question if we account for acclaimed physicist and cosmologist Stephen Hawking's haunting warning in 2010: "Abandon earth—or face extinction." Exponential population growth and the accompanying decrease of natural resources necessary for our survival without sufficient sustainable alternatives, risks such as nuclear disasters, and global climate change are all factors that make the warning appear reasonable.[63]

It may sound like science fiction to some, and indeed, science fiction has engaged the subject. In *Interstellar*, a lead scientist sends astronauts into space in the effort to save humanity, as Earth is dying. Instead of intending to send all humans into space, because of the seeming impossibility, his efforts are focused on the astronauts colonizing one of three

---

[62]David Brooks, "Love and Gravity," *New York Times*, November 20, 2014, www.nytimes.com /2014/11/21/opinion/david-brooks-interstellar-love-and-gravity.html.

[63]See "#5: Stephen Hawking's Warning: Abandon Earth—or Face Extinction," Big Think, July 27, 2010, https://bigthink.com/dangerous-ideas/5-stephen-hawkings-warning-abandon-earth-or -face-extinction; "Mankind Must Abandon Earth or Face Extinction: Hawking," Phys.Org, August 9, 2010, https://phys.org/news/2010-08-mankind-abandon-earth-extinction-hawking .html.

planets and repopulating the species with frozen embryos stored on their spacecraft.[64]

Appropriating the *Interstellar* imagery as a science fiction thought experiment on ethics, if you were faced with selecting a group of people from Earth's inhabitants or selecting a particular group of embryos to be transplanted, who would you choose to send and who would be left behind? Would the tickets to ride the spaceship go to the highest bidders? Would the tickets go to those with the "best genes"? What, then, would happen to those with disabilities or those with average (or "bad") genes? Recall the movie *Gattaca* discussed in the chapter on genetic engineering. In *Gattaca*, what is deemed "bad" (actually, ordinary) genes become the basis for discrimination against space travel rather than religion, race, or gender. In what follows, our entangled ethical framework entails exploring these questions from the perspective of both utilitarian and virtue ethics.

Before one decides for or against those with disabilities (Hitler went the latter route[65]), one should keep in mind that in space there is a sense in which everyone is disabled given that the environs are radically different. Outer space may become the great equalizer. Or perhaps some who are viewed as disabled here on Earth may be "super-abled" in space, as their predispositions and conditions could work to their advantage in very different environments. Moreover, consider that those who have had to cope and adapt with disabilities to survive and function in our society may have an advantage over the rest of us emotionally and mentally. They could be the most discerning and resilient in adapting to very different environmental conditions in outer space.

In view of the preceding reflections, it is worth noting that sometimes environments and not just bodies determine disabilities. As the article "Disability in Science Fiction" conveys, "The social model of disability insists that rather than being something inherent to the individual,

---

[64]"Interstellar: Plot," IMDB, accessed October 29, 2019, www.imdb.com/title/tt0816692/plotsummary#synopsis. *Interstellar* is about humanity's attempt (through NASA) to pursue survival in solidarity on another planet, not a competitive exercise where superpowers such as the US and the USSR competed for supremacy in outer space (which the movie references).

[65]"Hitler Authorizes Killing of Disabled," WW2 History, accessed October 7, 2019, http://ww2history.com/key_moments/Holocaust/Hitler_authorizes_killing_of_disabled.

disability is created by barriers in society which disable a person."
Through portrayals of various environments, "science fiction offers opportunities to depict the social model in action." The article suggests, "By
demonstrating that a person's, or community's, status can change from
impaired to non-impaired, and vice-versa, depending on the environment they are placed into, these texts show clearly that disability is
not only a matter of individual bodies, but about the relationship of
bodies to particular environments."[66]

This individual versus relational dynamic takes us back to Brooks's
metaphorical contrast involving the Newtonian cog in a machine versus
the Einsteinian particle and wave in a vast ecosystem. One cannot treat
an individual body as a replaceable cog. There is an inviolable connection
between the body and its environment. This relational connection extends to other bodies. No man or woman is an island, nor a solitary
planet or star, not even the ideal *Mensch*, who is Dr. Mann in *Interstellar*.
None of us can go it alone. Not even a group of individual or solitary
Übermenschen can go it alone on a given planet. Here we must account
for that most relational of emotions—empathy or compassion.

Do we wish for the related notions of empathy, compassion, and altruism to play a part in the world beyond—that is, in outer space?
Whether the time ever comes for us to have to make the determination
in outer space, we need to account for that possible determination here,
as it relates to genetic adaptations as well as other matters. Considerations of the great beyond involving astrophysics and astrobiology assist
us in discerning how we should live here below. If such noble qualities
as empathy, compassion, and altruism are bound up with evolutionary
adaptations to protect weak and suffering members of our communities,
would we wish to hamper or limit compassion's development by removing those "weak" and "suffering" individuals from our midst as we
depart for life in outer space?[67] If so, the move to exclude or remove the
disabled from habitats in space would alter the life-scape and disable us

---

[66]This quote was originally found at http://www.dadafest.co.uk/disability-in-science-fiction/. Unfortunately, the page was discontinued.

[67]See Jennifer L. Goetz, Dacher Keltner, and Emiliana Simon-Thomas, "Compassion: An Evolutionary Analysis and Empirical Review," *Psychology Bulletin* 136, no. 3 (May 2010): 351-74, for more on
the subject of compassion and evolution, and for more on the claim "that compassion evolved as

emotionally and ethically. To safeguard the cultivation of the better angels of our human nature, we must not exclude those with disabilities here below. We must also be sure to take them with us when we journey into outer space. Whether on earth or in the heavenlies, we who are able-bodied and affluent cripple ourselves emotionally and relationally when we do not include the disadvantaged and disabled.

We must also be aware that there is a sense in which even the advantages of wealth can disable people. A *Scientific American* article reports that the wealthy appear to be less prone to compassion. After noting the research methods and findings of Berkeley psychologists Paul Piff, Dacher Keltner, and their colleagues, the article concludes with the following assessment as to why wealth leads to less compassion:

> The answer may have something to do with how wealth and abundance give us a sense of freedom and independence from others. The less we have to rely on others, the less we may care about their feelings. This leads us towards being more self-focused. Another reason has to do with our attitudes towards greed. Like Gordon Gekko, upper-class people may be more likely to endorse the idea that "greed is good." . . . Wealthier people are more likely to agree with statements that greed is justified, beneficial, and morally defensible. These attitudes ended up predicting participants' likelihood of engaging in unethical behavior.[68]

Given such predispositions as emotional disconnect and greed for those suffering from affluenza, should we hold a drawing to decide who gets to escape a dying Earth for life in outer space? Or will the drawing be rigged by those in power? A drawing or lottery would require assurances that guard against cheating and bribing so the rich and those with the necessary financial means could not manipulate the lottery to their own advantage. Or perhaps, it would be better to select specific people from various social and economic classes, educational backgrounds and genders, ethnicities, religions, and genetic makeups, including the disabled.

---

a distinct affective experience whose primary function is to facilitate cooperation and protection of the weak and those who suffer" (351).

[68]See Daisy Grewal, "How Wealth Reduces Compassion: As Riches Grow, Empathy for Others Seems to Decline," *Scientific American*, April 10, 2012, www.scientificamerican.com/article/how-wealth-reduces-compassion/.

Why does it matter that we diversify habitation on other planets? The study above suggests that the rich and powerful are less likely than those on the opposite end of the spectrum to be compassionate. Unless such diversification is prized, perhaps it would be better to stay behind on Earth rather than try to survive on a planet such as Mars with the Gordon Gekkos of this world.

The Gordon Gekkos out in space may go so far as to argue that empathy, compassion, and altruism are like mineral commodities rather than muscles. They might also contend that it is important to conserve and ration out empathy rather than use it abundantly. That way, its value increases since it is in short supply. Moreover, they might claim that "excessive" exercise of empathy would deplete the remaining supplies.

But what if empathy is like a muscle rather than a mineral commodity? What if empathy expands with use? Contrary to those economists who warn people that altruism is depleted with use, altruism is enlarged with usage according to Michael Sandel, as well as Aristotle and Rousseau.[69] Aristotle argues that we become good by doing good: "By doing just things we become just; moderate things, moderate; and courageous things, courageous." The same principle would hold true for empathy or compassion.[70] If expansion results from the exercise of empathy, then it would benefit humanity to employ it and use it all the time rather than conserve and ration it.

My view of the importance of empathy and the inclusion of the disadvantaged and disabled for life in outer space includes utilitarian and consequentialist reasoning: limiting new planet habitation to the rich and powerful may not lead to the best results. From this perspective, making space for the more compassionate yet less well-off financially and seemingly less capable or presumably incapable may prove beneficial to societal well-being.

From a consequentialist perspective, we find that there are advantages to ensuring the disadvantaged and the disabled are among us so that we

---

[69]Michael J. Sandel, *What Money Can't Buy: The Moral Limits of Markets* (New York: Farrar, Straus and Giroux, 2012), 128. See also the book review by Peter C. Grosvenor: "What Money Can't Buy: The Moral Limits of Markets," *Humanist*, June 29, 2012, https://thehumanist.com/magazine/july -august-2012/arts_entertainment/what-money-cant-buy-the-moral-limits-of-markets.

[70]Aristotle, *Nicomachean Ethics*, trans. Robert C. Bartlett and Susan D. Collins (Chicago: University of Chicago Press, 2011), 27, line 1103b; see also 26, line 1103a.

are not disadvantaged socially. If, as Peter Singer claims, there is "an evolutionary advantage in being genuinely altruistic,"[71] we should choose altruistic souls as our traveling companions. They would include the poor and downtrodden, since they are generally more compassionate than those who are suffering from affluenza. Their compassion might even rub off on us. So just perhaps, the last—the less well-off and less naturally endowed—will be first in outer space, and the first—the rich and brilliant—will be last, not unlike the kingdom of God (Matthew 20:16). It puts a new twist on what is needed to prepare for life in the great beyond.

Now, if the rich and powerful were to clutch and grasp and gnash their teeth to ensure that they alone make it to Mars,[72] they would end up competing with one another. No doubt, some would win and some would lose, just as in our free-market society. Those who lose out might lose out even more there than here in that there likely would not be a safety net to catch them when they fall. Compassion would be in such short supply given how much all those in the country club of Mars lacked empathy here on Earth. Many of these elites would not be trained in the virtue of compassion if the research noted above holds true. Thus, it would take quite a long period of time for such virtues to permeate the habits and habitats of the "Earth refugees" who had migrated to another planet. By the time they would be prepared to catch the fallen in a safety net, those who lost out on positioning for power and influence may have already come crashing down. Given the amount of time and difficulty it would take for such virtues to be embodied, it might prove too, little too late in a natural environment already ill-suited to the survival of those who have not been acclimated to scarcity and suffering.

Speaking of the difficulty of fostering virtues, it is worth noting that virtue (*aretē*) entails such things as right intent (not simply right action). It is more than a habit. It is a disposition that goes all the way down to

---

[71] Peter Singer, "The Biological Basis of Ethics," in *The Expanding Circle: Ethics and Sociobiology* (New York: Farrar, Straus & Giroux, 1981), 23-53.

[72] This is not just a sci-fi fantasy. The wealthy can purchase trips to space with the new space-tourism industry that has started opening the final frontier for consumer consumption. Adam Mann, "So You Want to Be a Space Tourist? Here Are Your Options," NBCNews.com, July 21, 2017, www .nbcnews.com/mach/science/so-you-want-be-space-tourist-here-are-your-options-ncna784166.

the core of one's being. It is also more than an emotional state, for it entails practical wisdom (*phronesis*), which signifies that it takes a long time to cultivate and cannot be done by "children" who may possess emotions of compassion but who do not act virtuously, which entails practical wisdom cultivated over a lengthy period of time, as in the case of morally mature adults. Morally good people who are compassionate will not operate immorally. Such moral virtue constitutes *eudaimonia*, an ideal moral state of happiness or human flourishing. As such, it is not wanton pleasure or merely a subjective state of happiness: "Virtue ethicists claim that a human life devoted to physical pleasure or the acquisition of wealth is not *eudaimon*, but a wasted life."[73]

It is important to note that just because poor people often express a greater sense of compassion than the rich do, it does not follow that such compassionate activity always results from wisdom and virtue. While we may think all acts of compassion are virtuous, true virtue as embodied in compassion really arises from the ethical agent's personal moral being, intent, and disposition cultivated over many years. Thus, it is important that those given to more compassionate expressions and solidarity with the weak based on life circumstances and other factors train themselves in practical wisdom in the pursuit of true happiness or human flourishing.

Virtue ethics, at least Aristotle's model of virtue ethics, does not take us far enough. After all, Aristotle's ideal community was an elite group of educated males. Ultimately, Aristotle cannot lead us to where we need to go in this matter. From a Christian perspective, the holy, unconditional love of God embodied in Jesus and poured out through the Spirit is the necessary condition for the possibility of loving our neighbor, even the disadvantaged and disabled person. This necessary condition includes the needed motivation to love those we deem unlovable. Only the Spirit can energize us to love like God loves. As Martin Luther declares, God's love creates the attraction rather than responds or reacts to that which is often seen as attractive: "The love of God does not find, but

---

[73]Rosalind Hursthouse and Glen Pettigrove, "Virtue Ethics," in *Stanford Encyclopedia of Philosophy*, ed. Edward N. Zalta, Winter 2018, http://plato.stanford.edu/entries/ethics-virtue/.

creates, that which is pleasing to it. The love of man comes into being through that which is pleasing to it."[74]

We find here in this statement that God's love is not self-centered. It leads us to operate in a decentered manner toward others, which requires the cultivation of empathy toward our fellow humans. That same decentering is vital as we consider Earth in relation to the universe(s) at large. To this subject we now turn.

DECENTERED EARTH AND SPACE EXPLORATION

In this last section, we turn from consideration of a decentered deity and decentered humanity to reflect on a decentered view of Earth. This focus will involve consideration of property rights as well as our overarching priorities. Regarding property rights, we must ask whether it is ethical to own property in space and how we would engage intelligent life forms that do not own property. We must also consider questions of priorities in relation to space exploration. A proper comparative analysis of Earth and other planets helps us to safeguard against taking life here on Earth or on another planet for granted. Prudent comparative judgments will help us reframe our priorities so that we take better care of life here on Earth as well as not repeat the same mistakes of failed stewardship and waste here on this globe on planets in outer space.

Space exploration and property. Do rocks on the moon and Mars have inherent rights? And what about extraterrestrials? Can earthlings own the land and force the native population off land on planets such as Mars, if there are no property rights in existence there? Some might consider these questions and issues far-fetched, but they are only as far-fetched as the history of colonialism or the present-day aspirations to privatize domains in outer space.

Take for example this article in *Wired*: "Loophole Could Allow Private Land Claims on Other Worlds."[75] Private parties are looking for a loophole in the 1967 Outer Space Treaty, which does not allow a nation to claim

---

[74]Martin Luther, "Heidelberg Disputation," in *Martin Luther's Basic Theological Writings*, ed. Timothy F. Lull (Minneapolis: Augsburg Fortress, 1989), 48.

[75]Adam Mann, "Loophole Could Allow Private Land Claims on Other Worlds," *Wired*, April 5, 2012, www.wired.com/2012/04/moon-mars-property/.

sovereign rights to a body in outer space. Nations might not be able to do so, but what about companies and wealthy individuals? Depending on the answer, nations such as the United States might remove their support and withdraw from the treaty to sanction property rights to private interests. Such potential moves depend in part on whether they think the apparent gains to their economies outweigh the backlash from the global community.

A question arises at this point concerning the drive to colonize and privatize. Why must dominant cultural forces of the past and present seek to colonize or privatize nations and planets as property? It calls to mind C. S. Lewis's *Out of the Silent Planet*. The antagonist Weston, a colonialist expansionist from Earth, addresses the ruler of Mars:

> "It is in her right," said Weston, "the right, or, if you will, the might of Life herself, that I am prepared without flinching to plant the flag of man on the soil of Malacandra: to march on, step by step, superseding, where necessary, the lower forms of life that we find, claiming planet after planet, system after system, till our posterity—whatever strange form and yet unguessed mentality they have assumed—dwell in the universe wherever the universe is habitable."[76]

What is that supposed right of human life to plant humanity's flag on another planet's soil? No doubt, it is the same supposed right, or better, legal move, that makes it possible for us to take over land on other continents or islands on this globe in the past and present.

Think about Hawaii's beaches, which are public domain, as well as select tracts of land belonging to indigenous people, but that may now be up for wealthy people's grabs.[77] Dominant cultural forces introduced private property laws to Hawaii, which ended up eroding native Hawaiian sovereignty.[78] According to one account, "Before westerners came to Hawaii, stewardship of the land, or ʻaina, was a collective responsibility,

---

[76]C. S. Lewis, *Out of the Silent Planet* (New York: Macmillan, 1965), 137.
[77]Sophie Cocke, "How Famous Surfers and Wealthy Homeowners Are Endangering Hawaii's Beaches," ProPublica, December 5, 2020, www.propublica.org/article/how-famous-surfers-and-wealthy-homeowners-are-endangering-hawaiis-beaches. Consider also the fight over land in Hawaii: Jon Letman and Julia Carrie Wong, "Hawaiians Call Mark Zuckerberg 'the Face of Neo-colonialism' over Land Lawsuits," *Guardian*, January 23, 2017, www.theguardian.com/technology/2017/jan/23/mark-zuckerberg-hawaii-land-lawsuits-kauai-estate.
[78]Melody Kapilialoha MacKenzie, ed., *Native Hawaiian Rights Handbook* (Honolulu: Native Hawaiian Legal Corporation, 1991).

characterized by the familial relationship to the land. . . . Privatization came in 1848 with the Māhele, which began the process of divvying up parcels between the king, the government and the people."[79] Consider, too, the expansion of the continental United States, where First Nations people lost their land and water rights due to the doctrine of discovery, which "established a spiritual, political, and legal justification for colonization and seizure of land not inhabited by Christians."[80]

Why is it that Euro-American sojourners have so often failed to see themselves as guests rather than colonizers? The spirit of restlessness and a theology of conquest permeate our imagination. As we go in search of other planets, we should guard against staking our interest, our nation's interest, or our globe's interest there. We belong to the Earth. These planets do not belong to Earth, this or that nation, company, or wealthy individual.

Those who operate from a free-market ethical vantage point would possibly counter this argument and claim they seek to privatize land on other planets to maintain and increase its value. It is an easy move to make if we view life as a commodity. When economic value shapes humanity and creation's value, we cheapen life.

Speaking of value, how much value would there be if we were to extract nonreplenishable minerals and resources from other planets, as in *Avatar*, to bring back to use on Mother Earth, and in turn fill these planets or regions of space with garbage and waste from Earth? As far as garbage is concerned, the cost we would incur in energy used, pollution generated, and technology created and maintained to launch into space innumerable times to dump the incomprehensible amount of trash we generate would be astronomical.[81] Rather than reducing the debt associated with our carbon footprint and addressing our pollution problems here on Earth, we would only increase our liabilities and decrease our moral value as a species.

[79]Letman and Wong, "Hawaiians Call Mark Zuckerberg 'the Face of Neocolonialism.'"
[80]"Doctrine of Discovery," Upstander Project, https://upstanderproject.org/firstlight/doctrine. See also Robert J. Miller, *Native America, Discovered and Conquered: Thomas Jefferson, Lewis & Clark, and Manifest Destiny* (Lincoln: University of Nebraska Press, 2008).
[81]See for example Cain Fraser, "Why Can't We Launch Garbage into Space?," *Universe Today*, 2009, www.universetoday.com/25431/why-cant-we-launch-garbage-into-space/; John Wenz, "Here's Why We Can't Just Throw Our Garbage into the Sun," *Popular Mechanics*, February 29, 2016, www.popularmechanics.com/space/a19666/we-cant-just-throw-our-garbage-into-the-sun/.

Now, as to viewing life as a commodity, free-market ethicists may even go so far as to call for purchasing and selling alien life forms, even intelligent life forms. Why not, if the aim is to increase their value as commodities? Valuation results from commodification according to their moral ledger. Since such intelligent life forms are not human, what would be the problem with owning or enslaving them? Where should we turn for an answer? From a Kantian personalist perspective, humans alone are rational and moral ends in themselves, and not mere means. Then again, Kant only appeared to view White European men along such lines.[82] How do we go about protecting all intelligent life forms, no matter their planet of origin, as ends in themselves rather than as mere means?[83]

Let's think again. Perhaps we should not make equivalent rationality the guiding principle. We often assume we will find lower forms of life on other planets and so can subjugate them, as Weston sought to do in *Perelandra*. But what if we find intelligent forms of life on other planets that supersede us? In keeping with what H. G. Wells wrote about in *The War of the Worlds*,[84] why wouldn't superior forms of intelligent life on those planets have every right to colonize our planet, take away our property, and enslave humans? In fact, they would have more apparent justification than those "enlightened" White Europeans and Americans who grievously and mistakenly classified persons on the "Dark Continent," in India, and the Americas as less intelligent and civilized.

And what if, in our efforts in space exploration, we create superintelligent robots that exceed our capabilities? Should we bow the collective human knee to them? Some pioneers in space exploration fear that

---

[82]On Kant and racism, see Thomas E. Hill Jr. and Bernard Boxill, "Kant and Race," in *Race and Racism*, ed. Bernard Boxill, Oxford Readings in Philosophy Series (Oxford: Oxford University Press, 2001), 450.

[83]Science fiction abounds with compelling accounts for how to live and how not to live in a universe of multiple forms of intelligent life. See for example Michel Faber, *The Book of Strange New Things: A Novel* (New York: Penguin Random House, 2014). Many sci-fi TV shows manifest ethical concerns about space exploration. *Firefly* narrates humanity's survival on other planets after the earth is exhausted as a struggle between the haves and have-nots, the central planets versus the outer-rim planets. In *Doctor Who*, travel through time and space constantly raises questions about who has the right to dictate another (alien) race's survival and at what cost. Consider also the closing chapters of Walker Percy, *Lost in the Cosmos: The Last Self-Help Book* (New York: Picador, 1983). The concluding section reflects on some of the themes set forth in this chapter, such as how space exploration and habitation will not cure what ails us as a species.

[84]H. G. Wells, *The War of the Worlds* (New York: Modern Library, 2002).

humanity may not survive the appearance of superintelligence. Take for example space and AI technology business magnate Elon Musk. He worries that humanity may be the "biological boot loader for digital superintelligence."[85] Now, some will argue that Musk's fear is far-fetched, claiming that there is no need to be concerned about AI supplanting humanity in the foreseeable future. Perhaps they are right about the *foreseeable* future. Still, we should not avoid addressing such concerns, since today's possibilities often become the future's actualities.

Musk refers people to Nick Bostrom's work *Superintelligence*.[86] Bostrom claims that most experts believe scientists will create a "human-level AI" by the latter part of the twenty-first century. While the creation of this human-level AI may be inevitable, what is not inevitable is how we will construct and use it. He encourages those responsible to discern well how to build and employ such artificial intelligence. If our creations are not benevolent and well-inclined toward humanity, the results could be catastrophic.

Bostrom recommends Isaac Asimov's "Three Laws of Robotics" as critically important for providing the appropriate safeguards in this scientific venture. Asimov's tenets in order are (First Law) "A robot may not injure a human being or, through inaction, allow a human being to come to harm"; (Second Law) "A robot must obey the orders given it by human beings except where such orders would conflict with the First Law"; (Third Law) "A robot must protect its own existence as long as such protection does not conflict with the First or Second Law."[87] Not everyone accepts Asimov's laws,[88] while others maintain they need updating.[89]

---

[85]Refer to Ricki Harris, "Elon Musk: Humanity Is a Kind of 'Biological Boot Loader' for AI," *Wired*, September 1, 2019, www.wired.com/story/elon-musk-humanity-biological-boot-loader-ai/; James Vincent, "Elon Musk Says Artificial Intelligence Is 'More Dangerous Than Nukes,'" *Independent*, August 5, 2014, www.independent.co.uk/life-style/gadgets-and-tech/elon-musk-says-artificial-intelligence-is-more-dangerous-than-nukes-9648732.html.

[86]Nick Bostrom, *Superintelligence: Paths, Dangers, Strategies* (Oxford: Oxford University Press, 2014).

[87]Isaac Asimov, "Runaround," in *I, Robot*, Isaac Asimov Collection (New York: Doubleday, 1950), 40.

[88]Peter W. Singer, "Isaac Asimov's Laws of Robotics Are Wrong," Brookings, May 18, 2009, brookings .edu/opinions/isaac-asimovs-laws-of-robotics-are-wrong/.

[89]Mark Robert Anderson, "After 75 Years, Isaac Asimov's Three Laws of Robotics Need Updating," Conversation, March 17, 2017, https://theconversation.com/after-75-years-isaac-asimovs-three -laws-of-robotics-need-updating-74501; Christopher Salge, "Asimov's Laws Won't Stop Robots from Harming Humans, So We've Developed a Better Solution," Conversation, July 11, 2017;

Musk's concern, as well as Bostrom's and Asimov's reflections, calls to mind Kant's ethical system once again and how it might bear on whether humanity *should* seek to develop superior forms of artificial intelligence. If such artificial intelligence were to pave the way for our extinction, even while securing our legacy scientifically, how could Kant affirm such technological pursuits based on his categorical imperative? In the end, such technological achievements would give rise to collective suicide or humanity's demise. However, to the extent that Kant's categorical imperative involving the personalist principle of ends and means assumes or requires the presupposition or foundation that humans are the most intelligent creatures, then any intelligent life form, whether organic or artificial, that is higher than humanity could treat us as mere means. Why should humans maintain the upper hand, as Asimov's laws of robotics assume, if we are not the most intelligent entities at the end of the century? If, however, we do not equate esteemed status and dignity with superior intelligence but with being created in the image of God, then we are able to safeguard against exploitation of intelligent life forms of any kind, whether extraterrestrials, our terrestrial selves, or robots.

Space exploration and priorities in view of proper proportionality. Now we turn to what our ultimate priorities should be based on a comparative analysis of Earth and other planets. For one, in our search for other inhabitable planets, we may come to realize how unique this planet and life on this planet are. Such recognition and appreciation bound up with comparisons between Earth and other planets may move us to better cherish and steward life on Earth. As the "old" saying goes, the grass or vegetation always looks lusher on the other side of the universe, that is, until we land at our planetary destination. Moreover, we might sense the need to pursue peace rather than allow our grievances to give rise to war and bloodshed if we realized how unique we and our planet are. Carl Sagan speaks of how space exploration can help us move toward this realization in his work *Pale Blue Dot*.[90] We cannot afford to wage war with one another.

---

republished in *Scientific American*, www.scientificamerican.com/article/asimovs-laws-wont-stop -robots-from-harming-humans-so-weve-developed-a-better-solution/.

[90]Carl Sagan, *Pale Blue Dot: A Vision of the Human Future in Space* (New York: Ballentine Books, 1994).

Ironically or tragically, space exploration arose in the context of the Cold War. In fact, the tensions between the United States and Soviet Union shaped the race to space. The two superpowers could easily transfer research developed in the space industry to military uses. They also sought to demonstrate their superiority over each other through their race into outer space. One account puts it this way:

> The populations of both countries took a great interest in their respective space programs and it was a useful way for both superpowers to demonstrate their superiority. Nikita Khruschev, the Premier of the Soviet Union, used the country's early success in the Space Race to claim that the "economy, science, culture and the creative genius of people in all areas of life develop better and faster under communism." The American President John F. Kennedy, on the other hand, is quoted as saying "Everything we do ought to . . . be tied in to getting on to the Moon ahead of the Russians. . . . We hope to beat the USSR to demonstrate that instead of being behind by a couple of years, by God, we passed them."[91]

In contrast to the Cold War era, the movie *The Martian* gives us a science-fictional glimpse of how space exploration need not be divisive.[92] Indeed, even this fictional account may motivate us in the real world to move beyond sectional loyalties to those that embrace all peoples, as Martin Luther King Jr. envisioned during the Cold War: "Every nation must now develop an overriding loyalty to mankind as a whole in order to preserve the best in their individual societies." King adds, "This call for a worldwide fellowship that lifts neighborly concern beyond one's tribe, race, class, and nation is in reality a call for an all-embracing and unconditional love for all men."[93] It should even extend to include an all-embracing and unconditional love for all life/intelligent life forms on other planets.

In the movie *The Martian*, the Chinese assist NASA in seeking to rescue astronaut Mark Watney from the abandoned mission on Mars.

---

[91]"Space Race," Royal Air Force Museum, accessed October 7, 2019, www.nationalcoldwar exhibition.org/schools-colleges/national-curriculum/space-race/.

[92]"The Martian: Official Trailer," YouTube Video, 20th Century Fox, August 19, 2015, www.youtube .com/watch?v=ej3ioOneTy8.

[93]Martin Luther King Jr., "Beyond Vietnam," in *A Call to Conscience: The Landmark Speeches of Dr. Martin Luther King, Jr.*, ed. Clayborne Carson and Kris Shepard (New York: Warner Books, 2001), 160-61.

It is worth noting that one commentator indicates that the Chinese space program is a spinoff of the Russian space program "and uses similar modules to this day."[94] And yet, in contrast to the Russian and American Cold War space race that pitted the two world superpowers against each other, the whole world is invested collectively and collaboratively in the mission to Mars in this science-fiction movie, not just one or two nations.

The same kind of collective and collaborative venture is needed today between nations on the "pale blue dot." While we might think we cannot live with other nations, we really cannot live without them. Perhaps something similar could be argued, that by living abroad we would come to realize how unique we and our nation are and seek to cultivate peace within our own borders among those of various sectional loyalties, including ethnicities and classes. Life abroad often gives us a new perspective on life and people back home. In view of the risks of nuclear war, weapons of mass destruction, and gun violence in our midst, we must pursue just and lasting peace. Otherwise, the pale blue dot may become even paler and smaller, and then eventually disappear.

The universe is more mysterious than we imagined. Astrobiology accounts for its vastness and complexity and raises questions about meaningful existence in view of the conditions and possibilities surrounding life's origins and development wherever it may be found.[95] Decentering the Earth entails moving beyond solitary focus on Earth's biology. Interestingly, attention to astrobiology leads humanity to consider Earth's biology in fresh ways. The two fields mutually benefit each other.[96]

In seeking to detect life on other planets through a comparison with life on Earth, Carl Pilcher, director of the NASA Astrobiology Institute

---

[94]"The Martian: Trivia," IMDB, accessed October 7, 2019, http://m.imdb.com/title/tt3659388/trivia.

[95]Recent box office hits such as *Interstellar* and *The Martian* bear witness to the fascination many have with astrophysics, astrobiology, and their relation to questions of meaning and value. Refer to Aaron Gronstal, "The Martian Astrobiologist," Astrobiology at NASA, October 12, 2015, https://astrobiology.nasa.gov/news/the-martian-astrobiologist/.

[96]For treatments of astrobiology and interdisciplinary study, see David C. Catling, *Astrobiology: A Very Short Introduction*, Very Short Introductions (Oxford: Oxford University Press, 2014); Milan M. Ćirković, *The Astrobiological Landscape: Philosophical Foundations of the Study of Cosmic Life* (Cambridge: Cambridge University Press, 2012).

at Ames, states, "This work broadens our understanding of how life may be detected on Earth-like planets around other stars, while simultaneously improving our understanding of life on Earth." He goes on, "This approach—studying Earth life to guide our search for life on other worlds—is the essence of astrobiology."[97]

Similarly, attention to ethical considerations in our biosphere can assist with engaging ethics in relation to astrobiology. By decentering Earth and humans in the universe, theologians and ethicists can partner with astrobiologists and those in other disciplines to construct a framework for viewing life on Earth and life elsewhere in constructive, interplanetary terms. While ancient writings foreshadowed this perspective, it is largely a novel and prophetic enterprise, which will benefit the common good of all life forms wherever they may be found.

Comparisons between life on Earth and life in outer space should quicken us to guard against the two extremes of overaccentuating or discounting our uniqueness. Both extremes easily lead to global conflicts and reckless treatment of the earth. Regarding the latter, it would be good to remember that we are not lords over creation, only stewards. We do not own Earth, no matter how much private property we possess. As Karl Barth mused in meditating on humanity's relation to the beasts in Genesis 1, "Man is not their Creator; hence he cannot be their absolute lord, a second God. In his dignity and position he can only be God's creaturely witness and representative to them."[98] Such reflections should cause us to be more circumspect as our race searches for life on other planets. If we are not "absolute" lords on Earth, surely we are not absolute lords on other spheres.

If we do not account for our finitude and our fallen condition but seek to escape Earth for the heavenlies, we will lose the incentive to do all that is needed to preserve life here on Earth. Space exploration for the sake of habitation on other planets must never replace but complement rigorous exploration of ways to reduce pollution and the waste of life by

---

[97]Rob Gutro, "NASA Predicts Non-green Plants on Other Planets," Goddard Space Flight Center, April 11, 2007, www.nasa.gov/centers/goddard/news/topstory/2007/spectrum_plants.html.
[98]Karl Barth, *Church Dogmatics*, vol. III/2, *The Doctrine of Creation*, ed. G. W. Bromiley and T. F. Torrance (Edinburgh: T&T Clark, 1960), 187.

warfare over border disputes and related tensions on this planet. If we do not guard against an escapist mentality, the equivalent of global suicide will be the cataclysmic result. Moreover, we must get our own house in order here on Earth and put a check on our ambitions here below before taking up residence on other planets in keeping with what Maximus writes about our cancerous penchant to wreak havoc wherever we go. Otherwise, we may be to others the malevolent aliens many science-fiction writers such as Bradbury and Lewis and movie directors depict. Inhabitants of the pale blue dot would become the equivalent of the pale rider of John's Apocalypse.[99]

SPACE EXPLORATION: COSMOLOGICAL MONSTERS OR THE WHOLE PERSON

I am reminded here of Owen Gingerich's account of Copernicus discarding Ptolemy's astronomical model. Copernicus ultimately rejected the Ptolemian picture of the universe because it portrayed the universe as a cosmological "monster" of unrelated parts rather than as a whole person.[100] Not positivistic views of science and life but aesthetics launched Copernicus's investigation. The needed mathematical formulations and scientific data followed. As Gingerich observes,

> The debased positivism that has so thoroughly penetrated our philosophical framework urges us to look to data as the foundation of a scientific theory, but Copernicus' radical cosmology came forth not from new observations but from insight. It was, like Einstein's revolution four centuries later, *motivated by the passionate search for symmetries and an aesthetic structure of the universe.* Only afterward the facts, and even the crisis, are marshalled in support of the new world view.[101]

It is not simply the mathematical equations, empirical investigations, technological advances, or economic prospects that shape our perspectives of the world. Given our inviolable identity as human persons, none

---

[99]One of the four living creatures in Revelation announces, "I looked, and there before me was a pale horse! Its rider was named Death, and Hades was following close behind him" (Revelation 6:8).

[100]Owen Gingerich, "'Crisis' vs. Aesthetic in the Copernican Revolution," *Vistas in Astronomy* 17, no. 1 (1975): 89.

[101]Gingerich, "'Crisis' vs. Aesthetic in the Copernican Revolution," 90 (italics added).

of these factors go to the depths of our identity and longings. What we find most aesthetically appealing provides the greatest explanatory power for how to flourish as humans.

What aesthetic structures will help us view our universe as a whole and humans as whole personal beings rather than as disparate parts? What will aid us in moving beyond the mechanistic, market-driven, and despotic colonialist impulses accounted for in this volume that reduce our human identity to base things in isolation? Ethical debates will continue over what models provide the greatest staying power for human flourishing. Aesthetics is at the heart of that quest, and the personalism articulated and envisioned in this volume is one such moral portrait.

The Copernican revolution recentered our focus on God's grandeur, goodness, and mercy in cherishing microscopic humanity and the pale blue dot we inhabit. Scientific explorations in astronomy as well as astrobiology and astrophysics can aid us in recentering our gaze on humanity's and Earth's rightful place in relation to the universe. These scientific ventures can aid the Christian ethicist in accounting for the vastness and complexity, conditions and possibilities, surrounding life's origins and development wherever it may be found. Such considerations should quicken us to guard against the two extremes of discounting human uniqueness and overaccentuating it. Both extremes easily lead to international conflicts, the reckless treatment of Earth, and restless wandering throughout the universe bent on conquest. As we learn to decenter deity by discarding despotic notions of sovereignty and decenter humanity in a way that undercuts hubris and places restraints and checks on unbounded anthropocentrism, we will be in a better position to care for the human race, our environment, and life on other planets with profound dignity and respect as whole persons.

PART FOUR

JOURNEY'S END

13

REDISCOVERING PERSONS

Finding Our Way Home

WE HAVE TRAVELED A LONG WAY in this volume in search of missing persons. The journey has taken us from the beginning of life to its end, and we have crossed racial boundaries and national borders as well as raced across outer space. What we have sought to make clear at every turn is that humans are more than biological and sexual drives, market forces, consumer appetites, or cogs in a machine. Each chapter has sought to impress on us that we are more than things. To put the matter in aesthetic terms, following Copernicus's imagery noted at the end of chapter twelve,[1] humanity is not an assemblage of dismembered, disjointed parts that constitute a cosmic monster but rather whole persons in communion. God has made us for more.

Many traveling companions of various perspectives have helped us on our faith quest of entangled ethics. Confucius and Aristotle, Augustine of Hippo, Irenaeus of Lyons, Maximus the Confessor, Martin Luther, Jonathan Edwards, Immanuel Kant, Mahatma Gandhi, Karl Barth, Martin Luther King Jr., H. Richard Niebuhr and Reinhold Niebuhr, Jacques Ellul, Colin Gunton, Karol Wojtyla, T. F. Torrance, David Brooks, Karen Armstrong, the Dalai Lama, Tisha M. Rajendra, Christian Smith, Sarah Coakley, Alasdair MacIntyre, Melanie Harris, Peter Harrison, Wendell Berry, Willie Jennings, and Michael Sandel are some of those who have assisted us on our way. They are good conversation partners who have helped with directions at various points on the journey, even

---

[1]See Owen Gingerich, "'Crisis' vs. Aesthetic in the Copernican Revolution," *Vistas in Astronomy* 17, no. 1 (1975): 89-90.

when our personalist vision leads us to take separate routes in some cases along the way. None of us have a God's-eye or bird's-eye point of view. Each of us looks through a glass dimly. Not even Google Maps can help us find our way in moving from a culture of things to persons. We need the help of fellow humans in the quest for personhood. That is why it's never good to travel alone.

Our ecumenical quest, involving so many fellow pilgrims, does not lack a North Star. Jesus of Nazareth, who is God's embodied love, on whom the Christian community hangs its eschatological hopes, and for whom we long, serves as the guiding light. In the last chapter on space exploration, I drew attention to Psalm 8 and Hebrews 2 and how the Hebrews passage highlights the christocentric telos of biblical anthropology. The author of Hebrews argues that God has subjected the world to come to humans, not angels. Jesus as the telos or goal of our humanity has set the wheels in motion for that ultimate day:

> It is not to angels that he has subjected the world to come, about which we are speaking. But there is a place where someone has testified:
> "What is mankind that you are mindful of them,
>   a son of man that you care for him?
> You made them a little lower than the angels;
>   you crowned them with glory and honor
>   and put everything under their feet."
> In putting everything under them, God left nothing that is not subject to them. Yet at present we do not see everything subject to them. But we do see Jesus, who was made lower than the angels for a little while, now crowned with glory and honor because he suffered death, so that by the grace of God he might taste death for everyone. (Hebrews 2:5-9)

Jesus is God's ultimate declaration and confirmation that we were made for more: we are not to reduce our fellow humans and ourselves, equating one another with various drives, forces, appetites, and cogs, or think that we only have bit parts in God's drama of salvation. Jesus tasted death for everyone, not simply Aristotle's noble class of friends but also the widow, orphan, and alien in their distress, so that everyone might experience and participate in divine glory. Jesus is the model human we should strive to be more like and through whom God's Spirit invites us to experience abundant life.

Speaking of experiencing the abundant life, the experiential knowledge that God is love and loves us in Jesus through the Spirit provides confident assurance of faith and secure attachment. It frees us from inhumane positioning and posturing to be at the center of the universe. When we take matters into our own hands, we become what Augustine classified as tortured, cheated, and diseased souls.[2] When this happens, we are in danger of devolving into "cosmological monsters," to allude to Copernicus's repulsion over Ptolemy's picture of the universe noted in chapter twelve. In contrast, when we care deeply for one another and embody love in view of God's sovereign care, we are well on our way as human persons to our ultimate destination and eschatological hope. This destination and hope are not outer space but Jesus' eternal and blessed kingdom come to earth and our participation in his glorious life. His is the world to come.

Reminiscent of Augustine's reflections on the cheated soul noted in chapter two, C. S. Lewis informs us that we are too easily pleased. Rather than live in expectation of Jesus' promises and rewards of eternal life in the world to come, we settle for less, far less. As Lewis argues, it appears that "our Lord finds our desires not too strong, but too weak. We are half-hearted creatures, fooling about with drink and sex and ambition when infinite joy is offered us, like an ignorant child who wants to go on making mud pies in a slum because he cannot imagine what is meant by the offer of a holiday at the sea. We are far too easily pleased."[3] To use Augustine's language, we live as cheated souls.

We must give full weight to the desire for "our own far-off country."[4] We must not discount that desire, nor one another as humans. Rather than seek to avoid our present struggles and escape to outer space, we should live on earth in view of heaven's kingdom and bring heaven down to earth. We do so by taking one another's glory deep into our hearts. Lewis puts the subject of human glory in the following terms:

---

[2]Saint Augustine, *Of the Morals of the Catholic Church*, in *Nicene and Post-Nicene Fathers*, first series, vol. 4, ed. Philip Schaff, trans. Richard Stothert (Buffalo, NY: Christian Literature, 1887), III/4. Revised and edited for New Advent by Kevin Knight; http://www.newadvent.org/fathers/1401.htm.

[3]C. S. Lewis, *The Weight of Glory* (San Francisco: HarperSanFrancisco, 1980), 26.

[4]Lewis, *Weight of Glory*, 29.

The load, or weight, or burden of my neighbour's glory should be laid on my back, a load so heavy that only humility can carry it, and the backs of the proud will be broken. It is a serious thing to live in a society of possible gods and goddesses, to remember that the dullest and most uninteresting person you can talk to may one day be a creature which, if you say it now, you would be strongly tempted to worship, or else a horror and a corruption such as you now meet, if at all, only in a nightmare. All day long we are, in some degree, helping each other to one or other of these destinations. It is in the light of these overwhelming possibilities, it is with the awe and the circumspection proper to them, that we should conduct all our dealings with one another, all friendships, all loves, all play, all politics. There are no ordinary people. You have never talked to a mere mortal. Nations, cultures, arts, civilisations—these are mortal, and their life is to ours as the life of a gnat. But it is immortals whom we joke with, work with, marry, snub, and exploit—immortal horrors or everlasting splendours.[5]

As Lewis writes, "all day long" we are assisting each other to make it to one of two "destinations." Either toward amazing honor and beauty or horror and monstrosity. God has sought to barricade the latter possible destination by subjecting all things to humanity through Jesus, not celestial beings (Hebrews 2:5, 8-9). This affirmation of divine favor is flattering. So, we should honor one another more than we would angels from on high. While we do not yet see everything subjected to humanity (Hebrews 2:8), we should take to heart that Jesus did not become an angel but one of us. He who was made lower than the angels "for a little while" tasted death for everyone. He is "now crowned with glory and honor" and makes possible the greater destiny (Hebrews 2:9). In that light, we should look at no one "from a worldly point of view," as Paul writes, though we did look at Jesus this way for a time (2 Corinthians 5:16). As we "see Jesus" (Hebrews 2:9), we will see others differently. Rather than seeking to get the better of one another, we will consider others better than ourselves. We will bear one another's weighty glory on our backs and descend to greatness in the Spirit of Jesus (see Philippians 2:1-11).

---

[5]Lewis, *Weight of Glory*, 45-46.

To reflect back on chapter twelve again, our journey is not like a space race between superpowers, such as the former Soviet Union and the United States. This is not a competition, where only the first-place finisher achieves the crowning glory of personhood. Otherwise, we will not bear one another's glory on our backs but bear down on one other. Here we would be wise to remember Jesus' warning that the last will be first and the first will be last (Matthew 20:16). Only the humble can bear this glorious burden. Those who are proud will break their own backs.

Speaking of space races, we should not take too seriously those such as Nikita Khrushchev, who declared that the Russian cosmonaut returning from space did not find God. As C. S. Lewis argues, if one does not see God on earth, one will not see him in the heavens either.

> Looking for God—or Heaven—by exploring space is like reading or seeing all Shakespeare's plays in the hope you will find Shakespeare as one of the characters or Stratford as one of the places. Shakespeare is in one sense present at every moment in every play. But he is never present in the same way as Falstaff or Lady Macbeth, nor is he diffused through the play like a gas. . . .
>
> To some, God is discoverable everywhere; to others, nowhere. Those who do not find him on earth are unlikely to find him in space. (Hang it all, we're in space already; every year we go a huge circular tour in space.) But send up a saint in a spaceship and he'll find God in space as he found God on earth. Much depends on the seeing eye.[6]

Whether we are talking about God or human persons, so much depends on our perspective. If we do not discover a personal God or human persons here on earth but rather seek to discount or ignore them at every turn, we shouldn't expect to find them in the heavens or at the end of this ethical journey. If we prefer to focus on such things as the choices, functions, and exchanges we make as humans, or the appetites and interests we express, but not on the human persons who make rational choices, who function in various social systems, who exchange goods and services involving cost-benefit analyses, and who express certain tastes and cravings, we will never find personhood on the human or divine level.

---

[6]C. S. Lewis, *The Seeing Eye and Other Selected Essays from Christian Reflections* (New York: Ballantine Books, 1986), 226, 230.

But if that's the case, why should we be concerned with human rights and human emancipation? If we were consistent, we would seek to secure bureaucratic governmental authority and corporate shareholders' interests over the human masses at every turn.[7]

The journey to find "missing persons" and realize human personhood is long and arduous. We must take to heart those Amber Alerts and not get sidetracked and abandon the search. If we use our personalist moral compass at every turn, if we dedicate ourselves to cultivating an expansive and emerging sense of our embodied selves, and if we are able to see and take seriously every person's incommunicable and unrepeatable identity, inviolability, and dignity, we will reach our destination. In this light, we should live as "more than things" while looking for the far country. The great claim of the gospel is to live now in this world more fully as human persons, while expecting completion and perfection later in God.

Whether we believed in the triune God, who is supremely personal, at the beginning of the journey, if we value one another's supreme personal worth and help one another achieve the glory of human personhood, we will find what we are looking for. In the end, we may also come to the realization that as we traveled the heavens and the earth, the triune God was our copilot the entire way.

---

[7]Here I call to mind Christian Smith's answer to "Why Inquire About Human Being?" and his critical analysis of nonpersonalist quests in the social sciences in *What Is a Person?* (Chicago: University of Chicago Press, 2010), 2-4.

NAME INDEX

SUBJECT INDEX